# The Economics of Public Private Partnerships

# The International Library of Critical Writings in Economics

*Series Editor:* Mark Blaug

Professor Emeritus, University of London, UK
Professor Emeritus, University of Buckingham, UK
Visiting Professor, University of Amsterdam, The Netherlands

This series is an essential reference source for students, researchers and lecturers in economics. It presents by theme a selection of the most important articles across the entire spectrum of economics. Each volume has been prepared by a leading specialist who has written an authoritative introduction to the literature included.

A full list of published and future titles in this series is printed at the end of this volume.

Wherever possible, the articles in these volumes have been reproduced as originally published using facsimile reproduction, inclusive of footnotes and pagination to facilitate ease of reference.

For a list of all Edward Elgar published titles visit our site on the World Wide Web at
www.e-elgar.com

# The Economics of Public Private Partnerships

*Edited by*

## Darrin Grimsey

*Partner*
*PricewaterhouseCoopers, Melbourne*
*and Fellow*
*Australian Centre for Public Infrastructure, Melbourne University Private, Australia*

*and*

## Mervyn K. Lewis

*Professor of Banking and Finance*
*University of South Australia, Australia*
*and Fellow*
*Academy of the Social Sciences in Australia*

THE INTERNATIONAL LIBRARY OF CRITICAL WRITINGS IN ECONOMICS

**An Elgar Reference Collection**
Cheltenham, UK • Northampton, MA, USA

Published by
Edward Elgar Publishing Limited
Glensanda House
Montpellier Parade
Cheltenham
Glos GL50 1UA
UK

Edward Elgar Publishing, Inc.
136 West Street
Suite 202
Northampton
Massachusetts 01060
USA

A catalogue record for this book is available from the British Library



ISBN 1 84376 249 8

Printed and bound in Great Britain by MPG Books Ltd, Bodmin, Cornwall

# Contents

# Acknowledgements

The editors and publishers wish to thank the authors and the following publishers who have kindly given permission for the use of copyright material.

American Economic Association for article: Eduardo Engel, Ronald Fischer and Alexander Galetovic (1997), 'Highway Franchising: Pitfalls and Opportunities', *American Economic Review, Papers and Proceedings*, **87** (2), May, 68–72.

Blackwell Publishing Ltd for articles: David Campbell and Donald Harris (1993), 'Flexibility in Long-term Contractual Relationships: The Role of Co-operation,' *Journal of Law and Society*, **20** (2), Summer, 166–91; G. Owen and A. Merna (1997), 'The Private Finance Initiative', *Engineering, Construction and Architectural Management*, **4** (3), September, 163–77; S. Faruqi and N.J. Smith (1997), 'Karachi Light Rail Transit: A Private Finance Proposal', *Engineering, Construction and Architectural Management*, **4** (3), September, 233–46; Paul A. Grout (2003), 'Public and Private Sector Discount Rates in Public-Private Partnerships', *Economic Journal*, **113** (486), March, C62–C68; Oliver Hart (2003), 'Incomplete Contracts and Public Ownership: Remarks, and an Application to Public-Private Partnerships', *Economic Journal*, **113** (486), March, C69–C76.

Blackwell Publishing Ltd and David Mayston for article: David J. Mayston (1999), 'The Private Finance Initiative in the National Health Service: An Unhealthy Development in New Public Management?', *Financial Accountability and Management*, **15** (3 and 4), August/November, 249–74.

Dorset Engineering Consultancy for photograph on page 71 of article: G.J. Hodgson (1995), 'Design and Build – Effects of Contractor Design on Highway Schemes', *Proceedings of the Institution of Civil Engineers, Civil Engineering*, **108**, May, 64–76.

Elsevier for articles: S.C. Ward, C.B. Chapman and B. Curtis (1991), 'On the Allocation of Risk in Construction Projects', *International Journal of Project Management*, **9** (3), August, 140–47; J.J.A.M. Reijniers (1994), 'Organization of Public–Private Partnership Projects: The Timely Prevention of Pitfalls', *International Journal of Project Management*, **12** (3), August, 137–42; Paul G. Apen, Brian C. Benicewicz and Joseph R. Laia (1994), 'A New Model for Public–Private Partnerships', *Technology in Society*, **16** (4), 389–402; Christopher Hood (1995), 'The "New Public Management" in the 1980s: Variations on a Theme', *Accounting, Organizations and Society*, **20** (2/3), 93–109; Darrin Grimsey and Mervyn K. Lewis (2002), 'Evaluating the Risks of Public Private Partnerships for Infrastructure Projects', *International Journal of Project Management*, **20**, 107–18; David Parker and Keith Hartley (2003), 'Transaction Costs, Relational Contracting and Public Private Partnerships: A Case Study of UK Defence', *Journal of Purchasing and Supply Management*, **9** (3), 97–108.

Eno Transportation Quarterly, Washington, DC for article: Stephen C. Lockwood (1995), 'Public-Private Partnerships in U.S. Highway Finance: ISTEA and Beyond', *Transportation Quarterly*, **49** (1), Winter, 5–26.

*The Financier* (www.the-financier.com) for article: José A. Trujillo, Remy Cohen, Xavier Freixas and Robert Sheehy (1998), 'Infrastructure Financing with Unbundled Mechanisms', *The Financier*, **5** (4), Winter, 10–27.

Institute of Fiscal Studies for article: John Hall (1998), 'Private Opportunity, Public Benefit?', *Fiscal Studies*, **19** (2), May, 121–40.

Institution of Civil Engineers and G.J. Hodgson for article: G.J. Hodgson (1995), 'Design and Build – Effects of Contractor Design on Highway Schemes', *Proceedings of the Institution of Civil Engineers, Civil Engineering*, **108**, May, 64–76.

Institutional Investor Journals for articles: Raphael Henry Arndt (1998), 'Risk Allocation in the Melbourne City Link Project', *Journal of Project Finance*, **4** (3), Fall, 11–24; Anthony Forshaw (1999), 'The U.K. Revolution in Public Procurement and the Value of Project Finance', *Journal of Project Finance*, **5** (1), Spring, 49–54; Amira Mustafa (1999), 'Public-Private Partnership: An Alternative Institutional Model for Implementing the Private Finance Initiative in the Provision of Transport Infrastructure', *Journal of Project Finance*, **5** (2), Summer, 56–71.

International Monetary Fund for articles: David Haarmeyer and Ashoka Mody (1997), 'Private Capital in Water and Sanitation', *Finance and Development*, **34** (1), March, 34–7; Michael B. Gerrard (2001), 'Public-Private Partnerships', *Finance and Development*, **38** (3), September, 48–51.

Irish Bankers' Federation for article: Anne Ribault (2001), 'Lessons from the French Experience in Public and Private Partnership', *Irish Banking Review*, Spring, 49–60.

*Law and Policy in International Business*, Georgetown University Law Center for article: Martin Stewart-Smith (1995), 'Private Financing and Infrastructure Provision in Emerging Markets', *Law and Policy in International Business*, **26** (4), 987–1011.

NRC Research Press for article: A.M. Abdel-Aziz and A.D. Russell (2001), 'A Structure for Government Requirements in Public-Private Partnerships', *Canadian Journal of Civil Engineering*, **28** (6), December, 891–909.

Oxford University Press for articles: Michael Klein (1997), 'The Risk Premium for Evaluating Public Projects', *Oxford Review of Economic Policy*, **13** (4), 29–42; Paul A. Grout (1997), 'The Economics of the Private Finance Initiative', *Oxford Review of Economic Policy*, **13** (4), 53–66.

Sage Publications, Inc. for articles: Stephen H. Linder (1999), 'Coming to Terms With the Public-Private Partnership: A Grammar of Multiple Meanings', *American Behavioral Scientist*, **43** (1), September, 35–51; Joseph E. Stiglitz and Scott J. Wallsten (1999), 'Public-Private Technology Partnerships: Promises and Pitfalls', *American Behavioral Scientist*, **43** (1), September, 52–73; Anne Larason Schneider (1999), 'Public-Private Partnerships in the U.S. Prison System', *American Behavioral Scientist*, **43** (1), September, 192–208.

Paul Starr for his own article: (1988), 'The Meaning of Privatization', *Yale Law and Policy Review*, **VI** (1), 6–41.

Sweet and Maxwell Ltd for article: Nicholas Gould (1998), 'Dispute Resolution Mechanisms to Address Unforeseen Circumstances in Long Term BOT Contracts', *Constructional Law*, **9** (4), 133–6.

Taylor and Francis Ltd (www.tandf.co.uk/journals) for article: Simon Domberger and Stephen Rimmer (1994), 'Competitive Tendering and Contracting in the Public Sector: A Survey', *International Journal of the Economics of Business*, **1** (3), 439–53.

Thomas Telford Ltd for excerpt: A.J. Smith (1999), 'Philosophical Aspects of the Public/Private Sector Partnership', in *Privatized Infrastructure: The Role of Government*, Chapter 9, 129–45.

John Wiley and Sons, Inc. for article: Paulina Beato and Antonio Vives (1996), 'Private-Sector Participation in Infrastructure: Risk, Fiscal, and Efficiency Issues in Public–Private Arrangements for the Provision of Services', *Infrastructure*, **1** (3), 3–14.

University of Toronto Press, Inc. for article: Ronald J. Daniels and Michael J. Trebilcock (1996), 'Private Provision of Public Infrastructure: An Organizational Analysis of the Next Privatization Frontier', *University of Toronto Law Journal*, **XLVI** (3), Summer, 375–426.

Every effort has been made to trace all the copyright holders but if any have been inadvertently overlooked the publishers will be pleased to make the necessary arrangement at the first opportunity.

In addition the publishers wish to thank the Marshall Library of Economics, Cambridge University, the Library of the University of Warwick and the Library of Indiana University at Bloomington, USA for their assistance in obtaining these articles.

# Introduction

*Darrin Grimsey and Mervyn K. Lewis*

## Background

The literature on public–private partnerships (PPPs) is relatively new, and the earliest article we have included in the volume was published in 1988. However, the concept itself is not new. PPPs have been used in France to privately finance public infrastructure since the 17th century, when the French Concession Model was pioneered. The first concession contracts were awarded for the financing and construction of the 'Canal de Briare' in 1638 and 'Canal du Midi' in 1666. Later, in the second half of the nineteenth century, France extensively used PPPs to finance its infrastructure, and railways, water, electricity and tramways were all designed, constructed, financed and operated by private enterprises and banks. Most of these projects were realised under the form of long-term concession contracts, under which the property of the infrastructure was to return to the public entities at the end of the contract. This system was then generalised to numerous activities considered in France as 'commercial public services' such as water supply and sanitation, waste management or urban transportation. The concession system remains today one of the most popular modes of realisation and management of 'commercial' public services and public infrastructure in France, and in the case of water supply and treatment plants has led to the growth of the large, diversified French private utility companies such as Vivendi and Lyonnaise des Eaux (Suez-Lyonnaise).

While France can justifiably be seen as the founder of PPPs, the evolution of the PPP has been accelerated in the UK as the privatisation processes in that country gave way to different mechanisms for the delivery of public services by the private sector. PPPs have evolved differently in the United States, where they embrace policy-level partnerships (for example, highway assistance programs) and project-level partnerships (for example, private toll roads). As well as transport, PPPs in the US cover technology, energy and environmental policy, welfare and education, health care and criminal justice. In fact the PPP is evolving in different ways in each country in which the arrangements are being implemented.

As well as examining the recent experience of PPPs in the UK, United States and France, this collection has two other objectives. One is to consider the intellectual origins of the concept in terms of the changing market for public services, the private financing model and the concept of partnering. The other is to examine the organisational and risk management aspects of PPPs, especially in the case of construction-based activities such as roads, rail systems, bridges, tunnels, waste water treatment, private prisons, hospitals, courts, museums, sporting facilities, schools and government accommodation. From these examples, it is not difficult to see why the literature on PPPs straddles the economics–engineering divide, and we have drawn from both disciplines when preparing this collection. There is a large number of government reports and documents on PPPs, but for reasons of length and content (as they are aimed at practitioners and those submitting bids and tenders), these or extracts from them have been excluded. Also omitted are the numerous articles dealing with the accounting issues and tax treatment of PPPs. The interested reader is referred to articles by Heald and Geaughan (1997), Hodges and Mellett (1999, 2002) and Grimsey and Lewis (2002) as examples. To some degree, also, the literature on PPPs overlaps with that on public policy, and this becomes clear when we seek to define PPPs.

## PPPs Defined

Reflecting the engineering–economics heritage, PPPs can be defined as arrangements whereby private parties participate in, or provide support for, the provision of infrastructure, and a PPP project results in a contract for a private entity to deliver public infrastructure-based services. A fundamental feature is that the government does not own the infrastructure but, rather, contracts to buy infrastructure services and infrastructure-related ancillary services from the private sector over time. A common misconception about PPP projects is that they are principally about private sector financing of public infrastructure. This is not strictly correct. Financing is only one element of the calculation. The very essence of a PPP is that the public sector does not buy an asset; it is purchasing a service under specified terms and conditions. This feature provides the key to the viability (or not) of the transaction, since a PPP is at base a risk-sharing relationship, in this case to bring about certain desired public policy outcomes. A project needs to be structured to achieve optimal risk allocation.

Others would suggest that this emphasis on asset-based infrastructure is too narrowly based, and would define PPPs much more broadly. In the United States, as we have noted, PPPs have covered transport (for example, toll roads) and private prisons and detention facilities, but have also dealt with education policy priorities, welfare provision, health and medicinal services, and a range of community activities from schooling to urban regeneration and environmental policy, reflecting the distinction between policy-level partnerships and project-level partnerships. Linder in Chapter 5 of this volume begins by defining PPPs as 'a rubric for describing cooperative ventures between the state and private business'.

The reconciliation between these views turns in part also on how we define 'infrastructure'. Infrastructure can be classified into 'economic' or 'social' and within these into 'hard' or 'soft'. Roads, airports and telecommunications are 'hard economic', while 'soft economic' embraces vocational training, R&D facilitation and technology transfer. 'Hard social' involves water treatment, housing, childcare and prisons, whereas social security, community services and environmental agencies are 'soft social'. Much of the apparent difference between the two definitions disappears once we allow for the co-existence of the variety of forms that infrastructure can take. Nevertheless, since any relationship involving some combination of the private, voluntary and public sectors is prone to be labelled a 'partnership', it may be useful to clarify what is meant by a partnership in the context, and the relationships involved.

**Collaboration** PPPs involve a sharing of both responsibility and risk in a collaborative framework. They seek to draw upon the best available skills, knowledge and resources, whether they are in the public or the private sector, and deliver value for money in the provision of infrastructure.

**Focus on services** The emphasis is on services received by government, not government procurement of economic or social infrastructure. Government pays for services provided by the private party, which are delivered through privately owned or rented infrastructure as part of the service package.

**Length** The service provision needs to be long term and relational. A short-term contract for the provision of a good or service is presumably not a partnership – otherwise a partnership would be created every time a public sector organisation ordered a round of sandwiches for lunch from a private caterer.

**Trust** The partnership is a high-trust relationship. Underpinning the partnership will be a framework contract, which sets out the 'rules of the game' and provides the partners with some certainty. While this PPP contract provides the basic architecture of the arrangement, it does not (and cannot) specify all components and allow for all outcomes. A PPP has to be built on trust, like all successful partnerships.

**Whole-of-life costing** With a PPP there is the opportunity for a complete integration – under one party – of up-front design and construction costs with ongoing service delivery, operational, maintenance and refurbishment costs.

**Innovation** A PPP approach focuses on output specifications, providing enhanced opportunities and incentives for bidders to fashion innovative solutions in meeting these requirements.

**Risk allocation** Risk retained by government in owning and operating infrastructure typically carries substantial, often unvalued, cost. Transferring some of the risk to a private party, which can manage it at less cost, can substantially lower the overall cost to government.

**Type** While some partnerships are created for the purpose of policy formulation, priority setting, and coordinating organisations from the various sectors (for example, crime prevention strategies, educational action), our primary (but not exclusive) concern is with asset-based services and long-term service provision contracts related to 'hard' social and economic infrastructure. However, we do reproduce two chapters on technology partnerships (soft economic) and one chapter surveying the variety of partnerships in the United States.

In fact, the PPP model is very flexible and can allow for a variety of service outcomes and for a range of roles for the parties. In a hierarchy from a maximum to a minimum retention of service delivery by government, the various models are broadly as follows:

- Public sector delivery of services (considered to be essential public services) with private entities providing infrastructure-related services only (for example, policing);
- Public sector delivery of core services with private parties providing infrastructure and related ancillary services (for example, a courthouse);
- Public sector delivery of core services with private parties providing infrastructure and related ancillary services, together with some services to the community (for example, a sporting facility); and

- Private sector delivery of a full range of services to the community inclusive of infrastructure (for example, some transport projects).

When structuring the most appropriate approach, the focus should be on the output specifications, the public interest, the capabilities of both government and the private sector, the optimal risk allocation environment and commercial viability. The objective remains one of achieving effective and efficient 'value for money'. Value for money is not about cost-effectiveness alone, in isolation from the quality of the service, although it is fair to say that considerable controversy exists on this point, as will be apparent later.

Even more fundamental is the question of which (if any) part or parts of the proposed service is a service which government itself should deliver to its citizens. This is the essential or core services issue. Obviously if the whole service is considered to be core, there will be no scope for a PPP arrangement. Nevertheless, the application of a partnership policy is an opportunity to reassess the role of public services and the means through which they are delivered, for which the guiding principle should be a commitment to bring about desirable social, economic and environmental end results. Another merit of a partnership agenda is to determine the point at which the core ends and ancillary services begin. Yet the reality is that the precise boundaries are unclear, and the answer varies over time and from country to country. At one stage, steel production was widely seen as an essential public activity! In fact, there are no core functions that cannot be undertaken by the private sector and no activities for which public provision is infeasible. Not all public services provided to the community are necessarily core in the sense that government needs to provide these services itself. Moreover, core services are usually delivered in a context which does not preclude participation by private parties. For example, the services performed by police and judges within courts are widely regarded as ones which it is a function of government to provide. However, there is no reason, in principle, why supporting infrastructure and ancillary services within those service areas cannot be delivered by the private sector. 'Related ancillary services', in this context, encompasses a number of operational services including information technology services, accommodation services arising out of the infrastructure, building-related services such as maintenance, and some support services.

Changing attitudes on the public–private contribution and an associated re-assessment of what is really a 'core' service can be seen as one factor that has led to the development of PPPs. A PPP is simply a method of procurement (although of infrastructure services rather than the infrastructure itself) and as such falls into what has become known as the 'new public management' or 'marketisation' of the public sector. These terms embrace the corporatisation, privatisation, commercialisation, managerialism, outsourcing and downsizing of public sector activities. PPPs are one exemplification of these trends, and thus the first part of this volume focuses on the changing markets for public services.

In addition, in our view, two other factors have been instrumental in the growth of PPPs over the last decade. One is the refinement of the private financing model. The PPPs with which we are primarily concerned involve supplying whole-of-life infrastructure services to the public sector, and utilise project financing techniques in order to deliver the required private finance in a form which meets the risk-reward requirements of private financiers and suppliers of risk capital. Part II concentrates on this topic.

The third influence we identify is little known and probably poorly understood by most economic commentators. PPPs have been shaped by concepts of 'partnering' developed in the engineering construction industry. Here the literature overlap is between engineering and management. Our contention is that the partnering concept has provided an intellectual backdrop and support to the organisation of PPPs. Part III of the volume collects key analyses of the way PPPs are organised, beginning with the concept of partnering.

In the final three parts, the volume reproduces articles examining the application of PPPs. Part IV deals with the influential UK experience, while Part V examines the United States and France (illustrations from the Netherlands and Canada are discussed in Chapters 11 and 12). In the final part, VI, the focus is upon risk management. A PPP is a risk-sharing arrangement between the public and private sector, structured to obtain a desired public policy outcome in a cost-effective manner. Achievement of 'value for money' relies on obtaining an optimal transfer of risk because the entity in the best position to manage a particular risk should be able to do so at the lowest price. In Part VI, the conceptual treatment of risk in PPPs is considered, along with a number of case studies.

Before a review of the individual papers, one final point needs to be mentioned. Some of the articles are highly critical of PPPs. Our own position, as can be gathered from our contribution to this volume, is different. Nevertheless, our aim in the articles selected has been, first and foremost, to give readers an understanding of the major conceptual issues involved. Secondly it has been to present a range of views on the issues involved, rather than provide a polemic reflecting one particular viewpoint. We leave it to readers to decide how well we have succeeded in our aims.

## The Changing Market for Public Services

The volume begins appropriately with an article entitled 'Public-Private Partnerships' from the IMF's quarterly publication *Finance and Development*, although contributed by an outsider, Michael Gerrard from Partnerships UK, a body established by the UK government to accelerate the implementation of such projects. Like us, Gerrard uses the abbreviation PPPs (whereas many US authors use P-P partnership, perhaps to avoid confusion with Purchasing Power Parity, also invariably abbreviated to PPP), and defines them as arrangements which 'combine the deployment of private sector capital and, sometimes, public sector capital to improve public services or the management of public sector assets' (p. 49). The use of the word 'improve' might be seen as pejorative. Obviously, this is the aim of a PPP, but the PPP must be designed and executed properly to ensure that this is indeed the result. More recently, PPPs have been extended to incorporate not-for-profit organisations (or 'third sector') and this has long been a feature in the United States (Rosenau, 2000). In the case of urban regeneration, for example, PPPs are likely to involve community groups alongside private sector entities and government bodies.

Gerrard's PPP agenda includes the management of existing public assets as well as the construction of new infrastructure. Previously, PPPs were thought of mainly as vehicles for the provision of new public sector facilities through which services were provided to the public. This change of emphasis raises the question of whether, and how, PPPs differ from privatisation. One reason is that within a PPP the public sector acquires and pays for services from the private sector on behalf of the community and retains the ultimate responsibility for the delivery of the services, although they are being provided by the private sector over an extended period of time (that is, 25 years or longer). By contrast when a government entity is privatised, the private firm that takes over the business also assumes the responsibility for service delivery.

In the latter case, it would be wrong to say that the government is indifferent to the quality of services provided by the newly privatised entity. Rather two other mechanisms come into play, since the private firm is subject to disciplines from both product and capital markets, in the form of competition from other firms and competition when raising finance. Moreover, if these market constraints do not exist effectively, perhaps because the privatised firm has some form of natural monopoly, then the government would usually impose some type of regulatory regime, typically over price or rate of return. In this case, however, the regulation is quite different from that under a PPP, and this difference is another reason why PPPs are not privatisation in the usual sense, according to Gerrard. A PPP is a formal business arrangement between the public and private sectors. The nature of this business activity, the outcomes required, the prices paid for the services (and thus the scope for profits) along with the general rights and obligations of the various parties are specified in considerable detail in the concession agreement. Consequently, regulation does not come from some statutory regulatory agency or from unseen market forces, but is a direct result of an explicit contract subject to performance indicators and quality standards, with penalties attached to failure to maintain service standards on a continuing basis.

These two differences – the extent of government disengagement and regulation through contract – define much that is distinctive about a PPP. Nevertheless, PPPs might still be seen as privatisation in all but name, as they are by many public sector unions. At issue is how privatisation is defined, and this is the question addressed by Paul Starr in Chapter 2. He notes that privatisation has generally come to mean two things:

1. Any shift of activities or functions from the state to the private sector; and, more specifically,
2. Any shift of the production of goods and services from public to private.

The first, broader, definition of privatisation includes all reductions in the regulatory and spending activity of the state. The second, more specific, definition of privatisation excludes deregulation and spending cuts except when they result in a shift from public to private in the production of goods and services. This more focussed definition is the one preferred by Starr, so that privatisation means a shift in the locus of the production of services from public to private. Nevertheless, depending on whether one is talking about the locus of production or the forms of consumption, privatisation can mean rather different things. In regard to production, 'privatisation of health care' might mean a transfer of medical facilities from public to private ownership; regarding consumption, it might refer to a shift in expenditures from public health (environmental protection, vaccinations and so on) to individual medical care. Similarly, 'privatisation of transportation' might refer to the conversion of an urban bus system from public to commercial ownership; or it might mean a shift in usage from buses to private automobiles, regardless of whether the bus company is municipal or commercial. In general, however, it is argued that four types of government activities can bring about a shift in production from the public to the private sector. First, the cessation of public programmes and disengagement of government from specific kinds of responsibilities can represent implicit forms of privatisation. At another level, the restriction of publicly produced services in volume, availability, or quality may lead to a shift by consumers toward privately produced and purchased substitutes (called 'privatisation by attrition' when a government lets public services run down). Second, privatisation may take the explicit form of transfers of public assets to private ownership, through sale or lease of public land, infrastructure, and enterprises. Third, instead of directly producing some service, the government may finance private services, for example, through contracting-out or vouchers. Finally, privatisation may result from the deregulation of entry into activities previously treated as public monopolies.

None of these policies in themselves directly cover the example of PPPs. Some transfer of assets, especially by way of leasehold, forms a component of most PPPs, but it is not a defining characteristic. There is procurement, for sure, but normally under a PPP this is not simply an operations and maintenance (O&M) contract. Deregulation of entry is important for many PPPs, for example when a private toll operator is allowed to levy tolls, and utilise public law enforcement officers to enforce payment and impose fines. Yet a PPP allows for a contracting relationship between the public entity and private provider that far exceeds deregulation alone.

Thus in order to understand the distinctive contribution of PPPs, we need to consider a broader range of government business models in the context of the commercialisation or marketisation of the public sector. Hood in Chapter 3 considers the various dimensions of what has become known as the 'new public management', under seven changes. The seven elements are as follows. (1) A shift towards greater disaggregation of public organisations into separately managed 'corporatised' units for each public sector 'product' (each identified as a separate cost centre, with its own organisational identity. (2) A shift towards greater competition both between public sector organisations and between public sector organisations and the private sector. (3) A move towards greater use within the public sector of management practices which are drawn from the private corporate sector, rather than public-sector-specific methods of doing business. (4) A move towards greater stress on discipline and parsimony in resource use and on the active search for finding alternative, less costly ways to deliver public services, instead of laying the emphasis on institutional continuity, the maintenance of public services which are stable in 'volume terms', and policy development. (5) A move towards more 'hands on management' (that is, more active control of public organisations by visible top managers wielding discretionary power) as against the traditional style of 'hands off' management in the public sector, involving relatively anonymous bureaucrats at the top of public sector organisations. (6) A move towards more explicit and measurable (or at least verifiable) standards of performance for public sector organisations, in terms of the range, level and content of services to be provided, as against trust in professional standards and expertise across the public sector. (7) Attempts to control public organisations in a more 'homeostatic' style according to preset output measures (particularly in pay based on job performance rather than rank or educational attainment), rather than by the traditional style of 'orders of the day' coming on an *ad hoc* basis from the top.

Hood's analysis goes on to provide a useful summary of the various elements of the seven dimensions, including the justifications for the changes, the operational characteristics and the implications for accounting, especially in terms of the emphasis on the 'bottom line' and the adoption of private-sector accounting norms. These developments in turn have spawned a range of different public sector business models, which are as follows:

- Service Provision Contracts
- Outsourcing/Contracting

- Design and Construct (D&C)
- Sale and Leaseback
- Operate and Maintain (O&M)
- Operate Maintain and Manage (OM&M)
- Build Operate Transfer (BOT)
- Build Lease Transfer (BLT)
- Build Own Operate Transfer (BOOT)
- Lease Renovate Operate Transfer (LROT)
- Design Build Finance Operate (DBFO)
- Design Construct Manage Finance (DCMF)
- Design Build Finance Operate Manage (DBFOM)
- Build Own Operate (BOO)
- Franchise
- Concession
- Joint Venture (JV)
- Regeneration Partnership
- Outright Privatisation

Outright sale (or explicit privatisation in Starr's terminology) of public assets to private ownership is at one end of the scale. At the other end, in terms of Starr's schema, is 'contracting out' and this phenomenon is studied by Domberger and Rimmer in Chapter 4.

As we have seen, privatisation and contracting out are often used synonymously particularly in the USA. Elsewhere, and especially in the UK and Australia, privatisation refers to the transfer of ownership of physical assets from public to private ownership. The sale of a public utility via a share float constitutes straightforward privatisation in these terms. The privatised organisations may or may not operate in a competitive environment. In this respect, privatisation can be essentially independent from the promotion of competition. How much competition there is post-privatisation will depend largely on the structure of the industry and on government regulatory policy.

By contrast, contracting out involves opening up to competition a set of economic activities that were previously excluded from it. Organisations are invited to submit bids for contracts to provide particular services to the client. The distinctive feature of contracting out is the element of ex ante competition – competition for the market as opposed to competition in it. The market in this case is defined by the contract specification, and the bidding process resembles an auction. As Domberger and Rimmer argue, a formal contract binds the parties to an exchange of services of a pre-determined quality and quantity for agreed financial payments. The contract itself becomes the instrument through which relations between the parties are managed and regulated.

Domberger and Rimmer survey the type of activities outsourced, encompassing cleaning services and refuse collection predominantly but also air traffic control, buses and business services. Lengthening the term of the contract and widening its scope to incorporate operations, maintenance and management (OM&M) of the public facility over an extended period, say five years, would see some similarities emerge between contracting out and a PPP. Such a contract operates for the Haldimand–Norfolk, Ontario, Canada waste water treatment facility whereby the operator is responsible for all aspects of operating, maintaining and managing an existing facility, including decisions about personnel, energy, chemicals and sludge disposal. Yet there remains some gap between this OM&M contract and that of another water treatment project in Moncton, New Brunswick, Canada. This PPP incorporates two contracts, one for the design, building and finance of a new water treatment plant, the other a 20-year operations and maintenance contract for the facility, making a design-build-finance-operate (DBFO) project. Quite clearly, PPPs like these involve some elements similar to those involved in contracting out, but at the same time are much more complex in that intricate financing and organisational/ contractual issues are intertwined (Grimsey and Lewis, 2004).

Domberger and Rimmer survey the substantial evidence that has emerged since the mid 1980s suggesting that governments can save in the order of 20 per cent of expenditures on services by putting them through a competitive tendering process. The benefits are therefore substantial, and have been sustained by the growth of specialist private-sector firms providing a wide range of business and managerial services. Not surprisingly, the policy has gained currency as an instrument of public-sector reform – achieving better value for taxpayers' money. Because of their wider scope and sophistication, PPPs introduce many more elements into the equation, although achieving value for money is obviously an important issue, if not the overriding consideration. Drawing on the US experience of PPPs, Linder in Chapter 5 suggests six ways in which PPPs can introduce change into the public sector. First, PPPs are a tool for management reform. As such, PPPs can alter the way government functions by introducing market disciplines into public services. Second, PPPs encourage problem conversion, so that the task for public sector managers becomes one of re-framing constraints they face so as to facilitate the entry of private sector operators and their commitment of funds. The focus becomes one of the outcomes to be achieved, rather than the processes by which things are done. Third, once this is done, PPPs can produce a 'moral regeneration' by widening the number of stakeholders in the outcomes and building market experience for public service managers. Fourth, PPPs allow for financial risks to be shifted from public to private investors. This aspect is examined in Part VI of the collection. Fifth, partnerships can be a vehicle for restructuring public services, streamlining administrative procedures and substituting a private workplace for public servants. Sixth, as power sharing arrangements, PPPs can alter business–government relations in fundamental ways. One is that an ethos of cooperation and trust can replace the adversarial relations endemic to command-and-control regulation. Also, any relationship between partners will involve some mutually beneficial sharing of responsibility, knowledge, or risk. In most instances, each party brings something of value to the others to be invested or exchanged. Finally, there is an expectation of give-and-take between the partners, negotiating differences that were otherwise litigated. This is the essence of partnering considered in Part III below.

## The Private Financing Model

From the preceding discussion, it is apparent that PPPs can take different forms, including:

1. Contracting out or management contracts, where the private sector is only partially involved, for example it provides a service or manages without taking any risk;
2. Joint ventures, where the private and public sectors jointly finance, own and operate a facility;

3. Leasing, where part of the risk is transferred to the private sector;
4. BOT (Build Operate Transfer), where the private sector takes primary responsibility for funding, designing, building and operating the project. Control and formal ownership of the project is then transferred back to the public sector;
5. BOO (Build Own Operate), where the control and the ownership of the project remain in private hands.

A fuller listing was provided earlier of public/private business models, ranging from service provision contracts and outsourcing, at one end of the scale, to outright privatisation where the ownership of the asset is transferred fully to the private sector entity, at the other end. Traditional public procurement is covered by design and construct contracts, while sale and leaseback arrangements are often driven by taxation advantages, rather than any partnership motives (Grimsey and Lewis 2002). Most of the other models encompass some form of PPP arrangement. A wide variety are based upon some form of lease, franchise or fixed term concession, using different combinations of private sector resources to design, renovate, construct, finance, operate, manage and maintain facilities. Concession-based methods are some of the oldest forms of PPP. Except in the case of a BOO, when ownership remains with the private sector virtually for ever, at the end of a concession the public body usually takes over responsibility for the ownership, operation and management of the asset. Nevertheless, the public entity may then effectively extend the concession by means of an O&M, OM&M, or LROT (lease-renovate-operate-transfer) contract.

A feature of many of the PPP contract forms is the commitment of private sector finance to the construction or renovation of the facilities. Underpinning the development of the PPP concept has been an appropriate model for harnessing the supply of private finance for infrastructure projects. This model is the subject of Part II.

Traditional public sector procurement methods have generally resulted in the award of design and/or construct contracts. However, as Hodgson in Chapter 6 argues, 'the public sector's record in the design and construction of capital schemes is poor. Time and cost overruns are common. Part of the reason lies in the attitudes and culture of the public sector. In the construction sector this often results in conservative or over-engineered designs' (p. 68). Traditional methods also leave the government with a number of risks including that of asset ownership, the risk that the economic value of the asset either during or at the end of the contract term may vary from the value upon which the financial structure of the project is based.

The critical innovation of a design and build contract such as a DBFO road is that it is not a capital asset procurement policy but a service procurement policy. The infrastructure from which the contracted services and, where appropriate, the 'core services' are delivered belongs to the private party which is responsible for the creation of the infrastructure (design and construction risks), the life of the infrastructure (part of the operating risk) and, in many cases, the 'after-life' of the infrastructure (residual value and obsolescence risks).

As Hodgson notes, the DBFO concessionaire will have to assume substantial risk, the intention being that the government body will be buying a road service and not just a new road. Concessionaires will have to be capable of long-term commitment and, as a result, will need to be both robust and committed to quality of performance in this market. To encourage this high quality of service, the structure for the concessions will incorporate a payment system that includes both incentives and penalties. Achieving an appropriate transfer of risk is the primary aim and includes all or some of

1. Design risk
2. Construction risk
3. Opening date risk
4. Traffic risk
5. Legislative and force majeure risk and
6. Operational risk

These features, pioneered in the case of road schemes, have now become standard. Hodgson provides examples of the design and build approach including, the Dartford River Crossing, the second Severn River Crossing, the M8 St James Interchange, Glasgow and the Birmingham Northern Relief Road.

Stewart-Smith in Chapter 7 considers the applicability of private finance to infrastructure provision in emerging markets. As in developed countries, project-financing techniques hold the key and a mixture of instruments and methods, including asset-based financing, leasing, hire purchase, and the use of special purpose non-recourse financing vehicles. One major difference in emerging markets comes from the presence of country risk, and the need to take measures to mitigate this risk. Traditionally, these actions have involved the taking of guarantees and indemnities from the host government. However, other measures include legal and regulatory changes, along with financing from the World Bank group as outlined in the chapter. Further details can be found in the publication by the International Finance Corporation (1999).

If private bodies are to commit finance under PPPs for infrastructure, they need to be convinced that a viable revenue stream can be tapped. Beato and Vives in Chapter 8 argue that, in a public–private arrangement, revenues to the private firm can come from two sources, namely consumer payments or public entity payments (or some combination of both). The source is important because it determines (a) the incentives of a private firm to adjust the cost and quality to consumer willingness to pay for them, (b) the amount and timing of public expenditures, and (c) the nature of the risks to which revenues are exposed.

Ignoring the mixed case, Beato and Vives examine the two possible sources. When private entity revenues consist of prices or user fees (electricity prices, user charges, tolls), project revenues are governed by commercial risks, as in any market context, although the firm may be subject to regulatory risk if fees or rates of return are regulated. There are also collection costs and externalities to be taken into account. By contrast, if the public sector entity is the source of the revenues, there is little or no commercial risk, but there may be contractual disputes which result in a failure to pay. Add to this the difficulty of imposing financial conditions upon the public body, and either seizing the assets or suing the public agency involved, and there may be some reluctance on the part of the private firm – or its backers and investors – to bear public payment risk. In these circumstances, careful design of the contract is needed. Some of the conciliation and risk mitigation elements are considered in the other studies, in following sections.

Private–public arrangements can be classified according to who manages, owns and finances the infrastructure assets. Beato and Vives consider four different possibilities, which when combined with the revenue source (finance from consumers or public entity), produce a 4×2 matrix, which forms the basis of the authors' discussion. In general, they conclude that public–private arrangements in which revenues come from final end-users and the assets are owned, managed and financed by the private firm are the most conducive to increasing efficiency and reducing public expenditure. Many transport schemes and energy project have these characteristics.

Engel, Fischer and Galetovic in Chapter 9 agree that there are indeed benefits from having roads provided by private sector operators under DBFO-type arrangements, but recognize that there are some pitfalls that offset these benefits. Too often, they consider, governments feel obliged to offer guarantees to the promotors and also to bail out franchises that get into financial difficulties. The problem seems to be that in many applications (for example, developing countries), traffic volumes are hard to forecast when user charges are applied, generating considerable commercial risk to the operators concerned. However, Engel, Fischer and Galetovic argue that a change in the way the franchise is auctioned can ameliorate the situation. Usually the length of the franchise (for example, 30 years) is fixed in advance of the tender. This fixed-term concession can lead to demand risk for the franchise-holder; it is possible for the franchise to lose money even when the road is profitable in the long run simply because the term of the franchise may be too short given the state of demand. An alternative mechanism they advocate is to conduct a least-present-value-of-revenue (LPVR) auction. With such a system, the winner is chosen on the least present value to toll revenue required over the project lifetime. But the time span of the concession is not fixed in advance and can vary in response to economic conditions, ending when the present value of toll revenue is equal to the franchise-holder's bid. Thus an LPVR auction takes advantage of the fact that roads may eventually pay for themselves even when traffic turns out to be slower than expected by the device of allowing the franchise term to lengthen. Engel et al. develop a simple model which illustrates that, in comparison with the fixed-term franchise, the LPVR auction can eliminate demand risk (a more complete model is developed in Engel, Fischer and Galetovic, 2001). In fact, the institution of the LPVG auction technique for highway franchises in Chile has proven to be a workable solution to reducing the demand risk problem, lowering the cost of infrastructure investment (Engel, Fischer and Galetovic, 1997).

## Organisation of PPPs

This section is concerned with the structure and organisation of PPPs. Two themes recur in the articles collected here. One relates to 'bundling'. A characteristic of a PPP is the integration of the design, building, finance, operations and maintenance functions with one private sector entity. Several of the chapters examine the efficiency of this integrated structure with various 'unbundled mechanisms'. The other theme involves the concept of 'partnering' and the idea that long-term contractual agreements are essentially cooperative, effectively like partnerships. A PPP is necessarily relational rather than transactional, in the terms of Macneil (1974), and this feature provides the philosophical basis of PPPs.

Chapter 10 by Adrian Smith is called 'Philosophical aspects of the public/private sector partnership' and it discusses a number of issues relevant to PPPs, especially the need for a 'team' building approach, rather than a commercial supplier–purchaser relationship, and the nature of the concession agreement, including provision for non-performance and default.

Central to the analysis is the concept of partnering and the formulation of a 'partnering agreement' between the parties involved in a BOT, DBFO or PPP concession.

Partnering has its origins in the engineering and construction industry. It takes as its starting point that the construction industry is marred by adversarial relationships. Earlier contracting methods and project management practices, whether involving private or public sector projects, have had the effect of putting the participating parties – owner, designer and contractor – into adversarial situations in which common project objectives get lost. This failure of communication and cooperation leads to disruptive conflicts, the results of which are cost and schedule overruns, lost time, wasted money, low morale and ultimately litigation. Partnering, by contrast, centres around conflict management, team building, trust, commitment and mutual goals.

The concept of partnering was advocated in a number of articles published in the mid-1990s by the American Society of Civil Engineers, notably Crowley and Karim (1995) and Wilson, Songer and Diekmann (1995). The former article sees partnering as a means of resolving inter-organisational conflict, with two or more organisations maximising resource effectiveness in achieving common project objectives. The key elements introduced into the relationship are trust, commitment and a shared vision. Trust is important for confidence and encouraging a communication of ideas. Commitment allows for mutual improvements in technology and methods. A shared vision comes from consensus in realising objectives in common. A successful partnership is marked by openness, innovation, equity, shared risk and conflict resolution through problem solving. The latter article notes that partnering represents a significant cultural change for most organisations. A major hurdle is that project partnerships are single events and do not in themselves generate the cultural change mechanisms required for the partnering process. The authors seek to move partnering beyond a single event project arrangement, and investigate partnering from a strategic aspect of a partnering process embedded in an organisational change model in which strategic change is driven by a transformation leadership team responsible for defining the goals to be achieved from partnering, managing the partnering process and undertaking continual diagnosis, coordination and problem solving. The aim is to institutionalise change by placing common goals, trust and teamwork at the heart of all contractual agreements for construction.

A project partnering agreement of the form suggest by Smith in Chapter 10 fulfils this partnering role, since it would be signed not by the organisations but by the actual people directly involved in the project. Nevertheless, it is a non-contractual agreement, setting out the essence of the parties' mutually agreed obligations, and in this sense is non-enforceable. By contrast, the concession agreement itself is a legal contract, and is consequently enforceable through the courts. But this does not mean that it will be in the case of a dispute. As Campbell and Harris observe in Chapter 11, for long-term contracts such as those for a BOT or PPP project 'typically the classical law's remedies simply are not used by the parties' (p. 168), and disputes are frequently settled without reference either to the contract or to potential legal sanctions. The authors seek to develop the principles which should govern these exchanges. Their starting point is that efficient long-term contractual behaviour must be understood as consciously cooperative, if only because in practice all long-term contracts are necessarily incomplete, involving an element of irreducible uncertainty. Thus their governance requires an open-ended approach which leaves substantial ground for the variation or complete renegotiation of prior commitments. These negotiations rely on the cooperative efforts of each of the parties made in good faith so as to realise their joint objectives. In this respect, the contract should be seen not as a stand alone document but as part of a reciprocated relational web binding the parties together which is to be kept intact in all but the most acute circumstances.

PPPs draw on this heritage of 'partnering' and 'design and build', but add additional layers of complexity. These come from, first, the fact that many PPPs are of the DBFOM (design, build, finance, operate, manage) character, combining (limited) ownership, with operate and manage, and also design and construct. Second, PPPs cover many areas (for example, private prisons, hospitals, courts) where tolls, user fees etc, cannot be levied in the form of consumer payments, in the terminology of Beato and Vives (Chapter 8). Third, in some PPPs, such as those for regeneration and regional development, non-government organisations (NGOs) participate along with public and other private sector bodies, while for many projects the sponsoring parties are obliged to consult widely with community groups and other interested parties. For all of these reasons, the organisation of PPPs becomes a central issue, and the remaining articles in this section focus upon this aspect.

PPPs have been instituted in the Netherlands since the late 1980s, and Reijniers in a widely cited article, reproduced here as Chapter 12, draws on this experience. Not all projects are successful and 'the results are sometimes disappointing', in his words. He argues that the causes can be found in differences in the characteristics of the partnering organisations, in that there are conflicts in interests between the public and private sectors in terms of social benefits versus commercial benefits. At the same time, there are differences in corporate culture and working methods in relation to management approaches, perception of risks, decision-making processes, and time frames. Reijniers' review of previous PPPs suggests that adequate preparation for the project is the critical success factor. On this basis, he outlines what preparation is needed to realise a successful project. His recommendations are provided under five headings: assignment and objectives, planning, organisation and coordination, control and management.

Daniels and Trebilcock in Chapter 13 also look to the lessons from experience of PPPs, in this case from Canada. They begin by considering three case studies of projects involving PPPs for the development and operation of public infrastructure in Canada: a 69 km toll road in Toronto, a 13.5 km bridge across the Northumberland Strait to form the Prince Edward Island link, and the redevelopment of three airport terminals at Toronto's international airport. They then consider some of the common characteristics of these projects before focusing upon a number of key issues. A defining characteristic of PPPs is the integration within a private sector firm of all (or most of) the functions of design, building, financing, operating and maintenance of the facility in question, often in the form of a special purpose vehicle (or virtual corporation) created for the specific project. Like some other articles in this volume, Daniels and Trebilcock beg the question of why this extensive vertical integration or bundling of functions is an efficient solution. They discuss this issue at length, noting the possibility that there could be potential gains for the public sector in partly decoupling, say, design from other functions if a consortium with an inferior design but superior construction and other capabilities won the integrated bid. In principle, the government stands to realise efficiency gains from contracting out the design function and, effectively, creating a competition for ideas. After examining a number of relevant factors, the authors conclude that the case for bundling and vertical integration is much the same as that for the existence of firms in economic theory, and rests on the presence of contracting costs, information costs and economies of scale and scope. Essentially, the case for integrating design, construction, finance, operation and management is that firms can coordinate these functions at lower cost than can government.

Daniels and Trebilcock also address an issue which could be significant for the future of PPPs – namely, the potential for opportunistic behaviour. However, unlike some other articles in this collection, which are concerned about possible opportunism by the private party, Daniels and Trebilcock focus on the special status of the government as a party to the contract, which can pose distinct and quite vexing contractual difficulties. Two reasons are cited. First, governments can expressly abrogate contractual commitments and nullify contracts by passing legislation. Second, a whole range of government changes, for example environmental policy, health and safety provisions, transport, and regional development, can alter the franchise value of a concession to the private investor. The authors consider the implication of these potential sources for government interference, and argue that the conversion of PPPs from one-off events to repeated contracts by the institution of a continuous PPP programme would offer the best protection to non-government parties, since the government's reputation as a reliable contracting partner would lower the cost of future interactions and bring tangible future benefits.

Another solution involves the use of dispute resolution clauses in the contract, and this is the topic of Chapter 14, by Nicholas Gould. Dispute resolution mechanisms come into play when there is a change in circumstances, and involve three elements: 'in good faith' negotiations between the parties, determinations by an independent third party, and finally the right of parties to terminate the contract if the other provisions do not work, which, as Gould argues, may have consequences so severe as to encourage acceptance of third party recommendations. The issue of dispute resolution is particularly important in the case of contracts involving the public sector, as the service concerned is a public one, which cannot easily be interrupted while the negotiations are taking place. Thus the authority must step in, and in this respect retains ultimate responsibility for service delivery. As we noted earlier, this direct engagement makes a PPP different from conventional privatisation.

Trujillo, Cohen, Freixas and Sheehy in Chapter 15 explore the potential for 'unbundled mechanisms', a question considered in Chapter 13 by Daniels and Trebilcock and in Chapter 17 by Oliver Hart. Trujillo et al. focus on BOT-type projects such as toll roads, although they argue that many other PPPs could be developed with unbundled mechanisms. This is because the concentration of all responsibilities, such as design, building, management and financing, in a unique private entity (as in BOT toll roads) is a characteristic shared by conference centres, waste water treatment plants, communications systems, power facilities and so on. Such bundling of activities in a single entity or joint venture of several entities comes from the potential to realise economies of scale and scope along with innovations in design, pricing, risk sharing and so on when responsibility is assumed for the whole range of activities involved in a project. Often, however, the BOT concessionaires are joint ventures of a number of private companies which agree in advance to subcontract each of the different activities. The authors argue that two problems are thereby introduced. First, superior knowledge of one activity may not carry over to other activities; for example, good constructors may be teamed with not so good financiers. Second, competition is limited to those bodies which are part of the group. Companies, especially local entities, with, for example, good technical know how but poor financial capability, are unable to bid because the activities are jointly, rather than separately, auctioned. Transparency and competitiveness in the bidding process is lost, or more correctly traded-off for innovation opportunities, which they argue may not always be the most efficient solution.

Thus Trujillo et al. examine the case for unbundling. They argue that the costs of unbundling (for example, creating different entities, and monitoring the specifications in the different stages) may be considerable, but may be offset by an improved allocation of risk. This begs the question of how efficiently risks are allocated in practice with PPPs, considered in Part VI and discussed below. There is also the question of who is to handle the unbundling. The authors consider two possibilities. One is for a public sector agency to play the role of the concessionaire in BOT projects. In this case, competition is imposed when the various activities are subcontracted. However, the lack of qualified public sector institutions capable of articulating the project and supervising the private sector participants limits this option.

For this reason, the authors examine an alternative of expanding the role of the private sector in performing the coordinating function. In effect, the public agency, rather than carrying out the coordinating role itself, would appoint a private company to carry out the job. This private agent would, subject to the conditions established by the public sponsor, implement the process of subcontracting and monitor the contracts, while simultaneously structuring and launching the joint venture or special purpose vehicle needed for financing. That is, a private company acts as a service company for the project but without assuming the project risks. Of course, it can be argued that this 'unbundling' is essentially what happens in any case since the concessionaire rarely assumes all the project risks. Many are put out to a range of specialist providers, while the assumption of overall responsibility prior to this transfer gives the concession winner the appropriate incentives to do the job properly, which may not be present to the same degree when there is a nexus between principal (the public body) and the agent (the private sector service company coordinating entity). Also, a feature of PPPs is that risks are usually shared between the private sector and the public sector, with the government 'taking back' some risks for which private bodies would charge 'too much'. For this risk allocation process, the public sector entity might prefer to negotiate with a single body rather with a host of individual subcontractors, either directly or by proxy through the coordinating company. These are some of the issues examined in detail in later chapters, but the general framework is laid out in the next chapter.

The framework proposed by Abdel-Aziz and Russell in Chapter 16 revolves around rights, obligations and liabilities. This three-fold classification encompasses key features of any PPP project. Under the agreement, various rights are ceded to the private entity in return for it taking on and undertaking a specified set of obligations. One set of rights relate to possession, when the public sector transfers ownership of land and property in its possession to the private sector. The other right refers to revenues when the government entity gives the private sector body access to revenues during the operational stage of the contract. In return, the private firm is obliged to undertake certain functions. They relate *inter alia* to planning, design, construction, improvement, operation, maintenance, financing, environmental aspects (biophysical), labour issues and regional and other business impacts. Finally, the liabilities dimension refers to the actual and potential liabilities and risks shared or assumed by parties under the agreement. Included under this heading are general liability (tort, third party and facility damage), liability for taxation, and risk liabilities. The latter arises from the risk allocation process, and the risk 'take back' by the private sector, described earlier.

Using this framework, Abdel-Aziz and Russell examine a number of projects. These are the Channel Tunnel, the Second Severn Bridge (UK), the Western Highway Alignment, Nova Scotia (Canada), Northumberland Strait Crossing, New Brunswick (Canada), State Route 91, California (USA), and legislation for toll roads in Minnesota and Virginia. On the basis of their investigation, they provide a checklist of recommendations as to attributes of the three dimensions that need to be specified in documentation for PPPs. In particular, the authors stress the need for a clear articulation of government requirements in such documents and public–private partnership agreements in order to reduce the amount of supplemental materials issued to request for proposals, help consortia respond with proposals that can fit the requirements, and reduce the amount of time spent in negotiations and perhaps the need for contract amendments to reflect marketplace realities not considered at earlier stages. But, unlike in the traditional procurement process, in which all requirements are the responsibility of government, under a PPP the attributes of a requirement are temporarily or permanently assigned to another entity.

Chapter 17 returns us to the issue of 'bundling'. A defining characteristic of a PPP is not in fact private sector involvement in infrastructure, but 'bundling'. Under traditional procurement, it is possible for assets to be designed and built by the private sector under separate contracts, and then the management of the facilities outsourced to private entities under another contract. With a PPP, the asset and service contracts are combined, and there is integration within a private sector party of all (or most of) the functions of design, building, financing, operating and maintenance of the facility in question, often in the form of a special purpose vehicle created for the specific project.

Oliver Hart in Chapter 17 develops a theoretical model to examine the economic efficiency of 'bundling' from an 'incomplete' contracting perspective, in which imperfections arise because it is hard to forsee and contract about uncertain future events. PPPs are generally entered into for a lengthy period of time, and are developed in an environment of uncertainty. As such they exhibit the characteristics of 'incomplete' contracts, and their usefulness as integrated arrangements hinges on the nature of contracting costs. Hart's model compares a 'bundled' contract for facility construction and service provision with 'unbundled' conventional public procurement in which the government first contracts with a builder to construct the facility and then later contracts with another private sector party to operate and run the facility. The choice between the two alternatives, bundled versus unbundled, turns on whether it is easier to write contracts on service provision than on building provision. This leads to a straightforward result. Conventional provision ('unbundling') is better if the quality of the building can be clearly specified, whereas the quality of the service cannot. In contrast, PPP is better if the quality of the service can be well specified in the initial contract (or, more generally, there are good performance indicators that can be used to reward or penalize the service provider), whereas the quality of the building cannot.

Parker and Hartley in Chapter 18 start from transactions cost theory. What they add to this is the idea, discussed in earlier chapters of this section, that long-term contracting is necessarily relational. Reputation (based on past behaviour) and trust (based on expectations about future behaviour) are central to the economics of contracting, and acting in 'good faith' can to some degree substitute for detailed contractual control mechanisms. This framework is then applied to the case of PPP contracts in the UK defence industry, which has been a leading user of PPP/PFI initiatives since the mid-1990s. There are claims that PPP contracts for UK defence services have resulted in cost savings of between 5 per cent and 40 per cent compared with conventional public procurement. However, Parker and Hartley are concerned as to whether these apparent cost savings will be realised over the projects' whole-of-life due to the inherent uncertainties of long-term contracting. Notably, the UK is the market which has had the most intensive use of PPPs, and the study by Parker and Hartley leads us to the next section, which examines various perspectives on the UK experience.

## The UK Experience

The Private Finance Initiative (PFI) is the UK government programme to increase the involvement of the private sector in the provision of public services. Introduced by the Conservative government in November 1992, it continued under Labour in 1997. The scheme has been widely discussed and extensively examined in the literature. From its inception in 1992 until September 2001, 450 PFI contracts have been signed with a total value of just over £20 billion, with expenditure commitments extending well beyond 2026. PFI deals have ranged from small projects, such as the £100,000 Littlehampton Community School ITC facilities project in West Sussex, to mega construction projects, such as the London Underground. The Department of Health has signed the most PFI deals, 105, with a total value of just over £2.5 billion. The largest of these in monetary terms is the £404 million University College London Hospitals NHS Trust PFI project. In value terms 40 per cent of projects has been accounted for by the Department of Transport, Local Government and the Regions, which has signed contracts totalling £8.2 billion (Allen, 2001).

In Chapter 19, Owen and Merna consider the origins of the PFI and examine its conceptual basis. The PFI is a form of PPP. Like other PPPs it combines public procurement policies and long-term contracting out. Unlike many other PPPs, a PFI project has the private sector contractor arranging finance. Thus the most usual form of PFI is a DBFO under which the private sector designs, builds, finances and operates a facility according to 'output ' specifications determined by public sector contracting parties. With traditional procurement methods, the private sector builds most public facilities. The PFI enables, in addition, design, financing, operation and management to be carried out in the private sector. Nevertheless the public sector retains a substantial role in PFI projects, either as the main purchaser of services or as an essential enabler of the project. While the public sector does not own an asset, such as a hospital or school, it pays the PFI contractor a stream of committed revenue payments for the use of facilities over the contract period. Once the contract has expired, ownership of the asset either remains with the private sector contractor, or is returned to the public sector.

In effect, the essence of a PFI deal is in separating the asset from the service it produces. Procurement strategy was driven originally by the need to acquire the asset. But the government really only procured assets in order to get the flow of services from them. Political thinking nowadays places emphasis on the services supplied to the community rather than the asset, and PFI is about procuring a service. Having a private provider of a capital asset gives public bodies the option to purchase services without the need for the critical capital investment.

PFI, it has been noted, differs from some other PPPs, and traditional public procurement, by virtue of the requirement that the private sector finances the projects. Given that the extra cost of private sector funding *vis-à-vis* public borrowing is likely to be between 1 to 3 percentage points, some have argued that PPPs/PFI can never be good value for money. Others, while accepting that they can be value for money because the private sector is able to deliver cost savings in other aspects of the project (design, operation, management), nevertheless concede that private borrowing costs are higher.

Grout in Chapter 20 and Klein in Chapter 21 question this proposition. Both conclude that the 'lower government borrowing cost' argument is seriously flawed. Their argument runs as follows, and in some ways is analogous to the famous Modigliani-Miller theorem about the cost of capital. Modigliani and Miller argued that the 'true' value of a firm was independent of how finance was raised, and thus the capital structure of the enterprise. Somewhat analogously, both Grout and Klein argue that what is important is the 'true' risk of the project, which is independent of whether the public sector provides the funding. What differs is that the private provision of finance, that is, the PFI route, explicitly builds the risk into the cost of funds. By contrast, the traditional public procurement process masks the risk; the government can fund the project at a risk-free rate independent of the actual risk position. As John Kay (cited in Klein) has remarked: 'we would lend to the government even if we thought it would burn the money or fire it off into space' (Kay, 1993, p. 63).

But why can government borrow at a risk-free rate of interest? This reflects that (and again we quote John Kay) 'the cost of debt both to governments and to private firms is influenced predominantly by the perceived risk of default rather than an assessment of the quality of returns from the specific investment' (p. 63). For private debt there is a risk of default. For government debt, there is little or none (in the case of the UK government), because the government can raise the taxes to meet the obligation. The government is risk-free in the eyes of the investor lending funds because the risk is transferred to the taxpayers, who bear the cost through the risk of higher future tax payments and different consumption outcomes. In Klein's words, taxpayers have assumed a contingent liability for which they are not remunerated. This residual risk imposed upon taxpayers is a cost, which ought to enter into any cost–benefit analysis. If this were done, the real cost of government borrowing would be the same as the private sector, if the underlying risk of the projects were the same.

Grout goes on to consider the pricing of risk under PFI for the value-for-money test of public versus private provision (which test is argued to be biased against private sector provision) as well as the incentives to the private sector to build and provide the right type of service. He argues the case for the desirability of a system in which the same entity builds and sells the services, but is only remunerated for the successful supply of services, as opposed to an 'unbundled' structure in which one private body builds and another manages. However, this conjunction of activities requires that the service structure can be specified in advance. The PFI approach seems most appropriate where services contracts are relatively easy to write but build contracts are not due to design changes, uncertainty, unexpected events and a high level of disputation. As we saw earlier, these are circumstances which led to the concept of partnering in construction. But the more general implication is that PFI may not be for all sectors and project types.

In Chapter 22, Hall picks up the last point as well when he speaks of the 'PFI-ability' of projects. Those with high PFI-ability are those where the quantity and quality of output can be accurately measured and reflected either in actual or shadow revenue streams, while having low risk and complexity and being sufficient large in scale. Transport schemes satisfy these criteria, since user charges or shadow tolls can easily be applied. Health and education projects, he argues, do not meet such criteria, leading to concerns that the institution of the PFI regime will lead to under-investment in particular types of social capital.

Like other writers, Hall considers the implications of the higher borrowing costs of private sector bodies (while noting that private financing makes explicit costs that under public funding are 'hidden but no less real'). In these circumstances, achieving value for money relies on the private entities realising cost savings large enough to overcome their handicap. Hall seeks to ascertain whether this is indeed the case, in terms of innovation, competition and risk management. First, with respect to innovation, Hall finds evidence that private firms made much greater use of third party revenue sources to lower costs on PFI projects. Second, on the issue of whether PFI achieves value for money by introducing competition into public sector activities, the answer is more difficult. Certainly this would seem to be the case for the outsourcing of operation and maintenance contracts. But PFI, like outsourcing, introduces competition for the market as opposed to competition within the market, and there is the question of how many bids are enough. This problem, in Hall's view, is compounded by the high cost of bidding for PFI deals which means that inviting too many firms to submit bids may simply result in a large number of uncompetitive bids and reduce effective competition.

On the third point, that of risk management efficiencies, Hall argues that value for money from risk transfer comes from providing the private sector operator with the appropriate incentives to generate cost savings. Such incentives derive from payment mechanisms employed in an environment where the private contractor is left free to innovate in project design and strike an appropriate balance between construction costs and maintenance levels. The payment mechanism can encourage private firms to minimise lifetime costs, avoid delays in construction and commissioning, and undertake adequate maintenance. Evidence is presented which shows that such gains were obtained in many projects.

However, even strong supporters of PFI accept that not every project goes according to plan. The issue is whether there are systematic factors at work, and lessons to learn from the experience. Transport and health are two areas in which PFI projects have been most concentrated, and the next two articles focus upon these sectors.

Mayston in Chapter 23 looks at the impact of a PFI programme in the UK National Health Service, and has severe misgivings about a number of aspects. His concerns may be summarised as follows:

1. NHS decision-makers have not been able to choose freely between publicly and privately provided infrastructure, and have been corralled into more expensive PFI options because of cuts to direct public funding budgets.
2. There can be no presumption that private entities possess better design capabilities than the accumulated experience of the NHS itself, and no reason to assume that the chosen private contractor will be the most appropriate for facilities management or for providing finance (the 'bundling' issue).
3. The high degree of secrecy and confidentiality surrounding many PFI deals has hindered the process of public accountability and accounting for the contracts.
4. Involvement of major construction companies in the PFI creates a bias toward new building rather than maintenance and refurbishment of existing NHS capital facilities.
5. Tendering, negotiation, transactions (contracting) and monitoring costs are high relative to the value of many NHS schemes. Consultancy fees charged to the NHS add to the cost of PFI arrangements.
6. Payments under PFI schemes involve significant fixed payments to cover interest charges and capital repayment. These debt repayment charges introduced into the finances of health authorities limit the later flexibility of NHS bodies, by 'mortgaging the future' in return for immediate gains.
7. Insolvency of the special purpose vehicle created by private sector sponsors to deliver PFI services might result in lengthy litigation with no guarantee of financial redress, leaving the public authority to 'pick up the pieces'.

In considering these concerns, a number of general points can be made. First, as is emphasised in a number of articles included in this volume, PPPs separate service provision from asset ownership, and offer different financing options to public service managers, much as leasing facilities or hire purchase enable payments to be spread over time as asset services are consumed. The economic liberal will see these new instruments and options as welfare improving, in the sense that additional choices are now available, even if not all public sector managers make sensible decisions about their use. Second, the issue is not just experience and knowledge of NHS operations and practices but also importantly one of incentives. PPPs are no magic cure-all for public services provision but often simply a way of providing decision-makers with the appropriate economic incentives.

Third, Mayston raises many causes for concern but does not assess available evidence as to the overall success or failure of the PFI in health projects, although others (for example, Pollock et al., 1997, Pollock, 2000) have made case studies, arguing that the PFI has not delivered value for money in health services. In the case of PPPs in general, the National Audit Office has produced value for money reports on 15 projects, 7 of which (including a hospital project) were evaluated against a public sector comparator. On average, the cost saving was 20 per cent (NAO, 2001). Nevertheless, Allen (2001) considers that such averages conceal considerable differences across PFI types, with road and prison projects achieving 'reasonable efficiency gains', while those for schools and hospitals show 'minimal gains' (p. 32). This difference is attributed to two factors. The first is that for road and prison projects, there is no partition of core and ancillary services, enabling the private contractor to make design and build innovations since they will also operate and maintain services. In PFI health projects, core and ancillary remain segmented, perhaps reducing some of the potential for innovation. The other reason is that for roads and prisons there is a single, central government agency handling the contracting, whereas with health and education private sponsors must deal with a number of bodies, such as local education authorities and school governing councils.

Finally, it has to be appreciated that health and schooling continue to be highly charged political areas in the UK. Many people remain attached to the ideal of universal 'free' hospital and medical care, and look askance at the cost of private medicine in the United States. Mayston sees the PFI as a continuation of 'contracting out' in which the ownership and management of major capital assets such as hospitals will be in private hands. He sees parallels between PFI and earlier rounds of asset sales in the public sector under privatisation, and regards the PFI as a further step along the path that one writer described as the 'hollowing out of the state' (Rhodes, 1994). However, the dilemma that cannot be avoided is that public funding has not kept up with advances in medical technology, and this has led to a budgetary crisis in the system. In such an environment, if PFI can deliver genuine cost savings or efficiency gains then the experiment seems worthwhile. Yet PFI cannot overcome the basic issue of 'affordability', which arises because the 'Trusts' expectations exceed the realities of their budgets' (Grimsey and Graham, 1997, p. 220).

While the application of PPPs to the health sector in the UK seems likely to remain controversial, there is greater acceptance of the technique for transport, especially under the shadow toll schemes applied in the UK. Mustafa in Chapter 24 reviews the British experience of PPPs in this area. According to Mustafa, at least three problems have emerged. One is the failure of the technical innovative input by the private sector to reach its potential. This is because the private entity may be excluded from participating in the early stages of design when the parameters shaping the service are developed. Its input is then limited to the detailed design and use of material, rather than the overall conception. A second problem is that PFI proceeds on a project-by-project basis rather than on a sectoral level, making the current system more suitable for large one-off schemes. A third difficulty is the shortage of equity funds, resulting in financing with a high debt-equity ratio and greater associated risk. These are the three issues that Mustafa addresses.

Mustafa proposes a new framework based around what he terms the Public-Private Cooperative (PPC), aimed at the sector level rather than the project level. PPC is conceived as a joint arrangement between a public sector body (such as, in the case of roads, the Highways Agency), and a consortium of long-term investors. The investors are classified in two categories: those investors solely interested in long-term equity investment, for example, pension funds, and those investors that are interested in long-term investment in addition to having the technical skills in construction and/or operation of the facilities. The idea is that the investors set up an investment fund to make equity investments in specified types of projects within a particular sector. The investors and the department would be jointly involved in the early stages of project identification, planning, and feasibility study. It would thus provide an opportunity to assess which projects can and cannot be financed and provide a setting for a more realistic view of the risk apportionment between the public and private sectors at an early stage of a project's life. This would allow the PPC to facilitate a sound assessment of individual projects based on their business and economic merits, providing the opportunity of weeding out projects that are not fundable through PFI at an early stage. In this way more successful projects would be brought forward, while at the same time expanding equity funds in the projects.

In Chapter 25, the final article in this section, Grout examines at length an issue raised in his earlier contribution (Chapter 20), and that of Klein (Chapter 21), namely the discount rate used for evaluating public projects. What rate ought to be used for PPPs is a vexed question that raises issues of the treatment of risk and uncertainty in the cash flows being discounted and compared with those of the public sector comparator (the hypothetical measure of what it would cost if the project were to be conventionally procured). Risk can be allowed for either in adjustments to the cash flows (the numerator) or by incorporating a risk premium into the discount rate (the denominator). In the latter case, there is a tendency for governments to use the same discount rate for a project whether it is publicly provided or whether it is to be provided to the government by the private sector through a PPP. Grout argues that the standard practice of using the same discount rate in tests between public sector provision and PPPs is inappropriate because it prejudices private sector provision and leads to excessive reliance on public procurement. His argument runs as follows. When public sector provision is being valued a discount rate is applied to a cost cash flow. This cash flow represents the cost of building the facility if it is done in the public sector. In contrast, for valuing the private sector provision a discount rate is applied to a stream that constitutes an outlay for the public sector but is a revenue item to the private entity and is being valued from the revenue side. With a PPP, this revenue stream is not the equivalent cost of building the facility. It is the cash flow associated with the flow of benefits valued at the price in the contract. There is no reason to suppose that the risk characteristics are equivalent for these two cash flows. Indeed, Grout argues that there is every reason to suppose that they are not, because in general costs are less risky than revenues (particularly when the revenues depend on services of a suitable quality being provided). Under what appear to be plausible conditions, he contends that a higher discount rate should be used for the PPP than for the public sector equivalent. Failure to do so will suggest that private provision is less efficient than public since the present value of private provision will be overestimated relative to public procurement.

While Grout's argument is conducted at a theoretical level, his proposition hints at what are fundamental differences in terms of risk between the cash flows built up for the public sector comparator and those bid as service payments as a PPP. When comparing the two the public sector agency will need to make professional judgements as to the value for money to be derived from contracting with the private sector and the risks which that route involves, while not ignoring that there are also very large risks and considerable uncertainties in the public procurement route.

## Experience Elsewhere

Earlier we noted that the variety of forms that partnerships had taken in the US covering both 'hard' and 'soft' and 'economic' and 'social' applications. We begin this section of the volume with some examples from the US involving 'soft economic' (R&D, technology), 'hard social' (prisons) and 'hard economic' (highways).

The US government has a long history of involvement in supporting private sector activities in R&D, and PPPs are the latest manifestation of the involvement. Stiglitz and Wallsten in Chapter 26 explain the appeal of the partnership approach: there is a relationship with shared objectives in which each partner is assigned specific responsibilities and given incentives to fulfil those responsibilities. In the technology area, PPPs have taken two forms. One is government funding of industrial R&D. The other is when government and industry scientists work together for common aims. Underpinning both is the belief that government is not very effective in picking winners (that is, choosing good projects) and managing research. Hence the technology partnerships entail government giving support for research that is initiated and undertaken primarily by the private sector. The problem with this approach is that the government must still make a pick, in this case from projects thrown up to it. Stiglitz and Wallsten question the choice criteria that have been employed. Too often, they argue, government has funded the best proposals it receives. Instead it should be seeking to identify winning projects that would be privately unprofitable but socially beneficial because of high spillovers. That is, government should not choose the best projects, but fund the best from those that cannot be funded elsewhere. To this end, they provide a framework for evaluating the effectiveness of a partnership.

An alternative way around the 'picking winners' problem is outlined by Apen, Benicewicz, and Laia in Chapter 27. Drawing on a number of years' experience in managing government–industry collaborative research projects, they propose a new form of PPP – the establishment of a non-profit organisation to manage and operate a manufacturing or technology extension programme for a state or federal government. The PPP would act as an intermediary between private industry and federal laboratories by matching, acquiring, and efficiently utilising government-developed technologies for private industry. This effort could target medium to large businesses and require a cost for admission that could be paid in resources, such as manpower and facilities. Somewhat different strategies are required for small business enterprises. Nevertheless, they envisage that the federal or state government would directly award the intermediating PPP a contract for managing, operating, and coordinating a public–private initiative. The contract would include full funding and support for a series of projects to be subcontracted to laboratories and various R&D organisations, and the PPP would act as the project coordinator between private industry and the government and directly fund projects. Since the PPP would directly fund the project at the government facility, it would own the intellectual property generated. This feature is critical because it will enable the PPP to license the intellectual property to the participating company in a limited field-of-use arrangement. When the technology is successfully utilised by the private sector, a percentage of the revenues generated by the company would be returned to the PPP. Apen et al. see the advantages of having a broker between industry and the federally funded research institutions as being the proper management of the expectations of both parties, the careful evaluation of the applicability of government technologies to commercial markets, and the reduction of bureaucratic red tape.

Chapter 28 returns to the role of PPPs in transport infrastructure provision. PPPs have proven to be readily adaptable to this area. Nevertheless, the issue of financing remains. In Britain and some other countries, shadow tolls have been preferred over explicit charges upon users, with the stream of revenue to cover the service provision drawn from the general public purse. Fuel tax and other vehicle-related charges upon users are treated as general-purpose taxes. This is not the case in the United States, where motor fuel, vehicle excise taxes and licence fees are dedicated to highways. As revenues from these taxes have fallen behind demand for highway construction and improvements to infrastructure, governments have been led to examine a variety of methods to augment highway finance. Lockwood in the chapter reviews the various highway-financing methods and the characteristics of the different techniques, and gives examples of the innovative financing methods employed. PPPs feature extensively in these, involving build-own-operate (BOO), build-operate-transfer (BOT) and build-transfer-operate (BTO) arrangements. ISTEA (the Intermodal Surface Transportation Efficiency Act) gave emphasis to PPPs for the construction of toll facilities by enabling the co-mingling of state loans, grants or federal aid with private capital. Lockwood argues that this ability to combine federal aid and private investment produces a broadened range of funding options through loan/grant mixes to increase the feasibility of otherwise infeasible toll road projects. He sees this blending of credits, support mechanisms, and risk sharing as the future trend of US highway development.

The building and operation of prison facilities has been a feature of PPPs in a number of countries, including the US, UK, and Australia. However, there is a significant difference in the application in the US *vis-à-vis* the other countries. In the UK and Australia, for example, the construction and operation contract (for example, DBFO) is negotiated in advance between the private party and the relevant government body. Although some of the private prisons in the US have emerged as a result of contracts with the state in which they are located, the more common situation is that a private firm builds a prison in a state and simultaneously attempts to negotiate contracts with the home state – or any other state, county or federal entity – for prisoners. This is a point of some considerable resentment since most states cannot prevent a private business from building a prison in the state and contracting with the federal government or with other states to take their prisoners. Unless a state passes legislation prohibiting the prison business, it is subject to finding such a private prison within its borders at some point in the future. Then its citizens might bear the cost and inconvenience of prisoner breakouts resulting from the incarceration policies of adjoining states. Some state legislation requires that private prisons take out large insurance policies to reimburse state agencies that may have to intervene when an escape or a disturbance occurs.

Anne Schneider examines these, and other, aspects of the operation of private prisons in the US in Chapter 29. The remuneration to the private prisons comes from a per diem charge, either on the number of prisoners it houses for a particular entity or on the number of places it has reserved for that jurisdiction, so that the state pays the business to manage the prisoners. Most of the state contracts require that private firms offer the service at 5 per cent to 10 per cent below what it would have cost the state. Statistical studies surveyed by Schneider suggest that there is a cost advantage ('slight') of private prisons over state facilities. However as Schneider notes, the studies virtually never explain how or why the private prison manages to have lower costs even though they have the added responsibility of making a profit. There is a general perception that the reduced costs are at the expense of employee salaries, and this possibility makes them unpopular with the public sector unions – a feature shared with unions in the UK and Australia. Overall, Schneider is ambivalent about the phenomenon of private prisons, noting that there is something of a 'pendulum effect' whereby dissatisfaction with public prisons leads to experimentation with private prisons, and a few bad experiences with them leads away from private facilities. As she notes, a pendulum pattern in public and private delivery systems is perhaps only to be expected because prisons are institutions that cannot be managed as effectively as expected by the media, political entities, or the general public regardless of whether they are entirely under government control or whether they involve extensive privatisation.

Water and sanitation is another area that has featured in PPPs. A later chapter (36) considers a case study of a wastewater treatment facility in Scotland. Chapter 30 reviews the experience of PPPs involving water and sanitation in developing countries. It is found that a variety of models have been used, ranging from operation and management (O&M), to lease, to long-term arrangements such as build-operate-transfer (BOT) to build-own-operate (BOO). Then there are what is termed full-utility concessions and full privatisation by means of asset sale. Haarmeyer and Mody survey the allocation of responsibilities in the various approaches, along with the cash flow and risk profiles of the different models. They note that there is no one 'best' approach – a variety of models are available, depending on the political and economic circumstances. An important issue they raise is how PPPs involving water differ from those in other sectors. The authors argue that water projects are distinguished by there being little or no scope for introducing direct competition in any of the main operational aspects of treatment, transmission or distribution. Accordingly, they conclude that it is important to have a competitive and transparent tendering process to avoid political expropriation and contracting problems.

Water provision is the local public service with the greatest PPP element in France. Anne Ribault in Chapter 31 reports that 75 per cent of the population was in 1995 provided with water under PPP contracts. In fact, two PPP operators, Lyonnaise des Eaux and Vivendi, controlled 62 per cent of water distribution, 36 per cent of sewerage disposal, 75 per cent of urban central heating, 60 per cent of refuse treatment, 55 per cent of cable operation, and 36 per cent of refuse collection, all under PPPs. In most countries, these figures would be remarkable. They are not in France because PPPs have been around for a long time – dating back to the 17th century. Most of the railway network, water provision facilities and street lighting were developed under PPPs. In France, most PPPs are performed under *concession* contracts (essentially BOT and DBOT contracts) or *affermage* (lease) contracts (which cover design and building, or operation, but do not embrace project financing). Both have a long history, which shows strong growth until the 1930s, when they were supplanted by public utilities, some revival in the 1950s and 1960s, and a marked resurgence in the 1990s. Ribault surveys this experience and the current position in which almost all public services in France are subject to PPPs. On the basis of this analysis, she draws some conclusions, the main ones being that too little attention is given to evaluating incentives in contracts and incentives within contracts. For these reasons, she sees advantages in having a small government agency deal with PPP contracting. This is a lesson that has been learnt also by others. A central PPP unit has been instituted in the Netherlands and some of the Australian states.

## Risk Management

A PPP contract is a mechanism for allocating risks between the various parties to a project, and all need to be aware of the risks and have a risk management strategy in place. Of the five papers in this section, two look at general issues related to risk management while the other three consider risk management in practice based on three case studies.

Earlier in this introduction we argued that PPPs grew out of project financing and project management techniques employed in the construction industry, and were influenced by the concept of partnering developed for construction projects. It is thus appropriate that we consider first the treatment of risks in construction projects. Ward, Chapman and Curtis, in Chapter 32, start from the premise that project risk management is improved if risks are identified and evaluated in a systematic way, and then allocated to the parties best able to control them. They argue that willingness of contracting parties to take on risks is an important consideration in the allocation of project risks, and then go on to analyse in turn the general factors shaping the willingness of a contracting party to take on risks, the willingness of the client to retain risk, and the contractor's willingness to take on risks. In the case of the contractor, the willingness to assume risks is reflected in the premium charged for doing so, and in this respect the authors liken the contractor to an insurer and suggest pricing rules analogous to insurance practice.

Forshaw in Chapter 33 traces the development of the risk allocation process that lies at the heart of PFI in the UK to a reappraisal in the mid-1980s of the methodology of public procurement by means of design and build contracts, which required project appraisal to evaluate:

1. capital cost of any buildings or equipment that need to be replaced over the appraisal period;
2. residual values of capital assets at the end of the appraisal period;
3. operating costs over the whole term of the appraisal;
4. other costs or benefits which can be valued in money terms, in the form of revenues, cost savings or non-market outputs;
5. measures or descriptions of those costs or benefits that cannot be valued in money terms.

Once this agenda was instituted, public procurement necessarily became an instrument that also measured risk, since different outcomes had to be tested and examined. It was a short step to the conclusion that public procurement would benefit in value for money terms if certain risks could be transferred to other parties. But, at the same time, value for money would suffer if risk transfer was to be taken too far. The PFI risk transfer graph and the idea of an efficient extent of risk transfer was born. Achieving such an allocation requires a case-by-case analysis of the risks involved – risks relating to construction, operations, upgrades, quality, demand and the financing of the project. These elements feature in the three cases which follow.

The first case study project is a light rail transit (LRT) system in Karachi. The case study is provided by Faruqi and Smith, and is contained in Chapter 34. In the article, the authors first outline the nature of LRT systems and the major cost components. They then outline the revenue streams. Based on an examination of 48 urban mass transport systems, they find that on average 43 per cent of operating costs are recovered from user fares, the rest coming from grants, rents and taxes. In the Karachi case, the government proposed a 40 per cent grant. The contract was a BOT type concession contract, with a concession period of 30 years. Using simulation analysis, the authors investigate the risk to project returns from a number of cost and revenue factors identified as major sources of risk. The simulation results employ the now standard techniques of sensitivity analysis and Monte Carlo analysis. Overall, they find that the government provision of a grant in the form of a subordinated loan is vital for the project's viability, by reducing financing costs, and that delay to the delivery of the rolling stock posed the greatest potential risk to the project returns. On this basis, they recommend that the issues of vehicle design and specification be given attention early in the construction phase, so as to minimise this risk element.

In the second case study, Raphael Arndt in chapter 35 examines risk allocation in the Melbourne City Link Project (MCL). The project has a number of notable features. First, it is Australia's largest ever privately funded infrastructure project, and is undertaken on a BOOT basis. Second, it involves the construction of about 22 kilometres of road in central Melbourne, including a 6.5 km tunnel under the River Yarra. Third, operating under a 'user pay' system, collection of tolls is fully automated, using electronic tagging and e-payment systems. A feature of Arndt's case study is his detailed analysis of the project risks, and the allocation between the parties. Some earlier BOOT projects in Australia have been criticised for leaving too much risk with the public sector, and thus the taxpayer. Significantly, in this case, the operating company Transurban has explicitly accepted the risk of traffic demand, which is considered to be the most critical risk to the viability of the project post-construction. After comparing this project with others, Arndt concludes that the MCL agreement has shifted more risk to the private sector than in any previous Australian toll road. It has also created more symmetry in the acceptance of risk by the project parties.

Finally, in Chapter 36, Grimsey and Lewis provide a case study of a wastewater treatment facility in Scotland provided under PPP, effectively a DBFO, with a services contract over 30 years. Their study of the project explicitly considers the risks from the viewpoint of each of the major parties to the contract: the procurer, the sponsors, and the senior lenders. Sensitivity and Monte Carlo methods are used to assess the risk profiles of the different groups. From this analysis, it is concluded that the project delivers value for money to the procurer, provides reasonable likelihood of satisfactory returns to the sponsors, and is robust enough to generate the cash flows to pay off lenders.

## References

Allen, G . (2001), *The Private Finance Initiative (PFI)*, House of Commons Research Paper 01/117, House of Commons Library, December.

Crowley, L.G. and M.A. Karim (1995), 'Conceptual Model of Partnering', *Journal of Management in Engineering*, Sept/Oct, 33–39.
Engel, E., R. Fischer and A. Galetovic (1997), 'The Chilean Infrastructure Concessions Program – Evaluation, Lessons and Prospects for the Future', Universidad de Chile, Center for Applied Economics (CEA), Discussion Paper No 60 (September).
Engel, E., R. Fischer and A. Galetovic (2001), 'Least-Present-Value-of-Revenue Auctions and Highway Franchising', *Journal of Political Economy*, **109** (5), 993–1020.
Grimsey, D. and R. Graham (1997), 'PFI in the NHS', *Engineering, Construction and Architectural Management*, **4** (3), 215–31.
Grimsey, D. and M.K. Lewis (2002), 'Accounting for Public-Private Partnerships', *Accounting Forum*, **26** (3), 245–70.
Grimsey, D. and M.K. Lewis (2004), *Public Private Partnerships. The Worldwide Revolution in Infrastructure Provision and Project Finance*, Cheltenham, UK and Northampton, MA, USA: Edward Elgar.
Heald, D. and N. Geaughan (1997), 'Accounting for the Private Finance Initiative', *Public Money & Management*, **17** (3), 11–16.
Hodges, R. and H. Mellett (1999), 'Accounting for the Private Finance Initiative in the United Kingdom National Health Service', *Financial Accountability & Management*, **15** (3) & (4), August/November, 275–90.
Hodges, R. and H. Mellett (2002), 'Investigating standard setting: accounting for the UK's private finance initiative', *Accounting Forum*, **26** (2), 126–51.
International Finance Corporation (1999), *Project Finance in Developing Countries*, Washington DC: International Finance Corporation.
Kay, J. (1993), 'Efficiency and Private Capital in the Provision of Infrastructure', in *Infrastructure Policies for the 1990s*, Paris: Organisation for Economic Co-operation and Development, 55–73.
Macneil, I.R. (1974), 'The many futures of contracts', *Southern California Law Review*, **47**, 691–816.
NAO (2001), NAO Value for Money Reports on PPP/PFI, www.nao.gov.uk/publications/vfmsublist/vfm_ppp.htm, National Audit Office, 13 December.
Pollock, A.M. (2000), 'PFI is bad for your health', *Public Finance*, 6 October, 30–31.
Pollock, A.M., M. Dunnigan, D. Gaffney, A. Macfarlane and F. Azeem Majeed (1997), 'What happens when the private sector plans hospital services for the NHS: three case studies under the private finance initiative', *British Medical Journal*, **314**, 1266–71.
Rhodes, R. (1994), 'The Hollowing Out of the State: The Changing Nature of the Public Sector in Britain', *Political Quarterly*, **65** (2), 138–58.
Rosenau, P.V. (2000), *Public–Private Policy Partnerships*, Cambridge, MA: The MIT Press.
Wilson, R.A., A.D. Songer and J. Diekmann (1995), 'Partnering: more than a workshop, a catalyst for change', *Journal of Management in Engineering*, Sept/Oct, 40–45.

# Part I
# The Changing Market for Public Services

# [1]

# Public-Private Partnerships

Michael B. Gerrard

**What are public-private partnerships, and how do they differ from privatizations?**

PUBLIC-private partnerships (PPPs) are generally not "privatizations" in the sense that the latter term is most commonly used. (See Box 1.) A privatized business is one that was formerly owned by the public sector and is now owned by the private sector. It may operate in highly competitive markets—as, for example, an airline does—or it may hold a monopoly position and so require *active regulation* once it is transferred to the private sector—as a utility company does. In either case, the public sector is disengaged from the business.

By contrast, a PPP is a business relationship between the public and private sectors that is not patterned on either of these models. In the case of a Private Finance Initiative (PFI) project, the business is defined by a long-term contract in which public services to be delivered by the PPP—the *outputs*—are specified in great detail. In its form as an equity *joint venture* between the public and private sectors, a PPP is a business with certain public sector obligations set out in its constitutional documents or within contracts with the public sector.

In all cases, the scope of PPP business, and so its potential for profit, are constrained *contractually* rather than by market forces or the intervention of a statutory regulator. Normal private sector incentives for management still apply within a PPP, such as the need to earn an adequate return on capital, but the business is, in effect, *passively regulated* by virtue of the constraints placed upon it contractually and without the intervention of a regulator.

Moreover, within a PFI project, the public sector pays for services on behalf of the general public and retains ultimate responsibility for their delivery, whereas the private sector's role is limited to that of providing an improved delivery mechanism for the services. In the privatized utility model, by contrast, ultimate responsibility for service delivery is transferred to the private sector.

The essential role of the public sector in all PPPs—whether PFI project, joint venture, or other partnership structure—is to define the scope of business; specify priorities, targets, and outputs; and set the performance regime by which the management of the PPP is given incentives to deliver—and, in the case of PFI projects, also to pay for—the services. The essential role and responsibility of the private sector in all PPPs is to deliver the business objectives of the PPP on terms offering value for money to the public sector.

PPPs cannot always be well described as "partial privatizations." For example, there is an important distinction between, on the one hand, a private sector company in which the public sector holds a minority equity stake but has no influence on the objectives or operations of the company (which most would agree was well described as a *partial privatization*) and, on the other hand, a joint venture between public and private sectors whose business is constrained by public sector considerations or a service contract under which the public sector retains all its statutory functions. Both of these are forms of PPP.

The PPP model is very flexible and visible in a variety of forms. To date, most PPPs implemented in the United Kingdom have been concerned with the delivery of services to the public sector by a private sector partner under a long-term contract. Agreements for more than 400 such PFI projects, with a combined capital value of more than £19 billion, have now been signed in numerous sectors, including health, education, transport, defense, information technology, environmental protection, and government accommodation.

A successful PPP program will likely require a degree of reform by both the public and the private sector to create the right enabling environment. As such, there are clear drawbacks to a PPP approach to the extent that these reforms may delay implementation of investment. For the public sector, reforms would typically include a move from *input-* to *output-based* contracting, which may require significant investment in developing skills and guidance on best practices; enactment of enabling legislation—for example, to overcome issues of public sector vires (legal authority) and taxation of PPP contracts; and institutional reform to assist in prioritizing, providing resources for, and approving transactions. For the private sector, reforms may be required to build capacity in the provision of integrated whole-life-of-asset-based services to the public sector and to provide long-term (that is, 25 years or longer) project finance. Conversely, once the enabling environment has been established, the time taken to implement transactions and the fixed front-end implementation costs, for both public and private sectors, should steadily decrease, as has been the experience in the United Kingdom.

Box 1

**What is a public-private partnership?**

Public-private partnerships (PPPs) combine the deployment of private sector capital and, sometimes, public sector capital to improve public services or the management of public sector assets. By focusing on public service *outputs*, they offer a more sophisticated and cost-effective approach to the management of risk by the public sector than is generally achieved by traditional input-based public sector procurement.

The discipline of drawing up a PPP contract between a public sector client and a private sector contractor, on the one hand, obliges the public sector to articulate its long-term service needs (which could be the provision of, for example, transport, education, or health sector services) and, on the other hand, ensures that the private sector will not put its capital at risk to deliver these services unless and until it is satisfied about the PPP's long-term sustainable performance. As such, PPPs can be an effective antidote to the temptations of short-termism in both the public and the private sector.

Many build-operate-transfer–style concession agreements could be classified as PPPs, insofar as the public sector remains ultimately accountable for delivery to the public of the underlying services, which is the case under the U.K. government's Private Finance Initiative (PFI). Examples of such agreements within the United Kingdom include the provision of schools or hospital accommodations and supporting services under long-term contracts, where payment by the public sector client (authority) to the private sector service provider (contractor) is spread over the term of the contract (for example, 30 years) and, furthermore, where payment is made only to the extent that the required outputs (service standards) are maintained, year after year.

PPPs are certainly not an easy procurement option for the public sector, nor do they offer a universal solution. However, they do provide a flexible framework within which the skills and resources of the private sector can be mobilized to provide better-quality, sustainable, and more cost-effective public services in the right circumstances. (See Box 2.)

Evidence to date within the United Kingdom, which shows new investments in public services made through PPPs being largely completed ahead of schedule and within budget, supports the conclusion that while it may initially be more demanding for the public sector to contract on this basis, very worthwhile gains are available.

Supplementing the flow of PFI projects in the United Kingdom are a growing number of PPPs designed to make more efficient use of *existing* public sector assets rather than deliver public sector services by constructing *new* assets. These PPPs concern assets—which could be tangible assets, know-how, or intellectual property—that have either a dual use or spare capacity. Sometimes, realizing their potential will require an equity joint venture between the public and the private sectors. These PPPs fall under the U.K. government's Wider Markets Initiative.

Between these two established forms of PPP—a *concessions-based business* (PFI project), on the one hand, and a *joint venture* (Wider Markets project), on the other—lies a broad spectrum of possible PPP structures having features of both. These *combination partnership structures* offer some of the greatest potential for future application of PPPs because of their adaptability to the specific needs of the public sector. For example, where the scope of future service delivery cannot be fully defined at the outset, greater emphasis on *joint-venture* mechanics and less on detailed *output* specifications may be required. Alternatively, a public sector authority may decide to hold a minority equity stake in a PFI project it has commissioned, to share in the profits generated by the business.

The spectrum of possible PPPs also extends from businesses almost entirely controlled by the private sector, at one end, to those almost entirely controlled by the public sector, at the other. Outside the United Kingdom, there are PPP businesses jointly owned by the public and private sectors, but with the majority ownership held by the public sector. Examples include water utility companies within continental Europe. The explanation of why the U.K. model of PPPs generally involves effective control by the private sector, if not majority ownership, lies largely in the role that private sector finance plays in creating the necessary management disciplines for a PPP and in achieving a transfer of risk that provides value for money. Even when day-to-day management of the PPP is firmly in the hands of the private sector, which is generally the case in the United Kingdom, the PPP must still operate at the boundary between the public and private sectors in a way that *privatized* companies generally do not—thus further highlighting its special character.

The *value* that a private sector investor seeks from a PPP is a return on its capital employed—as a management incentive, this is no different from what any other private sector business seeks. The private sector investor may also have contractual interests in the PPP, but these are normally free-standing and arm's-length. The public sector, by contrast, will apply a much wider concept of value to its participation as an investor in a PPP than simply the return on its capital employed—this could include other policy considerations.

**Michael B. Gerrard is Head of Public Private Partnerships at Partnerships UK, a firm established by the U.K. government to accelerate the development, procurement, and implementation of such partnernships. He is also a Visiting Lecturer at Imperial College Management School (London).**

Box 2

## Why are governments turning to PPPs?

PPPs generally spread the costs of procuring an asset over time and/or cause the associated capital expenditure to affect private firms' rather than the public sector's balance sheets. These objectives may be achieved by basing the procurement on the public services required—that is, upon *outputs*—rather than on the underlying assets, or inputs. Where public sector capital budgets are constrained, there are obvious advantages in adopting a PPP to deliver public services that might otherwise be unaffordable to a government.

At the heart of all PPPs is the deployment of private sector capital. Within a PPP framework, this can result in greatly improved value for money for the government in terms of the risks transferred to the private sector (in cases where the latter is better able to assess the risks) and powerful private sector incentives for the long-term delivery of reliable public services. These benefits are sufficient to ensure that PPPs often become the favored means of procurement, even where public sector capital constraints do not apply. In many countries, such as the United Kingdom, therefore, the motivation for making greater use of PPPs is to obtain increased value for money in the procurement of public services.

Much of the improved value for money comes from the fact that when private sector capital is deployed and is at risk—to, for example, the long-term performance of public service delivery—the right commercial decisions are made about design, operating regime, human resource planning, whole-life-of-asset costings, and so on. For a fuller analysis of the drivers of value for money, see *Value for Money Drivers in the Private Finance Initiative: A Report by Arthur Andersen and Enterprise LSE Commissioned by the U.K. Treasury Taskforce* (London: 2000).

PPPs operate at the boundary of the public and private sectors, being neither nationalized nor privatized assets and services. Thus, politically, they represent a *third way* in which governments may deliver some public services. Moreover, in a practical sense, PPPs represent a form of collaboration under contract by which public and private sectors, acting together, can achieve what each acting alone cannot. Numerous member countries of the Organization for Economic Cooperation and Development now have active PPP programs, as do a growing number of developing countries.

The rules by which a PPP operates must be clearly articulated within its constitutional documents or other contractual arrangements, so that the management team knows the constraints within which it must run the business. These constraints are also likely to be important influences on the human resources strategy of the business and will affect the PPP's approach to attracting and retaining the right management and staff.

To harness the potential of PPPs requires that their unique characteristics be acknowledged and exploited: first, their ability to provide a flexible framework within which the complementary roles and capabilities of public and private sectors can be combined; second, their operation at the boundary between public and private sectors, by which the public sector retains ultimate responsibility for delivering public services; and third, their status as a form of regulated business—in effect a business that is *passively regulated* by means of its constitution and the contracts it enters into with the public sector, without the intervention of a statutory regulator. These characteristics also explain why PPPs are generally not well described as privatizations or partial privatizations in the sense that these terms are commonly used. F&D

# [2]

# The Meaning of Privatization

Paul Starr*

Privatization is a fuzzy concept that evokes sharp political reactions. It covers a great range of ideas and policies, varying from the eminently reasonable to the wildly impractical. Yet however varied and at times unclear in its meaning, privatization has unambiguous political origins and objectives. It emerges from the countermovement against the growth of government in the West and represents the most serious conservative effort of our time to formulate a positive alternative. Privatization proposals do not aim merely to return services to their original location in the private sphere. Some proposals seek to create new kinds of market relations and promise results comparable or superior to conventional public programs. Hence it is a mistake to define and dismiss the movement as simply a replay of traditional opposition to state intervention and expenditure. The current wave of privatization initiatives opens a new chapter in the conflict over the public-private balance.

This Article attempts to clarify the meaning of privatization as an idea, as theory and rhetoric, and as a political practice. In the process I hope to explain why I generally oppose privatization, even though I favor some specific proposals that privatization covers. But apart from this political judgment, I take privatization seriously as a policy movement and as a process that show every sign of reconstituting major institutional domains of contemporary society.

## *I. Privatization as an Idea*

In the ideological world we inhabit, contesting interests and parties use "public" and "private" not only to describe but also to celebrate and condemn. Any serious inquiry into the meaning of privatization must begin, therefore, by unloading the complex

---



* Professor of Sociology, Princeton University. Work on this Article was supported by a grant from the Pew Charitable Trust for the study of "Public Sector Reform and Privatization." An earlier version was completed at the Institute for Advanced Study at Princeton, New Jersey and delivered at a conference there on "The Public Sector and Its Problems." The Article will also appear in a slightly different version in a volume on privatization and the welfare state edited by Alfred Kahn and Sheila Kamerman. I wish also to express my general debt to Stephen Holmes, Jeffrey Weintraub, the members of the Yale Legal Theory Workshop, and others from whom I received ideas and suggestions.

The Meaning of Privatization

freight that the public-private distinction carries. In this section I analyze, first, the general uses of the public-private distinction and, second, the recent political application of the concept of privatization.

*A. The Public-Private Distinction and the Concept of Privatization*

The terms public and private are fundamental to the language of our law, politics, and social life, but they are the source of continual frustration. Many things seem to be public and private at the same time in varying degrees or in different ways. As a result, we quarrel endlessly about whether some act or institution is really one or the other. We qualify the categories: This group is quasi-public, that one is semi-private. In desperation some theorists announce that the distinction is outdated or so ideologically loaded that it ought to be discarded, or that it is a distinction without a difference.[1] Yet the terms can hardly be banished nor ought they.[2] To speak intelligently about modern societies and politics without using the words public and private would be as great an achievement as writing a novel with the word "the." However, neither is necessarily the sort of achievement that other theorists or novelists would care to imitate.

The frustration with these ubiquitous categories partly arises because public and private are paired to describe a number of related oppositions in our thought. At the core of many uses are the two ideas that public is to private as *open* is to *closed*, and that public is to private as the *whole* is to the *part*. In the first sense, we speak of a public place, a public conference, public behavior, making something public, or publishing an article. The private counterparts, from homes to diaries, are private in that access is restricted and visibility reduced. The concepts of publicity and privacy stand in opposition to each other along this dimension of accessibility. Public is to private as the transparent is to the opaque, as the announced is to the concealed. Similarly, a person's public life is to his or her private life as the outer is to the inner realm.

On the other hand, when we speak of public opinion, public health, or the public interest, we mean the opinion, health, or inter-

1. *See, e.g.*, Klare, The Public/Private Distinction in Labor Law, 130 U. Pa. L. Rev. 1358 (1982); Kennedy, The Stages of the Decline of the Public/Private Distinction, 130 U. Pa. L. Rev. 1349 (1982); Freeman & Mensch, The Public/Private Distinction in American Law and Life, 3 Tikkun 24-30 (Mar./Apr. 1988).

2. Starr, A Response to Mensch and Freeman, 3 Tikkun 31 (Mar./Apr. 1988).

est of the whole of the people as opposed to that of a part, whether a class or an individual. Public in this sense often means "common," not necessarily governmental. The public-spirited or public-minded citizen is one concerned about the community as a whole. But in the modern world the concepts of governmental and public have become so closely linked that in some contexts they are interchangeable. The state acts for the whole of a society in international relations and makes rules binding on the whole internally. Public thus often means official. In this sense a "public act" is one that carries official status, even if it is secret and therefore not public in the sense of being openly visible. Indeed, according to the Oxford English Dictionary, private originally signified "not holding public office or official position." As Albert Hirschman points out, this is a meaning that survives in the army "private," that is, the "ordinary soldier without any rank or position."[3] Now, of course, private is contrasted with public to characterize that which lies beyond the state's boundaries, such as the market or the family.

These different contrasts between public and private lead to some apparent conflicts in defining what lies on each side of the boundary. One such conflict concerns the location of the market. To an economist, the marketplace is quintessentially private. But to a sociologist or anthropologist concerned with culture, the marketplace is quintessentially public—a sphere open to utter strangers who nonetheless are able to understand the same rules and gestures in what may be a highly ritualized process of exchange. While economists use the public-private distinction to signify the contrast between state and market, analysts of culture—particularly those concerned with the roles and relations of men and women—take the public sphere to include the market as well as politics and contrast them both with the private domain of the family. In this sense, the public-private distinction is sometimes taken to mark out the contested boundaries of the male and female worlds—a usage that takes us back to the notion of the private as being more closed, more shielded from contact and view, than the open encounters of public life.[4]

3. A. Hirschman, Shifting Involvements: Private Interest and Public Action 121-22 (1982).

4. *See, e.g.*, J. Elshtain, Public Man, Private Woman (1981); Rosaldo, Woman, Culture and Society: A Theoretical Overview, in Woman, Culture and Society 17-42 (M. Rosaldo & L. Lamphere eds. 1974); L. Imray & A. Middleton, Public & Private: Marking the Boundaries, in The Public and the Private 12-16 (E. Gamarnikow, et al. eds. 1983).

The Meaning of Privatization

From these varying uses of the categories come several contrasting conceptions of the public sphere. The public sphere may be conceived of as the open and visible—the sphere of public life, public theater, the public marketplace, public sociability. The public sphere also may be conceived of as that which applies to the whole people or, as we say, the general public or the public at large, in which case the public may consist of an aggregate or a mass who have no direct contact or social relation—the very opposite of a sphere of sociability. Or the public sphere may be conceived specifically as the domain circumscribed by the state, although exactly where to draw the state's boundaries may be difficult indeed.

The general meanings of privatization, then, correspond to withdrawals from any of these variously conceived public spheres. Historians and sociologists write about the withdrawal of affective interest and involvement from the sphere of public sociability. For example, in their work on the development of the modern family, Peter Willmott and Michael Young argue that as the modern household became equipped with larger homes, private cars, televisions, and other resources, more time and capital came to be invested in the private interior of the family and less in public taverns, squares, and streets.[5] Similarly, Richard Sennett suggests that since the eighteenth century modern society has seen a decline of public culture and sociability, a deadening of public life and public space, a privatization of emotion.[6] Such arguments shade into a second meaning of privatization: a shift of individual involvements from the whole to the part—that is, from public action to private concerns—the kind of privatization that Hirschman describes as one swing in a public-private cycle of individual action.[7] In this sort of public-to-private transition, the swing is not from sociability to intimacy but from civic concern to the pursuit of self-interest.

Privatization can also signify another kind of withdrawal from the whole to the part: an appropriation by an individual or a particular group of some good formerly available to the entire public or community. Like the withdrawal of involvement, privatization in the sense of private appropriation has obvious implications for the distribution of welfare.

From these meanings it is but a short step to the sense of privatization as a withdrawal from the state, not of individual involve-

5. *See* M. Young & P. Willmott, The Symmetrical Family (1973).
6. *See* R. Sennett, The Fall of Public Man 16-24 (1977).
7. *See* Hirschman, *supra* note 3, at 121-30.

ments, but of assets, functions, indeed entire institutions. Public policy is concerned with privatization at this level. But the two forms, the privatization of individual involvements and the privatization of social functions and assets, are certainly related, at least by ideological kinship. A confidence that pursuit of private gain serves the larger social order leads to approval for both self-interested behavior and private enterprise.

Thus far I have been talking about privatization as if both spheres, public and private, were already constituted. But in a longer perspective, their constitution and separation represent complementary processes. Much historical experience corresponds to Simmel's paradoxical dictum that "what is public becomes ever more public, and what is private becomes ever more private."[8] This is true specifically of the histories of the state and the family. The difference between patrimonial domination and modern bureaucracies, as Weber describes the two, is precisely that in the patrimonial state public and private roles were mixed and in the modern state these roles are more clearly distinguished.[9] The modern state distinguishes offices and persons. The office is public, and its files, rules, and finances are distinct from the personal possessions and character of individuals. As public administration and finance were separated from the household and personal wealth of the ruler, the modern state became, in effect more public; the person and family of the ruler, more private.[10] That the domestic sphere has generally become more private is one of the classic themes of modern sociology and the history of the family.[11]

The rise of the liberal state specifically entailed a sharpening of the public-private distinction: on the one hand, the privatizing of religious and moral belief and practice and of economic activity formerly regulated by the state; on the other, a commitment to public law and public political discussion. Classical liberalism is often represented as a purely privatizing ideology, but liberals were committed to suppressing markets in votes, offices, and tax collection, not to mention human beings. Strengthening the public character of

8. *See* G. Simmel, The Secret and the Secret Society, in The Sociology of Georg Simmel 337 (K. Wolff ed. 1950). *See also* Horwitz, The History of the Public/Private Distinction, 130 U. Pa. L. Rev. 1423 (1982).

9. M. Weber, 3 Economy & Society 1028-31 (G. Roth & C. Wittich eds. 1968).

10. *See, e.g.*, R. Braun, Taxation, Sociopolitical Structure, and State-Building: Great Britain and Brandenburg-Prussia, in The Formation of National States in Western Europe 243-46 (C. Tilly ed. 1975); C. Webber & A. Wildavsky, A History of Taxation and Expenditure in the Western World 148-51 (1986).

11. *See* P. Ariés, Centuries of Childhood 411-15 (1962).

the state is a continuity in liberal thought from its classical to contemporary phases. Moreover, as Stephen Holmes argues, the liberal effort to privatize otherwise rancorous religious differences promoted a civilized public order.[12] Some kinds of privatization are not the enemy of the public realm but its necessary support.

In liberal democratic thought, public and private are central terms in the language of claims-making. In particular, they provide a deeply resonant vocabulary for making claims against the state. These are of two kinds. First, the concept of a public government implies an elaborate structure of rules limiting the exercise of state power. Those who wield power are to be held publicly accountable—that is, answerable to the citizens—for their performance. Government decisions and deliberations must be publicly reported and open to general participation. In short, the citizens of a liberal state are understood to have a right to expect their government to be public not only in its ends but also in its processes. Second, when the members of a liberal society think of their homes, businesses, churches, and myriad other forms of association as lying in a private sphere, they are claiming limits to the power of that democratic state. The limits are not absolute—private property rights, for example, are not an insuperable barrier to public control or regulation—but when crossing from public to private the presumptions shift away from the state and any state intervention must meet more stringent tests of the public interest.

Public and private in liberal thought have become pervasive dualities—or, perhaps better said, polarities—associated with the state in one direction, the individual in the other. Intermediate entities, such as corporations typically have been divided between the two categories. Until the nineteenth century in the United States, there was no clear legal distinction between public and private corporations. Initially, cities were not sharply distinguished in the law from business enterprise; but in the mid-1800s cities became classified as agencies of the state, while business corporations came to be treated as individuals. As public agencies, cities were allowed only such powers as states delegated to them; as fictive individuals, private corporations came to enjoy rights protected by the Constitution.[13] This bifurcation between powers and rights lies at the foundation of

12. S. Holmes, Benjamin Constant and the Making of Modern Liberalism 241-52 (1984).

13. *See* Frug, The City as a Legal Concept, 93 Harv. L. Rev. 1059 (1980).

the contemporary legal distinction between the public and private sectors.

Behind the legal categories, of course, the boundaries are blurred. On the one hand, private interests reach into the conduct of the state and its agencies; on the other, the state reaches across the public-private boundary to regulate private contracts and the conduct of private corporations and other associations. Through tax preferences and credit guarantees, the state shapes private economic choices and relations. The state is immanent in the economy and society, but the degree of penetration varies, and the public-private system of classification is used to express these variations. So, for example, among private corporations, we distinguish those that are privately held from those that are publicly traded and subject to the regulations of the Securities and Exchange Commission. The latter are often called public corporations, by which we actually mean *public private* corporations. Among those public private corporations are some subject to more extensive regulation, such as the utilities, which are especially *public, public private* corporations. And since the utilities, in turn, have some lines of business defined as public and others as private, the public-private boundary runs within them as well as around them.

It is as if, on finding two boxes labeled public and private, we were to open the private box and find two more boxes labeled public and private, which we would do again—and again—opening ever smaller boxes until we reached the individuals far inside, whom we could then split into respective offices and persons.[14] Moreover, if the boxes have been assembled by reasonably competent lawyers, they may be extremely intricate and some will have misleading labels. But this complexity and the legal manipulation of the categories do not invalidate their usefulness or underlying meaning. To speak of a public corporation in the private sector ought really to be no more confusing than saying that North Carolina is in the South. Public and private give us relative locations.

A further source of frustration with the public-private distinction is that the terms do not have consistent meanings from one institutional sphere to another. In the United States, the difference between public and private schools is not the same as the difference between public and private television broadcasting. An American public school is public, not only in that it is state owned and fi-

14. I am grateful to Gerald E. Frug for this analogy.

nanced, but also because it is open to all children of eligible age in its area. Private schools can reject applicants, but public school systems are denied that option. Public is to private, not only as state is to nonstate, but as open is to closed. However, in television broadcasting, the viewing public has open access to commercial as well as public channels. The difference lies in financing and programming. The public channels receive government support and do not choose programming to maximize audience ratings, though in fact even public broadcasting now competes for private corporate sponsorship, and some public stations are legally organized as private nonprofit corporations.[15] To make matters still more complicated, the differences between public and private institutions do not follow parallel lines in other countries. To take broadcasting again, public television or radio in the United States is more dependent on private financing, less subject to control by political authorities, and less the symbolic voice of the state than the state-owned networks of other Western nations, not to mention the Soviet bloc and Third World.

To say public or private, therefore, is not sufficient to specify a form of organization or even its relation to the state. Consequently, it is extremely risky to generalize about public versus private organizations—and, therefore, about the merits of privatization as public policy—beyond a particular institutional or national context. No general theory about the performance of public versus private organizations is likely to succeed if it fails to distinguish among political systems and the structural variety of public and private institutions. Privatization describes a direction of change, but it does not denote a specific origin or destination. Its meaning depends on the point of departure—the public-private balance previously struck in a particular domain. And it is a critical question whether moving from public to private in the sense of state to non-state entails a movement in the other senses: from open to closed (in access to information) or from the whole to the part (particularly in the distribution of benefits).

### *B. The Political Meaning of Privatization*

The term privatization did not gain wide circulation in politics until the late 1970s and early 1980s. With the rise of conservative gov-

15. Powell & Friedkin, Politics and Programs: Organizational Factors in Public Television Decision Making, in Nonprofit Enterprise in the Arts 245-69 (P. Dimaggio ed. 1986).

ernments in Great Britain, the United States, and France, privatization has come primarily to mean two things: (1) any shift of activities or functions from the state to the private sector; and, more specifically, (2) any shift of the *production* of goods and services from public to private.[16] Besides directly producing services, governments establish the legal framework of societies and regulate social and economic life, and they finance services that are privately produced and consumed. The first, broader definition of privatization includes all reductions in the regulatory and spending activity of the state. The second, more specific definition of privatization excludes deregulation and spending cuts except when they result in a shift from public to private in the production of goods and services. This more focused definition is the one that I shall use here. It leaves open the possibility that privatization may not actually result in less government spending and regulation—indeed, may even unexpectedly increase them.

Several further points about my definition need clarification. First, the public sector here includes agencies administered as part of the state and organizations owned by it, such as state enterprises and independent public authorities like the British Broadcasting Corporation (BBC) or the Port Authority of New York and New Jersey. In the private sector I include not only commercial firms but also informal and domestic activities, voluntary associations, cooperatives, and private nonprofit corporations.[17]

Second, in the definition I am using, privatization refers to shifts from the public to the private sector, not shifts within sectors. Thus the conversion of a state agency into an autonomous public authority or state-owned enterprise is not privatization, though it may well put the enterprise on a commercial footing.[18] This was the objec-

16. E.S. Savas defines privatization as "the act of reducing the role of government, or increasing the role of the private sector, in an activity or in the ownership of assets." E. Savas, Privatization: The Key to Better Government 3 (1987). I see nothing wrong with this broad definition, so long as one realizes that some actions may reduce one role of government while increasing another. For example, selling government-owned utilities may result in establishing a new system of public regulation. Setting up a voucher plan for education and housing may produce more public regulation of private schools. In other words, policies conceived as privatization may have unintended consequences for other dimensions of state intervention.

17. On the ambiguities of such classification, see generally Musolf & Seidman, The Blurred Boundaries of Public Administration, 40 Pub. Admin. Rev. 124 (1980); A. Walsh, The Public's Business (1980).

18. Glade uses the term "simulated privatization" to refer to the effort to put a public enterprise on a commercial footing. Glade, Sources and Forms of Privatization, in State Shrinking: A Comparative Inquiry into Privatization 2, 12-13 (W. Glade ed. 1987). S. Henrique Abranches refers to the same process as "privatization of the logic of opera-

tive, for example, of the conversion of the United States Post Office into a public corporation, the United States Postal Service, in 1971.[19] Similarly, the conversion of a private nonprofit organization into a profit-making firm also is not privatization, though it, too, may orient the firm toward the market. Both of these intrasectoral changes might be described as commercialization; in the case of public agencies, commercialization is sometimes a preliminary stage to privatization.

Third, shifts from publicly to privately produced services may result not only from a deliberate government action, such as a sale of assets, but also from the choices of individuals or firms that a government is unwilling or unable to satisfy or control. In many countries, private demand for education, health care, or retirement income has outstripped public provision. As a result, private schooling, medical care, and pensions have grown to relatively larger proportions. This is *demand-driven privatization*. When privatization is a demand-driven process, it does not require an absolute reduction in publicly produced services. Stagnation or slow growth in the public sector may be the cause. In some socialist societies the growth of an "underground" economy represents a form of privatization that is not a planned development (though it may well result from development planning). In other words, as a process, privatization encompasses more institutional changes than those brought about by self-conscious privatization policies. It seems useful, then, to distinguish instances of privatization according to whether they are predominantly *policy-* or *demand-driven*.

Fourth, if one shifts attention from the sphere of production to the sphere of consumption, one may alternatively define privatization as the substitution of private goods for public goods. A public good, in the economist's sense, has two distinguishing properties: One person's consumption does not preclude another's; and excluding anyone from consumption is costly, if not impossible. The prototypical example is fresh air. A public good need not be produced by government. A broadcast television program is a public good even if it is provided by a commercially owned station; but videotape is not, nor is programming on subscription cable services. Any shift toward these forms of nonbroadcast television represents

tion" of state enterprises. Abranches, State Enterprise and Modes of Privatization: A Critical View Based on Brazilian Examples, in State Shrinking, *supra*, at 75, 79.

19. Willey, Taking the Post Office Out of Politics, Pub. Interest, Spring 1969, at 57-71.

a privatization of consumption, even if the local cable service is municipally owned.[20]

Depending on whether one is talking about the locus of production or the forms of consumption, privatization can mean rather different things. In regard to production, "privatization of health care" might mean a transfer of medical facilities from public to private ownership; regarding consumption, it might refer to a shift in expenditures from public health (environmental protection, vaccinations, etc.) to individual medical care. Similarly, "privatization of transportation" might refer to the conversion of an urban bus system from public to commercial ownership; or it might mean a shift in ridership from buses to private automobiles, regardless of whether the bus company is municipal or commercial. Strictly speaking, public transportation is not a public good, since exclusion is possible and only one person at a time can sit in a seat; however, because buses and trains are open to the public at large, common carriers are a distinctively public form of consumption compared to private cars. More generally, the historical process described by Willmott and Young—the concentration of consumption activities in the home—represented a shift toward more privatized forms of consumption. This shift has been the source of much criticism of contemporary society, as in John Kenneth Galbraith's famous contrast of private opulence and public squalor in *The Affluent Society*.[21] In this discussion, whenever referring specifically to a shift from public goods to private goods, or from common carriers to private carriers, I use the phrase "privatization of consumption." Otherwise, I take privatization to mean a shift in the locus of the production of services from public to private.

Four types of government policies can bring about such a shift. First, the cessation of public programs and disengagement of government from specific kinds of responsibilities represent an *implicit* form of privatization. At a less drastic level, the restriction of publicly produced services in volume, availability, or quality may lead to a shift by consumers toward privately produced and purchased substitutes (called "privatization by attrition" when a government lets public services run down). Second, privatization may take the *explicit* form of transfers of public assets to private ownership, through sale or lease of public land, infrastructure, and enterprises. Third, in-

20. Starr, Television and the Public Household, in Television in America's Future—A Search for the Right Public Policy (M. Rice ed.) (forthcoming).
21. *See* J. Galbraith, The Affluent Society 195 (3rd ed. 1976).

stead of directly producing some service, the government may finance private services, for example, through contracting-out or vouchers. Finally, privatization may result from the deregulation of entry into activities previously treated as public monopolies.

These forms of privatization vary in the extent to which they move ownership, finance, and accountability out of the public sector. The spectrum of alternatives runs from total privatization (as in government disengagement from some policy domain) to partial privatization (as in contracting-out or vouchers). As I define the term, privatization may include policies anywhere along this spectrum; however, the implications of privatization vary with its degree. In cases of partial privatization, the government may continue to finance but not to operate services, or it may continue to own but not to manage assets. Privatization may, therefore, dilute government control and accountability without eliminating them. Where governments pay for privately produced services, they must continue to collect taxes. Privatization in this sense diminishes the operational but not the fiscal or functional sphere of government action. By putting the delivery of services into the hands of a third party, governments may divert claims and complaints to private organizations, but they also risk seeing those third parties become powerful claimants themselves. Whether this sort of partial privatization achieves any reduction in government spending or deficits must necessarily be a practical, empirical question.

Even asset sales sometimes involve only the transfer of a partial interest. Often governments sell some voting stock in an enterprise but refuse to surrender control. In these instances, privatization may amount to little more than a revenue-raising measure, as there may be no change in management, management behavior, or the enterprise's relation to state authorities. Although it may seem odd, the product of privatization is not always a private firm: Privatization also yields hybrid enterprises with varying balances of influence.

The different techniques used to privatize assets affect what emerges from privatization. Among the methods used are sales to private bidders, sales by public stock offering, conversion to employee ownership, and transfer of title to the firm's current managers. In the case of unprofitable businesses, far from charging a price, governments sometimes guarantee the new owners future public contracts, tax benefits, or the monopoly on a franchise.

These variations in privatization policy complicate simple-minded predictions of the effects of privatization on economic efficiency.

Just as there are various methods for the divestiture of assets, so too, various methods are available for shifting from publicly produced services to publicly financed private provision. Governments face a basic choice as to whether state agencies or private parties will do the purchasing. If the state purchases the service, it may enter into contracts or grants. If, on the other hand, the government allows private parties to purchase services, it may distribute vouchers, offer tax credits or other tax preferences, indemnify beneficiaries directly for some proportion of their costs, or pay providers chosen by beneficiaries. (The latter shades into contracting-out if the transactions become routine.) To introduce yet a further complication, the private parties whose costs the government defrays in whole or part may be individuals (the consumers of services) or employers. Privatization policy might, for example, call for the use of tax preferences to induce a shift from publicly provided retirement benefits to benefits provided by employers or to benefits provided through individual retirement accounts.[22] When governments give up producing services, they can "empower" many different parties.

Privatization should not automatically be equated with increased competition. Two related processes, privatization and liberalization, need to be carefully distinguished. By liberalization one generally means a reduction of government control; in this context, it refers to the opening up of an industry to competitive pressures. Entry deregulation of public monopolies is a form of privatization that is also liberalizing. However, it is entirely possible to privatize without liberalizing. When the Thatcher government sold shares of British Telecom and British Gas, it substituted private monopolies for public ones and introduced new regulatory agencies to perform some of the functions previously undertaken through public ownership. The option of putting liberalization first—that is, encouraging greater competition—was expressly rejected, perhaps for fear that it

22. *See, e.g.*, Ferrara, Social Security and the Super IRA: A Populist Proposal, in Social Security: Prospects for Real Reform 193 (P. Ferrara ed. 1985); Goodman, Private Alternatives to Social Security: The Experience of Other Countries, in Social Security, at 103; O'Higgins, Public-Private Interaction and Pensions Provision, in Public-Private Interplay in Social Protection (M. Rein & L. Rainwater eds. 1986); Starr, Social Security and the American Public Household, in Social Security: Beyond the Rhetoric of Crisis (J. Mashaw & T. Marmor eds.) (forthcoming).

would reduce the share price of the companies.[23] Conversely, it is also possible to liberalize without privatizing—that is, to introduce competition into the public sector without transferring ownership. For example, governments may allocate funds to schools according to student enrollments where families are free to choose among competing public schools; or they may require public enterprises or operating agencies to compete for capital or contracts from higher-level authorities. Indeed, it is even possible to nationalize and liberalize at the same time, as the French socialists demonstrated in the early 1980s when they first nationalized banks and later liberalized financial markets.[24]

Finally, just as there are different routes out of the public sector, so there are numerous destinations in the private sector to which privatization may lead. The alternative possibilities may be classified according to organizational complexity and proprietary status: first, the personal, domestic, or informal sector, thought to exemplify the virtues of self-reliance, mutual aid, and sensitivity to individual preferences; second, the voluntary nonprofit, or "independent," sector, consisting of formal, complex organizations, thought to display the same virtues as the informal sector, plus the advantages of professional leadership and management; third, the small-business sector, acclaimed for entrepreneurship and revered as a fountain of new jobs; and fourth, the large-scale corporate sector, where hopes for improved performance rest not only on the profit motive but also on professional management and economies of scale. The first two of these destinations, the informal and nonprofit sectors, remind us that privatization does not necessarily mean a reliance on commercial markets. Indeed, instead of one destination and one map, the advocates of privatization have several, distinctly different conceptions of where they are going. I turn now to the theories that provide the movement with its logic, intellectual coherence, and rhetoric.

## *II. Privatization as Theory and Rhetoric*

The normative theories justifying privatization as a direction for public policy draw their inspiration from several different visions of

23. *See, e.g.*, Privatization and Regulation: The U.K. Experience (J. Kay & D. Thompson eds. 1987); Brittan, The Politics and Economics of Privatisation, 55 Political Q. 109, 116-21 (1984).

24. Francis, French Financiers Marvel at "Capitalists in Socialists' Clothing," Christian Sci. Monitor, June 20, 1985, at 21.

a good society. By far the most influential is the vision grounded in laissez-faire individualism and free-market economics that promises greater efficiency, a smaller government, and more individual choice if only we expand the domain of property rights and market forces. A second vision, rooted in a more socially minded conservative tradition, promises a return of power to communities through a greater reliance in social provision on families, churches, and other largely nonprofit institutions. Privatization, in this view, means a devolution of power from the state to ostensibly nonpolitical and noncommercial forms of human association. Yet a third perspective sees privatization as a political strategy for diverting demands away from the state and thereby reducing government "overload." This last view, identified particularly with recent neoconservative thought, does not necessarily conflict with the other two—indeed, some advocates of privatization draw on all three—but each vision suggests a different framework for analysis and policy.

*A. The Economic Theory of Privatization*

Even within the economic theory of privatization, there are some subtle but important differences between two approaches: the radical view of privatization as a reassignment of property rights and the more moderate, conventional view of privatization as an instrument for fine-tuning a three-sector economy.

*1. Economic Model 1: Privatization as a Reassignment of Property Rights.* Private ownership and competitive markets are normally thought to go hand in hand, but the two issues of ownership and market structure are often separate. For the economist devoted to both, the question then arises as to which object of affection is more beloved: private ownership or competition. Here a difference of opinion appears among economists that corresponds to a preference for either privatization or liberalization. Those who believe that efficient performance depends on private ownership per se favor privatization, even in cases generally regarded as natural monopolies. Conversely, those who see competition as the critical spur to efficiency are more skeptical about the benefits of privatizing monopolies and often put more emphasis on other policies, such as deregulation. In the case of a government telecommunications monopoly, for example, those who stress ownership may be willing to privatize the monopoly intact, whereas those who stress competition may prefer to break it up before sale or even to keep it in public ownership while allowing private firms to compete with it on equal terms.

Thus the perspective that unequivocally points to privatization as desirable policy holds that property ownership is the fulcrum of political economy. Curiously, the two unlikely bedfellows sharing this appreciation of ownership are marxism and Chicago economics, which draw from it opposite but equally strong conclusions about the overriding importance of getting ownership into the right sector. From the Chicago tradition come two closely related clusters of work: the theory of property rights and the theory of public choice. Both attempt to enlarge the conventional economic paradigm by treating the classical firm and modern package of property rights as only one of various possible institutional forms. In this enlarged model, public institutions merely represent an alternative property rights configuration, which, on theoretical grounds, the Chicago School predicts regularly will perform less efficiently than private enterprise.

As developed by economists such as Armen Alchian, Ronald Coase, and Harold Demsetz, the theory of property rights explains differences in organizational behavior solely on the basis of the individual incentives created by the structure of property rights.[25] In this view, property rights specify the social and economic relations that people must observe with each other in their use of scarce resources, including not only the benefits that owners are allowed to enjoy but also the harms to others that they are allowed to cause. A right of ownership actually comprises several rights, chiefly the rights to use an asset, to change it in form, substance, or location, and to transfer all or some of these rights. Insofar as the state restricts these rights, they become "attenuated." Thus the key issues for the theory are, first, to whom are property rights assigned? and second, how, if at all, are they attenuated?

Like other branches of microeconomics, the property rights school conceives of human action as purely individualistic. The more individuals stand to gain from tending to their property, the better will it be tended. Conversely, the more attenuated and diluted their property rights, the less motivated individuals will be to use property under their control efficiently. Private ownership con-

25. *See, e.g.*, Alchian, Some Economics of Property Rights, 30 Il Politico 816 (1965); Demsetz, Toward a Theory of Property Rights, 57 Amer. Econ. Rev. Papers & Proc. 347 (1967); E. Furubotn & S. Pejovich, The Economics of Property Rights (1974); Furubotn & Pejovich, Property Rights and Economic Theory: A Survey of Recent Literature, 10 J. Econ. Lit. 1137 (1972); De Alessi, Property Rights and Privatization, 36 Proc. Acad. Pol. Sci. 24 (S. Hanke ed. 1987) (volume entitled Prospects for Privatization).

centrates rights and rewards; public ownership dilutes them. The property rights school does not recognize any fundamental change in the working of private enterprise as a result of the separation of ownership and management in the modern corporation. To be sure, shareholders in large corporations cannot monitor management as closely as the owner of the classical firm could oversee his enterprise. However, in this view, the market generates the needed spur to prevent corporate management from dissipating value through excessive salaries or slack attention. If returns from the enterprise are low, shareholders will sell their stock and the price will be depressed. In the extreme case, the firm may be acquired by outsiders and the managers may lose their jobs. These crucial deterrents to inefficient management are missing from the public sector. Since "shareholders" (citizens) have no transferable property rights in public enterprise, they cannot sell stock as a signal of dissatisfaction with performance; even moving to another jurisdiction is costly. Moreover, there is no "market for corporate control": public enterprises cannot be taken over by bidders who believe that they can make more efficient use of the assets. Hence, according to the theory, there is no check on the dissipation of value by the management of public enterprises.

It is worth taking note of the premises and implications of the property rights approach. First, the theory holds that the form of ownership is the predominant explanation for the varying performance of different organizations. The theory gives no importance whatsoever to organizational characteristics such as size, centralization, hierarchy, or leadership. Nor does it recognize any variation in performance that might stem from task characteristics, such as poor information or ambiguity about goals. The theory does not even recognize the effects of economic incentives unrelated to property rights, such as those originating in various types of contracts. The theory does not point to any contingencies in generalizing about public-private differences; it does not identify any particular conditions or characteristics that might cause public institutions to perform well. The disease the theory diagnoses in the public sector is, so to speak, genetic and incurable.

Second, the theory takes the market as the standard for judging value and finds public institutions deficient because they fail to measure up to that standard, e.g., their "shareholders" cannot sell stock. Survival in the market, of course, depends on the capacity of organizations to produce a residual reward for the owners—a profit. This is not the standard that public institutions generally need to meet. The property rights approach says that society would be better off if, instead of meeting approval in the political process, public organizations or their assets were privately owned and had to meet the test of profitability.

Third, the property rights theory assumes that the market for corporate control is highly efficient and that the chief reason corporations are acquired is their management's poor performance. In the United States today, however, some corporations are acquired because they have built up large pools of cash, while other corporations avoid being acquired because their managers take preventive but inefficient measures, such as piling up debt. Frequently, behemoths with large cash flow but low returns on equity and other indicators of poor performance have taken over firms with much better records.[26] Virtue is not always rewarded in the market for corporate control; nonetheless, according to the property rights view, market discipline forces managers of private firms to be more efficient than public managers. The theory gives no weight at all to the monitoring capacities of the state, the public at large, and the various institutions of a liberal democracy, such as the press, that routinely scrutinize the performance of public institutions. The reasons for this dim view of public monitoring are spelled out in the theory of public choice.

"Public choice," ill-named because the only choices it recognizes are essentially private, is both a branch of microeconomics and an ideologically-laden view of democratic politics. Analysts of the school apply the logic of microeconomics to politics and generally find that whereas self-interest leads to benign results in the marketplace, it produces nothing but pathology in political decisions.[27] These pathological patterns represent different kinds of "free-riding" and "rent-seeking" by voters, bureaucrats, politicians, and recipients of public funds. Coalitions of voters seeking special advantage from the state join together to get favorable legislation enacted. Rather than being particularly needy, these groups are likely to be those whose big stake in a benefit arouses them to more effective action than is taken by the taxpayers at large over whom the costs are spread. In general, individuals with "concentrated" interests in increased expenditure take a "free ride" on those with "diffuse" interests in lower taxes. Similarly, the managers of the "bureaucratic firms" seek to maximize budgets, and thereby to ob-

26. The acquisitions by General Motors, U.S. Steel (now USX), and W.R. Grace corporations provide illustrations.

27. *See, e.g.*, J. Buchanan & G. Tullock, The Calculus of Consent (1962); W. Niskanen, Bureaucracy and Representative Government (1971); Budgets and Bureaucrats: The Sources of Government Growth (T. Borcherding ed. 1977).

tain greater power, larger salaries, and other perquisites. Budget maximization results in higher government spending overall, inefficient allocation among government agencies, and inefficient production within them. In addition, when government agencies give out grants, the potential grantees expend resources in lobbying up to the value of the grants—an instance of the more general "political dissipation of value" resulting from the scramble for political favors and jobs.

Thus, like the theory of property rights, the public choice perspective indicts public ownership and management across the board. The exponents of these views have developed their position through studies of the public management of land, forests, water, and other natural resources and comparative analyses of public and private enterprises in a variety of industries, including airlines, fire protection, and solid waste disposal.[28] The property rights view of natural resource management exemplifies application of the theory. Public ownership, in this view, inexorably leads to what Garrett Hardin has called "the tragedy of the commons."[29] Acting out of rational self-interest, individuals abuse and ultimately destroy the commons but take good care of their own private property. Thus publicly managed grazing land and forests purportedly suffer from worse management than privately owned land and forests. Moreover, the public agencies responsible for resource management, such as the Forest Service, dissipate value through self-aggrandizing expansionary policies. Consequently, privatizing the public domain would better ensure its conservation and efficient use.[30] One plan for "privatizing the environment" calls for the sale to private investors of federal lands, including national parks, or their transfer to private associations such as the Audubon Society; the same author even recommends solving the problem of endangered species by creating new property rights in wildlife.[31]

In short, starting with an individualistic model of human behavior, the public choice school makes a series of empirical claims: (1) that

28. *See, e.g.*, Ahlbrandt, Efficiency in the Provision of Fire Services, 16 Pub. Choice 1 (1973); Davies, The Efficiency of Public Versus Private Firms, the Case of Australia's Two Airlines, 14 J. Law & Econ. 149 (1971); Bennett & Johnson, Public Versus Private Provision of Collective Goods and Services: Garbage Collection Revisited, 34 Pub. Choice 55 (1979).

29. Hardin, The Tragedy of the Commons, 162 Science 1243 (1968).

30. *See, e.g.*, Forestlands: Public and Private (R. Deacon & M. Johnson eds. 1985); Hanke & Dowdle, Privatizing the Public Domain, 36 Proc. Acad. Pol. Sci. 114 (S. Hanke ed. 1987) (volume entitled Prospects for Privatization).

31. *See* Smith, Privatizing the Environment, 20 Pol. Rev. 11 (1982); Smith, Resolving the Tragedy of the Commons by Creating Private Property Rights in Wildlife, 1 Cato J. 439 (1981).

democratic polities have inherent tendencies toward government growth and excessive budgets; (2) that expenditure growth is due to self-interested coalitions of voters, politicians, and bureaucrats; and (3) that public enterprises necessarily perform less efficiently than private enterprises.

A thorough analysis of the claims of the public choice school would be a book in itself, but the general lines of criticism may be at least briefly suggested. First, while the theory presents voters as narrowly self-interested, considerable evidence suggests that, even on economic issues, voters identify their interests with the overall performance of the economy, rather than simply voting in line with their private experience.[32] Voters, in other words, are capable of recognizing a collective interest apart from their own. Indeed, the whole point of "government by discussion" is to discover and express common interests not easily voiced or achieved in the private sphere. The public choice approach simply does not comprehend this preference-shaping function of political democracy. It also neglects the restraints built into the architecture of liberalism. While the theory holds that government is systematically biased toward dissipating value and increasing expenditure, it disregards the checks and balances among branches of government and within them. The scrutiny of spending programs by Congress and the Office of Management and Budget is an example. According to the theory, spending programs get approved because they have concentrated benefits and diffused costs; however, the same arguments apply to tax reductions for specific interests (that is, tax expenditures). Thus "fiscal illusions" should be symmetrical on the spending and tax sides of the budgetary process and cannot explain long-term tendencies toward higher tax levels. The "Leviathan theorists," as Richard Musgrave calls them, also overstate the historical trend toward higher government expenditure; the evidence does not show an accelerating increase as a proportion of national income.[33]

The empirical evidence comparing efficiency in public and private organizations is also more complex than the property rights and public choice schools acknowledge. To take the example of resource management again, Carlisle Ford Runge points out that the evidence suggests that federally owned rangeland is in better condi-

32. The evidence against the public choice view of political behavior is summed up in Orren, Beyond Self-Interest, in The Power of Public Ideas 13 (R. Reich ed. 1988). *See also* Kelman, Why Public Ideas Matter, in The Power of Public Ideas, *supra*, at 31.

33. Musgrave, Leviathan Cometh—or Does He?, in Tax and Expenditure Limitations 77 (H. Ladd & T. Tideman eds. 1981).

tion than nonfederal rangeland.[34] In one of the few relevant studies of forestland, a survey in Minnesota indicates that extremely few private purchasers of tax-forfeited public forests did anything whatsoever to maintain them.[35] The "tragedy of the commons" argument confuses resources in common ownership with resources in public ownership; it fails to give any credit to the democratic process or to professional management in raising the time horizons of voters, politicians, and bureaucrats to a level higher than that prevailing in the marketplace. Many observers have noted the propensity of American managers for concentrating on short-term profits; the property rights school, by contrast, bravely asserts that private firms have sufficient incentive to preserve wildlife and wilderness for future generations.[36]

The rhetoric of the public choice school is a kind of hard-nosed realism. The theory dismisses as naive civic ideals such as public service; it denies the capacity of voters or politicians to act on the basis of a national interest wider than their own private aggrandizement. Rather like marxism, public choice theory claims to face up to the self-interested basis of democratic politics and therefore treats all claims of higher purpose as smoke and deception. And also like marxism, the theory presents itself as a scientific advance over earlier romantic and idealized views of the state. But rather than being an advance of science over intuition, the appeal of the public choice school is precisely to those who are intuitively certain that whatever government does, the private sector can do better. Together, the property rights and public choice schools show only that, if you start by assuming a purely individualistic model of human behavior and treat politics as if it were a pale imitation of the market, democracy will, indeed, make no sense.

2. *Economic Model 2: Privatization as a Relocation of Economic Functions.* Compared to the right-wing schools that condemn the public sector as irredeemably inefficient, policy analysts trained in conventional microeconomics tend to have a more qualified, though still highly critical, view of public institutions. Rather than attribute the performance of public organizations to the incentives created by public ownership per se, mainstream policy analysts generally think of designing the right incentives within the framework of public or-

34. Runge, The Fallacy of "Privatization," J. Contemp. Stud., Winter 1984, at 3,12.
35. Ellefson, Palm, & Lothner, From Public Land to NonIndustrial Private Forest: A Minnesota Case Study, J. Forestry, Apr. 1982, at 219.
36. Krutilla, et al., Public versus Private Ownership: The Federal Lands Case, 2 J. Pol. Analysis & Mgmt. 548 (1983).

ganization. Of course, the overwhelming consensus is that private ownership is more efficient in providing private goods in competitive markets; hence it is rare to find any respectable opinion in favor of government ownership of factories producing high-performance sports cars. Mainstream views do vary, however, about the proper role of public institutions in producing public goods and managing natural monopolies. Viewing competition as the critical issue, the neoclassically trained are inclined to favor privatization insofar as it represents a move toward competition under conditions when markets should be expected to work efficiently. However, in recent years the requirements for efficient markets have come to be understood more liberally, while the reputation of public enterprise has markedly declined. Hence, the prevailing consensus in economics and policy analysis has become more sympathetic to privatization than it was two or three decades ago.

While the property rights view is parsimonious and unambiguous in analyzing the basis of public-private differences, the more conventional approach is a patchwork of theories about the conditions under which the market, the state, and the nonprofit sector fail to perform efficiently. In this tradition, the theory of market failure is the historical point of departure. According to the received neoclassical wisdom, imperfect information, externalities, increasing returns to scale, and (in some versions) inequalities of wealth prevent the market from achieving optimal performance; it is then a short—though not a necessary—step to say that where the market fails, some form of public ownership or regulation is justified. (The theory says nothing about the choice between regulation and ownership.) However, two recent developments have suggested more caution about public intervention. First, markets need not be perfectly competitive to perform efficiently; they only need to be contestable—and the requirements for contestability are more easily met.[37] Second, public choice theory has successfully raised the challenge that where markets fail, so, too, may government; indeed, the theory suggests that government's performance will only be worse. Attempting to state the argument symmetrically, Charles Wolf, Jr., has spelled out a series of conditions for "nonmarket failure."[38]

These twin theories of market and nonmarket failure have, in turn, suggested a role for the nonprofit sector; for if states and markets have peculiar weaknesses, perhaps philanthropy can be ex-

37. W. Baumol, J. Panzar & R. Willig, Contestable Markets and the Theory of Industry Structure (1982).

38. Wolf, A Theory of Non-Market Failures, Pub. Interest, Spring 1979, at 114.

plained as an attempt to fill the void.[39] But, rather than define the voluntary sector as residual, Lester Salamon has argued that in the United States nonprofits are the "preferred" mechanism for delivering public services and that government programs arise to meet the problems of "voluntary failure."[40] The upshot is a theoretical amalgam that defines the limits of the three sectors and suggests in what form different kinds of activities are most efficiently organized. From this perspective, privatization becomes a way to move activity from a less efficient to a more efficient form—a tool of economic adjustment rather than radical reconstruction.[41]

The expanded theory of sector failure is a kind of ecological approach to institutional choice. The various sectors provide alternative environments, and the problem is to decide whether a particular set of tasks is best carried out in one or more locations. However, the theory does not exhaustively assign all activities. No sector gets high marks for performing tasks for which there is poor information. The theory is also ahistorical; it makes no allowance for sunk investments in organizational capacity. Relocating an industry in a different sector is not, after all, a costless exercise. However, the most serious defect of this approach is that, like all the economic models, it is principally concerned with efficiency and has little to say about the effects of organizational design on other values. To subject an organization to market forces is to push it to maximize the returns to residual claims holders; perhaps it will generate those returns more efficiently, but as George Yarrow has observed, some activities have been turned over to the public sector precisely to be protected from such pressure.[42] The economic models cannot say whether or not that is a sensible choice.

### *B. Privatization as Community Empowerment*

A different set of arguments, not chiefly concerned with efficiency, comes from a more sociological theory of privatization that emphasizes the strengthening of communities. In the most noteworthy exposition of this position, Peter Berger and Richard Neuhaus propose that government "empower" voluntary associations, com-

39. J. Douglas, Why Charity? (1983).

40. Salamon, Partners in Public Service: The Scope and Theory of Government-Nonprofit Relations, in The Nonprofit Sector: A Research Handbook 99, 113 (W. Powell ed. 1987).

41. For an analysis of this perspective, see Young & Brodkin, The Political Economy of Privatization, in Privatization and the Welfare State (S. Kamerman & A. Kahn eds.) (forthcoming).

42. Yarrow, Privatization in Theory and Practice, 2 Econ. Pol'y 324, 331-32 (1986).

munity organizations, churches, self-help groups, and other less formal "mediating" institutions that lie between individuals and society's "alienating megastructures."[43] In their view, the modern liberal state has undermined these "value-generating," "value-maintaining," "people-sized institutions" by establishing service bureaucracies that take over their functions. Berger and Neuhaus are not opposed to the provision of social welfare, but they urge that, wherever possible, public policy rely on mediating institutions for the delivery of publicly financed services.

The view of privatization as community empowerment stands in sharp contrast to the conception of privatization as an extension of property rights. Berger and Neuhaus emphatically reject a narrowly individualistic view of human motivation. Indeed, they criticize liberalism precisely for defending individual rights over the rights of social groups to assert their own values; for example, they defend the capacity of neighborhoods to sustain "democratically determined values in the public sphere" by exhibiting religious symbols in public places.[44] They also suggest that attacks on the ideals of voluntary service "aid the expansion of the kind of capitalist mentality that would put a dollar sign on everything on the grounds that only that which has a price tag has worth."[45] Their concern is not to expand the domain of the profit motive but rather to strengthen local, small-scale forms of social provision. This is privatization with a human face, and it bears some resemblance to left-wing interest in community organizations and cooperatives.[46]

Although I find the community empowerment view more attractive than the property rights perspective, the Berger and Neuhaus claim that the liberal state undermines mediating institutions ignores the historical partnership between the two. The history of social provision in the United States does not, in fact, betray a disregard for the virtues of voluntary institutions. Salamon points out that the twentieth-century expansion of social spending in the United States has been largely a growth of what he calls "third-party" government (the third parties including local government as well as private nonprofit agencies).[47] Many nonprofit community

43. P. Berger & R. Neuhaus, To Empower People: The Role of Mediating Structures in Public Policy (1977).

44. *Id.* at 11.

45. *Id.* at 36-7.

46. *See, e.g.*, Donnison, The Progressive Potential of Privatisation, in Privatisation and the Welfare State 45 (J. LeGrand & R. Robinson eds. 1984).

47. Salamon, *supra* note 40, at 110.

organizations have depended for their survival on government subsidies. Moreover, today there is often a division of labor between the public and voluntary sectors. A still greater reliance on the non-profit sector might pose serious problems for the voluntary institutions themselves. To be sure, privatization is taking place in many social services, but the growth is chiefly of new for-profit organizations that are far from the local "people-sized" institutions envisioned by Berger and Neuhaus. Some of them, like the national chains of nursing homes, are every bit as alienating as other corporate "megastructures." It is probably an illusion to think that a major shift toward private social services would lead to a proliferation of community organizations, if only because the private institutions would need much more capital than they traditionally have had available. If not supplied by the state, the capital must be supplied by the financial markets. In health care, the demand of capital formation is one of the principal pressures producing a shift from non-profit to commercial organization, often national in scale.[48] Community empowerment might be a good idea, but if it is to come at all, it will come from more government intervention, not from privatization.

### C. *Privatization as a Reduction of Government Overload*

A final theory justifying privatization holds that privatization is desirable for its likely political effect in deflecting and reducing demands on the state. In the 1970s, some critics suggested that the Western democracies were suffering from an "overload" of pressure, responsible for excessive spending and poor economic performance.[49] In that framework privatization represents one of several policies encouraging a counterrevolution of declining expectations. In a similar vein, Stuart Butler of the Heritage Foundation has argued that privatization can cure budget deficits by breaking up the kind of public spending coalitions described by public choice theory. Privatizing government enterprises and public services, in this view, will redirect aspirations into the market and encourage a more entrepreneurial consciousness.[50]

The political theory of privatization has several different, overlapping elements. First, the privatization of enterprises is a privatiza-

48. Starr, Social Transformation of American Medicine (1982).

49. S. Huntington, M. Crozier & J. Watanuki, The Crisis of Democracy 163-64 (1975).

50. S. Butler, Privatizing Federal Spending: A Strategy to Eliminate the Deficit 43-62 (1985).

tion of employment relations. The advocates of privatization hope to divert employees' wage claims from the public treasury, with its vast capacity for taxing and borrowing, to private employers, who presumably will have more spine in resisting wage demands. Moreover, the proponents hope for a trickle-down of entrepreneurship from the newly privatized managers to the workers; for that very reason, privatizers often are perfectly willing to sell to the workers, at an advantageous price, whole enterprises or at least some proportion of the shares. In addition, by shifting to private contractors even in a few selected areas, government might signal a harder line on wage concessions and thereby weaken public employee unions.

Second, the advocates of privatization hope also for a privatization of beneficiaries' claims. Instead of marching outside of government offices when things go wrong, the privatizers want them to direct their ire to private service providers—or better yet, simply to switch to other providers. In other words, privatization could mean a wholesale shift, in Hirschman's terms, from "voice" to "exit" as the usual and preferred tactic of coping with dissatisfaction.[51]

Third, the privatization of public assets and enterprises is also a privatization of wealth. Advocates such as Margaret Thatcher want privatization to increase the proportion of the population who own shares of stock and therefore take a more positive view of profit-making.[52] "People's capitalism" is an old idea, but using privatization of public assets to bring it about is new. Moreover, by privatizing other assets such as public housing and Social Security trust funds, privatizers hope to turn public claimants into property owners and engender in them a deeper identification with capitalism. They expect the worker who receives a retirement income from a private pension or individual retirement account to have a more conservative view of the world than that of the worker who depends on rent subsidies and a government check every month.

This political theory of privatization, like the economic and sociological theories, contains empirical predictions as well as normative judgments. The predictions concern the probable effects of privatization on political consciousness and action; the normative judgments concern the desirability of weakening the political foundations of public provision. Empirically, it seems unlikely that contracting-out, vouchers, and other arrangements for paying pri-

51. A. Hirschman, Exit, Voice, and Loyalty (1970).
52. Francis, Britain Pushing "People's Capitalism," Christian Sci. Monitor, July 17, 1985, at 21; Smith, The British Scene, 64 Foreign Aff. 923, 930-31 (1986).

vate providers will reduce pressure on government spending; the contractors are as likely as public employees to lobby for larger budgets.[53] However, some forms of privatization may, indeed, change the underlying political values, understandings, and capacities for action in society. Turning public tenants into private homeowners, public employees into private employees, and Social Security beneficiaries into investors in private retirement accounts could very well change their frame of social and political thought. These prospects raise rather different issues from the usual efficiency-minded discussions of privatization; they demand that we consider the meaning of privatization not only as a theory but also as a political practice.

### *III. Privatization as a Political Practice*

I said earlier that the structural variety of public and private organizations, political systems, and national contexts makes it difficult to generalize about public-private differences and the effects of privatization. The task of generalization is still more complex because the forms of privatization vary so greatly. In this section, I spell out some of the contextual factors and critical choices that shape what privatization means in practice and that help to explain why political practice often conflicts with theory.

#### *A. The Political Contexts and Uses of Privatization*

The meaning of privatization depends in practice on a nation's position in the world economy. In the wealthier countries it is easy to treat privatization purely as a question of domestic policy. But where the likely buyers are foreign, as in the Third World, privatization of state-owned enterprises often means denationalization—a transfer of control to foreign investors or managers. Since state ownership often originally came about in an act of national self-assertion, privatization appears to be a retreat in the face of international pressure. In that sense, national memory colors the meaning of privatization. However, even in the United States, privatization would be understood rather differently if public assets up for sale or contracts up for bid were likely to be taken over by the Russians or even the Japanese. The more dependent a nation is on foreign investment, the greater the likelihood that privatization will raise the

53. Starr, The Limits of Privatization, in 36 Proc. Acad. Pol. Sci. 124, 128 (S. Hanke ed. 1987) (volume entitled Prospects for Privatization).

prospect of diminished sovereignty and excite the passions of nationalism. Where privatization raises such issues, it is often blocked, or citizens and domestic firms are reserved exclusive rights to publicly offered assets, shares, or contracts. In many Western countries, state ownership owed more in the first place to nationalist than to socialist sentiment; hence it is scarcely surprising that nationalism is liable to derail or distort privatization plans.

Throughout the world, the privatization of enterprises with strategic military or economic significance raises especially sensitive questions of sovereignty and security. In most oil-producing countries, for example, no government is likely to try to privatize the state oil companies because of the likely domestic political reaction. Even in Great Britain, the prospective sale of a helicopter company to an American company caused a political stir.[54] Despite its commitment to free markets, the Reagan Administration intervened in 1987 to prevent the sale to a Japanese corporation of a private American semiconductor company with important defense contracts.[55] On the other hand, the Reagan administration has sought to privatize some of NASA's satellite launch operations partly in the hope of strengthening the private American space industry in its competition with the Europeans.[56] Yet this case only reinforces the general point: The conflict between privatization and national interests depends on the relative power of a given state in the world system—the weaker the state, the more likely the conflict. Economically strong nations, knowing that they can privatize without jeopardizing their sovereignty, lecture the weak on the perils of state enterprise and restrictions on investment.

Like national interests, the more parochial concerns of politically dominant racial and ethnic groups may also confound privatization plans. In many countries, ethnic minorities, such as Indians in East Africa, make up disproportionate numbers of the potential domestic buyers of public assets. When a country's bureaucratic and entrepreneurial classes differ in ethnic composition, privatization may be understood as a transfer of wealth and power from one group to another and be politically resisted for that reason. Even if privatiza-

54. Marshall, Copter Firm's Bail-out Splits British Cabinet, L.A. Times, Dec. 31, 1985, § 4 at 2, col. 5.

55. Rempel & Walters, The Fairchild Deal: Trade War: When Chips Were Down, L.A. Times, Nov. 30, 1987, § 1, at 1, col. 1.

56. Broad, Space Drive's Tilt to Industry Gains Wide New Impetus, N.Y. Times, Jan. 24, 1988, § 1, pt. 1, at 1, col. 4.

tion is adopted, the field of potential buyers may be so restricted that potential gains from more efficient management evaporate.

The larger point in these examples of "distorting" influences on privatization is that private sectors are not only characterized by private ownership in the abstract. The potential private owners of public assets and contractors for public services represent specific interests and groups. Privatization is unlikely to be carried out with indifference to those social facts.

In general, the political uses of privatization are bound to compromise the avowed efficiency objectives. Governments that are in a hurry to sell state-owned enterprises may make concessions to current managers, whose cooperation is instrumental in divestiture. Privatization then becomes an occasion for managerial enrichment and entrenchment. It is striking that in Great Britain, France, and other countries that have privatized state-owned enterprises, privatization usually brings about little or no change in top management.[57] Moreover, governments commonly offer assets and enterprises up for sale to political allies. Some of these properties, such as broadcasting stations, are not simply economic but political assets; the incumbent government gains obvious advantage by placing them in the hands of political allies. The same patterns have long been evident in the contracting of public services; indeed, contracting is the *locus classicus* of the political pay-off. Even public offerings are not immune from political use. When governments underprice shares—as has been the overwhelming pattern in Britain[58]—they may be seeking to ensure not only that privatization is successfully realized, but also that happy shareholders have the opportunity to repay the government at the next election. Indeed, rather perversely, one could turn the whole force of public choice analysis on privatization itself: The logic of concentrated benefits and diffuse costs makes it altogether likely that the diffuse efficiency gains of privatization will be sacrificed in the effort to satisfy the big stakeholders—incumbent politicians and bureaucrats and their allies and supporters.

Politically inspired privatization is all the more likely because privatization attracts support not only from economists with a disinterested belief in liberalized markets but also from a privatization

57. Seminar with Helène Ploix, Executive Director, International Monetary Fund, Privatization Successes in Developed and Developing Countries, Princeton University, Jan. 14, 1988.

58. Mayer & Meadowcroft, Selling Public Assets: Techniques and Financial Implications, in Privatization and Regulation: The U.K. Experience, *supra* note 23, at 322.

The Meaning of Privatization

lobby consisting of investment banking firms, government contractors, and other corporations whose businesses stand to benefit if the public sector cedes ground. Rather than being an escape from interest group influence and the politicization of resource use, privatization typically provides a prime example.

I do not want to suggest, however, that the view of politics as pure self-interest captures all that is going on, even in the case of privatization. Privatization is a worldwide policy movement carried along by a combination of objective forces, imitative processes, and international financial sponsorship. Many countries whose public sectors expanded sharply in recent decades now find themselves confronted by rising debt and strong resistance to higher taxes. Privatizing state-owned firms promises to bring some fiscal relief, particularly where the treasury has been heavily subsidizing unprofitable enterprises. Privatization may help both to cut expenditures and boost revenues, and, by converting debt to equity, states may improve the overall financial structure of their economies and reduce pressure for even less palatable austerity measures. Privatization is not the only possible response, but as in other institution-shaping movements, like the postwar spread of public enterprises, organizational forms spread by imitation. Institutional models are disseminated through a variety of political networks and the direct influence of international lending organizations. Privatization is now one of the policies that the International Monetary Fund promotes in negotiating loans with developing countries.[59]

Of course, proponents of privatization see the process more as learning than as imitation or imposition. In their view, the poor performance of public enterprise and, more generally, overexpanded public sectors has simply taught that privatization makes sense. But experience is never so transparent. Even where state enterprises are generally agreed to be highly inefficient, it is not necessarily clear that privatization will be a remedy. Moreover, the performance of some state-owned enterprises—for example, in Malaysia and France—has been excellent, and it is simply not true that

59. *See, e.g.*, Brooke, International Report: Guinea Booms as Markets Replace Marxism, N.Y. Times, Dec. 28, 1987, at D8, col. 1; Killen, West Africa Turns to Private Sector for Efficiency, Reuter Bus. Rep., Sept. 4, 1987 (BC cycle); IMF Approves $1.7 Billion Standby Loan for Mexico, 47 Wash. Fin. Rep. (BNA) No. 21, at 880 (Dec. 1, 1986). However, see also Gains From Privatization May Be Small Without Measures to Boost Competition, IMF Survey, March 23, 1987, at 82.

as public sectors grow, rates of economic growth fall.[60] To be sure, the record of central government planning is dismal, but that experience cannot simply be extrapolated to all publicly owned organizations, particularly in states with more autonomous forms of public sector management.

The property rights approach predicts politically imposed inefficiency on the basis of public ownership alone, but the variety of public sectors and state-owned enterprises in the world suggests instead that performance may be contingent on political culture, the structure of the state, and public policy toward enterprises. In some countries public management is well-established, professional, and prestigious, whereas in others the political party in power expects to give its own people jobs at every level. The mode of public sector control depends also on the structure of political-administrative relationships. It is a mistake in this context to view the state as a unitary actor. Public sectors often comprise a vast sprawl of organizations in public ownership, many of them, like public universities in the United States, only loosely connected to the centers of political decisionmaking. A great array of institutional devices, such as independent governing boards with self-perpetuating membership and earmarked financing, can serve to insulate public organizations from political intervention. In their legal status, public organizations variously include agencies under direct political authority, independent authorities incorporated under public law, state-owned enterprises incorporated under private law, and private companies in which the government has some ownership. Of course, the legal differences may or may not matter; autonomy is never guaranteed purely by formal structure. Finally, as a matter of policy, governments may or may not require public enterprises to be run on a commercial, business-like basis. Privatization may have little impact on the efficiency of organizations already operated on a commercial basis, and the effect of privatizing more politicized organizations depends on their previous political uses, some of which may be eminently defensible.

Political culture and preexisting administrative capacities are not unreasonable bases for choices about state versus private ownership. Where the state is the only domestic institution capable of sustaining the confidence of foreign creditors or administering large

60. *See generally* Saunders, Public Expenditure and Economic Performance in OECD Countries, 5 J. Pub. Pol'y 1 (1986); R. Kuttner, The Economic Illusion: False Choices Between Prosperity and Social Justice (1984).

undertakings and where it has demonstrated management competence, the case for state enterprise may be correspondingly strong. On the other hand, in some regimes the penchant for political intervention produces endemic overstaffing, poor location of plants, extravagant wages, and prices far out of line with market levels. Like alcoholics unable to cut down except by quitting altogether, these governments may be unable to avoid disrupting public enterprises, except by privatizing them altogether. Moreover, in much of the world, state enterprise gives the dominant elites too powerful a grip over civil society. For example, the Argentine military is said to use its huge network of industrial enterprises as an instrument of patronage and power.[61] In such cases, privatization may well be justified as a means of releasing society from bureaucratic domination.

Whether the advanced capitalist societies suffer from too strong a bureaucratic grip is, of course, exactly where the right and left disagree. In this respect, the United States, which has never nationalized industry in the first place, stands in a position fundamentally different from the Western European countries with extensive public enterprise sectors. The sphere of public ownership in the United States has been so limited that I find implausible the view that Americans suffer from an oppressive government role in the production of goods and services. The relations between the public sector and political leadership are drastically different in the United States from those prevailing in Latin America, the Soviet bloc, and even many Western European countries. If political meddling is the chief problem in public sector organizations, the United States has an effective alternative to privatization in the establishment of public corporations (often called public authorities in the United States). Their insulation from political control, the independence of the judiciary, and the decentralization of power in the federal system prevent public authorities from being easily bent by political caprice.

Indeed, the problems of the American public sector seem to be of the opposite kind. So deeply entrenched are the barriers to unitary control that legitimate interests in coordinated management are thwarted. American public institutions at all levels of government suffer from rampant credentialism and proceduralism that hamper the ability of managers to hire and fire, reward, and motivate their subordinates. Ironically, many of these rigidities result from previous reforms, passed in the name of curbing corruption. For a vari-

61. Fontana, Armed Forces and Neo-Conservative Ideology: State Shrinking in Argentina, 1976-81, in State Shrinking, *supra* note 18, at 62-74.

ety of reasons, public organizations also do not respond quickly to change, such as the emergence of new technologies and consumer demands. The long lead times required by the appropriations process often prevent agencies from adapting quickly. Privatization is one route out of the procedural thicket; however, we might achieve some of the same ends by making public administration more flexible and giving public managers more independent authority.

To be sure, government cannot be run "just like a business" in part because its more elaborate procedures are meant to produce something else besides the specific services that the private sector provides. Reviews by advisory committees and congressional hearings, designed to increase accountability or to give a fair hearing to complaints by clients, contractors, or employees, cannot be dismissed simply as a source of inefficiency. Democratic government cannot narrowly concern itself with getting the job done, which is one reason why it should not concern itself with all the jobs that need doing. Privatization is a legitimate tool for sharpening the focus of government on those activities most important to the general welfare, but it is never simply efficiency that is at stake in such decisions.

### B. *Privatization as a Reordering of Claims*

Privatization needs to be understood as a fundamental reordering of claims in a society. As I indicated earlier, in the liberal world the terms public and private sum up a whole structure of rules and expectations about the proper conduct and limits of the state. To say some activity is public is to invoke claims of public purpose, public accountability, and public disclosure. To say something is private is to claim protection from state officials and other citizens. The theory of property rights sees privatization as a reassignment of claims to the control and use of assets, but it misses the special claims of the public sphere in a democratic society—claims for greater disclosure of information, which should improve the social capacity to make choices, and for rights of participation and discussion, which permit the discovery and formation of preferences that are more consistent with long-term societal interests. As a general movement of institutional design, privatization undermines the foundation of claims for public purpose and public services.

This reordering of claims holds distributive implications. It shifts power to those who can more readily exercise power in the market. It also may shift income and wealth, depending on the specific form that privatization takes. Some forms of privatization do not logically require a reduction in public benefits to the poor. It is hypothetically possible to conceive of a privatization program with highly progressive effects on income distribution. Imagine, for example, a program involving the sale of heavily subsidized, poorly managed public enterprises; the conversion of a publicly budgeted health service, covering only a minority of employed workers, into a voucher system covering the whole population; and the empowerment of local nonprofit, grassroots organizations with funds stripped from elite-dominated central bureaucracies. Taken together these steps would redistribute benefits to previously excluded or short-changed groups.

In practice, however, a progressive effect on income distribution seems highly improbable. The same political forces that support privatization generally also support cutbacks in public spending for social welfare; the same arguments about incentives and efficiency used in favor of privatizing public services are also cited by those who want to terminate public financing for the services altogether. In addition, private service providers often maximize profits by seeking out the least costly clients or by employing lower-wage workers, often on a part-time basis. Since wages tend to be more equal in the public sector, privatization is likely to skew the income distribution in the direction of greater inequality. Furthermore, while unions have lost ground in the private sector, they have generally made advances in organizing public employees. Privatization tends to undermine those gains—an effect not overlooked by advocates of privatization.

In the extreme case, privatization is an instrument of class politics. Where privatization is used to break up public employee unions and reduce the provision of services, it effectively represents a means of reordering class relations. Privatization in Chile in the mid-1970s had this character. A vast shift in wealth took place with the privatization not only of industry but of the financial assets of the social security system, which ended up concentrated in the hands of a few private financial groups.[62] At the other extreme, privatization is a relatively modest tool of public management. In many cases of contracting, the private firms receiving contracts are as unionized as the public sector and there is no change in wage levels. When New York City privatized its school busing, the drivers

62. A. Foxley, Latin American Experiments in Neoconservative Economics 106-07 (1983).

continued to be represented by the same union, and service costs did not change.[63] But this is scarcely the kind of example that privatization advocates hope to imitate. Once again, while privatization hypothetically does not mean wage reductions, the intentions behind the policy raise strong and entirely reasonable suspicions that it will.

Privatization is not only a policy; it is also a signal about the competence and desirability of public provision. It reinforces the view that government cannot be expected to perform well. If, to many Americans, private means better, it is partly because of long-existing restrictions on the scope and quality of public provision. We commonly limit public services to a functional minimum and thereby guarantee that people will consider the private alternative a step up. This niggardliness shows itself in ways large and small. In the 1960s, one congressman who was indignant over the costs of a public housing program succeeded in persuading his colleagues specifically to forbid flower boxes as an unnecessary extravagance.[64] The restricted quality of public provision is a self-reinforcing feature. Because the poor are the principal beneficiaries of many programs, the middle-class public opposes expenditures to produce as high a quality of service as they must pay for privately; and because the quality is held down, the poor as well as the middle class develop a contempt for the public sector and an eagerness to escape it. The movement toward privatization reflects and promotes this contempt, and therein lies part of its political danger.

Some individual proposals for privatization have considerable merit, but the overall message is clearly to call into doubt the nation's capacity and need for collective provision. The possibilities for change being discussed are not symmetrical. Privatization advocates raise questions exclusively about the adequacy of the public sector; the comparable questions about the private sector do not receive the same attention. Even though privatization is logically distinct from questions of distributive justice, the privatization debate puts the advocates of more generous public programs entirely on the defensive. This one-sidedness is why I am opposed to privatization. I am opposed to the political consequences that are likely to flow from pursuing privatization as a solution to the difficulties of administering democratic government.

63. Bailey, Uses and Misuses of Privatization, 36 Proc. Acad. Pol. Sci. 138, 145-46 (S. Hanke ed. 1987) (volume entitled Prospects for Privatization).
64. Talk by Lester Thurow, Williamsburg, Va. (Dec. 1984).

## The Meaning of Privatization

Privatization, as some advocates themselves point out, represents an effort to alter the conditions of political competition by breaking up the coalitions supporting public provision and by promoting more market-oriented political values. In other words, it is an attempt to fix in place the conservative orientation that has emerged forcefully in the 1980s. No one need doubt that public institutions, like private ones, are bases of wealth and power. They are environments that encourage those who work within them to develop different political orientations. To alter the public-private balance is to change the distribution of material and symbolic resources influencing the shape of political life. Privatization ought to be frankly recognized as part of an effort of conservatives to reinforce their own power position. Since I do not share the values for which that power is deployed, I distrust privatization. Ultimately I fear that one form of privatization does entail another—that as we move public provision into the private sector, we move from the realm of the open and visible into a domain that is more closed to scrutiny and access. And in the process, whether or not intending to change, we are likely to narrow our involvements, interests, and vision of a good society and a good life.

Pergamon

*Accounting, Organizations and Society*, Vol. 20, No. 2/3, pp. 93–109, 1995
Elsevier Science Ltd
Printed in Great Britain
0361–3682/95 $9.50+0.00

0361–3682(93)E0001–W

# THE "NEW PUBLIC MANAGEMENT" IN THE 1980s: VARIATIONS ON A THEME*

CHRISTOPHER HOOD
*London School of Economics and Political Science*

**Abstract**

Changes in public sector accounting in a number of OECD countries over the 1980s were central to the rise of the "New Public Management" (NPM) and its associated doctrines of public accountability and organizational best practice. This paper discusses the rise of NPM as an alternative to the tradition of public accountability embodied in progressive-era public administration ideas. It argues that, in spite of allegations of internationalization and the adoption of a new global paradigm in public management, there was considerable variation in the extent to which different OECD countries adopted NPM over the 1980s. It further argues that conventional explanations of the rise of NPM ("Englishness", party political incumbency, economic performance record and government size) seem hard to sustain even from a relatively brief inspection of such cross-national data as are available, and that an explanation based on initial endowment may give us a different perspective on those changes.

Over the 1980s, there was a move in a number of OECD countries towards the New Public Management (NPM). Central to this change in modes of public management was a shift towards "accountingization" (a term coined by Power & Laughlin, 1992, p. 133).[1] This development can be claimed to be part of a broader shift in received doctrines of public accountability and public administration. At the same time, accounting changes formed an important part of the assault on the progressive-era models of public accountability (cf. Halligan & Wettenhall, 1990).

For progressive public administration,[2] democratic accountability depends on limiting corruption and the waste and incompetence that are held to go with it (cf. Karl, 1963, p. 18). The assumption is that politicians are inherently venal, using their public office wherever possible to enrich themselves, their friends and relations, and that reliance on private-sector contracting for public services inevitably leads to high-cost low-quality products, either because of corrupt influence on the contract-awarding process or because the public contract market will come to be controlled by organized crime, or both. Whether these assumptions can be safely dispensed with in the wealthy OECD countries of today is a matter for debate.

From those assumptions, the accountability paradigm of progressive public administration (hereafter PPA for convenience) put heavy stress on two basic management doctrines. One of those doctrines was to keep the public sector sharply distinct from the private sector in terms

* This paper was presented in an earlier form to the Workshop on "Changing Notions of Accountability in the U.K. Public Sector", LSE, December 1991, and to the EIASM Workshop on Accounting, Accountability and the "New European Public Sector", Helsinki, September 1992. I am grateful for comments and criticisms received on those occasions, and particularly to Peter Miller for helpful suggestions.

[1] Broadly, "accountingization" means the introduction of ever-more explicit cost categorization into areas where costs were previously aggregated, pooled or undefined.

[2] That is, the style of public administration that emerged in the "progressive era" of the late nineteenth and early twentieth centuries.

of continuity, ethos, methods of doing business, organizational design, people, rewards and career structure. The aim, in Beatrice Webb's words (Barker, 1984, p. 34), was for a "Jesuitical corps" of ascetic zealots. The other doctrine was to maintain buffers against political and managerial discretion by means of an elaborate structure of procedural rules designed to prevent favouritism and corruption and to keep arms-length relations between politicians and the entrenched custodians of particular public service "trusts".[3]

This organizational model attracts more derision than analysis today (cf. Osborne & Gaebler, 1992). In fact, it reflects an underlying metaphor of trustee and beneficiary (John Locke's metaphor for government) and involves a complex mix of high-trust and low-trust relationships, with the accompanying accounting rules reflecting degrees of trust. Within the "Jesuitical corps" of the public service were many high-trust relationships (for example, in conventions of mutual consultation or action on the basis of word-of-mouth agreements across departments), the costs of which were not accountingized. The implicit assumption is that such high-trust, non-costed behaviour lowers transaction costs within the public sector and makes it more efficient than it would be if each action had to be negotiated and costed on a low-trust basis. However, PPA also embodied many low-trust relationships, particularly in areas where the Jesuitical corps faced the corrupting forces of the world outside, notably the award of contracts, recruitment and staffing, as well as the handling of cash, where distrust prevailed and elaborate records had to be kept and audited.

In the place of the PPA model came New Public Management or NPM (cf. Aucoin, 1990; Hood, 1987, 1990a, b, 1991; Dunsire & Hood, 1989; Hood & Jackson, 1991; Pollitt, 1993; Pusey, 1991). NPM involved a different conception of public accountability, with different patterns of trust and distrust and hence a different style of accountingization. The basis of NPM lay in reversing the two cardinal doctrines of PPA; that is, lessening or removing differences between the public and the private sector and shifting the emphasis from process accountability towards a greater element of accountability in terms of results. Accounting was to be a key element in this new conception of accountability, since it reflected high trust in the market and private business methods (no longer to be equated with organized crime) and low trust in public servants and professionals (now seen as budget-maximizing bureaucrats rather than Jesuitical ascetics), whose activities therefore needed to be more closely costed and evaluated by accounting techniques. The ideas of NPM were couched in the language of economic rationalism, and promoted by a new generation of "econocrats" and "accountocrats" in high public office.

The term NPM was coined because some generic label seemed to be needed for a general, though certainly not universal, shift in public management styles. The term was intended to cut across the particular language of individual projects or countries (such as the French "*Projet de Service*", the British "Next Steps", the Canadian "Public Service 2000"). The analogy is with terms like new politics, new right, and new industrial state, which were invented for a similar reason.[4]

As with the disappearance of the dinosaurs, there is no single accepted explanation of this alleged paradigm shift. In fact, emerging explanations roughly parallel the major contending theories of the dinosaurs' extinction. Some

[3] An organizational structure which could clearly be classed as "hierarchist" in the cultural theory of Mary Douglas (1982) and her followers (Thompson *et al.*, 1990).

[4] The term "new" does not imply that NPM doctrines appeared for the first time in the 1980s (any more than the "New Learning" of the fifteenth and sixteenth centuries involved the first discovery of Latin and Greek). Many NPM doctrines repackage ideas which have been in public administration since its earliest beginnings. Nor must NPM be confused with the "New Public Administration" movement in the U.S.A. in the late 1960s and early 1970s, which achieved no real mainstream influence (see Marini, 1971).

accounts stress "habitat loss" for the old style arising from post-industrial technology, producing a wholly new model of public administration built around electronic data handling and networking, providing many new niches for accountingization and lowering its direct costs (see Taylor & Williams, 1991, p. 172; Taylor, 1992). Some see the demise of the old model as the result of a sudden shock, with New Right ideas about organizational design coming as a meteorite from out of the blue (as in Quirk's, 1988, idea-centric account of 1980s' deregulation). Some see PPA's fate as a self-induced extinction, as older control frameworks and accounting practices came to degrade the values which they were designed to promote (see Painter, 1990, p. 77; Hirschman, 1982). And yet others interpret the change as caused by a new set of predator interests, such as accounting firms and management consultants, hunting PPA into extinction (see Dunleavy, 1985, 1986, 1991).

However, before such "extinction science" can be developed, we need to be satisfied that some general extinction has actually taken place, and that the new life-form of NPM is everywhere supplanting PPA. Such claims are indeed commonly made both by practitioners and by academic commentators. Aucoin (1990, p. 134), for instance, asserts that: "What has been taking place in almost every government in developed political systems and highly institutionalized administrative states is a new emphasis on the organizational designs for public management ... This internationalization of public management parallels the internationalization of public and private sector economies." Similarly, Osborne & Gaebler (1992, pp. 322–330) write of NPM as a new "global paradigm", claiming that transition to the new paradigm is inevitable "just as the transition from machine rule to Progressive government was inevitable" (p. 325).

If we accept such claims, we would expect to see a process of international convergence and diffusion of NPM ideas in public administration. But this paper argues that the internationalization of the NPM model at least contains important variations, and that no account of the shift from the progressive public administration model to NPM can be satisfactory unless it can account for international leaders and laggards.

## NEW PUBLIC MANAGEMENT; THEMES AND VARIATIONS

### *Themes*

The doctrines of public sector management encompassed by NPM have been variously described by different commentators (such as Aucoin, 1990; Hood, 1991; Pollitt, 1993), and some have identified different phases in the development of NPM. However, there is still a good deal of overlap among the different accounts of what NPM entailed. For example, the idea of a shift in emphasis from policy making to management skills, from a stress on process to a stress on output, from orderly hierarchies to an intendedly more competitive basis for providing public services, from fixed to variable pay and from a uniform and inclusive public service to a variant structure with more emphasis on contract provision, are themes which appear in most accounts.

Most commentators have associated NPM with approximately seven dimensions of change, which are summarized in Table 1, together with their associated doctrines, and some speculative ideas about their implications for accountingization. The elements relate to the two cardinal elements of PPA already noted, in that the first four elements of Table 1 relate to the issue of how far the public sector should be distinct from the private sector in its organization and methods of accountability, and the last three broadly relate to the issue of how far managerial and professional discretion should be fenced in by explicit standards and rules. The seven elements are as follows.

(1) A shift towards greater *disaggregation* of public organizations into separately managed "corporatized" units for each public sector "product" (each identified as a separate cost centre, with its own organizational identity in

TABLE 1. Doctrinal components of new public management

| No. | Doctrine | Typical justification | Replaces | Operational significance | Some possible accounting implications |
|---|---|---|---|---|---|
| *PS distinctiveness* | | | | | |
| 1. | Unbundling of the PS into corporatized units organized by product | Make units manageable; and focus blame; split provision and production to create anti-waste lobby | Belief in uniform and inclusive PS to avoid underlaps and overlaps in accountability | Erosion of single service employment; arms-length dealings; devolved budgets | More cost centre units |
| 2. | More contract-based competitive provision, with internal markets and term contracts | Rivalry as the key to lower costs and better standards; contracts as the key to explicating performance standards | Unspecified employment contracts, open-ended provision, linking of purchase, provision, production, to cut transaction cost | Distinction of primary and secondary public service labour force | More stress on identifying costs and understanding cost structures; so cost data become commercially confidential and cooperative behaviour becomes costly |
| 3. | Stress on private-sector styles of management practice | Need to apply proven private-sector management tools in the public sector | Stress on PS ethic fixed pay and hiring rules, model employer orientation centralized personnel structure, jobs for life | Move from double imbalance PS pay, career service, unmonetized rewards "due process" employee entitlements | Private-sector accounting norms |
| 4. | More stress on discipline and frugality in resource use | Need to cut direct costs, raise labour discipline, do more with less | Stable base budget and establishment norms, minimum standards, union vetoes | Less primary employment, less job security, less producer-friendly style | More stress on the bottom line |
| *Rules vs discretion* | | | | | |
| 5. | More emphasis on visible hands-on top management | Accountability requires clear assignment of responsiblity not diffusion of power | Paramount stress on policy skills and rules, not active management | More freedom to manage by discretionary power | Fewer general procedural constraints on handling of contracts, cash, staff; coupled with more use of financial data for management accountability |
| 6. | Explicit formal measurable standards and measures of peformance and success | Accountability means clearly stated aims; efficiency needs hard look at goals | Qualitative and implicit standards and norms | Erosion of self-management by professionals | Performance indicators and audit |
| 7. | Greater emphasis on output controls | Need for greater stress on results | Stress on procedure and control by collibration | Resources and pay based on performance | Move away from detailed accounting for particular activities towards broader cost centre accounting; may involve blurring of funds for pay and for activity |

Source: adapted from Hood (1991, pp. 4–5).

fact if not in law, and greater delegation of resource decisions, in a movement towards "one-line" budgets, mission statements, business plans and managerial autonomy). The corporatized style contrasts with the PPA style of providing all public services through "semi-anonymized" organizations within a single aggregated unit, with detailed service-wide rules, common service provision in key areas of operation, detailed central control of pay bargaining and staffing levels.

(2) A shift towards greater *competition* both between public sector organizations and between public sector organizations and the private sector. The aim for a more competitive style contrasts with the PPA style of ascribing semi-permanent "ascribed" roles to public sector organizations; that is, captive markets which are indefinitely assigned to particular "prestige" producers.

(3) A move towards greater use within the public sector of management practices which are broadly drawn from the private corporate sector, rather than PPA-style public-sector-specific methods of doing business. Examples of the latter include "model employer" aspirations to set an example to, rather than to follow the lead of, private-sector employers in matters of pay and conditions of employment (for example, in equal opportunity or employment of disabled persons) and the traditional "double imbalance" pay structure of public administration, in which lower-level staff tend to be relatively highly paid compared to their private-sector counterparts and top-level staff are relatively low-paid (cf. Sjölund, 1989).

(4) A move towards greater stress on *discipline and parsimony* in resource use and on active search for finding alternative, less costly ways to deliver public services, instead of laying the emphasis on institutional continuity, the maintenance of public services which are stable in "volume terms" and on policy development.

(5) A move towards more *"hands-on management"* (that is, more active control of public organizations by visible top managers wielding discretionary power) as against the traditional PPA style of "hands-off" management in the public sector, involving relatively anonymous bureaucrats at the top of public-sector organizations, carefully fenced in by personnel management rules designed to prevent favouritism and harassment.

(6) A move towards more *explicit and measurable* (or at least checkable) *standards of performance* for public sector organizations, in terms of the range, level and content of services to be provided, as against trust in professional standards and expertise across the public sector. The old PPA style involved low trust in politicians and managers but relatively high trust in professional expertise, both in a "vertical" sense (that is, up and down the organizational ladder, or between "principals" and "agents" in the new legal–economic language of the economic rationalists) and in a "lateral" sense (that is, across different units of the public sector; cf. Fox, 1974, pp. 72–84, 102–119).

(7) Attempts to control public organizations in a more "homeostatic" style according to pre-set *output measures* (particularly in pay based on job performance rather than rank or educational attainment), rather than by the traditional style of "orders of the day" coming on an *ad hoc* basis from the top, or by the subtle balancing of incompatible desiderata in the "collibration" style of control identified by Dunsire (1978, 1990) as central to orthodox bureaucratic functioning.

These doctrines of NPM link to recurrent debates about how public administration should be conducted, which stretch back at least as far as the major disputes between "legalists" and "Confucians" in the Chinese mandarinate over 2000 years ago (see Kamenka, 1989, pp. 38–39). How far the public sector should be insulated and clearly separated from the private sector in matters of handling business and staff, and how far business should be conducted by professional discretion rather than by pre-set rules or standards, are issues which go to the heart of most doctrinal disputes in public administration, including such major waves of classic public administration thought as the ideas of the German cameralists from the mid-sixteenth century (Small, 1909), the nineteenth-century British utilitarians (Hume, 1981) and the turn-of-the-century American progressives (Ostrom, 1974). Such doctrines also have profound implications for how public sector accounting is conceived, in the sense of what records are kept, how they are used, and what is costed and measured.

This summary list of course oversimplifies, and there are many interesting counter-trends. Examples of such counter-trends include: the unfashionability of the traditional public enterprise model in conventional market sectors of the economy, coupled with the vigorous adoption of that model for non-marketed public services in several countries; the weakening of older doctrines of metaphytic competition (i.e. public versus private providers; Corbett, 1965) as against doctrines of market testing by franchising; the weakening of trust in professionals while strengthening the hand of managers. Certainly, there is no logical necessity for a public management system to change in all of these seven respects at once. Many variations are possible.

*Variations*

There are no systematic cross-national studies showing degrees of variation in public management reform in a robust and reliable way. The literature in the area is long in anecdote and general commentary but short on systematic comparison, and comes close to being a data-free environment. There are only isolated fragments and relatively low-grade comparative data from sources like OECD public management reports and cross-national consultancy reports such as the Price Waterhouse/Cranfield study of comparative pay flexibility (Hegewisch, 1991).

But even such fragmentary sources are sufficient to show that not all OECD countries moved to adopt NPM principles to the same extent during the 1980s, and that there were marked differences even within similar family groups such as the English-speaking "Westminster-model" countries (cf. Hood, 1990c). It is particularly notable that some of the OECD's showcase economies, Japan, Germany and Switzerland, seem to have put much less emphasis on adopting NPM-type reforms (on the seven dimensions indicated in Table 1) in the 1980s than countries like Sweden, New Zealand or the U.K. But it would be hard to argue that those countries were closest to the NPM model at the outset, particularly in respect of use of private sector-style management practices, hands-on management or output controls.

For example, the NPM tendency to decentralize personnel management (such as hiring and job classifications) to operating units away from central oversight agencies was not a marked tendency in Japan, where the National Personnel Authority was if anything strengthened rather than weakened over the 1980s. Administrative reform received much attention, in the form of the three reform commissions over that decade (modelled on the famous 1937 U.S. "Brownlow" Committee on Administrative Management), but the accent seems to have been more on privatization, deregulation and tax reform than on the principles of NPM, with the exception of a small measure of corporatization in the form of more freedom for Ministries to reorganize themselves without specific authority from the Diet. And whereas doctrines of "pay for performance" took a strong hold in countries such as Sweden, Denmark, New Zealand and the U.K., there was no equivalent movement in Germany (partly because pay for performance potentially conflicts with the Basic Law doctrine of equality of pay across particular grades in the public service). Indeed, neither Germany nor Switzerland made any major changes in their public administration at federal level in the 1980s; rather, *Verwaltungspflege* (a quiet period of cultivation after the reforms of the 1960s which embraced policy evaluation) was a common watchword in Germany over that decade.

But even within the group of countries in which more emphasis seemed to be placed on public management reforms, it is not clear that the direction of change was the same. For instance, the "free commune" experiment in Norway in 1987 and the French move to far-reaching territorial decentralization in 1983 contrasts sharply with centralizing tendencies in the U.K. over the 1980s. Late 1980s reforms in the U.K. and New Zealand were aimed at separating policy setting and service provision (on the grounds that Ministers were not equipped to be managers), while the Australian Commonwealth government took measures intended to strengthen the capacity of Ministers to manage.

Any scoring of variations in the adoption of NPM in the seven dimensions discussed above must necessarily be highly impressionistic. Ideally, we would need both a reliable method of locating a country's initial state at the start of the period in question and the extent of movement over the period (given that a "backward" case might show dramatic change, and yet still be behind an apparently "static" country which started from a higher initial emphasis on the NPM style). At present, we do not have a cross-national information source which could reliably show either sort of variation.

From the fragmentary literature on public management reform over the 1980s, the high NPM group in the OECD countries would be likely to include Sweden, Canada, New Zealand, Australia and the U.K. with France, Denmark, the Netherlands, Norway and Ireland also showing a number of marked shifts in the direction of NPM. At the other end, the low NPM group would be likely to include Germany, Greece, Spain, Switzerland, Japan and Turkey.

These impressions are consistent with the country reports submitted to the OECD's survey of public management developments in 1988 and 1990, supplemented in 1991 (OECD 1988, 1990, 1991). Obviously, these reports are seriously contaminated in a number of familiar ways, mainly because they reflect what the correspondents used by OECD in each country thought it relevant or politic to record (although there was, of course, a general check-list issued by PUMA for these exercises), rather than what a single overall observer might have noted. Moreover (until such time as the OECD's public management profiles are greatly developed), it indicates what was on the government agenda for change rather than the "initial endowment" of each system.

Even so, OECD public management reports can give us a rough indication of the officially perceived agenda of public management change in the 1980s, and serve as a starting point for discussion of variations. The country reports for 1988 and 1990 were carefully examined, and a rough score awarded to each country under each of the seven points of public management doctrine which were mentioned above as components of new public management. A score of 2 was given for developments reported as being in place on each of the dimensions, 1 for developments under active discussion or experimentation and 0 for nothing reported in the area.

Clearly, such an exercise is only useful for identifying outliers, and not for making any fine differentiations. The extremes were taken as cases whose overall scores (summed across all seven dimensions) were more than one standard deviation away from the mean. The high and low cases identified in this way fitted sufficiently well with other impressionistic views of variation in NPM over the 1980s to serve as a basis for a discussion as to what might be responsible for putting a country at one or other of the extremes.

## WHY THE VARIATIONS?

As noted earlier, there are several different possible ways of explaining the rise of NPM. This section explores four conventional accounts of public sector change (relating such change to "Englishness", party politics, government size and macroeconomic performance) before suggesting a further interpretation couched in terms of institutional endowments.

### *"English awfulness"?*

Some commentators (notably Pollitt, 1993) have implied that NPM was mainly an Anglo–American phenomenon of the Reagan/Thatcher era. But this view seems difficult to sustain. If nothing else, it ignores the high degree of emphasis placed on NPM in South Africa, Hong Kong, Australia and New Zealand (for the latter, see Pusey, 1991; Scott *et al.*, 1990; Yeatman, 1987).

However, it might be possible to broaden the view of NPM as an Anglo–American preoccupation to the idea that it reflects what Castles ironically calls "the awfulness of the English". By this phrase, Castles means the relatively poor economic performance and arrested development of welfare state policies which, he claims, characterize the English-speaking countries (Castles, 1989; Castles & Merrill, 1989, pp. 181–185). It is, for example, noticeable that the high scorers on NPM emphasis are mostly English-speaking countries (and hence clearly candidates for "English awfulness" *à la* Castles). The low scorers, in contrast, are all non-English-speaking countries.

TABLE 2. NPM emphasis and political incumbency

| NPM Emphasis | Political incumbency emphasis "Left" | "Centre" | "Right" |
|---|---|---|---|
| Hi | Sweden | Australia<br>Canada<br>NZ | U.K. |
| Medium | France | Austria<br>Denmark<br>Finland<br>Italy<br>Netherlands<br>Portugal<br>U.S.A.[5] | |
| Lo | Greece<br>Spain | Germany<br>Switzerland | Japan<br>Turkey |

Sources: analysis based on OECD PUMA reports and on political incumbency data for OECD countries drawn from Gorvin (1989) and *Keesing's Contemporary Archives*.

Moreover, an "English awfulness" explanation might fit with a view of NPM as representing international convergence on a common public management style. On Castles' analysis, the English-speaking countries lost their formerly distinctive "high-direct employment" feature of public management between the 1960s and the 1980s, and NPM could be interpreted as part of that process of coming into line with non-English-speaking countries. Particularly with respect to the practice of accounting techniques and management consultancy, diffusion of the new NPM ideas might have been expected to spread more readily across countries with the same language and similar legal traditions.

But it seems too simple to attribute NPM to English awfulness alone. For example, Sweden appears as a high scorer on NPM emphasis, which would be particularly damaging for an interpretation built on a Castles-type English awfulness factor. Moreover, Denmark, the Netherlands and France are also cases which score relatively high on NPM emphasis, and two of them (Denmark and the Netherlands) reported strong development of variable pay in recent years to the 1990 Price Waterhouse/Cranfield project (Hegewisch, 1991, Table 3). NPM seems to be more than just another "English disease".

*Party politics*

Some commentators explain PPA's demise in rather similar terms to the predator theorists of the dinosaurs' extinction. The notion is that the old structure has been subverted by the development of "New Right" interests who stand to benefit in various ways from dismantling the PPA model.

At one level, the demise of traditional PPA is often attributed to the advent of New Right government in the 1980s and particularly to the influence of Ronald Reagan and Margaret Thatcher, who aimed to roll back big government and state-led egalitarianism and welfarism, and to remould what was left of the public sector in the image of private business (see Pollitt, 1993). If NPM was sparked by such figures, we would expect its development to be most marked in countries which were governed by right-wing parties during the 1980s.

[5] It is obviously debatable whether U.S.A. should be scored as "centre" or "right" for these purposes. In many "does party matter" studies, it is excluded, on the grounds that it is essentially unclassifiable. Given its separation of powers, it is here counted as a centre–left coalition for 1980, a centre–right coalition for 1981 to 1986 and a centrist coalition for 1987 to 1990.

Table 2 gives a rough indication of the extent to which OECD countries were governed during the 1980s mainly by parties on their left, their right or their centre. For this exercise, a score of +1 was given to each OECD country for each year of incumbency in government by a political party to the right of *that* country's political spectrum, and a score of −1 for each year of incumbency by a party to the left of *that* spectrum; 0.5 was given for each year of incumbency by a centre–right coalition and −0.5 for each year of incumbency by a centre–left coalition, with 0 for a grand coalition (as in the Austrian case). Countries which score hi (more than 1 S.D. above the mean) are taken as "right" in incumbency terms, and countries which score lo (more than 1 S.D. below the mean) are taken as "left" in incumbency terms. "Centre" scorers are the rest.

NPM scorings are based on the country reports to OECD on Public Management (1988 and 1990), with a maximum, score of 2 on each of seven dimensions of doctrine, as described earlier. "Hi" scorers are those whose overall score is more than 1 standard deviation (S.D.) above the mean score; "lo" scorers are those whose overall score is more than 1 S.D. below the mean score. "Medium" scorers are the rest.

This exercise is useful only for first approximations, and it may be that a better test would be a series of "before" and "after" looks at cases of *changes* in government. Scoring political incumbency involves problems which are familiar in the "does politics matter?" debate over macroeconomic policy in political science. There is no established method for comparing degrees of "rightness" and "leftness" *across* countries, and there are clearly different "*qualities*" of rightness and leftness (for example, participatory versus hierarchical emphases in socialism). Presidential and federal systems clearly cause complications (for example, the U.S. would count as "right" only in Presidential terms for the 1980s). Coalition/PR system cases tend to bunch in the middle, so that the outliers tend to be non-PR systems like France and Japan, which may get disproportionate weight in the analysis. All that such a scoring exercise does is to give us a first cut as to whether OECD countries were governed during the 1980s mainly by parties on their left, their right or their centre.

Crude as the data are, however, Table 2 shows up the difficulties in the popular idea that NPM was closely associated with incumbency by "right" governing parties in the 1980s. Sweden is the most obvious misfit for such an idea. It is a country which shows apparently high NPM emphasis during the 1980s, but also scores fairly high for left political incumbency with eight years out of the decade under Social Democratic governments. Indeed, Sweden is conventionally taken as the leading case of the social democratic alternative to liberal capitalism. And at the other extreme, there are unambiguously "right" cases, like Japan and Turkey, which seem to score distinctly low on the NPM emphasis scale.

Of course, such results are only surprising if we expect the incumbency of different political parties to lead to different public policy outcomes. Other analyses of party competition might lead to different expectations. An example is Scharpf's (1987) "nested game" model of the dynamics of party competition, in which two rival "left" and "right" parties compete for the fickle favours of floating middle-ground voters against a set of variant macroeconomic conditions produced by a game between incumbent governments, labour unions and central banks. Modifying that framework only slightly, we could posit a "party competition" game played between right and left wing parties (*á la* Scharpf) and a "public management game" played between incumbent governments and public managers/top bureaucrats or professionals (substituted for Scharpf's macroeconomic policy game played between governments and labour unions). In the second game, incumbent politicians choose between tough and tender approaches to public managers, and the latter choose between a cooperative and uncooperative approach to politicians. Table 3 outlines such a game. Clearly, politicians would prefer to be in cell (1), bureaucrats and managers in

TABLE 3. Politician–bureaucrat public management game

| Bureaucrats/ managers/ public servants | Politicians | |
|---|---|---|
| | Tender | Tough |
| Cooperative | (1) Outcome: smooth running medium cost public management | (2) Outcome: politicians exploit public service ethos for cheap and effective public management |
| Noncooperative | (3) Outcome: bureaucrats exploit politicians' goodwill for high cost public management | (4) Outcome: high cost administrative chaos |

cell (3); such a game therefore has a tragic bias away from cell (1) and towards cell (4).

If such a model of party competition is adopted, it becomes quite conceivable that incumbent social-democratic governments (such as those in Sweden or New Zealand in the 1980) might go just as far as "bourgeois" governments (and possibly even further) in moving towards a tough approach to public management, because they have nowhere else to go, and need to work harder to establish credibility in this area with wavering middle-class voters (adapting Scharpf's ideas of asymmetrical choice by the middle socioeconomic group).

From such evidence, it would seem that if the rise of the New Right influenced the demise of the old PPA model, it was not simply through right-wing parties holding office. It looks more like a general process of policy diffusion than a process in which policies vary with party incumbency. A modified version of the rise of the New Right explanation would therefore need to place more stress on the eclipsing of the old public administration coalition (particularly the public service labour unions) by an NPM coalition drawn from accounting firms, financial intermediaries, management consultants and business schools, along the lines of Patrick Dunleavy's (1986) account of how policy booms develop through a coalition of professional and corporate interests.

Alternatively (perhaps additionally), the change might be attributed to the recolonization of the public service from inside rather than to an assault from outside. Some contemporary commentators on the rise of NPM, notably Yeatman (1987, pp. 350–351) and Pusey (1991) have applied a form of "new class" analysis to the process, in the tradition of Burnham's (1942) analysis of managers as a new class. They claim that the upper echelons of the public service are increasingly being occupied by a new class of "econocrats" (and perhaps "accountocrats", certainly in the New Zealand case), who were not fired up into public service ideals by close experience of the rigours of ordinary life in the depressed 1930s or Word War II and whose education in narrow neoclassical economics (uncontaminated by the humanities or even by the other social sciences) in élite universities is claimed to make them natural sympathizers with New Right ideas.

It may be too that such a new generation of econocrats and accountocrats would be much more prone to "bureau-shaping", as analysed by Patrick Dunleavy (1985, 1991); that is, the propensity of top public managers to aim for high-status analytic work in collegial élite units and to distance themselves from front-line supervisory roles in favour of a "super-control" position which offers more job satisfaction and less tedious routine. Once bureaucrats adopt such preferences, there is nothing against their interests in enthusiastically cutting service delivery budgets down the line, or in breaking up and deprivileging the world of public service delivery, so long as the power and status of central agencies is retained or augmented.

*A response to fiscal stress and poor macroeconomic performance?*

Another common way of interpreting the demise of the old PPA model is to link it with changing social conditions, akin to the "loss of habitat" theory of dinosaur extinction. NPM is often interpreted as a response to fiscal stress and resistance to extra taxes. Underlying the onset of such fiscal stress may be the changes in income level and distribution, weakening the "Tocqueville coalition" for government growth in the electorate; that is, an electoral majority of voters at below-average incomes who stand to benefit from increasing public spending financed from income taxes. A move towards a more diamond-shaped income distribution pattern lays the conditions for a new tax-conscious winning electoral coalition, and NPM can be represented as the approach to public management which fits this new tax-consciousness in marginal electorates; for example, by keeping the overall public-sector pay bill down by means of performance pay rather than by across-the-board pay rises in the traditional style.

However, if NPM is best explained as a response to fiscal stress and government overload, we might expect NPM to be most strongly developed in those countries which score highest on government spending and employment and/or have a history of relatively poor macroeconomic performance on the conventional indices of GDP growth, public debt levels, inflation and unemployment rates (such as Greece or New Zealand).

Indeed, NPM has frequently been interpreted (for example, by trade union critics) as little more than a means of slimming down big government, and saving on resources in the public sector. If slimline public management is what counts in competition among industrial (or post-industrial) states for economic advantage, we would expect to see convergence, with the countries which are least slimline at the outset making the most dramatic strides in adopting NPM doctrines (because those are the countries which would have the most to worry about in terms of comparative advantage). Equally, countries with small-sized public bureaucracy might have proportionately less to gain from putting greater stress on such doctrines.

Finding useful indicators for government size is no easier than arriving at robust measures of the nature of party political incumbency. Indeed, it is commonly observed that coventional measures of government size can conceal as much as they reveal (Peters & Heisler, 1983). But if we look at four conventional measures of government size (that is, government employment as a percentage of total employment, government expenditure as a percentage of GDP, social security expenditure as a percentage of GDP and tax revenue as a percentage of GDP), it does emerge that the two most slimline governments within OECD (Japan and Turkey) placed a low degree of emphasis on NPM during the 1980s, just as would be expected. But not all outsize governments in OECD placed high emphasis on NPM in the 1980s, and the medium-sized governments also varied considerably in the emphasis which they laid on NPM. So if government size plays a part in determining NPM emphasis, it is probably a subsidiary one rather than the single determinant.

Similarly, the link between macroeconomic performance and the degree of emphasis on NPM seems to be far from clear-cut. NPM is often interpreted as a reflection of 1970s' economic chickens coming home to roost (i.e. the record of past or current economic performance), and a return to hard-headed realism. But there appears to be no automatic relationship between the emphasis placed by different OECD countries on NPM and their level of performance on the four conventional macroeconomic indicators in the post-oil shock era of the 1970s, i.e. 1974–1979.

Table 4 gives some indicative data on this point. It is true that some of the macroeconomic success stories of the 1970s are found in the low NPM emphasis group, as might be expected. Countries like Japan and pre-1990 Germany are in this group. But not all of the high performers of the 1970s are in that group, and nor are all the economic "basket cases" of the 1970s (in terms of overall scores on GDP growth per head, CPI growth and unemployment) in the high NPM emphasis group. And even if we relate degrees of NPM emphasis to *current* economic performance (on the same basis) over the 1980s, the same puzzles arise, as can also be seen from Table 4. It seems that macroeconomic

TABLE 4. NPM emphasis and economic performance 1974–1979 and 1980–1988

| Economic performance category | NPM emphasis 1980s | | | | | |
|---|---|---|---|---|---|---|
| | Hi | | Medium | | Lo | |
| Econ era | 1974–1979 | 1980–1988 | 1974–1979 | 1980–1988 | 1974–1979 | 1980–1988 |
| Hi | | | | | | Japan |
| Medium Hi | Sweden | Sweden (4) | France Austria (1) Norway | Austria Norway Finland | BRD Japan | BRD |
| Medium and Mixed | NZ (4) Aus | Canada Aus (4) UK (4) | Ireland | | Greece (4) Spain Turkey (1) (3) (4) | |
| Medium Lo | U.K. Canada | | Italy Port. | Italy Port. (4) Ireland (4) | | Greece (4) Spain (4) Turkey (4) |
| Lo | | NZ (1) (4) | | Switz. (4) | | |

Source: analysis based on *OECD Historical Statistics*.

Key to economic performance indicators:
Hi = all available indicators in hi category;
Lo = all available indicators in lo category;
Medium hi = 25% or more of available indicators in hi category and no indicators in lo category;
Medium lo = 25% or more of available indicators in lo category and no indicators in hi category;
Medium and mixed = (a) all available indicators in medium category; (b) available indicators distributed across all three categories (hi medium and lo).

Notes:
(1) No indicator available for unemployment rates for this case for this period.
(2) No indicator available for GDP growth per head for this case for this period.
(3) No indicator available for CPI growth for this case for this period.
(4) No indicator available for government debt relative to GDP for this case for this period.

performance alone is not sufficient to explain the rise of NPM.

As with Table 2, the placings are indicative and "broad-brush". NPM scorings are as described on p. 101. Economic performance scorings are based on OECD Historical Statistics 1974–1979 and 1980–1988. Four conventional series were used: average unemployment rates as a percentage of total labour force; average rates of growth in real GDP per capita; average growth rate in consumer price index; and average public debt levels as a percentage of GDP. For each of these indices, the countries were divided into "hi", "medium" and "lo" scorers by the method used as before (i.e. more than 1 S.D. away from the mean counted as "hi" or "lo", and the remainder "medium"), except that for the CPI index two outliers (Turkey and Iceland) were taken out, in that both had scores more than twice the mean and the effect of including them was to put almost all countries in the "medium" category.

*Initial endowment*

Popular wisdom notwithstanding, there seem to be important cases which do not readily fit standard explanations for why NPM developed in the 1980s. Another possible explanation is the baseline, or initial endowment from which different administrative systems start.

Specificially it could be argued that for an administrative system to move signficiantly towards NPM, it must be set up at the outset in such a way as to provide both *motive* and *opportunity* (conventional elements of detective fiction) for incumbent politicians to want to shift the administrative system sharply in that direction.

We could argue that *motive* in this case might be expected to consist mainly in the promise or hope of resource saving from the adoption of NPM measures, and could therefore be expected to be proportionately higher in a context of outsize government and/or acute fiscal stress associated with poor macroeconomic performance than in the context of slimline government and/or strong macroeconomic performance. *Opportunity* might be expected to depend on the existence of some "Archimedean point" from which would-be reforming politicians can influence the public sector as a whole. For instance, in a country like Switzerland, where even the number of Ministries (seven) in the federal government is set out in the constitution and has not changed for 150 years, the opportunity for politicians or top officials to reshape public administration is relatively slight, because there is effectively no difference between constitutional reform and administrative reform. But in countries like the U.K., where there is no constitutional check to administrative reform and politicians at the centre can change the entire system, opportunity is much greater. It would therefore seem that a crucial variable for opportunity is the extent to which there is an integrated public service controllable from a single point and without significant jurisdictional breaks (for example, without independent public bodies beyond the reach of control by a single set of elected politicians, like the German Bundesbank).

TABLE 5. Public management baseline styles and propensity to shift NPM-wards: a tentative hypothesis

| Stress on integration of public service | Stress on collectivism in service provision: Lo | Stress on collectivism in service provision: Hi |
|---|---|---|
| Hi | (1) 'Japanese way' Motive for switch: lo Opportunity: hi | (2) "Swedish way" Motive for switch: hi Opportunity: hi |
| Lo | (3) "American way" Motive for switch: lo Opportunity: lo | (4) "German way" Motive for switch: hi Opportunity: lo |

Table 5 puts these two aspects of initial endowment together to identify four polar types: what is labelled the "Japanese way", where public service integration in this sense is high but collectivism (in the sense of the relative size of the public sector in spending and employment) is comparatively low; the "Swedish way", where both public service integration and collectivism are high; the "American way", where both integration and collectivism are low; and the "German way", where collectivism is high but integration is low. These labels are used as convenient shorthand terms, and it is not suggested that each of these countries exactly corresponds to the stereotype in all particulars.

On this basis, some countries would be much more likely to move NPM-wards than others, at least in the first round of public management reforms. For the polar type labelled the "American way", there would on these assumptions be neither motive nor opportunity to make a major shift NPM-wards. No one would be in a position to order the changes, and in any case the gains would be expected to be less than in an outsize government system. For the "Japanese way", there would be opportunity but again little motive because the system is starting from the "small government" box. And for the "German way", there would be motive, but no opportunity.[6]

Only in the polar type labelled the "Swedish

way" would there be *both* motive and opportunity: motive, because outsize government makes resource saving of key importance in conditions of growing fiscal stress, and opportunity, because there are central points of leverage over the entire public service. Hence it might be argued that countries in the "Swedish way" box (like the U.K., France, the Scandinavian countries and possibly the Netherlands) would be the type most prone to make rapid strides towards the development of NPM in the 1980s.

A "variable diffusion" model of this kind can help to explain what more generalized explanations of NPM on their own cannot: namely, why a number of key OECD countries under governments of different political stripes shifted to NPM in the 1980s while others moved relatively little in that direction. All of the OECD countries which seem to have placed the highest stress on replacing PPA with NPM during the 1980s started from the "Swedish way" box in Table 5 at the baseline, and some of the countries which put medium-to-high stress on NPM, such as France and Denmark, also started as "Swedish way" cases in this sense. Of course, such an explanation is not independent of habitat-change accounts stressing the effect of fiscal stress and tax-consciousness, but it does explain why a similar habitat change might produce different effects in different institutional systems.

## CONCLUSION

Compared to the voluminous literature on deregulation and privatization, accounts of the rise of NPM are less developed and sparser. We still lack clear measuring rods for comparing public management style, and the discussion here is relatively speculative. Distinguishing surface change from deep change will always be difficult in public organizations. However, four tentative conclusions can be drawn from this highly exploratory exercise.

First, *pace* Aucoin, Osborne and Gaebler and other "global change" interpretations, it is not clear that the old PPA model of accountability has collapsed everywhere, or to the same extent. Even though we do not know how to measure cross-national differences finely, there do appear to be leaders and laggards in the process, and it is interesting that some of the notable laggards are leading countries in the international economy, posing something of a challenge for the view that public management internationalization parallels economic internationalization. If a policy dinosaur is going into extinction here, the process is still far from complete. Hence the possible relevance of a variable diffusion model based on initial institutional endowment, as discussed in the last section. And if the different institutional endowments lead to permanent differences (rather than simply governing the speed of PPA extinction), we may need to be cautious about assuming that changes in public sector accounting are likely to be global.

Second, the conventional explanations of change in the public sector do not on their own seem fully to explain observed variations in the degree to which NPM reforms were taken up by OECD states in the 1980s. For instance, ideas such as the view that NPM is all about right-wingers in office, slimming down outsize government or responding to macroeconomic failure (in the past or present) all come up against awkward cases which do not seem to fit expectations when we look across the OECD countries. But that does not of course rule out such items as part of a broader multi-factor explanation of the shift to NPM.

Third, there appears to be no simple relationship between macroeconomic performance levels and the degree of emphasis laid on NPM.

[6] Indeed, Germany itself is an ambiguous case, since its "large government" character derives more from high public spending than high public employment. If size of public employment is the key to NPM motivation, there would therefore be no more motivation than under the "American way".

A working hypothesis might be that the showcase economies were not under strong pressures to shake up their public management systems and that the more "basket-case" economies lacked the capacity to do so, so that those making the biggest strides with NPM are likely to be those in the medium-to-poor macroeconomic performance bands.

Fourth, there seems to be no simple relationship between the political stripe of governments (in so far as that can be gauged) and the degree of emphasis laid on NPM. Are we to assume that Downs' (1957) classic ideas about policy convergence in party competition better explain apparent concensus on NPM than Hibbs' (1977) ideas about policy divergence? Or could it be that apparently similar measures have been adopted in different political circumstances for diametrically different reasons and with quite different effects? After all, such things often happen in administrative reform. Perhaps the classic historical case is merit hiring for civil servants, which, according to Hans Mueller (1984), was adopted by eighteenth-century Prussia to bring the middle class into the public bureaucracy and by nineteenth-century Britain to keep them out.

On similar lines, it might be argued that NPM has been adopted in some contexts to ward off the New Right agenda for privatization and bureaucide and in other countries as the first step towards realizing that agenda. Much of NPM is built on the idea (or ideology) of homeostatic control; that is, the clarification of goals and missions in advance, and then building the accountability systems in relation to those preset goals (cf. Dunsire, 1990). But if NPM has *itself* been adopted for diametrically opposite reasons in different contexts, it may, ironically, be another example of the common situation in politics in which it is far easier to settle on particular measures than on general or basic objectives. That too may suggest that we should be cautious about assuming that public-sector accounting is likely to enter a new age of global uniformity, at least in the sense of the wider public management context within which it operates.

## BIBLIOGRAPHY

Aucoin, P., Administrative Reform in Public Management: Paradigms, Principles, Paradoxes and Pendulums, *Governance* (1990) pp. 115–137.

Castles, F. G., Big Government in Weak States: The Paradox of State Size in the English-speaking Nations of Advanced Capitalism, *Journal of Commonwealth and Comparative Politics* (1989) pp. 267–293.

Castles, F. G. & Merrill, V., Towards a General Model of Public Policy Outcomes, *Journal of Theoretical Politics* (1989) pp. 177–212.

Corbett, D., *Politics and the Airlines* (London: Allen and Unwin, 1965).

Douglas, J., Review Article: The Changing Tide — Some Recent Studies of Thatcherism, *British Journal of Political Science* (1989) pp. 399–424.

Douglas, M., Cultural Bias, in Douglas, M., *In the Active Voice*, chapter 9, pp. 183–254 (London: Routledge, 1982).

Dunleavy, P. J., Bureaucrats, Budgets and the Growth of the State, *British Journal of Political Science* (1985) pp. 299–328.

Dunleavy, P. J., Explaining the Privatization Boom: Public Choice versus Radical Approaches, *Public Administration* (1986) pp. 13–34.

Dunleavy, P. J., *Democracy, Bureaucracy and Public Choice* (London: Harvester, 1991).

Dunsire, A., *Control in a Bureaucracy* (Oxford: Martin Robertson, 1978).

Dunsire, A., Holistic Governance, *Public Policy and Administration* (1990) pp. 3–18.

Dunsire, A. & Hood, C. C., *Cutback Management in Public Bureaucracies* (Cambridge: Cambridge University Press, 1989).

Fox, A., *Beyond Contract: Work, Power and Trust Relations* (London: Faber and Faber, 1974).

Gorvin, I. (ed.), *Elections Since 1945: A Worldwide Reference Companion* (Harlow: Longman, 1989).

Halligan, J. & Wettenhall, R., Major Changes in the Structure of Government Institutions, in Power, J. (ed.), *Public Administration in Australia: A Watershed*, pp. 17–40 (Sydney: RAIPA/Hale and Iremonger, 1990).

Hegewisch, A., Public and Private Sector Trends in Remuneration Policies and Contract Flexibility in Europe, Paper presented at seminar *International Comparisons of Public Sector Pay in 10 Countries: 1990 Results from the Price Waterhouse/Cranfield Survey* (London: Public Finance Foundation, 5 September 1991).

Hibbs, D. A. Jr, Political Parties and Macroeconomic Policy, *American Political Science Review* (1977) pp. 1467–1487.

Hirschman, A. O., *Shifting Involvements: Private Interest and Public Action* (Oxford: Blackwell, 1982).

Hood, C. C., Public Administration, in Bogdanor, V. (ed.), *The Blackwell Encyclopaedia of Political Institutions*, pp. 504–507 (Oxford: Blackwell, 1987).

Hood, C. C., Public Administration: Lost an Empire, Not Yet Found a Role, in Leftwich, A. (ed.), *New Directions in Political Science*, pp. 107–125 (Aldershot: Elgar, 1990a).

Hood, C. C., Beyond the Public Bureaucracy State? Public Administration in the 1990s (Inaugural lecture, London School of Economics, 16 January 1990b).

Hood, C. C., De-Sir-Humphrey-fying the Westminster Model of Governance, *Governance* (1990c) pp. 205–214.

Hood, C. C., A Public Management for All Seasons?, *Public Administration* (1991) pp. 3–19.

Hood, C. C. & Dunsire, A., *Bureaumetrics* (Farnborough: Gower, 1981).

Hume, L. J., *Bentham and Bureaucracy* (Cambridge: Cambridge University Press, 1981).

Kamenka, E., *Bureaucracy* (Oxford: Blackwell, 1989).

Karl, B. D., *Executive Reorganization and Reform in the New Deal* (Cambridge, MA: Harvard University Press, 1963).

Marini, F., *Toward a New Public Administration* (Scranton, PA: Chandler, 1971).

Martin, J., *A Profession of Statecraft? Three Essays on Some Current Issues in the New Zealand Public Service* (Wellington: Victoria University Press, 1988).

OECD, *Public Management Developments* (Paris: OECD, 1988).

OECD, *Public Management Developments* (Paris: OECD, 1990).

Osborne, A. & Gaebler, T., *Reinventing Government: How the Entrepreneurial Spirit is Transforming the Public Sector* (Reading, MA: Addison-Wesley, 1992).

Painter, M., Values in the History of Public Administration, in Power, J. (ed.), *Public Administration in Australia: A Watershed*, pp. 75–93 (Sydney: RAIPA/Hale and Iremonger, 1990).

Peters, B. G. & Heisler, M. O., Thinking About Public Sector Growth: Conceptual, Operational, Theoretical and Policy Considerations, in Taylor, C. L. (ed.), *Why Governments Grow: Measuring Public Sector Size*, pp. 177–197 (Beverly Hills: Sage, 1983).

Piore, M. J. & Sabel, C. F., *The Second Industrial Divide* (New York: Basic, 1984).

Pollitt, C., *Managerialism and the Public Services: The Anglo-American Experience*, 2nd Edn (Oxford: Blackwell, 1993).

Power, M. & Laughlin, R., Critical Theory and Accounting, in Alveson, N. & Willmott, H. (eds), *Critical Management Studies*, pp. 113–135 (London: Sage, 1992).

Pusey, M., *Economic Rationalism in Canberra* (Cambridge: Cambridge University Press, 1991).

Quirk, P., In Defense of the Politics of Ideas, *Journal of Politics* (1988) pp. 31–41.

Scharpf, F. W., The Political Calculus of Inflation and Unemployment in Western Europe: A Game-Theoretical Interpretation, *Journal of Public Policy* (1987) pp. 227–258.

Scott, G., Bushnell, P. & Sallee, N., Reform of the Core Public Sector: New Zealand Experience, *Governance* (1990) pp. 138–167.

Sjölund, M., *Statens Lönepolitik 1966–1988* (Stockholm: Allmänna Förlaget, 1989).

Small, A. W., *The Cameralists* (Chicago: Chicago University Press, 1909).

Sturgess, G., First Keynote Address, in Carey, G. & Ryan, P. (eds), *In Transition: NSW and the Corporatisation Agenda*, pp. 4–10 (Sydney: Macquarie Public Sector Studies Program/Association for Management Education and Research, 1989).

Taylor, J. A., Information Networking in Public Administration, *International Review of Administrative Sciences* (1992) pp. 375–389.

Taylor, J. A. & Williams, H., Public Administration and the Information Polity, *Public Administration* (1991) pp. 171–190.

Thompson, M., Ellis, R. & Wildavksy, A., *Cultural Theory* (Boulder: Westview, 1990).
von Beyme, K., Do Parties Matter? The Impact of Parties on the Key Decisions in the Political System, *Government and Opposition* (1984) pp. 5–29.
Yeatman, A., The Concept of Public Management and the Australian State in the 1980s, *Australian Journal of Public Administration* (1987) pp. 339–353.

# [4]

*International Journal of the Economics of Business, Vol.1, No. 3, 1994* 439

# Competitive Tendering and Contracting in the Public Sector: A Survey

SIMON DOMBERGER and STEPHEN RIMMER

ABSTRACT *This paper is a survey of the role and impact of competitive tendering and contracting (CTC) policies in the public sector. The paper examines the theoretical rationale for introducing competition in the provision of public services and the methodology by which contracting decisions are reached. It investigates the extent of implementation and nature of outcomes in several countries. A broad sweep of the empirical findings suggests that CTC generates substantial cost savings. Lack of adequate data makes an assessment of the effect on quality more troublesome, and further research is needed.*

*Key words:* Competitive tendering; Contracting-out; Public sector management; Competition policy.

*JEL classifications:* L14, L33.

## 1. Introduction

Competitive tendering and contracting (CTC) is becoming an important management tool in both the private and the public sectors. Also known as 'outsourcing' or 'contracting-out', it defines the process of search and selection of suppliers of services traditionally produced in-house within an organisation. The process involves competitive tendering or informal market testing to determine which is the preferred supplier on the basis of price and non-price criteria. The formal contract that is entered into then binds the parties to the exchange of services of a pre-determined quality and quantity for agreed financial payments. The transaction typically spans a period of a year or more, and the contract becomes the instrument through which relations between the parties are managed and regulated.

The fundamental principle underlying CTC is deceptively simple: essentially a 'make or buy' decision is involved. Yet it is evident that the issue is far from straightforward in practice. In the private sector, the growing use of CTC has rekindled questions about the boundaries of the firm. Firms derive economic benefits from the specialisation that is facilitated by contractual arrangements. Such

Simon Domberger, Bowater Professor of Management, Graduate School of Business, University of Sydney, Sydney, NSW 2006, Australia, and Stephen J. Rimmer, Acting Director, Industry Commission, Canberra.

The views expressed here are those of the author and not necessarily those of the Industry Commission.

specialisation can enhance economies of scale in certain industries such as car component manufacturing. Consequently it has been suggested that contracting is making it "increasingly difficult to tell whether some firms are big or small" (*The Economist*, 11 June, 1994: 74).

In the public sector, CTC continues to be a politically charged issue. It is sometimes seen as a thinly disguised attempt to 'privatise' the provision of public services. In recent years the debate has converged on three critical matters: the effects of CTC on prices, on quality and whether competition is more important than ownership in determining performance.

This survey article takes a broad sweep of the literature on competitive tendering, with special emphasis on empirical evidence and policy developments in the public sector. Its purpose is to summarise the state of knowledge in the field and suggest priorities for further research. In Section 2, we begin by providing a theoretical framework underlying CTC. This is followed, in Section 3, with a summary of current policy across a range of countries where CTC is employed. Section 4 proceeds to assess the empirical evidence on cost and quality taking an international perspective. Finally Section 5 concludes with an assessment of policy implementation to date and a review of the research agenda.

## 2. Theoretical Framework

As was suggested in the introduction, if the organisation of production is governed purely by economic considerations then the make or buy decision appears trivial: use whichever mode of supply is cheaper. However, in the public sector economic considerations are not always dominant. Social objectives, accountability, equity considerations and security of supply are often given as reasons why public production is preferred to private.

Consider a specific illustration. In New South Wales (Australia) the government enlarged its office cleaning operations at the end of World War I in order to provide employment for war widows. The business grew in scale and scope over the years to reach A$180 million turnover by 1993. Yet it was neither an efficient nor profitable business and was finally privatised in 1994. This is but one example of the way in which the public sector may expand in-house economic activity even when it is not productively efficient to do so.

Much of the post-2nd World War expansion of the public sector in the industrialised world had a similar character. This is true of in-house activities both at local and central government level. From school meals to the provision of hospital cleaning, public production became the norm in countries such as the UK and Australia. In the words of the UK politician, Herbert Morrison, those who directed such activities were not simply business managers but the 'high custodians of the public interest'.

The turning point came in 1979 with the election of the Conservative administration in Britain. The Thatcher government was committed to 'rolling back the frontiers of the State'. It also sought to buttress public sector accountability in economic decision making and encouraged the use of market forces in the provision of public goods and services (see *inter alia*, Vickers and Yarrow, 1988; Kay *et al.*, 1986).

Public sector reform in Britain was spearheaded by privatisation: the transfer of ownership of public assets to the private sector. Less prominent in the early stages of the reforms, but equally far reaching in the long run, was CTC policy. The realisation that local governments were slow to introduce competition in the provision of services to their rate-payers, despite compelling evidence that significant savings could thereby be generated, led the government to make competitive tendering compulsory. Legislation was introduced in 1988 in the form of the "*Local Government Act*".

Gradually, a growing number of administrations in the industrialised countries came to view CTC as a means of reducing budget deficits and improving the management of public sector activities. Politically, CTC offered a convenient half-way house between public production and private ownership. By retaining public sector control over the activity whilst simultaneously introducing commercial discipline through a formal contracting process, many of the political and industrial relations difficulties associated with privatisation could be avoided. This approach has been reinforced recently by the work of Osborne and Gaebler (1992) who argued that the role of government should be confined to policy formulation. In the provision of services, it should not extend beyond the co-ordination and facilitation of production.

For economists, the question of contracting—the make or buy decision—verges on the trite. To quote Prager (1994: 177) "Simply put, business firms contract out when it is not cost-effective to produce internally". The difficulty starts when more explicit questions are asked concerning the determinants of optimal firm structure and size. Clearly, decisions about contracting are an important part of the answer. For a theoretical framework in which such decisions are made one must turn to Coase's seminal contribution on the nature of the firm. Coase (1937) argued that the size and structure of the firm is essentially endogenous, based on economic considerations of efficiency. Specifically Coase's analysis focused on the identification of circumstances where market transactions were likely to fail and required internal organisation instead. This insight was subsequently developed by Williamson (1985) who articulated further the conditions under which exchange in the marketplace would be eschewed in favour of internal production arrangements. This approach became known as transaction cost economics.

We draw on this theoretical framework to briefly analyse the contracting decision. Our approach highlights economic considerations and is therefore applicable directly to profit-maximising firms. But it is also applicable to public sector organisations that are motivated by efficiency considerations. It can also be suitably modified if other non-economic factors need to be taken explicitly into account.

We analyse the decision to contract in terms of the economic evaluation that must precede it. This is specified and illustrated by the decision tree in Figure 1. It describes three steps that must be taken in order to determine whether the decision to contract a service is economically sound, in other words, whether it is an efficient and effective method of service delivery. Although they are conceptually distinct, the steps need not follow the sequence implied in the diagram and could be treated as simultaneous.

The first step concerns the identification of potential suppliers. The economic rationale for conducting a preliminary search is to establish whether contracting is likely to be feasible. Private sector firms that produce final goods and services are rarely fully integrated. Many intermediate inputs, the resources that are needed for final production, are supplied by outside contractors. The optimal level of integration of productive activity becomes the key issue. It depends in part on whether efficient and effective suppliers of the intermediate goods and services exist. The contracting organisation must apply these criteria to determine whether outside

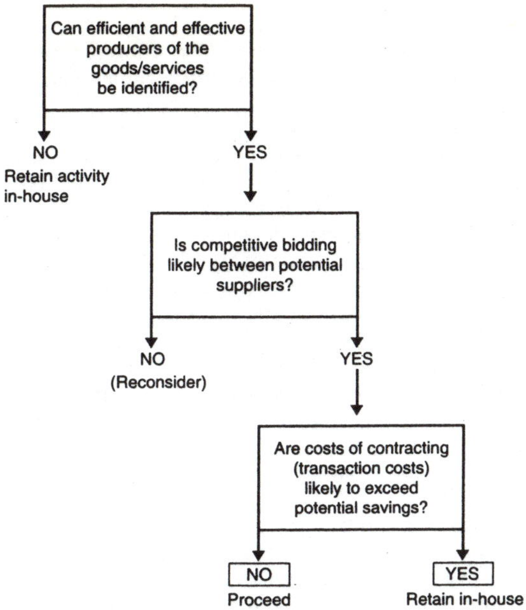


**Figure 1.** Competitive tendering and contracting decision tree.

contractors are likely to have the necessary experience and expertise to supply its requirements.

The second step in the contracting decision concerns the extent to which provision can be made competitive, or more precisely, contestable. Public sector organisations in particular, frequently express concern at the prospect of uncompetitive or collusive bidding behaviour by contractors. Yet private sector firms are often prepared to negotiate contracts directly with suppliers, without going through a bidding process. The properties of alternative competitive bidding schemes have recently attracted much attention from economists (see, for example, McAfee and McMillan, 1987). The bid price outcomes depend on the strategies adopted by individual bidders, their valuations of the contracts subject to tender which in turn will depend on their expectations of costs and revenues, and finally on the type of auction mechanism used. Although the literature focuses primarily on pure auctions such as those used for works of art, the analysis is useful in unravelling the complexities involved when bidding for service and other supply contracts (for a recent, practical application of auction theory see McMillan, 1994).

In most cases of competitive tendering the sealed tender bid system is used. But even in the public sector and where contracts for services are involved, it is no longer mandatory to accept the lowest bid. Trade-offs are increasingly made between perceived or expected quality of service and the tendered price. Public sector contract managers are expected to apply 'value for money' criteria when awarding contracts (see, for example, Domberger *et al.*, 1993a).

The client organisation needs to establish whether a competitive bidding process is essential and if so what form it should take. Formal tendering is usually required of public sector bodies for reasons of probity and accountability. In the private sector, firms do not always go through formal tendering processes, as suggested above, because they expect to get satisfactory results without incurring the costs of setting up and evaluating tenders.

The third element of the contracting decision involves the actual costs of contracting—the transaction costs. These include not only the costs of organising and assessing the bids but also the costs of contract design and negotiation as well as the monitoring and enforcement costs. Many commentators have suggested that the costs of contracting can sometime offset or even exceed the savings generated from competitive tendering (see, Walsh, 1992; Prager, 1994, for discussion). They argue that the monitoring and enforcement of contractors is more intensive than that required of in-house provision.

This argument is puzzling. It implies the optimal level of monitoring is greater when contractors are employed than when in-house production is involved. It also implies that the likelihood of opportunistic behaviour by contractors is correspondingly greater, perhaps because contractors are motivated by profits and therefore have an incentive to 'cheat'. The result is an expectation that contractors will attempt to shade quality unless deterrence is made effective through intensive and costly monitoring activity.

But it is not obvious that differences in monitoring costs between in-house providers and contractors arise from divergent incentives rather than from the inability to specify requirements and design contracts. Nonetheless, when evaluating in-house versus external provision, the organisation must weigh up the total costs of contracting against the savings likely to be obtained, as implied in Figure 1. Although somewhat simplified, this captures the essence of a rational decision making approach to contracting.

Public sector organisations typically incur greater contracting costs because of the need to ensure transparency and accountability (Domberger *et al.*, 1993a). Yet this need not skew decisions in favour of in-house provision. The degree of specialisation in the market and the competitiveness of potential suppliers is what ultimately determines the mode of provision.

Where technology and market characteristics are such that contracts would confer natural monopoly status on the suppliers, franchises are used as the preferred contractual mode. A franchise is a particular type of contract which gives the supplier the right to sell services in the marketplace on terms that are regulated by the franchisor. Several economists, most notably Demsetz (1967) favour franchising as superior to regulation of privately owned utilities. However others, most notably Williamson (1976) argue that franchising in practice differs little from conventional forms of regulation and suffers from some additional shortcomings. In recent years franchising has been used for award of television licenses in the UK and cable TV in the US. For detailed discussion of some issues see Domberger and Middleton (1985) and Domberger (1986).

## 3. The Extent of Use of Contracting

The extent of use of CTC by public sector agencies can be measured in several ways, including the number or proportion of public sector organisations using this method of sourcing inputs and delivering services, or the proportion of total spending allocated in this manner. A review of the literature illustrates that information about the extent of use of contracting by governments and private sector organisations is incomplete. Most studies focus on particular types of contracting, specific jurisdictions or a small number of activities. In addition, the extent of its use changes constantly over time. Nevertheless, a considerable number of studies were published in the late 1980s and early 1990s, focusing primarily on its use by local government.

### 3.1. Europe

The use of CTC has a long history in most Western European countries.[1] For instance, in France in the early 1800s, the rights to build and operate railways and water storage and distribution facilities were auctioned by competitive tender (Schmalensee, 1979; Veljanovski 1989). By the late 1980s its use ranged from police services in Switzerland, to cleaning, refuse collection and the operation of slaughter houses in Germany, and fire and ambulance services in Denmark (Fixler, 1988; Walsh and Davis, 1993).

By contrast, in the UK the use of CTC by governments was limited until 1979 when the victory of the Conservative Government heralded a substantial increase in its use by the central and local governments (Ascher, 1987). The UK government has mandated that a number of specific functions be put to competitive tender. The Central Unit on Purchasing has overseen a substantial increase in contracting and market testing, as part of the UK Government value for money purchasing policy. In 1988 compulsory CTC was introduced for all central government cleaning, laundry, security and maintenance. By 1986/87, approximately 7.3% of central government and 5.6% of National Health Service purchasing was allocated through competitive tender (Confederation of British Industry, 1988). In addition, UK Government legislation now requires local councils to contract out a variety of local government activities such as refuse collection, cleaning, catering and road construction and maintenance, town planning and tax collection.

### 3.2. America

In the US, CTC has been used for transport and energy generation and reticulation since the early 1900s (Bauer, 1939). Since 1955 the Federal Government A-76 Program has required governments to routinely tender for commercially available services. By 1987 approximately $200 billion of Federal Government spending was allocated through private firms, including defence and prisons (Report of the President's Commission on Privatization, 1988). In addition, State Governments use CTC for a wide range of services, including recreation and protection of the environment, human services, employment and training programs and public transport (Allen *et al.*, 1989).

The use of CTC in US local government administration is more extensive than in most other Western countries. In addition, its use increased dramatically in the 1970s and 1980s. Indeed, most local councils now use contracting for the provision of various medical, educational, infrastructure and welfare services (Clarkson, 1989). For instance, by the mid-1980s approximately 50% of councils contracted out 13 or more functions (Poole, 1988). Also, by the mid-1980s 62% of local councils had contracts with other levels of government (Savas, 1987). In the US contracting is particularly extensive for road construction, waste collection, building maintenance, security, grounds maintenance and legal services.

Its use by central, state and local governments in Canada is also substantial for a variety of activities. For instance, local councils often use contracting for the provision and maintenance of physical infrastructure, waste collection, community services and administration (McDavid, 1988). Little is known about its use in Central and South America. However, foreign aid to this region often requires governments to use CTC to build roads and provide some welfare and housing services (Burke, 1990).

### 3.3. *Asia*

In Japan CTC has been widely employed since 1945, particularly at the local government level. Activities often provided through CTC include public housing, refuse and tax collection (Ascher, 1987). In other countries in this region its use ranges from refuse collection in Malaysia to the operation of public transport in Thailand (McMaster, 1991; Dhiratayakinant, 1991).

In the Peoples' Republic of China (PRC) the use of competitive tendering and contracting increased dramatically after the introduction of market led reforms in 1988. The management and operation of a wide variety of publicly owned assets has been contracted out, including millions of small enterprises producing agricultural and industrial goods and services for consumption by governments and the public (Findlay and Watson, 1989). By the late 1980s CTC was employed by governments in most sectors of the economy, allowing market forces to operate alongside state ownership and regulation of physical and productive assets (Dewei, 1991).

### 3.4. *Oceania*

CTC has been used by governments in Australia since the turn of the century. In recent years there has been a steady acceleration in its use by the public sector. While the full extent of its scope is unknown, by the early 1990s approximately 5% of central government spending was allocated through competitive tender, particularly for defence procurement, maintenance, legal services and recreation services (Rimmer, 1991; Management Improvement Advisory Board, 1992). During the late 1980s and early 1990s State Governments increased their use of CTC. Activities most commonly contracted by Australian State Governments include information technology services, cleaning, building maintenance, library services and auditing (Domberger *et al.*, 1993b). In addition, up to 20% of spending by State trading enterprises—providing energy, transport and water services—is allocated by competitive tender (Domberger and Farago, 1994).

Its use by local government in Australia is also extensive, covering most local government activities such as protection of the environment, road construction and maintenance, and provision of recreation and welfare services (Rimmer, 1993). The New Zealand Government and some State Governments in Australia have announced that local councils will now be required to increase their use of competitive tendering, in some cases allocating up to 50% of their spending in this manner.

### 3.5. *World Overview*

This survey illustrates that information about the use CTC by government is limited and incomplete. Nevertheless, it is clear that its use by public sector organisations is extensive, especially for the provision and maintenance of physical infrastructure, defence procurement, community services and protection of the environment. In the 1980s most governments extended their use of CTC, particularly in the US, PRC and the UK. It is used extensive by in both free market and socialist economic systems. Most public sector organisations are free to implement this approach if they believe that they will benefit from its use. However, central governments in the US and UK require some jurisdictions to implement CTC and certain activities to be delivered through contract.

## 4. Evidence on Cost and Quality

### *4.1. Contracting and Service Costs*

Analysis of the impact of CTC on service costs can be a complex exercise. There are often practical difficulties in obtaining high quality cost data. Indeed, the quality and type of accounting systems employed by governments can vary substantially, making comparisons between jurisdictions using contracting with those using in-house provision difficult. In addition, accounting systems often change after the introduction of CTC, making before and after cost comparisons difficult. Comparisons of costs are also made more difficult when only part of a function or activity is subjected to CTC.

When assessing the impact of CTC on costs it is important that all costs are accounted for, including direct service costs and transaction costs, which are incurred through the implementation and monitoring of CTC over the duration of the contract. In practice, costs are measured in a variety of ways, including changes in average costs and median costs. In addition, multiple regression analysis can be used to take into account the impact on costs of factors such as demography, level of inputs and geography.

Many of the studies reviewed herein—including Walsh (1991) and Hensher (1989)—measure and compare costs before and after use of CTC. This approach has various advantages and disadvantages. For instance, this approach can allow for precise measurement of changes in costs. However, costs can vary over time because of changes in input prices, demand or technology. In practice, it can be difficult to distinguish between cost changes over time resulting from CTC and changes resulting from other factors not related to the use of CTC.

Other studies reviewed herein—including Savas (1977), Rimmer and Webb (1990) and Albin (1992)—compare costs of organisations using CTC with those of organisations not using CTC. Comparison of the costs of organisations using CTC with those employing in-house provision could produce spurious results where organisations using CTC have key characteristics in common, such as large populations. In such cases, cost variations could be explained by other factors—such as economies of scale and scope—rather than the use of CTC. For this reason, most of these studies are based on surveys of local councils, whose relatively large numbers reduce the risk of sample bias. Greater weight should also be attached to those studies based on multiple regression analysis, which allows for several factors which might impact on costs to be included in the analysis.

A review of the literature illustrates a broad consensus that CTC usually leads to substantial reductions in service costs (Table 1). While the level of cost changes varies greatly—between + 6 and − 68%—average reductions of 20% are usually attained by its use. These studies employ a variety of techniques to measure and compare costs for a wide variety of activities, ranging between central government

**Table 1.** Summary of evidence: costs

| Study | Activities and jurisdiction | Change in costs (%) | Remarks |
|---|---|---|---|
| Millward (1986) | 103 local councils in Switzerland in 1970, refuse collection | − 20 | Multiple regression, change in costs per tonne |
| Berenyi (1981) | 10 US local councils, 1971 to 1977, refuse collection | − 7 to − 50 | Cost reductions obtained when private or public sector won contract |
| Savas (1977) | 315 US cities in 1975, 4 functions | − 15 to − 29 | Random sample of cities, savings obtained when public and private sector won, regression analysis illustrated cost savings greatest for larger cities |
| Edwards and Stevens (1978) | 77 US cities in 1975, refuse collection | − 10 to − 41 | Employed econometric and regression models, savings greater for larger cities |
| Kramer and Terrell (1984) | 81 local councils social and welfare services in San Francisco area in 1980–81 | Usually reduced | Changes in costs not quantified |
| Mehay and Gonzalez (1985) | 53 local councils and county governments in the US in the early 1980s, 3 functions | − 9 to − 20 | Study of contracting between levels of government, based on multiple regression analysis |
| McDavid (1985) | 126 local councils in Canada in 1981–82, refuse collection | − 24 to − 29 | Multiple regression, cost reductions usually larger where contract won by private sector rather than mix of private and public contractor |
| Domberger *et al.* (1986) | Refuse collection by 305 local councils in the UK in 1983–84 | − 20 | Employed multiple regression analysis |
| Domberger *et al.* (1987) | Domestic Services in a sample of over 2000 hospitals in the UK | − 20 to − 30 | Multiple regression analysis employed |
| Pirie (1986) | 55 UK local councils, several functions | − 20 to − 40 | Based on survey, but unclear whether sample was representative |
| Hartley & Huby (1986) | 213 UK local government councils and national health services | Average − 26<br>+ 28 to − 68 | Based on 1985 survey with 52% response rate. Data and methodology sound |
| Moore (1987) | US Federal Government defence and air traffic control, early and mid-1980s | − 30 to − 50 | Review by US Administration of defence contracts and air traffic control operations |
| Confederation of British Industry (1988) | Range of UK central government, national health service and local councils in mid-1980s | − 17 to − 28 | Cost reductions 23% for central government, 17% national health service and 28% local government |
| Hensher (1988) | London buses in the mid-1980s | Average − 20 | Change in costs compared to public monopoly levels prior to competitive tendering |
| Pack (1989) | 15 US councils, several functions from early to mid-1980s | − 5 to − 60 | Initial cost reductions of − 5 to − 60 declined over a 5-year period |
| Walsh (1991) | Survey of 40 UK local councils in 1989–90, several functions | Average − 6 to − 7<br>+ 6 to − 17 | Government supported study, high quality data, change in costs after 1 year of compulsory CTC |
| Rimmer and Webb (1990) | 127 local councils in Australia in 1986, 5 functions | − 10 to − 24 | Difference in average costs between councils using CTC and those using in-house provision |
| ERC (1990) | 460 local councils in Australia in 1989, large number of functions | Usually increased | Based on observations of survey respondents. No statistical analysis quantifying impact of CTC on costs |
| Albin (1992) | 58 cities in Australia in 1990–91, functions not specified | Usually reduced | Bivariate regression analysis, cost reductions not quantified |

**Table 1.** *continued*

| Study | Activities and jurisdiction | Change in costs (%) | Remarks |
|---|---|---|---|
| Domberger *et al.*, (1993b) | 65 State Government agencies in Australia in 1993, several functions | − 4 to − 51 | Cost reductions vary according to function, with building and vehicle maintenance yielding the highest savings, while transport and catering produced less savings |
| Rimmer (1993) | 327 Local Councils in Australia, several functions | Commonly no change | Multiple regression, some cost reductions in city councils but not in rural |
| Farago and Domberger (1994) | 1993 survey of government business enterprises in Australia | − 8 to − 46 | Enterprises providing water, sewerage, gas and electricity services |

defence procurement to local government cleaning and refuse collection. The period covered by these studies is approximately 20 years, between the early 1970s and 1990s. The levels of cost reductions resulting from the use of CTC does not appear to have changed over this period of time.

The level of cost reductions is similar for each level of government and for each of the countries reviewed. Cost reductions are attained where both public and private sector organisations win contracts. This suggests that the process of competitive bidding, rather than simply transferring functions from the public to the private sectors, is the key source of widespread efficiency gains.

### 4.2. *Contracting and Service Quality*

The quality of goods and services provided by markets can be measured by the price consumers are prepared to pay. By contrast, the measurement of quality of publicly provided services is more complex. Perceptions about quality can vary between service providers, voters, elected officials and consumers. There is an absence of generally accepted measures of quality (Hall and Rimmer, 1994).

In practice, in-house service quality is usually measured and controlled through the bureaucracy. By contrast, where contracting is used quality is controlled through a legally binding specification in a contract. There are also different techniques for measuring quality, including surveys of users, changes in inputs, the range or number of outputs and performance indicators, such as a systematic assessment of user complaints. These different approaches to measuring quality mean that there is a shortage of accurate data about changes in quality over time, both within and between organisations and jurisdictions. In addition, governments rarely use quality specifications prior to CTC. This means that there is a lack of accurate data about the impact of CTC on service quality. Many of the studies reviewed herein use incomplete and narrow measures of service quality.

Analysis of the impact of contracting on service quality highlights two key questions. First, does contracting lead to different expectations about service quality? Some studies claim that CTC leads to a greater focus on service quality and the development of quality specifications (Walsh, 1991). Second, where CTC is employed, are quality specifications adhered to by service providers? The ERC (1990) claims that CTC usually leads to service providers ignoring specifications so that profits can be maximised.

A review of the literature indicates that while there is a broad consensus that CTC usually leads to reductions in costs, there is less consensus about its impact on service quality (Table 2). Some studies—including Ascher (1987) and ERC (1990)—claim that CTC leads to clear reductions in service quality, with contractors providing services below the specifications outlined in the contract. Other studies conclude that CTC does not have a measurable impact on quality, including Stevens (1984), Domberger *et al.* (1986) and Albin (1992).

Some studies argue that the impact of CTC on quality varies depending on the nature of the activity (Pack, 1989). For instance, one study found that in the UK in the mid-1980s service quality sometimes improved, yet some 25% of local councils surveyed had also invoked penalty clauses in contracts because of lower than expected service quality (Hartley and Huby, 1986). By contrast, some studies, including Savas (1977) and Domberger *et al.* (1994) found that CTC can enhance service quality.

A review of the literature shows that there is no consensus about the impact of CTC on service quality (Table 2). Care needs to be taken when interpreting each study, as conclusions are often based on small samples or based on incomplete measures of quality. Most of the studies reviewed here assess whether contractors adheres to specifications. However, where quality is affected, it is often unclear whether the contractor was not adhering to specifications or whether a policy decision has been made to use CTC as a mechanism to change quality. Overall, there is an absence of good, disaggregated data and more research is needed to resolve how CTC impacts on quality.

**Table 2.** Summary of evidence: impact of contracting on quality

| Study | Activities and jurisdiction | Impact on quality | Remarks |
|---|---|---|---|
| Stevens (1984) | 121 local councils in the US in 1974–75, 8 functions | No change | Several measures of quality used, quality variation smaller than variation in costs |
| Savas (1977) | City of Minneapolis 1971–75, refuse collection | Improved | Indirect measure, changes in the number of telephone calls |
| Savas (1982) | 25 health, welfare, transport and refuse collection functions in the early 1980s in the US | No change | Based on review of case studies |
| Hartley and Huby (1986) | Several local government functions in the UK in the mid-1980s | Reduced in 25% of cases | Analysed whether contractors adhered to specifications |
| Domberger *et al.* (1986) | UK study of refuse collection by 305 local councils in the early to mid-1980s | No change | Several measures of quality used |
| Ascher (1987) | UK local government in the mid-1980s | Usually reduced | Functions not specified, based on review of literature and several case studies |
| Pack (1989) | 15 local councils in the US between 1983 and 1987 | 33% of local councils dissatisfied | Some councils experienced problems with contract implementation |
| ERC (1990) | 44 local government activities in Australia in the late 1980s | Usually reduced | Based on observations of local government managers surveyed |
| Albin (1992) | 58 local councils in Australia in 1990–91 | No change | Functions not specified, used range and number of services as a measure of quality |
| Domberger *et al.* (1994) | 61 cleaning contracts in NSW (Australia) in 1993 | No change or improves | High quality data analysed through regression model |

## 5. Conclusion

The results of this survey suggest that the introduction of CTC has yielded significant benefits in the provision of public services. The effect of competition on costs and prices is unambiguous and the weight of evidence indicates that substantial savings are typically achieved—in the order of 20%. The evidence on quality is less clear cut and its interpretation is rendered more difficult by data problems. Generally the more precise and objective the measurement of quality, the less ambiguous are the findings (see, for example, Domberger *et al.*, 1994).

Two important implications emerge from this survey. The first is that whilst cost savings translate into economic benefits, these do not accrue in equal measure to producers and consumers of the services. In other words, competitive tendering generates winners and losers. The winners are the tax payers whose services cost less whilst quality is maintained or even enhanced. The losers are the producers—the employees of the public sector organisation—who work harder and/or smarter under the new regime. Often some employees will be made redundant as manning levels are reduced post-CTC.

However, the level of benefits associated with the introduction of CTC is such that there remains ample scope to compensate the losers. This is already being done in many cases. Some public sector organisations require their contractors to re-employ a significant proportion of the work force. Those who are not taken on can be given redundancy pay-outs and/or be re-trained and re-deployed elsewhere within the organisation (see, Hall and Domberger, 1992, for a specific case study). The emerging evidence also suggests that even where restrictions are placed on the employment policies of contractors, the savings achieved remain substantial (Jensen and Liebenberg, 1994).

The second issue concerns the vexed question of compulsory competitive tendering. Should public sector organisations be forced to go out to tender or should the decision be left to their discretion? This would not be an issue if incentives to adopt the most cost effective method of provision were sufficiently powerful. But evidence suggests that the decision to contract can be affected by non-economic considerations. It is for this reason that some jurisdictions have introduced legislation forcing public authorities to introduce competition. The UK 1988 Local Government Act has already been mentioned in this context but there are other examples. In 1994 the government of Victoria (Australia) legislated for compulsory competitive tendering in all local councils within the state. However, the legislation takes a gradualist approach: councils are required to put 20% of their service expenditure to tender in the first year, rising to 50% by the third.

Compulsory competitive tendering has disadvantages for both parties to the transaction. For the client organisation it creates an environment where compliance is what matters. It does little to instil a commercial outlook and may even delay its adoption. In the first round of contracts for UK local government services following the 1988 Act, 80% of decisions went in favour of the in-house teams. The private sector cried foul, but it remains an open question whether the market was sufficiently well developed to take on the volume of business that was contestable for the first time.

In general, compulsion ought to be the last resort. Changes in the governance structure of public sector administrators could be an alternative way forward. It may be feasible, for example, to introduce incentive schemes that align the interests of public sector managers with the efficiency and effectiveness of service provision.

This is not the place to consider these issues in detail. But it should be noted that most of the evidence reported in this study related to voluntary competitive tendering. Research on the impact of compulsory competitive tendering is still in its infancy and comprehensive results are yet to emerge.

Turning to the agenda for further research, it is both extensive and challenging. The measurement of quality will continue to be a costly area of research but it is a vitally necessary one if convincing findings are to emerge in this difficult area. It is encouraging to note that a wide range of performance indicators are now publicly available. This will ease the problems of investigation in this field.

Other questions that need to be addressed are: do savings fall over time as contractors get better established and competition more stable? How sensitive are bid prices to the number of bidders? And there are other issues that are peripheral to those considered in this survey but that merit further study. They include the effect of contracting on public sector accountability and on the industrial relations system. What is clear is that the public sector is undergoing a major transformation world-wide and that competitive tendering and contracting is making a major contribution to that process. Our broad conclusion is that on the evidence available thus far the change has been a positive one.

## Note

1. Little information is available about its use in former Eastern-bloc countries.

## References


Albin, S., "Bureau-Shaping and Contracting Out: The Case of Australian Local Government", *Public Policy Program Discussion Paper*, No. 29, Australian National University, Canberra, January 1992.

Allen, J., Chi, K., Devlin, K., Fall, M., Hatry, H. and Masterman, W., *The Private Sector in State Service Delivery: Examples of Innovative Practices*. Washington DC: The Council of State Governments and the Urban Institute Press.

Ascher, K., *The Politics of Privatisation: Contracting Out Public Services*. London: Macmillan Education, 1987.

Bauer, J., "Modernising the Public Utility Franchise," *Public Management*, August 1939, 21, 235–40.

Berenyi, E., "Contracting Out Refuse Collection, The Nature and Impact of Change," *Urban Interest*, Spring 1981, 3, 30–42.

Burke, M., "Private versus Public Construction in Honduras: Issues of Economics and Ideology," in D. Gayle and J. Goodrich, eds., *Privatization and Deregulation in Global Perspective*. London: Pinter, 1990, chapter 14.

Clarkson, K., "Privatisation at the State and Local Level," in P. MacAvoy, W. Stanbury, G. Yarrow and R. Zeckhauser, eds., *Privatisation and State-Owned Enterprises: Lessons from the United States, Great Britain and Canada*. Boston, MA: Kluwer, 1989, 143–94.

Coase, R., "The Nature of the Firm," *Economica*, 1937, 4, 386–405.

Confederation of British Industry, "The Competitive Advantage," *Report of the CBI Public Expenditure Task Force*. London, 1988.

Demsetz, H., "Why Regulate Utilities," *Journal of Law and Economics*, 1967, 11, 55–6.

Dewei, L., "Reform of Public Enterprise in PRC," in G. Gouri ed., *Privatization and Public Enterprise: The Asia Pacific Experience*. Hyderabad: Asian and Pacific Development Centre and the Institute of Public Enterprise, 1991, chapter 34.

Dhiratayakinant, K., "Privatization of the Bangkok Metropolitan Transit Organisation: A Case Study," in G. Gouri, ed., *Privatization and Public Enterprise: The Asia Pacific Experience*. Hyderabad: Asian and Pacific Development Centre and the Institute of Public Enterprise, 1991, chapter 22.

Domberger, S., "Economic Regulation through Franchise Contracts," in J. Kay, C. Mayer and D. Thompson, eds., *Privatisation and Regulation: The UK Experience*. Oxford: Oxford University Press, 1986, 269–83.

Domberger, S. and Farago, S., "Competitive Tendering and the Performance of Government Trading Enterprises in NSW," *Working Paper Series*, No. 01–94, Graduate School of Business, The University of Sydney, February 1994.

Domberger, S. and Middleton, J., "Franchising in Practice: The Case of Independent Television in the UK," *Fiscal Studies*, 1985, 6, 1, 17–32.

Domberger, S., Meadowcroft, S. and Thompson, D., "Competitive Tendering and Efficiency: The Case of Refuse Collection," *Fiscal Studies*, 1986, 7, 4, 69–87.

Domberger, S., Meadowcroft, S. and Thompson, D., "The Impact of Competitive Tendering on the Costs of Hospital Domestic Services," *Fiscal Studies*, 1987, 8, 4, 39–54.

Domberger, S., Hensher, D. and Wedde, S., "Competitive Tendering Policies in the Public and Private Sectors," *Australian Journal of Public Administration*, 1993a, 52, 4, 401–11.

Domberger, S., Farago, S., Hall, C. and Li, E., "Competitive Tendering and Contracting in the NSW Budget Sector: The 1993 Survey Findings," *Working Paper Series*, No. 11–93, Graduate School of Business, The University of Sydney, December 1993b.

Domberger, S., Hall, C. and Li, E., "The Determinants of Price and Quality in Competitively Tendered Contracts," *Working Paper Series*, No. 03–94, Graduate School of Business, The University of Sydney, February 1994.

Economist, The, "Does Size matter?" 11 June 1994, 331, 74.

Edwards, F. and Stevens, B., "The Provision of Municipal Sanitation Services by Private Firms: An Empirical Analysis of the Efficiency of Alternative Market Structures and Regulatory Arrangements," *Journal of Industrial Economics*, December 1978, XXVII, 2, 133–47.

ERC, *Breach of Contract: Privatisation and Management of Australian Local Government*. Sydney: Evatt Research Centre in association with Pluto Press, 1990.

Farago, S. and Domberger, S., "Competitive Tendering and Contracting in NSW Government Trading Enterprises: A Survey," *Working Paper Series*, No. 2–94, Graduate School of Business, The University of Sydney, February 1994.

Findlay, C. and Watson, A., "Risk and Efficiency: Contracting in the Chinese Countryside," Paper presented at the *Economic Society of Australia Conference*, July 1989.

Fixler, P., *A Privatization Program for State and Local Officials*. Santa Monica, CA: The Reason Foundation Local Government Centre, 1988.

Hall, C. and Domberger, S., "Competitive Tendering for Domestic Services: A Comparative Study of Three Hospitals in New South Wales," Graduate School of Business, The University of Sydney, September 1992.

Hall, C. and Rimmer, S., "Performance Monitoring and Public Sector Contracting," *Australian Journal of Public Administration*, 1994, 53, 4.

Hartley, K. and Huby, M., "Contracting-Out Policy: Theory and Evidence," in J. Kay, C. Mayer and D. Thompson, eds., *Privatisation and Regulation: The UK Experience*. Oxford: Clarendon, 1986, chapter 15.

Hensher, D., "Competitive Tendering in the Transportation Sector," *Economic Papers*, March 1989, 8, 1, 1–11.

Jensen, P. and Liebenberg, B., "The Sale of the NSW Government Cleaning Service," Mimeo, Graduate School of Business, The University of Sydney, 1994.

Kay, J., Mayer, C. and Thompson, D., eds., *Privatisation and Regulation—The UK Experience*. Oxford: Oxford University Press, 1986.

Kramer, R. and Terrell, P., *Social Services Contracting in the Bay Area*. Berkeley, CA: Institute of Governmental Studies, University of California.

Management Improvement Advisory Board, *Contracting for the Provision of Services in Commonwealth Agencies*. Canberra: Australian Government Publishing Service, December 1992.

McAfee, R. P. and McMillan, J., "Auctions and Bidding," *Journal of Economic Literature*, 1987, 25, 2, 699–738.

McDavid, J., "Privatizing Local Government Services in Canada," in M. Walker, ed., *Privatisation: Tactics and Techniques*. Vancouver: The Fraser Institute, 1988, 101–20.

McMaster, J., *Urban Financial Management: A Training Manual*. Washington, DC: World Bank, 1991, 161–9.

McMillan, J., "Selling Spectrum Rights," *Journal of Economic Perspectives*, 1994, forthcoming.

Mehay, S. and Gonzalez, R., "Economic Incentives Under Contract Supply of Local Government Services," *Public Choice*, 1985, 46, 79–86.

Millward, R., "The Comparative Performance of Public and Private Ownership," in J. Kay, C. Mayer and D. Thompson, eds., *Privatisation and Regulation: The UK Experience*. Oxford: Clarendon, 1986, chapter 6.

Moore, S., "Contracting Out: A Painless Alternative to the Budget Cutter's Knife," in S. Hanke, ed., *Prospects for Privatisation, 36(3)*. New York: Academy of Political Science, 1987, 60–73.

Osborne, D. and Gaebler, T., *Re-inventing Government: How the Entrepreneurial Spirit is Transforming the Public Sector*. Reading, MA: Addison Wesley.

Pack, J., "Privatisation and Cost Reduction," *Policy Sciences: An International Journal Devoted to the Improvement of Policy Making*, 1989, 22, 1–15.

Pirie, M., *Privatisation: In Theory and Practice*. Sydney: Adam Smith Institute and Centre 2000 Limited, 1986.

Poole, R., "The Limits of Privatisation," in M. Walker, ed., *Privatisation: Tactics and Techniques*. Vancouver: The Fraser Institute, 1988, 79–98.

Prager, J., "Contracting Out Government Services: Lessons from the Private Sector," *Public Administration Review*, 1994, 54, 20, 176–84.

Report of the President's Commission on Privatisation, *Privatization: Towards More Effective Government*. Washington DC, March 1988.

Rimmer, S., "Estimated Savings from Competitive Tendering," *Assistance Evaluation Branch Staff Working Paper*, No. 1, Industry Commission, Canberra, April 1991.

Rimmer, S., "Aspects of Competitive Tendering and Contracting in Local Government Administration," PhD Thesis, The University of New England, Armidale, 1993.

Rimmer, S. and Webb, G., "Greater Efficiency Through Competitive Tendering," *Economic Papers*, December 1990, 9, 4, 51–60.

Savas, E. S., "An Empirical Study of Competition in Municipal Service Delivery," *Public Administration Review*, November/December, 1977, 37, 6, 717–24.

Savas, E. S., *Privatizing the Public Sector: How to Shrink Government*. New Jersey: Chatham House, 1982.

Savas, E. S., *Privatization: The Key to Better Government*. New Jersey: Chatham House, 1987.

Schmalensee, R., *The Control of Natural Monopolies*. Lexington: D. C. Heath, 1979.

Stevens, B., "Comparing Public- and Private-Sector Productive Efficiency: An Analysis of Eight Activities," *National Productivity Review*, Autumn, 1984, 395–406.

Veljanovski, C., *Privatisation and Competition: A Market Prospectus*. London: Institute of Economic Affairs, 1989.

Vickers, J. and Yarrow, G., *Privatisation: An Economic Analysis*. Cambridge, MA: MIT Press, 1988.

Walsh, K., *Competitive Tendering for Local Authority Services: Initial Experiences*. London: Department of Environment, February 1991.

Walsh, K., "Quality and Public Services," *Public Administration*, 1992, 69, 40, 503–14.

Walsh, K. and Davis, H., *Competition and Service: The Impact of the Local Government Act 1988*. London: Department of the Environment, 1993.

Williamson, O., "Franchise Bidding for Natural Monopolies—in General and with Respect to CATV," *Bell Journal of Economics*, 1976, 7, 1, 73–104.

Williamson, O., *The Economic Institutions of Capitalism: Firms Markets and Relational Contracting*. New York: Collier-Macmillan, 1985.

# [5]

# Coming to Terms With the Public-Private Partnership

## A Grammar of Multiple Meanings

STEPHEN H. LINDER
*University of Texas, Houston*

*This essay critically examines the multiple meanings that the term,* public-private (P-P) partnership, *assumes in contemporary discussions. A brief deconstruction of this term not only clarifies these meanings, but also exposes to scrutiny their underlying premises and ideological commitments. Six distinct uses of the term are identified and linked to their respective meanings in neoconservative and neoliberal ideologies. Instead of focusing on partnership's conceptual definition, the term's strategic uses by political actors are attended to, consistent with the author's interest in partnership as a political symbol and policy tool. Accordingly, the claims of these actors about partnerships receive primary attention here. Their actual partnership practices and the distributional effects that partnering has on power and resources are left for others to consider.*

**The P-P partnership**, as a rubric for describing cooperative ventures between the state and private business, currently enjoys remarkable acclaim in both official and scholarly circles. Organizations ranging from the European Union to Canadian Heritage not only endorse the partnership idea but actively employ it as a programmatic tool for adapting to what they perceive as changing needs and circumstances (Kinnock, 1998; Canadian Heritage, 1996). Further, its advocates tout it as the epitome of a new generation of management reforms, especially suited to the contemporary economic and political imperatives for efficiency and quality. Despite momentum gathered since the late 1980s, and its present status as a de rigueur reform, the partnership is not new to governance. More than a decade earlier, without the fanfare or reformist cachet, partnerships were deployed by the federal government in the United States as a tool for stimulating private investment in inner-city infrastructure. Likewise, partnerships were key to coordinating federal initiatives in regional economic development. The record of these devices through the 1970s is at best mixed (Stephenson, 1991). How can we account for its reincarnation in the 1990s as a reform on the bleeding edge?

AMERICAN BEHAVIORAL SCIENTIST, Vol. 43 No. 1, September 1999 35-51

The simple answer in this instance raises only an unsatisfying irony. The P-P partnership is frequently viewed as a derivative of the privatization movement, which captivated conservative leaders in western liberal regimes on both sides of the Atlantic throughout much of the 1980s. Public asset sales, outsourcing (e.g., procurement contracts), and load shedding (e.g., divestiture) that occurred in these regimes was nominally intended to discipline the provision of services with competitive market pressures (Kettl, 1993). The rationale was that private providers would provide higher quality goods and services at lower cost, and the government sector of public providers would shrink accordingly. Conversely, the hallmark of partnerships is cooperation—not competition; the disciplining mechanism is not customer exit or thin profit margins, but a joint venture that spreads financial risks between public and private sectors. Joint-venture arrangements actually stabilize volatile markets and work to mitigate competitive pressures, not exploit them. Rather than struggling to redefine the boundary between public and private, with the former typically ceding territory to the latter, partnering works to blur them (Starr, 1990). It remains, then, an anomaly relative to contemporary ways of separating public from private.

The idea of government and business partnering for some common purpose evokes images of wartime solidarity and memories of small town life in America, where business and local government shared talent and community responsibilities. It seems to draw on communal traditions of cooperation that are, at once, vaguely familiar and socially valued. Of course, when we scratch the surface of these arrangements over the past century, the spectacle of machine politics, of graft and corruption, shines through. Part of the impetus for the growth of the liberal state was to inhibit these kinds of cooperative ventures by carefully defining and then policing the boundaries between public and private (Starr, 1990). This entailed both an elaborate overlay of administrative law on public sector activity, and a burgeoning regulatory apparatus to protect the public interest from private ones. For some, notably the critics of interest-group pluralism, the overlay was inadequate to the task. Nevertheless, the resulting partisan alignments, at least in the Anglo-American experience, were basically contests over the hegemony of one sector over the other (Jacobs, 1997). In this context, the movement for privatization in the 1980s endorsed the existence of a clear boundary separating the two sectors by contesting the division of responsibility between them. The partnership idea represents a different set of conceptual premises altogether.

## FROM PRIVATIZATION TO PARTNERSHIP

According to its proponents, partnerships (among other things) require actors from each sector to adopt characteristics and points of view that once defined and stabilized the identities of their counterparts. Government actors would need to think and behave like entrepreneurs, and business actors would need to embrace public interest considerations and expect greater public accountability. Here, the elaborate demarcations that defined roles and set the rules of engagement between business and government since the Progressive Era are, in large part, elided, removing the impetus for the adversarial character of their interactions. Moreover, the legal doctrine that professionalized the civil service in western liberal regimes and institutionalized public accountability through administrative procedure is being altered in certain states to support partnering arrangements. In Italy, for example, civil service reforms are eliminating many of the features of public sector careers that distinguished them from private sector employment (Supiot, 1996). Rulemaking procedures, once at the heart of command-and-control regulation in the United States, have been amended to center on negotiation among stakeholders (Negotiated Rulemaking Act, 1990). In short, the ground appears to have shifted under the postwar contest between the liberal state and its free-market opponents. Rapprochement of a sort lurks behind the partnership rhetoric.

More generally, the points of reference defining the binary separation of public from private, in welfare economics and liberal political doctrine alike, have been confounded by complex, variegated views of multiple sectors, including civil, intimate and dialogical realms, anchored to distinctive notions of social relations and political order. Use of the terms, public and private, now suggests any of a variety of social differentiations, not all of which translate into bipolar struggles for hegemony (Weintraub, 1997). To say that partnerships are yet another antiliberal effort to shrink the state by privatizing its functions is to misconstrue the significance of the partnership idea. First, figuratively stretching one sector by shrinking the other simply no longer applies (if it ever did) because the meaning of the sectors themselves is shifting (Feigenbaum, Hamnett, & Henig, 1998). Second, partnership advocates talk of new roles and innovative tools for the public manager, leveraging private capital for policy initiatives. The earlier privatization rhetoric of inefficient government and wasteful programs has largely faded from view, although its partisans remain active (Jack, Phillips, & The Robert Phillips Group, 1993). Part of the enthusiasm surrounding the rebirth of the partnership notion reflects a sense of new possibilities and changing alignments. As I will argue later, this sense reflects, albeit unconsciously, larger changes in the ideological, as well as the conceptual, landscape of governance.

The drive for privatization as a programmatic movement is typically attributed to free-market advocates and conservative politicians, joined in common cause against the liberal welfare state (Starr, 1988). Partnerships arise as a derivative reform in areas where full privatization seems less tractable, perhaps due to technical problems attending the assignment of property rights. If statist responsibilities must extend to certain goods and services, so the logic goes, then the delivery should be through business-mediated arrangements. Complications set in, however, once these ideologies are considered in detail. Part of the force behind privatization came from its status as a portmanteau idea, bringing together pragmatic reformers and ideologues of different stripes. As we unpack the various lines of reasoning among the constituent ideologies, we find distinctive commitments that partnerships are intended to embody. The more prominent among these ideologies draw upon neoconservative and neoliberal ideas. These will be explored as sources of meaning attached to partnerships. Consequently, the concept of the partnership itself will appear protean, making it less amenable to simple technical or programmatic definition.

Besides the loss of sector boundaries and its accompanying logic, and the ideological splits along new fault lines, the third influence on the rhetoric and significance of the P-P partnership comes from the advocates of management reform. They are providing the operational details and organizational processes for altering traditional governance in fundamental ways. The scope of these initiatives rivals the postwar efforts to reform the civil service. The Public Service Ministry in Britain refers to the partnership idea as central to the New Public Management, perhaps to distance itself from the ill-fated Tory experiment in quasi-autonomous governmental organizations (i.e., quangos; British Council, 1997). In the United States, the reform campaign underway is to reengineer government; the premises and rhetoric can be found in the promotional material of major management consultancies (Reijniers, 1994; Jack et al., 1993; Apen, Benicewicz, & Laia, 1994). Again, governmental and business organizations appear alike in their need to adapt to a global economy, new communications technologies, and growing client pressure for quality. The prescriptions are largely the same, flexible structure, results-oriented processes, and a client-service ethic (Canadian Council for Public-Private Partnerships, 1996; National Council for Public-Private Partnership, 1997). Partnering then becomes a vehicle for jointly overcoming the few remaining insoluble differences. Once we add an ideological backdrop, however, these forward-looking reforms appear less prescient and more instrumental and opportunistic.

My argument so far links the contemporary renewal of the partnership idea to three kinds of changes. At the most abstract level, there has been extensive theoretical work critically elaborating on, and extending the complexity of, the traditional binary division of sectors into public and private on economistic grounds. This thinking opens up public discourse on distinctive institutional realms and stimulates new ideas about social orderings. In effect, the old compartmentalization of public and private loses its natural appearance and assumes the features of an outmoded artifact of an earlier era (Wolfe, 1997). At a lower level of abstraction comes the influence of political values and commitments that animate contemporary ideological cleavages, at least among liberal constitutional regimes bordering the North Atlantic. The ascendancy of conservative leadership in these regimes throughout the 1980s added status and practical experience to their doctrinal base (Giddens, 1994). These, together with official responsibilities and error, helped splinter the movement into factions but, at the same time, multiplied the plausible alternatives to Progressive-era ideals and to the centrist methods of the postwar welfare state. Finally, at a pragmatic level, trends in management reform by the early 1990s had turned away from leadership and behavioral principles and toward more structural emphases on flexibility and innovation—reinforcing partnership ideals (Reijniers, 1994).

## THE MULTIPLE MEANINGS OF PARTNERSHIP

With these contextual features in place, we can now attempt to sort out the welter of meanings that P-P partnership assumes in contemporary discussions. As the title suggests, a form of deconstruction is adopted here to unpack the various meanings of the term and expose at least some of their underlying premises and ideological commitments to critical scrutiny. A deconstructive strategy was implicit in the preceding argument's attention to contexts—conceptual, ideological, and pragmatic—to clarify the production of meaning. My intent in the remainder of the piece, however, is much more modest than a full-blown post-structuralist analysis would admit. I prefer to rely on discursive uses of the term by certain actors rather than on narrative images and stories that evoke the term, because my interest inclines more toward political ideas and policy tools than to representational strategies. Likewise, claims about partnership will receive attention rather than partnership practices, because, at this point at least, I am more interested in conceptual clarification than in the workings of power or patterns of exclusion that partnerships may entail (see Handler, 1996). Finally, my efforts at clarification will not extend much beyond the level of value commitments. Questions of ontology and metaphysical pedigree are left for another time.

To map the discursive terrain, we must first identify some landmark usages that can serve as reference points, and then orient them relative to several fixed ideological projections. The meaning of each usage, not to strain the metaphor too much, comes from clarifying its location relative to other usages and knowing its ideological bearings. For the term, P-P partnership, as a policy device, there are at least six distinct usages that can serve as reference points. These are not mutually exclusive, definitional categories that might serve some taxonomic purpose, but rather are simple meanings attached to the use of the term by certain actors in making claims for its application or adoption. The next step is to orient these relative to several ideologies and identify their most likely attachments.

## THE IDEOLOGICAL REFERENTS

The two ideologies represented here both have *neo* prefixes, indicating a self-conscious split from their respective, institutionalized forms that have been well elaborated in the western political experience. Perhaps with a touch of irony, both neos are reversions to centuries older and, in their view, purer forms. Neoliberalism defines itself in opposition to, what it calls, welfare-state liberalism, the liberalism of the postwar European labor parties and New Deal democrats. Although aligned philosophically with Lockean individualism, it appears indebted to Scottish enlightenment notions (due to Smith and Hume) of moral regeneration through ownership and market exchange. Its faith in the spontaneous social coordination fostered by market incentives owes much to Hayek. Yet, it is distinguished from contemporary libertarianism by its apparent commitment to progress—material and technological—and a Deweyian pragmatist's sense of agency.

This sense of agency draws, not so much on the perfectibility notions espoused by the radical left and right, as on faith in human ingenuity and its role in social betterment. Although hardly collectivist and understandably wary of paternalism, neoliberalism bears an intriguing resemblance to the liberalism that Crowley (1987) found in the Progressive Era work of the Webbs, which was typically consigned to the ranks of utopian socialists. Progress, for the Webbs, depended upon innovation, and innovation would come from social experimentation. The neoliberals would agree that social change could be engineered through organizational means, but would prefer Hayek's entrepreneur in the marketplace to Beatrice Webb's industrial planner. Still, both see the devising of novel organizational mechanisms, not community solidarity, civic virtue, or individual training, as the key to progress. And both, in varying degrees of course, turn to government as the sponsor or referee.

The second ideology is neoconservatism, formed in part out of disaffection with the anticapitalist sentiments and religiosity of traditional conservatism. Although the neo view of conservatism shares Burkean roots with its parent, it represents an odd amalgam of deference to the sedimented knowledge that tradition conveys, with a Lockean liberal's faith in self-reliance and commerce as guarantors of human freedom. In doctrinal terms, this translates into an effort to strengthen the local cultural institutions that inculcate traditional values—the family, community churches, and civic associations—while opposing concentrations of power (economic or political) that undermine these values or the social order they reproduce. The liberal welfare state, in its substitution of entitlement for desert, of legalism for virtue, and of paternalism for self-initiative, effectively erodes the cultural basis of social order. Likewise, the mass marketing of large corporations to promote limitless consumption substitutes immediate gratification for self-restraint, celebrity lifestyles for prudent ways of living, and possessive egoism for community service. To be sure, either the state or the corporation can be an ally, should it choose to promote the appropriate cultural attachments and institutions or simply choose to withdraw its substitutions.

Both neo ideologies are typically lumped together under the banner of the New Right, as espousing traditional values and free markets. Ironically, the two claims are contradictory. In historical terms, the market, if anything, has been a de-traditionalizing force, advancing social change, not stability. Participants in unfettered exchanges in the global marketplace are likely to be exposed to sentiments and practices that prove corrosive to their values. Moreover, the sovereign consumer seeking to satisfy her appetites behaves quite differently than the citizen fulfilling community obligations. We expect the consumer to look outward for opportunities and price signals, and the citizen to look inward to a moral compass pointing the way. There is no guarantee that the two views will coincide. The New Right's formulation pits virtue against appetite and trusts that the former will triumph. In this context, the market can only make things tougher.

Certainly, one aspect of modernity is a belief that the self can be both citizen and consumer, that we adapt to complexity and social differentiation by proliferating ourselves to suit our social roles. Liberalism in the modern era offers two other solutions that complement this. First, moral sentiments can be fashioned from tastes rather than from virtues, deftly removing one side of the contradiction. This was Bentham's gift to the modern self. Second, social life can be divided into separate domains, a private one for money and consumption and a public one for power and citizenship; we appear to owe the genesis of this separation to natural law theories of contract (Gobetti, 1997). The New Right takes comfort in neither solution.

To simplify, neoconservatives split with neoliberals over which side of the traditional-values/free-markets contradiction they are willing to entrust with the task of securing a stable social order. Again, neoliberals side with Hayek and the invisible hand; neoconservatives prefer to rely on Berger's mediating institutions. Contrasting views about the role of the state follow. Collective activity, planned and undertaken by the state, appears to be the antithesis of the private orderings of the market; accordingly, neoliberals presume that it typically interferes (the exception occurs when the state acts to prop-up a failing market or to police market agreements). Similarly, to the extent that state transactions fail to mimic market ones, they are presumed to be inefficient. For neoconservatives, the state has a legitimate role to play in the acculturation of its citizens. The problem with the welfare state is not that it tried to instill a regime of social discipline on the needy, but rather that it was inadequate to the task. Other institutions, especially local ones, in their view, are more suitable and competent. The problem with the state is that it is overextended and it tries to do too much, and consequently, it does not do many things well. Neoliberals want to privatize the state because it is intrinsically inefficient. Neoconservatives want to privatize because the state is perpetually overburdened and underdisciplined; it can control neither its giveaways to the undeserving, nor its appetite for more tax dollars.

## SIX OF THE MEANINGS

Partnerships have been viewed as a retreat from the hard-line advocacy of privatization. From this perspective, they serve a strategic purpose, enlisting the support of more moderate elements that are less opposed to state action on principle. Partnerships are accommodationist; they hold back the specter of wholesale divestiture and, in exchange, promise lucrative collaboration with the state.

Unfortunately, this picture assumes that everyone sees partnerships in the same way—as a political tool—and that fear of privatization brings the state and its supporters to partner with the privatizers and their beneficiaries, whose successes of late have dwindled. Yet, once we deconstruct the partnership idea, attending to the discursive claims made on its behalf and to the premises that support them, the meanings proliferate. They convey not just strategic aims but normative ones as well.

There are at least six distinctive uses of the term, P-P partnership. Each use makes a claim about what partnerships are and conveys an understanding of their intended purpose and significance. Moreover, each use invokes certain premises about what the relevant problems are to be solved and how best to solve them. The premises of interest here are the ideological ones that form a coherent but largely unassailable set of beliefs and commitments. All six meanings, in my view, can be plausibly related to either neoliberal or neoconservative ideologies. This, of course, matters much more to those would-be supporters of partnerships, who take serious issue with these ideological premises, than it would to their ideological kindred. For those skeptical of partnerships, the discussion to follow may clarify the grounds for their skepticism.

*1. P-P partnership as management reform.* Partnerships, in this instance, are severed from their historical roots in community voluntarism and urban economic development and linked instead to the privatization movement's quest for efficiency gains. Accordingly, neither of these other roots will be explicitly treated here. (In fact, the link to voluntarism in the United States is quite complex; it typically evokes either traditionally conservative service obligations on the Right, e.g., the Junior League, or progressive ideals of citizen activism, e.g., Volunteers in Service to America, and not-for-profit community projects on the Left.) Nevertheless, as a management reform, partnerships are promoted as an innovative tool that will change the way government functions, largely by tapping into the discipline of the market. To do this, managers of government programs must formally enlist the collaboration of profit-seeking firms that (presumably) already enjoy the benefits of such discipline.

The collaboration, however, resembles more of a mentoring relationship than a joint undertaking. The flow of know-how appears asymmetric. Government managers are expected to become more like their business counterparts, than vice versa. This implies that business managers, at some earlier time, were reformed themselves, perhaps chastened by the fires of free-market competition or educated by management consultants in the ways of cost-efficiency and quality improvement. Government managers, in contrast, are taken to have grown flabby without competitive pressures and to be mired in the inefficiencies of red tape and bureaucratic organization. Such overstatement is typical of the rhetoric of the Reason Foundation, Coopers and Lybrand, or the Canadian Center for Management Development (Apen et al., 1994; Rodal & Wright, 1997; Gratias &

Boyd, 1995). The conduct of the promotion itself follows the regimen of the management consultancy. The National Council for Public-Private Partnerships (1997) in the United States and the Canadian Council for Public-Private Partnerships (1996) both have official government sanction (the former displays President Clinton's photograph in its materials). There are networks of prospects awaiting partners, databases of experienced exemplars, corporate underwriters, fee-for-service consultations, a speakers bureau, workshops, conventions, and of course, membership fees.

The imperatives for transforming government agencies to resemble profit-seeking businesses come from the hard lessons learned by firms that had their profits squeezed by more intensive competition, rapidly changing markets, and more demanding customers. The core presumption is that the skills needed to find new markets, enhance productivity, and stay ahead of the competition can also improve the way government works. Partnerships are viewed as the best vehicle for accomplishing this. Government managers learn by emulating their partners, as they adapt to the rigors of competition. If successful, they will become more entrepreneurial and flexible, occupied with deal making and attracting capital rather than with administrative procedure. The premises of this construction are prototypically neoliberal. The market stands as the superior source of production and service efficiencies, and its competitive character stimulates innovation and creative problem solving. Rather than divesting government altogether, however, its culture and operations can be changed with the right kind of intervention. Partnership, as management reform, is meant to serve this purpose.

*2. P-P partnership as problem conversion.* A variation on the management reform, partnerships are viewed from this perspective, not as a tool for changing managerial practices, but rather as a universal fix for most problems attending public service delivery. The task for government managers shifts from getting their own practices in line with entrepreneurial mores to reframing the problems they face in a way that will attract profit-seeking collaborators. In other words, commercialize problems to bait the marketplace. Here, the manager's duty is not to reform herself or himself but to induce others, wise to the ways of the market, to perform government's tasks for less money. The intent of the United Nations Development Program for the Urban Environment (1996), for example, is to accelerate private sector involvement by creating business opportunities out of gaps in infrastructure. Private firms bring their know-how and their capital. Government eases the regulatory and tax burdens and may add funds. The public gets its roads and water treatment. What distinguishes this venture from the machine politics of a century ago, in part at least, is the promoter's apparent obliviousness to the temptations of kickbacks and patronage. Will prospective partners be judged on noncommercial grounds? Where there is substantial money to be made, commercializing public problems can raise special difficulties with oversight. The other major difference comes from the partnering mechanism replacing the standard procurement-by-contract with some kind of joint-investment arrangement.

This commercialization idea bears some resemblance to the European Union's effort to attract private capital for a TransEuropean road network (Kinnock, 1998). The distinction between them becomes obvious only at the level of their premises. The European Union wants to supplement public funds to add projects that would otherwise not be affordable; it plans to take on partners, as it needs them, either for their expertise or for their capital. Nonetheless, government managers remain in charge. There is no effort to alter their public service ethic, or to change the way they manage. Instead, there is official sanction given for opportunistic partnerships as a supplemental tool for the financial management of complex, large-scale projects. In contrast, the United Nations depicts partnerships as the principal means of obtaining sustainable development in urban areas. Sustainability, in this context, appears to coincide with commercial viability; one must attract enough businesses that are not only willing to stay put, but able to shoulder the costs of infrastructure development largely on their own. Here, the government manager assumes the role of investment broker, putting deals together and attracting entrepreneurs and private capital to cooperative ventures on a project-by-project basis. Again, neoliberalism inspires confidence in the capital markets and enthusiastically propels the government manager beyond the bounds of contracting for services and into the promotion of private business growth and equity-based commercial transactions.

*3. P-P partnership as moral regeneration.* Each of the foregoing usages depicts partnership as a vehicle for bringing government closer to the market, either as a deal maker or as a pseudoentrepreneur. In both instances, competitive market exchanges appear as a model deserving emulation. The neoliberal's faith in the superiority of market-mediated relations helps reinforce whatever other influences are at work driving government to embrace market incentives. Similarly, it takes a neoliberal's sense of agency, holding that change for the better can be engineered through properly organized efforts, to inspire the confidence in partnership arrangements displayed here. Neoconservatives, in contrast, are more likely to view partnerships as a middle ground between public and private, rather than as a comprehensive tool for remaking government in the market's image.

A more subtle distinction becomes apparent when we consider the effects that partnerships are intended to have on the people involved. Performance aside, there are certain features of government provision that convey official sanction, desert, entitlement, or worth that are largely absent from anonymous market exchanges, mediated by money rather than eligibility. In rejecting government for some forms of the public's business, the neoliberal is implicitly also taking exception to the noncommercial differentiations that government programs rely upon. These are thought to have a corrosive influence on those served, as well as on those doing the serving. Of course, the opportunity costs of (unreformed) government programs and their tax implications are always a prominent concern. And yet, consider the efforts of the Clinton Administration to link welfare to work. Without work, the argument goes, welfare cultivates dependency and, at the same time, generates bureaucratic waste. Part of the impetus behind welfare reform can be found behind management reform. Commercial bases for doing the public's business are less fraught with moral judgments and are thus less corrosive to the human spirit. Hence, getting government managers involved as market participants, say through partnering arrangements, should have a salutary moral effect on them as well.

Taking this a step further, it is not just the relief of moving away from the effects of government service programs that matters to the neoliberal, it is the movement toward market-inspired traits of character. Self-reliance, initiative, hard work, integrity, prudence, and so on, all of which are familiar from Weber's characterization of the protestant ethic, are all thought to accompany participation in property holding and commercial enterprise. When Prime Minister Thatcher denationalized British utilities, shares were sold below par value with the intent of giving as many people as possible a chance for ownership. The idea was not to liberalize the industries (the regulatory regime remained in place), but to give the public a direct stake in an important national enterprise (and to raise some cash) (Starr, 1988). Like property ownership, partnerships accomplish this moral purpose in a way that direct privatization would not have. Government managers are drawn into entrepreneurial activities via partnerships that strengthen their characters and stimulate their creative problem-solving skills.

The interesting irony here is that although neoconservatives promote virtue and wish to nurture the institutions that do so, neoliberals are the ones who find virtues in the market. Character is built through self-initiative and entrepreneurship, that is, through market experience. The place of other institutions is less central. For the neoconservative, on the other hand, the market offers expression to certain values but cannot be their principal source.

For the three usages that follow, the tone and perspective shifts subtly. In place of the neoliberal's commitment to the market as the wellspring of social order, we have the neoconservative's more reserved endorsement of market incentives as a partial means of devolving and decentralizing public sector responsibilities.

*4. P-P partnership as risk shifting.* The usage here portrays partnering as a means of responding to fiscal stringency on the part of the government. The program's advocates are typically speaking from official positions within government and express concerns about leveraging public capital for infrastructure and other capital-intensive projects. From the government's perspective, the partnership arrangements are a means of getting private interests to sign on, and they promise profit potential for doing so. The British Treasury's Private Finance Initiative (1997) encourages government managers to refashion property-rights assignments to attract private capital to shoulder start-up costs. Through special lease-purchase arrangements, private investors assume the financial risks of ownership, once the projects are complete. The rhetoric in this instance is similar to that coming out of the European Union, as mentioned earlier. It follows the logic of load shedding but stops short of full privatization. In effect, government is exhorted to do more with less.

This usage fits squarely in neither one ideological camp nor the other, because we also find this kind of thinking in the New Deal liberal's support for funneling public money directly to cities for redevelopment partnerships with local developers and business interests. In the latter case, it represents a pragmatic coalitional strategy for ensuring sufficient support for these projects in business-dominated jurisdictions. In more colorful terms, it promises enough pork to go around. The neoconservative's construction, however, puts business on the check-writing side. When partnering works the way it is supposed to, business partners help bring fiscal restraint to these projects and insure their financial viability. Certainly, reinforcing the support that business traditionally offers conservative parties may play a role in the push for partnering. Nevertheless, the idea of heightened vigilance over public investments squares with the neoconservative's efforts more generally to restrain government spending, especially for service programs, and to scale back its service commitments.

On the surface, there are obvious parallels between risk shifting and problem conversion, both of which are depicted here as separate meanings assigned to partnership. The two meanings appear to differ more in degree than in kind; risk shifting might be seen as a prelude to more elaborate efforts to transform a public problem wholly into a private one. Nonetheless, as our deconstruction shows, their ideological premises differ. The rhetoric of problem conversion valorizes commercial activity and market discipline, placing government in a supporting, subordinate role. In contrast, risk shifting assigns the supporting role, not to government, but to commercial interests. Furthermore, the exhortation is for business to join in cooperative ventures of some sort to leverage government's resources, not displace them. The purposes remain public, even though the resources are eventually mixed.

*5. P-P partnership as restructuring public service.* Part of the neoconservative's objection to government reflects concerns about its growth. Recent thinking about the engines of this growth continues to owe a debt to Lowi (1979) for singling out interest-group liberalism as the culprit. In his scenario, government agencies are set upon by legions of interests demanding money and services. The agencies respond, having been given (in error) the discretion and authority to do so. The regrettable result is government out of control, overburdened and overextended. The two putative solutions are to take the discretion away (Lowi's) or to devolve the responsibilities to other levels of government more used to saying no. Several decades later, we have two unintended consequences of these fixes. First, the administrative procedures intended to structure agencies' discretion have restricted their ability to adapt to changing circumstances. Second, those local agencies, expected to say no, have been less able to cope with demands from the inside. Public sector employees in the United States have unionized in record numbers. Partnerships can address both.

In theory, partnerships can not only relieve projects of some of the weight of administrative procedures, at least on the private partners' side, they can also move from a public to a private workforce, one that is disciplined by the labor market. In conventional labor-management relations, the management's efforts to shift work outside a unionized plant to nonunion employees (also called outsourcing) is reason enough to strike. For public employees who are typically prohibited from striking in the United States, the recourse is less clear. Partnerships can serve as a means for effectively deregulating employment relations through the substitution of unorganized workers (Supiot, 1996). The approach of labor and liberal governments might well be the reverse. Partnerships could also be used to control labor standards via formal agreements on wages, as well as noncommercial features, such as gender and racial discrimination. This has been a recent trend in international trade agreements and contracting in some large cities. In this case, partnerships appear to provide a vehicle that can move in either direction.

*6. P-P partnership as power sharing.* Although privatization has been promoted by some as empowerment because it devolves control vertically downward toward the consumer, partnerships, according to this sixth usage, spread control horizontally, especially in regulatory matters where control has been concentrated in the government. Partnerships as power sharing can alter business-government relations in fundamental ways. First, an ethos of cooperation and trust replaces the adversarial relations endemic to command-and-control regulation (Ghere, 1996). Second, any relationship between partners will involve some mutually beneficial sharing of responsibility, knowledge, or risk. In most instances, each party brings something of value to the others to be invested or exchanged. Third, there is an expectation of give-and-take between the partners, negotiating differences that were otherwise litigated. For the neoconservative, power sharing can take the teeth out of regulation, making it less rigid, punitive, and arbitrary. Although the neoconservatives are not opposed to the government using force and coercion to preserve order, using coercion to force firms to change the way they make their business decisions is objectionable. The neoliberal typically goes further and supports commercialization of environmental problems, as opposed to the liberalization of compliance schedules and control requirements.

What kinds of control are shared in practice is another matter. The U.S. Environmental Protection Agency (EPA; 1998a, 1998b) operates extensive partnership programs for each of its major areas of responsibility. Some are promotions to provide technical assistance for recycling or waste disposal on a voluntary basis. Others enlist firms in programs that promise reductions in reporting and control requirements for those willing to demonstrate higher abatement levels and share their control strategies with their competitors. The market lure is cost savings, technical assistance, and flexibility in monitoring and enforcement. The agency, on the other hand, gains an opportunity for intensive social marketing, roughly analogous to the Salvation Army's exchange of soup for sermons. Here, the partnership falls under the rubric of reengineering government, stimulating innovation and cost savings. Nevertheless, regulatory control in EPA's case seems to be parceled out very sparsely and only to trusted firms. This seems to have little to do with the neoconservative's preference for loosening regulatory controls. As with the usage of partnerships as restructuring public sector employment, the power sharing idea can harbor a liberal's intent behind its neoconservative face.

## TWO REMAINDERS

The grammar of meanings that has structured my treatment of partnerships assumes six distinct, but sometimes overlapping, ways of understanding and talking about partnering. Each of these six ways, in turn, depends upon a set of normative premises that have been linked to one of two major neo ideologies. Although many more ideologies are influential in the industrialized West, these two continue to play a central role in provoking and inspiring the reform of the welfare state before the century's end. There are, however, two significant remainders—meanings excluded from our grammar. Both entail very different takes on partnering. One connects it with traditional modes of not-for-profit collaboration, and the other treats it as simply a new face on conventional forms of privatization. A brief consideration of these remainders follows.

The grammar of partnerships fashioned in previous sections has purposely excluded the variety of day-to-day, public-spirited partnerships that have gone on in various localities for years, often with progressive intent. Partnerships among nonprofit organizations, schools, churches, and civic organizations, for example, often fill gaps in the social service safety net left by fiscal austerity and neoliberal thinking about government. Not-for-profit service organizations may partner with advocacy groups and local government to serve the needs of certain neighborhoods or vulnerable groups. Money may be raised locally, contributed by fund-raising organizations, such as the United Way, or charitable foundations; in the United States, this is indirectly subsidized by the tax code. These classes of service partnerships deserve their own deconstructive treatment for several reasons.

First, unlike the P-P partnerships discussed above, these *public-public* or *private-private* partnerships may have historical roots in their communities that extend across generations. In effect, they are woven into the fabric of civic life and may not easily be distinguished from the communities that they serve. Second, the ideologies that they are premised upon represent very different traditions in public thinking from the ones treated here. The rhetoric of these partnerships is typically a moral one tied to meeting communal needs. Finally, the absence of profit motives among the participants changes the dynamics of the partnership itself—who participates and why—as well as the bases of cooperation.

Among these local institutions, rights-based liberalism or communitarian notions direct objectives away from commercial interests and profit seeking, and toward service ideals and civic responsibilities. Traditional conservatism may play a role in directing aims, as in some organizations based on religious affiliation or upper-class voluntarism. From across the ideological spectrum, social democratic ideology may appear in grassroots organizations, partnering in coalitions to oppose for-profit corporate projects or practices. In either instance, opposition to a legitimate government presence or advocacy of market solutions—the core of our neo ideologies—play a negligible role.

The second remainder omitted from our grammar consists of those treatments that construct partnerships as a rubric to cover most ongoing forms of privatization. Here, the term seems to function as a euphemism for privatizing the functions of government without assailing its legitimacy. Attention to partnerships between government and for-profit firms, in North America at least, has intensified over the last decade, on the heels of the privatization campaigns of the 1980s. The central messages of these campaigns, their open animosity toward government and strident assurances of superior service and no waste, have been tempered somewhat in the promotional literature that disguises privatization as partnering. Hence, partnering appears as privatization's logical successor, but a more refined and domesticated version, perhaps one better adapted to the less doctrinaire 1990s. Partnerships in this genre seem to offer a more palatable, less prickly, form of packaging around the contents of a government's shifting functions to commercial enterprises.

The more circumspect academic pieces that attempt to assess the performance of contemporary partnerships as a policy tool can easily be caught up in this symbolic succession. Accordingly, partnering, in this literature, is distinct from privatization in name only. Further, what passes for partnerships, because of the term's connotation of cooperativeness and its reformist cachet, can extend from indirect subsidies to traditional procurement contracting. Lost to these treatments is the basic idea that partnering, in some of its guises, can represent a fundamental departure in the post-Cold War relationship between public and private sectors. This idea is the premise behind the grammar of multiple meanings presented here.

## REFERENCES

Apen, P. G., Benicewicz, B. C., & Laia, J. R. (1994). A new model for public-private partnerships. *Technology in Society, 16*, 389-402.

British Council. (1997). Restructuring government. In *Issue 1: Law and governance* [On-line]. Available: http://www.britcoun.org/governance/briefing/iss1res.htm.

Canadian Council for Public-Private Partnerships. (1996). *About the council* [On-line]. Available: http://www.inforamp.net/~partners/index.html.

Canadian Heritage. (1996). *Partnership resource kit* [On-line]. Available: http://www.beyondgov.ca/kittoc.html.

Crowley, B. L. (1987). *The self, the individual, and the community: Liberalism in the political thought of F. A. Hayek and Sidney and Beatrice Webb.* Oxford, UK: Clarendon Press.

Environmental Protection Agency. (1998a). *Partners for the environment* [On-line]. Available: http://www.epa.gov/partners/.

Environmental Protection Agency. (1998b). *Review of the common sense initiative, executive summary* [On-line]. Available: http://www.epa.gov/epahome/.

Feigenbaum, H., Hamnett, C., & Henig, J. (1998). *Shrinking the state: The political underpinnings of privatization.* New York: Cambridge University Press.

Ghere, R. K. (1996). Aligning the ethics of public/private partnership: The issue of local economic development. *Journal of Public Administration Research and Theory, 6,* 599-621.

Giddens, A. (1994). *Beyond Left and Right: The future of radical politics.* Stanford, CA: Stanford University Press.

Gobetti, D. (1997). Humankind as a system: Private and public agency at the origins of modern liberalism. In J. Weintraub & K. Kumar (Eds.), *Public and private in thought and practice: Perspectives on a grand dichotomy* (pp. 103-132). Chicago: The University of Chicago Press.

Gratias, F.X.A., & Boyd, M. (1995). *Public/private partnerships: A tool to right-size government. Discussion notes.* [On-line]. Available: http://www.cyberus.ca/~ppp/ccmd.html.

Handler, J. F. (1996). *Down from bureaucracy: The ambiguity of privatization and empowerment.* Princeton, NJ: Princeton University Press.

Her Majesty's Treasury. (1997). *Private finance initiative* [On-line]. Available: http://www.treasury-projects-taskforce.gov.uk/contacts/pppp.htm.

Jack, M., Phillips, R., & The Robert Phillips Group. (1993). Public-private partnership organizations in health care: Cooperative strategies and models. *Hospital & Health Services Administration, 38,* 387-400.

Jacobs, B. (1997). Networks, partnerships and European Union Regional Economic Development Initiatives in the West Midlands. *Policy and Politics, 25,* 39-50.

Kettl, D. F. (1993). *Sharing power: Public governance and private markets.* Washington, DC: Brookings.

Kinnock, N. (1998). *Using public-private partnerships to develop transport infrastructure* [On-line]. Available: http://europa.eu.int/en/comm/dg07/speech/sp9837.htm.

Lowi, T. (1979). *The end of liberalism* (2nd ed.). New York: W. W. Norton.

National Council for Public-Private Partnership. (1997). *Partnership forum* [On-line]. Available: http://www.ncppp.org.

Negotiated Rulemaking Act of 1990, 5 U.S.C. § 561 *et seq.* (Lexis Law Publishing, 1999).

Reijniers, J.J.A.M. (1994). Organization of public-private partnership projects. *International Journal of Project Management, 12,* 137-142.

Rodal, A., & Wright, D. (1997). A dossier on partnerships. *Optimum, the Journal of Public Sector Management, 24,* 1-4.

Starr, P. (1988). The meaning of privatization. *Yale Law and Policy Review, 6,* 6-41.

Starr, P. (1990). The new life of the liberal state: Privatization and the restructuring of state-society relations. In J. Waterbury & E. Suleiman (Eds.), *Public enterprise and privatization* (pp. 22-54). Boulder, CO: Westview Press.

Stephenson, M. O., Jr. (1991). Whither the public-private partnership: A critical overview. *Urban Affairs Quarterly, 27,* 109-127.

Supiot, A. (1996). Work and the public/private dichotomy. *International Labour Review, 135,* 653-663.

United Nations Development Program for the Urban Environment. (1996). Program information. In *Public-private partnerships for the Urban Environment Program* [On-line]. Available: http://www.undp.org:81/undp/ppp/listserver/index.html.

Weintraub, J. (1997). The theory and politics of the public/private distinction. In J. Weintraub & K. Kumar (Eds.), *Public and private in thought and practice: Perspectives on a grand dichotomy* (pp. 1-42). Chicago: The University of Chicago Press.

Wolfe, A. (1997). Public and private in theory and practice: Some implications of an uncertain boundary. In J. Weintraub & K. Kumar (Eds.), *Public and private in thought and practice: Perspectives on a grand dichotomy* (pp. 182-203). Chicago: The University of Chicago Press.

# Part II
# The Private Financing Model

[6]

# Design and build — effects of contractor design on highway schemes

*Proc. Instn Civ. Engrs, Civ. Engng*, 1995, **108**, May, 64–76

*Civil Engineering Panel*

*Paper 10644*

*Written discussion closes 15 June 1995*

*G. J. Hodgson*, BSc, ARICS

Contractor design of highway schemes is possibly the most significant and challenging innovation affecting the UK civil engineering profession since the introduction of the first edition of the *ICE conditions of contract* in 1945. The days of project design and supervision being separate from construction are numbered — and a major culture change will have to be accommodated by all those involved. This paper examines the philosophy and rationale behind contractor design in all its guises and considers the likely effects that these changes will have on consulting engineers.

*Fig. 1. Dartford Crossing*

Design and build procurement in civil engineering is not new. The UK Government became seriously interested nearly ten years ago with the award of the first major privately financed project to design, build and operate the Dartford–Thurrock Crossing (Fig. 1).

Dartford River Crossing Ltd (Trafalgar House with Kleinwort Benson as advisors) were given a maximum 20-year concession period to operate the crossing. Costs at 1986 prices were £86 million and the project took five and a half years to design and build with no recourse to Government funds.[1]

The second major privately financed design and build project was the Second Severn Crossing (Fig. 2). During the period prior to April 1990 when the proposal from Severn River Crossing plc (John Laing, GTM Entrepose, Bank of America and BZW)[1] was selected, new procurement initiatives were thought necessary and desirable to the extent that a completely new form of design and build contract was required.[2] The results of these procurement initiatives have formed the basis for the Government's philosophy regarding design and build, which is now embodied in the new Highways Agency.

Contractor design is not limited to design and build contracts per se, but is also to be found in the new Department's seventh edition *Specification for highway works* and fourth edition *Method of measurement for traditional procurement*, collectively known as the *Manual of contract documents for highway works*. The

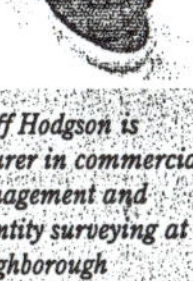

*Geoff Hodgson is lecturer in commercial management and quantity surveying at Loughborough University of Technology*

*Fig. 2. Second Severn Crossing under construction*

*Specification* introduces design of the permanent works by the contractor for structures and structural elements.[3] This undoubtedly affects the way the compiler of contract documentation specifies goods and materials. It inevitably limits the choice of goods and materials that in the past have been at the discretion of the consulting engineer. Choice will effectively be transferred to the contractor who will be free to secure the most economically advantageous goods and materials from within the European Union. This raises important questions relating to the employer's requirements, which previously could be specified by proprietary name. This approach is now considered discriminatory within the boundaries of European law.

### European legislation

The procurement change became necessary to comply with EU legislation and in particular, Directive 83/189. The Directive stipulates that 'technical regulations' be notified to the European Commission, which in effect validates the documentation as being free from restrictive trade practices. In complying with this Directive the UK Department of Transport realized that its existing *Specification* (the 'brown book'), still relatively new, would have to be redrafted to remove barriers to trade that were expressed or implied in its clauses.

A barrier to trade is a breach of Article 30 of the Treaty of Rome which states

> Quantitative restrictions on imports and measures having equivalent effect shall, without prejudice to the following provisions, be prohibited between member states.

It has been established that qualitative restrictions also contravene Article 30 and in cases considered by the European Courts of Justice it is the words 'all measures having equivalent effect' that have been elaborated to establish what constitutes a barrier to trade.

The most often quoted legal example is *Commission* v *Ireland* (Dundalk water supply) (Case 45/87R). In this case a contract was to be let by Dundalk Urban District Council for the construction of a water main. The contract documentation specified an Irish standard for the pipes. Only one manufacturer could comply — an Irish company. A tender for pipes manufactured in Spain was not considered. The Commission found this to be contrary to Article 30 and sought an interim order to ensure no contract was concluded pending further settlement or final judgment between the

Commission and Ireland.[17]

The Treaty of Rome was signed in 1957 but it was not until June 1985 that the Commission sent a white paper to the European Council entitled *Completing the internal market* as a result of which the Single European Act (SEA) came into force on 1 July 1987. This states *inter alia* that a single market would exist from 31 December 1992. It was for this reason that the Department's seventh edition *Specification* had to be implemented by 1 January 1993.

Further Directives govern the procurement process. The Public Works Directive[4] regulates the tendering process for building and civil engineering works and specifies the procedure and awarding criteria for contracts to be let. Public procurers for building and civil engineering works are required to publish various notices in *The Official Journal of the European Communities* which include invitations to tender, notices of award and information regarding future procurement requirements.

## Why design and build?

Design and build is a generic term and can encompass a number of different definitions including contractor design, design and construct, design build finance and operate (DBFO)

*Fig. 3. Average cost increases on Department of Transport contracts completed between 1986–87 and 1990–91*

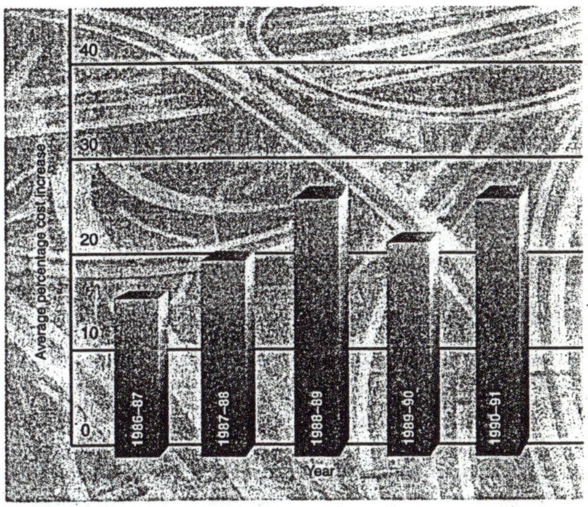


*Fig. 4. Range of cost increases on completed contracts between 1986–88 to 1990–91*

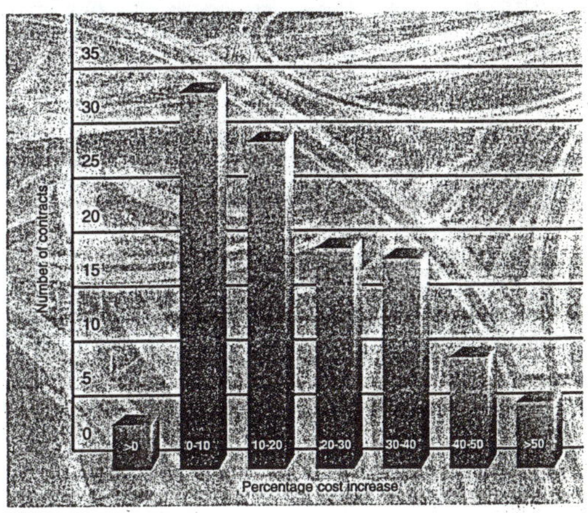

**Table 1. Contracts completed between 1987–88 and 1990–91 with cost increases over 50%**

| Contract | Tender price: £ | Estimated final cost at end of maintenance period: £ | % cost increase | Main reason for increase |
|---|---|---|---|---|
| A6 Chapel-le-Frith and Whaley Bypass | 17 030 885 | 36 400 000 | 113 | Ground conditions and design failures |
| A47 Dualling at Postwick to Blofield | 744 130 | 1 411 224 | 89·6 | Changes to design |
| A38 Belvedere Cross Improvement | 772 683 | 1 320 015 | 70·8 | Changes required by DoT |
| A303 South Petherton Broadway (Illminster Bypass) | 12 860 606 | 20 600 757 | 60·1 | Earthworks and drainage problems |
| A65 Settle to Gigleswick Bypass Main Works | 7 010 094 | 10 848 144 | 54·7 | Earthworks and drainage problems |

and design and refine.

It would be prudent of any professional to ask the simple question 'why?' The traditional form of procurement has been in existence for many years and while not perfect has been the main spar underpinning the competitive tendering process for UK highway schemes.

Two major influences are at the centre of a need for change. The first is the report by the 1992 National Audit Office[5] which revealed that average cost overruns on construction projects in 1988–89 were a massive 28%. This contrasts sharply with Department of Transport's own targets of attempting to reduce cost overruns from 18% in 1985–86 to 15% in 1988–89.

Figure 3 illustrates the average cost increases on Department contracts completed between 1986–87 and 1990–91. It can be seen that the Department achieved its target in 1986-87 but this then escalated to 28% in 1988–89 and 1990–91.

Further statistics show that out of 35 contracts, 28 had increased by more than 30% and five had increased by more than 50% (Fig. 4). Table 1 provides a breakdown of the five contracts with cost increases over 50%. The largest increases, between 70% and 113%, are due to Department changes, design changes, design failures and ground conditions.

The National Audit Office report sampled 17 out of 26 completed major projects. The main causes of increased costs were cited as unforeseen ground conditions (£18·1 million), changes to design (£4·2 million) and additional Department of Transport requirements (£2·2 million). Design errors were also examined. One example cited by the report was a bridge designed with insufficient headroom for the British Rail track underneath requiring the road to be raised after the work on the bridge had begun. The total cost of rectification was £0·4 million. It was revealed that only one of the Department's nine regions requires consulting engineers to classify each variation order according to the main cause.

In order to obtain a balanced view the National Audit Office consulted 29 companies for their reasons as to cost overruns. The results of the questionnaire confirmed that unforeseen ground conditions, changes to the original design and problems with statutory undertakers were the main causes (Fig. 5). In conclusion the report said it was important for the Department to underpin its contract arrangements with reliable estimates to assess the competitiveness of tenders, comprehensive systems for quality assurance and procedures to identify cost increases and their causes. Without this the Department would not be able to verify any benefits of its new forms of contract.

Further comment of interest is to be found in a report from the Committee of Public Accounts (PAC) [6] which in June 1993 examined the National Audit report and took evidence from the Department of Transport. The PAC were not satisfied that the Department had been sufficiently positive and vigorous in its efforts to avoid increases in the cost of contracts. However the PAC noted the measures being taken to improve value for money and recognized the desirability of transferring more risk to contractors with a recommendation to the Department that it press forward with the wider introduction of design and build contracts. Placing more risk on the contractor would bring a significantly greater proportion of the cost increases within the framework of direct competitive tendering.

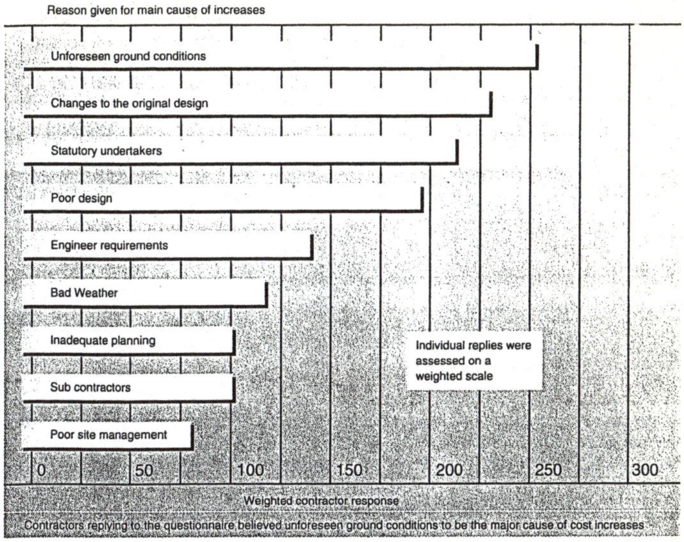


*Fig. 5. Main causes of cost increases as recorded by contractors replying to the National Audit Office questionnaire*

The second influence is the Department's active and enthusiastic participation in the Government's private finance initiative[8] which has, as one of its chief aims, the transfer to the public sector of private sector management skills. The private finance initiative was launched by Norman Lamont in his Autumn Statement in November 1992 and essentially has two fundamental requirements

(*a*) the private sector must genuinely assume risk

(*b*) value for money must be demonstrated for any expenditure by the public sector.

There are no hard-and-fast rules as to how a private sector project is dealt with by individual Government departments but Fig. 6 shows the progress of a typical project.[8] It can be seen from this flow chart how the Government and industry would develop a privately financed road project.

The public sector's record in the design and construction of capital schemes is poor. Time and cost overruns as we have seen above are common. Part of the reason lies in the attitudes and culture of the public sector. In the construction sector this often results in conservative or over-engineered designs. Clearly there is a growing need to create a new strategy for the procurement of the road network to take the UK into the next millennium.

## Design and build contracts for roads

Design and build for roadworks has been growing steadily in the UK and especially through the Scottish Office. The Scottish Office has been the pioneer in design and build and commenced the first contract on a design and build basis in the mid-1970s. This was the Kessock Bridge crossing the Beauly Firth just north of Inverness. In 1989 the largest UK design and build road project valued at £30 million was tendered for the M8 at St James Interchange near Glasgow Airport (Fig. 7). It was designed and built by Balfour Beatty with a 0·5% outturn overspend. However, difficult ground conditions, resulting in more piling, cost the contractor more than planned. Balfour Beatty's civil engineering director Brian Osborne, commented in *New Civil Engineer* in November 1993 that 'The biggest downside with design and build is pricing the risk'.

The M74 in south west Scotland is a scheme designed by Scott Wilson Kirkpatrick, and although not strictly design and build, it is nevertheless a progression in that direction. The philosophy behind this is aptly put in a report titled *A distinctive approach* by Scottish Office director of roads John Dawson, who says

> We have trialled various arrangements to allow the contractor to have greater flexibility and for him to gain or share the rewards from innovations and cost savings arising during construction of the contract.

The scheme will be built under at least three different forms of contract each one including different degrees of risk to be accepted by the contractor. The contract is for more than 34 km of new dual three-lane motorway, valued at over £110 million and split into four phases. Two of the four phases have already been awarded to Balfour Beatty.

In England the first design and build trial was the A35 Yelloham Hill to Troytown, estimated at £5·1 million with a tender accepted at £4·3 million (Fig. 8). Tender invitations were made to four contractors rather than the normal six and tender assessment was based on a points scale for quality of design, time and cost. One scheme was rejected owing to a less than satisfactory bid, the remaining three were equal on quality of design, but the successful bid was won on a time and cost basis. The contract was awarded to Fairclough/Acer in a joint venture. The second design and build was the A11 Thetford to Bridgham, a 3·2 km length of dual carriageway. The tender value was £2·2 million and was constructed within the Department's budget. The contract was awarded to May Gurney in April 1992 and was completed in December 1992.[9]

## DBFO contracts for roads

The Government announced in November 1992[9] that, as a possible transition to motorway charging, private sector companies might be invited to bid for Department of Transport contracts under which they would design, build, finance and operate (DFBO) roads. The full extent and details to which this participation will be implemented is still in the consultative stage, but the principles were set out in the Green Paper *Paying for better motorways* issued in May 1993.

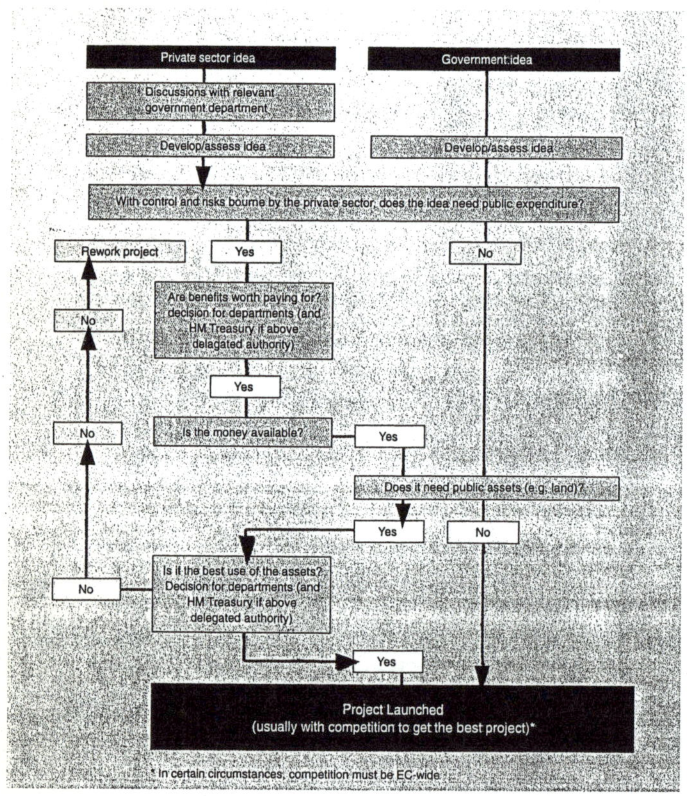


*Fig. 6. Private finance decision flow chart*

DBFO concessions are designed to encourage the development of a road operating industry with a view to increasing the scope for private sector involvement in road provision and operation.

The DBFO concessionaire will have to assume substantial risk, the intention being that the Department will be buying a road service and not just a new road. Concessionaires will have to be capable of long-term commitment and, as a result, will need to be both robust and committed to quality of performance in this market. To encourage this high quality of service, the structure for the concessions will incorporate a payment system that includes both incentives and penalties.

The transfer of risk is the primary aim of the Department, in keeping with the private finance initiative, and could include all or some of

(*a*) design risk
(*b*) construction risk
(*c*) opening date risk
(*d*) traffic risk
(*e*) legislative and *force majeure* risk and
(*f*) operational risk.

The extent of DBFO as of June 1994 is limited. The Birmingham Northern Relief Road was won in competition by Midland Expressway Ltd (a joint venture of Trafalgar House and Iritecna)

*Fig. 8. A35 Yelloham Hill to Troytown*

in 1991.[1] The scheme comprises a 48 km motorway as an alternative route to the M6 through the West Midlands. MEL will have a 53-year concession from when the Department grants possession of the site. Cost is estimated at £270 million (1991 prices) with a construction period estimated at three years due to commence in 1996.

The Birmingham Western Orbital Route is still under consideration. Competition started in February 1992 but doubt has been expressed by some bidders as to whether this scheme is suitable for DBFO.[1] Estimated cost is £500 million. Further schemes being studied are a Lower Thames Crossing and a new Mersey Crossing.

## The changing role of the engineer

With the traditional role of procurement undergoing radical change and the introduction of design and build, the status and position of the professional consulting engineer will markedly change. Traditional procurement now embodies EU legislation designed to prevent barriers to trade between member states. This changes the design procedure and the way consulting engineers can specify, but retains the overall separation of design and supervision from construction.

Design and build on the other hand attempts to remove this separation and in so doing creates new roles with different philosophies for the consulting engineer. Under the current framework this can be the contractor's designer, employer's agent and site representative or the contractor's planners. Extending design and build to finance and operate will create additional opportunities for professional advice to the concessionaire on the liabilities and risks regarding whole-life costing.

The Department of Transport's *Manual of contract documents for highway works* introduces permanent works to be designed by the contractor. This requires the consulting engineer to adopt a novel approach to the design and specification of certain structures that are an integral part of a highway scheme. The structures that have been identified by the Department that warrant this innovative approach are those for which the design solution is best provided by a proprietary system[12] and therefore if specified by a proprietary name would constitute a barrier to trade.

It is accepted that, common to all highway schemes, the design will generally comprise many elements that need not be a unique structure designed by the consulting engineer. Design elements can, therefore, be grouped into three.

*Group (a)* A unique design by the consulting engineer that is most suitable for the site conditions and will be designed utilizing materials that are not of a proprietary nature, e.g. reinforced concrete or structural steel.
*Group (b)* A design where the solution to the design problem can best and most economically

HODGSON

*Fig. 9. Design procedures when adoption of a proprietary manufactured structure is a possibility*

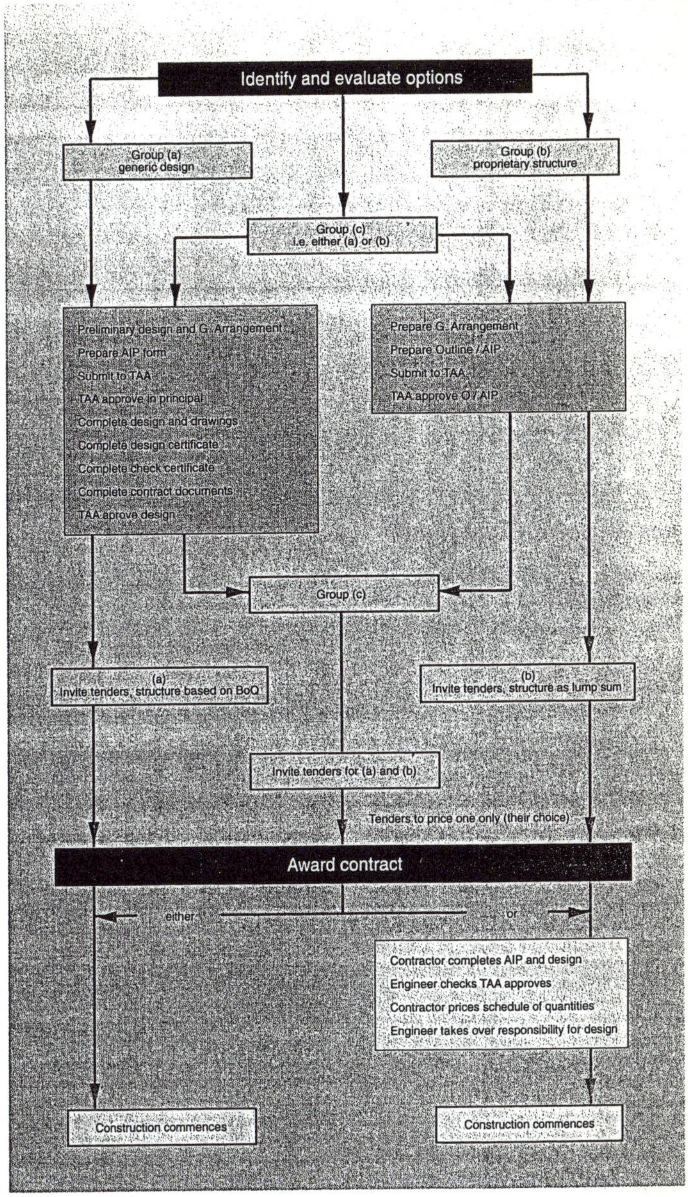

be satisfied by a proprietary product, e.g. reinforced earth structures, precast concrete culverts, corrugated steel culverts and an array of expansion joints and bridge bearings.

*Group* (*c*) Structures where the advantages of a proprietary structure in preference over a unique design are marginal, and both could be used as a design solution.[10]

The traditional route followed by the consulting engineer when considering a group (*b*) or (*c*) structure has been to prepare a general arrangement drawing, based on a particular proprietary structure, and with 'or equivalent' added, or to prepare a fully detailed design in non-proprietary materials but be prepared to accept an alternative by the contractor, based on a proprietary product. Both of these procedures are not conducive for contractors to prepare alternative designs. Design during the tender period is cost significant with no chance of recovery for the unsuccessful tenderers, and contractors cannot be certain of the cost implications of post-contract design approval procedures. Clearly then the particular materials or products specified enjoy an advantage over others that offer similar levels of performance.

If trade barriers are to be truly removed then the specification must provide a mechanism whereby tenderers can freely choose an appropriate product with financial impunity.

The seventh edition of the *Specification* has addressed this problem by providing an outline approval in principle form (O/AIP) with the tender documents as a contractual requirement. The O/AIP is in effect a performance specification for a structure for which the design solution is considered to be best provided by a proprietary product.

The design procedure when adopting a proprietary manufactured structure is illustrated in the flow chart shown in Fig. 9.[11] The consulting engineer is at some liberty to consider which structures fall into this category and guidance is offered through notes for guidance to the *Specification*.[12] Failure to identify proprietary products as design solutions could risk litigation from a manufacturer in a member state, claiming that the employer was discriminating and had therefore created a barrier to trade.

Clearly the O/AIP will have to contain sufficient information to allow the tenderer to be able to offer a product that satisfies the design requirements in addition to where it goes and how it links with other parts of the works.

The Department considers that an O/AIP should contain

(*a*) location
(*b*) operational dimension/levels
(*c*) highway loading requirements
(*d*) other loading requirements
(*e*) relevant Department standards, British Standards, codes of practice, etc.
(*f*) GA drawings including a designated outline
(*g*) geotechnical data
(*h*) appearance of the structure
(*i*) environmental factors
(*j*) constraints and control during construction
(*k*) operational or user requirements
(*l*) special maintenance requirements
(*m*) other essential requirements

The successful contractor is required to complete the O/AIP form and forward it for acceptance. Under an amendment to clause 8 of the *ICE conditions of contract* (5th edition) the consulting engineer has to accept responsibility for the contractor's design after the check procedures and notify the contractor of the date of acceptance.[13] In addition the same amended clause states that the employer will bear the cost of checking the contractor's design proposals.

Typical structures which have been given as examples by the Department as suitable for contractor design are environmental barriers, crib walling, precast concrete box culverts (up to 8 m span), corrugated steel buried structures (0·9 m to 8 m span), reinforced earth structures. anchored earth structures, footbridges, small span under bridges (up to 8 m span) and drains (exceeding 0·9 m diameter).[12]

Difficulties will arise in drawing preparation as to the means of identifying a structure to be designed by the contractor. The current method being adopted by the Department is to provide a 'designated outline' (DO) on the drawings.[11] The DO is effectively a 'shaped outline' which contains no indication of the nature of the structure. To indicate in any manner in a DO a preferred solution would be considered discriminatory.

The selection of the DOs on the drawings should be carefully considered by the consulting engineer. Each DO should be sufficiently large to include the non-proprietary design (where appropriate) and all the possible options the contractor may put forward in accordance with the design specification. The main requirement for the DO is that it should be clearly defined and fully enclosing.

The DO is important for payment as it delineates, for measurement purposes, the limits of the structure to be designed by the contractor. The tenderer is provided with a single item to price in the bill of quantities for the structure enclosed by the DO.

However, where possible, the DO should exclude common items such as pavements, kerbing, safety fencing, service ducts, cables, headwalls and the like. Where these features cannot be excluded from the DO a schedule should be provided to list the features which pass through or into the DO and which are therefore to be excluded from the contractor's price for the design. Such items should not include integral parts of the structure to be designed.

A new section in the *Method of measurement for highway works* sets out the measurement rules.[14] In order for the contractor to obtain an interim value and for the engineer to assess the value of an ordered variation for work carried out to a structure in a DO, there is a contractual requirement for the contractor to provide a schedule of rates.[11] The schedule must total to the sum inserted by the contractor against the item in the bill of quantities. Clearly, therefore, there could be some concern that this sum will not be sufficient to cover the post-contract design approvals and amendments, none of which could have been known at the time of tender.

During the pre-contract tender evaluation stage the employer will be unable to identify the exact nature of the design solution offered by the contractor. The implications of this are that there may be maintenance problems when the employer is not in control of the design.

### The effects on consulting engineers

Design and build in its many forms is still in the early stages of development, the ultimate roles of the consulting engineer are yet to emerge. Various consultative documents are being circulated for comment by the Highways Agency.

Senior consultants concur that the challenge of designing for the contractor will be invigorating. The process of design would loose some of the constraints imposed by the Department but still offer confidence and integrity. Equal partnerships will enhance and consolidate teamwork now so necessary for survival in this era of change.

Partnering is a recommendation by Latham in his report *Constructing the team*,[19]

> Such a system can be very effective in large programmes where it is desirable to build up expert teams and keep them together.

Recent trends have indicated that contractors are placing more and more reliance on subcontractors for everything from bulk earthworks to white lining. Concern among the consultants is that as the process of design and build becomes more established the relationship between the contractor and his designer will be reduced to that of a sub-contractor, providing just another service. Fees will be on a 'pay when paid' basis and the status and position of the consultant will become marginalized.

The supervisory role of the consulting engineer under traditional procurement is now in the hands of the contractor and his designer. Previously the consulting engineer would have a site staff of clerks of works to monitor the day-to-day activities of the contractor. With the predominance of sub-contractors and a design and build contract this supervision could rest largely with the representatives of those subcontracting companies, but overseen by the main contractor. In the opinion of a senior consultant, contractors may find it difficult to adopt a more rigorous approach to supervision owing to the previous management philosophy. This in turn raises serious questions over liability and the demarcation of responsibilities between the designer and the contractor. The Department *Conditions of contract for design and build* imposes an obligation on the designer to examine the works through various certifications provided by clause 7 — review procedures. To assume the employer's agent and site representative will take on full supervisory duties does not accord with the philosophy of transfer of risk and, as such, the duties of this agent will be limited to a watching brief. Conditions of engagement for the employer's agent are in the process of being drafted.

Within the *Conditions of contract for design and build* it could be argued that there is an inference that the contractor's designer is acting as a quasi resident engineer and therefore client's representative. This is particularly so with respect to payment certificates. Clause 60.1 requires a certificate from the designer to be accompanied by the application for payment. This will inevitably exert a pressure on the consultant, as a contractor's designer, to certify that the works have been constructed and completed in accord with the design data. The payment of the designer's fees could depend on a successful application by the contractor.

A response to the issue of supervision was succinctly put by a director of a construction company, who was of the opinion that if the workmanship — in the opinion of the designer — was unsatisfactory and no remedial action taken, then liability for a subsequent failure would not lie with the designer. The whole philosophy of design and build has to be one of teamwork and trust and, as a consequence, professional opinions by the designer as to workmanship have to be taken very seriously.

The transference of risk, its quantification and pricing are the major concerns of the contractors tendering under this form of procurement. David Neale, construction director of May Gurney, outlined a risk analysis matrix in a paper delivered to the IHT Cambridge '94 symposium but commented that all the risks that they had attempted to identify and price did not, ironically, materialize but instead something totally unforeseen happened. His concluding remarks focused on the sharp reality of risk assessment.

**Table 2. National Audit Office analysis of causes of cost increases**

| Cause of increase | Total: £ million | Percentage |
|---|---|---|
| Unforeseen ground conditions and earthworks | 18·1 | 44 |
| Necessary variations to the main carriageway and structures | 2·2 | 5 |
| Changes in the DoT's requirements | 4·2 | 10 |
| Measurement changes | 1·7 | 4 |
| Cost price fluctuations | 8·9 | 22 |
| Other | 6·1 | 15 |
| Total | 41·2 | 100 |

Source: National Audit Office analysis of 17 completed contracts

> Although the risk analysis we carried out gave some comfort to the tender team, in reality it was a totally useless exercise and I urge any contractors in the audience not to try it as it is like running an insurance company with only one premium payer. Unless you have another 40 or so jobs to cross balance the risks - you have no protection at all. It's all very well assessing probability but if the 1,000 to 1 chance comes up your provision of £1,000 has become a loss of £1 million. Contractors should concentrate on their activities - design and construction - they should not be persuaded to gamble or to operate insurance companies.

Risk analysis affects the consulting engineer in the commercial decision-making process of which contractors they are prepared to form an alliance with in a bid for a contract. Will consultants operate on a no bid, no fee or negotiate a reduced fee for initial bid designs and then expect an enhanced fee for post-contract design?

## Conclusion

This paper presents the current situation regarding the effects of contractor design on highway schemes but it is recognized that this may alter with respect to DBFO as the Department of Transport is currently refining the various contract documentation. Even under the Department's design and build contract there is still no published version and changes can be expected. With regard to traditional procurement, the current version of the *Manual of contract documents* is now the August 1993 amendment which completely replaces volumes 1 and 2 and substantial parts of volume 4. Due to unfortunate timing the amended volume 0 *Model contract documents*, generally available from February 1994, is to be used with the December 1991 specification and not with the amended August 1993 specification.

There is now a new set of documents with many technical changes, updated references, new advice, separate model contract documents for the different overseeing departments, new specification requirements for Wales, Scotland and Northern Ireland and appropriate measurement rules for the changes. Problems with the measurement of contractor designed structural elements have sadly not been addressed by the Department and will continue to provide confusion.

It is worth noting that the interim Latham report[18] confirms many of the fears and hopes of the consultants and contractors who have expressed their opinions through this paper. The interim report indicates that there is a mood for change but that the industry has a deeply engrained adversarial attitude. The report goes on

> The traditional separation of design and construction has long since been a source of controversy in the industry, though some of the newer procurement routes seek to bring these functions closer together.

The report further advocates that trust and money are the two vital concerns and are inextricably linked. The report offers some warnings. On the role of the consultant it states that

> professions which feel under-remunerated, marginalised, and with their historic and proud role changed to that of design services sub-contractors, will be sucked further into adversarial stances.

Will contractor design give the Department of Transport what it wants? Is price certainty the overriding priority of the Highways Agency in order to satisfy its political masters? If this is so, then more detailed pre-contract information with specific attention to geotechnical data may achieve this at lower cost than opting for design and build. The National Audit Office analysis shows that only 44% of cost increases are due to unforeseen conditions and earthworks, the bulk of the remaining 56% are due to cost price fluctuations, Department changes and necessary variations (Table 2).

The role of the employer's representative under the Department's design and build contract is one of a watching brief with very limited powers and it is arguable that the employer will have lost, in part, the independence and professionalism that the consulting engineer offered under a traditional form of procurement.

## Acknowledgements

The author would like to thank H. Blackwood, partner of Scott Wilson Kirkpatrick; E. Clarke, Hambros Bank; J. Dawson, director of roads at the Scottish Office; J. A. Green, director of Burks Green & Partners; J. Innes, head of engineering and procurement at the Scottish Office; W. R. Kemp, partner of Scott Wilson Kirkpatrick; D. E. Neale, managing director of May Gurney; D. Ogden, managing director of Shephard Hill; I. Sharman, Department of Transport; and T. R. Wells, regional surveyor at Balfour Beatty. The opinions they expressed and which were used in preparing this paper were not necessarily those of the organisations they represent. Thanks are also due to Bill Money, my colleague who read and advised me on the text.

The photograph of the A35 Yellham is published by kind permission of Martyn Thresh, Dorset Engineering Consultancy.

## References

1. Department of Transport, CF Division. *Private Sector Funding of Transport Projects*, Update May 1994. DoT, London.
2. Key, R. Minister for Roads. IHT Cambridge '94 Symposium.
3. Department of Transport. *Manual of Contract Documents for Highway Works*, Vol. 1. DoT, London, 1991.
4. European Commission. Public Works Directive 71/305/EEC (OJ L185, 25.8.71) as amended by 89/440/EEC (OJ L210, 21.7.89), EC, Brussels, 1989.
5. European Construction Institute. *Guide to Community Directives*. ECI, Loughborough University, 1991.
6. National Audit Office. *Department of Transport Contracting for Roads*. Report by the Comptroller and Auditor General, HMSO, London, 1992.
7. Committee of Public Accounts. *Contracting for Roads, Session 1992–93*. 43rd Report, House of Commons, London, 1993
8. HM Treasury. *The Private Finance Initiative Breaking New Ground*. Central Information Office, London, 1993.
9. May Gurney (Construction) Ltd, Norwich. Personal Communication, 1994.
10. Department of Transport. *Design, Build, Finance and Operate Concessions for Trunk Roads and Motorways*. A Preliminary Note, DoT, April 1994.
11. Department of Transport. *Manual of Contract Documents for Highway Works*, Vol. 0, SD4/92. DoT, London.
12. Department of Transport. *Manual of Contract Documents for Highway Works*, Vol. 2. Series 100, Clause 106. DoT, London.
13. Department of Transport. *Manual of Contract Documents for Highway Works*, Vol. 0. SD5/92. DoT, London.
14. Department of Transport. *Manual of Contract Documents for Highway Works*, Vol. 4. Section 2, Series 2500, Para. 1. DoT, London.
15. Department of Transport. *Manual of Contract Documents for Highway Works*, Vol. 4. Section 1, Series 2500. DoT, London.
16. Department of Transport. *Manual of Contract Documents for Highway Works*, Vol. 4. Section 1, Chapter III, Preambles to Bill of Quantities. DoT, London.
17. Oliver P. *Free Movement of Goods in the EEC*. European Law Centre, 1988.
18. Latham M. *Trust and Money*. Interim Report of the Government/Industry Review of Procurement and Contractual Arrangements in the United Kingdom Construction Industry. December 1993.
19. Latham M. *Constructing the Team*. HMSO, London, 1994, 6.44.

# [7]

# PRIVATE FINANCING AND INFRASTRUCTURE PROVISION IN EMERGING MARKETS

MARTIN STEWART-SMITH*

## I. INTRODUCTION

This Article addresses the key policy, legal, and regulatory issues that arise in the private financing and provision of infrastructure in emerging markets.[1] Many of these issues have their genesis in the experiences of developed countries. However, the need in developing countries to increase the overall quantity of infrastructure stocks and to improve the quality of infrastructure services justifies a focused treatment of the financing instruments and the key legal issues, as well as of the more complex requirements of industry structure, competition, and regulation specific to emerging markets.

New investment in infrastructure in developing countries represents four percent of their national output and one-fifth of their total investment, that is, some US$200 billion a year.[2] At stake is not just the sustainable availability of these large amounts but also efficiency in investment and in delivering services. The role of the private sector both in providing and in financing infrastructure development is growing rapidly. As the private sector takes greater responsibility and the role of government is redefined, the stability and nature of the legal and regulatory framework become important factors in the risk equation.

Infrastructure development and the financing of infrastructure present a number of formidable challenges. Existing poor performance has to be tackled, not only in terms of the lack of maintenance but also in terms of the gross over-staffing of many government service providers. For example, almost half of the labor in African railways is superfluous.[3] But perhaps more importantly, the amount of investment required to

---

* Energy & Major Projects Group, Ashurst Morris Crisp, London (formerly counsel at the World Bank, Washington, D.C.).

1. This Article draws mainly on two texts: WORLD BANK, WORLD DEVELOPMENT REPORT 1994: INFRASTRUCTURE FOR DEVELOPMENT (1994) [hereinafter WORLD DEVELOPMENT REPORT], and MARTIN C. STEWART-SMITH, INDUSTRY STRUCTURE AND REGULATION (World Bank Policy Research Working Paper No. 1419, 1995) [hereinafter STEWART-SMITH].

2. WORLD DEVELOPMENT REPORT, *supra* note 1, at 1. The World Development Report defines developing countries to include both low-income countries (GNP per capita of $675 or less in 1992) and middle-income countries (GNP per capita of more than $675 but less than $8356 in 1992). *Id.* at x.

3. WORLD DEVELOPMENT REPORT, *supra* note 1, at 1.

meet present demand is beyond the capabilities of governmental resources, making private sector participation and private financing essential to sustaining many countries' economic development. This participation involves tapping both domestic and foreign capital sources in order to make substantial investments in infrastructure. At present, taking all developing countries together, about ninety percent of financing is channeled through government sponsors,[4] which in turn bear the project risks. Nonetheless, the emergence of private sector participation in infrastructure sectors using innovative financing techniques is having a marked effect. Furthermore, the gap between the amount of investment needed to meet present suppressed demand alone (excluding demand growth) and the amount of available funds from government sources will mean that private capital and these financing techniques will play an increasingly important role.

This Article will address these issues by: (a) looking, in Part II, at regulation and regulatory instruments and at some of the key policy decisions that surround the development of a sustainable regulatory system; (b) providing, in Part III, an overview of various financing and project development techniques employed and, in particular, the contractual matrix forming the typical project financing in infrastructure sectors; and (c) examining, in Part IV, sources of external financing such as World Bank Group financing. While the Article does not attempt to cover all legal issues raised by the financing and provision of infrastructure, it tackles and emphasizes those issues particularly relevant to emerging markets.

## II. Regulation and Regulatory Instruments

The need for regulation does not acutely arise when infrastructure is provided on a monopoly basis by a government or a government-owned institution. The provider of infrastructure in such cases either provides it according to its own rules or applies it according to rules imposed by legislation or decree as part of the system of government. Thus, regulation in this situation is subsumed within state ownership as a control mechanism.

The situation differs, however, when infrastructure is to be provided in whole or in part by the private sector. In such cases, as the role of the government moves from that of service provider to that of supervisor of those providing the service, some form of a regulatory framework will be required. The instruments forming the new regulatory framework may

---

4. *Id.* at 89.

constitute an authorization or contract between the government (or a public entity) and the service providers, typically in the form of a license or a concession contract. Apart from these instruments of regulation, the institutional arrangements that form part of the new regulatory framework also need to be designed to give the private sector comfort that the government is seriously committed to sustained private participation. Depending on the practice in each country, either a governmental regulatory agency or an autonomous regulatory commission may be established as an institution to administer these instruments in a manner that demonstrates commitment and credibility to the reform. In the process of granting a license or concession to a private entity, the government is essentially redefining its role from provider to regulator.

### A. *Contractual Forms and the Need for Sector-Wide Regulation*

The concession contract, under which operators are specifically authorized to construct the facilities and operate them under stated terms and conditions, is the typical contractual form of regulation. On the other hand, a license—which similarly stipulates operational terms and conditions, performance standards, system roll-out obligations, prohibitions against undue discrimination, tariff formulae, and third party access obligations—may or may not be of a contractual nature, depending on the legal tradition of the country. Whether or not a concession or license is characterized as an "authorization" or a "contract"[5] is important. An authorization may be revocable or amended by the grantor at will without prior consent, whereas a contract will usually only be alterable by agreement between both parties. This is a significant issue in terms of the "bankability" of the license or concession for the purposes of raising private finance.

The terms of the license or concession contract will prima facie need to be satisfactory to the private sponsors and to the government—the two "contracting" parties. Yet because additional parties, such as financiers, are normally involved, the concerns of others will have to be met as well. In other words, the commercial and financial terms need to be capable of financing, or "bankable," by the financial markets. Conse-

5. If the instrument is characterized as an authorization, it is essentially an administrative act of government governed by administrative law and can be unilaterally revoked or amended by the grantor at will. However, where the instrument is characterized as a contract, the government as grantor is acting in a commercial capacity such that general commercial and contract law could apply, as a consequence of which revocation or amendment normally cannot be effective without consent of both parties.

quently, regulatory reform is a corollary to private sector participation in infrastructure.

Other regulatory instruments that might be employed by governments as part of the overall framework include unilateral instruments approved or issued by a governmental agency, such as grid codes and distribution codes in electricity, statutory instruments, or other decrees made under enabling legislation. Some developed countries have also employed sector-wide contractual arrangements. Similar to the pooling and settlement agreements established in 1990 in the context of the British electricity privatization program, these sector-wide contractual regimes would apply to a sector under which there is an agreed regime of resource and liability sharing. For example, in the electricity sector, dispatch and financial settlement can be undertaken under contract on the basis of a pooling of generated output.

Despite analytical differences between licenses and concessions[6]—and their many contractual variations—they are in fact little more than different legal instruments establishing the rights and obligations of the "contracting" parties. Choices about the location of the rights and obligations of service providers in the legal hierarchy—whether in primary legislation, government decree, agency regulation, license, or concession agreements—will largely depend on the overall institutional capacity of the regulatory administration and legal traditions of the country in question. However, contractual regimes do not by themselves eliminate the need to establish effective institutions to carry out the supervisory function.[7] The need for effective sector-wide regulation therefore remains, and contract-based regulation provides only a temporary solution pending the establishment and implementation of a functional regulatory institution.

---

6. Typically, a license only touches upon the *activity* of the regulated business and not the assets. To simplify, a driving licence permits a person to carry on the activity of driving an automobile and does not stipulate whether that automobile is to be owned, leased, or hired. Concessions, however, generally touch upon not only the activity but also the underlying assets of the regulated business.

7. This is because, inter alia, (a) it is practically impossible in any contract to adequately foresee every possibility or regulatory need that might arise in the longer term and (b) the "regulator" may need to be party to the arrangement to ensure enforcement unless the legislation determines otherwise. This is particularly the case in common law jurisdictions where the doctrine of privity of contract excludes the possibility of third parties who benefit (*i.e.*, consumers) enforcing contractual obligations on the private operator to the government or municipal authority. It is perhaps less the case in certain civil law jurisdictions where the principle of *ius quaesitum tertio* may apply, under which a contract entered into for the benefit of a third party may be enforced by that entity even though it was not directly party to that contractual arrangement.

B. *The Interrelationship Between Sector Structure and Regulation*

Apart from the form and status of regulatory instruments and the nature of any regulatory institution established to oversee the implementation of these instruments, the policy maker will assist with the creation of an effective regulatory regime by using the tools of competition and sector restructuring.

Experience from both developed and developing countries over recent years has shown the importance of two key ingredients to secure sustainable sector reform. The first is the *structure* given to the industry in the course of the reform process, including the nature of competition in the sector concerned. The second is a clear identification of the *objectives* of regulation, including the development of a well-defined separation between the functions of policy making, policy implementation, and operation. The extent to which competition can be harnessed to assist regulation in terms of both efficiency and effectiveness varies according to the intrinsic technical characteristics of the sector concerned. In addition, the factors giving rise to the reform itself influence the shape and extent of the regulatory design by policy makers. Each of these decisions, in turn, has an effect on the viability of the regulatory regime in the face of a threat of political and commercial regulatory capture.

The starting point in the process of regulatory design is a thorough analysis of the structure of the industry to be reformed or privatized. This is the key not only to understanding the present standing of the sector and how each of the services are packaged together, which goes to comprehending its technical aspects, but also to understanding fully the implications for regulation of a particular model.[8] This analysis of industry structure also means that policy makers will need to have a clear vision of what the sector structure should look like in both the medium and long term. Too often, regulatory failure is caused not by a failure of the regulatory processes themselves but by a lack of attention to detail in the appraisal of sector structure and in addressing these issues in both the law and regulation, *i.e.*, a failure to tailor the regulatory regime to the adopted industry structure. The process of regulatory design is also crucial to balancing the interests of the various actors in the sector: government, industry, investors, lenders, and consumers. One model that has been relatively successful is the combination of new entry, unbundled services, and an unambiguous set of

8. For example, in electricity, the "single buyer" model as opposed to one under which generators may sell directly to consumers or distributors.

legal rights and duties—applicable to both public and private service providers alike—administered by an autonomous regulatory authority.

### 1. Assisting Effective Regulation with Economic Incentives

Adopting a particular sector structure, even if it remains unchanged, will have real implications for the type and style of regulation and its long-term effectiveness. The interrelationship between the type or style of regulation and sector structure is exemplified in natural gas transportation.

The economic incentives felt by a gas pipeline operator that is prohibited from trading in gas on its own account are very different from the incentives felt by a gas pipeline operator that is allowed by law to do so. In the first case, the pipeline operator will welcome requests for transportation services, because this will be its only source of revenue. If, however, the operator also trades in gas, it will be in the commercial interests of that operator not to allow third-party access, or at least not to allow access without attempting to discriminate between itself—as gas trader—and third-party users.

The policy-maker must decide, therefore, whether to require the unbundling of trading and transportation. This decision needs to be made with a full appreciation of the likely consequences for effective regulation. Broadly, if the transporter is permitted to trade in gas on its own account, the regulatory regime will need to be more invasive and proactive in order to ensure compliance with any open access obligations imposed. Also, the regulatory authority will need greater institutional capacity to be able to deliver under the terms of its brief. This example illustrates the trade-offs between the amount of sector unbundling undertaken and the resultant impact on the type of regulation that needs to be instituted.

Taking this illustration a stage further, cross-ownership structures at the shareholder level or nominee shareholdings will have the same economic effect as allowing a pipeline operator to trade directly in gas. This then raises complex questions as to what limitations should be placed on cross-ownership and how they should be policed—whether by the regulator or by merger controls in the country's antitrust laws.

### 2. Competition and Industry Structure

In the process of regulatory design, however, a balance within the industry must be struck between sector restructuring—or unbundling—and economies of scale. Some industries call for special consideration as to structure due to the type of service they provide. In electricity generation, for example, as a general rule little or no economies of scale exist in packaging power stations together.

This general inapplicability of economies of scale is true even where the combination involves a mix of generation sources such as hydro and thermal plants, although greater fuel diversity is advantageous to generating companies because it reduces total exposure to market fluctuations of any one particular fuel both in terms of price and availability. In addition, certain technical aspects of the industry relating, for example, to the economic despatch of a plant, do call for central control at a technical and operational level rather than the allocation of these functions to several competing private entities.

There are, however, aspects of the power sector where one entity is preferable to several competitors. For example, an interconnected high-voltage power grid has real technical efficiencies—due to the role an interconnected transmission system plays—in terms of both the security and reliability of the entire power sector. A sudden loss of load on one part of the interconnected power system, due to generator failure or transmission line outage, can cause significant disequilibrium to the entire system. Responsibility for system integrity may have to be assigned to one entity that controls the central dispatch function to minimize the risk of such occurrences. These technical efficiencies therefore place limitations on the extent to which the sector may be divided, and the extent to which competition is introduced must be compatible with these technical constraints.

Despite these concerns, however, the introduction of competition in the functions of generation and supply through an open access regime is possible without threat to the integrity of an interconnected power system. In some cases, liberating entry to the market may actually *increase* system security because new private entrants may carry out higher levels of capital investment than were possible in the public sector. Whether or not this benefit arises depends, of course, upon the particular configuration of the power system in question. Furthermore, from the perspective of private generation developers, an open access regime offers the private generator the possibility of accessing more creditworthy customers, provided that those benefits are not eroded through imbalanced charging for transmission services. The terms and conditions for wheeling power must be reasonable by reference to the industry standard, which should be supervised by the government or regulatory commission for that country and its regions in order to send the correct pricing signals to the private developers.

### C. *The Interrelationship Between Competition and Regulation*

The feasibility of introducing competition requires careful consideration in public utility sectors such as water, sewage, roads, electric power, and telecommunications. Where the policy maker wishes to introduce competition, two basic questions arise: how far should competition be introduced into the sector, and how should that competition be introduced. These are not just critical questions for the policy maker; they may also impact the viability of certain non- or limited-recourse greenfield[9] infrastructure projects. For example, when the incumbent state-owned provider is not creditworthy, the project sponsors will want to place third-party access obligations on the incumbent provider to allow the project company to access directly the large, creditworthy users. To that extent, the project sponsors will want competition to be introduced. On the other hand, if the viability of the project depends on demonstrating "captive" customers for the life of the financing (which is typical of distribution networks), the sponsors will wish to resist retail competition.

The answers to these fundamental questions will shape the future of the sector. For example, with telecommunications, should the introduction of competition be limited to value-added services only, or should it include basic telephony? In electric power, should competition be limited to generation, or should it be extended to distribution? If so, to what level? In finding answers to these sorts of questions, the policy-maker will need to consider the particular nature or technical characteristics of the relevant sector, simply because the introduction of competition is likely to be inherently easier in some sectors than in others. Even within a particular sector, competition may be easier to introduce in certain parts of the sector than in others. The relative ease with which competition in generation may be allowed in the power sector as against the provision of other services, such as transmission and distribution, is a classic example.

In the past, academics and politicians have emphasized that effective competition in a market reduces the need for external regulation—principally because strong competition constitutes a self-regulating system that ensures the elimination of excess profits.[10] Competition in

9. *I.e.*, a completely new development—such that before the construction of the project, there was only a "green field" on the site.

10. *See, e.g.*, statement of Michael Heseltine, President of the Board of Trade and Secretary of State for Trade and Industry, in relation to the new Gas Bill for the introduction of greater competition in the privatized gas industry in Great Britain, 256 PARL. DEB. (HANSARD) 574 (Her Majesty's Stationery Office, Mar. 13, 1995).

the market drives firms to reduce their costs as much as possible to minimize loss of market share to competitors, and it spurs innovation, research, and development. Furthermore, where many players exist in the market, opportunities for collusive and anti-competitive behavior are severely limited.

In comparison, the argument goes, regulation is often difficult to establish, cumbersome, costly, and prone to neutralization by capture. For these reasons, some analysts have proposed that regulation in infrastructure is a transitory phase, to be replaced by competition once sufficient entrants are operating in the market.[11] However, while the extension of competition undoubtedly serves to assist regulation, experience shows that regulation in infrastructure is still required to allow competition to be effective.

In infrastructure, transition in regulation applies more to the style of regulation employed than to its elimination. The type of regulation employed should vary as the number of significant market participants increases. When there is little or no competition, regulation needs to be proactive and intrusive in its style in order to be effective. This is because the utility being regulated will be in a position to exercise the power of market dominance and control of information, and it has little or no incentive to improve performance. Whether public or private, the temptation of monopoly profits is usually too great to resist. As new competitors enter the market and create effective competition, the need for proactive and heavy regulation is thereby diminished, and the market becomes more reactive. In practice, however, as competition is introduced it is difficult to "down-size" regulatory bureaucracies to tailor them to the actual needs of regulation, which points to the importance of ensuring that sufficient competition is introduced in the sector at the time of the reform or privatization.

Models for industry structure may exclude competition, contain a mix of competition and a dominant national provider, or permit extensive competition through radical restructuring. The regulatory framework that results will depend directly on the nature of the model adopted. Nevertheless, the regulatory processes and institutions that result are also dictated by the existing political, social, and legal realities of the country.[12]

---

11. *See generally* Stephen C. Littlechild, *Ten Steps to Denationalisation*, *in* PRIVATIZATION AND COMPETITION: A MARKET PROSPECTUS 15 (C. G. Veljanovski ed., 1989).

12. *See generally* Brian Levy & Pablo T. Spiller, *Regulation, Institutions and Commitment in Telecommunications: A Comparative Analysis of Five Country Studies*, *in* PROCEEDINGS OF THE WORLD BANK ANNUAL CONFERENCE ON DEVELOPMENT ECONOMICS 1993 215 (1994) (on file with *Law and Policy in*

### D. *The Process of Regulatory Reform*

#### 1. Deregulation

Regulation is, of course, not new. It has long been a tool of policy makers, used alongside ownership as a means of control. Historically, regulation was often used to erect barriers against new entrants to the market, thus preserving the monopoly position enjoyed by the state-owned enterprise. The scope of this old-style regulation varies quite markedly from country to country. Where direct control is exercized by government over such matters as the capital investment decisions of the enterprise, prices, and staffing levels (matters that would otherwise be dealt with by management in a truly competitive market), regulation often deals with little more than setting technical standards that operate to prohibit, or at best significantly hinder, competition. Even when prices are within the scope of regulation, substantial cross-subsidization is common and the relevant ministry retains the right to intervene when deemed politically expedient. This, however, just leaves enterprise management in doubt as to the scope of its authority in decision making, a dilemma that becomes particularly acute if management is expected to behave in a commercial manner. In designing regulatory reforms, it is important to determine the scope of any old-style regulation that touches upon the sector before devising a new regulatory regime. In other words, it is important to understand the substance of existing old-style regulation in order to be fully apprised of how the existing law must be amended.

#### 2. Institutional Capacity

Before embarking on *re-regulation*, an important prerequisite to effective regulatory design is analysis of the overall institutional capacity of the country concerned. This analysis is necessary because the choices available to policy makers in the design of regulation are restricted by the institutional capacity of, and the interrelationships among, the legislative, executive, and judicial branches of government.[13] This reflects the formal procedures for law-making, the bodies of government that implement and enforce the laws, and the relationship among those functions.

---

*International Business*). This paper illustrates—by reference to Argentina, Chile, Jamaica, the Philippines, and Great Britain—the importance of designing regulations to fit the local environment.

13. *Id.* at 221–23.

The institutional capacity existing within a country will also shape the placement of the core regulatory rules within the spectrum of available mechanisms. While the goal is to achieve a balance between flexibility and certainty in implementing regulatory policy, primary enabling legislation that establishes the principles and parameters within which regulatory institutions may exercise delineated discretionary powers is usually necessary. Granting significant discretionary powers to independent quasi-governmental agencies is, however, uncommon outside the major Western industrial economies. Governments are often quite reluctant to allow an agency to have wide discretion in approving prices or service standards for public services. Where a distinct separation of powers between the legislative and executive branches exists, an alternative (although perhaps sub-optimal) option is to set out the rules in detail in the primary legislation that create the regulatory scheme. Chile and Peru are successful examples of this approach.[14]

Conversely, where the executive is dominant and commonly makes arbitrary administrative actions, a legislative-based solution is unlikely to be viable. In such cases, it may be possible to create an enclave body of rules in the license or concession. However, this mechanism will not satisfy the concerns of investors as to the stability of the contractual regime without a capable and independent judiciary to arbitrate disputes between the government and the service provider.[15] The courts must have a reputation for impartiality and enforcement of private property rights and contracts—including enforcement against uncompensated government expropriation. Other important factors include the role of informal rules of custom and social interest that serve as restraints on arbitrary action by individuals and institutions.

Notably, however, reliance upon project-specific rules embodied in the license or concession—concerning pricing, quality of service, and competition—carries some risk in emerging markets. This is clearly the case when the government lacks the skills and bargaining leverage to ensure that the "regulatory contract" fairly balances public and private inter-

14. *See, e.g.*, Ley General de Telecomunicaciones [General Telecommunications Law] (Chile), No. 18,168 (1982) (as modified and amended through 1994) (on file with *Law and Policy in International Business*). An example from Peruvian law is the Ley de Concesiones Electricas [Law on Electrical Concessions], No. 25,844 (1992) (on file with *Law and Policy in International Business*) and the implementing regulation, Aprueban el Reglamento de la Ley de Concesiones Electricas [Approval Regulation of the Law on Electrical Concessions], No. 009-93-EM (1993) (on file with *Law and Policy in International Business*).

15. *E.g.*, STEWART-SMITH, *supra* note 1, at 29 n.60 (citing WORLD BANK, VENEZUELA: JUDICIAL INFRASTRUCTURE PROJECT, July 15, 1992 (Staff Appraisal Report 10635-VE, publication forthcoming)).

ests. If the contract is unbalanced, the government may face public pressures in the future to protect the public interest by utilizing other tools such as taxation, price controls, or even unilateral termination. The "stabilization clauses" often included in such contracts to guard against changes unilaterally introduced by government may not always be an effective safeguard against future legislative or administrative action, usually under the doctrine of sovereign immunity and related arguments on sovereignty.

This risk is particularly great when periodic, negotiated revisions of the contract are not envisaged. Greater stabilization can be ensured through economically balanced contracts and through better definition in these arrangements of the public interest grounds for review. In addition, where domestic courts are weak and politicized, reference to international arbitration in the contract may provide a useful impartial forum for dispute settlement.[16]

### 3. Re-Regulation

In conjunction with the deregulation process, the development of new regulatory regimes and institutions will facilitate competition and set the new environment for the industry by emulating market mechanisms within the confines of accepted policy. The re-regulation process necessitates reallocating responsibility for the supervision of technical and safety regulation, usually from the national service provider to the regulator. This reallocation process includes the complete separation of the previous regulatory functions from the operational functions of the national service providers. This is a key step in the reform process for private sponsors and their financiers. Without the separation of these functions, the new entrant in effect will be regulated by its competitor.

The re-regulation process will normally involve passing primary legislation establishing the regulatory authority and giving it industry watchdog powers as a quasi-judicial entity with a high degree of sectoral orientation.

The private provision of infrastructure involves a complex interplay between industry structure, regulation, and competition. Regulation is necessary to maintain effective competition, if only to prevent market concentration and the abuse of a dominant market position by any operator. Regulation is also needed to monitor open access and interconnection in sectors such as electricity and telecommunications. In other

16. However, the efficacy of international arbitration may be illusory where the local law requires that a decree arbitral must be reviewed by the domestic courts before it can be enforced.

words, competition is not an alternative to regulation but rather is its beneficiary.

## III. Financing Instruments and Project Development Techniques

### A. *Financing Instruments for Private Providers*

The financing of government-owned infrastructure providers is normally accomplished through equity provided by the central or local government combined with direct borrowing by, or with the guarantee of, that government. These arrangements do not raise particular legal problems; financiers in most cases rely on the credit of the host government, accepting the sovereign risk or taking out insurance against it. The situation—already complicated by private sector involvement in the provision of the services—is becoming more complex as new innovative private financing techniques emerge and are proven effective in emerging markets.

The present marked trend toward private participation and risk bearing in infrastructure provision has led to the development of various innovative financing techniques and instruments.[17] These include: (a) asset-based financing; (b) other forms of financing such as leasing, hire purchase and conditional sales, acceptance credit facilities, and debt factoring—none of which involve conventional borrowing; and (c) different project financing structures, whether on a limited or non-recourse basis, of individual projects. Project financing will often include some of the instruments mentioned in (b) above. One example is the recent re-emergence of leases for the financing of project assets within independent power projects that are project financed.[18]

From a policy-maker's perspective, a key benefit of these financing techniques, and of project financing in particular, is the way they afford governments the opportunity to develop regulatory experience as they make the transition from being the provider of services to being the regulator of others who provide them. A further benefit is that the technique of project financing brings better financial and managerial discipline to bear upon the ongoing activities of the project company. The tightly defined roles of the actors are spelled out in the project

17. WORLD DEVELOPMENT REPORT, *supra* note 1, at 89–90.

18. For a discussion of the commonality of leasing in low and middle-income countries, see *id.* at 60.

documentation and are supervised by the financiers. In this regard, project financing is more likely to deliver better and more sustainable projects than conventional government financed projects, even though the initial transaction costs and failure rate are high. At the same time, such projects provide the private sector with new opportunities to take a direct role and obtain greater experience of operating in the emerging markets where the legal and regulatory environment is usually more risky than the comforts of the known regulatory system of the U.S. or north-west European markets.

Project finance is a broad term used to refer to a wide range of possible financing structures. However, they all have one important feature in common: those providing the senior debt place substantial reliance on the viability of the project rather than on external comfort provided through third party guarantees or through mortgages and the like. Reliance is mainly placed on the project's revenue stream and thus on the performance of the project. As a result, the financing is not primarily dependent upon either the credit support of the sponsors or the guarantee of third parties.

In limited-recourse asset-based financing, the security structures provide the primary recourse by reference to the proceeds of sale of specific property secured through charge or mortgage. Conversely, project finance techniques primarily look to the revenue stream, even though it is normal practice for security interests to be taken over the project's tangible assets as additional security. Consequently, closer attention is paid to the feasibility of the project and its sensitivity to adverse factors that might negatively affect the flows of revenue to the project. In the course of the development of the project and its appraisal, both technical and financial tests are strictly applied. The technical test will normally entail a technical feasibility study carried out by independent experts, such as consulting engineers, with an emphasis on proven technological solutions. The financial test will involve cash flow forecasts to show that revenues will be sufficient to cover debt service, taxes, and other costs, plus a contingency and surplus for the project to meet its target return on equity.

Financiers commonly draw a distinction within the contractual matrix for the project (see below) between the construction phase and the operational phase. The financing of the construction phase is not normally provided on a non- or limited-recourse basis. Once the commissioning tests are undertaken, and the plant is operational, the project enters the operational phase, and the commercial private loan facility typically takes on the non- or limited-recourse characteristic.

## B. *The Contractual Matrix*

The financing techniques bringing about the benefits of better financial and operational management are essentially based on the degree of risk and the way that that risk is allocated between the different parties: the sponsors, the suppliers, the customers, the financiers, and, in certain cases, the host government.

If the sponsors wish the financing to be on a non-recourse basis, the matrix of project agreements that anticipates the likely requirements of both domestic and overseas lenders and other investors is critical to minimizing the difficulties of financing. For example, in the context of independent power projects, this matrix of contracts will usually include a *power purchase agreement*. This will contain "take or pay" obligations on the part of the purchasers of the generated output—a concept that has been effective over many years in the oil and gas industry—as well as a division within that agreement of the power tariff between capacity costs and energy costs. Such a division ensures that the fixed costs of the plant are covered at all times. Secondly, the contractual matrix will include a *fuel purchase agreement* and the associated *transportation agreements* which, respectively, secure the supply of fuel and arrange for its transport from the source to the plant. Other contracts in the matrix include the *construction contract*, which is usually on a turnkey basis, the *operation and maintenance agreement*, and, when the technology has not been fully proven, *technology support agreements*. An *implementation agreement* may also be utilized, requiring that the host government grant the key permissions and authorizations necessary for the implementation of the project, thereby giving the advantage of "one-stop shopping" to the project developers in terms of obtaining the requisite governmental authorizations from various ministries or agencies.

The key to the success of this technique of project development is that the risks of late- or non-performance are clearly allocated between the actors, ideally resting on those best placed to manage the risk. The terms of the project agreements are therefore focused on specifics, rather than placing reliance on general guarantees provided by the government or the project sponsors.

If the risks cannot be allocated, guarantees may be used for additional support, and the project may proceed on a limited-recourse rather than a non-recourse basis. Nevertheless, even when limited recourse is required, the guarantee will be restricted to specific and identifiable risks. Typically these will be matters outside the control of any of the actors, such as the grant of permits and approvals from governmental authorities, compensation guarantees in the event of expropriation, and guarantees in relation to foreign exchange and transfer risks. The project finance technique is therefore likely to deliver greater financial discipline within the project as well as to appropriate management responsibility.

These financing techniques also form an integral part of the Build, Operate, and Transfer (BOT) and the Build, Own, and Operate (BOO)[19] projects employed in South Asia, closely coupled with a concession contract or license.

Following the creation of the project documentation, the financing documents for the project are likely to include a *credit facility agreement* that may be an individual loan or co-financing agreement between the borrower and a number of lenders. Where applicable, equity *subscription agreements* between the lenders, the project company, and the project sponsors will also be included. A *security agreement* will provide for: (a) mortgages or charges over the land, the fixed plant, and machinery; (b) an assignment of the project company's rights under all project contracts, performance bonds, and project insurances and reinsurances; (c) charges over the project company's bank accounts and book debts; (d) a floating charge over all other assets of the project company; and (e) provision for both on- and off-shore bank accounts and escrow accounts to control and retain cash flows relating to the project.

The extent to which non-recourse and limited-recourse project financing techniques can be employed in infrastructure development depends to a large degree upon the nature of the contemplated infrastructure project. Compared to an independent power project with a limited number of actors, the application of these financing techniques to the development of toll roads has proven to be more difficult. This difficulty is principally due to the lack of contractual certainty of the revenue stream. Nonetheless, a number of such projects have been successfully concluded in recent years: for example, the Guangzhou-Shenzhen-Shunhai Superhighway Project in China (the highway from Guangzhou to the Hong Kong border) at a project cost of US$1 billion.[20]

Apart from the wider use of project financing techniques for infrastructure development, another interesting trend is the changing mix of

19. BOT projects are, typically, projects where the private developers build and then operate an infrastructure facility for a number of years under license or concession. At the end of such time, the ownership of the asset is transferred to the public sector, usually for nil payment. Other structures, such as BOOs, Build-Transfer-Operate projects (BTOs) and Build-Own-Operate-Transfer projects (BOOTs) are variants on this theme. Conversely, Rehabilitate-Operate-Transfer projects (ROTs) relate to the taking over of an existing asset by the private developers for rehabilitation or upgrading, followed by commercial operation.

20. WORLD DEVELOPMENT REPORT, *supra* note 1, at 97.

investors. Non-utility private investors are playing an increasing role, particularly in power generation. While this trend is most marked in the OECD countries, despite the intense interest expressed by various project sponsors it has yet to develop to the same extent in developing countries. A key reason for this gap between expressions of interest and financially closed projects is difficulty in securing debt financing and the scarcity of these funds.

Scarcity of funds is largely due to perceptions of country risk. Lenders fear that the host government will take arbitrary action jeopardizing the repayment of the loans to the project. These issues go not to the project contracts themselves, which tend to be similar in form in both developed and developing countries, but rather to the environment in which these contracts are to operate. This environment is composed of such factors as the predictability of government decisions, the enforceability of contracts, the regulatory framework, and its transparency (especially with regard to the process for setting tariffs and their review, currency convertibility, and money transfers). Because these areas produce typically non-commercial or political risks in which governments have the greatest discretion, lenders attach particular attention to them and are likely to require guarantees or other sources of comfort to cover them.

### C. *Comfort Letters, Guarantees, and the Mitigation of Risk*

Until recently, the private investor approach to mitigating project or country risks was to require certain guarantees or indemnities of the host government through guarantee instruments. However, if the host government is unwilling to ensure that the state-owned utility will adhere to its obligations in the underlying project contracts, one cannot be certain that the government will respond to claims on such guarantees.

The evolving approach to dealing with these risks first involves its mitigation, primarily through economic reform. Clearly, this has to be government-led. This reform process also involves reform of the legal and regulatory framework at a much wider level than the scope of the particular project. In this area, the various multilateral and bilateral development finance agencies have played a significant role. Legal technical assistance that facilitates new entry and private sector development is only one part of this process. The strengthening of institutions that will act in a transparent and more predictable manner goes hand in hand with the reform of the legal and regulatory environment. For example, the judiciary is important in the enforcement of contracts, and regulatory institutions that will administer the regulatory scheme in a consistent manner should be developed. Far-reaching reforms of both the legal and institutional framework are required to make these financing techniques and private sector provisions sustainable over a significant period of time. In addition, capital markets must be nurtured to ensure efficient channelling of savings into investment.

In addition to these actions in the mitigation of country risk, new and innovative contractual mechanisms may be developed to reduce the exposure of the project to certain kinds of risk. For example, if the local power utility that would normally purchase electricity generated by the independent power project is not particularly credit-worthy, the electricity may be sold to local industrial or commercial users. Wheeling arrangements may be concluded with the utility for the use of its transmission system to transport the power to those users. Also, if the local currency is not convertible, special arrangements may be made with the central bank to ensure availability of foreign exchange for spares, debt service, and dividends.

Finally, lenders can obtain cover from third parties for remaining country risk. Export credit agencies provide guarantees in this regard. International financial institutions may also provide cover. For example, the International Finance Corporation (IFC), a member of the World Bank Group, has developed instruments such as the "B" Loan to give commercial creditors comfort.[21]

To deal with other risks, lenders employ a number of other instruments to provide a degree of recourse to the project sponsors or others. The legal nature of these undertakings varies. For example, project sponsors might grant a comfort letter in favor of the commercial banks in a non-recourse project financing saying that, as parent companies, they generally support their subsidiaries. Comfort letters, of course, may be merely statements of present intention rather than instruments creating legal obligations. Nonetheless, they can be just as effective in terms of instilling moral obligation in a large multinational corporation to support its floundering special-purpose project company. Where an intention to create legally binding obligations exists, a parent company guarantee or the guarantee of a foreign or international financing institution may be required for specified risks in particular circumstances. This Article next deals with the latter source of comfort in the following Part.

---

21. Peter F. Fitzgerald, *Overview of Risks in International Financing*, *in* PROJECT FINANCING FROM DOMESTIC TO INTERNATIONAL—BUILDING INFRASTRUCTURE PROJECTS IN DEVELOPING MARKETS 1995 7, 15 (Practicing Law Institute Comm. Law & Practice Course Handbook Series No. A4-4460, Robert Thornton Smith & Peter F. Fitzgerald eds., 1995).

## IV. External Financing

### A. *Alternatives to Domestic Governmental Financing*

Except for the least developed countries, most countries mobilize the funds for investment in infrastructure domestically. This is true even though the relatively large sums involved in infrastructure projects make the need for external financing more self-evident. Until recently, external and domestic private financing were minor complementary sources of funds compared to those provided by both central and local governments through budgetary allocation.

A strategy for tapping both foreign and domestic sources of capital must accompany a sustained infrastructure program. To meet the needs of municipal governments in particular—which are responsible for large and growing urban infrastructure—one option available to developing countries is to seek to revitalize existing local lending institutions, such as infrastructure development banks.[22] However, the creation of a new specialized domestic institution may be justified "only if the value of business warrants it and if the concomitant technical and managerial capabilities exist."[23] A more practical alternative suggested by the World Development Report may be to "develop and improve upon existing commercial and development banking channels."[24]

Several governments, including those of Mexico, the Philippines, and Jamaica, have created or are contemplating creating specialized infrastructure funds designed as transitional mechanisms to provide long-term finance for private infrastructure development until local capital markets are better developed. The number of private funds for developing country infrastructure is also growing. This is particularly true of funds that channel international capital, including private placements from institutional investors.[25] Such funds serve the commercially useful purpose of diversifying investor risk. Both types of funds allow government resource leveraging or official development assistance by attracting co-financing from private sources. They can also create credit histories for borrowers currently perceived as risky. In time, it is expected that these borrowers can secure direct access to capital markets.[26] Indeed, broadening and deepening domestic capital markets is

22. World Development Report, *supra* note 1, at 102–04.

23. *Id.* at 103.

24. *Id.*

25. *Id.* at 104.

26. Examples of countries that have successfully accessed these markets include Chile, Argentina, and Indonesia through the issuance of American Depository Receipts (ADRs) for selected utilities on the New York market.

the long-term goal because they can be "efficient and reliable conduits for infrastructure finance."[27] Domestic financial intermediaries, through appraisal and underwriting functions, may play an important role in furthering the development of capital markets.[28]

Foreign financing of infrastructure in developing countries is obtainable through official and private sources. The official sources include bilateral donor agencies and multilateral development banks, although over recent years the level of official funding has been small compared to total private capital flows. Private sources include direct borrowing from bond markets, borrowing from commercial banks, and equity investment by foreign investors and contractors.

The role of multilateral development banks and the growing linkage between this role and private sector financing deserve elaboration. This is particularly true in view of recent developments in this area, as illustrated by the recent activities of the World Bank Group.

### B. *World Bank Group Financing*

The International Bank for Reconstruction and Development (IBRD) and the International Development Association (IDA) have traditionally financed infrastructure more heavily than other sectors,[29] although the share of infrastructure in total lending has declined somewhat in recent years due to the rise in adjustment lending and human resource development loans. Among the different types of infrastructure projects, energy and transport have always figured prominently, not only in World Bank financing but in official development finance generally.[30]

Until recently, the World Bank financing of infrastructure, much as the financing by other official development finance agencies, was directed almost exclusively to governments or government-owned entities. On the one hand, until recently the prevailing practice in borrowing countries had been to reserve the provision of infrastructure and public utilities to the public sector. On the other hand, the IBRD lending requirement of obtaining a governmental guarantee in case the borrower is not a member country[31]—and the very concessional nature of

---

27. WORLD DEVELOPMENT REPORT, *supra* note 1, at 104.

28. *Id.* at 108.

29. *See id.* at 149 (table A.3, entitled *IBRD and IDA Commitments*, comparing IBRD and IDA spending on infrastructure to their respective total spending).

30. *Id.* at 90, figure 5.1. As an illustration, World Bank commitments to infrastructure reached almost 50% of total commitments in 1980 (US$6361 million out of US$12,240 million), compared to 37.5% in 1993 (US$8887 million out of US$23,696 million). *Id.* at 149.

31. Articles of Agreement of the International Bank for Reconstruction and Development,

IDA credits—made IBRD loans or IDA credits to private enterprises impractical in most cases.

This situation is changing, however, as countries resort to various forms of privatization of public utilities in response to the limited success that public ownership has achieved in the vast majority of cases. In addition, private funds are flowing more readily to emerging markets for investment purposes, including long-term investment for infrastructure projects. Latin American countries in particular are currently considering infrastructure initiatives, where large private funds are projected to finance a broad array of infrastructure projects with various forms of financial support,[32] mainly including guarantees and extension of loan maturities from the IBRD, the International Finance Corporation (IFC), the Multilateral Investment Guarantee Agency (MIGA), and the Inter-American Development Bank (IADB).

The governments of some of these countries may also play a crucial role in the financing of these projects, in collaboration with the private sector. For instance, Mexico was until recently considering the establishment of an infrastructure fund that would have used proceeds of privatization to provide loans and guarantees to private operations. Other countries such as the Philippines are actively pursuing this whole-sale method toward facilitating new infrastructure development.[33]

Because of the long-term nature of infrastructure investments, private investors often seek co-financing or guarantees from the World Bank Group or similar institutions. The co-financing may take the form of direct lending on a joint or parallel basis, and it may be limited to extending the maturities of private loans by refinancing them on a definite or contingent basis. Guarantees may also take one of several forms of credit enhancement.[34]

---

Dec. 27, 1945, art. III, § 4(1), 60 Stat. 1440, 1444, 2 U.N.T.S. 134, 144, *amended* Dec. 16, 1965, 16 U.S.T. 1942 [hereinafter IBRD Articles].

32. *See, e.g.*, *Brazil Builds IT Infrastructure*, OPEN SYS'S. COMM., Feb. 23, 1994, *available in* Westlaw, ALLNEWS Database; *World Bank Prepares for New Lending Tasks*, LANGIAPPE LETTER, Oct. 14, 1994, *available in* Westlaw, ALLNEWS Database.

33. Recent discussions between the World Bank and the Government of the Philippines have resulted in a program for the rationalization of guarantees and the setting up of approval procedures. These programs will be coupled with technical assistance for the development of an infrastructure fund to be supported under the World Bank's new guarantee policy in conjunction with co-financiers.

34. For example, partial credit guarantees that allow for longer maturities than would otherwise be possible or partial risk guarantees that would cover political or possibility regulatory risks.

In the case of the IFC, such financing raises no particular problem, because the IFC was established to provide finance to private enterprises without government counter-guarantee. In the case of the IBRD, however, the issue is complicated by the requirement that any IBRD loan or guarantee to a non-member entity must be made with the guarantee of the member in whose territory the project is located.[35]

The Executive Directors of the World Bank recently approved a policy paper advocating the more extensive use of the Bank's guarantee powers in its operations regarding private sector participation.[36] These loans, according to previous experience, are likely to be made mostly for the financing of infrastructure projects. Most of these guarantees are likely to be performance guarantees rather than repayment guarantees, envisaged to protect private equity and loan investors against adverse governmental action rather than against commercial risks.

In practice, however, the scope of expansion of such operations will probably depend upon the recipient countries' willingness to give the Bank the required sovereign counter-guarantee. Such willingness is likely to be limited to the cases where the country sees obvious benefits in the private financing of infrastructure (with a Bank guarantee and a government counter-guarantee) over direct borrowing by the government or its public enterprises—assuming the availability of public funds for such purposes. Recent actual and projected private financing of power projects in countries such as the Philippines, China, and Pakistan, with co-financing and a guarantee by the World Bank, demonstrate that this is a promising trend, especially for large infrastructure projects.[37]

IDA financing of private enterprises is more problematic, however, for policy rather than legal reasons. Under its Articles of Agreement, IDA can make credits to private enterprises with or without a government guarantee.[38] This flexibility has not resulted in the IDA financing of a single private enterprise. The fact that IDA credits are given without interest and for maturities of thirty-five to forty years made providing such soft credits directly to private entities unthinkable for policy

35. IBRD Articles, *supra* note 31, art. III, § 4(1), 60 Stat. at 1444, 2 U.N.T.S. at 144. Although the IBRD Articles allow for the guarantee by the central bank or comparable agency of the member, instead of the guarantee by the member itself, the Bank's practice has consistently required the member's guarantee even when the loan was made to the Central Bank.

36. World Bank Press Release No. 95/F08, Sept. 12, 1994 (on file with *Law and Policy in International Business*); *see also* WORLD BANK, WORLD BANK'S GUARANTEES: CATALYSTS FOR PRIVATE CAPITAL FLOWS 2 (1994) [hereinafter WORLD BANK'S GUARANTEES].

37. WORLD BANK'S GUARANTEES, *supra* note 36, at 6–11.

38. Articles of Agreement of the International Development Association, Jan. 26, 1960, art. V, § 2(d), 11 U.S.T. 2284, 2293, 439 U.N.T.S. 249, 264–66 [hereinafter IDA Articles of Agreement].

reasons. IDA credits to governments have been made, however, on lent on semi-commercial terms to financial intermediaries. The issue is further complicated by the fact that IDA's authority to make guarantees without an explicit authorization by the sources of its additional subscriptions and supplementary contributions is not free from doubt.[39] No such authorization has been made so far in any IDA replenishment resolution.

Conversely, MIGA was specifically created to provide guarantees against non-commercial risks to foreign investors, including those who invest in infrastructure projects. Its guarantees are limited, however, to equity interests, including medium- or long-term loans made or guaranteed by holders of equity in the enterprise concerned, and may be extended, by a special majority decision in MIGA's Board, to any other medium- or long-term loans only if they are related to a specific investment covered or to be covered by MIGA. In addition, MIGA's guarantee capacity is limited both on country and operational grounds.[40]

## V. Conclusion

The private development of infrastructure has raised particular institutional, policy, legal, and regulatory issues that go beyond the general requirement of implementing a framework of rules, processes, and institutions to ensure that a country's resources will be managed

39. The IDA Articles of Agreement list among its "Miscellaneous Operations" the power to "in special cases, guarantee loans from other sources for purposes not inconsistent with the provisions of these Articles." *Id.* art. V, § 5(iv), 11 U.S.T. at 2294, 439 U.N.T.S. at 266. However, another section in Article V, after providing that "[f]inancing by the Association shall take the form of loans," authorizes other forms of financing only in two situations: either out of subscription funds (and funds derived therefrom) "if the authorization for such subscriptions expressly provides for such financing" or, "in special circumstances, out of supplementary resources furnished to the Association, and funds derived therefrom if the arrangements under which such resources are furnished expressly authorise such financing." *Id.* art. V, §§ 2(a)(i)–(ii), 11 U.S.T. at 2293, 439 U.N.T.S. at 264.

40. MIGA's cover is limited at present to $50 million per project and $150 million per country. For percentages used in calculating these monetary amounts, see Operational Regulations of the Multilateral Investment Guarantee Agency, June 22, 1988, para. 3.60, 27 I.L.M. 1228, 1247. However, the latter limit is expected to be increased soon. Under the MIGA Convention, the aggregate amount of contingent liability under MIGA's cover was initially limited to 150 % of MIGA's subscribed capital and reserves plus a portion of its reinsurance cover as its Board determines. Multilateral Investment Guarantee Agency, Oct. 11, 1985, art. 22(a), 24 I.L.M. 1605, 1615. This limit was increased in 1994 and could be further increased in 1995. MIGA's Council, acting by special majority, can increase the aggregate limit up to five times the amount of subscribed capital, reserves, and "such portion of its reinsurance cover as may be deemed appropriate." *Id.*

efficiently and responsibly. Infrastructure provision raises specific questions related to the industry structure, competition, and regulation—as well as to the interplay among these important factors. These inquiries in turn raise questions concerning financing documents, the planning of infrastructure systems, the pricing of the services rendered, and the allocation of risks. These issues are all directly relevant to successful private infrastructure investment financing. Factors that have given rise to the use of a wide range of regulatory instruments and financing techniques include the recent trend toward globalization, the large increase of the flow of private funds to certain emerging markets, and the ongoing reforms in many such countries.

Due to the large sums of money involved and the multiplicity and transnational character of the parties, a great variety of financial and regulatory instruments and institutions relevant to infrastructure sectors exist. The matrix of contracts and other legal instruments needed for the appropriate packaging of financial arrangements and for the subsequent project execution and delivery of services are particularly complex in the case of infrastructure. This Article has, at the risk of some oversimplification, attempted to portray major aspects of these complex issues in the context of emerging markets. Of particular note is the increased participation of the private sector, not only in the financing and delivery of infrastructure but also in the regulatory reform such participation brings to bear.

Contracts are being used increasingly, both as regulatory tools—as in concession agreements—and as efficiency tools for the delivery of public services by private enterprises—as in the contracting out of certain public services. Contracts are also the main instruments for the financial, construction, and operation arrangements required in each infrastructure project involving the private sector.

The financing techniques employed in the private delivery of public utilities not only give governments the opportunity to develop regulatory experience but also to introduce a greater measure of financial and managerial discipline to each sector. In allocating risks among the different players—the sponsors, suppliers, consumers, creditors, and government—such techniques pay particular attention to the non-commercial or political risks and their effects, especially on debt-financing by non-utility private investors.

The role of domestic banks and infrastructure funds—and of long-term domestic financial institutions generally—is complemented by a broad array of external financiers, private investors and creditors, bilateral donors, and international financial institutions. The complexities involved in the latter's infrastructure financing portrayed in various parts of this Article illustrate the new realities of private and public cooperation in the funding and delivery of public services. They point in particular to the potential of a growing use of external guarantees against sovereign risks by institutions like the World Bank and its affiliates.

The regulatory framework, similar to the other institutional aspects involved, does not flow solely from the varied political, social, and legal realities of each country; it depends on the models chosen for the sector structure. The design of a regulatory framework should thus be based on the chosen sector structure, an honest assessment of the scope of the "old style" barriers to market entry with a view to reducing them, and a focus on the separation of the functions of policy making and policy implementation from operations in that sector. The design of a regulatory framework should also take into account the institutional capacity of the country as well as the pattern of relationships among, and the degree of efficiency of, the various branches of government. Inadequate attention to any of these factors will have a direct, negative impact on the effectiveness of the regulatory framework.

Apart from the demonstrable improvements in performance and system expansion in many countries following private sector entry, the creation of a multi-operator environment and the separation of the regulatory functions and the operational functions have indeed been useful by-products of increasing private sector involvement. The realization that competition is an important ally to optimal regulation has also been important. Appropriate regulation, competition, and restructuring are mutually supportive. While appropriate regulation fosters competition, competition allows the sector to respond to market forces, resulting in market-driven sector restructuring.

The above-mentioned separation of policy making from policy implementation involves the need for deeper institutional reform within government, as the supervisory function of government is transferred to the regulators. Again, multilateral agencies—such as the World Bank and other similar organizations—are in a particularly advantageous position in terms of providing technical assistance and information on the experiences of particular organizational structures and methodologies adopted in other countries. Furthermore, the provision of financial support for these reforms is becoming a common component in many World Bank projects.

The author is now Partner, Energy and Project Finance, Orrick Herrington and Sutcliffe (www.orrick.com)

[8]

# Private-Sector Participation in Infrastructure: Risk, Fiscal, and Efficiency Issues in Public–Private Arrangements for the Provision of Services

**PAULINA BEATO AND ANTONIO VIVES** *Infrastructure and Financial Markets Division, Inter-American Development Bank*, 1300 New York Avenue, Washington, DC 20577*

## INTRODUCTION

Although most infrastructure assets were privately owned, financed, and managed in the 19th century, over time many countries nationalized most infrastructure companies,[1] so that by the middle of the 20th century, public agencies owned, financed, and managed most infrastructure assets. Construction of infrastructure works was usually the only relevant private-sector participation in the provision of infrastructure services, and most of the time this took place under a contract from a public agency. Although private firms have maintained ownership and management of some infrastructure assets in some countries, these are more the exception than the rule, especially in developing countries.

**Over the past decade, the role of the public sector in infrastructure services has been changing worldwide, from one of owning and managing infrastructure assets to one of planning and regulating privately owned and managed assets to balance the interests of consumers and private-sector firms.**

Over the past decade, the role of the public sector in infrastructure services has been changing worldwide, from one of owning and managing infrastructure assets to one of planning and regulating privately owned and managed assets to balance the interests of consumers and private-sector firms. The forces that have led to these changes in infrastructure provision are rooted in both fiscal and efficiency issues. Public deficits and increasing social demands have led governments to privatize infrastructure assets to increase revenues, reduce public-sector participation in new investments, and decrease public expenditures resulting from public-enterprise losses. State-owned enterprises have traditionally performed poorly in three areas: meeting growing consumer demand, upgrading technology, and providing adequate customer services. The main causes of this are inadequate pricing, poor financial management, and the lack of appropriate incentives.

Although private-sector participation in infrastructure provision may increase efficiency and reduce fiscal pressures, infrastructure assets have features that require some degree of public-sector involvement. The high level of investments, economies of scale and scope, externalities, and the nontradable nature of the output of infrastructure assets are features that demand public-sector involvement to avoid monopolistic behavior or other market failures. Governments usually wish to ensure that infrastructure services do not jeopardize economic growth. Thus, private-sector participation in infrastructure provision requires an arrangement between the private and public sectors. The public sector regulates the provision of the service and, in some cases, may be involved in some aspects of the provision of the service, as will be seen below. Such public-sector involvement introduces other noncommercial risks for the private sector, risks that must be adequately dealt with.

* The findings, interpretations and conclusions contained in this paper are the authors' own responsibility and should not be attributed to the Inter-American Development Bank, its Executive Board of Directors, or any of its member countries.

[1] For a discussion of nationalization and privatization waves, see Klein and Roger [1].

Infrastructure, Vol. 1, No. 3, pp. 3–14 (1996)


CCC 1081-7174/96/030003-12

The objective of this article is to characterize different institutional arrangements involving the public and private sectors in infrastructure provision and analyze their efficiency and fiscal features.[2] Risks to the private sector derived from the public–private arrangement are also analyzed. In order to draw some policy recommendations for multilateral institutions and the public sector, and to guide the actions for effective private-sector participation, the article gives special attention to these main topics:

- Private–public arrangements in which a private firm has the responsibility for financing infrastructure assets.
- Regulatory risk derived from decisions of regulators about prices of infrastructure services.
- Credit risk derived from the public entity's failure to pay.[3]

Arrangements that strike the proper balance between the needs of consumers, minimum cost, good quality, and the interests of the private sector are likely to be sustainable in the long run. Therefore, the design of the role and behavior of the public and private sector should set incentives for the private firm to minimize the cost of infrastructure services, but should also establish attractive conditions for private investors.

The remainder of this article is organized in five sections. In order to analyze the efficiency and fiscal implications of arrangements, Section 1 proposes a characterization of them using two features of public–private arrangements: the *source of revenues* to the private firm and its *responsibilities over the assets.* Section 2 discusses arrangements in which a public entity assumes responsibility for owning and financing the assets, and a private firm manages them. Given the important implications of private-sector financing, two sections of the article are dedicated to arrangements in which a private-sector firm is responsible for financing assets. Section 3 examines arrangements in which a private-sector firm finances the assets but the firm revenues come from a public entity. Section 4 elaborates on arrangements in which the private firm is responsible for financing assets and revenues stem from final consumers. A summary of major conclusion is given.

## SOURCE OF REVENUES AND ASSET RESPONSIBILITIES OF PRIVATE FIRMS IN PUBLIC–PRIVATE ARRANGEMENTS

Private participation in infrastructure services requires that a government make the decision of allowing private-sector involvement and establish some schemes to balance the interests of users and producers. Many institutional arrangements have been devised. The choice depends on factors that range from the country's legal framework to financial resource requirements, and from the nature of macroeconomic adjustments to demand or supply characteristics. Each institutional arrangement has advantages and disadvantages for dealing with the provision of a specific infrastructure service; therefore, an analysis of an individual arrangement should be made in each case. Nevertheless, a simple characterization of private–public arrangements is useful to identify the relevant issues.

Although an institutional arrangement for providing infrastructure services may be defined by a multiplicity of features, this article proposes to characterize such arrangements using only two: the source of revenues and asset responsibility of the private firm. The first criterion has been used by the World Bank in its World Development Report [3]. The second has been used by Guislain and Kerf [4]. Using both allows us to identify the problems derived from the combination of both features which, as will be seen, is critical to understanding the efficiency and fiscal issues underlying the arrangement.

### Sources of revenues of private firms

The source of revenues is a relevant feature to consider when assessing public–private arrangements for providing infrastructure services. The source determines (a) the incentives of a private firm to adjust the cost and quality to consumer willingness to pay for them, (b) the amount and timing of public expenditures, and (c) the nature of the risks to which revenues are exposed.

In a public–private arrangement, private-firm revenues may come from consumer payments, from public-entity payments, or from both. To simplify matters, this article only addresses the two pure cases. Nevertheless, because mixed cases share features of the pure cases, they may be evaluated by using the relative participation of final consumers and the public agency in the private-firm revenues.

[2] This article focuses on public-private arrangements for infrastructure provision in emerging markets. However, many conclusions can be applied to mature markets.

[3] Other political risks of infrastructure projects, such as expropriation, inconvertibility, or foreign-exchange risk, are not addressed in this article as they are not exclusive of infrastructure projects, and insurance schemes are commonly available and discussed elsewhere. See, for example, Bensman [2].

***Private-firm revenues stemming from final users***

When private-firm revenues stem from final users they are the result of quantities and prices. The market consumption quantity results from decentralized decisions by consumers that are determined by prices, consumer preferences, service quality, and the existence of other substitute services. Thus, consumption levels are subject to variability and expose the firm's revenues to commercial risk. However, the private-firm revenues are also a function of prices or user fees; prices can be set independently by the firm or by regulation. For instance, in most countries the private firm is free to set user prices of cellular telephone services, but in general the government fixes or regulates electricity prices. When prices are set by competitive markets, project revenues are only exposed to commercial risk; however, if regulators set or control prices, private-firm revenues are also exposed to the decisions of regulatory authorities. This introduces regulatory risk.

The possibility of a change in revenues due to public authorities' decisions about user prices is called regulatory risk.[4] There are three main differences between regulatory and commercial risks. First, commercial risk derives from the decisions of many different economic agents, whereas regulatory risk derives from centralized decisions, which may be discretionary and unrelated to firm choices. Second, managers can rationally forecast and manage commercial risk, but there are no standard techniques to do so with regulatory risk. Although managers may reduce regulatory risk through lobbying and the public media, investors do not like controlling regulatory risks in this manner. Finally, commercial risk is the result of continuous changes in different directions, whereas regulatory risk is usually the result of a random shock.

There are three important points to bear in mind with respect to arrangements in which all revenues come from final users. First, revenue providers are not a legal party in the contract that set the conditions of the private–public arrangement. Second, collecting from final users may be difficult, so operators must have tools for enforcing payment, such as stopping service. Third, private–firm decisions usually minimize the internal cost of infrastructure services, but the resulting prices and quantities may not be appropriate from a social standpoint in the presence of externalities, increasing returns, and other market failures. Therefore, regulation is usually required.[5]

***Private-firm revenues arising from a public agency***

In some cases where private-firm revenues come from a public agency, the private-firm provider of infrastructure services sells the output to a public entity (e.g., independent power producer selling to a national utility). In other cases, the private firm provides services to final consumers, but receives payments from a public entity (e.g., solid-waste service in some localities). Payments from the public agency are directly or indirectly public expenditures and will therefore have a negative impact on the fiscal budget. The degree to which these arrangements may (or may not) reduce fiscal pressures depends on the cost of the provision of the services through a pure public-sector arrangement relative to the payments made to the private firm by the public agency.

In addition, if a public agency makes the payments to the private firm, the direct relationship between consumers and private firms is lost. As a result, private-sector involvement is less likely to solve the problems of unattended demand and poor-quality service. Operational efficiency may or may not improve with private-sector involvement. Other features of a public–private arrangement, such as management and ownership of assets, should also be considered in analyzing operational efficiency.

Revenues originating from a public agency are not usually exposed to commercial risk. They are, however, dependent on the willingness and capacity of the public agency to make the payments. Failure to pay may be seen as a contract failure, similar in nature to a regulatory failure. A distinction between regulatory and payment commitments should nevertheless be made, because the fulfillment of a regulatory commitment does not depend on the financial capacity of the public entity, and because schemes to mitigate and share the risks derived from both types of failures may be different.

There are three reasons private investors may be unwilling to accept public-payment risk. First, investors cannot usually impose conditions on the public entity to ensure its financial soundness. Second, cumbersome procedures are usually required to sue a public agency. Finally, public assets are often not subject to seizure.

[4] Regulatory risk may also derive from the decisions of regulatory authorities on the prices of substitutive services. For example, a gas subsidy may reduce the revenues of firms that distribute electricity.

[5] For a discussion of these issues, see [5, Chap. 11].

### Private-firm responsibilities for infrastructure assets

Responsibilities for and rights over infrastructure assets can be assigned between the public and private sector in many ways. Private–public arrangements can be classified according to who owns, manages, and finances infrastructure assets. The four cases that present themselves are discussed below.[6]

#### *A private firm owns, finances, and manages infrastructure assets*

A private infrastructure firm has the same rights over the assets as any private industrial or commercial firm has over their productive assets. Most power-generation plants in Chile and Argentina are owned, managed, and financed by private companies, and the public sector regulates the relationships between them and consumers.

#### *A private firm finances and manages infrastructure assets but a public agency owns them*

The private firm manages and operates the assets for a fixed period of time, after which assets are transferred back either to the public sector or to another private firm. Concessions fall into this group. These schemes are socially demanded for natural monopoly infrastructure assets, because the community members are willing to maintain public ownership over these assets to ensure long-term service quality. Two groups can be distinguished, depending on the conditions at the time of setting the arrangement. In the first case, existing assets were financed by the public sector but a private firm finances new assets (this is the case in most potable water and sanitation concessions). In the second case, all assets are financed by the private firm, either because they were purchased as a part of a privatization or because there were no assets before the arrangement (green-field projects, as in the case of some concessions for electricity distribution). For the purposes of this analysis, no distinction will be made between the two cases.

#### *A private firm manages assets, but the public sector finances and owns them*

The private firm may manage all or part of the assets owned by the public sector. For instance, private-sector management contracts for operating a public utility (potable water in Mexico City is provided through an arrangement of this type) fall into the first group. Arrangements in which a private firm manages commercial services, such as billing, collection, or customer service, fall into the second group (commercial water and sewerage services will be provided by a private firm in Guayaquil, Ecuador, with water itself being provided by the public firm).

#### *A private firm owns and finances infrastructure assets but the public sector manages them*

These are rather unusual cases in which the private firm owns infrastructure assets but leases them to a public entity. Examples of these arrangements are some thermoelectric power-generation plants. In these cases, the private sector cannot provide operational efficiency, as its involvement is limited to financial responsibility and, in some cases, to asset construction.

### A characterization of arrangements

For the purposes of analysis, a characterization of public–arrangements is made by using both the source of private-firm revenues and the distribution of responsibilities over infrastructure assets. In Figure 1, the participation of user fees in private-firm revenues is represented on the horizontal axis, and the assignment of rights and responsibilities between the private firm and the public sector over infrastructure assets is represented on the vertical axis. The combination of the two criteria, source of revenues and assignment of rights and responsibilities over assets, generates eight classes of arrangements.

The top area of Figure 1 (Zones I, II, III, and IV) represents arrangements in which a relevant private-sector involvement occurs whereby a private-sector firm manages and finances infrastructure assets. These are at the core of the new model of infrastructure provision being instituted around the world. The middle area of Figure 1 (Zones V and VI) corresponds to arrangements with limited private-sector involvement in the provision of services, since the private firm does not manage assets.[7] The lower area of Figure 1 (Zones VII and VIII) represents arrangements in which the public entity is responsible for financing infrastructure assets and a pri-

[6] The case where a public entity owns, finances, and manages infrastructure assets is not considered a public–private arrangement, because all asset responsibilities lay in the public sector. Such a case is called a pure public-sector provision. For the purposes of analyzing fiscal and efficiency issues of each public–private arrangement, they will sometimes be compared with the case of pure public-sector provision.

[7] If a private firm owns infrastructure assets and a public entity manages them, the source of private-firm revenues is usually the public entity. Therefore, arrangements of Zone V, in which the sources of private firm revenues are final consumers, do not exist in practice, and as such they are not addressed in this article.

Infrastructure Asset Responsibility

| | | |
|---|---|---|
| **MOF** Private firm manages, owns and finances infrastructure assets. | Zone I | Zone II |
| **MF** Private firm manages and finances infrastructure assets, but a public entity owns them. | Zone III | Zone IV |
| **OF** Private firm owns and finances infrastructure assets, but a public entity manages them. | Zone V | Zone VI |
| **M** Private firm manages infrastructure assets but a public entity owns and finances them. | Zone VII | Zone VIII |
| | Private firm revenues from final consumers. | Private firm revenues from a public entity |

Source of private firm revenues

**FIGURE 1. Public–private arrangements.**

vate-sector firm manages them. This last type is often used as a preliminary step leading to a larger private-sector participation. The arrangements shown in Figure 1 are analyzed in more detail in the sections that follow, proceeding in inverse order of the degree of private-sector involvement, that is, from the bottom to the top of Figure 1.

## PRIVATE INVOLVEMENT BY MANAGEMENT: A PUBLIC ENTITY OWNS AND FINANCES INFRASTRUCTURE ASSETS

In countries where political and economic risks are high, private firms may not be interested in financing a new infrastructure asset or may request a very high risk premium in return for their participation. This may be the case of water and sanitation in countries without a regulatory framework in place or where public opinion is not ready for private ownership or private-sector concession. It could also be the case where rates must be set so low that private-sector interest in any form of ownership or concession does not exist, as is the case of rural water systems. In these circumstances, private-sector involvement may be limited to management, with the public sector financing and owning the assets (Zones VII and VIII of Figure 1). This arrangement may eventually lead to larger private-sector participation. An implication of these arrangements is that the duration of contracts between the public and private sector may be relatively short as compared with the life of the assets under management, and mistakes can thus be easily corrected by contract modifications. As already mentioned, water provision in Mexico City is an example of an arrangement falling into Zone VIII, in which private-firm revenues come from a public entity and a public entity owns and finances assets. The provision of water in Guinea is through an arrangement in which private-firm revenues are derived from final consumers and assets are owned and financed by a public entity (arrangements in Zone VII).

**In countries where political and economic risks are high, private firms may not be interested in financing a new infrastructure asset or may request a very high risk premium in return for their participation.**

### Fiscal Issues

To analyze fiscal issues, a distinction is made between two types of public expenditures:

public investment and current public expenditures. Public investment in these arrangements are larger than in arrangements in which a private firm owns, finances, and manages infrastructure assets. Although in these cases assets are financed by a public entity, as in the case of provision without private involvement, public investments may be smaller with management contracts than with a pure public-sector provision. The reason is that efficiencies in management may translate into a lower level of assets, thus reducing the need for new public-sector investment. Nevertheless, because the cost of assets is borne by a public entity, the new investments under management contracts (arrangements in Zone VII and VIII) will increase fiscal pressures, for they imply public expenditures.

As for current public expenditures, if private-firm revenues were to derive from consumer payments (Zone VII), there would be no current public expenditures derived from the arrangement. If the private firm pays a fee to the public sector for the exploitation of the assets, then public revenues will be generated. The current fiscal impact of a change from pure public provision to a contract arrangement will depend upon the operational results under pure public provision. If operational losses occurred before the management contract, private-sector involvement would reduce fiscal pressures.

If revenues were to come from a direct management fee from the public sector (Zone VIII), the arrangement generates public expenditures to fund fee payments. In arrangements with public payments, the public-sector entity may receive payments attached to services from consumers that may be larger or smaller than payments to the private firm. Usually, payments from consumers to the public entity are smaller than payments to the private firm from the public entity; therefore, they increase fiscal pressures.

In summary, the overall fiscal impact of a change from pure public-sector provision to contract management is usually very limited, because the cost of assets remains in the public sector. The fiscal impact of operational losses of an infrastructure service provided by a public entity are usually reduced through management contracts in which the sources of private-firm revenues are consumer payments.

### Efficiency issues

From an efficiency point of view, private-sector involvement may have an impact on customer service and meeting demand, depending on the features of the contract, but it will not significantly improve the problem of lagging technology, as new technologies are usually introduced in a productive process through new long-term investments, which in this case are the responsibility of the public sector.

In arrangements in which private-firm revenues come from final users, the private firm has incentives to manage assets to meet demand and improve quality. These incentives are more difficult to find when private-firm revenues come from a public entity, for they may be independent of consumer satisfaction. Schemes relating public payments to fulfillment of consumer preferences may be envisioned, but they are difficult to implement in most cases, because benchmarks for consumer satisfaction are difficult to establish and measure, and they tend to be a source of conflict, not of benefits.

### Issues derived from regulatory risk and failure of public-entity payments

Private-sector revenues are exposed to regulatory risk or the risk of nonpayment by the public entity, depending on the source of private-firm revenues. Nevertheless, because the private firm does not have long-term investments that need to be recovered, it has higher mobility. Thus the task of mitigation of risk appears as less relevant than in the cases where there is a long-term commitment. Both issues, regulatory risk and the risk derived from a failure of public entity payments, are discussed in the corresponding section dedicated to arrangements in which a private firm finances the infrastructure assets. However, because management arrangements are used as a stepping stone to larger private-sector involvement, a contract failure, whether regulatory or financial, will jeopardize future private-sector involvement.

## PRIVATE INVOLVEMENT BY PRIVATE FINANCING: PRIVATE-FIRM REVENUES FROM A PUBLIC ENTITY

These arrangements correspond to zones II, IV, and VI in Figure 1. Arrangements of Zones II and IV, where assets are managed by the private sector, may generate some public expenditures, but are likely to improve efficiency. Arrangements of Zone VI, in which assets are managed by a public entity, do not have incentives either for reducing fiscal pressures or improving efficiency. Examples of arrangements with private financing and private firm revenues from a public entity are some power plants in Guatemala and Mexico (Zone II or Zone VI) and the water service in Puerto Vallarta, Mexico (Zone IV).

### Assets managed by a public entity: fiscal issues and efficiency issues

These arrangements are likely to have a negative fiscal impact compared to a pure public-entity provision. In these arrangements a private-sector firm builds an asset and leases it to a public entity for the entire length of the asset life. The public entity saves the cost of investment, but has to pay a lease during the asset life. The present value of lease payments will be larger than the cost of investment under pure public-sector provision. The reasons for this are the higher rates of interest that a private firm would have to pay compared to the public sector. Private firms will pay higher interest rates because normally they are perceived as riskier than the public sector that hosted the project, and revenues coming from the public sector may not be accepted as guarantees for bonds or other debt.

It is worthwhile to consider the timing of the fiscal impact. Arrangements with private financing and revenues from a public agency, even though they may have an overall negative fiscal impact relative to arrangements with pure public provision, allow a public expenditure to be postponed and spread out over the life of the assets. This may give the public sector time to correct a temporary fiscal deficit or overcome liquidity restrictions.

Private-sector involvement will not improve efficiency, because assets are managed by a public entity. The private-sector role is limited to financing and construction. However, financing infrastructure assets through a private firm will, in general, be more expensive than direct public financing. The benefits of private involvement during the construction period can be achieved through other methods, for instance, competitive bidding for turnkey contracts. An additional problem that may arise from these arrangements, is the lack of transparency regarding the real level of public debt because public payments to private firms financing infrastructure payments are in many cases not accounted for as public debt; thus, they are often used to overcome public-debt restrictions.

### Assets managed by a private firm: fiscal issues and efficiency issues

The fiscal impact of these arrangements compared to a public provision is better analyzed by disaggregating it into three components: public saving from private financing, public saving from reducing the need for new assets, and public saving from operational efficiency. The first component is the difference between the cost of financing an asset by a public entity and the cost of financing by a private firm. The impact of this component will be negative, because interest rates for private financing will be higher than those for public financing. The second component is usually positive, because asset management improvement will reduce the need for new investment (for instance, private management of power plants in Chile has increased utilization by around 40%). The third component is usually also positive, because payments from public to private sector are usually smaller than the cost of operating and maintaining assets by the public entity. The overall fiscal impact will depend upon the relative size of the three components.

In these types of arrangements, a private firm will generally have an incentive to operate efficiently, but it may not have incentives for meeting demand or improving quality. The reason for this is that the private firm does not derive its revenues from consumers; therefore revenues are not tied to consumer satisfaction. The degree to which incentives work depends upon each specific contract. If it is a "take-or-pay" contract, where the agency pays even if it does not buy, there are few incentives to provide good service or even for good maintenance. For instance, consider the case of a country that has ample gas reserves and wants to introduce gas consumption. A gas pipeline would be extremely risky for a private firm in the face of uncertain consumer demand. As a result, to ensure that the project is undertaken, the government may need to guarantee payments, even if consumer demand fails to materialize. In this case there is little incentive for efficient performance, except that derived from some contractual clauses specifying asset availability.

This is not to say that contracts with take-or-pay or similar clauses should not exist. It does point out, however, that the contract should carefully evaluate costs and benefits and incorporate the proper incentives. In the previous example, the contract between the private and public sectors may have a phasing out of the take-or-pay clause so as to incorporate market demand in the incentives for the private firm. Contracts with take-or-pay clauses during the initial phase of the project are appropriate for infrastructure projects that generate their own demand. For example, a government willing to introduce competition in the electricity sector through electricity imports may use an arrangement with the following conditions:

1. A private firm builds and operates a transmission line joining two countries.
2. At the beginning of project life when there is no electricity market between the countries, the public sector makes payments to the private firm.
3. Later, when the market develops, the government reduces the payments to the private firm.

Thus, because revenues after an initial period come from final consumers or electrical distribution firms and depend upon the electricity imports, the private firm has incentives to support competition in the electricity sector. The project also does not entail public expenditures after the initial period.

### Failure of public-sector payments

Private-firm revenues are exposed to the willingness and capacity of the public agency to make payments. As a result, the financial soundness of the public agency is a relevant issue in financing projects under these arrangements. The following tools may be used to reduce or mitigate the risk of payment failure by a public entity.

***Transparent Accounting Rules.*** Even though public entities in most countries are required to report future contractual commitments, in some countries the rules of public enterprises and public accounting may allow long-term contracts to be ignored in the financial statements or in budgets of the central government or municipalities. For instance, in many countries capital leases may be treated as operational leases for accounting purposes. In many cases, capital leases are done without reporting them, not even in the notes to the financial statements. Accounting for the present value of future contractual payments as on-balance-sheet debt in financial statements and public budgets gives a better picture of the capacity of the public entity to carry on additional debt. This introduces an element of control and thereby reduces the probability of default. Nevertheless, it does not mitigate the risk derived from poor management or a reduction in the public agency's future revenues.

***Trust Funds and Escrow Accounts.*** The use of externally managed trust funds and escrow accounts for mitigating contract failure risks should be explored to mitigate the risk of public-payment failure. A fund would be used to make payments on behalf of the public agency in case of default. To be efficient and acceptable, a fund of this sort should meet the following requirements:

1. The fund or account should be fed by contributions made by the agency that has to pay the revenues to the infrastructure project; otherwise the public agency would not be motivated to meet its commitments.
2. The size of the fund or account and the payments from the public entity should be jointly determined in the public bid that awards the project to the offer that minimizes both periodic payments and the size of the trust fund.
3. The funds should be managed independently of the public entity making the commitment.

As an alternative to using multilateral loans to finance directly the full cost of infrastructure investments, multilateral financial institutions should explore the possibility of providing financing to the public entity to fund these escrow accounts. With a significantly lower amount they could help mobilize private-sector financing for a project perceived as risky because revenues come from a public entity.

***Multilateral Bank Guarantees.*** The use of multilateral bank guarantees may also mitigate this risk. However, they may be less flexible than the above-mentioned funds to be integrated in a bid process. From a transparency standpoint, funds would be better than guarantees, because contributions from a public agency to the fund would be accounted as public debt, whereas the accounting standards of guarantees are not always clear. Furthermore, guarantees on the full face value of the private-sector financing would be more expensive than funds used to cover only a predetermined portion of the revenues.

## INVOLVEMENT BY PRIVATE FINANCING AND MANAGING: PRIVATE-FIRM REVENUES FROM FINAL CONSUMERS

These arrangements correspond with Zones I and III of Figure 1. Arrangements in both zones have similar features, and they have the best properties to deal with efficiency and fiscal issues. Arrangements for the provision of phone services in most countries are in Zone I, whereas the provision of water in Buenos Aires is made with an arrangement in Zone III.

**Efficiency, fiscal, and risk issues**

In Zone I a private firm owns, finances, and manages assets, with revenues coming from final users. A private firm providing infrastructure services with an arrangement in this area has strong incentives for balancing asset costs and quality improvements. Providing infrastructure services under these arrangements does not generate public expenditures, and incentives for proper asset maintenance are present. Assets and revenues can be used as guarantees or collateral for financing, allowing for greater flexibility in the management of risks. These cases are very close to the noninfrastructure or industrial cases. Investors bear the commercial risk and, depending on the price-setting mechanism, they may or may not bear the regulatory risk. If the market is truly liberalized, regulatory risk may be minimal, but in most cases it will still be present.

For example, in many countries the cellular telephone service falls into this zone, because a private company owns, finances, and manages the assets, and revenues come from final users. In some countries, regulatory risk exists, because service prices are set by regulations. In others, where there is competition, regulatory risk does not exist, as each firm is free to set its own price. In most countries, electricity distribution to the general public bears a regulatory risk, as the service is a monopoly and some regulatory agency must approve changes in rates.

In Zone III, a private firm manages and finances the assets, but does not own them, with revenues coming from final users. Arrangements in this zone have fiscal and efficiency effects similar to those in Zone I. Revenue risks are also similar in both zones. The relevant differences that derive from the lack of private ownership of assets in Zone III are the following:

1. Fixed assets cannot be used as collateral or as guarantees, making infrastructure financing harder. Only customer revenues and receivables may be used for this.
2. There is a lack of incentives to carry out appropriate maintenance or provide good service during the years prior to the transfer back to the public sector or to another firm winning the reconcession. However, if asset life is close to the concession period or if there are good chances of it winning back the concession, then the private firm has incentives to maintain the assets properly and provide quality service.

This arrangement is generally the case of potable water concessions, where old assets belong to the public sector and even new investments, financed by the private sector, may not be used as collateral, because they become part of the concession and belong to the public sector.

**Regulatory frameworks**

These arrangements usually rest on a regulatory framework to balance the interest of consumers and producers. A regulatory framework may reduce the incentives for the private firm to seek efficiency, and it introduces regulatory risk. Some guidelines for avoiding efficiency problems and ways of mitigating regulatory risk are discussed below.

If competition is present in the provision of an infrastructure service, the regulatory framework should focus on maintaining competition and ensuring that consumers receive appropriate information. Prices should be mainly set through the markets.

The presence of externalities and public goods may generate service allocations (quantity and prices) that are not efficient from a social point of view. For example, the consumption of electricity in rural areas will be less than optimal if electricity prices are set to cover the total cost of providing the service to those areas. In these cases, the government may be willing to provide some subsidies. However, if an infrastructure service is provided in a competitive market, subsidies may destroy the efficiency derived from competition. Direct subsidy schemes usually do not destroy competition, but their implementation is very expensive. Governments should balance the loss of efficiency from a reduction of competition and the cost of implementation with the equity gains from subsidy schemes.

Lack of competition in the provision of an infrastructure service requires that a regulatory framework set service prices to protect consumers from monopolistic behavior. Regulatory systems that rely heavily on the actual costs of the private firm for setting prices should be avoided. Otherwise, regulatory price systems may destroy incentives for the private firm to reduce costs.[8]

Prices of infrastructure services are far below cost in many developing countries where private-sector involvement is sought. However, private-sector involve-

[8] For a discussion of this point, see Smith and Klein [6].

ment requires that prices cover total costs and generate profits. Thus, at the beginning of its activities, a private firm may face social rejection and problems in collecting bills because of the price increases required to fill the gap between costs and prices. Regulatory frameworks should provide the private firm with tools to enforce consumer payments and include transitional systems that allow a gradual increase in prices.

### Mitigating regulatory risk

In public-private arrangements with private-firm revenues coming from final consumers, private revenues are usually exposed to regulatory risk because of a lack of competition in infrastructure markets. As previously discussed, private investors are not willing to accept this risk. Therefore, in designing these arrangements, authorities should contemplate schemes to reduce it, and, if at all possible, to introduce competition.

A well-functioning regulatory commission is one tool for reducing regulatory risk. A regulatory commission is a public entity of the central government with a certain degree of independence. The independence can be achieved by requiring that commission members have high professional qualifications and a term of office usually longer than that of the government. Most existing regulatory commissions in emerging markets are relatively new and, therefore, it is too soon to evaluate their actual performance in mitigating a long-term regulatory risk. However, they are appropriate for reducing regulatory risk under certain institutional arrangements. The following guidelines can be used to assess the capacity of a regulatory commission to reduce regulatory risk:

1. When the responsibility for supplying the infrastructure service is at the national level (telecommunications, energy generation, major highways), revenues come from final user prices, and when sponsors and operators are private firms with good reputations, regulatory commissions should be useful in mitigating regulatory risk. The presence of a private firm with a good reputation moves members of the regulatory commission to balance the interest of users and infrastructure firms. When prices are set at the national level, local governments cannot reject the decisions of the regulatory commission.
2. When primary responsibility for the infrastructure service is local (water, electricity distribution in some countries), a central regulatory commission may not be very useful. Conflicts between the central commission and the local government usually arise. In addition, the central commission often lacks the skills and staff necessary to evaluate many different infrastructure companies. For instance, a central regulatory commission for water and sewerage in an institutional environment in which service responsibilities rest mainly with municipalities may not be appropriate.
3. Investors in emerging markets tend not to trust regulatory commissions, whereas investors in mature markets rely on them. The reason for this is that mature markets have clearer rules than emerging markets on how authorities make decisions on the prices of infrastructure services, and the rules are designed to make decisions less centralized and less discretional. In mature markets, investors are able to appear to the judicial system if a regulatory decision is inappropriate. Investors usually trust judicial decisions in mature countries. Although many emerging markets have taken steps to make the decisions of regulatory authorities less discretionary, it takes time to gain the trust of investors. As the judicial systems are slow in emerging markets, investors feel that an erroneous regulatory decision may not be changed within a reasonable amount of time.

Most investors in emerging markets would like to have insurance for regulatory risk, but this is a limited option in the real world. Although existing political-risk insurance schemes cover currency inconvertibility risk, war, and expropriation or confiscation risk, they seldom cover regulatory risk. Specialized public agencies from developed countries are the main suppliers of political-risk insurance; these public agencies provide broad coverage for that portion of the project associated with exports or investments from each agency's home country, but they do not cover regulatory risk, although many agencies are allowed to do so. The Multilateral Investment Guarantee Agency of the World Bank (MIGA) provides political insurance in developing countries for those niches that bilateral agencies do not cover, but MIGA does not usually cover regulatory risk. Some private companies supply political-risk insurance, including traditional political risk and some form of insurance for regulatory risk, but premiums are extremely high and terms very short.

The promotion of regulatory-risk insurance is a challenge for developing countries attempting to increase private-sector participation and for multilateral financial institutions supporting these efforts. In promoting a market for insuring regulatory risk, the following points should be considered:

1. Distortion of financial markets should be minimized, and incentives for countries to comply with their regulatory framework should be established.
2. Regulatory-risk insurance can be supplied jointly with more conventional types of political-risk insurance, but it can also be supplied independently. The second route seems more promising because the skills required to assess both types of risks are different, and conventional political-risk insurance markets are mature, whereas regulatory-risk markets are new.
3. Regulatory-risk insurance requires simple, clear, and enforceable regulatory frameworks. Future prices are more predictable if they are set through a concession contract than if they are set through legislation. Concession contracts are more specific than regulatory laws because concession contracts have a more limited domain. In addition, the private firm may also impose conditions on a concession contract. Last, concession contracts are outside the political process, whereas regulatory laws are political in nature.

## CONCLUDING REMARKS

This article has analyzed different public–private arrangements for infrastructure provision and developed some guidelines to evaluate their capacity to reduce fiscal pressures and increase efficiency. As pointed out in the Introduction, these have been the leading forces for increasing private-sector participation. Some recommendations for mitigating the risk derived from public involvement, regulatory risk, and failure of public payments have been also established.

The following is a summary of the guidelines for assessing public–private arrangements and recommendations for mitigating risk.

1. **Public–private arrangements in which private firm revenues come from final users and assets are owned, managed, and financed by a private firm are the most conducive to increasing efficiency and reducing public expenditures. Therefore, if feasible, they should be preferred to other arrangements. Mitigation of regulatory risk is one relevant issue of these arrangements.**

Private infrastructure investors in these arrangements bear regulatory risk in addition to other risks (commercial risk, exchange rate risk, inconvertibility risk, expropriation risk, etc.). However, if some degree of competition is present, the regulatory risk will be less than would be the case without competition, because a natural monopoly requires price regulation, whereas services provided in a competitive market do not.

The mitigation of regulatory risk requires clear rules for regulators to make decisions and systems to ensure that regulators follow established rules and procedures. However, although clear rules and enforcing systems may be in place, time is required for investors to trust in them. Therefore, the multilateral development institutions should be prepared to promote coverage of regulatory risk.

2. **Public–private arrangements in which private-firm revenues come from a public agency and a private firm finances assets should be carefully designed to avoid or minimize negative fiscal impacts and efficiency problems. These arrangements often raise efficiency problems and increase public expenditures compared with other arrangements. Private investors bear a risk derived from the payment failure of the public entity. Schemes for mitigating this risk without enticing the public entity to default (moral hazard problems) need to be developed.**

These arrangements should meet the following requirements to mitigate fiscal and efficiency problems:

1. Proper accounting standards should be used to make sure that these arrangements are not used to overcome restrictions on public debt or to artificially enhance debt capacity.
2. Projects should be awarded through competitive bidding or other schemes to ensure that the present value of all public payments, including the cost of guaranteeing the public payments, is the minimum required for a private-sector involvement.
3. The private firm should manage the assets. If assets are managed by the public agency, the private-sector role is merely financial. Therefore, if acceptable, the present value of all public payments, including tax incentives, should be smaller than the financial cost of public-sector investment through a turnkey contract. However, this acceptability criterion is unlikely to hold.

3. **Public–private arrangement in which the public sector owns and finances assets and the private firm manages do not reduce significantly public expenditures, and private involvement is very limited. Nevertheless, they may improve operational efficiency in relation to arrangements in which a public agency undertakes all activities.**

These arrangements are used as a prior step for a larger private-sector involvement in countries where investors perceive a high political or economic risk. They are also used as a vehicle to subsidy consumption in cases where positive externalities are present. In such cases, the public sector finances infrastructure assets through taxes and the private firm covers operating and maintenance costs through payments on final consumers.

To conclude, two remarks should be made. The first one is that social acceptance is needed for a public–private arrangement to be sustainable in the long term. This acceptance depends upon its efficiency and capability to reduce fiscal pressures, but also upon other social values. Thus, an arrangement may be more socially acceptable than others with better efficiency and fiscal properties. However, the efficiency and the fiscal implications should be evaluated for a rational social decision. The second remark is that real-world arrangements for the provision of infrastructure services are complex. The most appropriate arrangements for one infrastructure service depend on the economic and social conditions of each country and on the features of each specific infrastructure service. Therefore, the analysis should be made on a case-by-case basis and no general rules should be applied. Nevertheless, problems and advantages of a real-life arrangement may be evaluated with references to the relatively simple arrangements presented in this article. ■

## REFERENCES

1. Klein, M., and Roger, N., 1994, "Back to the future: The potential in infrastructure privatization," in R. O'Brien (Ed.), *Finance and the International Economy*, Oxford University Press, pp. 42–68.
2. Bensman, M., 1995, October, "Forging the missing link," *Inst. Inv.*, 113–126.
3. World Bank, 1994, *World Development Report 1994: Infrastructure for Development.* Author, Washington, DC.
4. Guislain, P., and Klerf, M., 1995, "Concessions—Overview of PPI techniques," Draft FDP Note, World Bank, Washington.
5. Mas-Colell, Whiston, M.D., and Green, J., 1995, *Microeconomic Theory.* Oxford University Press, New York.
6. Smith, W., and Klein, M., 1994, "Issues and options for East Asia," World Bank, Infrastructure Regulation, Working Paper, Washington DC.

# [9]

# Highway Franchising: Pitfalls and Opportunities

*By* EDUARDO ENGEL, RONALD FISCHER, AND ALEXANDER GALETOVIC*

Most developing countries urgently need massive highway construction programs. For this reason, a growing number of countries are auctioning highway franchises to the private sector. In these auctions, it is usual for the regulator to fix the length of the highway franchise, say, for 20 years, and for firms to bid on the toll. The benefits from privatizing highways are well known by now: gains in efficiency, avoidance of "white elephants," easier access to financing, and fewer political pressures to reduce tolls. Assigning the franchise in a competitive auction should lead to the same outcome that would be obtained in a competitive market: competition *for* the field rather than *in* the field (Edwin Chadwick, 1859). Nevertheless, worldwide experience shows that there are some important pitfalls that offset these benefits. Most prominent among them are (a) the frequent use of government guarantees, thereby reducing incentives to control construction costs, and (b) government bailouts for almost every franchise that faces financial trouble.[1] Underlying this unhappy experience is the fact that traffic forecasts are notoriously imprecise, making the highway business very risky. This fact, combined with informational asymmetries, implies that there may be important welfare differences between alternative auction systems (Oliver Williamson, 1985).

In this paper we present a simple framework for evaluating different mechanisms for awarding franchise contracts. We argue that many of the problems stem from the fact that franchises are typically awarded for a fixed period whose length does not depend on demand realizations. We present a simple auction that implements efficient contracts, least-present-value-of-revenue (LPVR) auctions. We will argue that this type of auction solves many of the difficulties that have plagued highway franchises around the world.

This paper originated in work performed for the highway construction and improvement program currently underway in Chile. Investments of more than U.S. $3 billion (6 percent of GDP) in new and existing highways will be auctioned between 1996 and 1999. The importance of this program cannot be overstated: one of the major threats to Chile's solid economic performance in the last decade is the lack of adequate infrastructure, particularly highways. There are early signs pointing toward the problems mentioned above: the government is providing generous guarantees (70 percent of building costs), and there is pressure to renegotiate the terms of one of the existing franchises (the "El Melón" tunnel, inaugurated in 1995). Furthermore, many of the international firms participating in the auctions have previous experience renegotiating contract terms to the detriment of governments, taxpayers, and toll users.

## I. A Simple Model

For simplicity assume that demand is constant and completely inelastic. Demand may be high ($Q_H$), with probability $\pi_H$, or low ($Q_L$), with probability $\pi_L$, where $\pi_L = 1 - \pi_H$ and $Q_H > Q_L$.[2] The cost of building the highway is the same for all firms and equal to $I$, which is common knowledge among firms, but unknown to the government. There are no maintenance or operation costs, and the toll is

* Centro de Economía Aplicada, Departamento de Ingeniería Industrial, Universidad de Chile Av. República 701, Santiago, Chile; Engel is also affiliated with the NBER. We gratefully acknowledge the support of the Mellon Foundation. We thank Alvaro González, who first suggested that we study the properties of an auction based on least total revenue, a special case of the LVPR mechanism with a zero discount rate.

[1] For evidence substantiating both statements, see the case studies in José Antonio Gómez-Ibáñez and John Meyer (1993).

[2] These and other simplifying assumptions are relaxed in Engel et al. (1997).

equal to $P$. After the franchise ends, tolls fall to zero. All firms are identical, risk-averse expected-utility maximizers, with preferences represented by the strictly concave Von Neumann-Morgenstern utility function $u(\cdot)$.[3] Auctions are competitive, and the planner's objective is to minimize the expected value of tolls paid by users subject to the constraint that firms be willing to build the highway.

### A. *Socially Optimal Auctions*

It is useful to start by considering the problem solved by a social planner who knows $I$. Denote the present value of the income received by the franchise-holder with high and low demand by $\text{PVI}_H$ and $\text{PVI}_L$, respectively. Then,

$$\text{(1)}\quad \text{PVI}_i \equiv \int_0^{T_i} PQ_i e^{-rt}\, dt = \frac{PQ_i(1-e^{-rt})}{r} \qquad i = \text{H, L}$$

where $r$ is the discount rate common to all firms and $T_H$ and $T_L$ denote the length of the franchise when demand is, respectively, high or low. The planner chooses $T_H$, $T_L$, and $P$ to minimize the expected value of toll payments $\pi_L\text{PVI}_L + \pi_H\text{PVI}_H$ subject to the constraint that firms be willing to participate, that is, $\pi_L u(\text{PVI}_L - I) + \pi_H u(\text{PVI}_H - I) = u(0)$, where $u(0)$ is the level of utility attained by a firm not undertaking the project.

It is easy to see that $\text{PVI}_L = \text{PVI}_H = I$ solves the planner's problem. Since the franchise-holder is risk-averse, it is efficient to insure her completely. To do so, the planner fixes a toll high enough to ensure that the franchise-holder loses no money when demand is low (i.e., $P \geq rI/Q_L$). It then follows from (1) that, since $Q_H > Q_L$, the planner chooses $T_H < T_L$ (the term of the franchise is shorter when demand is high). Note that users pay the same amount in both states of nature and thus face no risk.

When the planner does not know $I$, consider the following auction, which we call least-present-value-of-revenue (LPVR) auction, in which (a) the regulator fixes a toll $P$ larger than $rI/Q_L$;[4] (b) the franchise is won by the firm that asks the least present value of toll revenue; (c) the franchise ends when the present value of toll revenue is equal to the franchise-holder's bid; and (d) the rate used to discount toll revenue is equal to $r$. In a competitive auction, firms offer PVI such that $\pi_L u(\text{PVI} - I) + \pi_H u(\text{PVI} - I) = u(0)$; that is, $\text{PVI} = I$. Thus, we have shown that an LPVR auction implements the social optimum even when the planner ignores key data such as $I$, $\pi_i$, or $Q_i$.[5] Moreover, note that equilibrium bids are a function of $I$ only. Demand data such as $\pi_i$ or $Q_i$ do not affect a firm's bid. It follows that there is no winner's curse.

### B. *Fixed-Term Franchises*

Almost all mechanisms that have previously been used to auction highway franchises around the world fix the franchise term in advance.[6] In the mechanism currently in use in Chile, the regulator fixes the term $T$ and allocates the franchise to the firm that offers to charge the lowest toll. Competition among firms implies that the winning bid $P$ will satisfy

$$\text{(2)}\quad \pi_L u[P\cdot \text{PVQ}_L(T) - I] + \pi_H u[P\cdot \text{PVQ}_H(T) - I] = u(0)$$

where $\text{PVQ}_i(T)$, $i$ = L, H, denotes the present value of vehicle flow when the franchise lasts $T$ years and demand is, respectively, low or high.[7] Note, first, that in this case

[3] In our experience, potential bidders are risk-averse. One explanation may be the substantial percentage of building costs that must be financed by the firm itself.

[4] We assume that the planner has an upper bound on $rI/Q_L$.

[5] In this example, the result continues to hold if the planner is risk-averse.

[6] We are aware of no exceptions.

[7] The same equation holds when the regulator fixes $P$ and the franchise is allocated to the firm asking the shortest term $T$.

$P \cdot PVQ_L(T) < I < P \cdot PVQ_H(T)$: the franchise-holder loses money when demand is low and thus does not receive full insurance, leading to $\pi_L PVI_L(T) + \pi_H PVI_H(T) > I$, so that users pay more on average. Second, in the aggregate, users also face risk, as in present-value terms they pay more when demand is high. Third, the winning bid is a function not only of $I$, but also of demand data $\pi_i$ and $Q_i$. Thus the winner's curse is likely to occur.[8]

## II. Comparison

### A. *Risk*

An important defect of fixed-term mechanisms is that they impose demand risk on the franchise-holder and make users pay more on average. In Engel et al. (1996), we estimate that the savings from switching to LPVR auctions in Chile are 33 percent of the value of investment.

The intuition behind these results is quite simple: a fixed term makes it possible for a franchise-holder to lose money even when the road is profitable in the long run because the term of the franchise may be too short given the state of demand. In fact, as shown by the previous analysis, in a fixed-term auction, firms will bid tolls that result in losses in some states. These losses are compensated by states where the term is more than long enough to pay for the road. In contrast, an LPVR auction takes advantage of the fact that roads may pay for themselves even when traffic grows slower than expected, provided that the franchise term be longer. In doing so it improves bad states and worsens good states, thereby reducing the risk borne by franchise-holders. Moreover, given that revenue from tolls is paid by users and that they pay the same amount in all states, they bear no risk. An LVPR auction eliminates demand risk![9] The general lesson is that, when the timing of revenues is uncertain but the present value of the income stream is sufficient to pay building costs in all states of the world, a contract with a state-independent term creates unnecessary risk for both parties. Thus, risk is not exogenous, but depends on the type of contract.

Under pressure from firms and financiers, the high risk in highway franchising has led governments to provide guarantees. The magnitude of the demand risk facing the owner of a fixed-term franchise is illustrated in Table 1 for the Chilean case. This table shows the rates of growth for the number of motor vehicles paying tolls during the past decade at the three busiest highways near Santiago. Despite the fact that the past decade has been Chile's most stable during this century, with no recessions and with GDP growing 6 percent on average per annum, traffic growth rates have fluctuated considerably, both across years and across roads in a given year. High demand risk and the use of fixed-term auctions explain why the Chilean government has pledged to cover any difference between actual toll income and the sum needed to pay for 70 percent of the government's expected construction costs. These guarantees are undesirable, not only because of government budget constraints, but also because one of the main virtues of private franchises is the reduction in the likelihood of white elephants. Since white elephants are

TABLE 1—VEHICLES PAYING TOLLS: GROWTH RATES IN PERCENTAGES

| | Highway | | |
|---|---|---|---|
| Year | Angostura | Zapata | Lampa |
| 1987 | 8.8 | 21.5 | 3.8 |
| 1988 | 15.0 | 14.4 | 13.4 |
| 1989 | 11.7 | 13.1 | 15.9 |
| 1990 | 4.5 | 8.1 | 8.9 |
| 1991 | 8.7 | 7.2 | 6.8 |
| 1992 | 12.4 | 5.2 | 18.0 |
| 1993 | 6.7 | 2.9 | 8.8 |
| 1994 | 7.8 | 3.9 | 16.2 |
| 1995 | 9.4 | 4.9 | 12.5 |

*Notes:* The rates correspond to the growth in the flow of vehicles from one year to the next. For example the vehicle flow through the Angostura tollbooth in 1987 was 8.8-percent larger than in 1986.
*Source:* Ministry of Public Works, Chile.

[8] Firms participating in road auctions in Chile may have been victims of the curse. When the "El Melón" tunnel was auctioned in 1993 to the firm offering the highest annual payment for 20 years, the winner's bid was more than three times the second-highest bid.

[9] Whether this is desirable depends on the source of demand uncertainty. For details see Engel et al. (1997).

usually the result of pressures by interest groups that are better represented in the political process than taxpayers, they should be easily detected by private firms. Thus, it is desirable that franchise-holders bear the risk associated with constructing a road that cannot finance itself. Finally, guarantees reduce the incentives of financiers to screen firms and projects, creating a standard moral-hazard problem.

### B. *Renegotiation*

Franchises suffer renegotiation problems due to the incompleteness of contracts. Under fixed-term franchises, future income projections are highly subjective and cannot be inferred from accounting data, which worsens the problems. Opportunistic renegotiations become more likely for several reasons. First, as equation (2) suggests, competition leads to losses in some states of nature. Second, the taxpayer or user is unable to estimate the wealth transfer to the franchise-holder that often results from a renegotiation. Thus governments bear a lower political cost if they cave in to franchise-holders. Third, fixed-term auctions encourage lowballing in the expectation of renegotiation, favoring firms with political connections, not the most efficient firms. Fourth, the lack of an objective standard facilitates expropiation of the franchise without fair compensation, or the lowering of tolls to reap political benefits by arguing that the franchise-holder is making ''excessive'' profits. While such takings are not frequent, this risk has discouraged franchising in some countries (see Gómez-Ibáñez and Meyer, 1993).

An LPVR auction reduces the problems caused by contract incompleteness. This is partly due to the fact that the term of the franchise depends on the state of demand. Big losses (prompting franchise-holders to ask for renegotiation) and big profits (which may encourage governments to change the contract to prevent ''excessive'' profits) are less likely. In addition LPVR auctions reduce the scope for renegotiations. Under fixed-term franchises, renegotiations usually concern raising tolls or extending terms. In contrast, under an LPVR auction the effect of raising tolls is just an earlier end to the franchise, and term extensions are impossible by definition. This means that any renegotiation involves an explicit wealth transfer. The winning bid reveals the revenue required by the franchise-holder to obtain a normal profit; it is a clear benchmark for any wealth transfer. Since such a simple figure is easier to understand than a calculation of expected future revenue, government actions can be scrutinized by public opinion. Thus opportunistic renegotiations favoring a franchise-holder have a higher political cost, and it is easier to contest an arbitrary regulatory taking before a court.

### C. *Flexibility*

The flip side of opportunistic renegotiation is that there are plausible circumstances under which it becomes socially desirable to modify the contract. Consider the case where traffic grows much faster than expected and it is desirable to widen the highway. In such circumstances there is a potential Pareto improvement in modifying the original contract. Under a fixed-term franchise, however, it is difficult to strike an agreement, because both parties can argue endlessly about the ''fair'' compensation for early termination. Under an LPVR franchise the winning bid minus the (discounted) toll revenue received is a fair compensation for ending the franchise. If the regulator desires to widen the road she can end the franchise, pay the fair compensation, and auction the new project. Similarly, raising or lowering tolls does not affect the franchise-holder's revenue, since the term of the franchise automatically adjusts.[10]

### D. *Effort*

A real limitation of LPVR franchises is that incentives favoring efficient marketing are smaller than when the term is fixed. The reason is that with LPVR mechanisms, any marketing effort that translates into higher demand shortens the term of the franchise but does not change profits. This implies that under LPVR

[10] This analysis ignores maintenance and operating costs. These are relatively small in comparison to the cost of the projects and are fairly easy to estimate.

auctions franchise-holders have fewer incentives than under fixed-term franchises to invest in demand-increasing features such as road quality and maintenance or speedy attention at toll booths. For this reason, LPVR auctions probably need to be supplemented with institutions that determine and enforce minimum quality standards on the franchise (see Jean Tirole, 1997).

### E. *Congestion*

In Section I, we showed that LPVR auctions replicate the social planner's auction conditional on the self-financing constraint (i.e., it is a "second best"). For the case in which there is enough traffic for optimal congestion tolls to finance investment in the highway, it is clear that LPVR auctions achieve the first-best solution to the social planner's problem. The reason for this is that LPVR auctions decouple the financing problem from the optimal toll-setting problem. This property is especially relevant for urban projects.[11]

## III. Conclusion

The massive highway construction program recently launched in Chile illustrates the pitfalls and the opportunities facing governments that privatize roads. Brazil and Argentina are embarking on similar programs, and other developing countries are expected to follow suit. It is too early to tell whether current interest in infrastructure privatization is part of one more privatization–nationalization cycle (see Michael Klein and Neil D. Roger, 1994), or the beginning of a definitive trend toward privatization. The latter possibility is more likely if franchises are flexible and can avoid white elephants, undesirable renegotiations, and government guarantees (explicit or implicit). In this article we have argued that LPVR auctions are much better suited to achieving these goals than are fixed-term auctions.

[11] According to recent press reports, Chile's Ministry of Public Works is planning to use the LPVR mechanism to auction urban highway projects.

## REFERENCES

**Chadwick, Edwin.** "Results of Different Principles of Legislation in Europe." *Journal of the Royal Statistical Society*, Series A, 1859, 22.

**Engel, Eduardo M. R. A.; Fischer, Ronald D. and Galetovic, Alexander.** "A New Method to Auction Highway Franchises." Documentos de Trabajo CEA Nr. 13, Department of Industrial Engineering, University of Chile, 1996.

______. "Auctioning a Road by Income." Documentos de Trabajo CEA Nr. 21, Department of Industrial Engineering, University of Chile, 1997.

**Gómez-Ibáñez, José Antonio and Meyer, John.** *Going private: The international experience with transport privatization*. Washington, DC: Brookings Institution, 1993.

**Klein, Michael and Roger, Neil D.** "Back to the Future: The Potential in Infrastructure Privatisation," in R. O'Brien, ed., *Finance and the international economy*, Vol. 8. Oxford: Oxford University Press, 1994, pp. 42–68.

**Tirole, Jean.** "Highway Franchising in Chile: A Comment." *Estudios Públicos*, 1997 (forthcoming; in Spanish).

**Williamson, Oliver.** *The economic institutions of capitalism*. New York: Free Press, 1985.

# Part III
# Organization of PPPs

# [10]

# Philosophical aspects of the public/private sector partnership

## Introduction

It is considered axiomatic, in the development of public/private sector partnerships, that both parties wish to maximize the chances of project success; to achieve what has been termed a 'win–win' outcome. In order that this may be achieved however the structure of the partnership and the working relationship between the people involved requires very careful consideration and, as Mody[1] points out, establishing such a partnership requires a clear understanding of the relative strengths and weaknesses of both parties in addition to an understanding of their histories. On the one hand government often believes that it can only fulfil its functions by maintaining close control over all aspects of the project, but on the other hand this process may be perceived by the private sector partner as an unwarranted interference with the way he wishes to run his business. Hurst,[2] for example, writes that

> Even in most developed states such as the United Kingdom, there is a tendency for government to retain control of projects through a complex approvals procedure, especially where design and construction of projects is concerned. In private-sector electricity projects, especially in Asia, the state is often involved at every stage of the project, going far beyond the usual 'planning' rules, treating the private-sector generators as though they were part of the public sector.
>
> This extends to requiring the right to review and approve all design drawings, the specifications for each item of equipment, the right to act as an additional *de facto* project manager during the construction phase of a project, the right to receive hundreds of 'as-built' drawings for every aspect of the station, and the right to visit and inspect the station. Vast quantities of corporate information on the project company and/or the sponsors are often required ...

*Privatized infrastructure: the role of government*

The same point is also made in connection with the first two prisons to be commissioned under the British government's Private Finance Initiative programme. Price and Ivison[3] comment that, although the focus of the contract was on the provision of a custody service rather than on the construction of a building, and thus the design and construction risk lay solely with the private sector partner, none the less government insisted on the appointment of an independent engineer, who expected to have an input into design matters. The situation was apparently only resolved when the role of the independent engineer was redefined such that:

> ... government [had] the comfort of an independent adviser who was familiar with its concerns doing an initial design-check of the prison and monitoring construction on site, but also enabled the consortium to be innovative in its design and construction methods.

The privatized infrastructure developer's ideal market would probably be one in which they were able to provide services to, or on behalf of government, to a captive market, at prices to be fixed solely by themselves, whilst at the same time being subject to an absolute minimum of regulatory or governmental control. Unfortunately, however, history shows that this kind of *laissez-faire* approach does not work very well.

The major rationale usually put forward for governmental regulation and control of projects is that the government may, at some stage, become owner or operator of the utility, either because ownership of the project assets falls to be transferred to the host government at some stage during the concession or, in the event of default by the concessionaire or project operator, government may be forced to take over operation of the utility in order to preserve some essential public service. While these may in some cases be genuine concerns, it is obvious that any increase in government 'interference' is likely to increase project risk and thus project costs and in turn therefore the cost to the user. Government is therefore faced with a considerable dilemma. The latter concern basically envisages some failure of the concessionaire to perform his obligations. This concern might well be real, but as a starting position it seems somewhat negative. It is not in anyone's interest for these schemes to fail financially or otherwise once they are operational. A financial failure, or indeed any failure of the operator to deliver the required level of service which is serious enough for government to terminate the concession contract early, is bad news for all of the parties involved. Operation of the utility by the government itself is often the very eventuality which government wished to avoid, and may be the reason for privatized operation in the first place.

Smith and Walker[4] have identified those high-level factors in which success appears to be necessary in order that each of the major project participants in a BOT infrastructure project have the maximum chance of achieving their goals. They are:

(*a*) A genuine desire for a win–win solution with common agreement between the parties as to their mutual and individual objectives. These objectives must be explicit, realistic and achievable.

(*b*) A complex BOT requires a strong, persistent, persuasive and politically skilled project leader willing and able to fight for the scheme.

(*c*) Adequate and accurate data and risk assessment of both the procurement and operational phases, with responsibility for managing the risks placed with the party best able to control them.

(*d*) An honest and accurate calculation of the project economics, including the length of the concession, which incorporates probability assessments of the influence on income and expenditure of the risks and uncertainties previously identified.

(*e*) Choice of the correct procurement methodology for the construction phase.

The 'mechanics' of the government role have been examined in earlier chapters, and although the exercise of these largely regulatory functions does not in itself *demand* a partnership approach, the additional factors outlined above, coupled with the need for governments to offer increasing degrees of comfort and support of various kinds in order to persuade financiers and investors to fund any one particular project in preference to another, means that a true partnership in which government takes a share of the responsibilities, in exchange for a share of the benefits, in both the constructional and operational phases of the project, would appear to be in the interests of both parties. The question which then remains is what form this partnership should take and how it is to be facilitated.

It is also important to remember that governments often come and go within relatively short time periods. The life of a particular administration may represent only a small fraction of the length of the concession itself, and subsequent governments have been known to wish to revisit agreements made by their predecessors. Two examples, the Dabhol power project in India and the Bangkok Second Stage Expressway in Thailand are reviewed in Chapter 10. In at least one of these projects the primary reason for wishing to revisit the original negotiations centred around allegations of corruption. In order that allegations of this kind may be refuted, it is plainly essential to ensure a high degree of public accountability in all government action and decision making. The initial negotiation process must therefore be both totally transparent and accurately documented.

There are evidently significant philosophical issues here which require detailed and careful consideration, and it is suggested that a 'team' approach involving shared perceptions and shared goals between the public and private sector representatives is likely to be more effective than the very commercial customer/service-provider relationship envisaged by the United Kingdom government's Private Finance Initiative, or the more conventional purchaser/supplier or 'pseudo-agency' approaches commonly used elsewhere. Reijniers[5] analyses the working of just such a partnership in Holland.

Different patterns of partnership formed with different kinds of people may be required at different stages of the process. During the initial stages, prior to the appointment of the concessionaire, particularly if a competitive tendering process is involved, governments must obviously maintain a proper distance between themselves and their tenderers, and must be seen to be impartial to all of the competitors, but once the concession is signed then it can be convincingly argued that government should perhaps take on a much more active partnership role during the construction and operational phases. It is however important here that government is seen to be actively contributing to the *success* of the project and not merely interfering in the affairs of its private sector partners.

## Team building for major projects

Hurst,[2] writing about the construction of private power plants, reports that

> Governments are not always well-advised in structuring their private infrastructure initiatives, with the result that the structure and method proposed to encourage private-sector investors into infrastructure projects has led to confrontation between developers and governments over an unnecessarily complex, and restrictive, privately financed infrastructure project regime in which governments remain intimately involved at every stage and level.

This situation is plainly not conducive to achieving the required win–win outcome, and it would appear likely that better results would be obtained from a more integrated approach. There is now considerable research evidence (see, for example, Albanese[6]) to suggest that successful project outcomes are more likely to be achieved if time is spent on building an integrated project team early in the process. Although project team building in construction has generally been studied mainly at the operational level, for example in order to facilitate more effective construction project procurement, construction planning, or construction processes, nevertheless some of the objectives of the conventional team-building process would appear to be equally applicable to the public/private sector partnership itself. Objectives such as developing a project based culture, which places the highest value on *project* goals rather than *individual* or *organizational* goals, diffusing the project culture, together with the authority to make decisions, to project managers and others who are in a position to directly facilitate project results, and providing ongoing support to maintain the project culture appear to be directly applicable to concession contracts for infrastructure.

A team building approach embodying shared goals requires trust, and this in turn means that each party has to be prepared to be honest and open about its own organizational goals and objectives. The chances of overall project success are improved if all parties have a stake in the successful completion of the project, but this is all meaningless unless the team ethos is carried down through all levels of the organization. Hurst[2] also writes that:

> It is not uncommon for developers to encounter resentment in negotiations with governments; entrenched bureaucracies, especially those used to running state monopoly utilities, are notoriously reluctant to surrender any control to private developers, and thus sometimes strongly resist the entry of private developers, regardless of what their ministers say.

Shields,[7] whilst discussing road and bridge projects, makes the same point:

> I believe that most of us will have experienced the schism between those politicians (and senior civil servants) who embrace the privatisation concept and others who adopt unhelpful attitudes. Such persons are often found typically at lower levels in the administration/civil service, but nonetheless are not lacking in negative controls on project progress.

The historically bureaucratic and strictly hierarchical organization which typically characterizes most public bodies is well recognized and all too familiar, but has no place in a culture where the *project goals* are paramount. None the less Wilson *et al.*,[8] reviewing some contemporary American experience, make the point that introducing partnership concepts into organizations which have a long experience in operating in an adversarial way poses a major management problem. Overcoming entrenched adversarial attitudes may be a long and painful process.

*Privatized infrastructure: the role of government*

It might, at first sight, appear that the establishment of an inter-organizational project team is very easy, and is simply a matter of each party appointing personnel to work together in managing the project, but Albanese,[6] in a study of American practice, points out that the results from this type of approach are rarely satisfactory. He goes on to postulate that a structured team building process is required, the purpose of which:

> ... is a project focused process that brings together key stakeholders in the project's outcomes ... Its purpose is to improve project results by developing a common mission statement of shared goals, building and developing trust and commitment, resolving differences, removing road-blocks, creating interdependence and accountability among team members, and developing problem solving skills.

Cowan[9] recommends a three step team building strategy:

(*a*) establish top-level relationships between the participants' organizations
(*b*) identify all of the problems which might be expected to occur during the project
(*c*) build a project team that responds quickly to critical issues.

Similar ideals have been formalized in other areas requiring complex contractual relationships, particularly where the parties involved are more concerned with maximizing the chances that the contract will be concluded satisfactorily and to the advantage of all parties than in attempting to provide legal remedies when the contract has already been breached and the project is already on the road to failure. Such an approach requires a fundamental shift in attitude by all of the parties involved, away from the traditional contractual, confrontational and litigious approach, and towards an approach based on common goals and shared obligations and responsibilities, with problems being resolved through discussion and negotiation rather than by recourse to law. Such an arrangement requires trust, and a willingness to compromise on detailed points so that the contract can be substantially performed to everyone's advantage.

This is not always easy to achieve, even when both parties are keen that it should be so. Reijniers,[5] for example, while discussing Dutch experience with such projects over a period of some eight years, reports that differences in the corporate culture, objectives, and political responsibilities between the public and private sector partners more often than not means that the common goals are not as common as they might appear at first sight. He reports that an analysis of a number of projects indicates the following common major problem areas:

(*a*) A mutual lack of confidence of the partners in each other, often coupled with a lack of clarity about objectives and working methods and a lack of clarity about the distribution of authority. This is made worse by a lack of experience in working together.
(*b*) Conflicting interests and power struggles.
(*c*) Exaggerated expectations and a lack of clarity about the distribution of input, risks and benefits.
(*d*) Political changes during implementation and a laborious political decision making process.
(*e*) Inadequate project management.

The obligations, responsibilities and rights of the various parties must, of course, be enshrined in some form of formal contract or project agreement. The kind of 'project oriented' organization envisaged above however leads to the view that the contract might itself embody the essence of this alternative business approach. This specific issue is considered later in the context of the concession agreement.

Reijniers[5] goes on to identify the following critical success factors for successful public/private sector partnerships:

(*a*) key decision makers form part of the project team from the beginning
(*b*) measurable results are essential and this demands clear goals and well organized phasing
(*c*) a 'goal-directed' project but with a focus on results
(*d*) good progress monitoring and control
(*e*) an independent project team with an independent leader reporting to a steering group of senior management
(*f*) early agreement on the assignment of political and economic risks
(*g*) the private sector must be allowed to fulfil its entrepreneurial role
(*h*) mutual confidence.

These factors, coupled with the objectives referred to above, lead to consideration of the management approach which has commonly come to be known as 'partnering', something which has been the subject of considerable construction industry research in America and in Australia in the recent past.

## Partnering

Crowley and Karim[10] summarize the theoretical basis upon which the ideas of partnering are built. They define partnering as '... a means of resolving interorganizational conflict', and they see partnering as a device for removing those inter-organizational barriers which tend to prevent project success. Organizational barriers constitute the boundaries which limit a company's organization and culture, and which define and segregate the organization from others. These organizational barriers may, in theoretical terms, be to some extent both flexible and permeable. Flexibility and permeability tend to be greater in private sector organizations, whereas in public sector bodies the boundaries tend to be both rigid and impermeable. Partnering centres attention on the project not the individual parties involved, and the resultant project-centred culture requires that these organizational barriers must be modified. Overcoming the rigidity and impermeability inherent in the traditional organizational structure of public organizations is extremely difficult, involving as it almost always does, strongly entrenched attitudes, established and rigid codes of behaviour, a hierarchy which has often historically discouraged personal initiative, and a consequent unwillingness for individuals to assume personal responsibility. Finding a solution to these problems is however essential if such bodies are to successfully enter into effective partnering agreements with commercial organizations.

Crowley and Karim go on to define the partnering process as creating an organization which:

> ... implements a cooperative strategy by modifying and supplementing the traditional boundaries that separate companies in a competitive climate. In this way partnering wraps the major project participants into an alliance that create a cohesive atmosphere for the project team members to openly interact and perform.

Hellard,[11] writing about partnering in construction, sums up the partnering ethos very well:

> The partnering concept is not a new way of doing business – some always conduct themselves in this manner. It is going back to the way people used to do business when a person's word was their bond and people accepted responsibility. Partnering is not a contract, but a recognition that every contract includes an implied covenant of good faith.

A partnering approach is usually supported by a written partnering agreement, a non-contractual agreement, signed not by the organizations but by the actual people who will be directly involved, which sets out the essence of the parties' mutually agreed obligations. There is considerable evidence that the act of negotiating and writing down the terms of the partnering agreement helps to fix them in the minds of the participants, and it is therefore fundamental to the success of the process that these terms should be developed and written by the actual members of the project team. It is however common for the parties to employ an outside facilitator to aid the process. The role of the facilitator is simply to help the parties to develop the required 'team ethos', to develop the partnering agreement, and to help the parties to stick to the bargain they have made; ownership of the whole process must rest unconditionally with the parties themselves. One possible form of partnering agreement for a BOT tolled road concession might look something like that shown in Box 9.1.

*Box 9.1 Example project partnering agreement*

**Partnering Agreement**

We, the partners of the Blanktown Bypass toll road concession, agree to work together for the whole period of the concession in such a way as to ensure the design, construction and operation of a high quality project. We hereby affirm that we are one team, and that we are jointly committed to achieving the following objectives:

- Design, construct and operate a high quality scheme to the continuing satisfaction of all concerned.
- Achieve or better all programme targets.
- Maintain an effective team relationship.
- Operate effective communications systems.
- Resolve any contentious issues at the lowest possible level in a timely and progressive way.
- Achieve or better all environmental objectives.

We also jointly agree to use our best endeavours to develop specific action plans to improve problem resolution procedures and to ensure successful completion of the project.

Signed:

## The operation phase

The operational phase of the project, so far as government is concerned, is usually seen as revolving around ensuring that the concessionaire maintains the levels of service and charges set out in the concession agreement. In many projects this is relegated to a monitoring and inspection role, with perhaps an auditing role where the project agreement included a mechanism for profit sharing or toll increase.

*Privatized infrastructure: the role of government*

There are many parallels here with facilities management contracts. The operation of a toll road is not conceptually very different from operating a railway, a hospital or a prison, in that all must provide specified services to a guaranteed and measurable standard within a predetermined budget, although there are obvious differences in the level of difficulty and the kind of expertise required. Smith[12] identifies three options for facilities management contracts for health care buildings:

(*a*) An integrated facilities management contract with a single commercial partner delivering both management and services. In this model the commercial partner takes full and complete responsibility for providing management, services, and maintenance facilities in accordance with detailed and measurable objective standards as set out in the contract.

(*b*) Contract facilities management services working alongside in-house management. In this option the commercial partner provides services and maintenance at an agreed cost, with management being provided by the host organization.

(*c*) Collaborative ventures between National Health Service trusts and a commercial partner. Here representatives of the host organization and the commercial partner establish an independent joint venture company in which both parties must accept their share of the project responsibilities. Such arrangements usually rely upon complete trust and transparency, and frequently incorporate management partnerships and open-book accounting.

All these generic models are equally applicable to infrastructure projects. In practice however, to date, most infrastructure agreements most closely resemble option (*a*), with the private sector operating company being solely responsible for providing a service as specified in the original project agreement. But this model has severe deficiencies, perhaps the greatest of which is that government needs to establish and maintain some kind of monitoring system in order to ensure that the private sector operator fulfils his obligations. In the case of infrastructure perhaps the most crucial areas of operation are those to do with safety and maintenance, and there is a real danger that, in these areas, the enforcement of government's inspection and supervisory role can easily lead to a deterioration in the relationship thus leading to a classic 'us and them' conflict.

It is at least possible, and it is certainly within the ethos of the partnering ideal, that this problem may be eased by the use of operations contracts closer in form to option (*c*) above. This model comes closest to the ideas of partnership and commitment to shared project goals outlined earlier. In this model government and the private sector partner work together to ensure not only that the operator provides the levels of service set out in the original agreement, but also to ensure that government does not actively obstruct the private sector operator from making a reasonable profit. Agreements such as the modified toll adjustment formula as used in recent Hong Kong projects (see Chapter 8) begin to move towards this model, but there is scope for much more joint participation to better ensure the desired win–win outcome. Smith[12] does however again point out the need for changes in the conventional style of thinking of many public sector bodies if participative models of this type are to work effectively. These changes will include the need for public sector staff to accept the demands of a business culture, to accept that it is not in some way immoral for the operator to make profits, and to accept the need for devolution of management control and decision making.

## The concession agreement

The document in which the roles of the two main parties involved in the project, the host government and the concessionaire, are summarized and formalized is the project concession agreement. This document, usually with a number of appendices and supporting documents, establishes the concession rules and sets out formally the various contractual rights and obligations of the main parties. There is, of course, a whole network of subsidiary contracts between all of the other parties involved (e.g. the funders, the construction contractors, the equity shareholders), but the project concession agreement is the main plank upon which the entire enterprise will stand or fall.

The concession agreement is a contract, and is thus enforceable through the courts, and one of its main purposes will be to stipulate how the various project risks are to be divided between the parties. It is as well to remember that the host government, being the granter of the concession, is usually regarded as being in the strongest bargaining position when it comes to negotiation of the terms of the contract, but this is not always the case and the true balance of negotiating power will often depend upon just how important the project is to the host government and how keen is the competition among potential concessionaires.

Vintner[13] proposes the following as the principal issues which ought to be covered by the concession agreement:

(*a*) The nature and length of the concession, scope of the works, and operation of the completed utility.

(*b*) A specification of what is to be provided.
(*c*) The extent of permitted variations to the specification.
(*d*) The performance standards to be achieved together with any warranties required and penalties which might be applied for non-conformance.
(*e*) Any undertakings made by the granter of the concession (e.g. property development rights, ensured revenue agreements, income from existing utilities, etc.).
(*f*) The tolls, prices or other payments to be charged, together with any arrangements for subsequent adjustments.
(*g*) General legal 'stabilization' provisions to ensure the concessionaire's rights in the event of subsequent changes in legislation, etc., and any payments which might accrue therefrom.
(*h*) In the event of concessions which have the benefit of political risk cover, for example through export credit guarantees, etc., an undertaking by the government not to take any unjustifiable action, for example unjustified withholding of consents, etc.
(*i*) Provisions to be applied in the case of *force majeure* (i.e. completely unforeseeable events which are beyond the control of either party).
(*j*) Provisions for termination of the contract.
(*k*) The circumstances in which the granter of the concession will be permitted to take over the concession, and the rights of the parties should this occur before the end of the concession period.

## Issues of particular concern in concession agreements

The drawing up of concession agreements is plainly a very skilled task. However the following have been identified[13] as some of the more important questions of principle which need to be considered by governments when carrying out this task:

### What provisions should government include in the agreement to safeguard itself against non-performance by the concessionaire? How should disputes be resolved?

It has already been established that governments would normally be wise to only consider early termination of a concession in the direst of circumstances. To do so would usually bring upon government more problems than it would solve. Vintner[13] therefore suggests that it may therefore be more sensible, if the government wished to be able to penalize the concessionaire in some way, for the concession agreement to incorporate a system of fines, or alternatively a system of penalty points linked to some graduated reduction in revenue.

The length of concession contracts often poses a major problem, in that the contract periods are often so long as to make it virtually impossible to predict, and thus to provide for, all of the possible changes in circumstances which may arise. This issue has been considered by a number of eminent legal writers who have questioned whether the classical approach to contract drafting, embodying fixed remedies for breach, is truly applicable. Macniel[14] in his seminal essay on the subject, draws attention to the differences in the kind and scope of various types of contractual relationship. He makes a firm distinction between what he terms 'transactional' contracts such as buying a newspaper, which are essentially short-term, where the action is affected by no past events and concerned with no future ones, and upon the basis of which the classical law of contract has developed, and 'relational' contracts where the parties anticipate a lengthy relationship and where the contract generally attempts, to some extent, to predict the future.

Campbell and Harris[15] go further, and maintain that the foundation of classical contracting, which is based on the principle of presentation (in other words an assumption that one can predict the future with some degree of accuracy, and that a contract can be drawn up which adequately apportions the consequent risks and assigns strict liabilities for breach) is totally inappropriate for relational agreements. Their review of the available literature leads them to believe that, where long-term contracts do include strict liabilities for future breaches, the contracting parties frequently compensate for their inadequacy by ignoring them when disputes arise in favour of '... a repertoire of extra-legal strategies when the liability arises'. They therefore assert that:

> Efficient long term contractual behaviour must be understood as conciously co-operative. We see a long term contract as an analogy to a partnership. The parties are not aiming at utility-maximisation directly through performance of specified obligations; rather, they are aiming at utility-maximisation indirectly through long-term co-operative behaviour manifested in trust and not in reliance on obligations specified in advance.

One consequence of the increasing acceptance of the distinction between transactional contracts and relational contracts has been the increasing inclusion in relational contracts of various types of alternative dispute resolution (ADR) provisions. These mechanisms (for example mediation, negotiation, adjudication, etc.) go beyond the boundaries of classical contract law by recognizing that the parties may not be in a position, when they sign the initial agreement, to foresee all of the possible consequences and to make provision for them. ADR therefore attempts to provide a mechanism for settlement of disputes in such a way that the parties are not necessarily rigidly bound by the terms of the original contract. Such settlements may involve modifying, or even in some cases setting aside, specific provisions in the original contract in the interests of settling the dispute quickly and, hopefully, to everyone's advantage in the light of changing circumstances. Campbell and Harris[15] however point out that, in order to make these provisions work, they must be supported by an attitude of trust and a willingness to co-operate, and this again reinforces all of the arguments already made above.

It would appear however that such options are only used reluctantly if at all. Gould[16] reviews the various dispute resolution mechanisms commonly used in BOT contracts. The only options reported in his review are an obligation to negotiate 'in good faith' in an attempt to reach agreement on the changed circumstances, reference of the dispute to an independent third party whose decision may or may not be binding, and, in exceptional circumstances, the right of one party or the other to terminate the agreement.

## How detailed should the specification be?

It has already been shown that many governments are apparently uncomfortable unless the works to be constructed, and the way in which they are to be operated, are closely specified in the concession agreement. The argument for doing this, particularly in the case of concession contracts, are usually twofold. Firstly government will argue that at some point they will have to take over responsibility for operation of the facility, and they therefore need to know that it will meet whatever standards they have set, and secondly because government needs to ensure that, at the end of the concession, the facility will still be an asset and will not be either time-expired or in need of extensive, and very probably expensive, maintenance. Concessionaires complain that detailed specifications of this sort severely restrict their freedom to provide innovative solutions to problems and thus limit their competitive edge. Whilst this argument may appear to have some superficial appeal, in truth there is, usually, little really innovative engineering in BOT projects, because innovation normally involves risk, and the concessionaire will normally do all he can to limit the project's exposure to technological risk.

Allowing the concessionaire the freedom offered by a performance specification, especially for a complex project, may not always be wise. Performance specifications for complex projects need to be written very carefully, with no loose ends left undone, if the host government is not to leave itself open to disappointment. In some types of facility, for example a power station, it is possible for the concessionaire to compromise the efficiency and energy saving characteristics of the plant in the interests of economy. Walker and Smith[17] provide a good example with a case study of the Shajiao B power station in China which was provided under a BOT contract. In discussing the technical aspects of the plant they write that:

> The [Shajiao B] station appears to typify control of the technological risk factors through the use of design and construction methods which are both well tried and economic, although without some of the frills which might be expected in stations constructed elsewhere ... The general impression of the plant was that it was relatively simple and old fashioned. The turbine is designed with a relatively low basic level of efficiency and requires more frequent and extensive overhaul maintenance than up-to-date turbine technology.

On the other hand it is, of course, much easier to specify the operation phase of the concession in performance terms, and here government should be prepared to allow the concessionaire much more freedom of action while still safeguarding standards of service.

The British government, in its PFI deals, has opted for this approach, generally specifying the *service* which it expects the private sector to provide rather than the *facility* to be constructed. In other words government is quite happy to prepare a performance specification, leaving the detailed means of providing the required service to the concessionaire. This is perhaps most appropriate where there is to be no transfer of the completed facility to government at the end of the concession.

## To what extent should the concessionaire's bankers be given the rights to take security over the concession agreement in the event of default on their loans?

Generally the host government will, of course, want to control the identity of the party providing services to it under the concession agreement, and it will therefore usually be reluctant to allow bankers rights of this kind. Nevertheless in many schemes the funding will not be forthcoming unless the banks have this level of security. The usual form for arrangements of this type is a direct supplemental 'step-in' agreement between the concession granter and the banks, where the bank itself agrees to take over the concessionaire's responsibilities under the main concession agreement. Vintner[13] points out that, in setting up such an agreement, the following points merit special attention:

(*a*) The supplemental agreement should provide specifically for the banks to step-in, rather than a nominee, and must require them to take over *all* of the concessionaire's obligations.

(*b*) Provision must be made for the banks to be released from their obligation at some point after their debts have been repaid, and government needs to consider very carefully how it will approach the task of maintaining the service provided by the facility when this point is reached.

(*c*) Under this type of agreement both the banks and the government may have rights to take over operation of the project. It is obvious that some provision must be made in the agreement to regulate this position and to establish who has priority rights in the event of a default.

(*d*) It may be that the banks are still required to make payments into the project after their step-in rights have been exercised. Some provision must therefore be made in the agreement to establish the legal status of such payments.

### Should compensation be payable to the banks in the event of termination of the agreement by the host government?

This question is very difficult, both as to principle and as to amount. As regards the principle, it can be argued firstly that this is one of the risks the bank assumes when it undertakes no-recourse or limited recourse financing, and secondly that the government should not be placed in the position of having to pay a lump sum in compensation when the whole purpose of the exercise was to avoid substantial capital expenditure. On the other hand the banks argue that not to pay compensation would leave the government holding a substantial asset for which it had paid nothing whilst the banks would lose everything. Vintner[13] sets out a number of legal observations upon this issue, but it will probably only be finally resolved through a legal test case.

## References

1. MODY A. Infrastructure delivery: new ideas, big gains, no panaceas. In *Infrastructure delivery: private initiative and the public good*, A. Mody (ed.). The World Bank, Washington, DC, 1996.

2. HURST P. BOT, BOO, BOOT – what is a true private-sector project? *Private Finance Int.*, Asian Survey, Oct. 1994, 14–16.
3. Price R. and Ivison A. DCMF prisons – a case of maximum security. *Project Finance Int.*, 14 Feb. 1996, No. 90.
4. SMITH A.J. and WALKER C.T. BOT: critical factors for success. In *Investment strategies and management of construction. Proceedings of the East meets West international conference, Brijuni, Croatia*. Society of Croatian Construction Managers, Zagreb, 1994.
5. REIJNIERS J.J.A.M. Organisation of public–private partnership projects: the timely prevention of pitfalls. *Int. J. Project Manage.*, 1994, **12**, No. 3, 137–142.
6. ALBANESE R. Team building process: key to better project results. *J. Manage. Engng*, 1994, **10**, No. 6.
7. SHIELDS G. Bridging the gap. *Project Finance Int.*, 27 Mar. 1996, No. 93.
8. WILSON R.A., SONGER A.D. and DIEKMANN J. Partnering: more than a workshop, a catalyst for change. *J. Manage. Engng*, 1995, **11**, No. 5, 40–45.
9. COWAN C.E. A strategy for partnering in the public sector. In *Preparing for construction in the 21st century*, L.M. Chang (ed.). American Society of Civil Engineers, New York, 1991.
10. CROWLEY L.G. and KARIM M.A. Conceptual model of partnering. *J. Manage. Engng*, 1995, **11**, No. 5.
11. HELLARD R.B. *Project partnering principle and practice*. Thomas Telford, London, 1995.
12. SMITH D. Changing roles and responsibilities in health-care facilities management. *Facilities*, 1995, **13**, No. 1.
13. VINTNER G. Recent developments in concession agreements. In *Project finance international yearbook 1996*. Private Finance International, London, 1996.
14. MACNIEL I.R. The many futures of contracts. *S. Cal. Law Rev.*, 1974, **47**, 691–816.
15. CAMPBELL D. and HARRIS D. Flexibility in long-term contractual relationships: the role of co-operation. *J. Law Soc.*, 1993, **20**, No. 2, 166–191.
16. GOULD N. Dispute resolution mechanisms to address unforeseen circumstances in long term BOT contracts. *Construct. Law*, 1998, **9**, No. 4.
17. WALKER C. and SMITH A.J. (eds). *Privatized infrastructure: the BOT approach*. Thomas Telford, London, 1995.

# [11]

JOURNAL OF LAW AND SOCIETY
VOLUME 20, NUMBER 2, SUMMER 1993
0263-323X

# Flexibility in Long-term Contractual Relationships: The Role of Co-operation

DAVID CAMPBELL* and DONALD HARRIS**

## INTRODUCTION

A very substantial body of empirical and theoretical literature now exists[1] which purports to show that the explanation of long-term contracts by means of the classical law of contract is most problematic. The classical law, and its economic corollary in relatively unsophisticated forms of neo-classical economics, assume contractual promises to be the legal expression of the intentions of rational, utility-maximizing individuals making discrete exchanges in perfectly competitive markets. There is a strong implication bound up in this assumption that the parties to a contract would rapidly alter their allocative decisions should changed circumstances offer them the possibility of realizing profits in excess of those to be realised by performance of the existing contract.[2] This implication is contradicted by the widely corroborated empirical finding in the case of long-term contracts that such shifts, even when of recognizable and quantifiable benefit to the potentially breaching party, typically are eschewed in order to realize what is assessed as the greater utility of the preservation of a long-term contract or wider long-term relationship. Indeed, short-term individual maximizing behaviour is rejected as opportunistic.[3]

At first glance, it would seem that very serious shortcomings of the classical law are exposed by these empirical findings, and we will argue that this is so.

* *Reader in Law, Department of Law, City Polytechnic of Hong Kong, 83 Tat Chee Avenue, Kowloon, Hong Kong, and Research Associate, Centre for Socio-Legal Studies, Wolfson College, Oxford*
** *Director, Centre for Socio-legal Studies, Wolfson College, Oxford OX2 6UD, England*

This paper was read to the seventh annual conference of the European Association for Law and Economics at Libera Universita Internationale degli Studi Sociali in Rome in September 1990. We would like to thank many participants at that conference, and in particular Gerrit de Geest, for comments which have been of great help in our subsequent revision of the paper. We should also like to thank Tony Dugdale, Paul Fenn, Roger Halson, and Stuart Schwab for their similarly helpful comments. The typical disclaimer that these colleagues are not responsible for the views expressed in this article is of more than ritual status in this case. Further thanks are due to the British Council in Hong Kong.

However, in our opinion the way in which long-term contractual behaviour is to function as counter-evidence to the classical law has not hitherto been sufficiently clearly formulated. Defences of the classical law which can, to some extent, be successful in their claims that this law can account for the rejection of opportunism have been and may continue to be mounted.[4] This possibility rationally[5] arises because there is a continuing lack of clarity about the exact nature of the shortcoming of the classical law at issue.

We will argue that this shortcoming is fundamental. It is the implicit psychological and sociological assumption in the dominant law and economics literature of rational economic behaviour as narrowly *individual* utility-maximization that has run out of explanatory productivity in the case of long-term contracts and must be regarded as false. Efficient long-term contractual behaviour must be understood as consciously co-operative.[6] We see a long-term contract as an analogy to a partnership. The parties are not aiming at utility-maximization directly through performance of specified obligations; rather, they are aiming at utility-maximization indirectly through long-term co-operative behaviour manifested in trust and not in reliance on obligations specified in advance. The co-operative mechanism by which utility is achieved in a long-term relationship is radically different from that in the paradigmatic, short-term, specified contract. The precise conduct required by future long-term co-operation is necessarily unable to be specified in advance and the shares in the joint product of that co-operation are equally often not specified in advance. The parties accept a general and productively vague norm of fairness in the conduct of their relationship.

In this paper, therefore, we use two paradigms, which we would like to keep distinct, of individual utility maximization and co-operative utility-maximization (which we shorten to 'co-operation'). We wish to use them to say, as bluntly as clarity requires, that the explanation of long-term contracts requires the rejection of immediate *individual* self-interest as the measure of economic rationality and its replacement by common interest as this measure. One may put it this way, that the adequate form of self-interest in long-term contracts is co-operation. In so doing, it is essential to recognize that the individual utility-maximizer taken as a rationally discussable theoretical concept is now so unproductive that it must be rejected in the explanation of long-term contracting and in this there is entailed a very strong criticism of the heart of the classical law.

Our argument will be pursued along two lines, one of which we trust that this paper will complete but the second of which can only be outlined here and which will be the task of future work to complete. First, in a brief review of the existing literature on long-term contracting, the problems which this literature seems to pose for the classical law will be set out. In essence, these problems are the typical agreement of contractual documents of so open-ended a character that they simply cannot be regarded as fixing strict liabilities in respect of risks of non-performance. Even more, particularly when documents do purport to fix such liabilities, they typically are ignored by a repertoire of extra-legal strategies when the liability arises. This degree of flexibility seems to make the classical law more or less irrelevant to these contracts.

The more powerful of the still broadly classical law's responses which have been and can be made to its apparent irrelevance will then be taken up. We will argue that the more sophisticated transaction cost accounts of forms of governance do not take sufficient distance from the classical law.[7] Though the very substantial contribution of these accounts must be recognized, this contribution has now run up against the limits to which it can be developed. Transaction cost accounts of governance now involve theoretically unscrupulous variations of what is meant by the concept of the individual utility-maximizer. Nothing but the extent of ingenuity can limit the unscrupulous defences which may be made of a concept. But, if assessed as part of an explanatorily progressive programme, then the maintenance of individual utility-maximization must make some determinate claims about the empirical attitudes of contracting parties. Once these claims clearly are recognized, then it will be seen that they are not supported by the empirical evidence of the attitudes of the parties to long-term contracts.

Pursuing this will bring us to the second line of argument we will wish to develop. We will attempt to set up a testable model of the co-operative attitudes and behaviour of the parties to long-term contracts which formalizes some of the explanatory advances in contract theory associated in particular with the works of Macaulay, Macneil, and Williamson which it is our intention to examine in future empirical work. For the present, we offer the model as a potentially more powerful explanation of the behaviour of parties to long-term contracts than the individual utility-maximization model and thus as itself a good reason, apart from the difficulties attendant on the maximization concept, for the rejection of the classical law in the explanation of long-term contracting.[8]

## THE FEATURES OF LONG-TERM CONTRACTUAL BEHAVIOUR

The problems posed for the classical law by long-term contracts seem clear and very profound. The classical law regards the contractual remedies which are open to an individual utility-maximizer faced with a breach as the principal resources that party has to protect her or his contractual expectations. What should at once be said about this is that typically the classical law's remedies simply are not used by the parties to long-term contracts. The evidence we have shows the contracting parties disregarding the remedies they may have even when these clearly would win them a short-term gain. The evidence available entirely supports Macaulay's early observation that:

> Disputes are frequently settled without reference to the contract or to potential or actual legal sanctions. There is a hesitancy to speak of legal rights or of threats to sue in . . . negotiations.[9]

If the legal remedy is not pursued when it is available, then the contract itself is not of the first importance. One does not need a contract to exchange goods – one needs the contract to get a state-underwritten guarantee of a remedy in the event of a breach. If there will be no necessary recourse to the remedy, then the form of the contract has less importance. Accordingly, there is considerable empirical evidence that long-term contracts will be formed even when there is less than even readily available clarity about the terms of those contracts, clarity being rejected in favour of a productive ambiguity.[10] As Beale has clearly expressed it in relation to a manufacturing industry:

> ... formal use of contract remedies to settle disputes was unusual. Court proceedings were very rare except for enforcing uncontested debts and arbitrations were uncommon. Claims were not settled out of court on the basis of contractual rights ... when a contract was being made ... the planning was far from complete ... the exchange of paper produced no legally enforceable contract. Manufacturers were usually aware of this but do not seem to be very worried by it.[11]

This non-use of contracts turns on a rejection of the classical understanding of contract as a form of economic allocative mechanism. The classical law of contracts centrally turns on the goal of presentiation, the goal of making a present decision about all – including future – aspects of a contractual relationship.[12] The parties to a contract determine all its terms at the time they agree. This point is to be identified by the acceptance of the offer. Such an agreement turns on the assumption that the parties' judgements about the nature of the world at the time of agreement, including judgements about the way the world will develop during the time of performance, are correct: this, of course, involves an element of risk. The strict liability of contractual obligations is a presentiated way of dealing with those risks. The party undertaking an obligation is strictly liable for its performance or non-performance, and in this sense the risk is allocated under the contract to that party.[13]

In long-term contracts, where the margin of such risk is considerable, a party will be loath to contract on a strict liability basis. Accordingly, the market may be eschewed as a way of dealing with this margin of risk:

> ... where contracts are peculiarly difficult to draw up and an attempt to describe what the parties have agreed to do or not to do ... would necessitate a lengthy and highly involved document, and where, as is probable, a long-term contract would be desirable, it would be hardly surprising if the emergence of a firm ... was not the solution adopted.[14]

This reason for the emergence of the vertical integration of production has not always been described in the clearest way. It is not really that the transaction costs of attempting rationally to allocate all risks are lowered by integration. It is that the firm overcomes the residual risk which remains for those making the commitment to production even after they have decided to enter into some sort of relationship *and which cannot be eliminated.*[15] Were all risks capable of being presentiated, there would be no residual risk. The question for the organization of production would be simply which governance structure involves fewest transaction costs. But this typically is not the entire question. The problem is that presentiation is a quite illusory goal and all long-term contracts must in practice be incomplete.[16] There must be a margin of irreducible uncertainty at *any* particular point of 'acceptance', uncertainty which produces this residual risk. In this sense, it is market *failure* that produces integration through the firm.[17]

One can say that the market fails in the sense that the transaction costs of the adjustment of long-term commitments are less through the firm and, as part of this, one must recognize that, as market transaction costs are infinite for large-scale projects,[18] the firm can do things that simply cannot be done by the market conceived on the lines of the classical law. This situation follows, from the point of view of our present concerns, because within the firm there is an organizational structure of co-operation which deals sequentially with the contingencies of long-term projects in a hierarchical but nevertheless co-operative way involving a 'corporate culture' of general commitment to the goal of the firm's success.[19] It is this unanimity of purpose which provides the framework within which problems will be typically dealt with in such a way as to minimize their cost consequences.

Freed of non-rational considerations, the choice of how to deal with the governance of long-term commitments should boil down to the choice of the governance structure which keeps transaction costs to a minimum.[20] This choice may be of a long-term contract rather than integration, because, of course, the firm has its own organizational costs[21] and these may well outweigh its benefits to the contracting parties.[22] The point which follows from the above comments on the nature of the firm, however, is that the long-term contracts themselves cannot begin to look like the discrete exchange paradigmatic to the classical law or the firm would be the most cost-effective form of governance even in these areas (or the commitment would not be made). The long-term contract equally has to reject the fruitless goal of complete presentiation even for market governance and does so by incorporating an 'open-ended' approach which leaves a great margin for the variation or complete renegotiation of commitments or even eschews attempting to give those commitments any definite form at the outset but awaits the circumstances to arise which will allow such definition. This is co-operation within the market which is analogous to the co-operation organized within the firm.

A very wide repertoire of planning devices for long-term contracts now exists which to some extent are specific to particular enterprises and on which more work would be welcome but from which some general legal[23] and economic[24] principles can be drawn. Those principles eschew presentiation and really turn on a commitment to the co-operative efforts of each of the parties made in good faith (or to the acceptance of independent third party adjudication) to realize their joint and several goals.[25] It is an entirely natural claim that this renunciation of presentiation is a fundamental contradiction of the remedy and formation doctrines of the classical law.[26] The situation is summed up adequately by Atiyah:

> The modern commercial transaction is, in practice, apt to include provision for varying the terms of the exchange to suit the conditions applicable at the time of performance. Goods ordered for future delivery are likely to be supplied at prices ruling at the time of delivery; rise and fall clauses in building or construction works are the rule and not the exception;

> currency-variation clauses may well be included in international transactions . . . . The rewards and penalties for guessing what the future will bring are no longer automatically thought of as being the natural consequences of success or failure in the skill and expertise of business activity.[27]

We have omitted the following from the above quotation from Atiyah:

> And even when such [explicit variation] provisions are not included in the contract itself, business people are in practice often constrained to agree to adjustments to contractual terms where subsequent events make the original contract no longer capable of performance on a fair basis.

We believe this is also accurate, but it raises a different point. Here we are dealing not with the extension of long-term contract planning formally to provide for uncertain contingencies but with a co-operative response to failures in that planning. The classical law is clear about the response that should follow any such failure. This is liability and, indeed, efficient liability, because a firm that cannot make correct long-term decisions should be driven out of business. However, what Atiyah is postulating, and what the evidence we have shows to be the case, is that failures under these circumstances lead rather to extra-legal strategies to keep the long-term relationship alive in all but the most acute circumstances.

There is a rather good example of this, widely known and discussed, based on Westinghouse's difficulties over uranium supply contracts in the 1970s. Westinghouse undertook very large long-term uranium supply contracts whilst leaving themselves without full cover of their own supplies. Shifts in the costs of all energy sources – in which the successful cartelization of oil prices by the Organization of Petroleum Exporting Countries (OPEC) played some part, made these contracts potentially ruinous, even for a corporation of the size of Westinghouse. So desperate was the industry as a whole that litigation was instituted by Westinghouse's buyers which Westinghouse tried to defend by a plea of commercial impracticability under UCC 2–615.[28] Joskow has shown that Westinghouse made a number of what one might politely term 'non-optimal decisions' over these supply contracts, and, relying on an analysis of impossibility in contract derived from Posner,[29] he became rather warm in saying that Westinghouse should not be excused performance but should bear the costs of its non-optimal decisions.[30] When, it would seem, the court's adjudication denied Westinghouse relief under 2–615, this was welcomed thus by Maughmer, who shared Joskow's reasoning and amplified his tone:

> The extension of relief to Westinghouse via section 2–615 would have created serious inroads in contract law from both a legal and an economic viewpoint. By applying strict tests and cautious interpretations to the elements of section 2–615, courts are able, as a matter of policy, to protect the legal and economic functions of contracts.[31]

Thus the law on 2–615 is now authoritatively stated to be that commercial impracticability is basically a dead letter, for if Westinghouse going bust in order to perform a contract is not a case of commercial impracticability, then nothing ever can be,[32] and Joskow's analysis is taken to be evidence of the value of the Posnerian defence of the classical law of presentiated risk allocation.[33]

All this is very fine, except that a consultation of the list of corporations wound up for insolvency in the United States of America in the 1970s will not yield Westinghouse's name and, indeed, none of the heralded protection of the function of contracts took place. When the court seemed to declare the UCC irrelevant to the solution of this crisis in the energy economy of the United States of America,[34] Westinghouse reached a set of completely renegotiated contracts of supply with its buyers on terms as favourable as the generally adverse business conditions allowed and things continued much as before (though in a changed international energy economy).[35] What one imagines happened is that the buyers realized that they could gain no possible advantage from the liquidation of Westinghouse for, as even Joskow recognized, Westinghouse's pricing and supply policies were designed in good faith to encourage its buyers and thus expand the nuclear energy industry.[36] No alternative more favourable supplier could conceivably become available, especially not after Westinghouse's trauma. Once freed from the panic of the oil crisis and the competitive suspicion and hostility into which the mutually destructive idea of holding Westinghouse to its contracts or of Westinghouse abandoning its buyers led, a sensible co-operative adjustment to the changed circumstances took place.[37]

We have clearer evidence of these non-legal strategies in respect of other long-term supply contracts which suffered strain during the recession in the 1970s. Daintith's example[38] of iron ore contracts is particularly significant, for the contracts he examined were very poorly drafted, their weakness following from their drafters' obvious commitment to presentiation. Even prices were fixed over long periods. It would be hard to exaggerate the depth of the shortfall in demand for steel production over the period that these contracts were to run, and yet virtually none of the formal legal remedies under those contracts were taken up. By a series of entirely extra-legal negotiating strategies, the relationship between the buyers and sellers of ore was renegotiated and, indeed, in a strong sense the contractual relationship was maintained. But the contracts had all been transformed into more flexible forms, with prices, quantities, and delivery dates becoming open to subsequent determination. The point is that the original form of the documents did not facilitate or even allow for this factor, but this form proved irrelevant as the document was changed by extra-legal negotiation. This example is corroborated by such evidence as we have.

In sum, then, long-term contractual documents eschew pursuit of the goal of presentiation in order to leave open-ended the parties' ability to deal with contingencies during the course of their performances. Furthermore, the parties' typical recourse to extra-legal strategies when their documents fail to provide for a reasonable resolution of such difficulties as do occur shows a commitment to flexibility far in excess of that which could conceivably be provided for by any document in order to avoid having to pursue formal remedies.

## THE PROBLEM OF LONG-TERM CONTRACTUAL CO-OPERATION: THE PARTIES' ATTITUDES TO THE ADJUSTMENT OF THEIR COMMITMENTS

The conclusion that should be drawn – but which has not been sufficiently strongly drawn from what we know of long-term contract planning and extra-legal strategies – is that classical contract should be completely rejected as an explanation of long-term contracting. Risk allocation through presentiation simply is not the mechanism long-term contracting parties use. But presentiation is the corollary of regarding contracts as the expression of the intentions of the parties and this in turn is the legal corollary of assuming a market composed of rational, utility-maximizing individuals.[39] It is an explanatory requirement of a proper understanding of long-term contracting that we carry through our rejection of presentiation to the rejection of the classical assumptions of the behaviour and attitudes of the contracting parties. These parties do, of course, typically rationally gauge their utilities, but not as discrete individuals.

Open-ended documents and extra-legal dispute resolution are not in themselves sufficient to account for the form of long-term contracting. For such readily observable non-classical phenomena do not really go to the heart of the method of risk allocation going on in the long-term contract. Let us consider open-ended contract planning over, say, price and quantity adjustment. One might have such formal provisions, but they do not themselves really speak directly to the point at issue. We do not mean by this that formal provisions can never be perfectly flexible, though this is so. We mean that the open-ended provisions might themselves be interpreted narrowly in a competitively hostile fashion and that there is nothing in the formal document that could prevent this. Just as the static and purportedly fixed allocations of risk under presentiation turn on competitive bargaining between rational utility-maximizing individuals, so the plausibility of writing contracts in an open-ended fashion turns on assuming a co-operative attitude to the resolution at the appropriate time of the problems initially left open-ended. Without a shift in attitude, formal provision for flexibility is fruitless, for one cannot create a co-operative attitude by writing down that such an attitude will be taken to contingencies as they arise. One needs the attitude to make the writing have any meaning (though the writing then reinforces the attitude, as under UCC 1–102).

This really is to say that explanation of the open-endedness of long-term contractual documents and the prevalence of extra-legal strategies to preserve long-term relationships require a fundamentally different set of assumptions about the unit of the analysis of exchange. The classical law cannot describe the mechanisms for dealing with risk in long-term contracts because the assumption of the purely individual utility-maximizer does not capture the co-operative stance which is fundamental to those mechanisms.

This strong claim for the lack of explanatory power in classical contract seems to involve three empirically testable hypotheses about the nature of long-term contracting, the last of which is the real heart of any claim that co-operation is a more explanatorily valuable model of long-term contracting behaviour than pure individual maximization. The first hypothesis is that the form of long-term contracts as documents will tend to be open-ended and to display a rejection of the goal of presentiation in favour of explicit flexibility. The second hypothesis is that, in addition to the explicit sophistication of these documents, there will be a co-operative recourse to extra-legal strategies to resolve problems which cannot be handled under these documents. The third hypothesis, which is the foundation of the plausibility of formally providing for flexibility and of turning to extra-legal strategies when necessary and thus is of more fundamental interest, is that the parties to the contract will, in all but the most extreme cases,[40] adopt a co-operative rather than narrowly maximizing, opportunistic attitude to their own and others' performance.

## THE NATURE OF TRANSACTION COST ANALYSIS

There is considerable empirical work on all of these hypotheses, so much in the first and second cases that, though further evidence would be most welcome, particularly in respect of the specific contract planning and extra-legal strategies of particular enterprises, we regard them as already being borne out by the evidence briefly discussed above. Amongst this evidence, we would draw particular attention to the writings of Macaulay, Macneil, and Williamson because – hardly uniquely – we regard these as representing the best of the available resources in the 'law and economics' literature for the examination of long-term contracts. In particular, their accounts of the open-endedness of long-term contractual documents and the parties' recourse to extra-legal strategies set up the third hypothesis, that the parties' conduct will be consciously co-operative, as a requirement for the explanation of long-term contractual behaviour.

Macaulay's discussions of extra-legal strategies all reveal co-operative attitudes to the contract[41] and these findings have, we feel, been more or less corroborated. However, though Macaulay has utilized his findings to set up very compellingly the necessity of a rival to the classical contracting model, he has not really advanced such a model in an explicitly coherent way. On the basis of this type of finding, Williamson already has asked explicit questions about the behavioural assumptions informing the classical law and criticisms of it.[42] Macneil's work contributes to this questioning and takes the issue further by hazarding a number of schemata of co-operative contractual norms setting out the behavioural assumptions apposite for long-term contracting.[43] We now intend to reformulate Williamson's and Macneil's behavioural questions in such a way as to stress the necessary element of co-operation, consider the classical responses to this problem of co-operation, and then advance our model of the co-operative attitudes of long-term contracting parties.

Williamson's discussion of 'the behavioural assumptions imputed to contractual man'[44] in the chapter of *The Economic Institutions of Capitalism* on 'Contractual Man' is conducted by recognizing two such assumptions as central to transaction cost economics. These are 'bounded rationality and opportunism'.[45] These assumptions are established polemically, being intended to show the heuristic superiority of transaction cost economics in comparison with neo-classical economics. As against the assumption of rational decision-making in perfect markets, transaction cost economics 'acknowledges limits on cognitive competence'[46] as 'bounded rationality is the cognitive assumption on which transaction cost economics relies'.[47] With respect to individual utility-maximization, whereas 'neo-classical man confronts self-interested others across markets [and] bargains are struck on terms that reflect original positions',[48] transaction cost economics 'substitutes subtle for simple self-interest seeking'.[49] An apparatus of levels of rationality and degrees of self-interestedness are developed which extend the transactional apparatus for the analysis of boundedness and less direct maximization into the institutional accounts of the different governance structures which Williamson develops.

Without wishing to detract from the enormous productivity of Williamson's work, we must say that the stylistic form of this chapter on 'Contractual Man', entirely representative of the style of that work, recalls to mind nothing so much as Bentham.[50] A powerful insight is broadened through a plethora of classification and concept formulation focusing on idiosyncratic investment and asset specificity, but in this breadth there is something of a sacrifice of depth. The transaction cost apparatus is extended, in *The Economic Institutions of Capitalism*, to cover the whole of the advanced capitalist economy, but only in the form of a set of boundary conditions, of which bounded rationality is the most important, to the still retained assumptions of individual maximization. This can go on only to a certain extent. The point must come when one has to ask fundamental questions about the heuristic power of a basic unit of analysis which can be applied only with a vast number of *ceteris paribus* ('other things being equal') clauses having to be entered for it.

Bounded rationality functions as an exception for Williamson:

> . . . but for bounded rationality, all economic exchange could be effectively organized by contract. Indeed, the economic theory of comprehensive contracting has been fully worked out.[51]

What sort of an exception is it that is of far greater importance than the so-called normal case? What plausibility can be given to the normal case if it only exists through its exceptions, or through 'concessions to human nature as we know it', as Williamson says.[52] We do not know of any case discussed in the modern philosophy of science that can begin to compare with the tenacity of the retention of problematic core assumptions in neo-classical economics and its more sophisticated refinements. But the tenacity is not without cost. By the time Bentham has finished classifying all the circumstances which, say, influence penal policy – such as the chance of getting caught, the hardiness of the offender to be punished, and so on – there is nothing left of his basic idea that punishment should be proportionate to the mischief of the offence. By the time Williamson has given his full institutional account of the conditions of economic behaviour, surely there is equally nothing left of the basic intuition of individual utility-maximization in long-term relationships.[53]

This questioning of core assumptions is not a line actively pursued in Williamson, because dwelling on the discussion of information costs can apparently do a great deal to save the initial individual maximization approach. If we see relationships being preserved rather than terminated despite the occasion for legal termination arising, this might be redescribed as the parties simply adjusting their view of their self-interest as the development of their relation over time yields progressively more information and expands the bounds of their rational pursuit of that self-interest. 'Co-operation' can thus be reduced to the constant 'renegotiation' of self-interest along lines initially developed by Alchian and Demsetz in the context of the labour relationship:

> To speak of managing, directing, or assigning workers to various tasks is a deceptive way of noting that the employer continually is involved in renegotiation of contracts on terms that must be acceptable to both parties.[54]

What one is tempted to do in the context of the labour relationship when one actually knows something of the concrete nature of that relationship is to say that this account is just wrong. One useful way of distinguishing between the good, reliable labour relationship and a bad one is to identify just what Alchian and Demsetz leave out – a type of attachment between the parties that cannot be reduced to a contract-nexus – or, even worse, a cash-nexus.[55] Now, this would be right, for Alchian and Demsetz do make hermeneutic errors of a type we will examine in Coase, of just missing what is essential to the relationship between the parties because of an unshakeable commitment to (mis-)describing that relationship in strongly individualistic ways. However, for the moment, it is perhaps better to acknowledge this type of reasoning and see what costs of theoretical integrity it involves.

When one follows the contractual applications of transaction cost analysis, one has the curious feeling of the tail wagging the dog. Transaction costs are to be minimized in order to approximate to the perfect discrete exchange, but the way in which this exchange works as a goal is in theoretical terms entirely perverse. One can assume zero transaction costs, but the actual securing of that assumption takes a great deal more effort than is actually repaid when it is secured. The main focus cannot be the residual assumption, for the whole account shows it is not even remotely applicable but, rather, attention is concentrated on the boundary conditions which are its corollaries. Of course, there is a great deal about the explanatory form of neo-classical and transaction cost economics which is expressed in this. Williamson is a little shamefaced about discussing behavioural assumptions, because he recognizes that in economics there is 'a widely held opinion that the realism of the assumptions is unimportant'.[56] This agnosticism about the realism of assumptions really does place serious limits on what can be achieved even by economic explanation of Williamson's type and something must be said about this here.

For there is, of course, a sense in which the most interesting developments in the economics of contracting (and much else) are, as it were, focusing on what we have referred to as Williamson's boundary conditions and do so to such an extent as effectively to question the realism of the basic underlying assumptions. An obvious example is those game theoretical accounts of mutual interdependence which, moving beyond the prisoner's dilemma games probably most widely known in the 'law and economics' literature,[57] now contain highly sophisticated accounts of firm structure[58] and seem to offer considerable potential for a wide range of institutional analyses[59] through more sophisticated modelling.[60] Such modelling is an example of the clear pursuit of realism in institutional economic analysis in an emerging 'behavioural economics',[61] 'economic sociology',[62] or even 'political economy'[63] which may, indeed, radically question neo-classical assumptions.[64] These movements are highly welcome, but their productive utilization in the explanation of contracting will, in our opinion, have to take a strict stand against the form of 'realism' which presently dominates transaction cost analysis, particularly in the 'law and economics' literature. As it is Coase who has determined the nature of this 'realism', it is against him that our criticism should be pursued.

This criticism of a lack of realism seems a remarkable one to bring against Coase, for, of course, the power of his work lies, in an important sense, in its claims *to be* realistic: 'Modern institutional economics should study man as he is, acting within the constraints imposed by real institutions. Modern institutional economics is economics as it ought to be.'[65] Coase's explanations of institutions purport to be of real structures, classically of course, of the firm:

> It is hoped to show . . . that a definition of a firm may be obtained which is . . . realistic in that it corresponds to what is meant by a firm in the real world . . . the definition we have given is one which closely approximates to the firm as it is considered in the real world.[66]

Although the reasoning involved did not become clear until 'The Problem of Social Cost' was published, Coase's account of 'The Nature of the Firm' puts forward a paradigmatic transaction-cost explanation, the firm being described (against some contemporary contributions that are now not widely read) as a cheaper way of dealing with the risks of complicated production than the market.

In transaction cost analysis after Coase generally, a hypothetical discrete exchange carried out with zero transaction costs is assumed[67] and then the costs ancillary to establishing the exchange are added in as – to put it in a way of which Coase would not approve – externalities. The object of the exercise is to keep such costs to a minimum, for they obstruct or prevent the exchange. Hence the conclusion is the establishment of the least costly appropriate governance structures. This may mean regulating the market through congenial principles of contract or integrating through the firm (or even state governance).[68]

By setting up transaction cost analysis in this way, Coase generated a serious bias which has characterized that analysis ever since. There is a very strong separation between the realism of his statement of boundary conditions, the transaction costs, and the unrealistic nature of his assumption of the transaction at zero cost. Coase recognizes that transactions at zero cost could never take place but does not really see what this means. He thinks there will be a problem of residual ineliminable costs but he does not see why. The negotiating, information gathering, organizing, and so on within which transactions take place are not *only* costs, they are also the social relations which are essentially facilitative of the transaction. All actions, including all transactions, can take place only within a constitutive social system. If one really took away *all* the costs of exchanging, the exchange would not take place cost-free. It simply would not take place at all.

However, this is absolutely *not* what Coase wants to say. At the hands of Coase, transaction cost economics has, seemingly as a result of its technique but actually because of certain social and political positions he adopts, closed off all possible explanations of human nature and social relationships other than the most thorough-going individualistic ones. Coase does believe – and claims to identify this belief in Adam Smith[69] – that there is some residual quality about human beings as such that makes them exchange, or – as Coase's more modern synonym has it – choose. 'Economics', Coase says, is 'the science of human choice'.[70] This is like saying that physics is the science of forces and objects, in that whilst it is in a sense true, it is so utterly abstract as to be useless. But Coase is quite sanguine about 'the acceptance by economists of a view of human nature so lacking in content',[71] indeed he celebrates not only that economics might be applicable not only to all human phenomena[72] but to the 'animal behavior' of 'the rat, cat and octopus'.[73]

If we are to do anything with this idea, we must have some idea of concrete preferences, and, permeating his claims for generality, this is just what Coase has:

> I believe that human preferences came to be what they are in those millions of years in which our ancestors (whether or not they can be classified as human) lived in hunting bands and were those preferences which, in such conditions, were conducive to survival.[74]

This identification of the preferences effective in contemporary economies – and Coase really has in mind the United States of America – with some general idea of human preferences as such is complete nonsense which receives no corroboration from any philosophic or sociological work on the determinate features of human preferences of which we are aware,[75] other than the really quite suspect discipline of sociobiology, which Coase significantly cites in his support to the exclusion of all other social theory.[76] Ignorance of social theory's conclusions about the nature of human agency and social structure[77] is essential to Coase. His position, which is a common enough one,[78] rests entirely on a mistaken identification of capitalism, a specific economic form with a clearly delimited historical provenance,[79] with 'choice'.

It is obvious that on this basis Coase could not possibly give an accurate account of the origin or the nature of the capitalist (or indeed any) economic system, nor can he do other than grudgingly acknowledge the structural properties of that specific system.[80] These are very serious shortcomings which prevent any attempt to extend Coase's work into a general account of the modern economy. Coase correctly observes that 'in mainstream economic theory, the firm and the market are, for the most part, assumed to exist and are not themselves the subject of investigation'[81] and his own work undertakes such an investigation. But his accounts are based on the very assumption of a perfect market – of transactions at zero cost – which he is trying to refine, and there is a self-defeating circularity about this:

> What differentiates [my writings] is not that they reject existing economic theory, which... embodies the logic of choice and is of wide applicability, but that they employ this theory to examine the role which the firm, the market and the law play in the working of the economic system.[82]

Coase's objection to assuming markets to exist is not that he wants to explain the market's existence, for he himself makes this assumption. He objects to assuming the market to exist everywhere and he goes on to explain instances of its non-existence (forgetting that this is all instances) as a departure from the normal case. The institutional thrust of Coase's work really is rather undercut in this way for a principal economic institution, the free market, is never itself explained. Rather than being regarded as a governance structure itself requiring explanation, the market is given the status of being *the* natural form of life, neither requiring nor permitting explanation.

What is most important to us here is that determining whether individual utility-maximizing assumptions still hold for contemporary long-term contracting behaviour[83] simply cannot be an issue for Coase. He thinks that this assumption holds for all times and indeed for all creatures. If one is a little less ambitious about one's claims and is at pains to understand what attitudes and behaviour actually inform specific contractual phenomena, then the type of general applicability Coase claims must be viewed not as a strength but as the weakness of a theory now making claims which are so wide as to have no particular descriptive value for long-term contracting behaviour (or, indeed, for any particular behaviour). We believe that an accurate account of the attitudes and behaviour of the parties to long-term contracts requires a more realistic description of their *co-operation*, rather than the accumulation of the facts of co-operation as exceptions to individual utility-maximizing assumptions. Our point at the moment, however, is that this question cannot even arise for Coase. All institutions are the products of responses to a given human nature which functions as the assumed basis of explanation in his work when rather that nature – individual utility-maximization – is itself an empirical hypothesis which should be tested.

In the way Coase sets up transaction cost economics, it is immune from criticism. Its essential assumption of individual rational utility-maximization is stated so widely that it can never be attacked[84] and all the power comes from the reality of the boundary assumptions. One can keep adding boundary assumptions indefinitely, but the theory which allows this can never be wrong, and this is the most profound failing a theory can have.[85] Coase's retention of the basic unit of neo-classical explanation in transaction cost economics should rather be viewed as an unscrupulous accumulation of boundary conditions – transaction costs – which have the theoretical form of exceptions to the essential form – neo-classical maximization – of that explanation. The acceptability of a form of explanation which generates such exceptions as a condition of the basic plausibility of the explanation is entirely suspect.[86] What should be at issue is an assessment of the accuracy of the psychological and sociological assumptions of purely individual utility-maximization as the basis of explanations.

Williamson, we believe, generates more than enough evidence about the necessity of inventing concepts to save individual utility-maximization to show that it should not be saved but, remaining within a broadly Coasean notion of transaction cost analysis, does not attempt the necessary theoretical innovation. It is, however, to Macneil's enormous credit that he attempts to go beyond this type of explanatory structure. His account of long-term contracting behaviour attempts to make co-operative relations central to the explanation, avowedly working against any basic stress on the rational, utility-maximizing *individual*; we will consider this account now. Macneil explains the boundary conditions of transaction cost analysis not as costs (which should be minimized) but as essential relations which must be fully integrated into the account because their heuristic value in explaining long-term contracting massively dwarfs the purely abstract and obstructive notion of individual utility-maximization.

Macneil's crucial departure from the transaction cost approach lies in his depiction of the phenomena transaction costs describe as costs not as costs but as facilitative relations. The goal of the perfect discrete exchange, even as a remote abstraction, must be eschewed because it is inconceivable outside the relations which constitute even that exchange. Achieving zero transaction costs would not leave the perfect allocations of the rational utility-maximizer. It would leave nothing, because those allocations take place only through the relations described as costs. Neo-classical and transactional analysis:

> . . . assumes the existence of very complex relations between the parties – relations established through society generally, language, law, and societal economic organization. But once such relations are assumed, the impact of those relations on the analysis is typically ignored. *Ceteris paribus* conquers all. . . . Because economic analysis is the analysis of social behavior, economic man is necessarily in society at all times . . . potential fallacy lurks in all social analysis starting from the non-social, relation-omitting model of neo-classical economics.[87]

As Macneil puts it in an economic fashion: 'Because it is impossible to conduct exchange without transaction costs . . . they are every bit as much a factor of production as capital and labour.'[88] Macneil continuously stresses a facilitative relational basis in explaining the content of contracts. He argues that this content is not arrived at by negotiations composed of perfect discrete exchanges conducted within transactional boundaries, but is the product of negotiations *whose very form* is constituted by external and internal relations.

Macneil's account of the co-operation between long-term contracting parties runs essentially as follows. The self-interest of the individual utility-maximizer must bring about a certain element of co-operation between the parties if their separate goals are to be realized through mutual performances.[89] However, such co-operation does not require commitment to the goal of the other party and indeed may, within prudential limits, be inimical to it. The transaction cost analysis describes the structures which set these prudential limits (and other boundaries), but they are to be kept to a necessary minimum in order to give as free a rein as possible to the rational individual allocation of resources by the parties. The exchange remains predicated on narrow self-interest: the elements of co-operation are considered to be an external structure.

For Macneil, the recognition that 'all mutual planning in transactions . . . is conflict laden', and indeed may involve 'the most brutal kinds of in-fighting',[90] is coupled with a description of co-operation which gives it a rather more central place than that of 'external material . . . of little interest'.[91] The common sociality essential for all human activity[92] and the political limits to self-interest which prevent economic competition from decaying into war[93] or parasitism,[94] are described, and their elements of co-operation are made central to the relational account. Furthermore, crucially, Macneil then goes on to argue that 'law contributes more than general stability, it is directly facilitative in [that] it provides for the accomplishment of co-operation [and the] continuation of interdependence'[95] through external and internal[96] 'values of contract behaviour . . . generated . . . in billions of contractual relations'.[97]

External norms or values are imposed, not only, nor even necessarily most importantly,[98] by 'the positive law of the sovereign, but also from many other sources [including] private law, such as that imposed on . . . businesses by trade associations'. Not only are there such relatively 'vertical impositions', but there is also the 'more horizontal imposition of external values, such as those arising from . . . customs of a trade'.[99] These foster co-operation by reducing the 'choice of a party which is reciprocating too little, is too powerful, is terminating relations, or is following arbitrary or other procedures viewed as inadequate'.[100] Finally, internal norms or values orient 'both [the] actual behaviour and [the] principles of right action'[101] of contracting parties. In the latest formulation, a set of ten common contract norms[102] underpin all contracting by generating a co-operative attitude which respects 'solidarity and reciprocity',[103] setting the boundaries within which legitimate negotiation and competition are allowed. A range of relatively discrete and relatively relational norms[104] operate within the common norms, but essential co-operation emerges at this internal level as well as at all other external levels. Any legitimate competition is bounded by an integral acceptance of co-operation as operative within the contract:

> The word 'solidarity' (or 'trust') is not inappropriate to describe this web of interdependence, externally reinforced as well as self-supporting, and expected future co-operation. The most important aspect of solidarity . . . is the extent to which it produces

> similarity of selfish interests, whereby what increases (decreases) the utility of one participant also increases (decreases) the utility of the other. . . . Seldom, if ever, is this merger of interests complete, but it is omnipresent, immensely significant, and, in a vast range of circumstances, complete for most practical purposes. . . . [S]imilarity of interests may be produced by external forces such as sovereign law. But . . . solidarity may and does arise internally in relations.[105]

Macneil's analysis of contractual behaviour shows conduct which is predominantly so modelled *with this element of co-operation in the minds of the parties* that a contract 'no longer stands alone as in the discrete transaction, but is part of a relational web'.[106] All the negotiating tactics adopted by parties, concerning formation,[107] performance,[108] variation,[109] termination,[110] and application of remedies,[111] are explained as being informed by this attitude, so that, at the heart of the analysis, it is no longer possible to work with the assumptions of perfect discrete exchange, for they cannot plausibly be attributed to an economic actor. Such an attribution 'postulates individuals acting as if the relations in which those individuals exist had no effect on their behaviour'. [112] Transaction cost analysis treats parties as separate individual maximizing units and then concerns itself with 'the prevention of their *subsequently* acting as separate maximizers, the limiting of opportunism'. But, crucially, we should note that in contracts:

> . . . there can be present a 'sense of productive increase from the relationship which can dwarf variations in expectation, or of long-term anticipations of mutual benefit that dwarf variations in shares received by parties'. This anticipatory, commonly held 'sense' of the parties may virtually obliterate any present separation as maximizers, thereby making them effectively a single maximizer.[113]

There are certain elements in Macneil's work which, in our opinion, rather undercut the power of this notion of contracts as 'instruments for social co-operation'.[114] These turn on a failure to appreciate the limits to the co-operation which can be brought about by contracts properly understood as the legal expression of *capitalist* exchange.[115] The nature of the co-operation arrived at through capitalist competition is, of course, overlaid by many themes of conflict.[116] However, in terms of showing that co-operation is an essential and irreducible element of *efficient* long-term contracting behaviour, we regard Macneil's work as a foremost contribution to the social theory of the modern economy. It requires, however, empirical examination and possible factual corroboration of its co-operative hypothesis if its status is to be accepted.

In sum, the transaction cost analysis of contracting holds, in our opinion, the greatest promise for the examination of the difficult empirical case of long-term contracts. However, the predominant line of transaction cost analysis in the 'law and economics' literature is still so heavily dominated by Coase's quite unshakeable commitment to an assumption of individual utility-maximization as the unit of analysis that the realization of this promise faces serious handicaps. Much transaction cost analysis and other developments in institutional economics are beginning to question this commitment. Such questioning is essential if the principal feature of efficient long-term contracting, conscious co-operation, is to be properly appreciated and therefore such contracting be adequately explained.

## THE CO-OPERATIVE ATTITUDES OF PARTIES TO LONG-TERM CONTRACTS

Having shown the necessity of replacing long-term individual utility-maximization with long-term mutually-reinforcing co-operation as the unit of the analysis of efficient long-term contractual behaviour, we should now like to formalize this idea of co-operation and indicate how we intend to operationalize it in future work, and do so in Figure 1 below.

| A<br>Party 1's analysis of the benefit of the relationship to it | |
|---|---|
| 1<br>Party 1's incentive to continue the relationship | 2<br>Party 1's disincentive against terminating the relationship |
| Party 1's expectation of an undefined share in the joint gains to be generated by the relationship (which share is expected to be larger than any gain achievable by it independently) | (i) The loss of any idiosyncratic investment made in the relationship<br><br>(ii) The potential cost to Party 1 of developing a new relationship and making an idiosyncratic investment in it |
| **B**<br>Party 1's assessment of the value which Party 2 places on the relationship | |
| 1<br>Party 2's incentive to continue the relationship | 2<br>Party 2's disincentive against terminating the relationship |
| Party 2's expectation of an undefined share in the joint gains to be generated by the relationship (which share is expected to be larger than any gain acheivable by it independently) | (i) The loss of any idiosyncratic investment made in the relationship<br><br>(ii) The potential cost to Party 2 of devoping a new relationship and making an idiosyncratic investment in it |

*FIGURE 1: Model of self-interested behaviour which consciously adopts co-operation as the optimal long-term strategy*

This model assumes that the continuance of a long-term relationship does not depend on the sanctions provided by the law nor on direct market pressures but rather on a package of incentives and disincentives established through a continuing co-operative relationship. 'A' in this model represents the package of reasons for Party 1's wish to continue in the relationship. These are determined by a – perhaps informal or even implicit but in long-term contracting often highly formalized – cost-benefit analysis of the value of continuing the relationship rather than terminating it and of the costs of terminating it rather than continuing it. Party 1 expects to gain more from the continuing co-operation than from any alternative commitment of resources. 'B' in this model provides the justification for Party 1 continuing to rely on Party 2's future co-operation. *This relationship of trust, we believe, is the crucial feature of our model.* It gives Party 1 the incentive to make further idiosyncratic investment in the relationship and it gives that party some protection against Party 2 acting in an opportunistic way to exploit the bilateral monopoly created by the relationship. So long as Party 2 continues to value the relationship more than any alternative commitment of its resources, Party 2 will not intentionally act in such a way as to risk Party 1 deciding to withdraw from the relationship.

Exactly the same model will apply to Party 2's analysis of the relationship. The relationship will continue so long as each party's analysis concludes that continuance is more advantageous than termination *and this essentially requires that each side can continue to trust with confidence in the other's co-operation.* The model requires reciprocity in making this evaluation and in relying on the other party's self-interest in continuance.[117]

The thinking of the parties we are trying to drive at runs essentially like this: 'I calculate that I shall be better off in the longer term if I continue my relationship with you instead of terminating it; and I also estimate that you similarly have calculated that you will be better off if the relationship continues.' The first stage of our model, A, is the self-interested appraisal of its own position conducted by each party. The second stage, B, is the estimate which each party makes of the cost-benefit analysis carried out by the other party. Let us expand this reasoning.

1. *Party 1's analysis of the value of the relationship to it*

(a) Incentive on Party 1 to continue the relationship

The obvious starting-point is each party's assessment of the net advantages expected to be gained from continuing the relationship, namely, the surplus of the expected benefits over the expected costs. Unlike a partnership, in which the proportionate shares of the net profit are determined in advance, in a long-term contractual relationship the 'shares' which each party will gain are not determined in advance, because each party operates as an independent profit centre. However, each party expects (i) the relationship to generate joint profits which will exceed the sum of the net profits which each party could produce independently; and (ii) that those joint profits will be divided in a way which exceeds the net profits of independent production. The relationship maximizes the joint profit and thus maximizes each party's own expected profits. Unless the jointly produced profit meets this standard of being so large as to be likely to yield more than independently produced profits, either party will terminate the relationship, as indeed either will if the division of the joint profit does not in fact yield excess profit. This cost-benefit analysis is not a once-and-for-all calculation: it will be a continuing assessment updated in the light of current information available to the parties.

(b) Disincentives on Party 1 against terminating the relationship

A second part of each party's own assessment will be the calculation of the expected costs of terminating the relationship. Williamson has identified the importance of idiosyncratic asset-specific investment which is made in a long-term relationship, namely, the investment of resources which could not be transferred to any other use or to any other relationship.[118] If a party were to withdraw, it could not adequately salvage the investment which has been committed to developing the existing relationship. This is an investment which the party expects to generate gains within the existing unique relationship, but which cannot do so elsewhere.

There may be a further cost to terminating, which is the cost of developing a substitute relationship with another party if that is desired. This cost of developing an alternative relationship will, in a long-term contracting situation, often be substantial. In an empirical study of the relationship between car manufacturers and car dealers in the United Kingdom,[119] the manufacturers said that the cost of replacing a dealer would be high. It would take a long time to search for a suitable dealer, with only one in fifty applicants being suitable in the opinion of the dealership manager of one manufacturer. Even if the manufacturer could find a suitable applicant with suitable premises, it would take the new dealer a considerable time to learn about a new range of cars, about the manufacturer's distribution network, servicing standards, supplies of spare parts, and so on. The cost of finding and training a new dealer clearly was a very powerful disincentive to terminating an existing dealership.

2. *Party 1's estimate of the value which Party 2 places on the relationship*

In considering the maintenance of the relationship, each party takes into account an estimate of the cost-benefit analysis which it expects the other to be conducting. Each party estimates the benefits which the other expects from continuing the relationship and estimates the costs which the other would expect to incur from terminating the relationship. Each party relies on the incentive which arises from the other party's expectation of joint excess profits as the outcome of continuing co-operation, and on the disincentive to terminate which arises from the other party's expectation of costs consequent upon the ending of the relationship. From each party's point of view, these

In all, we are trying to model the fundamental reciprocity of concerns between the parties, where each identifies its own best interest so closely with the interest of the other that it is inaccurate to view them as individual maximizers. They are joint maximizers. Whilst the parties remain separate profit centres and thus a hypothetical point at which their relationship could be terminated does exist, their typical behaviour is co-operative. If we may partially repeat ourselves, one could say that this is merely sophisticated self-interest. There is no objection to this, if the burden of individual utility-maximization is separated from what is meant by self-interest. We believe that clarity is better served by seeing co-operation and individual utility-maximization as rival explanations.

## HYPOTHESES TO BE TESTED IN EMPIRICAL STUDIES

We are investigating various types of long-term business relationships where we can gain access for observation and interviews with key personnel. For this purpose, we have developed a number of hypotheses which we propose to test on the basis of the data to be gathered from actual business relationships.

By 'long-term relationship', we refer to a business relationship in which the parties (firms or individuals) have made an idiosyncratic investment of resources for which no substitute relationship is readily available, namely, any alternative relationship would involve (i) substantial search costs to find a suitable 'partner', and (ii) a considerable period of time before the parties could achieve the degree of understanding and co-operation already achieved in the existing relationship. The hypotheses which we have developed and hope to test in empirical studies are:

That the parties to a long-term relationship will continue to co-operate in maintaining and developing the relationship so long as:

(i) (*the incentive*) each party calculates that, in the long run, the benefits which it expects to receive as a result of the co-operation will exceed the benefits which it could derive from any alternative use of its resources; and

(ii) (*the disincentive*) each party is unwilling to abandon the idiosyncratic investment which it has made in the relationship; (the disincentive will be increased if a party would wish to develop a new relationship with a third party, should the existing relationship terminate); and

(iii) (*the reciprocal trust*) each party feels confident that a similar incentive and disincentive are operating upon the other party, so that it may rely on the continuing co-operation of the other.

If the hypothesis in (iii) above is established by empirical findings, it is likely to carry with it the negative finding that the parties to a long-term relationship do not rely on either legal remedies or on market factors to preserve the relationship.

Our contribution to the analysis of long-term relationships is centred on the emphasis on factor (iii) above, the reciprocal trust. The incentive and disincentive in our hypotheses are obviously based on the work of others, but we believe that an important additional factor is trust in the way these factors work on the other party.

It will be clear enough that our model draws heavily on transaction cost analyses, not least of all Williamson's, and in conclusion it is as well to state again what we hope to add to those analyses. The substantial findings of transaction cost analyses presently exist, at the very best, as a very unwieldy collection of exceptions to a basic assumption of individual utility-maximization. What is worse is that to the very large extent that they serve to shield that assumption from criticism when it is at odds with the appreciation of the co-operative features central to the long-term contract, they are explanatorily regressive. Following Coase, transaction cost economics has largely cast its explanations in terms of narrowly individual interest when the issue which seems to be of most importance at the moment seems to be the explanation of an emergent relationship of co-operation based on mutual trust. We hope, following Macneil, to place the insights of transaction cost analysis in a more productive framework by setting up those insights not as a protective barrier of exceptions around *individual* utility-maximization but as counter-evidence to holding that assumption to be the only possible basis of the investigation of long-term contracting.

## NOTES AND REFERENCES

1 D. Campbell and S. Clay, *Long-term Contracting: A Research Bibliography* (forthcoming).

2 One form of this idea is the notion of the efficient breach. The rejection of the possibility of coming to any general conclusion about the efficiency of breach because of the impossibility of quantifying the full costs of such a breach to the non-breaching party is one example of the type of rejection of individual utility-maximizing behaviour as a tenable explanation of contractual relations that we will pursue in general here. I. R. Macneil, 'Efficient Breach: Circles in the Sky' (1982) 68 *Virginia Law Rev.* 947; D. Harris, 'Contract as Promise' (1983) 3 *Int. J. Law and Economics* 69; and I. R. Macneil, 'Contract Remedies: The Need for a Better Efficiency Analysis' (1988) 144 *J. Institutional and Theoretical Economics* 6.

3 T. J. Muris, 'Opportunistic Behaviour and the Law of Contracts' (1981) 65 *Minnesota Law Rev.* 521.

4 David Campbell has analysed why and how this can be the case in 'The Undeath of Contract: A Study in the Degeneration of a Research Programme' (1992) 22 *Hong Kong Law J.* 20.

5 One is obliged to say that many such defences are irrational in that they are not really defences at all; they simply fail to acknowledge the problems involved. We will examine below one of these cases concerning long-term uranium sales.

6 We do not claim, of course, that all parties involved in long-term contracts act co-operatively. Purely individualistic attitudes are common enough. We do claim that those parties which contract efficiently act co-operatively.

7 Developing an argument made in D. Campbell, 'The Social Theory of Relational Contract: Macneil as the Modern Proudhon' (1990) 18 *Int. J. Sociology of Law* 75.

8 There is a sense in which this work attempts to challenge individual utility-maximization as a description of long-term contracting behaviour in the way that the concept of satisficing behaviour did (H. A. Simon, *Administrative Behavior* (3rd ed. 1961), and evolutionary theory is doing (R. R. Nelson and S. G. Winter, *An Evolutionary Theory of Economic Change* (1982)) for maximization goals in corporate planning.

9 S. Macaulay, 'Non-contractual Relations in Business' (1963) 28 *Am. Sociological Rev.* 55.

10 H. Beale and T. Dugdale, 'Contracts Between Businessmen' (1975) 2 *Brit. J. Law and Society* 45.

11 H. Beale, *Remedies for Breach of Contract* (1980) 4–5.
12 I. R. Macneil, 'Restatement (Second) of Contracts and Presentiation' (1974) 60 *Virginia Law Rev.* 592–5.
13 A. M. Polinsky, 'Risk Sharing Through Breach of Contract Remedies' (1983) 12 *J. Legal Studies* 427.
14 R. H. Coase, *The Firm, the Market, and the Law* (1988) 116 (compare pp. 39–40).
15 Within the sense of 'eliminated' we mean to include complete shifting through insurance.
16 Macneil, op. cit., n. 12; Campbell, op. cit., n. 7, pp. 84–86.
17 O. E. Williamson, *Economic Organization* (1986) 88–98.
18 A. D. Chandler, *Scale and Scope* (1989).
19 D. M. Kreps, 'Corporate Culture and Economic Theory' in *Perspectives on Political Economy*, eds. J. E. Alt and K. A. Shepsle (1990) ch. 4.
20 Coase, op. cit., n. 14, pp. 114–9; and O. E. Williamson, *The Economic Institutions of Capitalism* (1985) prologue.
21 O. E. Williamson, *Markets and Hierarchies* (1975) ch. 7.
22 Coase, op. cit., n. 20, chs. 7–8.
23 I. R. Macneil, 'A Primer of Contract Planning' (1975) 48 *Southern California Law Rev.* 627. This article provides the essential structure for Macneil's casebook, *Contracts: Exchange Transactions and Relations* (2nd ed. 1978), and thus the casebook usefully provides a catalogue of the planning devices he describes.
24 Williamson, op. cit., n. 20, ch. 3.
25 H. Collins, *The Law of Contract* (1986) ch. 10.
26 I. R. Macneil, 'Contracts: Adjustment of Long-term Economic Relations Under Classical, Neo-classical, and Relational Contract Law' (1978) 72 *Northwestern Univ. Law Rev.* 854, and Williamson, op. cit., n. 17, ch. 7.
27 P. S. Atiyah, *The Rise and Fall of Freedom of Contract* (1979) 714.
28 *In re Westinghouse Elec. Corp. Uranium Litig.* 405 F Supp 316 (1975).
29 R. A. Posner and A. M. Rosenfield, 'Impossibility and Related Doctrines in Contract Law' (1977) 6 *J. Legal Studies* 83.
30 P. L. Joskow, 'Commercial Impossibility, the Uranium Market and the Westinghouse Case' (1977) 6 *J. Legal Studies* 119.
31 J. T. Maughmer, 'Commercial Impracticability as a Contractual Defence' (1979) 47 *Univ. Missouri-Kansas City Law Rev.* 665.
32 J. J. White and R. S. Summers, *Handbook of the UCC* (2nd ed. 1980) 131–33.
33 R. A. Posner, *Economic Analysis of Law* (3rd ed. 1987) section 4.5. Joskow's analysis is excerpted in *The Economics of Contract Law*, eds. A. T. Kronman and R. A. Posner (1979) 143–49. It is most regrettable that neither of these texts makes any editorial reference to the developments in the Westinghouse case subsequent to Joskow's article which we are about to mention.
34 A more valuable decision, though universally excoriated in classical accounts of 2–615, was *Aluminium Company of America* v *Essex Group Inc.* 499 F Supp 53 (1980), which used the impracticability plea as a basis for the reasonable renegotiation of energy supply contracts. One should note, however, that even this was extra-legal as even the most relaxed reading of frustration remedies under the common law or the UCC could not yield this renegotiated outcome.
35 J. P. Dawson, 'Judicial Revision of Frustrated Contracts: The US' (1984) 64 *Boston Univ. Law Rev.* 25–26. Dawson expands this into an account of the irrelevancy of the plea of impracticability and sets up an account of frustration along similar lines. But it is not the practice of adjustment that is irrelevant, it is the ridiculous legal plea that will not even recognize the practice.
36 When one is a little appreciative of the distance between the oligopoly economy of giant corporations desperately seeking to expand typically moribund effective demand by large-scale planned ventures and the neo-classical economy of buyers who should never commit themselves without being covered, as envisaged by Joskow, then one can readily imagine that Westinghouse's active encouragement of its buyers was at least arguably rational. The

alternative would have been the conclusion that the nuclear energy programme could not have been developed privately or, more generally, that the enterprise would stagnate.

37 The episode is accurately evaluated in S. Macaulay, 'Elegant Models, Empirical Pictures, and the Complexities of Contract' (1977) 11 *Law and Society Rev.* 515–17; S. Macaulay, 'An Empirical View of Contract' (1985) *Wisconsin Law Rev.* 475–76; T. M. Palay, 'A Contract Does Not A Contract Make' (1985) *Wisconsin Law Rev.* 561; and S. W. Halpern, 'Applicability of the Doctrine of Commercial Impracticability: Searching for the "Wisdom of Solomon" ' (1987) 135 *Univ. Pennsylvania Law Rev.* 1123.

38 T. Daintith, 'The Design and Performance of Long-term Contracts' in *Contract and Organization*, eds. T. Daintith and G. Teubner (1986) 164–89.

39 J. Adams and R. Brownsword, *Understanding Contract Law* (1987) ch. 8.

40 Macaulay's reading of all the reported US appellate contract litigation of the two decades up to 1985 yielded examples of the litigious dissolution of long-term relationships only when 'prompted by major shocks to the world economic system' (Macaulay, op. cit., n. 37 (1985), p. 472).

41 Macaulay, op. cit., n. 9, and 'The Use and Non-use of Contracts in the Maufacturing Industry' (1963) 9 *The Practical Lawyer* 13, and op. cit., n. 37 (1977), and op. cit., n. 37 (1985)).

42 Williamson, op. cit., n. 20, ch. 2.

43 Those of Macneil's writings which are particularly important in this respect are *The New Social Contract* (1980) ch. 2 and 'Values in Contract: Internal and External' (1983) 78 *Northwestern Univ. Law Rev.* 340.

44 Williamson, op. cit., n. 20, p. 44.

45 Id., p. 45.

46 Id., p. 44.

47 Id., p. 45.

48 Id., p. 49.

49 Id., p. 45.

50 Anything of Bentham's will convey his elephantine pedantry, but perhaps *An Introduction to the Principles of Morals and Legislation* (1970) chs. 12–14 provide a particularly clear example.

51 Williamson, op. cit., n. 17, pp. 140–41. The fully worked out theory to which Williamson refers is, of course, the Arrow-Debreu model.

52 Williamson, op. cit., n. 20, p. xiii.

53 And in fact what happens is that one of Williamson's behavioural assumptions plays so much the inferior role to the other, bounded rationality, that it really falls out of consideration. This is a mistake, because, as R. Cooter in 'The Cost of Coase' (1982) 11 *J. Legal Studies* 1 points out, strategic bargaining is an obstruction to contracting *theoretically distinct from and in addition to* imperfect information. Our work is an attempt to state this insight as strongly as its full appreciation in the context of long-term contracting requires. It is a typical feature of Posner's work that he has a very brief way with this. Difficulties are typically explained away in this corpus by being redefined in such a way as to confirm Posner's initial position, and so, in this instance, strategic bargaining is a transaction cost (Posner, op. cit., n. 33, pp. 54–55). This is a perfect example of what is called 'concept stretching' in the modern philosophy of science, a strategy for defending original positions at the cost of any actual explanatory growth.

54 A. A. Alchian and H. Demsetz, 'Production, Information Costs, and Economic Organization' (1972) 62 *Am. Econ. Rev.* 777. The type of reasoning involved is extremely clearly presented in R. Townsend, 'Optimal Multi-period Contracts and the Gain from Enduring Relationships Under Private Information' (1982) 90 *J. Pol. Economy* 1166. Alchian would seem to have withdrawn from this position subsequently: A. A. Alchian, 'Specificity, Specialization, and Coalitions' (1984) 140 *J. Institutional and Theoretical Econ.* 38–39.

55 A. Fox, *Beyond Contract* (1974).

56 Williamson, op. cit., n. 20, p. 44.

57 R. D. Lucce and H. Raiffa, *Games and Decisions* (1957). Lucce and Raiffa try to come to terms

(pp. 97–107) with the counter-intuitive non-co-operative result that tends to be produced by finite horizon prisoners' dilemma games. Now, extremely sophisticated reformulations of game theory avoiding these problems can, no doubt, be produced (for example, D. M. Kreps et al., 'Rational Co-operation in the Repeated Prisoner's Dilemma' (1982) 27 *J. Econ. Theory* 245) but just how far this type of remodelling to produce an intuitive result known in advance is actually productive is a prime example of the type of question we are trying to raise.

58 M. Akoi, *The Comparative Game Theory of the Firm* (1984) Part 2.

59 J. Sutton, 'Implementing Game Theoretic Models in Industrial Economics' in *Recent Developments in the Theory of Industrial Organization*, ed. A. Del Monte (1992) ch. 1.

60 D. M. Kreps, *Game Theory and Economic Modelling* (1990).

61 B. Gilad et al., 'From Economic Behaviour to Behavioural Economics' (1984) 13 *J. Behavioural Econ.* 1.

62 R. Swedberg et al., 'The Paradigm of Economic Sociology' in *Structures of Capital*, eds. S. Zukin and P. DiMaggio (1990) ch. 3.

63 P. C. Ordeshook, 'The Emerging Discipline of Political Economy' in Alt and Shepsle, op. cit., n. 19, ch. 1.

64 G. P. Brockway, *The End of Economic Man* (1986).

65 R. H. Coase, 'The New Institutional Economics' (1984) 140 *J. Institutional and Theoretical Econ.* 231.

66 Coase, op. cit., n. 14, pp. 33–34, 54.

67 Id., pp. 97–114.

68 Id., pp. 114–19.

69 R. Coase, 'Adam Smith's View of Man' (1976) 19 *J. Law and Econ.* 529.

70 Coase, op. cit., n. 14, p. 2. Coase bases his view of economics as choice on L. Robbins, *An Essay on the Nature and Significance of Economic Science* (2nd ed. 1935) 16.

71 Coase, op. cit., n. 14, p. 5.

72 Id., p. 2. Coase has in mind the work of G. S. Becker, *The Economic Approach to Human Behaviour* (1976).

73 Coase, op. cit., n. 14, p. 3. Coase refers to J. H. Kagel et al., 'Demand Curves for Animal Consumers' (1981) 96 *Q. J. Econ.* 1.

74 Coase, op. cit., n. 14, p. 4.

75 The most productive lines of contemporary development are expressed in R. Harre, *Social Being* (1979) and R. Bhaskar, *The Possibility of Naturalism* (2nd ed. 1989).

76 Coase, op. cit., n. 14, pp. 4–5.

77 A. Giddens, *The Constitution of Society* (1984).

78 S. Lukes, *Individualism* (1973) chs. 11–13, 18–20.

79 I. Wallerstein, *The Capitalist World Economy* (1979).

80 To the extent that this is so, Coase's work represents a substantial failure to pursue a number of highly productive lines from Veblen which were taken up by a number of other institutionalists, including obviously Commons but represented principally by the sadly relatively little-known Clarence Ayres. For example, see C. E. Ayres, *Science: The False Messiah (1927) and Holier than Thou: The Way of the Righteous (1929) in One Volume with a New Introduction: Prolegemenon to Institutionalism* (1973) xi-xii. The empirical richness to be found in Ayres is a very different type of 'realism' from that of Coase.

81 Coase, op. cit., n. 14, p. 5.

82 Id.

83 As is being undertaken by, for example, M. Taylor, *The Possibility of Co-operation* (1987).

84 Coase is quite happy to say, in *The Firm, the Market, and the Law* (p. 2) that utility is 'a non-existent entity which plays a part similar, I suspect, to that of ether in the old physics'.

85 K. R. Popper, *The Poverty of Historicism* (1987) chs. 1–2.

86 I. Lakatos, *Philosophical Papers* (1978) Vol. 1, ch. 1.

87 Macneil, op. cit., n. 2 (1982), p. 961.

88 I. R. Macneil, 'Economic Analysis of Contractual Relations: Its Shortfalls and the Need for a "Rich Classificatory Apparatus" ' (1981) 75 *Northwestern Univ. Law Rev.* 1022.

89 I. R. Macneil, 'Whither Contracts?' (1969) 21 *J. Legal Education* 405.

90 I. R. Macneil, 'The Many Futures of Contract' (1974) 47 *Southern California Law Rev.* 780.
91 Macneil, op. cit., n. 43 (1980), p. 91.
92 Ibid., p. 1.
93 Id.
94 Ibid., p. 42.
95 Ibid., p. 93.
96 Ibid., pp. 36–37; and Macneil, op. cit., n. 43 (1983), p. 367.
97 Ibid., p. 351.
98 Macneil, op. cit., n. 43 (1980), p. 37.
99 Macneil, op. cit., n. 43 (1983), pp. 367–68.
100 Ibid., p. 379.
101 Macneil, op. cit., n. 43 (1980), p. 38.
102 Macneil, op. cit., n. 43 (1983), p. 347. Compare Macneil, op. cit., n. 90, pp. 808–809; op. cit., n. 28, p. 895; and op. cit., n. 43 (1980), p. 40.
103 Macneil, op. cit., n. 43 (1983), p. 348.
104 Macneil, op. cit., n. 43 (1980), ch. 2.
105 Macneil, op. cit., n. 88, p. 1034.
106 Macneil, op. cit., n. 12, p. 595.
107 Macneil, op. cit., n. 89, pp. 726–35, 753–80; op. cit., n. 23 (1975), pp. 666–67; and op. cit., n. 88, pp. 1044–46.
108 Macneil, op. cit., n. 89, pp. 780–82; op. cit., n. 23 (1975), pp. 651–56; and op. cit., n. 88, pp. 1047–48.
109 Macneil, op. cit., n. 88, pp. 886–98.
110 Macneil, op. cit., n. 89, pp. 750–53; op. cit., n. 26, pp. 899–900; and op. cit., n. 88, pp. 1041–43.
111 Macneil, op. cit., n. 23 (1975), pp. 676–702.
112 Macneil, op. cit., n. 2 (1982), p. 969.
113 Macneil, op. cit., n. 88, pp. 1023–24. (Macneil is quoting from a letter sent to him by S. T. Lowry.)
114 I. R. Macneil, *Contracts: Instruments for Social Co-operation* (1968).
115 Campbell, op. cit., n. 7.
116 J. R. Bowman, *Capitalist Collective Action* (1989).
117 But the incentives and disincentives of the parties need not be of equal weight, as long as they are each of sufficient weight to generate confident mutual reliance. One party's expected share of the joint gains may be greater than the other's. Nevertheless, each will have an incentive to continue so long as it expects its share to be greater than any profit it could make from any alternative commitment of resources. Similarly, one party may have made a heavier idiosyncratic investment in the relationship than the other. Nevertheless, each party is under a disincentive to terminate if it has made an investment of such a size that it is loath to lose it.
118 Williamson, op. cit., n. 17, pp. 105–10.
119 H. Beale et al., 'The Distribution of Cars: A Complex Contractual Technique (English Report)' in *Contract Law Today: Anglo-French Comparisons*, eds. D. Harris and D. Tallon (1989) ch. 7.

# [12]

*International Journal of Project Management* 1994 **12** (3) 137–142

# Organization of public–private partnership projects

## The timely prevention of pitfalls

**J J A M Reijniers**
*Coopers & Lybrand, Churchilllaan 11, 3527 GV Utrecht, Netherlands*

**Public–private partnership (PPP) projects are a special type of project which has lately become of increasing interest to both the public and the private sectors. For such projects (e.g. a bridge, tunnel or industrial area), both sectors are the joint principals. Owing to the fact that these joint partners often have conflicting interests, the organization of this type of project requires special attention. This conclusion was reached after analysis of both the project-management issues and several PPP projects in the Netherlands. To avoid pitfalls during the execution phase of a PPP project, more attention should be paid during the preparation phase to the causes of these pitfalls. Lessons learned on this subject from other types of projects must be put to use. A PPP project also requires a specific organization structure so that the conflicts of interest can be managed. The structure should focus on the constraints and on one common (agreed-upon and accepted down to the last detail) goal. The paper analyses the causes and effects of the problems which arise (pitfalls) when PPP projects are organized and managed. A number of practical recommendations are made to prevent the pitfalls identified. The necessity and importance of PPP projects are not explicitly discussed.**

Keywords: project preparation, project organization, public–private partnership projects

The parliamentary coalition in the Netherlands first mentioned public–private partnerships (PPPs) in 1986 in the light of the rationalization operation and increasing government effectiveness. Since then, PPPs have increasingly constituted an instrument that provides the government with a solution to reduce the financing deficit, and private investment companies with new investment markets. Active cooperation in the form of PPP projects between the public and private sectors also takes place abroad.

Many initiatives have been taken in this field since then. Small local PPP projects are already operational, and turn out to be successful. Various large projects are still in the preparatory phase. The durations of large-scale infrastructural and urban investment projects, for instance, are often quite extensive, as infrastructural projects affect town and country planning to a considerable extent.

However, not all of these projects are always a success. Unexpected major problems usually arise during the operational implementation phase of the project, these are problems which jeopardize the achievement of the goal ultimately envisaged by the participants.

The expectations of PPP projects are high ('PPP projects are a must; they do our country good'), the investments are also high, and yet the results are sometimes disappointing.

One of the causes of these disappointments can be found in the non-goal-directed preparation of PPP projects. The fundamental differences in the participants' characteristics are not considered adequately in advance in the preparation of the project's organization.

### PPP projects: a survey

The true *raison d'être* for a PPP project is two-fold:

- solving the government's financing deficit by cutbacks in investment expenditure, and looking for possibilities of financing the projects from other sources;
- finding new markets for investment companies, as they are faced with a decrease in one of their investment objectives because of cutbacks in the government's financing deficit.

0263–7863/94/030137–06 

In addition, there are the following reasons:

- a more business-like operation by the public sector (the public sector is increasingly forced to manage its funds more efficiently, and a market incentive may prove to be the right boost here);
- more active involvement of the private sector in government decisions.

Before discussing the functioning of PPP projects in greater detail, it would be useful to provide further notes on the definitions of a project in general, and a PPP project in particular. A PPP project can be seen as a special type of project with specific and unique characteristics.

A project is characterized by five features:

- It brings about a change (effecting a technical or organizational change).
- It has complex objectives (the participants may also have 'hidden' objectives).
- It is unique (not only in terms of the objectives, but also in terms of the organizational context).
- It is limited in terms of time and scope (there should always be a balance between time, cost and quality objectives).
- It requires the efforts of a variety of people and funds (and therefore requires the proper skills, responsibilities and authorities to realize the project objective).

A *PPP project* may be defined in various ways. The definition which can best be used in analysing the organizational pitfalls is as follows:

> Bringing about, maintaining, managing and operating provisions and activities by means of a project-wise approach by the public and private sector, starting from a joint risk acceptance as regards estimated costs and expected returns, aimed at the joint realisation of commercial and social objectives.[1]

This means cooperation in a project in which both the public and private sector work together to realize commercial (corporate) and public (social) goals, equally spreading the risks and revenues.

Each PPP project consists of four main phases: the generation of ideas, a feasibility study, the preparation and actual implementation, and operation and management.

Each of these phases has unique features and objectives, and should be considered as a project in itself. The involvement of the participants varies for each of these main phases. The following aspects are important in the definition of a PPP project:

- There is an interaction between the public and private sectors.
- A PPP project is aimed at synergy in the realization of a unique goal.
- Both social and commercial features are involved.
- The identities and responsibilities of the participants are maintained.

Potential pitfalls are hidden in the above aspects of the definition of PPP projects, which will be analysed in more detail in this section. For example, there are a number of essential differences between PPP projects and nonPPP projects. The common goal is not as common as it seems to be at first, and, consequently, the efforts of people and the funds differ. Moreover, there are two different principals. The differences ensue from the different interests of the public and private sectors, such as the nature of the participants on the one hand, and the differences in the corporate culture on the other hand, leading to differences in the method of working.

*Differences in interests*

The interests of the *public sector* are concerned with

- legislation, regulations and authorities;
- political opinion and political influence;
- democratic decision-making processes;
- the minimization of risks;
- the realization of a social goal.

The public sector therefore has its own objectives and its own political responsibilities. It should be borne in mind that, usually, in politics, a balanced compromise between all the interested parties involved needs to be arrived at. Legislation in the field of involvement is conducive to the concept of compromise.

Hardly any government objective is quantifiable (can be expressed in a performance figure, for example). In addition, the public sector is suspicious of the requirement for a private company to make money on an investment, and is hardly aware of the fact that losses may also be suffered.

The public sector is not homogeneous either. Local authorities may have their own set of rules and regulations, which may be in conflict with the national interest.

The interests of the *private sector*, on the other hand, are aimed at

- achieving returns on the invested funds;
- daring to take business risks;
- having to anticipate market and competitive developments;
- realizing a corporate goal.

The compromise concept mentioned above never goes as far for the private sector as it does for the public sector. The laws of business economy apply to the private sector. For the private sector, it is vital that the nonrealization of the business objectives, or the inability to realize them, is always immediately felt. It sometimes results in the discontinuance of the business operations.

## Differences in corporate culture

There are some typical differences between the public and private sectors in relation to working methods:

- There is a difference in management approach. 'Management by objectives' and 'a deal is a deal' should come to mind here.
- There is a difference in the perception of risks and their consequences.
- There is a difference in decision-making processes. Hierarchy in decision making, consultative structures, and involvement procedures should come to mind here.
- There is a difference in opinion about the time factor.

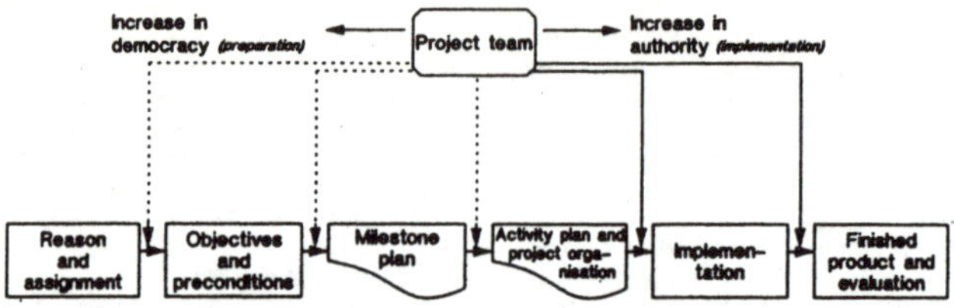


**Figure 1** One principle of project preparation: involve performers in planning process

In short, it can be said that the above-mentioned differences in interest and corporate culture between the public and private sectors may create a tension that can be considered the basis of the problems that arise during the preparation and implementation of PPP projects.

The pursuit of social benefits (by the public sector) and the pursuit of commercial benefits (by the private sector) are simply not features which go together naturally.

In the initial phase of a PPP project, such tensions do not as yet have an impact, since the participants are eager to work together. After some time (and definitely after the contract has been signed), changes in the principles, objectives and preconditions of the project sometimes lead to far-reaching (financial) consequences.

## Organization of project

Before the detailing of the organization of a PPP project, the organization of projects in general is explained. *Projectivity* comes first in such projects: preparing and managing projects efficiently and effectively[2]. Naturally, this is also true for PPP projects.

Practical experience has shown that adequate preparation for a project is *the* critical success factor. A phased approach should be adopted, incorporating

- the reason for and definition of the assignment;
- a definition of the objectives and preconditions;
- a definition of the milestones to be attained;
- a definition of activity plans, project organization, responsibilities and authorities;
- the implementation of the project;
- an evaluation.

*Figure 1* shows such a phasing.

An analysis of a large number of projects already carried out* shows that project management has many pitfalls. These can be divided into five categories: assignment and objectives, planning, organization and coordination, control, and management. Examples of the most common pitfalls are as follows.

*Objectives:*

- The project is not adequately supported by company management. The project plans are not in line with the company plans or principles, and the project's policy lines are not described.
- The project is not well defined, because only the technical changes have been described, because cultural implications have been forgotten, or because the scope of the project has not been established accurately.

*Planning:*

- The level of planning has not been divided evenly. The management is inundated with details, while the project team is provided with too little information.
- The tools intended for planning are impractical. People are more interested in the extensiveness of the aids than in their effectiveness.
- The planning technique discourages creativity.
- The time and cost estimates are too optimistic.

*Organization:*

- The organization of the project is not efficient; it is too heavy and bureaucratic.
- The distribution of authorities is not described.
- The cooperation principles are unclear.
- The key staff and line managers are not motivated; they are not sufficiently interested in the project and its objectives.

*Control:*

- The project team does not understand the necessity of progress control.
- The plan and the progress reports are not integrated; they do not provide a useful standard for further progress of the project.
- Changes in the plan or in the specifications are left unmonitored.
- The objectives of the project are out of balance with the practical implementation.

*Management:*

- The project manager has the responsibility, but not the formal authority.
- The project manager is a technocrat, and not a manager. He/she is unable to delegate, coordinate and control.

Further analysis of projects with problems that arose during the implementation phase has shown that the problems arose in the preparatory phases. A comparison of these results with other surveys described in various publications on the subject leads mostly to the same conclusion. *Figure 2* shows the results of the analysis.

* This was carried out by Coopers & Lybrand Management Consultants in the Netherlands. The projects varied greatly in nature and in terms of different environments.

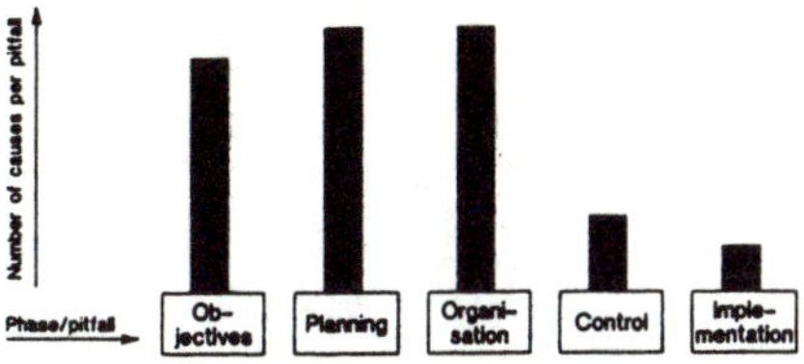


**Figure 2** Problems arising during the implementation of a project often originate in the preparatory phases
[*Source:* Coopers & Lybrand desk research (104 projects).]

To be able to realize a successful project, and prevent the pitfalls mentioned above, a systematic approach which aims at achieving the objectives is needed. During the preparatory phases, the active involvement of the participants is necessary (a democratic process), whereas, during the implementation phase, a consistent execution of the (adequately prepared) plans is needed (i.e. an increasingly authoritarian process to make sure that the plan is executed in a goal-directed manner).

The outlined approach is based on four principles:

- *Results-directed:* The project manager focuses on what has to be achieved (objectives) and not on *how* this is to be achieved (tasks).
- *Describing both the cultural and technical objectives:* This should result in a consistent solution for the tensions that may occur during the project.
- *Providing leadership and not just plans:* The project manager should compile a framework for the project, within which the plan is only a tool.
- *Keeping the project documentation simple and accessible.*

These principles are the key characteristics of the Goal Directed Project Management approach[2].

The essence of successful project management is in the preparation: 'think before you act'. The organizations of projects described in general are also of importance to a PPP project.

## Analysis of some Dutch PPP projects

Some investment projects undertaken in the Netherlands which could be designated PPP projects are the tunnel under the river Noord, Parkeerschap Den Bosch, Parking Amsterdam, the Westerschelde bank connections, the Betuwe railway, high-speed train tracks, Fokkerweg Schiphol-Oost, the Maastricht Sphinx plan, Zeedijk Amsterdam, and the Amsterdam IJ bank project.

A number of these projects have been assessed* in terms of their organizational project problems. The methodology described in the preceding section has been used as a working model.

The problems identified all arose during the implementation phase. The cause can often be found in an earlier project phase (see *Figure 1*). The problems are given below, and classified by their cause for each pitfall category:

*Assignment and objectives:*

- the fact that small-scale projects are much more successful than large-scale projects;
- problems with the financial structure and the formation of consortia in the case of large-scale projects;
- little confidence in each other (no basis for a lasting relationship);
- lack of clarity about objectives and working methods;
- conflicting interests of the public and private sectors;
- uncertainty about future developments;
- lack of clarity about the distribution of authority;
- lack of experience with PPPs;
- exaggerated expectations;
- lengthy duration, and inability to respond to market developments;
- lack of clarity about the distribution of input, risks and benefits;
- no arbitration procedures.

*Planning:*

- insufficient phasing.

*Organization and coordination:*

- little experience of doing business together;
- no adequate distribution of responsibilities and authorities;
- laborious political decision-making process;
- difference in working methods and knowhow;
- long-lasting noncommitted attitude;
- influence by third parties;
- inadequate project organization structure;
- insufficient 'internal' project coordination;
- power struggles.

*Control:*

- political changes during implementation;
- absence of progress-control methodology.

*Management:*

- absence of management skills;
- absence of independent project manager.

Upon further elaboration, it was established that project-management problems can, in fact, be traced back to the conflict of interests between the public and private sectors: social benefits *versus* commercial benefits. As long as there is no balance, it is impossible to resolve the tensions. To avoid this pitfall, the government sector should manage issues such as revenues and speed, and the private sector should act upon governmental rules and laws, and use a democratic process.

With large-scale PPP projects in particular, such as in the field of infrastructure and urban investment projects, the implications of introducing changes during the implementation phase are not sufficiently taken into account. As the project preparation or implementation continues, the consequences relating to costs/benefits may be considerable.

## Practical recommendations

To prevent the pitfalls outlined in the preceding section,

* By the author.

the following recommendations* are made for the organization of PPP projects. The recommendations are structured according to the categories in *Figure 2*.

*Assignment and objectives:*

- clarity about the actual principals/clients;
- a 'champion' with evident decision-making power;
- commitment in relation to the goal of and approach to the project;
- risk analysis and feasibility tests;
- project objectives in line with the business plans of both the public and private sectors;
- an unambiguously described final objective;
- a clearly defined project scope;
- a definition of interim results (milestones) aimed at the final objective;
- formulated quantifiable measuring points;
- intensive kick-off discussion with 'key' decision makers aimed at a formulation of the objective, confidence, and the application of creativity; private sector involved from the beginning;
- adequate decision documents available;
- 'teaching' of one another about working methods and style of management;
- 'technical specialists' not allowed to participate in the kick-off discussion too soon, the chance of slipping into procedural details being too large;
- preparation of an arbitration protocol;
- clarity about the distribution of input, risk and yield (costs/benefits and the level of compliance of each participant).

*Planning:*

- at least two planning levels prepared;
  - o *milestone plan: what* must be achieved;
  - o *activity plan: how* to achieve it;
- creativity in preparing the plans;
- thorough preparation and realistic planning;
- risk management embedded in planning;
- phased approach.

*Organization and coordination:*

- responsibilities and authorities laid down in a responsibility chart;
- project organization organized 'practically' and 'conveniently';
- commitment as to personnel and funds;
- preconditions and goal formulated for each project phase in line with the milestone plan;
- project manual compiled for all project participants;
- adequate consultative and communication structures set up;
- goal and work agreements unambiguously laid down;
- 'kick-off' meeting convened with all project participants.

*Control:*

- integrated planning and progress reports;
- tight monitoring of changes in the original plan;
- involvement of many activated by progress reports and the provision of information;
- bottlenecks detected at an early stage;

* These are partly based on experience with the Coopers & Lybrand method Goal Directed Project Management.

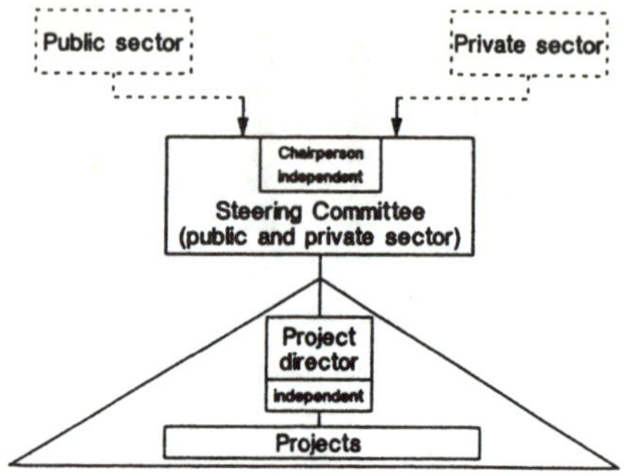


**Figure 3** Organization of PPP project: practical and well organized

- each project phase always evaluated as well as the completion of the project (audit).

*Management:*

- balanced responsibilities and authorities for the project manager;
- outsider as independent project manager;
- project manager recruited on the basis of leadership skills.

*Figure 3* shows a proposed organizational structure for a PPP project.

## Summary and conclusions

For a PPP project to be successful, it is important to bear in mind that, if the public sector is a participant, it must act as a private company in terms of management (i.e. effectively and efficiently, focused on the realization of goals with the funds available, within the time set and with accepted revenues). An additional advantage for the public sector may consequently be that projects are actually completed on time. The public sector should be aware of the public rules and regulations, and also have an understanding of the democratic decision-making process.

However, the public sector must also fulfil its obligations. Continual changes of policy do not constitute a basis for cooperation with the private sector. If the public sector (or the political establishment) wants to introduce changes in principles, objectives and preconditions, then it must provide financial compensation for the ensuing consequences.

Every entrepreneur will require a risk surcharge for projects which entail (large) risks. The public sector should take this for granted.

The core problem with PPP projects is the level of compliance with the benefits and the agreements on financial compensation if the targets are not achieved (beyond the level of compliance of the private sector).

In view of the impairment risk with PPP projects, it should be established, before such a project is begun, whether the added value of the combination (public–private sector) is greater than if each of the individual parties were to carry out the project independently.

Small-scale PPP projects usually derive their success because they are orderly, they have hardly any cross-relationships with other fields (of policy), the entrepreneurial risks can be reasonably well estimated, and the entrepreneur is capable of independently exerting influence on the benefits.

Some critical success factors for successful PPP projects are as follows:

- 'Key' decision makers form part of the project team right from the start of the preparation of the project (the project 'kick off').
- Measurable results are available to enable active monitoring of the progress (clear goals and well organized phasing).
- There is a focus on results, and the project is goal-directed.
- There is active periodic progress monitoring during implementation.
- There is an independent project team and an independent project leader, who report to a steering committee consisting of top representatives from both the public and private sectors (project organization).
- The political and economic risks are distinctly spread at an early stage.
- There are adequate and clear working methods and agreements.
- The private sector is allowed to fulfil its entrepreneurial role.
- There is mutual confidence.

In addition to the solutions to the pitfalls mentioned above, some major recommendations are as follows.

- Start the 'kick-off' meeting at an early stage. Focus on becoming familiar with the participants' methods and objectives via
  - o teaching each other;
  - o intensive consultations about the project objectives, preconditions, risks and the role of the participants.
- Compile a milestone plan and responsibility chart.
- Ensure that the participants in the 'kick-off' meeting are officials at a strategic level with decision-making authority.
- Keep decision-making procedures short.
- Establish a convenient project organization at a high corporate level.

## References

1 Knoester, T 'Publiek-private samenwerkingsvormen vinden steeds meer toepassing' *Harvard Holland Rev.* No 15 (1988) pp 100–107 (public–private cooperation is being applied increasingly)

2 Andersen, E S, Grude, K V, Haug, T and Turner, J R *Goal Directed Project Management* Kogan Page (1987)

## Bibliography

Bakker, R 'Gereedschap voor Publiek–Private Samenwerking' *ESB* (8 Jul 1992) pp 676–678 (tools for public–private cooperation)

*Het Financieele Dagblad* (1991) and (1992) (several PPP articles)

Kohnstamm, P P and Uittenbogaard, L B 'Publiek–Private Samenwerking en stedelijke vernieuwing' *ESB* (25 Sep 1991) pp 964–966 (public–private cooperation and urban development)

Reijniers, J J A M 'Doeltreffend projectmanagement' *Harvard Holland Rev.* No 22 (1990) pp 77–82 (Goal Directed Project Management)

*Jacques Reijniers MBA is a partner at Coopers & Lybrand in the Netherlands. He is responsible for both the interim management department and the project-management business area. He is also the director of the Coopers & Lybrand European Centre of Excellence for Project Management, and a part-time associate professor of project management at Brunel University/Henley Management College, UK. His background is in mechanical engineering, logistics and marketing. He has been responsible for a large number of projects in the areas of logistics, marketing, and organization in various business environments.*

[13]

Ronald J. Daniels
Michael J. Trebilcock*

# PRIVATE PROVISION OF PUBLIC INFRASTRUCTURE: AN ORGANIZATIONAL ANALYSIS OF THE NEXT PRIVATIZATION FRONTIER†

## I *Introduction*

Constrained by severe, ongoing fiscal pressures and sensitive to concerns over bureaucratic inefficiency, policy-makers in a number of countries are re-evaluating both the goals and instruments of the modern state. In doing so, some have endorsed the need for government 'reinvention,' a term that is admittedly susceptible of a broad range of meanings, but which nonetheless contemplates a significant shift away from reliance on governmental provision of goods and services in favour of provision by the for-profit and third sectors.[1] Although not uncontroversial, the claim is that, in comparison with governmental supply systems, both for-profit and third sector modes of delivery offer a superior means for organizing productive activity because of the greater incentives that exist within these organizations for lower-cost, innovative production. Although the claim has been made in a number of different policy contexts, we focus on its salience in the context of government's role in supplying traditional physical infrastructure projects such as roads and highways, bridges, dams, water and sewage systems, and airports.

Physical infrastructure offers a useful litmus test for evaluating the sundry claims that have been made in favour of government reinvention. First, there is a growing level of concern in both the developed and developing world with the adequacy of existing levels of investment

* Both of the Faculty of Law, University of Toronto.

† We acknowledge the invaluable research assistance of Lesley Arbus, Philip Panet, and Randy Cass in the preparation of this article. We also wish to thank Ian Ayres, Gillian Hadfield, George Priest, Pablo Spiller, Oliver Williamson, and Ralph A. Winter, as well as participants in workshops at the American Law and Economics Association annual meeting (May 1995), the Canadian Law and Economics Association annual meeting (September 1994), the University of California (at Berkeley), and the University of Pennsylvania, for comments on an earlier draft.

1 See David Osborne and Ted Gaebler *Reinventing Government* (New York: Plume 1993); The National Performance Review (*Gore Report on Reinventing Government*) (New York: Random House, Times Books 1993); Michael Trebilcock *The Prospects for Reinventing Government* (Toronto: C.D. Howe Institute 1994).

in infrastructure.[2] In part, concern over infrastructural investment can be traced to economic studies that have asserted a strong linkage between infrastructure investment and national productivity. Perhaps the leading proponent of this view, David Aschauer, has argued that declining levels of investment in infrastructure accounted for declining productivity growth in the G-7 countries during the 1970s and 1980s.[3] Although the magnitude of the purported correlation between infrastructure investment and growth has been questioned in subsequent research, that research has tended to confirm that such a relationship does exist,[4] and, further, that societal welfare gains could be realized

2 The World Bank has recently undertaken an extensive study of infrastructure investment in the developing world: World Bank report *Infrastructure for Development* (New York: Oxford University Press 1994). The report notes that developing countries currently invest $200 billion a year in new infrastructure, an amount equal to 4% of their national output and a fifth of their total investment, a level which is expected to increase to 7% of total output by the year 2000. While private investment in infrastructure now constitutes only 15% of the total investment, given fiscal pressures, that level is expected to grow in the near future.

3 David Aschauer 'Is Public Expenditure Productive?' (1989) 24 *J. of Monetary Econ.* 177; 'Does Public Capital Crowd Out Private Capital?' (1989) 24 *J. of Monetary Econ.* 171; and 'Public Investment and Productivity Growth in the Group of Seven' (1989) 13 *Econ. Perspectives.* Aschauer's results were based on regression analysis on a standard Cobb Douglas aggregate production function which generated predictions of the effect of infrastructure investment on productivity. On the basis of Aschauer's research, it is possible to attribute fully 100% of the productivity slowdown in the United States over the last several decades to declining levels of infrastructure investment. Indeed, Aschauer has claimed that returns to core infrastructure expenditure may be as much as 20 times that of private capital. (David Aschauer 'Why Is Infrastructure Important?' in Alicia Munnell (ed.) 'Is the Public Capital Stock Too Low?' Chicago Fed. Letter, Federal Reserve Bank of Chicago, October 1987, No. 2.) On the basis of this work, Aaron projected that a $500 billion increase in the 1988 stock of public capital would translate into a productivity gain of 14.0 to 14.8%. (Henry J. Aaron, Discussion of 'Why Is Infrastructure Important?' in Alicia Munnell, supra, 51–63.) Similarly, Robert Reich has invoked Aschauer's work to suggest that a one-time $10 billion increase in new infrastructure investment would support a permanent $7 billion increase in US GNP. See Robert Reich 'The Real Economy' (February 1991) 267 *The Atlantic* 35 at 46).

4 For instance, invoking cost function analysis, Catherine Morrison has found that 20% of productivity growth in the United States could be attributed to infrastructure investment. (Catherine J. Morrison *A Microeconomic Approach to the Measurement of Economic Performance: Productivity Growth, Capacity Utilization, and Related Performance Indicators* (Springer-Verlag Press 1992); 'Macroeconomic Relationships between Public Spending on Infrastructure and Private Sector Productivity in the U.S.' in J. Mintz (ed.) *Infrastructure and Competitiveness* (Ontario: Queen's University 1995). Specifically, Morrison has concluded that 'the cost-benefits from infrastructure investment at the margin appear positive, significant, and often larger than the

by reallocating public and private investment away from other expenditures towards infrastructure.[5]

A second reason for focusing on physical infrastructure projects relates to the challenges in designing workable institutional arrangements that permit public goals to be vindicated in a setting of enhanced private sector involvement. These issues are particularly acute in physical infrastructure projects where an amalgam of efficiency and distributional goals – public goods, natural monopolies, externalities, coordination problems – have traditionally furnished support for public intervention of some kind. To the extent that these rationales enjoy some continued force, the question is whether and how enhanced levels of private sector or third sector involvement can be reconciled with a role for the state.

A final reason for focusing on physical infrastructure relates to the distinct properties of these projects and the challenges posed for devising optimal institutional arrangements. These properties include: (1) the large, up-front investments required by physical infrastructure projects (given asset lumpiness, investors often cannot make incremental investments, and typically these projects have high minimum-efficient scales); (2) the longevity of infrastructure assets (implying that the life span of the asset will often exceed the term of the project contract, which creates contracting problems discussed below); (3) the sunk investment in such assets (given the location and use-specific nature of these assets, investors will not be able to recover the value of their investment through the redeployment of assets to next-best uses); (4) the anticipatory character of the investment (the final value of physical infrastructure projects is hard to determine ex ante because

associated costs even when only manufacturing benefits are taken into account' (in Mintz, supra). It should be noted that Aschauer's recent work, which is based on an expanded framework, yields results that are consistent with Morrison's.) Other economists, relying on project-specific cost-benefit analyses, have also demonstrated significant gains from targeted infrastructure investment. For instance, David Lewis argues that fully audited benefit-cost studies of investments in new runways for Minneapolis–St. Paul and Vancouver international airports yield reported rates of return in excess of 100%. (David Lewis 'Infrastructure and Economic Growth' in Mintz, supra.) He also cites studies respecting other infrastructure projects that indicate significant benefits from public infrastructure investment: highway maintenance projects (30 to 40%), new highway construction in urban areas (10 to 20%), and modernization and expansion of air traffic control systems (20 to 25%). For a summary of these studies, see World Bank, supra note 2, 15.

5 See, for instance, Douglas Holtz-Eakin 'Public Sector Capital and the Productivity Puzzle' National Bureau of Economic Research, Working Paper No. 4122, July 1992.

the services they provide are dependent upon the value of downstream goods and services); and (5) the status of government as a party to infrastructure projects with the private sector and the difficulties in devising effective contractual commitments against ex post opportunism by government.

In this article, we canvass the scope for enhanced private sector involvement in the provision of public infrastructure by focusing on several different projects that have been recently initiated or completed in Canada: airports (Terminal 3 and the aborted redevelopment of Terminals 1 and 2 at Toronto's Pearson International Airport), toll roads (Highway 407 north of Toronto), and bridges (the fixed link between Prince Edward Island and New Brunswick). The structure of these projects is based on an allegedly innovative set of organizational arrangements: the so-called public/private sector partnership. The stated purpose of these projects is to increase the level of private sector participation in designing, building, and operating projects that service public goals.

We develop two central themes in the article. First, while tangible efficiency gains can be realized by remitting responsibility for infrastructure development to the private sector, we argue that these gains can easily be offset by losses that derive from faulty design of both the selection process and the contractual arrangements used for implementation. Second, and greatly complicating matters, are the contracting problems posed by the status of government as a party to the public/private partnership. Because of its inherent powers of legislative fiat, governments can abrogate contractual undertakings without having to compensate parties for the loss of their expectation profits. The existence of this power places understandable limits on the willingness of private sector developers to invest risk capital in these projects, thereby depriving government of at least some of the benefits from private sector involvement. In general, we conclude that insufficient attention to the complexities of the institutional challenges raised by highly integrated public/private sector infrastructure partnerships has led to uncritical enthusiasm for them by many of their proponents. The recent World Bank report *Infrastructure for Development* strikingly exemplifies this tendency: while emphasizing the magnitude of present and prospective investments in infrastructure by developing countries and the potential for a much enlarged role for the private sector in infrastructure development and operation, very little attention is paid to the design of the institutional processes surrounding public/private sector infrastructure partnerships or the complex contracting problems that they present. However, the difference between success and failure of these projects in terms of the welfare gains over traditional modes of infrastructure development resides in the institutional details that we analyse herein.

## II *Three recent Canadian case studies involving public/private partnerships*[6]

### A. INTRODUCTION

The public/private sector partnerships in the development and operation of infrastructure that are proliferating around the world vary widely in both scale and nature. According to the World Bank, the average size of such projects in low-income countries has been $440 million and that of projects in the planning stages has been even higher, at $640 million. In middle-income countries average project size is more than 25% smaller.[7] However, even in developed economies, some projects are of very large scale, the best-known being the private financing, construction, and operation of the Channel Tunnel between England and France involving a capital investment of about $US11 billion.[8] By contrast, a number of public/private infrastructure partnerships relate to relatively small-scale activities, often at the local or municipal level, such as water and sewage treatment facilities, often entailing capital investments of a few million dollars. The sectors where these partnerships have emerged also vary widely and include telecommunications, power generation, power distribution, gas distribution, railroads, road infrastructure, ports, airport facilities, and water and sewage treatment plants.[9] The nature of the arrangements involved also varies widely. Some involve public ownership with private operation through lease contracts, concessions, or management contracts, while others involve full private ownership and private operation. Yet others involve non-profit operation through local community organizations.[10]

In this part, we briefly discuss the structure and salient features of three recent Canadian case studies involving public/private partnerships in the development and operation of public infrastructure that are the basis of the organizational analysis we develop in this article:

6 A detailed description of the case studies is developed in a draft manuscript on file with the authors.

7 World Bank, supra note 2.

8 See Robert Tiong 'Comparative Study of BOT Projects' (1990) 6 *J. of Management in Engineering* 107, 108.

9 World Bank, supra note 2, 64.

10 Ibid. 8 and 9.

Highway 407; The Prince Edward Island Fixed Link; and the redevelopment of Pearson International Airport in Toronto.

B. HIGHWAY 407

Highway 407 is a 69 km toll highway that is designed to alleviate traffic congestion in the northern region of the Greater Toronto Area at a cost of $929.8 million.[11] Although the provincial ministry of transport was initially committed to developing the project as a non-toll highway through the traditional procurement model, government budget constraints would have dictated the project's completion over a twenty-year period. By structuring the project as a public/private partnership, the government was able to expedite the project's development to four-and-a-half years.[12] Further, by vesting ownership of the highway for a term in the private sector, it can be presumed that government's direct responsibility for the imposition of the tolling charge (a revenue generation device used infrequently in Canada on public highways) would be attenuated.

Responsibility for the selection of a project developer was vested in a Crown corporation, the Ontario Transportation Capital Corporation (OTCC).[13] The OTCC used a three-stage selection process, involving an initial request for expressions of interest and qualifications, a value engineering exercise,[14] and a closed-bid request for proposals. Three consortia participated in the first round of the selection process, but one consortium was disqualified early on, and only two bidders sub-

11 Employment benefits are estimated at 3,000 jobs in the first year and 20,000 jobs over the life of the construction project. jobsOntario: Capital, news release, 8 April and 11 May 1994.

12 Under the public/private partnership model, the project would take only four-and-a-half years rather than the twenty years necessary under the traditional model. Conversation with L. Brian Swartz, legal counsel, MTO, 1 June 1994.

13 The OTCC was established in 1993 for the purpose of financing and implementing major public transit and highway construction projects, encouraging private sector investment and participation, and focusing on user-pay financing methods. jobsOntario news release, 10 February 1993. The actual nature of the relationship between the OTCC and the provincial government is unclear, and the Crown corporation seems to be an attempt by the Ontario government to shift infrastructure financing off-budget, even though OTCC debt remains a liability of the provincial government. Although the OTCC is structured as a mechanism which dedicates toll revenues to financing highway construction, it also seems to be able to finance construction at least in part by borrowing against the general provincial credit through government guarantees.

14 See discussion in note 48, infra.

mitted final bids. While it was initially anticipated that the project would be privately financed, concerns by the remaining bidders with the risks of low traffic volumes led to demands for government financial guarantees. Ultimately, however, the government concluded that the benefits of private sector financing did not outweigh the costs of such guarantees, and the project was financed entirely through an OTCC public debt issue. At the end of the selection process, the OTCC selected Canadian Highways International Corporation to design and build the project. As of June 1996, the operation and maintenance contracts had not yet been executed.

### C. THE PRINCE EDWARD ISLAND FIXED LINK

The Prince Edward Island Fixed Link is a federally sponsored project to build a 13.5 km bridge across the Northumberland Strait, which would constitute the first permanent crossing between PEI and the mainland. The fixed link would serve as a substitute for the existing ferry service between the mainland and PEI, which, in accordance with a constitutional obligation, was required to be subsidized by the federal government. The principal avowed benefit of the project was a significant reduction in the time necessary to travel to and from the province, resulting in enhanced local business competitiveness and increased Island tourism.[15] As well, by contracting out the obligation to link the mainland and PEI, the federal government sought to reduce the financial level of its constitutional obligation.

The project was initiated in 1985, when the federal government received several unsolicited private sector proposals for the development of a fixed link between PEI and the mainland. The project was subject to extensive public review for social (particularly environmental) benefits before and after the selection process was commenced.[16]

15 The economic value of the reduced travel time is estimated to be $398.4 million (1993$) (*A Benefit-Cost Analysis of the Northumberland Strait Crossing Project*, prepared by Gardner Pinfold Consulting Economists Limited, September 1993 at p. 4). The fixed link is also expected to have additional indirect benefits on economic activity in PEI and the Atlantic provinces, since construction of the bridge creates a large, front-end-loaded job creation stimulus in the Atlantic economy, which is currently suffering from a severe decline in the Maritime fishery – perhaps as many as 1,500 direct-hire jobs annually over the life of the project. (William G. Reinhardt 'PEI Bridge Project Essentials' (November 1993) 68 *PWFinancing* 23.)

16 The initial cost-benefit study conducted by PWC (Economic Feasibility Assessment for the Northumberland Strait Crossing, Draft Final Report, July 1987, Fiander-Good Associates Ltd.), which found a net benefit of close to $500 million (1987$), has been criticized on methodological grounds (Peter Townley 'The Weakest Link'

Indeed, so intense was public concern with the social impact of the project that nearly six-and-a-half years transpired between the publication of the initial request for expressions of interest and the execution of the contract between Strait Crossing Inc. (SCI)[17] and the federal government.[18]

As with Highway 407, the government used a multi-stage selection process, in this case involving an initial request for expressions of interest and qualifications, a request for proposals, and a request for more complete proposals (including a financial plan). Initially, twelve different consortia expressed interest in the project. However, by the final stage of the selection process, only three bidders remained. The winning bidder, SCI, was selected on the basis that, inter alia, it required the lowest level of federal financial assistance to develop the project: $40.6 million annually for a term of 35 years.[19] The subsidy conferred by the federal government on the project operators graphically underscores the persistence of government risk sharing in these projects.[20] Having selected SCI, sixteen months of negotiations were required before the government and the consortium were able to

(July/August 1992) 13(6) *Policy Options* 15; and *A Review of the Benefit-Cost Analysis of the Northumberland Strait Crossing Project*, prepared by Gardner Pinfold Consulting Economists Limited, September 1992). However, a subsequent cost-benefit study conducted by one of the critics found a net benefit of $263.6 million (1993$) (Gardner Pinfold, supra note 15; note that this 1993 study was commissioned by Public Works Canada). The main difficulties in the cost-benefit studies were the valuation of travel savings, the treatment of corporate taxes, and the determining of the social opportunity cost of labour.

17 SCI is a joint venture owned by four firms: Strait Crossing Inc. of Calgary (15%); Northern Construction Co. (35%); GTMI (Canada) Inc. of Montreal (30%); and Ballast Nedam (20%). Consultation with Strait Crossing office, Charlottetown, 26 August 1994.

18 Such searching social review is a necessary complement to whatever private sector certification occurs through the financing process, as the latter is predicated on private, not social, costs and benefits.

19 The federal government's obligation to supply $41.9 million a year in indexed funding to the project developers was then used to support a debt issue of $661 million by the developers in exchange for rights to the subsidy. After the 35-year period, the government's subsidy would end, and the project developers would be required to recover ongoing maintenance costs entirely from toll revenues.

20 In addition, the federal government assumed a number of different exogenous risks related to the project, in some cases agreeing to compensate SCI for costs of delay related to war, earthquakes, nuclear events, government regulation specifically affecting the project, and environmental injunctions.

conclude a contract.[21] To safeguard SCI's franchise, the contract between the federal government and the developer limited the government's ability to compete with the project by providing ferry service or by constructing an additional bridge or tunnel within 25 km of the fixed link or by any means that would significantly reduce traffic volumes. However, in the light of the monopoly power conferred on the operator by this restriction, the contract imposed limits on permissible increases in bridge tolls by the operator to 75% of CPI.

### D. THE REDEVELOPMENT OF PEARSON INTERNATIONAL AIRPORT

The Pearson International Airport project was a staged public/private project designed to redevelop Toronto's congested international airport by securing private sector involvement in the design, construction, and operation of two new terminal facilities. The first, Terminal 3 (T3), involved the construction of a new terminal building, parking garage, and adjacent hotel and office complex, while the second, the redevelopment of Terminals 1 and 2 (T1T2), involved the replacement of the airport's two existing (and somewhat dilapidated) terminals with a single new terminal which would have had 55 gates in total by the year 2000.[22] Several reasons were advanced for enlisting private sector involvement in the project, including higher levels of revenue likely to be generated for the federal government by the project (as opposed to a scenario of continued federal government ownership and operation), the need to ensure the timely introduction of new capacity, and the superior organizational efficiency of the private sector.[23] The T3 project was announced in 1986 and was based upon a two-stage selection process: an initial request for expressions of interest and qualifications, and then a second-stage request for proposals. As in other projects, the criteria used to determine success in the first-round tournament for design ideas were fairly broadly defined: Transport Canada merely identified that the objectives of the project were to: provide a 'world-class' terminal in the shortest period of time; provide a financial return

21 The primary factors in this delay were the two environmental challenges pursued in the Federal Court against the minister of public works.

22 According to a 1987 Transport Canada study, Pearson International Airport has a $4 billion direct economic impact on the economy of Ontario and is directly and indirectly responsible for over 56,000 jobs. Referred to in the Nixon Report, infra.

23 According to Transport Canada, the purposes of the Terminal 3 development were to (1) provide a world-class air terminal facility; (2) reduce government investment in airport facilities; (3) increase private sector participation; and (4) provide a financial return to the federal government. See LBPIA–General Distribution, p. 6.

to the Crown; and maintain acceptable levels of safety and security to air travellers in Canada. Requests by the bidders for information with respect to the actual weighting of each of these factors by the project evaluation team were refused. Eight bids were submitted in the design tournament, and, of those, five consortia were qualified to proceed to the second stage. Of these, only four consortia submitted final proposals, and, at the end of June 1987, the federal government awarded the project to Airport Development Corporation (ADC). Within five months, the government was able to execute a contract with ADC for the project based on a 40-year lease (with a 20-year period of renewal) with required annual lease payments that would vary directly with gross revenues and with the time since project completion. Although the project was expected to cost $350 million, an expansion in capacity to accommodate an expected increase in traffic load of the terminal's principal tenant, Canadian Airlines, increased costs to $550 million. The project was completed within 32 months of commencement.

Whereas the rapid completion of the T3 project was viewed as a model for public/private partnerships, the T1T2 redevelopment project was much less so. Almost from the outset, the project was embroiled in controversy. The first reason for controversy was based on the federal government's decision, apparently motivated by revenue goals, to depart from its stated policy preference for vesting responsibility for the development of federal airports in local airport authorities – not-for-profit organizations which would be governed by, and accountable to, local interest groups.[24] The second principal reason for controversy was the decision to proceed with the project by way of a single-stage selection process rather than the multi-stage selection process that had been used in other projects. Concerns over the process were compounded by the decision to allow only 90 days (later extended to 125 days) for the submission of formal proposals. However, given the long (one-and-a-half-year) period of delay between the time when the government announced its intention to seek private sector participation in the T1T2 project and the call for proposals, the accelerated time

24 The decision to proceed with a private developer was motivated by the desire to ensure the rapid development of the project (specifically with a view to increasing local construction employment) and by infighting among local politicians over the composition of the local airport authority designated for the Greater Toronto Area. It was also alleged by some that patronage considerations affected the decision (see, for instance, Nixon Report at 9). The federal government's preference for the local airport authority concept was set out in *Guiding Principles* (Ottawa: Ministry of Transport 1987) and elaborated upon in *Supplementary Principles for the Creation and Operation of Local Airport Authorities* (Ottawa: Ministry of Transport 1989).

period may not have visited serious hardship on interested bidders. In any event, three bids for the project were ultimately submitted, of which two were deemed to be within the stipulated terms of reference. Of these two, the government awarded the contract to Paxport Inc. However, soon after the contract was awarded, Paxport was required to merge with the losing bidder, Air Terminal Development Group,[25] because the former lacked the financial resources to develop the project on its own.[26]

In August 1993 (eight months after the contract was awarded), a general agreement for the project was concluded between the merged consortium, Pearson Development Corporation (PDC), and the federal government. As in the case of Terminal 3, the arrangement was structured as a long-term lease (57 years) involving sliding-scale lease payments. Similar to the PEI Fixed Link, the contract with the developer limited the government's ability to undertake actions which would directly debase the operator's franchise, by, for instance, permitting an airport to be built within 25 kilometres of the airport if it would reduce passenger volume by more than 1.5 million passengers a year.[27] However, the T1T2 contract did stipulate limits on the prices that retail concessionaires and parking lot operators could charge customers[28] and provided constraints on the strategic use by occupant airlines of the airport gates to forestall entry by competitors.[29] Further, as in other projects we surveyed, in both the T3 and T1T2 airport developments, the federal government agreed to a scaled rental formula that resulted in a de facto sharing of the risks of low gross revenues with the developer/operator.[30] These were supplemented in the case of T3 by a $70 million loan guarantee contingent on low passenger volumes.[31]

25 ATDC was substantially the same consortium that had developed and was operating Terminal 3.

26 Apparently, the federal government failed to consider financing capability when reviewing prospective developers for the project.

27 However, once a stipulated threshold level of passenger volume was exceeded, the constraint would no longer apply.

28 Prices charged could not exceed 115% of the prices charged for comparable goods and services in downtown Toronto.

29 Through 'use them or lose them' requirements.

30 It also consented to the airport developer utilizing a cost-based rental formula in respect of the rental obligations of the retail concessionaires and airlines, which, given the monopoly properties of the airport, can best be understood as an enforced sharing of developer/operator risks with these parties.

31 While such a guarantee was not provided for in the T1T2 project, the government did make an allowance for a maximum $33 million deferral of rental payments incurred by the developer in the first three years of the project.

Given the intense concern expressed by the press and others during the 1993 fall federal election campaign with the terminal development, Jean Chrétien's newly elected Liberal government requested a review and report of the transaction from Robert Nixon, a prominent Liberal party member and former provincial cabinet minister. His report, completed in a mere 30 days, found that the contract with the consortium was severely flawed and should be cancelled, subject only to minimal levels of compensation (for expenditures made to the date of cancellation) being provided to consortium members.[32] On 3 December 1993 the government cancelled the contract. However, issues of compensation for PDC could not be resolved through negotiation, and in April 1994 the government introduced legislation which would permit it to impose a settlement of approximately $30 million on the developers, but without the attendant procedural safeguards that normally accompany the public power of confiscation.[33] The legislation has not yet been adopted by Parliament because of the determined

32 Nixon concluded that the project 'fell far short of maximizing the public interest' (at 9). The recommendation that the deal be abrogated was based on perceived infirmities in both the selection process and the contracts designed to implement the transaction. In terms of the former, Nixon focused on the fact that the privatization of the terminals contradicted stated government policy in favour of local airport authorities; on the single-stage, abbreviated selection process that led to an enormous advantage to ATDC (which had gained previous experience through its successful participation in the Terminal 3 contract); and on the lack of a financial pre-qualification requirement. Nixon further alleged that the selection process was sullied by patronage – three individuals in the consortium were closely identified with the Progressive Conservative party. The report also alleged a number of substantive shortcomings in the contracts. Among the most serious was the length of the lease term, which Nixon characterized as being 'difficult to fathom' given that 'with an asset as moved by technological change as an airport, the length of this obligation does not serve the public interest' (at 11). In Nixon's view, the rental formula was flawed because future government revenues from the project would be highly dependent on aggressive pricing conducted without appropriate governmental control and at the risk of making the airport uncompetitive with other airports in Canada and the United States (at 11). It is, of course, not self-evident why the private developer would adopt operational policies that would make the project uncompetitive. Finally, Nixon expressed concern with the broadly phrased performance obligations that bound PDC, noting that it would be difficult for the Government of Canada to determine when such obligations are breached. Because the government's remedies for breach are so Draconian (cancellation or seizure and operation), Nixon speculated that the government would be unlikely to exercise such powers (at 12).

33 Bill C-22: An Act respecting certain agreements concerning the redevelopment and operation of Terminals 1 and 2 at Lester B. Pearson International Airport (First Session, Thirty-Fifth Parliament, 42–3 Elizabeth II, 1994).

resistance of the Progressive Conservative–controlled Senate to the measure, fuelled by growing public apprehension regarding the bill and by a judicial determination that the government had breached its contractual obligations.[34] The matter was remitted to a special Senate committee on the Pearson Airport agreements for a public inquiry, which divided along partisan lines in its 1995 report.

E. SUMMARY: THE CHARACTERISTICS OF PUBLIC/PRIVATE PARTNERSHIPS

Following the standard pattern for large-scale infrastructure projects, each of the projects we examined contained several common characteristics. First, each of the projects entailed large, up-front, sunk investments by bidders that were not compensated for by direct ex ante government subsidies (ranging from approximately $6 million incurred by the bidders who submitted proposals for the Highway 407 project to $30 million incurred by SCI in developing its bridge proposal[35]). Second, each of the projects implicated a range of public policy concerns which could not be sidestepped by the decision to develop the project through a public/private partnership. As illustrated by the PEI Fixed Link, concern over the effectiveness and transparency of levers that the state would be able to wield during and after the construction of the project led to heightened public apprehension around the project's merits and resulted in considerable delay. Indeed, review of the contracts concluded between sponsoring governments (or their agents) and the project developers disclosed considerable attention to these public policy concerns. In some cases, specific contractual limitations were placed on the operator's ability to charge monopoly prices for access to the goods and services under consideration. In the T3 airport project the contract went even further, explicitly incorporating by reference federal, provincial, and municipal laws, and making non-compliance with these laws an event of default under the contract. Of course, given developer concerns over sunk, up-front investments in

34 This finding was in the context of a claim made by the consortium against the federal government for unspecified damages but apparently alleging losses, including forgone profits, in excess of $200 million: *T1T2 Limited Partnership* v. *Canada* [1995] OJ No. 137, Court File No. 94-CQ53762 (Ontario Court of Justice General Division, per Borins J) (plaintiffs have provided evidence which satisfies me that the defendant committed a breach of the airport contracts on 3 December 1993, at paragraph 4). See also 'Developers Sue Over Loss of Airport Deal' *Globe and Mail*, 17 September 1994.

35 Apparently the bidding costs were fifteen times higher than originally projected by SCI. William G. Reinhardt 'The High Cost of Building Bridges' (November 1993) 68 *PWFinancing* 18, 26.

specific assets, the desire to incorporate sensitivity to broadly defined public policy concerns often was in direct tension with the need to provide credible assurances to the developer/operator (as an inducement to investment) that the franchise value of the undertaking would not be debased ex post by direct governmental action. Third, with the exception of the T3 airport project, the process used to award the infrastructure franchise involved multiple stages, typically an initial tournament for design ideas followed by a final competition for the construction and operation contract for those bidders successful in the first stage.[36] One notable feature of the selection process used in each of these cases was the small number of bidders who actually progressed to the final stage of the tournament.[37] A fourth common characteristic of these projects was the lengthy period of time (ranging from several months in the case of T3 to well over a year in the case of the PEI Fixed Link) between the time of the formal award of the franchise and the actual consummation of the written contract necessary to implement the project, which probably attenuated the impact of the competitive bidding process on the winning bidder's post-selection performance incentives. Fifth, despite the characterization of these projects as being based on the efficiency benefits associated with private sector finance and risk bearing, virtually all of these projects revealed some significant role for the government in this area, ranging from government-backed public financing of the entire project, in the case of Highway 407; to provision of a long-term governmental subsidy that was used to fund the lion's share of the project costs, in the case of the PEI Fixed Link; to revenue-based ground lease payments that rendered government a quasi-residual claimant, in the case of the airport terminals. Sixth, as is true of long-term contractual relationships generally, the contracts executed between sponsoring governments and franchise operators disclosed considerable reliance on elaborately designed adjustment formulas (in respect of pricing and maintenance obligations) and governance structures to deal with problems of contractual incomplete-

36 Information respecting the structure of these projects was derived principally from an extensive set of interviews conducted over the summer of 1994 with public and private sector experts involved in the projects and from inspection of the various contracts used to implement the projects.

37 In Highway 407, three bidders expressed initial interest, but only two progressed to the final stage of the bidding process; in the PEI Fixed Link, twelve bidders expressed initial interest, but only five progressed to the final stage; in the T3 airport project, eight bidders started out, but only four progressed to the final stage; while in the T1T2 project, only three bidders submitted proposals.

ness.[38] Significantly, when governance mechanisms were utilized, the mechanisms were based on standard arbitration models used in the private sector. To the extent that it has been argued by Goldberg and others that the adjustment mechanisms used by public utility commissions to administer regulatory contracts are functionally equivalent to the contractual provisions embedded in long-term public franchise contracts, this claim is thus only partially correct in the context of the contracts we examined.[39] In contrast to the public utility model, public franchise contracts reveal only limited opportunity for meaningful levels of transparency or public participation, thereby raising fundamental accountability concerns.

## III *Analysis of the organizational structure of public/private infrastructure partnerships*

### A. INTRODUCTION

In order to appreciate the distinctive features of many of the public/private partnerships that have emerged in the infrastructure setting, particularly with respect to larger projects, it is important not to draw too sharp a dichotomy between the respective roles of the public and private sectors. With many publicly owned and operated infrastructure facilities, such as airport terminals, many of the functions have traditionally been contracted out, for example, catering, security services, airplane refuelling, baggage handling, retail concessions, and janitorial services. Moreover, even with respect to the initial construction of these facilities, governments rarely, if ever, build these facilities themselves through public sector employees, but rather tender out the construction through a competitive bidding process against a detailed set of tender specifications that the government has developed either internally or through consulting arrangements with external design specialists,

38 For instance, concerns over asset degradation through chiselling on required maintenance – one of the principal contractual difficulties involving assets having an expected life that exceeds the term of the franchise contract – were dealt with through a number of different mechanisms, including: general exhortatory duties on the developer/operator to maintain assets in an appropriate condition, stipulated expenditures on asset maintenance (expressed as a percentage of annual gross revenues), annual contributions to an asset reserve fund, periodic inspections by third-party monitors, and provision for resolution of disputes over the breadth of this obligation through binding arbitration.

39 Victor Goldberg 'Regulation and Administered Contracts' (1976) *Bell J. of Econ.* 426. See also George Priest 'The Origins of Utility Regulation and the "Theories of Regulation" Debate' (1993) 36 *J.L.E.* 289.

with the winning bidder in turn subcontracting out various aspects of the construction to specialized third parties, often through a competitive bidding process of its own.

The most distinctive feature of many of the larger public/private sector infrastructure partnerships that are now emerging is the integration within a single private sector firm or consortium of all (or most of) the functions of financing, designing, building, operating, and maintaining the facility in question (subject again to further subcontracting out). The bundling of these functions reflects a form of vertical integration on the part of the private sector provider of these services. Because the functions involved are often highly specialized and entail deployment of quite different bodies of complementary expertise and resources, private sector providers are, however, typically not vertically integrated firms in a conventional sense but consortia ('virtual corporations') that are formed to develop and operate a particular infrastructure facility. This arrangement reflects the often relatively sui generis requirements of that facility, usually involving as participants engineering and project management firms, construction firms, financial underwriters, and specialized operating firms. While the consortia typically incorporate their joint venture as a corporation for the project in question, they have a higher degree of malleability or transitoriness relative to the conventional firm. The partners often maintain substantially independent activities, although there are clear reputation and learning curve advantages for consortia in preserving some stability of membership where there are opportunities for bidding on similar infrastructure projects in what is rapidly becoming a global market for these services, and in these cases consortia may evolve permanent corporate structures.[40]

In this section of the article, we explore the potential efficiency gains to be made, at least in principle, from extensive integration, or bundling of financing, design, construction, operation, and maintenance functions in a single provider. At the same time we examine a range of institutional problems relating to the design of the bidding process, the contract negotiation process, and contract monitoring and enforcement processes which these new arrangements give rise to and which may substantially attenuate potential efficiency gains from this particular form of privatization of public sector activities. The problems of

40 In the T3 airport project, the principal construction firm, Huang and Danczkay, sold its interests once the terminal was completed, illustrating the fluid nature of these relationships.

creating and preserving a genuinely competitive bidding and rebidding process, the long-term nature of the contracts entailed and hence the difficulties of writing complete contingent claims contracts, the large-scale sunk costs typically involved, and the financial sensitivity of these projects to changes in the governmental policy environment all raise special challenges. We also briefly consider distributional and political considerations that may influence a government's decision to privatize infrastructure services and the form that the privatization arrangements may take. We then analyse the particular problems of credible commitments raised by the central fact that the government is a party to these contractual arrangements.

### B. POTENTIAL EFFICIENCY GAINS FROM VERTICALLY INTEGRATED PRIVATE SECTOR INFRASTRUCTURE PROVISION

#### *1. The traditional procurement model*

In assessing the potential efficiency gains that may be realized from vertically integrated private sector providers (consortia) of infrastructure services, it is important to be clear as to the comparative reference point against which these arrangements are being evaluated. For major road, bridge, or airport facilities of the kind on which this article focuses, governments traditionally have themselves identified the need for the project, often reflecting pressures for or against particular projects by politically salient constituencies, and sometimes tested more objectively through benefit-cost analysis. Whether the project proceeds or not has been, to an important extent, contingent on the relevant level of government's fiscal capacity at the time (in many countries in recent years increasingly constrained by severe budget deficits) and on the revenue-generating capacity of the project, which in turn in part depends on where it is situated on the public-goods/private-goods continuum in terms of meeting the criteria of rivalry and excludability that distinguish private goods from public goods, and in part on distributional and political considerations that may dictate that the services in question should be provided free or at subsidized rates to some or all user classes, even where efficient user charges for the services in question could be devised. Assuming that a decision is made to proceed with the project, typically government will draw up a set of comprehensive technical specifications for the initial construction of the facility, in part relying on already developed technical standards or manual specifications for the class of facility in question, or, to the extent the facility presents novel features, through project-specific specifications developed by internal technical personnel or outside specialized consultants such as architectural or engineering firms, or some combination thereof. Once these detailed specifications have been fully developed, government departments or agencies would then typically advertise for tenders for the construction of the facility in a competitive bidding process. In order to qualify as bidders, firms may be required to demonstrate relevant credentials such as financial and technical capacity, and past experience and performance records on similar projects. The contract with the winning bidder will specify completion date, security and penalties for non-completion or other defaults in performance, and provide for a schedule of payments to the construction firm reflecting satisfactory completion of sequential stages of the project as determined either by staff of the government department or agency concerned or by some agreed third-party certification agent. Broadly speaking, contracts could be cost-plus, fixed-price, or incentive contracts.[41] With respect to cost-plus contracts, these provide few incentives for the private sector contractor to minimize construction costs and correspondingly entail greater risk for the public sector, which will attempt to minimize this risk by intensive but costly monitoring of the contractor's costs. Under a fixed-price contract, the contractor's costs will be of no direct concern to the government, so that less intensive monitoring will be required, although monitoring will still be relevant to non-price dimensions of performance. If construction costs are likely to be affected by technological uncertainties, climatic factors, variable input prices, or labour shortages or disputes, these risks, which the contractor will bear, will presumably be reflected in a risk premium embodied in the fixed price negotiated in the contract. Under incentive contracts, these risks may be shared in various ways. Any such risk sharing will involve risk-incentive trade-offs. Incentives on the contractor to minimize costs may be reduced, to the extent that he can control these factors, although the risk premium charged the government for risks over which he has little or no control is likely to be smaller. With respect to government-determined risks or entirely exogenous risks, the government may be the more efficient risk bearer, given its greater capacity to spread the risk. After satisfactory completion of the project, the government may choose to operate the facility entirely itself through government employees; or, depending on the nature of the facility, it may contract out, for limited periods of time, under a competitive bidding process, the performance of various functions.

41 See R. Preston McAfee and John McMillan *Incentives in Government Contracting* (Toronto: University of Toronto Press 1988).

*2. The vertically integrated private sector model*

*a) Project identification.* In comparison with this traditional model of the infrastructure development and operation process, the fully vertically integrated private provision model that is the focus of this article differs in important respects. First, the government may choose to invite private sector firms to identify potential infrastructure projects. For example, the California Department of Transportation (Caltrans) recently issued an open-ended public invitation for private sector firms to propose toll-road projects in California, which the government agency then evaluated.[42] Complete government detachment from the question of which projects should proceed is often impossible because of right-of-way and eminent domain issues, network externalities, other external impacts, and monopoly pricing concerns. The private sector, in identifying potential infrastructure projects, will of course be driven by a different set of considerations from the public sector in engaging in the same exercise. As noted above, the public sector is likely to respond to a mix of political pressures and may in addition undertake a benefit-cost analysis that weighs all relevant social costs and benefits associated with the project. Private sector proposals will be influenced only by the expected private rate of return on the project, which will disregard political pressures one way or the other, and are likely to also disregard external costs and benefits of the project that would be captured in a comprehensive social benefit-cost analysis. However, with a totally open-ended public sector invitation to the private sector to propose new infrastructure projects, the evaluation process that the public sector will subsequently have to undertake of these proposals will presumably implicate both political considerations and social costs and benefits, so that proposers are likely to attempt to anticipate, and to some extent accommodate, these considerations in their proposals, consistently with realizing an adequate private rate of return on the project. Unless most of the evaluation criteria to be employed by the government are rendered at least partly explicit and transparent, or other indications are provided in the invitation that to some extent define the range of projects in which the government may be inte-

42 See Jose Gomez-Ibanez and John Meyer *Going Private: The International Experience with Transport Privatization* (Washington, DC: Brookings Institution 1993); Ron Hirshhorn 'The Ownership and Organization of Transportation Infrastructure: Roads and Airports' Background Study Prepared for the Royal Commission on National Passenger Transportation: *Directions* (Ottawa: Supply and Services Canada 1992) 18.

rested, proposers are unlikely to invest significant resources, at least in the absence of subsidies, in developing proposals that may prove to be of no interest to the government. In any event, these proposals are likely to be framed at a largely conceptual level, leaving detailed design for the post-project identification stage.

Under the fully vertically integrated private provider model, once a project has been identified, at least at the conceptual level, either by the government itself or by the government in response to private sector proposals, in theory the government would call for integrated bids on the design, construction, operation, and maintenance aspects of the project. Each of these functions needs to be analysed both separately and in relation to the other functions in the bundle.

*b) Design.* With respect to the design function, the argument by proponents of the privatization of infrastructure provision is that unlike the traditional method of contracting out engaged in by government in the infrastructure context, where comprehensive specifications of project characteristics are provided to private sector parties, the government stands to realize substantial efficiency gains from contracting out the design function and, in effect, stimulating competition for ideas. Implicit in this view is the notion that governments should shift their focus from specifying inputs to specifying some desired outcome, leaving private sector providers with the opportunity of formulating means of realizing that outcome in the most cost-efficient way possible. Under the traditional contracting-out regime, government agencies would typically rely on standardized specifications or bureaucrats would develop design specifications for sui generis projects, but with few incentives to maximize service innovations or minimize costs, and disabled by major information asymmetries as to what may or may not be technologically feasible – expertise which is likely to be better known to private sector firms specializing in the technologies in question.[43]

43 In this respect, the multi-stage structure of the public/private partnership bears striking similarity to the model used by the US federal government for defence procurement. Because of long lag times between the development and production of defence weapons, defence production is characterized by severe demand and cost uncertainties and, as a consequence of required up-front investments in asset-specific research and production, is beset by endemic hold-up problems. One of the principal models used to resolve these difficulties is a multi-stage selection process that involves competition for a procurement contract on the basis of research ideas tendered in the first stage of the selection process. Interestingly, and in contrast to the structure typically used in the public/private partnership infrastructure studies

On the approach advocated by proponents of the vertically integrated model of infrastructure provision, it is critical that the government be able to specify some desired outcome or output against which competing designs can be evaluated. This may be more feasible in some infrastructure projects than others. For example, in designing a bridge or a toll road, the government could stipulate that the bridge or road must be capable of moving a given volume of traffic over given units of time. In other projects, such as designing airport facilities, the policy objective is much less easy to specify, involving the aggregation and reconciliation of many preferences;[44] in these cases private sector providers will face difficulties in determining what criteria their potential designs will be evaluated against, and government and public sector agents will have difficulty evaluating competing and perhaps sharply different design proposals without well-specified outcome measures, at least if the risk of appearing arbitrary, subjective, or politically motivated (or even corrupt) is to be avoided.[45] Obviously, the less clearly

we examined, the federal government will subsidize the development of designs in the first stage of the selection process. However, the subsidy covers only a portion of the costs actually incurred by bidders in the qualifying rounds of the project and so, as in the case of the infrastructure projects we examined, the bidders' decision to invest in research and development is based on a private cost-benefit analysis that compares the up-front costs incurred in design development with the probability of winning the project multiplied by its economic value. After the design proposals are submitted, the government will select two (or more) bidders (of the five or so initially qualified to enter the competition) to proceed to the second stage of the competition where a more detailed prototype of the weapon is developed for competition in the third and final stage of the selection process, wherein the winning bidder will then secure from government a cost-reimbursement-based procurement contract to supply the weapons. An excellent overview of the defence procurement process is provided by William P. Rogerson 'Economic Incentives and the Defense Procurement Process' (1994) 8 *J. of Econ. Perspectives* 65.

44 See David Sappington and Joseph Stiglitz 'Privatization, Information and Incentives' (1987) 6 *J. of Policy Analysis & Management* 567, 575.

45 Curtis Taylor ('Digging for Golden Carrots: An Analysis of Research Tournaments' (draft dated October 1993) forthcoming in the AER) argues that the golden carrot tournament solves for both the input monitoring and output specification problems associated with research: 'Competition among researchers trying to win the contest causes expending effort to be incentive compatible. Moreover, the only role of the courts is to ensure that the specified "prize" ... is awarded to one of the contestants at the conclusion of the contest. *It is not even necessary that a court be able to verify the rank order of the final entries since the sponsor typically has little incentive other than to exchange the prize for the innovation it values most.*' Nevertheless, given endemic accountability problems surrounding public officials, the application of this conclusion to competitions involving adjudication by public officials is somewhat problematic.

specified the project selection criteria, the greater the latitude that decision-makers have in selecting projects; hence the greater the vulnerability of the process to investment by bidding firms in socially unproductive influence activities.[46] As noted earlier, concern over these difficulties was centrally at issue in the Pearson International Airport redevelopment, where, in part, ambiguity in the definition of required outputs buttressed concerns over the potential for patronage.

The government could, of course, unbundle the design function from the other functions in the bundle and hold a separate design competition just for the ideas. Here again, however, the problems of stipulating with sufficient precision the outcome criteria against which competing designs are to be evaluated would arise. Indeed, government traditionally has often contracted out the design function for various public facilities, by hiring architectural or engineering firms to design public buildings or other facilities. In so doing, the government is able to utilize private sector firms with relevant technical expertise and significant investments in reputational capital, which reduce information asymmetries in the design process. However, in stimulating a vigorous competition for design ideas on an unbundled basis where the objective is to generate a detailed design which would then support a public tendering process of the traditional kind with respect to the construction of the facility that is the subject of the winning design, the government is likely to have to offer a large fee to the winning design proponent (given the 'winner takes all' nature of the competition), in order that participants in the design competition will find it rational to invest significant resources in developing a detailed design, given their expected return on this investment. In the context of defence procurement, William Rogerson speculates that public concerns over the magnitude (and scope for manipulation) of the ex post prize necessary to stimulate optimal ex ante investment in research supports a bundled tournament where this premium can be embedded in the production contract, thereby limiting public transparency of the prize.[47] Often in the past, government has simply approached several architectural or other design firms, depending on the nature of the facility, and sought preliminary ideas, and then committed itself to one designer to develop

46 The problem of influence activities in the context of a multi-stage auction process is briefly alluded to in Paul Milgrom 'Auctions and Bidding: A Primer' (1989) 3 *J. of Econ. Perspectives* 3, 20. For a discussion of influence activities, see Paul Milgrom and John Roberts *Economics, Organization and Management* (Englewood Cliffs, NJ: Prentice-Hall 1992) 192–4.

47 Rogerson, supra, 71.

a detailed design. It is not clear that this process generates an optimal supply of the best design ideas, particularly in large infrastructure projects where different features of different design proposals may be attractive and the optimal design may be a combination of features from a number of proposals. In this case, losing bidders have to contemplate the possibility that the government will use some of their design ideas in the ultimate design, but that they will not be compensated at all for these ideas (the problem of appropriability). Thus, in order to attract a significant number of detailed design proposals, only a large expected return reflecting an appropriate risk premium is likely to attract sufficient losing bidders from which to develop a combined set of design specifications. However, even in this case, bidders still face strong incentives to develop proposals that capitalize on their firm-specific advantages in production, even if the design that is ultimately produced is not least cost. In this way, bidders limit the capacity of government to transfer their design innovations to other bidders.[48]

An alternative approach to design production would be to commission the preparation of a number of design proposals, probably on a fixed-fee basis; but now government may face a larger pay-out than under the winner-takes-all approach and, more seriously, would create no incentives (beyond reputation effects) for proponents to invest resources in developing superior rather than inferior design proposals. Information asymmetries may subvert the capacity of government to determine the level of effort expended in design development.

The government faces many of these problems with the vertically integrated infrastructure provision model. That is to say, competing consortia are unlikely to have equal strengths across all the various functions in the bundle, yet the winning bidder must be chosen on the basis of some balance of strengths and weaknesses. Even if a number of the competing bidders have roughly equivalent strengths in the design function, for a large complex facility (such as an airport) it is unlikely to be the case that one consortium's design is superior in all respects to the others. Thus, ideally, the government would wish to combine the best features of the various competing design proposals. However, this

48 In this respect, investment in these firm-specific design features bears analytical similarity to the entrenchment problem related to excessive investment by managers in manager-specific investments so as to limit the gains from displacement. See Andrei Shleifer and Robert W. Vishny 'Management Entrenchment: The Case of Manager-Specific Investments' (1989) 25 *J. of Fin. Econ.* 123.

combination implies significant complications in the bidding and contracting process.[49] In this respect, the vertically integrated model exhibits obvious tied sales properties. One option is to partly decouple the design competition from the other functions in the bundle by requiring all qualified, vertically integrated consortia first to submit their design proposals, on the assumption that it will still be in their interests subsequently to bid on the winning design (which may be another consortium's design proposal or represent a combination of features of the competing designs). Presumably, the consortium with the winning or predominant design proposal may feel it has informational, technological, or other advantages over rival bidders in bidding on the remaining functions, and thus there is an incentive to prepare the design proposal which commends itself most to the government. Here again, as with an unbundled competition for design ideas, the cost of preparing a detailed design proposal for a large infrastructure project might be very substantial, but unlike an unbundled design competition there may be no direct compensation for the winning design. Moreover, by restricting the design function to consortia capable of bidding on the remaining functions, proposers in the design competition now face serious free-rider problems in that a rival consortium with an inferior design but superior construction and other capabilities may win the integrated bidding competition. These risks are likely to generate significant risk premiums in vertically integrated bids, given both the inherent costs of preparing such comprehensive bids and the appropriability problem with design innovations. They are also, as mentioned above, likely to result in

49 Some of these problems are revealed by the value engineering exercise that was incorporated into the Highway 407 selection process. After the first-stage design tournament, the government sought to pool the best design ideas submitted by each of the bidders into a baseline project description that could then serve as the basis for bidders to make more elaborate proposals in subsequent bidding stages. By increasing the common base of information available to bidders in a common values auction, uncertainty over the underlying value of goods is diminished, which should, in turn, enhance bidder competitiveness. Apart from its effect on competition, the exercise provided the public with an opportunity to express preferences over trade-offs in the design of the project, for example, between safety and cost. Nevertheless, value engineering is not unproblematic; recognizing that a bidder's best ideas will be appropriated for the benefit of all bidders in later-stage bidding over the production contract, consortium members have strong incentives to hold back their best ideas to protect their relative advantages. This effect may, however, be dulled by the fact that if a bidder withholds sound ideas from the first stage of the selection process, its ability to proceed to subsequent bidding stages may be jeopardized.

bidders making socially perverse investments that attempt to limit the ability of other bidders to exploit their design proposals.

An alternative approach to mitigating these problems would be to deal with them at the contracting rather than at the bidding stage of the process. That is to say, bids on all functions – design, construction, financing, operation, and maintenance – could be solicited in a single competition, but the winner of the competition would thereby win the right merely to attempt to negotiate a contract thereafter with the government, in the process of negotiating which the government would be free to introduce design or other features of losing bidders' proposals. The winning bidder would then have to decide whether to accept these proposed changes to its proposal. But again, various problems present themselves. First, suppose the winning bidder does not accept all or any of the changes to its bid proposed by the government. Presumably, in the absence of a concluded contract, the government would be free to withdraw from negotiations and perhaps reapproach one of the other bidders. Or the government may behave more strategically and play the winning bidder off against other bidders in the contract negotiations. Alternatively, the winning bidder could accept all or most of the changes proposed by the government and modify its bid, but losing bidders will not unreasonably complain that they should have been given a similar opportunity to modify their bids in the light of what is really a rolling or evolving set of contract specifications ('a moving target'). Moreover, once a government agency has pre-committed to a particular bidder before negotiating the detailed contract, competitive pricing discipline is likely to be attenuated.[50] Thus, extracting from private sector firms in the competitive bidding process an optimal supply of innovative design ideas without attenuating competitive pricing discipline presents serious difficulties.

Beyond eliciting an optimal supply of ideas, the arguments for bundling the design function with other functions have some force. Under more traditional modes of developing infrastructure projects (and indeed building other facilities), it has been a common complaint that separating the design function (and personnel) from the construc-

50 Once the government has publicly announced its selection of a winning bidder, it is subject to political embarrassment if it is forced to reopen the bidding process in the event that it is unable to come to terms with that consortium, especially in a setting where concerns over project timeliness explain government's decision to opt for the public/private partnership in the first place. Concern over these political costs creates undesirable lock-in effects which tip the post-selection balance of bargaining power in favour of the winning consortium.

tion function (and personnel) in different teams (hiring an architect to undertake the design of a building while contracting out its construction to another firm, for instance) increases the risk that the designer will be insensitive to 'constructability' problems presented by his design. Given that 80% of the costs of many large-scale construction projects are estimated to be determined by the design, dissonances between the design and construction teams may prove very costly,[51] although again it is not entirely clear why reputational markets for professional firms would not minimize these problems. In the vertically integrated infrastructure provision model, the design and construction teams form part of a larger team that is organized by the consortium undertaking the project, the premise being that the consortium is able to reduce coordination problems through internalizing these functions at lower cost than the public sector where it contracts out these functions separately. However, given that design and construction expertise are likely to reside in different groups of personnel and probably in different firms that are partners in the consortium, at most the coordination problems are minimized but not eliminated through this form of cooperation – presumably by more regular contact between the design and construction teams, by developing design and construction plans simultaneously and interactively rather than sequentially, and perhaps by repeat dealings between the two teams on different projects.

*c) Financing, design, and construction.* The construction function on large public facilities has almost invariably been contracted out to the private sector, and so the vertically integrated infrastructure provision model represents no change in this respect. However, it does affect various interdependencies between the financing, design, and construction functions by changing incentives in important ways. Most of these relate to how the project is to be financed and operated. If the private sector provider is itself to finance the construction of the facility and to recoup this investment and a return thereon out of subsequent user fees generated from operating the facility, the government has no direct concerns with the initial capital costs, provided that the design which the private sector provider has committed itself to, which will obviously reflect expected revenue constraints, is acceptable to the government. Alternatively, where the project is not to be financed at all or in its entirety from user fees, but wholly or in part from government

51 See Issaka Ndekugri and Adrian Turner 'Building Procurement by Design and Build Approach' (1994) 120 *J. of Construction Engineering and Management* 243.

subsidies, then the government, by stipulating a maximum size of subsidy, will create similar constraints on feasible design and construction options. In contrast, the government is vulnerable to opportunistic behaviour in this context from the private sector provider given the 'essential' nature of many infrastructure facilities and the likely political inability of a government simply to let such a facility fail, with the attendant disruption, pending government assuming full control of the facility or identifying another private sector operator. The private sector operator may well gamble that, notwithstanding an extravagant or misconceived design or excessive construction costs, it can coerce the government into relaxing constraints on user fees so as to permit monopoly pricing, or to raise the level of maximum committed subsidies. Thus, both the design and construction functions are highly sensitive to incentives created by the nature of the financing function.

The nature of these cross-function incentive effects (interdependencies) are key to understanding what superficially may appear to be one of the major mysteries of private sector financing of infrastructure projects. In most cases, private sector financing will carry a higher cost of capital than government financing, simply because the default risk on sovereign debt (given that governments have access to the entire taxpayer base) is obviously lower than for a private sector infrastructure provider, where the cost of capital will reflect both project-specific risks and its de jure or de facto limited liability. Thus, if the financing function were viewed in isolation from the other functions, given the lower cost of sovereign debt relative to private sector debt, we should see governments financing all activities in the economy. The fact that they finance very few of these activities, at least in a market economy, requires an explanation. In the present context, the explanation appears to lie in the fact that while the cost of capital to the private sector infrastructure provider will be higher than the cost of an equivalent amount of capital to the government (which has the same access to private capital markets), offsetting efficiency gains from the other functions performed by the private sector provider are influenced positively by virtue of the fact that it is bearing the financial risk on the project. However, this trade-off in turn depends upon how the capital investment is to be recouped. If the investment must be recouped from competitively determined revenues from the project, then this will create socially appropriate incentives with respect to the design, construction, operation, and maintenance of projects. While it may be true that governments and private sector infrastructure developers borrow capital from the same sources, lenders' incentives with respect to private sector project financing are sharply different. With the government as borrower, lenders can ignore project-specific returns, given that lenders ultimately have access to the government's entire tax and asset base. With project financing, project returns become central; lenders are likely to screen development consortia more carefully before lending, to insist on adequate security and financial penalties against non-completion or default, and to monitor performance more closely through the inclusion of numerous, tailored covenants than they would if they were lending to government which in turn then financed the project, thus significantly improving the performance of the infrastructure provider.[52]

However, with respect to most forms of infrastructure, the infrastructure operator is likely to possess some measure of market power and thus, in the absence of contractual restriction or regulation, may be able to charge monopolistic user fees. Given that even a monopolist has some incentive to maximize profits by minimizing costs, it is not obvious that this will change its calculus with respect to design, construction, operation, and maintenance costs or lenders' monitoring of these functions. However, if user fees are restricted or regulated by the government to prevent monopoly pricing, through some form of rate-of-return regulation, this may create incentives for the private sector provider to overcapitalize the project in order to expand the rate base or to exert weak controls over operating costs, given the cost-plus nature of this form of regulation.

Another argument that is sometimes made for private sector financing of infrastructure projects, notwithstanding the higher cost of private sector capital, is that this serves an economic certification or verification function, and that projects will only proceed that have a positive net present value to the provider, whereas the public sector in selecting projects will not necessarily feel so constrained. This argument has only qualified force. Obviously, a private sector provider, in making his calculus, will be influenced only by private costs and benefits. Where monopolistic setting of user charges is possible, a project may have a positive net value to him even though its social value may be negative, once the dead-weight social losses are taken into account. In contrast, if user charges were to be constrained by regulation to marginal cost (ideally marginal social costs, including congestion and environmental externalities), given the high ratio of fixed to variable costs entailed in

52 See Ronald Daniels and George Triantis 'The Role of Debt in American Corporate Governance' (Summer 1995) *U. of Calif. LR*; William Pearson, President, Agra Engineering Group, Toronto, interview with the authors 1 September 1994.

many infrastructure projects, revenues are unlikely to cover the costs of the project and to generate a positive net present value. A more complicated scheme of regulated prices, such as Ramsey prices, would permit price discrimination where prices are inversely related to elasticity of demand so that the marginal consumer is served, but average total costs are covered by charging inelastic demanders more than marginal costs. Thus, a private sector provider's judgement on the financial viability of a project is a useful check or discipline on a government's decision to proceed with such a project only if these pricing issues are clearly and appropriately resolved at the outset. Given that the government, albeit through negotiations with the private sector provider, will determine and administer these contractual or regulatory constraints on pricing, this to an important extent endogenizes government policy considerations in the private sector provider's calculus as to the economic viability of the project, and undermines this judgment as an independent second check on the social desirability of the project. Where a project is not to be financed entirely out of user fees, but partly or entirely from government operating subsidies, a private sector provider's judgment as to the financial viability of the project again is not an exogenous check on the government's decision to proceed with it, given that the government's decision over the nature and scale of the subsidies is endogenous to the private provider's calculus.

Apart from the necessary relationship between the viability of the initial capital investment and subsequent options with respect to the pricing of services or the nature and size of government operating subsidies, a private sector provider's judgement about the financial viability of a project will reflect only *private* expected costs and benefits and not expected social costs and benefits. With many large infrastructure projects, there are likely to be significant positive and negative externalities, which will not be reflected in this private calculus, but which government agencies overseeing the project may wish to consider in judging the social viability of the project or in containing or compensating for these externalities through other policies. A private sector firm's willingness to privately finance an infrastructure project may reflect a disregard for negative externalities. Conversely, an unwillingness to privately finance such a project may simply reflect an inability to capture or charge for the benefits of positive externalities. In both cases the private financing decision may not be congruent with a social welfare calculus.

*d) Operation and maintenance.* With respect to the operating function, this could, like prior functions, be unbundled and contracted out discretely. Indeed, this is sometimes done with infrastructure. Presumably in this case, the government could simply enter into a management contract for a fixed term, probably accompanied by a lease of existing facilities for the same term, to a private sector provider chosen through a competitive tendering process in very much the way that Demsetz has argued is feasible in creating competition for natural monopoly markets.[53] Several well-known problems present themselves with this option.[54] First, if the infrastructure facility has monopoly features to it entailing some degree of market power on the part of the operator, the government faces a choice between, on the one hand, maximizing the sale price of the franchise by allowing the operator to charge monopoly prices to users or, on the other hand, soliciting bids not on the basis of the highest franchise price but the lowest contractually permitted set of user prices. Presumably the latter is the social ideal, in that it avoids the dead-weight losses associated with monopoly pricing, although it imposes a much more substantial burden on the public sector in reviewing and approving initial bids and monitoring adherence to price commitments thereafter and may have less attractive political properties than maximizing the franchise price.

Under either form of competitive bidding, the winning bidder presumably has similar incentives to minimize costs over the period of the operating contract in order to maximize net profits. However, a major divergence between a private and social calculus in this respect relates to maintenance costs. Where the assets are long-lived, but the operating contract is of shorter duration, there are obvious incentives for the operator to skimp on maintenance or improvement costs where these will have little or no impact on the revenue stream until the post-contract period. This problem could, of course, be solved by making the initial operating contract the same length as the expected life of the assets, thus fully internalizing both the costs and benefits of expenditures on maintenance, although not necessarily capital improvements, replacements, or facility expansion where returns can only be realized thereon beyond the term of the contract. In many cases involving large-scale infrastructure, this internalization function may entail initial contracts of 50 or 60 years. Another advantage of integrating the design, construction, financing, and operating functions in these cases

53 Harold Demsetz 'Why Regulate Utilities?' (1968) 11 *J. of Law & Econ.* 55.

54 For a review of these problems, see Keith Crocker and Scott Masters 'Regulation and Administered Contracts Revisited: Lessons from Transaction-Cost Economics for Public Utility Regulation' *J. of Econ.* (forthcoming).

is that the private provider will have an incentive to minimize the life-cycle costs of the project. Where initial capital investments and ongoing maintenance are substitutes for one another, less initial capital investment results in higher subsequent maintenance and conversely. The optimal mix of the two functions is more likely to be selected by an integrated provider. However, technological uncertainties, uncertainties relating to market demand, and uncertainties relating to the durability or stability of surrounding government policies that may affect the costs or revenues generated by the project make these long-term contracts a much riskier proposition from the perspective of a private sector operator. In turn, the government will have committed itself for the life of the assets to a single operator, notwithstanding the possible subsequent emergence of superior operators. While the government may attempt, in a long-term operating contract, to specify all performance obligations of the operator, over a long-term contract these are very difficult to specify completely ex ante and in any event are likely to entail intensive and costly monitoring. Short-term contracts reduce some of these problems (the difficulty of anticipating all future contingencies) while exacerbating others (the incentive to degrade the assets, for example). Moreover, while there is at least the potential for periodic competitive retendering of the contract, as Williamson has pointed out, asset specificity – in this case, specialized human capital relating to the operation of a facility – may create considerable advantages for the incumbent at contract renewal junctures, and militate against the preservation of a competitive contracting environment.[55]

More generally, the case for vertical integration of operation and maintenance with design, construction, and financing functions in the provision of infrastructure is that firms can coordinate these functions at lower cost than can the government; that the cross-function incentive effects of bundling functions (interdependencies) yield superior performance to more discrete forms of contracting out, that is, that decisions affecting the design and construction functions will be influenced by operating obligations, all of which will be affected by financing obligations; and that economies of scale and scope can be realized through integration. The empirical evidence tends to suggest that indeed vertically integrated private providers of infrastructure services can complete initial infrastructure construction much more

55 Oliver Williamson *The Economic Institutions of Capitalism* (New York: Free Press 1985) chapter 13 ('Franchise Bidding for Natural Monopoly'); see also Crocker and Masters, supra.

quickly than can be done under the traditional mode of public provision with discrete contracting out of particular functions, in large part because of reductions in transaction and coordination costs through a more simultaneous and less sequential construction process and greater freedom from stringent government budget allocation and procurement regulations.[56] Yet, the value of this benefit should not be overstated; for instance, in the Highway 407 project, it was alleged that use of the public/private partnership model enabled the government to reduce the time necessary to complete the project from a projected 20 years through traditional procurement to 4.5 years. However, the principal factor behind the shortened construction period appears not to be any design or production efficiency but the government's decision to use off-budget financing to increase the funding for the project from the original on-budget allocation.

One important offsetting feature of vertical integration is likely to be a marked reduction in competition for infrastructure contracts, relative to more discrete or disaggregated contracting-out policies. Economies of both scale and scope are likely to be such that in bidding on large integrated infrastructure projects very few firms or consortia are likely to be able to assemble all the relevant specialized inputs.[57] These problems are, of course, exacerbated when sponsoring governments impose domestic content restrictions on prospective bidders. Thus, one would predict a very small number of bidders on many of these contracts. In contrast, by contracting out the various functions involved in providing and operating infrastructure in a discrete or disaggregated form, it seems likely that the competitive bidding process with respect to each function is likely to attract significantly more bidders and to be correspondingly more vigorous. Empirical evidence with respect to government procurement generally suggests that increasing the number of bidders from three to four can result in savings of up to 18%; from seven to eight, up to 4%; and from ten to eleven, up to 2%.[58] The World Bank's *Infrastructure for Development* report, in relation to what have hitherto been treated as natural monopolies (electricity and telecommunications, for example), argues strongly for unbundling these activities, vertically in the case of electricity by unbundling generation from transmission and distribution, and horizontally in the case of telecommunications by unbundling local from long-distance

56 Ndekugri and Turner, supra note 51, 250.

57 See Sappington and Stiglitz, supra note 44, 571, 572.

58 McAfee and McMillan, supra note 41, 151.

service and cellular or radio paging services, in order to stimulate greater competition.[59] While full vertical integration of the provision of major infrastructure facilities, which the World Bank appears to favour in other cases, may offer offsetting economic advantages, it may well entail highly attenuated competition at the bidding stage of the process (and even less at recontracting intervals), as well as monopoly provision of all services provided through the facility thereafter by the winning bidder or parties to whom it in turn has granted exclusive or monopoly sub-franchises. Nevertheless, if the production of new design ideas can impact materially on the final value of a proposed project, if the nature of those ideas cannot be easily specified in advance, and if explicit prizes for innovative designs cannot be awarded without attracting political controversy, then restrictions on the number of entrants competing in the selection process (by, for instance, insisting on bundled services) increase the value of the expected premium, and elicit increased research effort.[60]

### C. DISTRIBUTIONAL AND POLITICAL CONSIDERATIONS

Distributional considerations arising from the privatization of infrastructure services are likely to vary widely, depending upon the nature of the service in question. Where the services have previously entailed substantial cross-subsidies under public provision, for example to rural or low-income users, these are likely to disappear under an unconstrained, fully vertically integrated private provision model,[61] and thus will provoke resistance to the adoption of this model. Indeed, under such a model adverse distributional effects may be exacerbated if the elasticity of demand by these groups is low, reflecting the absence of choices, thus permitting monopoly pricing or price discrimination. The private sector provider may, of course, be required to maintain these cross-subsidies through ongoing contractual or regulatory constraints. However, these constraints are likely to make it less attractive for private sector operators to invest in such projects and, even where investment is feasible, will entail the government in complex, ongoing contractual or regulatory oversight. The empirical evidence suggests that at some

59 World Bank, supra note 2, 53, 54.

60 Curtis Taylor, supra note 45: 'Because equilibrium research effort by each firm increases with the size of the prize and decreases with the number of contestants, there is a one-to-one correspondence between choosing the optimal prize and entry fee and choosing the optimal number of contestants and equilibrium effort level.'

61 See John Vickers and George Yarrow 'Economic Perspectives on Privatization' (1991) 5 *J. of Econ. Perspectives* 111, 114.

point detailed regulatory oversight of a private utility or other infrastructure facility operator is likely to yield performance characteristics not sharply different from those of a public enterprise.[62] Thus, privatization may offer few advantages where the government is committed to maintaining existing subsidy policies (other than through direct transfers).

Other constituencies whose interests may be jeopardized by privatization of infrastructure services are members of public sector labour unions who have been employed in the operation of existing infrastructure facilities that are to be privatized. After privatization, they may face lay-offs, lower remuneration, less job security, and more flexible or more demanding job assignments.

Other constituencies that may be at risk from privatization are both commercial and retail customers, who face the risk of monopolistic pricing of user charges by the private sector service provider if not otherwise constrained either in the initial contract between the government and the provider or by ongoing regulation. Given the essential nature of many infrastructure services, demand for these services is often inelastic and is likely to support a significant degree of monopoly pricing.

Still another constituency that may perceive itself as prejudiced by the privatization of infrastructure services is environmental and related groups who may see private sector developers and operators of certain kind of infrastructure facilities, for example toll roads or airports, as being more likely than public sector providers to discount environmental and related negative externalities.[63]

A more general and amorphous constituency that may be opposed to the privatization of existing infrastructure facilities accompanied by the imposition of user charges are present users who perceive themselves as having already paid for the facility through various kinds of taxes and are unlikely to be impressed by arguments as to the efficiency of the price mechanism in rationing access to scarce or over-utilized resources.

All of these constituencies are likely to translate the distributional and other impacts that they are likely to bear from privatization into political resistance to the process. With a number of these constituencies (labour or users) the resistance is likely to be less in the case of the privatization of new infrastructure facilities than with existing infrastructure facilities. This is particularly likely to be the case where the govern-

62 Hirshhorn, supra note 42, 13, 21.
63 Gomez-Ibanez and Meyer, supra note 42, 205.

ment is able to persuade voters and interest groups that the facilities are unlikely to be built at all in the absence of privatization. However, the opportunities for profitable private development and operation of new infrastructure (highways, for example), especially in developed economies where most essential infrastructure already exists, may be very limited.[64] As well, development of new infrastructure facilities is likely to exacerbate the concerns of environmental and similar groups, relative to the privatization of existing facilities, given the incremental negative environmental impacts or at least 'Nimby' effects that additions to infrastructure are likely in many cases to generate.

On the other hand, privatization of infrastructure services offers some political attractions to government. The most prominent attraction is that it enables governments in a period of budget deficits and an environment of fiscal restraint in many countries to move major capital expenditures on new infrastructure off-budget or to capitalize existing infrastructure by sell-offs to the private sector. However, two important caveats are warranted in this context. First, as noted above, governments, even severely overcommitted governments, can typically borrow more cheaply than the private sector, so that from a social perspective, the case for privatizing infrastructure provision, including the financing function, necessarily turns on the various efficiency and incentive effects, described above, that flow from integrating the financing function with other functions to be performed by the private sector service provider. The second caveat is that the public sector technically is as capable as the private sector of imposing user charges for its services. Thus, if investment in an infrastructure project has a positive net present value, taking into account the revenues that it will generate, the net long-term worth of the public sector may not be enhanced, and could conceivably be reduced, by full privatization of an infrastructure facility.[65] Unfortunately, because of the manner in which public accounts are maintained by governments in many countries (cash rather than accrual accounting), moving the initial capital investment off-budget or capitalizing existing infrastructure, while not simultaneously reporting forgone future revenues, encourages a form of fiscal illusion which may fool some taxpayers and citizens concerned with the size of the current budget deficit.[66]

64 Hirshhorn, supra note 42, 1.

65 See Oliver Williamson 'Credible Commitments: Using Hostages to Support Exchange' (1983) 73 *Am. Econ. Rev.* 519.

66 See Jack Mintz and Ross Preston (eds) *Capital Budgeting in the Public Sector* (Kingston, Ont.: John Deutsch Institute for Study of Economic Policy 1993).

Another political attraction of privatization of infrastructure services is that it enables 'hands tying' or credible commitments with respect to a range of policy-related risks that relate to both the financial viability and in some cases social benefits of a project.[67] For example, the World Bank reports that failure to maintain existing basic infrastructure in many developing countries has proved a more costly policy shortcoming than failure to invest in new infrastructure, at least in terms of the return on the investments involved.[68] This shortcoming seems largely explained by the inability of governments to commit resources, on a long-term basis, to infrastructure maintenance in the face of more pressing day-to-day political or other demands on public resources. By privatizing, on a vertically integrated basis, the provision of infrastructure, an ongoing commitment to maintenance of the assets (subject to the difficulties noted above) can be built into the arrangement. Similarly, pricing and subsidy policies can be rendered more stable and predictable by embodying them in contractual commitments between the government and private sector providers, and thus made more resistant to the whims of the political process.[69] On the one hand, without strong ex ante commitments in these areas, private sector providers, having incurred large sunk costs in the initial capital investment, are vulnerable to opportunistic behaviour by government in changing the rules of the game ex post, which will increase risk premiums demanded ex ante or at the limit discourage more risk-averse firms from bidding at all.[70] On the other hand, in order to protect or enhance the private sector provider's revenue stream, the government may be tempted to make anti-competitive commitments which may enhance the government's return on the contract, for example, a commitment not to build other competitive facilities, or to permit monopoly pricing of user charges, or to relax environmental constraints, where in each case social welfare may be impaired. But the government, by distancing itself from service provision and tying its hands, short of legislating cancellation or modification of the contract and arguably risking claims for compensation, can deflect some of the political costs that it might otherwise have to confront if it pursued these policies itself as a public operator.

67 World Bank, supra note 2, 27, 29.

68 Ibid.

69 See Pablo Spiller 'Institutions and Regulatory Commitment in Utilities Privatization' (1993) 2 *Industrial & Corporate Change* 387.

70 Vickers and Yarrow, supra note 61, 114; Sappington and Stiglitz, supra note 44, 574 and 580.

Another political advantage of privatizing infrastructure provision in a period of fiscal constraint is that it permits employment creation in depressed labour markets without committing additional public resources to this objective (albeit again something of a fiscal illusion if the government is forgoing subsequent revenues from the facility). The empirical evidence suggests, as noted above, that fully vertically integrated private infrastructure providers can complete major infrastructure projects much more quickly than public provision under the traditional disaggregated form of contracting out. Thus, under privatization, jobs in the initial construction phase of the facility can be created more quickly than under public provision. Whether all of these jobs should be counted as net increments to the labour force may again be largely a fiscal illusion. Given that private sector infrastructure providers simply draw on existing sources of domestic and international capital and do not in themselves expand the pool of savings and capital in the economy, it should probably be assumed that most of these projects involve diverting capital from one activity to another where the expected private return is higher.[71] In terms of job creation effects, the net effect, while more concentrated and visible, may be quite ambiguous.

A final argument for privatization of infrastructure services is an infant-industry argument. By governments privatizing the provision of such services to domestic private providers or consortia, the development of the necessary qualities of specialized expertise and the resolution or minimization of coordination problems in large multidisciplinary teams can be advanced by a process of learning-by-doing. Given the size of the global market for infrastructure projects described by the World Bank in its recent report, providing infrastructure services may develop into a major export market. However, implicit in this argument is that governments in awarding infrastructure contracts should adopt an explicit preference in favour of domestic firms, even where foreign firms could provide a superior or cheaper service, thus 'taxing' domestic users or taxpayers, directly or indirectly, in the short run. As with infant-industry arguments that have been invoked over the past century to justify trade protectionism in various contexts,[72] such policies may promote and preserve firms or industries that have a long-term comparative *disadvantage* and the 'tax' on users or taxpayers equally

71 Gomez-Ibanez and Meyer, supra note 42, 101.

72 See Robert Howse and Michael Trebilcock *The Regulation of International Trade* (London: Routledge 1995) chapter 1.

becomes permanent. In addition, the increasingly stringent government procurement and foreign investment provisions that have been adopted in NAFTA and the Uruguay Round agreement of the GATT may in some cases elicit justifiable complaints by foreign governments or firms of discrimination.[73]

### D. THE STATUS OF GOVERNMENT AS A PARTY TO THE PARTNERSHIP CONTRACT

So far, we have emphasized the problems inhering in public/private partnerships owing to the nature of infrastructure assets, and the distinct design problems related thereto. However, as alluded to earlier, a fundamental problem for these partnerships relates to the status of government as a party to the contracts. Because of its inherent legislative powers, government involvement presents distinct and quite vexing contracting problems.[74] First, particularly in countries such as Canada that lack constitutionally entrenched property rights, governments are able to abrogate express contractual commitments through legislative fiat. In other words, even where the contracting parties have been able to anticipate and to contract ex ante for the risks of future acts of contractual opportunism by government, the ability of governments to nullify these contracts through express legislative amendment attenuates the degree to which private parties can rely on governmental contractual undertakings.[75] Consequently, the value of even an express contractual commitment to provide fair compensation in the event of a

73 Ibid. chapters 6 and 11.

74 The lack of institutional safeguards against government takings is interpreted by Douglass North as a critical constraint on the pace of national economic development. See Douglass C. North *Institutions, Institutional Change and Economic Growth* (Cambridge: Cambridge University Press 1990); and Douglass C. North and Barry R. Weingast 'Constitutions and Commitment: The Evolution of Institutions Governing Public Choice in Seventeenth-Century England' (1989) 49 *J. of Econ. Hist.* 803. See also Spiller, supra note 69, 387; Brian Levy and Pablo Spiller 'Regulation, Institutions, and Commitment in Telecommunications' in *Proceedings of the World Bank Conference on Development Economics* (Washington, DC: The World Bank 1994); and Pablo Spiller and Ingo Vogelsang 'The Institutional Foundations of Regulatory Commitment in the UK' draft paper dated 16 June 1994, on file with the authors.

75 This is the paradox of sovereignty. The 'greater the sovereign's ability to impel submission by citizens, the less the ability of a third-party arbiter to compel performance by the sovereign, and so the less the sovereign's ability to induce voluntary cooperation. *This paradox turns the sovereign's power into the sovereign's handicap.*' David D. Haddock 'Foreseeing Confiscation by the Sovereign: Lessons from the American West' in Terry L. Anderson and Peter J. Hill (eds) *The Political Economy of the American West* (Lanham, Maryland: Rowman & Littlefield 1994) (emphasis added).

'taking' is subject to doubt. Second, even where governments face constitutional or other institutional constraints on their power to confiscate outright the undertaking of a private owner/operator, considerable contractual design problems emanating from the breadth of governmental policy powers remain. Here, it is difficult ex ante for parties to anticipate the myriad ways in which governments can infringe the franchise value of the private investor. Simple cases, such as when government transfers title or establishes a competitor to the investor, can be anticipated in advance, and can be restrained by the judiciary. However, beyond these simple cases, the task of design is rendered much more difficult. For instance, in the case of an asset like an airport terminal, changes in transportation, environmental, occupational health and safety, or regional development policy could all adversely impact the franchise value of the undertaking. Not only is the range of possible 'takings' difficult to anticipate in advance, but it is also difficult to differentiate legitimate governmental actions from those actions which are nothing more than a thinly disguised attempt to debase the value of the investors' interests, leaving investors with little choice but to tender their interests in the project to government on exploitative terms.

The problem in differentiating permissible from impermissible governmental modifications of state contractual commitments is graphically illustrated by the experience of the United States Supreme Court in interpreting the Constitution's contract clause, which prohibits states from enacting laws impairing the obligation of contracts.[76] The clause was first interpreted by the Court in cases involving public grants, such as *Fletcher* v. *Peck*,[77] and *Dartmouth College* v. *Woodward*,[78] wherein the Court prevented state governments from abrogating contractual obligations that were explicitly made to private beneficiaries. However, by 1837, the Court began to retreat from an expansive interpretation of the contract clause, by, for instance, declining to incorporate into a toll-bridge charter an implied promise by a state not to authorize construction of a competing bridge, even though this would severely affect the value of the franchise that had been

76 Article 1, subsection 10 of the Constitution. Although there is no explicit constitutional provision that imposes a similar constraint on the federal government, it is arguable that the Fifth Amendment's due process clause may have (or had) this effect: see Laurence Tribe *American Constitutional Law* 2d ed. (Mineola, NY: The Foundation Press 1988) 613n1. See also *Bowen* v. *Public Agencies* 477 US 41 (1986).

77 6 Cranch (10 US) 87 (1810).

78 4 Wheat. (17 US) 518 (1819).

awarded.[79] By the late 1930s, the clause fell into virtual disuse, a situation which was not reversed until the Court's decision in 1977 in *United States Trust Co. of New York* v. *New Jersey*.[80] In that case, the Court prohibited New Jersey and New York from repealing a statutory covenant that earmarked certain revenues and reserves from rail transportation as security for state borrowings. The states sought to use the funds to subsidize rail passenger transportation. The Court held that the contract impairment was not reasonable and necessary to serve an important public purpose, in this case, state transportation, energy, and environmental goals.[81] Nevertheless, under the *US Trust Co.* doctrine, it is clear that cases involving more subtle debasement of the state contractual or quasi-contractual commitments could still withstand constitutional scrutiny where the end to be achieved could not be achieved through alternative means.[82]

In any event, as demonstrated by the federal government's decision to abrogate its contractual commitments to the Pearson Development Corporation in respect of the T1T2 development, it is clear that the scope for governmental modification (or abrogation) of state franchise contracts is more than speculative. This problem of government opportunism is, however, by no means novel in Canada. In an exhaustive analysis of the performance of long-term franchise contracts governing natural monopolies in a range of different industries (electricity, railways, telephony, tramways, water, and gas) from the mid-1800s to the 1930s in Canada, John Baldwin argues that infirmities in the institutional environment enabled governments to exploit opportunistically the sunk investment costs of franchise operators, ultimately leading to a general contractual failure that resulted in a form of vertical integration that linked consumers and suppliers, namely high levels of state ownership of such assets.[83] Baldwin cites several

79 *Charles River Bridge* v. *Warren Bridge* 36 US (11 Pet.) 420 (1837).

80 431 US 1 (1977).

81 In subsequent cases, the Court has emphasized that state abrogation of its own contractual commitments will attract considerably less curial deference than state legislative interference with private contracts generally. See, for instance, *Keystone Bitminous Coal Assn.* v. *deBenedictis* 480 US 470 (1987).

82 For an analysis of the revival of the contract clause see Bernard Schwartz 'Old Wine in Old Bottles? The Renaissance of the Contract Clause' in Philip B. Kurland and Gerhard Casper (eds) *The Supreme Court Review* (1979) 95–122; and Richard A. Epstein 'Toward a Revitalization of the Contract Clause' (1984) 51 *U. Chi. LR* 703.

83 John Baldwin *Regulatory Failure and Renewal: The Evolution of the Natural Monopoly Contract* (Ottawa: Economic Council of Canada 1989); see also Christopher Armstrong and H.V. Nelles *Monopoly's Moment: The Organization and Regulation of Canadian Utilities 1830–1930* (Toronto: University of Toronto Press 1986).

examples of contractual failure leading to nationalization: the decision by the federal Board of Railway Commissioners to limit the freight rates charged by private railways during a period of rapid price inflation, resulting in the demise and nationalization of two major railways;[84] the Manitoba legislature's threatened imposition of a discriminatory tax on Bell Canada's operations in the province as a prelude to nationalization by the province;[85] and the Ontario legislature's use of legislative amendments designed to abrogate contractual and legislative commitments made to investors in power generation and distribution, electric tramway, and electric lighting franchises; all in an effort to bolster the prospects of a newly created provincial electric utility – Ontario Hydro.[86] Baldwin's claim is that the source of the failure of private franchise contracts in Canada resides in weak judicial traditions (specifically, a failure to regard governmental action other than an outright taking of title as a taking) and the absence of constitutional protection for property rights.[87] Had the institutional regime been structured differently, Baldwin speculates that private ownership subject to regulatory oversight would have been a viable substitute for nationalization – a course of evolution more typically followed in the United States.[88]

Interestingly, many of the franchise contracts concluded during the period of Baldwin's study had properties strikingly similar to the public/private partnerships observed today. The contracts were long term, involved durable assets in areas where technology and demand conditions were changing or, at least, somewhat uncertain, and often contemplated government equity interests in the project through a fixed or varying level of participation in gross revenues. Further, the contracts, at least in the initial stages of their evolution, specified the obligations of the parties in vague, aspirational terms, a feature which ultimately forced the parties to develop more elaborate contractual mechanisms (through more detailed specification of terms and the creation of arbitral governance mechanisms) that would deal with

84 Grand Trunk and Canadian Northern. See discussion in Baldwin, supra, chapter 4.

85 Baldwin, supra note 83, 73–4.

86 To be fair, the government's actions followed a series of failed attempts to compel the electric rail and lighting franchisees to abide by the terms of their earlier contract. See discussion in Baldwin, supra note 83, chapter 10.

87 Many of these same themes are developed by George Priest 'The Origins of Utility Regulation and the Theories of Regulation Debate' (1993) 36 *J. of Law & Econ.* 289.

88 See also George Priest, supra. In contrast, Spiller argues that some countries were able to achieve significant levels of governmental commitment in respect of up-front private sector investments by relying on judicial enforcement of governmental licences. However, this mechanism imposed costs in terms of forgone adjustment to changing circumstances (Spiller, supra note 69).

adjustment to changing contracting conditions, both on renewal and before.[89] The question then arises as to whether the current institutional environment renders the contractual adjustment problems studied by Baldwin moot. While the role of the judiciary in constraining governmental opportunism through contractual interpretation is subject to debate, there is still no constitutionally entrenched contract or property rights clause in Canada, attenuating the constraints that could be imposed on government. Moreover, while certain international obligations (chapter 10 of the North American Free Trade Agreement, for example) constrain governmental actions in respect of procurement decisions, the constraints on ex post governmental action are much weaker.[90]

Given the dearth of formalized institutional constraints on governmental opportunism, what constraints will currently operate to ensure governmental fidelity to contractual undertakings set out in the public/private partnerships? One possibility is that governments will provide hostages to support the initiatives.[91] For instance, to the extent that private sector operators have developed considerable expertise in the operation and maintenance of the projects as a result of learning, then the decision to expropriate the franchise may imperil these human capital investments. Alternatively, depending on the operation of reputational markets, a decision by the government to expropriate the undertaking may damage its reputational investment, and raise the costs to it of contracting with subsequent parties.[92] Of course, to be effective, third parties must be able to observe the government's conduct and discern that it is opportunistic in character. To the extent that public/private partnerships are not one-off affairs, but rather are a frequent and predictable component of government policy-making, then the costs to government opportunism, in terms of forgone future benefits, should be correspondingly increased. In this respect, it is arguable that the *current* costs to government of impairing its obliga-

89 The same point is made by Priest, supra note 87, who argues that the theories used to explain the role of regulation in natural monopolies (public interest or industry capture) ignore the functional similarity between regulation by public commission and several contractual innovations found in long-term franchise contracts.

90 See Evan Atwood and Michael Trebilcock 'Public Accountability in an Age of Contracting Out' *Can. Bus. LJ* (forthcoming).

91 Oliver Williamson 'Credible Commitments: Using Hostages to Support Exchange' (1983) 73 *Am. Econ. Rev.* 519.

92 For a general discussion of the operation of reputational markets, see David Charny 'Nonlegal Sanctions in Commercial Relations' (1990) 104 *Harv. LR* 373.

tions to holders of debt of public/private partnership are much greater than to the equityholders. In the former case, whether expressly guaranteed or not, impairment of a debt obligation associated with a public/private partnership could have dramatic and severe effects on government's capacity to finance its broader borrowings.[93]

Yet reputational mechanisms alone may not be a sufficient constraint on governmental opportunism.[94] One possible response is to develop institutions that are capable of augmenting the restraints imposed by reputational markets. That is, at the time of contract formation, government could commission an arm's-length review of the contract to certify the integrity of the selection process, the contract's congruence with the proposal submitted by the winning bidder (recall the lock-in problems relating to the lag period between the decision to award the contract and the actual execution of the contract), and the compatibility of the project with applicable public goals and concerns. Alternatively, and less ambitiously, the evaluation panel that oversaw the selection process could be required to write and release publicly a summary of their evaluations of the competing bids and their reasons for preferring the winning bidder over the remaining bidders. Assuming that a project has been vetted and vindicated through such a review process, the costs to government abrogation of the contract on grounds of alleged process or substantive frailties should be magnified considerably. Another option is to limit independent review to ex post evaluation – that is, only those cases where government decides to renege on its contractual undertakings. While such review might economize on the costs of certification, these savings would come at the cost of heightened private sector uncertainty respecting the status of the contracts. In any event, if government does opt for a regime predicated on ex post review, the process would have to be considerably more rigorous and objective than the highly politicized process invoked by the federal government to analyse the T1T2 airport deal.

93 Interestingly, the interests between equity and debt holders in respect of a confiscation of an infrastructure undertaking may diverge quite radically, to the extent that government appropriates the equity investment only. In this case, the default risk to debt holders will be reduced by having government more closely associated with the undertaking, thereby enhancing the underlying value of debt. Conversation with Duncan MacCallum, Gordon Capital, October 1994.

94 Jeremy Bullow and Kenneth Rogoff 'A Constant Recontracting Model of Sovereign Debt' (1989) 97 *J. of Pol. Econ.* 155 (more complex institutional arrangements necessary to support state opportunism than reputation alone).

In considering the desirability of these measures, it is important to stress that ex post constraints on government conduct, such as mandatory compensation based on expectation damages, may prove efficacious only in respect of relatively stark types of governmental opportunism. For more subtle types of impairment, that is, takings through generalized policy initiatives, the case for conferring explicit protection on parties making infrastructural investments seems no different in kind from the case that obtains for actors having made investments in other industries, the value of which are subject to change as the result of government policy changes. In these cases, Kaplow has argued persuasively that government compensation for losses occasioned by regulatory change is undesirable as it would distort incentives for market-based risk management.[95] But so long as government continues to own infrastructure assets that are similar in character to those subject to public/private partnerships, then the incentive for opportunistic expropriation through generalized (non-targeted) initiatives is reduced.[96] This is because government will suffer losses on its infrastructure investments similar in character to losses sustained by private infrastructure investors.

Nevertheless, for relatively stark takings, the case for some type of protection through expectation damages or injunction is more robust. To the extent that legal and non-legal sanctions are inadequate, investors will rely on the pricing mechanism to protect their interests – that is, by impounding the expected cost of confiscatory action by government into the price that the investor is willing to pay for the franchise. Under this scenario, the costs of future expected opportunism are reflected back onto government in the form of a lowered rate of return to government from the proposed infrastructure project or a higher expected risk premium. Alternatively, private investors may need

95 Lewis Kaplow 'An Economic Analysis of Legal Transitions' (1986) 99 *Harv. LR* 509. Contrary views of the scope of government obligation in respect of generalized takings are developed in M. Graetz 'Legal Transitions: The Case of Retroactivity in Income Tax Revision' (1977) 126 *U. Pa. LR* 47; and J. Mark Ramseyer and Minoru Nakazato 'Tax Transitions and the Protection Racket: A Reply to Professors Graetz and Kaplow' (1989) 75 *Va. LR* 1155.

96 This, of course, assumes that governmental actors respond to financial incentives in the same way that private actors do. See discussion in David Cohen 'Regulating Regulators: The Legal Environment of the State' (1990) 40 *UTLJ* 213; and 'Suing the State' (1990) 40 *UTLJ* 630 (government officials have only weak incentives to minimize costs, as excess costs can be transferred to taxpayers or to different institutions of government). However, for a contrary view, see H. Kee 'Incentives and Rewards in the Public Sector' (1986) 29 *Can. Pub. Admin.* 545.

to be induced into making up-front investments by government subsidies (perhaps in the form of transfers of assets having an ongoing stream of earnings) and/or financing guarantees to generate needed equity funds. Both of these responses result in more highly leveraged capital structures that induce excessive risk taking by project managers.[97] A final pricing-related strategy is for project managers to compress the payback period for investment, which may have distortionary effects on risk taking and/or on capital structure. In any event, it is important to stress that from the perspective of a government that is intent on keeping its promises, the inability to credibly commit its intent is costly, and heightens the importance of devising workable and durable institutional mechanisms that are responsive to this problem.[98]

## IV *Conclusion*

A central theme of this study has been the considerable complexity entailed in the use of public/private partnerships designed to realize productive efficiency gains in the development and operation of physical infrastructure projects. In all of the case studies we explored, the details of the institutional and contractual framework proved central in determining whether the infrastructure projects were likely to generate welfare gains over alternative modes of organization. Since, save for one of the projects we examined, all of the case studies developed in the study are in the design or construction stages, the task of evaluating the long-term efficiency consequences of these arrangements is somewhat speculative. Nevertheless, examination of the incentive effects of both the selection processes and the contracts involved in these projects provides a foundation upon which reasonably robust conclusions can be drawn about the likely performance of these projects, and the broader implications for policy-makers seeking to enhance the efficient delivery and operation of physical infrastructure, both in developed and developing countries.

Commencing with the project selection stage, a first important lesson concerns the premium that policy-makers should place on responsible project selection through explicit and searching cost-benefit analysis. Whatever the merits of arguments which purport to link infrastructure

97 Importantly, because of explicit or implicit government guarantees, creditors may be indifferent to socially excessive levels of risk taking, and will not devise restrictive covenants on project managers.

98 See Spiller, supra note 69.

with productivity more broadly, it is clear that in a setting of scarce resources, policy-makers will be required to make choices among competing infrastructure projects. While some have advocated the use of public/private partnerships as a means of certifying or confirming the alleged welfare properties of proposed projects, the design of the arrangements governing the projects analysed in the case studies demonstrates the limited value of such an enterprise. Each of the projects studied reveal important – albeit sharply varying – levels of embedded public financial assistance. As argued earlier, once the state insinuates itself into these projects by, for instance, providing assurances of annual subsidies or of subsidies conditioned on the project's underlying financial performance, the market's capacity to undertake an independent valuation of the project is compromised. The problem with relying on private markets to make these quintessentially public choices was graphically illustrated in the study of the PEI Fixed Link, where policy-makers misleadingly touted the private sector's interest in the highly subsidized project as objective and tangible evidence of its societal value. Yet in the light of the various rationales for intervention enumerated in the first part of this study, the market's capacity to make legitimate judgments respecting the underlying social value of these projects, even when unclouded by state financial assistance, is of dubious value.

Assuming that threshold problems of general project selection can be surmounted (that is, that the most valuable projects are selected for development in descending order of their social value), and further that a public/private partnership model constitutes the best means of organizing the project, then the next challenge is to devise a process that can identify the most deserving project and/or developer/operator, while ensuring fidelity to political legitimacy concerns. In considering this issue, it is important to emphasize the role that auctions play in economizing on endemic information problems when valuing highly idiosyncratic assets. In all of the infrastructure projects that were examined, there were no obvious benchmarks that policy-makers could invoke to determine what the minimum return necessary was to entice private developers to deliver and operate these projects; hence, the attraction of the competitive auction.

Nevertheless, the traditional information revelation function of auctions is best served when the good subject to allocation is stable and well defined. But, the highly bundled character of most public/private partnerships poses formidable problems for the design of a competitive bidding process. On the one hand, through reliance on vague and nebulous project definitions and standards, bidders will have the latitude necessary to propose novel solutions in response to the government's request. Under a more rigid bid structure, the prospect that these ideas would be created and then developed into a concrete proposal would be rendered much more remote. Quite simply, if the narrow and quite detailed standards enumerated in traditional government procurement competitions were to be used to develop large-scale infrastructure, the room for private sector innovation and creativity would be very considerably circumscribed. On the other hand, the less crystallized the project, the more expensive it will be for bidders to participate in the process. This expense derives from the out-of-pocket costs that bidders must incur in incorporating a creative design component into the proposal process and the risk that decision-makers will evaluate proposed projects on factors unrelated to the underlying merits of the proposal. As these ex ante bidding expenses increase in magnitude, so too does the need for ex ante compensation necessary to entice bidders to participate in the process in the first place. In other words, ideas matter, but the government will have to pay for them one way or another, and the question really is how that price is best paid.

So far, the merits of the multidimensional auction process for public infrastructure projects has been viewed from a strictly efficiency perspective. But given the high levels of public funding typically involved in these projects, it is important to be cognizant of the important political legitimacy values that are implicated. One need only recall the rather intense outpouring of public sentiment surrounding the redevelopment of the Pearson terminals to realize the centrality of these values in this area. Here, it is apparent that even if there are tangible efficiency gains that can be realized through a multidimensional bidding process, the public's inability to monitor systematically the selection process involved in the allocation of projects costing upwards of a half a billion dollars becomes salient.

Assuming that infrastructure projects can be allocated to the most deserving bidder through the auction process, the next, and most daunting, problem relates to the contractual design mechanisms used to alleviate the opportunism problems inhering in these projects. One of the major problems that must be confronted in these partnerships relates to asset degradation, which reflects the fact that these physical infrastructure projects typically have expected lives which extend well beyond the term of the lease, and which thus create troubling incentives for chiselling on asset maintenance. The costs of devising and enforcing contractual solutions to temper these problems must be balanced against the efficiency gains sought to be realized through the public/private partnership.

In determining whether the public/private model is a suitable means for organizing production of a specific physical infrastructure project, it is useful to highlight what these precise efficiency gains are. As discussed earlier, the principal benefit of the public/private partnership over traditional procurement models in the delivery of physical infrastructure resides in the bundling or integration of the finance, design, construction, and operating functions. Integration promotes the formation of cross-functional expertise and also ensures more disciplined performance of these functions than would be observed were government required to separately contract for the performance of each function on its own. Nevertheless, the case studies developed in this article raise doubts surrounding the likelihood of these benefits being realized on the scale contemplated by their proponents.

The most significant problem stems from de facto unbundling of the bundled partnership. Again, a striking, indeed recurrent, feature of the public/private partnership is the high degree of government financial assistance. The simplest explanation for the assistance relates to the need to subsidize public goods or to compensate for positive externalities. Yet, if these goals were the exclusive motivation for government assistance, we would expect to see simple one-time subsidies being funnelled to project developers instead of the more complex financial risk-sharing contracts that are documented in this study. Why, given the loss of integration benefits entailed by such financing, do governments decide to intervene in the provision of infrastructure in this way?

Perhaps the most important factor explaining the persistence of public financing relates to the risks of governmental contractual opportunism faced by private developers in the development and operation of physical infrastructure projects. In a first-best world, the risks embedded in the development contract might be divided between the government and the contractor in a manner that makes the private developer responsible for the endogenous production risks and the government responsible for risks of infringement through policy changes. Each party is the least-cost avoider of the risks that it has been assigned. Exogenous risks, that is, risks that neither party can control, should be transferred to the least-cost insurer, in this case, the government, owing to its superior risk-bearing capacity.[99] Unfortunately,

99 The claim that government constitutes the lowest-cost insurer, hence the best risk bearer, of exogenous risks is criticized by George Priest in the context of losses caused by catastrophic events: see 'The Government, the Market, and the Problem of Catastrophic Loss' (paper presented at the Conference on Social Treatment of

however, the first-best contractual allocation of risks is not realizable in this setting, given problems of contractual design. Put simply, a fully contingent contract outlining the limitations on governmental conduct cannot be specified owing to endemic foreseeability problems. But, even if such a contract could be devised, it is, of course, apparent that in the light of political and constitutional realities, government contractual commitments in respect of risks over which it has direct control would be virtually impossible to specifically enforce. Its inherent legislative and regulatory jurisdiction makes the contract susceptible to unilateral ex post opportunism by a government which has changed, or which has changed its mind. The problems of unanticipated government action are, of course, pervasive in the modern regulatory state, but what makes these problems particularly acute in the case of physical infrastructure are the higher level of risks that reflect the sunk costs, anticipatory, and asset lumpiness properties of such investments.

It is the combination of government inability to credibly commit to non-confiscatory measures, combined with high probabilities (and accompanying costs) of such intervention, that makes the first-best contractual solution unattainable, and which remits parties to the second-best world. It is here that the sundry financial arrangements observed in the various public/private partnerships become more readily understandable. In the absence of nuanced contractual risk-allocation mechanisms, government risk-bearing through the supply of financial capital will attenuate the apprehensions of private developers over future governmental action. So doing will ensure that projects that might otherwise be negative net present value decisions will be undertaken by the developer. At the limit, government will supply all of the risk capital and the private developer will work on a cost-plus basis. But while this contract saves the developer harmless from the costs of future government action, it does so at too high a price; in terms of the optimal balance between incentives and insurance, the arrangements provide excessive insurance, increasing the likelihood of developer moral hazard, which impairs the productive efficiency gains that motivated the use of the bundled organizational form in the first place; hence, the value of more complex intermediate financial arrangements that do not dampen developer incentives for cost containment but do

Catastrophic Risk, Stanford University, Lucas Conference Center, draft dated 21 October 1994). Among other claims, Priest argues against government superiority in risk bearing on grounds of government's inability both to evaluate and to sort risks to ensure a pooling of independent (not variant) risks.

provide some element of insurance. All of the projects surveyed in this study contain hybrid levels of financial risk sharing, whether achieved through well-specified subsidies or performance-based rental payments.

In this respect, it should be noted that the financial structure dictated by optimal risk bearing may also coincide with some of the imperatives of the tournament-based selection process. The auction theory literature, for instance, distinguishes between private and common values auctions. Whereas in the former, the underlying values relied upon by bidders to frame a bid are solely a function of the bidder's own costs, in the latter case a bidder can improve his underlying valuation of the good subject to auction by learning his competitors' valuations. Given the role of exogenous factors – such as the level and direction of network externalities, trends in customer demand, and government policy changes – the multi-stage tournament for the franchise is most accurately characterized as possessing both common and private values properties. McAfee and McMillan argue that where common value elements are present in an auction, conditioning payment for the good on a royalty payment will generate more competitive bidding because the significance of inherent differences in bidder valuations is reduced.[100]

It is well known that contractual equilibria are conditioned on a number of external factors, one of the most important being the institutional framework for contractual enforcement. In Canada, the unfortunate events surrounding the abrogation of the Terminals 1 and 2 project, a related decision, amidst the public uproar over the Terminals 1 and 2 contract, to abandon a proposed private runway development project at Pearson International Airport after bids were received but not opened, and the ex post modifications to the terms of the Highway 407 bidding process, have all contributed to legitimate concerns over government motivations, creating an environment which is becoming less congenial to these projects. To remedy this situation, supplemental institutions will have to be created which will support durable government commitments.

In a thoughtful article on the relationship between institutions and government commitment making and keeping, Levy and Spiller have expressed caution with the degree to which institutional arrangements designed to support public commitment can be successfully transferred

100 R. Preston McAfee and John McMillan 'Auctions and Bidding' (1987) 25 *J. of Econ. Lit.* 699, 717–9.

across countries.[101] The claim is that if underlying social, political, and constitutional factors – so-called institutional endowments – are not supportive of restrictions on governmental action, then the imposition of complex institutional arrangements designed to fetter arbitrary governmental action will be ineffectual. In this setting, other options, involving, inter alia, innovative transactional engineering, widespread public investments and monitoring by supra-national institutions are required. In the case of public/private infrastructure partnerships, the often sui generis nature of the projects, the difficulty of specifying clear outputs, the capacity of governments to confer broad gains on ratepayers by imposing price restrictions on investor operators, the need for project flexibility, all combine to subvert the capacity and cost-effectiveness of domestic regulatory or judicial remedies aimed at constraining governmental opportunism.[102] In this setting, greater reliance may need to be placed on supranational institutions, such as the GATT, regional trading blocks, or the World Bank. One possibility is for the bid protest and expropriation provisions currently set out in the North American Free Trade Agreement to be enlarged to include domestic as well as foreign firms. Alternatively, international public and private lending agencies could agree to condition the provision of investment on governmental adherence to independent arbitral decisions made in respect of alleged governmental takings.

In any event, if the public/private partnership is to realize the expectations of its proponents, a more systematic and objective means of reconciling government's need for policy flexibility with the market's need for certainty must be devised. The ad hoc and politically motivated inquiry, such as that undertaken by Robert Nixon to evaluate the merits of the Pearson redevelopment project, will simply not suffice to allay market fears over capricious government action in respect of these investments. Nor, on the other hand, are conventional forms of judicial review of government actions likely to possess the institutional expertise to evaluate credibly the integrity of the decision-making process entailed in such large and complex projects.[103] In the absence of such

101 Levy and Spiller, supra note 74.

102 And while ex ante certification procedures may assist in resolving these problems around the time of project construction, as soon as the project commences operation, several explicit or implicit modifications will be made to the formal contract which, in turn, will subvert the value of the earlier certification exercise and render the owner/operator susceptible to a charge that these changes are in bad faith and abusive.

103 See Atwood and Trebilcock, supra note 90.

institutional innovations, one cannot dismiss the possibility that the current wave of enthusiasm for private sector development of public infrastructure in both developed and developing economies may turn out to be little more than a form of political 'cycling' that will replay the demise of the municipal franchise contract in Canada and the United States early in this century. Let us hope that we will not be condemned to repeating the errors of history by neglecting that history.

# [14]

# DISPUTE RESOLUTION MECHANISMS TO ADDRESS UNFORESEEN CIRCUMSTANCES IN LONG TERM BOT CONTRACTS

**Nicholas Gould**
***Lovell White Durrant***

**Difficulties arising from changes in circumstances during the life of a BOT(build, own, transfer) contract may be catered for by way of contractual adjustment mechanisms, but are not always easily resolved, particularly in linked contracts. The author considers dispute resolution options in such cases.**

The length of many a BOT contract exposes the parties to the risk that circumstances existing at the time of the making of the contract will change substantially during its life, with adverse effects on one or more of the parties. The nature of the project and the risk which the contractor is typically required to bear in connection with infrastructure projects dependant on project finance make this issue particularly important to the parties involved in such projects, including the financiers.

**Changes in circumstances**

Changes in circumstances may come about as a result of a change of mind or policy on the part of the contracting authority – the authority may require a different level of service to that envisaged originally; it may require a different physical infrastructure. In these cases carefully thought through adjustment mechanisms can usually provide for appropriate adjustments to be made to the contractor's income and to other terms of the contract where necessary.

*adjustment mechanisms*

But changes in circumstances can also come about as a result of *force majeure* or other events not the fault of either party to the contract. Those changes give rise to the same issues as changes of mind by the contracting authority, but without the same moral feeling that the authority should pay for them or suffer the consequences of them. This is especially the case when the change comes about against the wishes of both parties, and wholly independently of either of them. In such cases it is not likely that the parties will reach agreement on who should bear the cost of coping with the necessary changes to the contractor's obligations, or on changes to the terms of the contract itself. The purpose of this article is to consider what mechanisms a contract might incorporate to resolve the dispute which is likely to result in such a situation.

**Dispute resolution mechanisms**

*Negotiate and agree*

Quite commonly, contracts require the parties to negotiate and agree the consequences of a change in the obligations or rights of a party, and sometimes they require that to be done "in good faith". A simple obligation to agree is, at least under English law, unenforceable. An obligation to negotiate may be enforceable in principle, but is too vague to be of practical use. An obligation to negotiate in good faith is more readily enforceable, but in circumstances where the objective interests of the parties can be seen to be different the obligation is probably of no use.

*"in good faith"*

*Independent third party*

Contracts often include a provision whereby an independent third party can be brought in to decide on the contractual consequences of a change in circumstances when the parties themselves cannot agree. The independent third party is sometimes an individual, with a specified skill, and sometimes a board or panel. Sometimes the third party is given power to reach decisions which will be binding on the parties, and sometimes they just make recommendations which the parties can adopt or ignore. Their remit might be limited to determining the financial consequences of the change in circumstances or it might extend to making adjustments to substantive contractual provisions.

It is tempting for the parties, at the stage of negotiating their contract, to provide for the third party to make recommendations and not binding decisions. This is partly because they normally do not know who the third party will be at that stage, partly because they optimistically expect to be able to reach agreement on a change when the need for it arises, and partly because they do not fully think through the consequences of failing to reach agreement or failing to agree to implement the non-binding recommendations of the third party.

*Right to terminate*

*"Russian roulette"*

However, some contracts do think through those consequences, and apply a form of "Russian roulette": if the recommendations of the third party are not adopted then one or both parties have the right to terminate the whole contract. This may well be appropriate if the change required is so drastic that it cannot be accommodated within the walls of the existing contract. In other cases, the thinking behind these provisions is presumably that termination is such a Draconian course, and would have such awkward consequences on other linked contracts, that neither side will want it to happen, and will adopt the recommendations of the third party rather than bring it about.

*considerable losses before termination*

Nevertheless, termination is unlikely to work equally badly for both parties. The change in circumstances which led to the involvement of the third party is likely to have been in effect for quite some time before its consequences became apparent, and the parties are likely to have attempted to negotiate a change before going to the third party, and the third party may have taken some time to arrive at their recommendations before announcing them. One party or the other will, therefore, probably have incurred considerable losses before termination can take effect, and the clauses providing for "Russian roulette" rarely, if ever, provide for the party suffering a loss to be compensated by the other – there is no necessary reason why they should do so if the change in circumstances which brought the problem about was the result of "neutral" forces and not the actions or fault of the parties.

In the Arlandabanan project now underway in Sweden, *force majeure* can lead to termination in certain circumstances, but if it does and the government then takes over the completed works the government will only pay compensation equal to the then outstanding debt, and not to the value of the assets as they then stand.

**Unforeseen events**

The difficulties attached to the "Russian roulette" solution lead the parties and their advisors to attempts to foresee the future and make provision for change in advance. This in turn leads to a temptation to include a clause saying that anything not foreseen and dealt with will be ignored. If something unforeseen then does occur, the parties are left to the provisions of the relevant governing law, whatever it may be.

134

The way in which the provisions of the governing law will apply to an unforeseen event is uncertain, and that in turn makes it tempting for the parties or the financiers behind them to stipulate that the risk of unforeseen events which are not expressly dealt with by the contract must be assumed by one or other of the parties.

*ambiguity inherent*

These attempts to foresee the future are made even more difficult by the ambiguity inherent in the exercise: are the parties attempting to anticipate specific future events, or only the possibility of a change in circumstances? The difference can be illustrated by the common form of clause found in engineering contracts, to the effect that the contractor is deemed to have allowed in the rates or price for all ground conditions which are foreseeable, or sometimes which are "reasonably" foreseeable. In that context "foreseeable" does not mean the complete range of geological conditions known to science, but only those conditions which the circumstances indicate are likely to be found or may well be found.

The distinction between circumstances which are likely to or may well happen, and the full range of all possible circumstances which could happen, should be borne in mind by those drafting BOT contracts if they include a provision to the effect that the risk of unforeseen events will be assumed by one of the parties.

**Public sector**

It is particularly important to cater for possible future changes in public sector BOT contracts because those contracts are for the provision of a public service and it is generally of paramount importance that the service be maintained. The projects dealt with in such contracts are also often large scale, so that it is not practical for replacement contractors or operators or financiers to step in and replace the original ones at short notice.

**Coordinating dispute resolution between linked contracts**

This is a particularly important and difficult topic. The nature of infrastructure projects means that there are likely to be a number of contracts linked to the contract most immediately affected by the change in circumstances and the interests of the parties to those contracts may be different from those of the parties to the first contract. Also a material change in the obligations of the contractor, or an event of *force majeure*, may affect a linked contract differently from the way in which it affects the first contract.

*First contract*

*corresponding changes*

The simplest way of dealing with this is for all contracts after the first to have a provision stipulating that they follow the first contract, and that any changes to that contract must be reflected in corresponding changes to the later contracts. In project finance that simplest way is seldom acceptable to the financiers and others, and it can in any event be difficult to decide what the knock-on consequences are.

*Third party remedy*

An alternative approach, as used in the contracts relating to the new motorway in Hungary, is for the concession company (as the party common to the greatest number of contracts) to undertake to pursue whatever remedies it may have against a third party. This concept is likely to be of limited use in many project finance schemes because the obligations under one contract will often bear only a conceptual relationship to rights under a linked contract.

*Representations to expert*

In the financing arrangements for the Hub River project in Pakistan there appears to be no automatic change to linked contracts as a result of a change to the underlying concession agreement. On the contrary, the financiers are, in certain circumstances, given the right to make representations to an expert appointed under the concession agreement, but the exercise of that right does not seem to exhaust or limit the rights of the financiers.

*Tripartite arbitration*

A number of concession contracts include a provision similar to that which is often found in construction subcontracts, whereby the parties agree that if the dispute between them is the same as or similar to a dispute between associated parties or to a dispute which arises under associated contracts, the parties agree to a form of tripartite arbitration in which the arbitrator has the same powers of joinder, and so on, as a court would have had. These provisions may solve, or go some way towards solving, the procedural difficulties otherwise involved in several parallel arbitrations, but they often fail to deal with the underlying substantive difficulty.

*procedural difficulties*

**Different obligations**

The underlying difficulty is that, whereas a construction subcontractor should be under exactly the same construction obligations as the main contractor, the financiers under a project finance scheme (to take just one example of the many different parties involved in a project financed deal) will be under quite different obligations to those of the concession contractor. In addition, the financiers will be most reluctant to assume in the loan documentation an obligation to lend any further sums which might be required by a change imposed on the concession contractor by the contracting authority, or an obligation to accept a delayed or lesser return as the result of an event of *force majeure*.

It follows that even if, procedurally, the financiers can be brought into the same arbitration as the concession company and the contracting authority, the underlying obligations will be different, and the concession company may have no substantive rights against the financiers which the arbitrator could enforce.

*no substantive rights*

In non-recourse finance, which would be the normal arrangement in project finance, the concession company and the other participants will probably have to rely more on the commercial common sense of the financiers than on strict legal rights against them.

[15]

© *The Financier* • Vol. 5, No. 4, 1998
*http://www.the-financier.com*

# *Infrastructure Financing with Unbundled Mechanisms*

**José A. Trujillo, *Titulización de Activos SGFT***
**Remy Cohen, *Cohen & Co.***
**Xavier Freixas, *Universitat Pompeu I Fabra***
**Robert Sheehy, *Bear, Stearns & Co. Inc.***

Concession schemes of the Build-Operate-Transfer (BOT) type for the development of infrastructure projects by the private sector are a means to address the shortage in public resources and the relative inefficiency of the public sector in the provision of certain services. However, such schemes have problems which are aggravated in the case of emerging economies. The issues that we present as problems affecting BOT mechanisms, and the proposals that we make based on unbundled schemes, refer to those projects where the required investment is relatively large in relation to the importance of the net cash flows generated by the infrastructure, after maintenance and operating costs. They also refer to projects whose revenues have a high degree of uncertainty. We argue that BOT schemes, defined by the concentration of all responsibilities (building, management and financing) in a unique private agent (or a joint venture of private agents) are inefficient in the case of projects with the mentioned characteristics (high relative investment and high uncertainty), and can be challenged on the grounds that the unbundling of these responsibilities is a more efficient alternative. More specifically, we argue that there are efficiency gains if financing is made through a neutral special purpose vehicle (SPV) sponsored by the public sector on behalf of the infrastructure users and payers.

## I. INTRODUCTION

During the last decade the role of the public sector in the financing of infrastructure projects has changed radically, both in developed and in emerging economies. On the one hand, budgetary constraints are now more restrictive. On the other hand, it is also widely accepted that the private management of public projects generates efficiency gains.[1] As a consequence, the role of the public sector is shifting from financier/owner/manager of projects to regulator and guarantor, and its involvement in the productive economy is shrinking. Simultaneously, private sector initiative is invading areas that were previously considered in the exclusive domain of the public sector. Such a situation has required a new dimension for public-private arrangements to allocate responsibilities, risks and profits.

The generalized response to this new environment has taken the form of arrangements in which private initiative is empowered to construct and finance the projects, retaining their ownership temporarily. In some cases, depending on the nature of the project and on the management capabilities of the public sector, the infrastructure is publicly operated on a lease basis, as is the case of some power plant projects.[2] Alternatively, the private sector operates the infrastructure under a concession contract, as is the case with the majority of toll roads. These arrangements, which are referred to as Build-Lease-Transfer (BLT) and Build-Operate-Transfer (BOT), respectively, have proved to be an efficient approach to develop infrastructure that the public sector by itself could not undertake.[3]

It should not be a surprise that BOT mechanisms have shown more success in developed and relatively stable economies, where they have a reasonable track record, than in less developed countries. However, when the available experiences are examined in greater depth, in many cases we encounter the long and generous hand of the public sector behind the projects, with a variety of subsidies, guarantees and barriers to competition, as has been the case with many privately operated toll roads in Europe. We encounter also numerous cases of contract renegotiation due to spectacular errors in demand prediction.[4] With the experience of the industrialized economies, and in the absence of a better alternative, the use of BOT mechanisms has expanded to emerging and deeply unstable economies. To attract the private sector to projects located in these more complicated environments the use of BOT mechanisms has required the support of multilateral agencies (MLA) and the introduction of risk sharing agreements between the public sector and private concessionaires. This has helped to solve, at least partially, the problems resulting from high levels of uncertainty.

We argue that such a generalized use of BOT schemes, whose main characteristic is the concentration of all responsibilities (building, management and financing) in a unique private agent (or a joint venture of private agents), could be challenged on the grounds that the unbundling of these responsibilities is a more efficient alternative. More specifically, we argue that there are efficiency gains if financing is made through a neutral special purpose vehicle (SPV) sponsored by the public sector on behalf of the infrastructure users and payers. This has led us to consider the desirable characteristics of such a financing scheme, and as a consequence the role of the public and private sectors, as well as that of the MLA.

The issues that we present as problems affecting the BOT mechanism, together with the proposals that we make based on unbundled schemes, refer to those projects where the required investment is relatively large in relation to the importance of the net cash flows generated by the infrastructure, after maintenance and operating costs. These are typically represented by toll roads, urban water distribution systems and, in general, by those services that can be defined as ***toll goods***. They include telecommunication systems, ports, airports, power transmission facilities, power distribution networks, etc. However, these are not the only type of projects that can be developed with unbundled mechanisms and financed by a neutral SPV. The proposal can be extended to other projects such as railways, urban transport, exhibition centers, wastewater treatment plants and solid waste management facilities. Nevertheless, in spite of the wide range of projects that could be developed by means of the scheme proposed in this paper, toll roads are the most representative example and the contents of this paper may be biased towards that particular case.[5]

Apart from the relative size of the required investment, we consider the presence of uncertainty as the fundamental issue behind the problems of BOT financing schemes. It is precisely the consequences of uncertainty that can be mitigated by unbundling the project and financing it by means of a neutral SPV.[6]

Once it is accepted that infrastructure projects can no longer be financed directly by the public sector, the project cash flows have to be the source of finance.[7] Such an assignment of costs to the beneficiaries, which may include others apart from the direct users, can be defended both in terms of equity and in terms of an efficient allocation of resources, in particular if it is possible to identify and price externalities. The use of cash flows as a source of financing is compatible with both BOT and unbundled schemes. Yet, unbundling may have some advantages when compared to BOT, because it yields a higher degree of freedom without requiring the public sector either to assume managerial responsibilities or to use public resources to finance the project. In addition, it will be shown that the use of a neutral SPV that allocates all costs directly to the beneficiaries mitigates the negative effects of uncertainty on the overall costs. Thus, in some cases (particularly in emerging economies) infrastructure development through BOT schemes may be an incorrect answer to public sector inefficiency and budgetary restrictions.[8]

Following Fishbein and Babbar (1996), there is a trade-off between two critical variables that are relevant in analyzing alternative approaches to private finance of infrastructure (toll roads in their example): on the one hand, the opportunities for innovation in design, pricing, risk sharing, etc., and on the other hand, the transparency and competitiveness of the concession process. BOT mechanisms can be implemented with a different degree of bias towards one or the other set of variables. Projects in environments and with characteristics that require opportunities for innovation, the authors say, should trade off transparency and

**Exhibit 1**

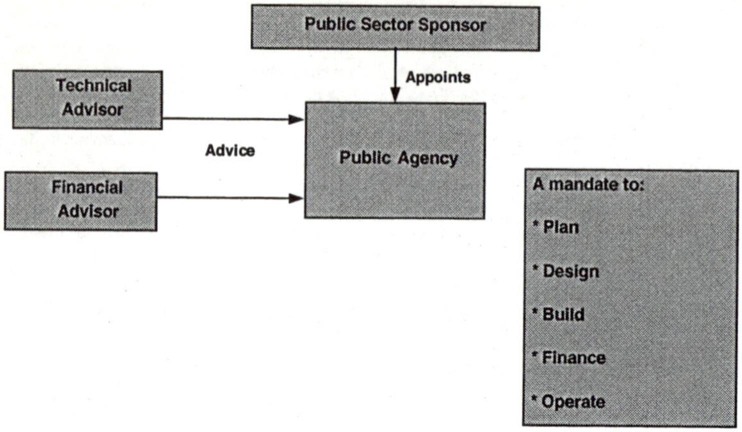


competitiveness for innovation opportunities. Such a trade-off exists also when the project is unbundled, but we claim that the possibility of defining each of the granting processes separately benefits the overall implementation process. In this case, however, a different trade-off may exist between the degree of independence of each of the contractual processes and the need for coordination by the public sponsor.[9]

## II. UNBUNDLED MECHANISMS

The alternative to BOT mechanisms that we favor has two basic characteristics: first, the activities involved in the project are unbundled and, second, the financing is carried out by means of a neutral SPV. Even though these two characteristics are shown to be conceptually independent, we will refer to the joint proposal as the *unbundled mechanism*.

### A. Unbundling

A project includes various parts: building, operating, maintenance and financing. The unbundling of a project into its different parts is efficient for two reasons. First, some agents have superior know-how of a particular aspect of the project, say, its construction, but poor knowledge of other activities, as for instance, its financing. Second, unbundling reduces the risks faced by private contractors (in particular, the financial guarantees of the contractor are lower when the project is unbundled) so that more agents, particularly local companies (with sufficient technological know-how but insufficient financial capability), will be able to bid for the project, which increases competition on bids. Very often, BOT concessionaires are joint ventures of private companies that have an agreement among themselves to subcontract each of the different activities of the project. For instance, a typical joint venture for a toll road may include construction companies, operating experts and, in some cases, banks. Therefore, given the composition of joint ventures, BOT concessionaires cannot be criticized on the grounds of lack of expertise in one or another activity. The point we make is that the requirement that all the activities be included in the "concession", and therefore jointly auctioned, limits competition. In addition, the risks and nature of each of the activities contaminate each other unnecessarily.[10]

For a large project (such as an infrastructure project) the costs of unbundling (such as creating different entities, monitoring the technological specifications during both the building and the operating stages, finding credit enhancement, etc.) may be high, but they will be offset by an improved allocation of risk. In such a way, project finance brings "better financial and managerial discipline" (Stewart-Smith, 1995).

In what follows we go over the characteristics of an unbundled mechanism to develop an infrastructure project. This unbundling or separation of the specific tasks can be pursued more or less deeply depending on the project (for instance, maintenance can be separated

**Exhibit 2.** Paying Construction

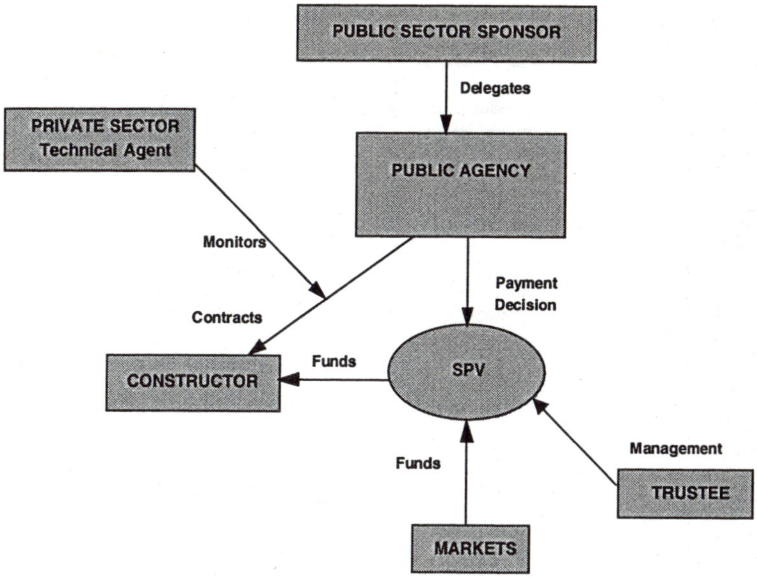


from operation). It also makes it possible to define contracts with different maturities for the different activities. We do not go any further into these details because they are project specific. Yet, we do assert that there is an optimal level of unbundling that makes BOT a suboptimal solution.

### B. The Concessionaire: A Public Agency

In the first place, we assume that the process requires the public sponsor to empower a public agency to plan, design, build, finance and operate the infrastructure (see exhibit 1). That is, from a legal point of view, a public agency plays the role of the concessionaire in BOT mechanisms, but in this case the competitive process is imposed at the level of the subcontracting of the various activities of the project. The public nature of the agency is not a requisite; in Section 5 we discuss the possibility of using a private company to play the role of the concessionaire without falling into the BOT mechanism.

The concessionaire is a vehicle that does not necessarily have a structure and whose purpose is to facilitate the contractual articulation of the operation, in particular if it is constituted as a commercial entity.

The agency, as concessionaire, is the owner of the concession and of the infrastructure until its transfer to the sponsor. The concessionaire contracts the construction, maintenance and operation of the project and constitutes the SPV as the financing tool. The agency is responsible for the preliminary technical, economic and financial studies that are necessary for proper definition of the subsequent contractual process.

The existence of the concessionaire, as distinct from the sponsor, facilitates the allocation of the separate parts of the price paid by consumers to each of the subcontracts and to the SPV. If this role were to be played by the sponsor, who is generally an administrative entity or a government body, the allocation of the components of the price may present legal problems, while at the same time it will be more difficult to avoid problems of commingling with other public resources.

In addition, it is easier to manage the contracts over time if the contracting party is not directly the public administration. This consideration is particularly important because there may be elements in the contract that have to be modified by the concessionaire over the life of the project, such as, for example, the term during which revenues from the concession are allocated to the SPV.

Another function of the concessionaire is the possibility of grouping the interests of various sponsors, as is the case when several municipalities undertake a common infrastructure project. Examples of such common projects are systems of solid waste treatment providing service to a group of communities or the development of regional highways, as is the case of the Foothill/Eastern Transportation Corridor in California.

#### 1. Formal Instrumentation of the Concession

A contractual instrumentation of the concession, as opposed to an administrative authorization, is important. The contractual form gives more legal guarantees to the concessionaire in case of amendments or breaches. At the same time, a contract facilitates the transfer to a subcontractor, if not of the concession itself, at least of certain guarantees and covenants of the concession contract. In relation to the latter point, the contract will explicitly stipulate the transferability of those guarantees and covenants, while leaving full responsibility to the concessionaire with respect to the sponsor, as regards the terms and conditions that define the concession in the concession contract.

### C. Construction

The construction contract should be a turnkey compromise granted by the agency through a competitive tendering (see exhibit 2). Implementation should take into account the above referred trade-off between innovation opportunities and transparency. The standard mechanisms of guarantee, insurance and fines, common to BOT concession contracts in relation with construction, should be applied in this case also.

The agency will require the assistance of technical advisors both through the granting process and to supervise construction. Typically, the role of such an agent is played by private sector engineering consultants, who carry out the preliminary technical studies and designs.

The construction contractor is paid by the SPV. The latter maintains the funds obtained from the market in an escrow account, and pays following standard procedures of control and supervision by the technical agent on behalf of the agency. The guarantee of payment on time should have a positive effect on the construction contract bidding process and reduce the construction bill.

The construction contractor may be required to participate in the SPV with equity or subordinated debt both as a means of improving the structure of incentives and to facilitate financing. However, it has to be taken into account that such a requisite is inherently inconsistent with the notion of unbundling.

Depending on the type of infrastructure the constructing contractor may be responsible also for maintenance. That activity, distinct from the post-construction responsibilities, should be treated as an independent contract, linked to the cash flows of the project.

### D. Operating

The proposed scheme (see exhibit 3) is compatible with the existence of two separate functions, construction and operation, and either unique or separate contractors.[11] However, separation (which certainly introduces elements of flexibility and can increase competition) may not be the most appropriate formula for certain types of projects or economies. For example, the relationship between construction and management of a highway may not be the same as for a water distribution system. There may be also a difference between the degree of involvement required from the sponsor for the management and control of the various contractors, depending on the project and according to the level of development of the country. Consequently, it may be an adequate choice in some cases that a unique entity assume jointly the responsibilities for construction and operation, or at least for a number of years after construction is completed. However, the convenience of unifying the responsibilities of construction and operation is in general difficult to justify on the basis of technical or management synergies, while, at least on a theoretical level, the separation of these two activities introduces elements of efficiency.

Nevertheless, even in those situations with a unique contractor, it is not advisable that the term of the operating contract be as long as that of the concession. Such equality (which is implicit in BOT contracts in order to permit the concessionaire to finance the construction) is neither necessary nor advisable in this case. This last consideration is important because it is reasonable that changes in circumstances may occur at some point during the necessarily very long period of the concession, that require modification of the terms of the management contract.

Operation has to be understood differently depending on the type of infrastructure. In some cases, operation includes management of the service, fee collection and maintenance. At least in theory, all these activities are

**Exhibit 3**

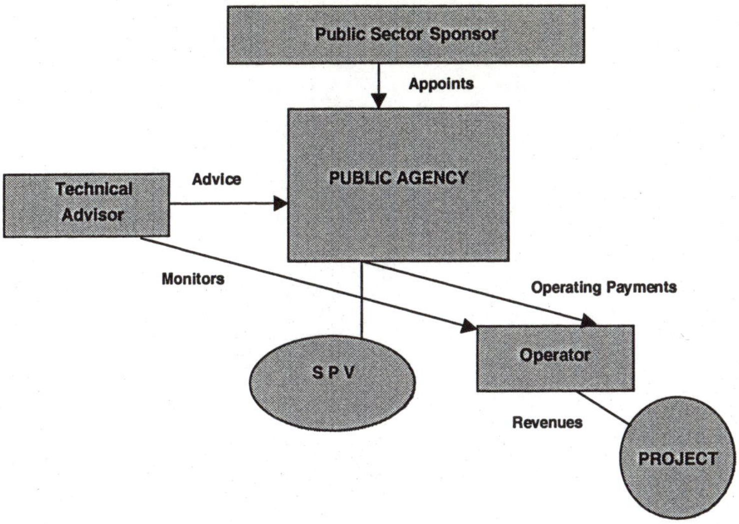


separable, but we are not implying that their unbundling gives rise to more efficiency in all cases.[12] Unbundling the project raises the issue of incentives, including those of other agents apart from the operating contractor. As an example, consider the effect of unbundling on consumers if they are unable to associate service quality and payment. We do not discuss these issues in this paper; on the contrary, to simplify matters, we consider the operating contract as comprehensive of all the aforementioned activities.

The revenues from the infrastructure, which are assumed to be collected by the operator, are considered to be the property of the agency (the concessionaire). Consequently, the concessionaire becomes responsible for paying the operator. Such payment may be defined either as fixed, as revenue dependent or based on a mixed formula. Once again, the incentive issue will be a determining factor in the selection of the payment structure. In addition, risk allocation considerations will have to be taken into account. In particular, the existence and conditions of recourse from the operator to the agency and the sponsor are crucial. In the case of non recourse and in the absence of guarantees, payments to the operator depend exclusively on project revenues, with all their characteristics of risk. Clearly, for the project to be self-sustaining, revenues have to exceed the cash flows needed for the operating contract; otherwise the project will have to be subsidized.

The characteristics of the contract granted to the operator can be independent of the financial parameters. Both the remuneration of the operator and the period of concession can be determined exclusively by the specific nature of the operating problems of the particular infrastructure. In most cases it will be possible to define a shorter maturity for the operating contract than for the concession, which at least will be as long as the life of the SPV. Such an independence allows for a flexible contractual policy which may take into account changing market conditions.

To enhance incentives and to facilitate financing, the operator should be required to subscribe a portion of the subordinated debt of the SPV. As was mentioned in the case of the constructor, such a requirement may be interpreted as contradictory to the objectives of unbundling, but it can be shown to be compatible. In that sense, notice that a major characteristic of unbundling, among other things, is that the characteristics of the operating contract, in particular the concession period, are not determined by the overall financing requirements of the infrastructure. The point is whether it is possible to attain such independence and still require the operator to invest in the project through the SPV. The answer depends on the characteristics of the SPV and, in particular, of the subordinated debt. The

**Exhibit 4**

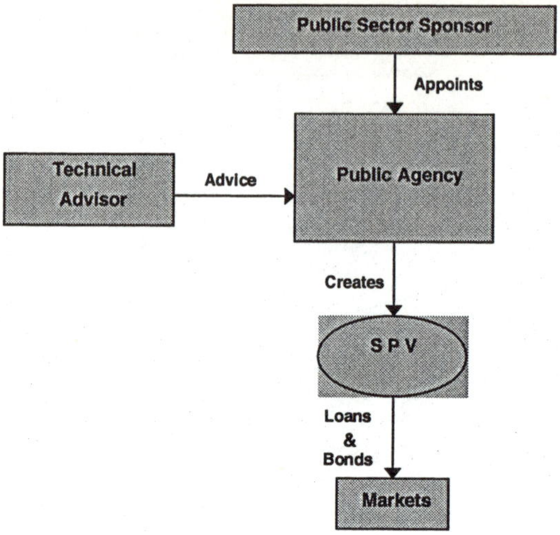


SPV that we propose and explain in the next section, has an open-ended right to the net cash flows of the infrastructure until all its liabilities are canceled, allowing for the definition of a subordinated debt tranche to be subscribed by the operator without influence on the characteristics of the operating contract.

### E. Financing

Project finance structures are better designed by the use of special purpose vehicles, a common legal technique used in the world of private financing to isolate and administer risks. An SPV is an entity with legal status that allows for a favorable treatment of accounting, fiscal, regulatory and financial issues. Typically, creating an SPV allows privately managed infrastructure projects, either at the stage of construction and/or operation, to enjoy some degree of isolation. In addition, in most cases the use of an SPV is a requirement imposed on the private agent by either the public sector, the financiers, the guarantors or the contractors of the project.

From a conceptual viewpoint we may distinguish between those vehicles that focus on the isolation of the project as a legal entity and those which are designed as a purely financial instrument. According to this distinction we may refer to the former as *special legal purpose vehicles* and to the latter as *special financial purpose vehicles;* with the understanding that, in all cases, the purpose of the vehicles, one way or another, is risk isolation, and that there is not always a clear cut separation between both types. Moreover, special legal purpose vehicles typically also play financing roles.

In the unbundled scheme described in this paper, a separation between legal and financial vehicles is proposed. The role of the *legal* vehicle is played by the concessionaire, which we have proposed to be a public agency. In its turn, the *financial* vehicle is a trust-like entity, sponsored by the concessionaire.

The financial SPV, as is herein proposed, can be considered as neutral, in the sense that it is an instrument to channel resources to the project, both from consumers and from the public sector, limiting undesired transfers to third parties.

The SPV, sponsored by the agency, will have its particular legal definition, *fideicomiso, patrimonio autónomo, fondo de titulización,* grantor trust, etc.) depending on the jurisdiction. In any case, what is required is a legal vehicle that, minimizing fiscal and operational costs, is capable of obtaining resources from the market, secured by the pledge of the cash flows from the infrastructure (see exhibit 4). The ideal SPV requires a legal framework that allows for tax neutrality, flexibility to design contracts and free access to products and markets. In all cases, a trust or similar juridical instrument is required.

**Exhibit 5. Cash Flows**

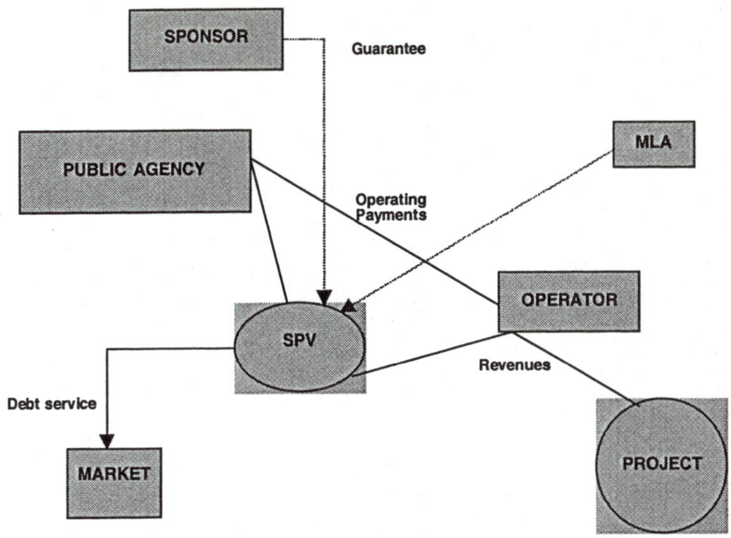


### 1. Assignment of Cash Flows

Future revenues from the infrastructure have to be ex-ante divided and assigned to cover ongoing costs and financial liabilities. That is, the price paid by consumers should be split in (at least) two basic parts: operating and finance. Such a partition could be explicit for the consumers, by reflecting in the corresponding instrument of payment (road toll, water bill, etc.) the different components of the price. Such information, which could include the existence of subsidies and which would show the intergenerational redistribution effect implicit in the financial part, may have a positive effect on the social acceptance of the burden of payment.

To simplify, we call "net revenue" the part of the cash flows which are left after payment of the ongoing commitments acquired by the agent in the operating and maintenance contracts.[13] These net revenues are pledged to the SPV to secure its liabilities. Depending on the characteristics of the operating and maintenance contracts, the commercial risks imbedded in the project cash flows will be shared one way or another between these contracts and the SPV (see exhibit 5). As was mentioned above, it may be desirable from an incentive point of view that the operator be paid on a revenue dependent basis, at least partially. In that case, the risk absorbed by the operator will result in an equal reduction of the risk assigned to the SPV.

The contract between the agency and the SPV will entitle the latter to receive the net revenues until all its liabilities are canceled. That is, the life of the SPV is undetermined and dependent on: *i)* the total revenue flow, *ii)* the economic conditions of the operating and maintenance contracts and *iii)* the financial conditions of the SPV's liabilities. Such a contract between the agency and the SPV turns out to be a contract between the infrastructure users and the SPV investors. Consequently, it is justified that the SPV be structured and its liabilities placed under strict competitive procedures.[14]

The characteristics of the net revenue flow, in particular its variable and uncertain nature, pass through the SPV determining the characteristics of its financial liabilities, taken as a whole. In most cases, such variability and uncertainty will require the liabilities to have principal payments that also vary. In turn, to reduce costs by minimizing interest rate risk premiums, the liabilities will generally have to be defined as floating rate instruments. Therefore, in the absence of alternative

**Exhibit 6**

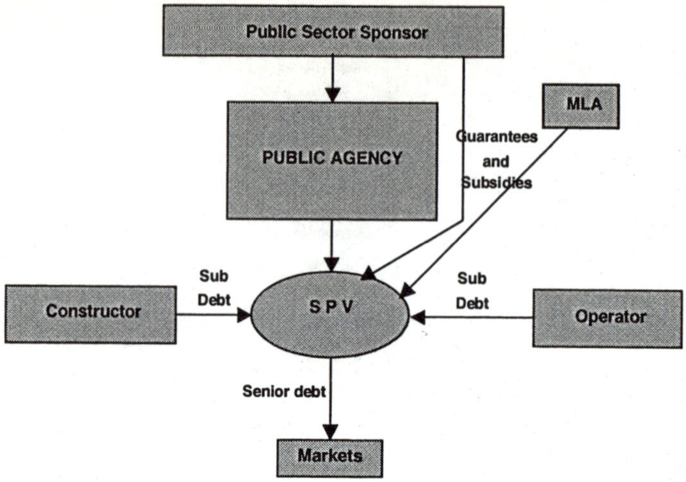


sources of revenues or subsidies, the life of the liabilities of the SPV, taken as a whole, will be determined by the net revenue flow and by interest rates (and currency exchange rates if funding is done in a foreign currency).

We are assuming that the SPV obtains its resources in the market. However, the expected life of the SPV may be excessive for investors, in particular in emerging economies. These are characterized by financial markets that are not sufficiently developed and by political, regulatory and general macroeconomic risk, affecting either the project or the financial investors. The importance of these risks increases dramatically with the time horizon of the investments, and it has to be taken into account that some projects may require financing for 25 years and beyond. To cope with that problem, the public sector sponsor should provide a guarantee that limits the maturity of the SPV. Such a guarantee does not imply a direct cost for the public sector, but rather the obligation to establish the necessary conditions to enable the liabilities of the SPV to be refinanced with a new SPV.

## III. INSUFFICIENT REVENUES

In the scheme described above, financing the infrastructure is equivalent to financing the SPV. The latter is assumed to be a non recourse entity, managed and represented by a trustee, with the right to the future net revenue flow as its unique source of income. The use of such a neutral vehicle does not guarantee the project's viability. The question remains as to whether the SPV is by itself capable of attracting market resources to finance the project.

We are assuming that the right to receive future revenue flows, granted by the public sector to the agency (as concessionaire) passes to the SPV and lasts until the latter pays back all its debts, that is, until financing has been completed. Such a condition would be difficult to implement if the special financing entity were privately owned. However, the SPV proposed is an instrument of the public sector, on behalf of the consumers, which does not generate either profits or losses.

Funding the SPV in the market will be more or less difficult, that is, more or less costly depending on the soundness of the expected revenue flow and the combination of project and political/regulatory risks passed to the investors. Success will result from the appropriate mitigation of those risks, when possible, or from their efficient allocation among the parties involved: the public sponsor, guarantors if any, the contractors, the SPV investors, the consumers (as toll payers), and the government as collector. We do not include either the agency (the concessionaire) or the SPV, since they are assumed to be neutral entities.

In principle, the financial package of a project is expected to be based on its future revenue flows, if these are considered sufficient to support the required debt and remunerate the capital invested. However, in many cases, at the time of structuring the project financing, future revenue flows may be considered insufficient in the absence of subsidies to cover operating costs and finance construction, and hence are incapable of attracting investors. Such a situation, caused either by the intrinsic lack of capacity of the project to generate sufficient revenues or as the direct consequence of an inefficient price policy, is aggravated by the uncertainty associated with the flow of revenues and by all the other various risks perceived by investors.

We define the revenues of a project as *insufficient* when the value of the resources required for construction, maintenance and operation exceeds the value of the expected future flows, discounted at market yields representative of the financial characteristics and risks assumed by investors. That is, an insufficient revenue situation is one in which the project is not capable of standing by itself. Such a definition of insufficiency implies that the assumption that revenues flow indefinitely to the SPV is not a guarantee for the project to stand by itself. In other words, an indefinite flow does not guarantee that its present value exceeds the resources needed for the project.

A situation of insufficient revenues relates basically to income generation capacity and to commercial risk, but it is also determined by the other risks affecting the project. All kinds of project risks influence the perception of the reliability of future revenues and the same has to be said in relation to political and regulatory risks, which are taken into account by investors when selecting the appropriate level of the discount rate. Therefore, if revenues assigned to the SPV are considered insufficient, as defined above, the project requires either subsidies to supplement market resources, or the mitigation of risk affecting investors, to either increase expected revenues or reduce discount rates.

At the limit, situations of insufficient revenue would include any situation where private investors are unwilling to finance the SPV in its totality, since, at least in theory, every perceived risk has been taken into consideration to define expected flows and appropriate discount rates. However, as earlier stated, it is useful to separate what can be considered as *pure* insufficient revenue situations, that is, those characterized by a poor expected performance of the project given its objective risks, from those problems caused by subjective risks of a political and regulatory nature, which could be mitigated under the right contracts. In most cases, these risks represent situations of extreme loss or whose economic consequences are unknown or, at least, very difficult to assess. As a result, exposure to these subjective risks is considered critical for the investment decision. If the particular risk is not completely eliminated or dramatically mitigated, the investor may not consider investing, independently of how favorable are other characteristics. An example of the latter is convertibility/ transferability risk, but we can include also the potential problems that may be caused by decisions of the sponsor affecting project cash flows.

In the rest of this section we cover the problem that we have denominated as of *insufficient revenues*, leaving aside the issues pertaining to regulatory risk.

### 1. Coping with Insufficient Revenues

The intervention of the public sector in a project, either by granting subsidies or by mitigating risks, may be justified either by the existence of positive externalities, by redistributive policies, or by other considerations of a political nature. We assume that the objective of the sponsor is to intervene to enhance the project up to the point at which it can be assumed by the market, minimizing the cost of the intervention. The mechanism of finance described herein allows for such an efficient intervention by the public sector, in particular if subsidies and guarantees are granted to the SPV (see exhibit 6). We describe several alternatives to enhance the project. First, we consider the use of equity or subordinated debt subscribed by the sponsor. Second, we mention the possibility of granting guarantees as an alternative to the disbursement of resources. Third, we describe enhancements in the form of options attached to the senior debt.

### A. Subsidizing by Means of Subordinated Debt

As a simple formula of direct subsidy, the sponsor could take a share of subordinate debt in the SPV. With a sufficient proportion of subordinate debt, the senior debt may be competitively placed with the sole guarantee of the expected future net revenue flow.

The subscription of subordinated debt by the sponsor, below market prices or when a market for such a debt does not exist, is a form of subsidy to the project with the inconvenience that it involves the disbursement of resources. Nevertheless, it has to be pointed out that the need for a subsidy, because *ex-ante* the project is not self-standing, does not imply that *ex-post* revenues may not prove to be sufficient to cover all costs and pay back the "subsidy" with interest. On the contrary, a subsidized project may provide revenues that the market was unable to foresee. If that is the case, subsidies will return to the sponsor; in other words, if eventually the project generates "excess" revenues, these will not be transferred to private parties. Subsidies given to the SPV are easily structured to facilitate their recovery as they become superfluous, but subsidies given directly to builders, operators and investors are more difficult to control and recover.

If public resources are available, the participation of the sponsor in the SPV by means of subordinated debt or equity is highly recommended, both from the point of view of the enhancement of senior debt and for risk mitigation purposes.

As mentioned above, the builder and the operator may be required to subscribe subordinated debt of the SPV. But such a requirement cannot be a solution to cope with a problem of insufficient revenues. This requires either external subsidies or risk mitigation. The investment in the SPV by the builder and the operator pursues a different objective; namely, reducing the proportion of resources obtained from the market and enhancing incentives. However, we have to account for the possibility that the benefits of requiring such investment are partially offset by an increase in the cost of construction in the competitive bidding process. An adequate yield assigned to the subordinated debt, including a premium representative of the risks of investing in the SPV, will reduce the distortion of construction prices.

### B. Guarantees

The sponsor may subsidize the project by means of a wide variety of guarantees granted to the SPV. A possibility is a guarantee of the minimum level of revenue received by the SPV. Alternatively, the guarantee could be designed to assure that the SPV is able to service its debt, and could be either granted directly to the vehicle or through a third party acting as liquidity provider. A guarantee to limit the maturity of the SPV (and refinance it by means of a new vehicle) is also a form of subsidy. In those cases in which the SPV incurs currency exchange risk, the subsidy could be the total or partial mitigation of that risk.

Instead of subsidizing by means of investing in the SPV or guaranteeing its income or senior debt, the sponsor may guarantee a subordinated debt share subscribed by a third party. However, in addition to the endorsement by the sponsor, if the subordinated debt is supposed to be taken by private investors, it must have characteristics and expected yield that justify the investment on a market basis. It is possible to assign a high yield, but in general it is difficult to define other attractive financial characteristics when the subordinated debt is the residual of the senior debt in an infrastructure project financing.

Subordinated debt may take various forms, depending on the characteristics of subordination, risk limits, risk premiums, etc. In all cases its basic role is to provide a cushion to protect senior investors, by absorbing indiscriminately all those risks affecting the SPV which have not been specifically covered. In that sense, guaranteeing subordinated debt has different implications, from a risk point of view, than granting guarantees to specific risks, as it may result in the coverage of all kinds of risks without distinction.

If the sponsor has a poor credit-risk rating, as likely to occur in projects sponsored by municipalities, it is important to avoid guarantees which eventually may require the disbursement of funds. In some cases it may be sufficient for the sponsor to guarantee the implementation of price policy changes.

### C. Using Put Options

As a form of subsidy, senior debt may be issued with an attached put option that, under predetermined circumstances, allows the investors to put their bonds to the sponsor or to an alternative guarantor. The circumstances under which the option can be exercised may refer to the evolution of project revenues or to precise events which may endanger SPV cash flows. In such a case, the credit risk of the option seller becomes the relevant issue.

An alternative to a put option that prepays senior debt is the possibility of putting the bonds in exchange for debt of predetermined characteristics, either issued by the sponsor or by a third party. Such a swap of risk could be definitive or temporary. That is, investors may have the option to return to the original debt if the solvency of the SPV is restored. Again, the risk of the issuer of the debt becomes the relevant risk for the investor.

## IV. THE BENEFITS OF UNBUNDLING

The positive effects of the *unbundled mechanism* (unbundling the project and SPV financing) on the overall cost of the project derive principally from the more efficient allocation of the *objective* risks affecting the project. Such a mechanism allows for the mitigation of the consequences of the uncertainty that typically characterizes both the revenue flow (demand) and the financial cost (interest rates and exchange rates). Also, this mechanism allows for a better treatment of *subjective* risks of a political and regulatory nature. In addition to the reduction of the overall cost (which in some cases can make a project economically viable), the *unbundled mechanism* provides the sponsor with a higher degree of flexibility, particularly in the characteristics of the operating and maintenance contracts and in pricing policy.[15]

Starting with the effect of risks on the construction contract, we argue that the isolation of the funds obtained by the SPV in an escrow account will guarantee the contractor that, upon satisfaction of the commitments of its contract, the payments will be received in due amount and time. Such a guarantee should result in less inflated contracts than those typical of BOT concessions.

In the case of the operator, we can assume that the uncertainty affecting its economic performance is limited to the commercial risk which has been left in the definition of its revenue policy. Indeed, with generality, we can assume that operating costs are much less affected than revenues by uncertainty. In addition, unbundling allows for a shorter contract maturity. The combination of less uncertainty and a shorter maturity reduces renegotiation risk and post-contract opportunism and, as a consequence, gives rise to more realistic bids.[16] It may not be possible, nor desirable, to eliminate all commercial risk from the operating contract; however, a reduction of the uncertainty affecting the contract may reduce the overall cost. Such a possibility, always at the expense of increasing the variability of the cash flows assigned to the SPV, could take the form of a risk sharing cap-floor agreement that leaves the revenue of the operator in a band. A shorter maturity of the operating contract, in relation to that required by a BOT mechanism, facilitates the implementation of such a guarantee.[17]

The effects of uncertainty on the cash flows assigned to the SPV are absorbed by the open-ended nature of the horizon and by structuring its liabilities with variable payments and floating rates. In addition, as was mentioned above, refinancing guarantees and liquidity facilities could be provided by the public sponsor. With such a financing scheme, an overestimation of revenues or higher than expected interest rates will be transformed into an extension of the period of financing and a longer period of payment by consumers. By contrast, underestimation of revenues or lower than expected interest rates will benefit either the consumers or the public sponsor, depending on the allocation of the excess revenues when financing concludes.

Another effect of unbundling is the possibility of having flexible price policies. On the one hand, such flexibility derives from the shorter maturity of the concession period for the operator, compared to BOT schemes. On the other hand, contracts may include admissible price modifications whose effect is automatically passed on to the SPV. In addition, the definitive structure and level of prices affecting consumers can be postponed to the termination of construction, allowing for a better adjustment of prices to market conditions, thus reducing the errors in demand estimates. In the case of BOT schemes, which require establishing the price policy for the complete time horizon before the concession is granted, the possibility of price flexibility is very limited. By contrast, the degree of flexibility with regard to pricing policies acceptable by the SPV investors may be larger.

The ***unbundled mechanism*** also makes the intergenerational distribution of costs more attainable. The period of financing can be extended independently of the operating concession, adapting the financing horizon of the infrastructure to its real depreciation and use. BOT mechanisms bias the redistribution of the burden of financing towards the present generation. This is notorious in the case of infrastructure projects that are built to last for decades if not for centuries. The problem is that under strictly private solutions, as is the case of BOT concessions, investors are unable to consider horizons beyond certain limits, a problem aggravated in emerging economies. On the contrary, "institutional" arrangements such as transfers among consumer groups can also be explicitly attained by allocating excess revenues of the infrastructure to other projects that yield a deficit.

The ***unbundled mechanism*** may be more efficient if subsidies and guarantees are given to the SPV. With such an intermediation, the public sector transfers will benefit consumers directly by, *ceteris paribus,* reducing either prices or the length of the period of financing. In addition, subsidies can be designed in such a way that they return to the public sector if eventually shown to be unnecessary. In any case, public sector transfers to consumers, granted through the SPV by means of subsidies, guarantees or subordinated debt, can be justified in terms of the future tax revenues to be generated by the project. By facilitating the viability of a project the public sector creates a source of future public resources.

In many cases and not only in emerging economies, there is social resistance to paying directly for the infrastructure service. We argue that payment by consumers will be socially more acceptable if the proposed SPV structure is implemented and appropriate information on the contents of prices is given. The alternative, from the point of view of the consumers, is that the infrastructure is fully paid either by its users or by all taxpayers (through public sector support). Consumers do not profit from the fact that a BOT concessionaire has underpriced a concession. Such a case always ends up either in the bankruptcy of the concessionaire, or in public subsidy or the renegotiation of contracts. Consequently, it is only a mirage to consider that the underpricing of a BOT may result in a permanent lower burden for the users or the taxpayers.

The ***unbundled mechanism*** may make financing in the local currency more attainable, thus reducing currency exchange risk and its corresponding cost. An SPV structure, secured by the open-ended contract with the infrastructure users, may be positively perceived from a risk point of view by local institutional long-run investors. However, in some emerging economies these sources of funding are very scarce.

## V. THE ROLE OF MLAS

From a theoretical point of view, the existence of multilateral agencies is justified because financial markets fail to provide an efficient allocation of funds. This could be either because of the existence of one of the traditional sources of market failure, such as externalities generated by the project, or, more likely, because of the asymmetric information problems typical of financial markets, particularly where multiple countries/currencies are concerned.

One of the major problems in financing infrastructure projects in emerging economies is the lack of domestic long-term capital. The absence of developed long-term domestic financial markets stems from a more fundamental financial market imperfection. In such economies, in our view, the key explanation for the lack of long-term funding that can be tapped by such projects is the excessive risk that investors attribute to the projects, an attitude justified by the intrinsic instability of institutions in general and the economy in particular, and the absence of the government's ability to commit to a stable regulatory policy.

More specifically, as noted by Barrientos (1995), "certain types of risks, particularly those concerning the maintenance of stable political and regulatory conditions over the long term, or the effective governmental or agency performance of contractual obligations remain difficult for the private sector to absorb or manage". This explanation is also consistent with two other characteristics of financial markets in emerging economies. First, government guarantees by themselves are generally not sufficient to attract long-term funding. Second, the success of privatization programs in some countries (for instance in Argentina) indicates that capital does exist that can be invested in long-term projects, provided that investors expect their profitability not to be impaired by political decision.

Traditionally, the role of multilateral agencies (MLA) has been to provide long-term capital in economies lacking such funds to projects generating long-term cash flows. In these operations, the MLA acts as a monitor of the project, but also of the government sponsoring it, which usually provides some guarantees. From that perspective, the role of the MLA is that of a bank, which lends long term, using its monitoring ability to identify the right investment opportunities. The MLA's access to the major financial markets complements this scheme by allowing it to obtain funds in the most efficient way.

Still, as the role of public and private sectors has evolved, the environment in which the MLA operates is bound to change.

### A. The New Financing Environment

Traditionally, MLA financing has been a source of funds for investment projects sponsored by the public sector. With the decreasing role of the public sector in the economy, this has begun to change. Private sector participation in providing equity to projects channeled through BOTs or BLTs has increased, but as Barrientos et al. (1995) point out, ". . .alternative avenues must be sought to mobilize additional private resources for the productive sector". Indeed, if the role of private sector funding in the project is mainly to provide equity, this may prove to be expensive, and even unreliable, since, even in developed industrial countries there may be a shortage of this type of funds.

In addition, the increased involvement of the private sector through equity participation, although welcome, raises a new issue because of the access of the project to (public) MLA financing. Indeed, the MLA support may result *ex post* in an unintended transfer of resources from the MLA to the private sector if the project is successful.

### B. The Use of Special Purpose Vehicle Financing

If the policy of the MLA is to provide support to the projects by means of loans, the use of a neutral SPV shows some advantages. In the first place, the MLA as a lender is better protected if financing is given to the SPV instead of the concessionaire.[18] On the other hand, the characteristics of lending, which may implicitly contain a portion of subsidy, can be designed to recover the subsidy part if the project eventually is self-sustaining. In addition, the "public" nature of the SPV makes it politically more acceptable for the MLA to transfer resources to the project. Moreover, financing given to the SPV could be conditioned on the guarantees of the public sponsor in relation to regulatory risks.

However, the role of the MLA may change, reducing its concentration on traditional lending activity and increasing two other types of activities: credit enhancement and strengthening the legal and regulatory framework.

The use of guarantees granted by the MLA to the SPV is an alternative to direct loans. Guarantees could be in the form of a line of credit (LOC) given to the SPV, limited both in its volume and in the circumstances under which it can be used. Alternatively, guarantees could be granted to a third party that issues the LOC. Such guarantees are less costly than loan disbursements and reduce currency exchange problems. Political and regulatory risks taken aside, the risk that the given guarantees result in the disbursement of funds by the MLA is mitigated by the open-ended nature of the SPV.[19]

By providing guarantees, the MLA may indicate that it has monitored the whole structure of the project, that each agent is able to perform its contractual obligations, that the incentive scheme reduces moral hazard and that, overall, the project is sound and correctly designed to produce the long-term cash flows the investors expect. The use of guarantees also enables the MLA to target more specifically the types of risk that it will cover, concentrating its resources more on systemic risks (e.g. currency convertibility) and avoiding coverage of risks related to purely commercial factors.[20]

The strengthening of the legal and the regulatory framework is a type of activity that MLAs already accomplish,[21] but which would be emphasized if the techniques of project finance were to be more deeply used. Indeed, the stronger the legal and regulatory framework, the easier it is for the sponsor to commit in a credible way to develop a stable regulatory policy. In the case of unbundled concessions, which require a high degree of coordination to implement the process, there is an additional role for the MLA. That role is as advisor for the preliminary financial and legal structures of the projects, supervisor of the contract granting processes and, during the life of the project, referee in the case of disputes over the effect of policy changes on the level and allocation of cash flows.

## VI. IMPLEMENTATION

Unbundling could be criticized on the grounds of the higher degree of difficulty which may be required to implement the projects, in relation to a BOT alternative. Indeed, we have mentioned that unbundling may give rise to a trade-off between the degree of independence of each of the contractual processes and the need for coordination by the public sponsor. Such a problem can be mitigated from the point of view of the public sponsor by means of two alternatives that amount to the transfer of responsibilities (at a cost) to the private sector.

In those cases in which it is advisable that the public sector minimize its responsibilities of coordination, two alternatives can be proposed. A radical proposal is that the role of the concessionaire, instead of being carried out by a public agency, is carried out by a private company. Such an alternative should not be confused with a BOT mechanism. The proposal is that a private agent, subject to the conditions established by the public sponsor, implement the process of subcontracting and monitor the contracts, while simultaneously structuring and launching the SPV. That is, a private company acts as a service company for the project but without assuming the project risks.

Alternatively, implementation could be simplified by requiring that private participants present a joint proposal that covers all the activities of the project: construction, operating and financial resources by means of the SPV, each activity under its independent contract and in all cases subject to the conditions established by the agency acting as concessionaire. This alternative reduces the problem of coordination for the public agency, but at the cost of reducing competition, and therefore losing one of the benefits of unbundling.

### 1. The Project Steps

The following is a list of the basic steps for project implementation and a short description of the contents of each step. The need for coordination and the importance of timing in the granting process are obvious.

i) Public Sector Decision

- Project identification
- Public/private agency appointment
- Instructions to the agency to initiate the project

ii) Preliminary Technical Studies

The agency appoints a technical agent to:

- Define technical characteristics
- Evaluate rights of way
- Perform environmental studies
- Perform preliminary cost approach: construction, operation and maintenance
- Make first traffic and revenue studies
- Define first proposals for toll policy

iii) Preliminary Financial Studies

The agency appoints a financial advisor to develop the preliminary SPV and design and assess the viability of the project. The preliminary cost and revenue results from the technical agent are used by the financial advisor as a basic input.

- Basic legal structure
- Cash flow analysis
- Viable sources of funds

- Role of MLA
- Credit enhancement proposals
- Need for subsidies or guarantees to mitigate market risks
- Mechanisms to mitigate regulatory risk

iv) The Bidding Process

The public agency with the technical agent and the financial advisor defines the parameters of the bidding process. The advisors are not permitted to participate or be related to the participants. They will act as advisors to the Public agency in the final decision.

*Parameters for the Bids*

- Design specifications
- Basic toll structure
- SPV basic principles
- Guarantees granted by the public sponsor
- Other third party guarantees (MLA, etc.)
- Limit on concession period (operating)
- Minimum structure of insurance, guarantees and fines

*Construction Bid*

- Construction specifications, schedule and costs
- Performance guarantees
- Participation in the SPV with subordinated debt

*Operation and Maintenance Bid*

- Operation and maintenance characteristics and costs
- Proposal for toll to be assigned
- Performance guarantees
- Participation in the SPV with the subordinated debt
- Traffic studies

*Financing Bid*

- Legal and financial structure of the SPV
- Regulations
- Source of funds
- Guarantees and credit enhancement
- Underwriting compromise: costs, characteristics and guarantees
- Dependence of the proposal on the definitive toll structure
- Expected cash flow analysis
- Pre-rating analysis

*Bid Selection Criteria*

- Design specifications and construction costs
- Operation and maintenance specifications and cost
- Support provided through subordinated debt and its costs
- All In Cost paid by the SPV
- Experience and strength of the contractors
- Strength of the underwriting compromise
- Toll policy flexibility
- Participation of local companies

v) Project initiation

- Adjudication resolved
- Licenses and rights of way available
- Contracts signed
- Trustee selected
- SPV launched
- Funds deposited in the SPV's escrow account
- Construction starts

## VII. FINAL COMMENTS

The disadvantages of BOT schemes are caused by the severe uncertainty affecting most projects and under which their contracts have to be signed. Those contracts incorporate unnecessary risk and have a high risk of renegotiation. High inflationary and unstable environments, common to most emerging economies, further complicate problems.

Schemes based on the unbundling of project activities and financing through neutral special purpose vehicles, created on behalf of the infrastructure users and payers, reduce risks and allow for an efficient use of public subsidies and guarantees, minimizing undesired transfers to the private sector.

The main criticism of these unbundled schemes is the lack of efficient public sector institutions to articulate the project and supervise the private sector participants. However, such a situation does not occur in some countries and, if necessary, it is possible to expand the role of the private sector to perform the coordinating role.

The problem of financing projects in domestic markets, and avoiding currency exchange risks, is common to both BOT and unbundled schemes. However, we argue that the latter are in a relatively more favorable position to attempt to find local long-run investors.

### END NOTES

[1]On the broader issue of the effects of deregulation, liberalization and privatization there is no such generalized consensus, as pointed out in the survey on eleven sectors reported in Kwoka (1996).

[2]A good example of a BLT is the SAMAYALUCA II project in Mexico, which is partially financed by the IDB. Private sponsors invest in the construction of a power plant that is leased to a public agency CFE ("*Comisión Federal de Electricidad*") to be operated. After 20 years the property is transferred to the CFE. This project is also a good example of the benefits of using a special purpose vehicle, in this case a trust, to solve legal problems.

[3]We do not include private arrangements of the type Build-Own-Operate (BOO) which we consider strictly private.

[4]In relation with toll road privatization, evidence and alternatives: Engel, Fisher and Galetovic (1996), Fishbein and Babbar (1996) and Gómez-Ibáñez and Meyer (1993)

[5]The type of projects that will be considered does not include those producing tradable goods which generate non domestic cash flows. Obtaining resources for such projects using as collateral the future flows or receivables denominated in hard currency is a well-known case with numerous examples in various emerging markets (Doetsch,1996).

[6]The mechanism here proposed has as a main feature the fact that the period of concession is ex-ante undetermined, mitigating the consequences of uncertainty. In that respect it resembles the concession mechanisms proposed by Engel, Fisher and Galetovic (1996) to auction highway franchises, which allocates the concession to the firm that bids the least present value of toll revenue. Otherwise, the similarity between both mechanisms is limited, since their proposal does not question the BOT scheme. In a follow-up paper by the same authors, their proposal is extended to unbundled schemes (1997).

[7]Where user-paid tolls do not exist, the use of so-called *shadow tolls* to define the level of the periodic payment by the public sponsor to the concessionaire is not more than a means of postponing payments to reduce current public expenses. However, shadow tolls can be criticized on the grounds that such a traffic dependent revenue incorporates artificial risk into the problem, increasing costs unnecessarily. Such payment mechanisms have been established in the case of two British toll roads developed by means of BOT procedures and there are plans to use a similar procedure in future concessions in Spain. Shadow tolls are criticized on different grounds in Fishbein and Babbar (1996).

[8]There is a major difference between the issues of "project finance" which we address here and those of "municipality finance", which we disregard. Of course, there are some similarities between both, because the sponsor of an infrastructure project is typically a municipality, and the credit rating of the municipality may be relevant if it acts as guarantor or enhances the project in any other way.

The distinction primarily stems from the fact that some projects are capable of generating revenues and some are not. The latter situation may arise either because services are provided free of charge, independently of the possibility of establishing a price system, or because the service is a public good which cannot be individually priced

If there are no revenues flowing from the project to back the issue of debt instruments, the financing problem is of a different nature. The public sponsor, say a municipality, may be fully responsible for the project, either because it assumes the total cost and subcontracts construction and management, or because it pays a concessionaire which in addition to construction and management assumes responsibilities for financing. In such cases the risk taken by the investors which provide financial resources is the credit risk of the public sponsor. Therefore, the risk is the same as the one imbedded in financing the public sponsor itself, a question not addressed in this paper. Financing a municipality and coping with the risks involved demands a different approach. The proposal contained in this paper shows that, in certain circumstances, it may be compatible for a municipality to sponsor a project and avoid both budgetary commitments and private sector recourse.

We limit our interest to situations where the infrastructure project generates revenues which constitute substantial value to back the financing, leaving aside those cases in which the project has to be financed directly by the sponsor or, if by a private party, requires a full guarantee.

[9]An anonymous reviewer points out that there is another trade-off that must be considered: the one between efficiency through specialization and the mitigation of the effects of information asymmetries by bundling the different components of a franchise. The following example is given as a case in which the franchise holder internalizes the effects of its actions: a construction company is required to maintain the infrastructure to absorb the costs of inadequate construction. We agree with the general argument raised and, in fact, we mention in the paper that unbundling may not be the most efficient alternative in all cases because of both incentives and information asymmetries. However, in some cases, and this applies to the example given, the effects of information asymmetries can be corrected by means of contractual responsibilities. For instance, in the example of the road, by requiring post-construction responsibilities, as is the case for housing developers in some countries for long periods after construction (ten years in Spain).

[10]The Foothill/Eastern System is an example of an unbundled project. It comprises two public toll roads in Orange County, California. A special purpose newly created public agency, the Foothill/Eastern Corridor Transportation Agency, was empowered by the State of California to plan, design, construct, and operate the toll roads. Each of these activities was subcontracted to specialists: engineering consultants, construction companies, management experts, toll collection specialists, etc. The agency obtains financial resources by means of revenue bonds issued by a grantor trust. The revenues from the tolls (net of maintenance and operational costs) are pledged to secure the bond. The bonds are issued without recourse to the agency or the sponsors.

[11]We do not refer to separation in subcontracts typical of most BOT concessionaires that take the form of joint ventures.

[12]An example of the complete unbundling of these activities is the Foothill/Eastern Corridor toll road. In other types of infrastructure, say, urban water distribution systems, separation may be more complicated.

[13]If the amount of revenues allows for it the costs of the agency could also be netted out.

[14]An example of such a competitive procedure in a very similar framework is the case of the securitization in 1996 of the rights resulting from the nuclear moratorium in Spain. An SPV, *Fondo de Titulización* under Spain's legislation, structured under the supervision of the government, publicly auctioned an amount approximately equivalent of six billion U.S. dollars in bonds and loan participations. For a description of that transaction see Trujillo (1996).

[15]An anonymous reviewer points out that ". . .*the advantages (of a public SPV) are not clear, since those that are claimed are counterbalanced by the incentive problems inherent to public agencies and by the disadvantages of an endless multiplication of public agencies.* An alternative scheme is proposed by means of the following example for a franchised road. . . .*a construction company builds and maintains the road, in exchange of a fixed (in present value) sum; an operating company working on a fixed term lease collects tolls, keeps a predetermined sum as payment for its services and gives the remainder to the construction company until the sum owed to the company is collected. Under such scheme, there is no need for the elaborate system of SPVs. The government must be able to check the revenues collected by the operator, but that has an order of difficulty easier than being an efficient operator of an SPV.*"

These comments show some confusion in relation to the role of the SPV and its public or private nature. On the one side, we may consider the concessionaire of our scheme as a kind of SPV, in the sense that it could be an ad-hoc agency set up to play the organizational and supervisory roles, previously described. Such an agency could be public or private and may perform other activities unrelated to the infrastructure under discussion. Most of the roles which we assign to the agency-concessionaire are played by the franchise holder of a BOT, but it is not clear who is playing those roles in the reviewer's example. On the other side, we have the financing SPV, which is a completely different kind of entity, both in its role and legal nature. The financing SPV (basically a grantor trust), is neither public nor private but a pure neutral instrument, technically owned by its investors and which we could, being somewhat liberal in terminology, consider the property of the infrastructure users. Comparing its role with the reviewer's example, the SPV receives the net revenues from the operating company and pays the investors, not the construction company. The latter received its payment at the termination of construction (hence no need for present value calculation). Therefore, the difference between proposals, in relation to financing, is that in the reviewer's example the burden of financing is for the construction company, that passes it to the infrastructure payers through its demand of a future cash flow (in present value), while by means of an SPV such a cash flow demand (its present value) is determined in the financial markets, where the SPV obtains its funding. We claim that the latter is necessarily more efficient.

[16]On this issue see also Engel, Fischer and Galetovic (1996).

[17]An example of such a guarantee can be found in the BOT concession of the Cali-Florida toll road in Colombia in 1996.

[18]In most cases, the MLA requires a counter guarantee of the government, making the argument of better protection unimportant. However, it has to be taken into account that in some cases the cash flows of the SPV have a higher credit quality than the local government itself.

[19]On the use of guarantees by the MLA see Barrientos et al (1995).

[20]The interest rate reduction obtained through the guarantees of the MLA can be spectacular as reported in Hass and Bender (1996,) for the case of Chile's Pan American Highway in which interest rates were reduced from 12% for a non-guaranteed project to 8% with the guarantees.

[21]See Rivas and Vives (1996) "IDB Group Support for Private Infrastructure".

## REFERENCES

Arca, E. (1996): Cross-Border Securitization. *The Review of Banking and Financial Services.* Standard & Poor's. February 1996.

Barrientos, M.E. (1995): Use of Bank Guarantees. *Inter-American Development Bank, Private Sector Department. Internal document.* July 1995.

Beato, P. and Vives, A. (1996): Risk, Fiscal, and Efficiency Issues in Public-Private Arrangements for the Provision of Services. *Infrastructure,* Vol. I, No.3, pp 3-14, Spring 1996.

Cohen, R., Comito, V., Dal Prato, L., (1995): La Gestione Finanziaria dei Progetti. *Guerini & Associati.* Milano

Doetsch, Douglas A. (1996): Emerging Market Cash Flow Securitization Take Off. *International Financial Law Review.* November 1996.

Engel, E., Fischer, R. and Galetovic, A. (1996): A New Mechanism to Auction Highway Franchises. Serie *Economía No. 13. Centro de Economía Aplicada. Facultad de Ciencias Físicas y Matemáticas. Universidad de Chile.* November 1996.

Engel, E., Fischer, R. and Galetovic, A. (1997): Revenue-Based Auctions and the Unbundling of Infrastructure Franchises. *Presented at the Conference "Alternatives to Traditional BOTs for Financing Infrastructure Projects", I.D.B.,* June 1997.

Hass, J.E. and Bender, C.S. (1996): The Problem of Attracting Long-Term Debt for Privately Financed Infrastructure. *The Journal of Project Finance.* Spring 1996

Fishbein, G. and Babbar, S. (1996): Private Financing of Toll Roads. *RCM Discussion Paper Series No. 117. The World Bank.* December 1996.

Freixas, X. and García-Fontes, W. (1995): Infrastructure Financing for Argentine's Provinces: Issues and Options. *Universitat Pompeu I Fabra.* Barcelona.

Israel, A. (1992): Issues for Infrastructure Management in the 1990s. *World Bank Discussion Papers. No. 171.* Washington D.C.

Kessides, Ch. (1993): Institutional Options for the Provision of Infrastructure. *World Bank Discussion Papers. No. 212.* Washington D.C.

Kwoka, J. (1996): Privatization, Deregulation, and Competition. *PSD Occasional Paper No. 27. The World Bank.* September 1996.

Roberts, D.L., Hayes, W.T. and Moran, M.T. (1996): Future Flow Securitization Rating Methodology. *Duff & Phelps Credit Rating Co.* Executive Summary

Sauvage, J.G. and Sheen, R. (1995): Pooled Project Finance Financings. *The Journal of Project Finance.* Spring 1995

Stewart-Smith, Martin (1995): Private Financing and Infrastructure Provision in Emerging Markets. *Law & Policy in International Business.* Vol 26 No 4. Summer 1995

Trujillo, J. (1996): Securitization of Tax Credits: The Spanish Nuclear Moratorium. *The Financier ACTM,* Vol. 3. No. 1, February 1996.

Trujillo, J. (1996): La Titulización de los Derechos de la Moratoria Nuclear. *Cuadernos de Información Económica. No. 112. FIES.* Madrid. July, 1996

Verzariu, P (1996): Investment Rating Enhancement on Small-Scale Infrastructure Projects in Developing Countries. *The Journal of Project Finance.* Fall 1996.

## ACKNOWLEDGMENT

A version of this paper was presented at the conference: *Alternatives to Traditional BOTs for Financing Infrastructure Projects,* sponsored by the Infrastructure and Financial Market Division of the Inter-American Development Bank, June 3, 1997 in Washington, D.C. It is a part of the research *Mitigating Regulatory Risk in Infrastructure Projects* produced by the authors for the IDB (CMO 960395). The authors are specially indebted to Paulina Beato of the IDB. They would also like to thank Fernando Bautista of *Garrigues & Andersen.* The comments of two anonymous reviewers are also acknowledged. The findings, interpretations, and conclusions expressed in the paper are entirely those of the authors and should not be attributed in any manner to the IDB.

**REMY COHEN** the founder of Cohen & Co., serves as consultant to Italian firms on project financing, both in Italy and abroad; he also represents Bear Stearns in Italy for its investment banking and capital market activity. Previously, he was CEO of Recchi Finanziaria and Central Director of Euromobiliare, where he oversaw mainly Project and Corporate Finance deals and Capital Market transactions. He has also been an economist in Washington at the International Monetary Fund. R. Cohen, after a degree with honors at Università Commerciale Luigi Bocconi has specialized in Monetary Economics attending Rochester University's postgraduate courses. He is author of many articles in the press and in specialized magazines and has taught numerous seminars on project financing at the Università Commerciale Luigi Bocconi.

**JOSÉ A. TRUJILLO** is Managing Director (CEO) and member of the board of directors of *Titulización de Activos SGFT, S.A.* (TDA), a management company (*Sociedad Gestora*) regulated by Spain's asset-backed securities laws, and a joint venture between seven Spanish banks and Bear Stearns Intl. Ltd., that specializes in the structuring, constitution and administration of special purpose vehicles in asset-backed transactions.

Mr. Trujillo received his Ph.D. from the University of Minnesota in 1980, and is a tenured professor (on leave) in the Department of Foundations of Economic Analysis of the *Universidad Complutense de Madrid, Spain.* He is co-author of books on economic theory and finance, with several papers published in professional journals. At present he specializes in asset-backed transactions and project finance, being a frequent participant in public seminars on these subjects. He has extensive experience in the finance industry, with responsibilities at the management level, and has experience as a consultant to the Spanish Public Administration, large industrial corporations, and financial institutions, which include the Inter-American Development Bank and various Spanish banks and savings banks.

**XAVIER FREIXAS** (Ph.D. Toulouse University 1978) is Professor at the Universitat Pompeu i Fabra in Barcelona (Spain) where he is Director of the Center for Financial Economics Research (CREF, Universitat Pompeu i Fabra). He is currently a Houblon Norman Senior Fellow at the Bank of England and Visiting Research Fellow, Financial Market Group, London School of Economics (July 1998-June 1999). Before joining his present position he was Joint Executive Director Fundación de Estudios de Economía Aplicada (FEDEA), 1989-1991 and Professor at Toulouse University. He has been invited lecturer at Ecole des Hautes Etudes, ENSAE (Paris), CEMFI (Madrid), The Wharton School, Harvard University and University of Illinois.

He has been associated with, Commissariat General au Plan (Paris) and a consultant for the World Bank, 1995, the Inter-American Development Bank and the Comisión Sistema Eléctrico Nacional.

He is Member of the Executive Committee of the European Finance Association, Associate Editor of *Journal of Financial Intermediation.* He is the author of articles in journals as Econometrica, Review of Economic Studies, Journal of Economic Theory, Journal of Financial Intermediation and is the coauthor with Jean-Charles Rochet of *Microeconomics of Banking*, MIT press, 1997.

**ROBERT L. SHEEHY** is a Senior Managing Director at Bear, Stearns and Co. Inc. He is head of the International Securitization Group which is responsible for the development of asset-backed and mortgage-backed securities outside the United States. Prior to becoming the Head of the International Securitization Group he was the President and General Manager of Bear Stearns Finance S.A., Paris , France. Before joining Bear, Stearns in 1990 Dr. Sheehy was an Assistant Director at the International Monetary Fund, Geneva, Switzerland. He received his Ph.D in economics from the University of Florida, Gainesville.

# [16]



# A structure for government requirements in public–private partnerships

**A.M. Abdel-Aziz and A.D. Russell**

**Abstract**: A spectrum of requirements for the procurement of public infrastructure under various public–private partnership arrangements has been communicated by governments to the private sector participants. This paper suggests a structure for these requirements and demonstrates how they have been realized in public–private partnership projects. Government requirements are categorized and described under a structure of three dimensions: rights, obligations, and liabilities. Each dimension is further defined and explained through a number of attributes. The structure provides insights as to the basis for the different modes under public–private partnerships such as build–operate–transfer, build–own–operate–transfer, and build–transfer–operate. The structure is used to examine government requirements in a number of public–private partnership transportation projects. The results show that, for each dimension and its related attributes, comprehensive and clear articulation of government requirements is generally needed. This will reduce the amount of supplemental materials issued for the request for proposals, help consortiums in responding with proposals that can fit the requirements and reduce the amount of time spent in negotiations and (or) the need for contract amendments to reflect marketplace realities missed earlier.

*Key words*: public–private partnerships, concessions, development agreements, franchise agreements, transportation projects.

**Résumé** : Plusieurs exigences pour l'obtention d'infrastructures publiques par le biais d'arrangements variés de partenariats entre le public et le privé ont été communiquées par les gouvernements aux participants du secteur privé. Cet article suggère une structure pour ces exigences et démontre comment elles ont été réalisées dans des projets de partenariats entre le public et le privé. Les exigences gouvernementales sont catégorisées selon une structure en trois dimensions: droits, obligations et responsabilités. Chaque dimension est définie et expliquée plus en détails par le biais d'un nombre d'attributs. La structure fournit des éclaircissements au sujet des fondations des différents modes de partenariats entre le public et le privé, tels que construction–opération–transfert (« build–operate–transfer »), construction–appropriation–opération–transfert (« build–own–operate–transfer ») et construction–transfert–opération (« build–transfer–operate »). La structure est employée afin d'examiner les exigences gouvernementales pour quelques projets de partenariats entre le public et le privé en transport. Les résultats montrent que, pour chaque dimension et ses attributs associés, une description complète et claire des exigences gouvernementales est généralement nécessaire. Cela réduira la quantité de matériel supplémentaire suivant la requête de propositions, aider les consortiums à répondre avec des propositions qui peuvent remplir les exigences, et réduire le temps passé en négociations et/ou le besoin d'amendements au contrat afin de refléter les réalités du marché qui ont été omises auparavant.

*Mots clés* : partenariats entre le public et le privé, concessions, ententes de développement, ententes de franchise, projets en transport.

[Traduit par la Rédaction]

## 1. Introduction

As public–private partnerships (PPP) have become a viable alternative to the traditional project delivery approach (U.K. Secretary of State for Transport 1989, 1993; Augenblick and Custer 1990; Price Waterhouse 1993; World Bank 1994), a spectrum of procurement modes has evolved allowing expanded roles for the private sector in infrastructure development. While the build–operate–transfer (BOT) mode is the one most frequently referred to, its variants such as build–own–operate–transfer (BOOT), design–build–finance–operate (DBFO), and build–transfer–operate (BTO) are used almost as frequently. Governments usually follow a multi-step process for project procurement under any of these modes; an important step in this process is the formulation of government requirements for the project. This paper focuses on these requirements, as they provide the basis for structuring PPP project documents and agreements.

Government requirements cover all of the contractual, technical, and financial aspects of a project. An example of a government requirement is project ownership; government may provide for specific forms such as public ownership, private ownership, or both where transfer of ownership may

Received January 2, 2001. Revised manuscript accepted August 22, 2001. Published on the NRC Research Press Web site at http://cjce.nrc.ca on October 22, 2001.

**A.M. Abdel-Aziz[1] and A.D. Russell.[2]** Department of Civil Engineering, The University of British Columbia, 2324 Main Mall, Vancouver, BC V6T 1Z4, Canada.

Written discussion of this article is welcomed and will be received by the Editor until April 30, 2002.

[1]Present address: SC Infrastructure Inc., Calgary, AB T2R 1K9, Canada.
[2]Corresponding author (e-mail: adr@civil.ubc.ca).

 DOI: 10.1139/cjce-28-6-891 

occur during the term of development. The domain of ownership can be the whole project or may be defined for parts of the project, e.g., real property (land), facility (improvements), movable and immovable properties, intellectual property rights, and airspace rights. Whether to allow specific forms of domain may have consequences for both government and developers, for example, on tax treatments, on the availability of rights or licenses to use a technology after the project is transferred to government, or on the ability to obtain private financing for the project. These consequences need to be addressed, otherwise they may produce conflicts. Lawson (1994) explained that conflict might arise between government's statutory power and the developer's interests in areas such as changes to design, safety standards, delay in land acquisitions, and provision of approaches/feeders for road concessions. Where government requirements are not made clear for such issues, private sector developers will try to secure the PPP environment through negotiating binding covenants on the government before drafting development agreements (Lawson 1994). Therefore, the use of PPP calls for government to address the range of terms or conditions necessary to stipulate each requirement and the consequences of each.

The objective of this paper is to identify government requirements for the various phases of a project and demonstrate how they have been addressed in PPP projects. To help identify and demonstrate these requirements, a structure is formulated to model all requirements in a PPP project. This structure helps (*i*) identify the possible range of terms and conditions for each government requirement, (*ii*) government in formulating project documents and agreements for PPP projects, (*iii*) identify the basic structure underlying the different PPP modes, (*iv*) government in reaching a balance in their requirements in PPP, and (*v*) developers gain a better understanding of government requirements and how they should structure themselves (range of expertise/experience required) in order to comply with these requirements. In Sect. 2, the suggested requirement structure is presented. Then, Sect. 3 uses the structure to investigate government requirements in a number of PPP projects in the U.K., Canada, and the U.S. as well as in some U.S. acts. Recommendations and conclusions are the subjects of Sects. 4 and 5.

## 2. Requirement structure

Based upon a detailed study of public domain information pertaining to several PPP projects and acts, we conclude that a useful structure for describing the key features of a PPP project has three major dimensions: rights, obligations, and liabilities. These dimensions along with explanatory attributes are shown in Fig. 1. The rights dimension describes the various rights given by government to a private entity in return for carrying out a specified set of obligations. The rights of possession of a facility and access to revenues constitute the primary attributes of the rights dimension. The obligations dimension represents the promises that the developer and the government agree to be bound to under the agreement. Obligations can be described by four attributes: development obligations (e.g., planning, design, construction, and improvements); operating obligations (e.g., operation and maintenance); environment obligations including related biophysical (e.g., air, marine, and terrestrial life) and socioeconomic (e.g., labor issues, regional benefits, and affected businesses) requirements; and financing obligations. The liabilities dimension covers the most controversial issues in PPP negotiations and includes three attributes: general liability (e.g., tort or third party liability and facility damage), risk liabilities, and tax liabilities.

For the traditional mode of project development, all requirements and associated attributes belong to, or are the responsibility of, government, as is ownership of a facility. Under PPP, a subset of attributes of a requirement can be temporarily or permanently assigned to another party. Therefore, various allocations of the attributes of the requirement structure can be assembled, which in turn leads to the spectrum of procurement modes commonly associated with PPP (e.g., BOT, BTO).

## 3. Projects and attributes description

The following subsections explain the projects and acts used for investigating government requirements and demonstrate all the dimensions and attributes of the requirement structure. For each attribute a general summary of the requirements is given, followed by a detailed description of attribute "values" assigned for the projects studied.

### 3.1. Projects and acts considered

The investigation on government requirements involved two BOT projects, two BOOT projects, one BTO, and a number of U.S. acts.

#### *3.1.1. The Channel Tunnel, U.K./France (BOT)*

The Fixed Link is a twin bored tunnel rail link with associated service tunnel under the English Channel between England and France. The approximately 50 km link was developed at a cost of U.S. $16 billion. The invitation to promoters (equivalent to a request for proposals) was issued in 1985 (U.K. DOT 1985) with no prior call for expressions of interest. Agreement with the successful developer was reached in 1986 (HMSO 1986*a*), and the project was legislated in the U.K. by the Channel Tunnel Act (U.K. DOT 1987).

#### *3.1.2. Second Severn Bridge, U.K. (BOOT, DBFO)*

The Second Severn Bridge is a 920-m cable-stayed bridge and has two 2000-m approach viaducts over the Severn Estuary between England and Wales with a total cost of £300 million. Through a notice and invitation for prospective tenderers (U.K. DOT 1988) and tender invitation (U.K. DOT 1989), the project was arranged as a DBFO one (design–build–finance–operate); however, it is known also as a BOOT project. Along with the provision of a new crossing, the government required the promoter to take over the responsibility for the existing crossing over the Severn Estuary, including its debt.

#### *3.1.3. Highway 104 Western Alignment, Nova Scotia, Canada (BOT)*

The Western Alignment is a 45-km four-lane highway that forms part of Highway 104 (Trans- Canada Highway) in Nova Scotia. The total capital cost of the project is Cdn

**Fig. 1.** Requirement structure.

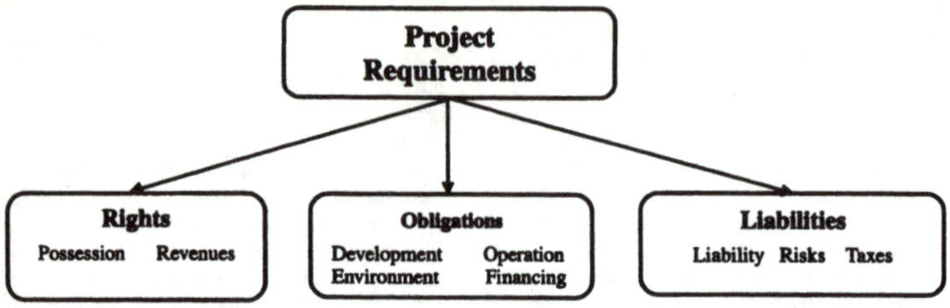


$113 million. The request for proposals, issued in 1995, was followed by six addenda (Nova Scotia DOTC 1995). The legislation required for the project forms the Western Alignment Act (W-A Act) (Province of Nova Scotia 1995). This act provided for the creation of the Western Alignment Corporation as a single-purpose corporate vehicle, not a public authority or crown corporation. This corporation was created to assist the developer (Atlantic Highways Corp., a subsidiary of Canadian Highways International Corp.) in contracting with the Province for the realization of the project, rather than the developer creating a project company.

*3.1.4. Northumberland Strait Crossing Project, New Brunswick/P.E.I., Canada (BOOT)*

The Northumberland Bridge crosses the Northumberland Strait between New Brunswick and Prince Edward Island, Canada. The estimated cost of the 13.5-km bridge was about Cdn $840 million, although the actual cost was in excess of this. After receiving unsolicited proposals for the project, the government issued a call for expressions of interest in 1987 (Public Works Canada 1987) followed by a call for proposals and six addenda in 1988 (Public Works Canada 1988). The project was legislated by the Northumberland Strait Crossing Act (Government of Canada 1993), and financial closing with the developer, Strait Crossing Development Inc., was made in 1993 after a number of environmental assessments and challenges in the courts. Some 39 separate agreements and 400 documents were executed, including a development agreement, a construction contract, a project security agreement, a project trust agreement, an operation agreement, and a regional agreement (FHWA 1996).

*3.1.5. State Route 91 median improvement, California, U.S.A. (BTO)*

The State Route 91 (SR 91) median improvement is one of four demonstration projects in California authorized by Assembly Bill 680 (Assembly Bill 1989). These projects were proposed by the private sector after issuance of guidelines for conceptual project proposals by the California Department of Transportation (Caltrans) (California DOT 1990). The SR 91 development franchise agreement (1993), signed in 1991, was granted to the developer, California Private Transportation Corporation (CPTC), with final approval of the agreement being contingent on meeting environmental requirements. The agreement was amended and restated in 1993 (California DOT 1993). The project consists of four new express lanes, electronically tolled, 10 miles long (16 km) within the center median of State Route 91. Construction started in 1993 and the project opened in December 1995. Estimated cost of the project was U.S. $126 million.

*3.1.6. U.S. acts*

Following California's initiatives as set out in Assembly Bill 680, several states enacted similar legislation for PPP projects. In Washington State, Substitute House Bill 1006 (SHB 1006) initiated BOOT/BTO procurements. It was later amended by SHB 1317 to provide for very comprehensive public involvement in the approval process. In Minnesota, Toll Road Enabling Legislation 1993 (TREL) (State of Minnesota 1993) was enacted to provide for BOOT/BTO projects through the TRANSMART request for proposals (Minnesota DOT 1995). Highway project TH 212, proposed following TRANSMART, was the first agreement signed by the government (Minnesota DOT 1996). However, during a 30-day voting period required by the Act for community approval, one of four cities on the proposed highway voted against it. In Virginia, the Public–Private Transportation Act (PPTA) (Virginia DOT 1995) was enacted to provide further refinements for the implementation of PPP projects following the earlier Virginia Highway Corporation Act of 1988 (Virginia DOT 1988) and the Qualifying Transportation Act of 1994 (Virginia DOT 1994). General consideration is given to these acts in this paper.

**3.2. Rights dimension: possession attribute**

The investigation of government requirements for this attribute shows an emphasis on the types of properties and requirements for the possession and transfer of property. Several types of properties have been mentioned in the selected projects and acts. These include

(a) land or real property needed for the project;
(b) improvements or the facility the developer agreed to construct on the land (e.g., highway, bridge, structure, movable and immovable properties, plant, equipment);
(c) airspace premises (e.g., over and under the right-of-way); and
(d) intangible properties needed for the development, operation, and ownership (e.g., intellectual property rights, patent rights, project documents, reports, drawings, plans, and specifications).

Generally, not all of these properties have been explicitly identified and defined in the request for proposals (RFPs) or agreements. Except for the U.S., governments seem to dislike explicitly stating that the developer will be the owner of the project. All-encompassing statements that treat the transfer of all properties at the expiration of the agreement, such as with the Second Severn Bridge (BOOT), are typically featured in agreements. When lease agreements are made for land or right-of-way, the reversion of the improvement (facility) may be treated explicitly such as with the Northumberland Strait Crossing Project (NSCP) (work is deemed to be a fixture to the land) or implied to occur with the reversion of the land at the end of the lease such as with the Channel Tunnel. The two BOOT projects, Severn Bridge and the NSCP, leased the land to the developer at an insignificant rent. For the Channel Tunnel and Western Alignment BOT projects, the first provided land at cost and the second was free.

Intangible properties such as intellectual property rights were the subject of transfer for the Channel Tunnel. However, for the Western Alignment, the request for proposals stated that it was to be under government possession at all times.

Table 1 provides a summary of the relevant characteristics of the possession attribute. Projects were generally required to be transferred or revert at no charge to the government at the end of the agreement. While this transfer requirement might be common in public–private partnership projects, exceptions can usually be found. For example, the Texas High Speed Rail project, a $5.6 billion project awarded in 1991 and cancelled in 1994 as a result of financial troubles of the consortium that spent $40 million on the project, had a requirement that at termination the government had the option to purchase the facility at its fair market value (State of Texas 1991).

*3.2.1. Channel Tunnel*

The Channel tender invitation stated that the chosen promoters would benefit from a concession to construct and operate the Link for a period of time, and the rights of the promoters would expire when the concession was terminated. The governments required the Link to be kept in the public domain (HMSO 1986*a*). The term Fixed Link was an all-encompassing term, defined to include a twin bored tunnel rail link with associated service tunnel, together with the terminal areas and dedicated facilities for control of, access to, and egress from the tunnels. The term also included plant, machinery, movable and immovable equipment, and railway shuttle rolling stock. Lands for the project were provided by the government through compulsory acquisition and (or) agreement and were leased to the developer.

Upon termination of the agreement, the Fixed Link was to be handed over to the two governments. Immovable property would revert to both governments and land leases would end. In respect of intellectual property rights, the government required the developer to grant a non-exclusive royalty free license to use or sub-license any intellectual property which would be vested in the government for purposes of construction and operation of the Fixed Link after expiration of the agreement.

*3.2.2. Second Severn Bridge*

The tender invitation (U.K. DOT 1989) stated that both crossings would be highways for which the Secretary of State is the highway authority. The Severn Bridges Act (S-B Act) (U.K. DOT 1992) granted the British Secretary of State the right to construct the new bridge and to delegate all relevant functions and power to levy tolls to a private promoter according to a concession agreement. The S-B Act authorized the acquisition of lands and to grant a lease or other interest in or right over any land according to a concession agreement. Such lease was to be provided at a peppercorn (insignificant) rent as mentioned by the tender invitation.

The tender invitation provided for the transfer by the promoter of both crossings to the government at the end of the concession period. The S-B Act provided for the transfer of all property, rights, and liabilities of the concessionaire with no explicit definition of property.

*3.2.3. Highway 104 Western Alignment*

The project as developed is part of the public highway system and the ownership of the project facility at all times is vested in the Province of Nova Scotia. All the needed lands were acquired and paid for by the government and made available to the project. The request for proposals provided for the project facility to include the road and all improvements, buildings, erections and structures, and all chattels, machinery, equipment, materials, tools, forming part thereof or used in the construction or operation. The first addendum provided for construction equipment not to be part of the facility during project operation. Along with public ownership of the facility, the request for proposals provided for the exclusive use and possession by the government of all project materials and information and their related patents, copyrights, and other industrial and intellectual property rights, including trade secrets. With such prior possession of the project by government, no transfer clause was included in the RFP.

*3.2.4. Northumberland Strait Crossing Project*

The federal government had as a main objective that the project be financed, designed, constructed, operated, and maintained by the developer under a long-term subsidy agreement. The 1988 NSCP proposal call explained that the development agreement would include a ground lease and a schedule of requirements, terms, and conditions. In this call, the project facility was described to include collectively the lands, the work complete in all respects, with all operation and maintenance systems in place, and any other improvements or structures located on the lands. The work means all improvements and all appurtenances, which the developer agreed to construct on the lands.

For project possession, the proposal call stated "the work shall be fixtures to the lands and shall become the absolute property of the landlord (Minister of Public Works) without compensation upon the expiration or termination of this lease." In the first addendum, the government explained further its intention by stating that the contract with the developer would be to build, to own, and to operate the facility for 35 years, after which it would be transferred at a nominal amount to the government. The second and third addenda explained that the nominal amount was meant to effect that the facility would revert to the government after the 35-year ownership period, and that alternative private sector ownership could be considered and be the subject of negotiation after selection. "Own" was defined by the third addendum to mean "to own the leasehold interest in the facility." In the

**Table 1.** Rights dimension: possession attribute characteristics for selected projects and acts.

| Project or act | PPP mode | Possession characteristics | Acquisition by | Property transfer at termination | Property reversion at termination |
|---|---|---|---|---|---|
| Channel Tunnel | BOT | Land and facility in public domain, land leased to developer at cost | Government, at cost to developer | Intellectual property rights, movable property | Immovable property, land leases to end |
| Second Severn Bridge | BOOT | Land leases, no explicit clause of private ownership; known as DBFO contract | Government, at peppercorn cost to developer | All properties, rights, liabilities | na |
| Highway 104 Western Alignment | BOT | Public possession at all times of facility, all improvements, patents, intellectual property | Government, at no cost to developer | na | Project to revert at expiration |
| Northumberland Strait Crossing | BOOT | Ground lease, work is fixture to land; own means to own leasehold interest in facility | Government, at peppercorn cost to developer | na | Work becomes absolute property of government at termination of lease |
| SR 91 and AB 680 California | BTO | Construction lease term, transfer of property at completion to government, operation lease term; airspace option lease | Developer; eminent domain is available, all at developer's cost | na | Surrender of real property and facility |
| PPTA Virginia 93 | BOOT | Developer to acquire, construct, improve, maintain, and (or) operate a facility | Developer/government; cost by developer | Project to be dedicated to public authority | na |
| TREL Minnesota 95 | BTO/ BOOT | Agreement to provide for any mode or procurement (BTO or BOOT) or operation | Developer/government; government sell, lease, or donate right-of-way | Facility titles transfer to government after expiration under BOOT | Facility titles under BTO transferred before operation and reverts at end of lease |

**Note:** na, not applicable.

sixth addendum, the government stated that for purposes of financing and taxation, the project was a private sector venture.

*3.2.5. State Route 91*

Assembly Bill 680 authorized Caltrans to enter into agreements for the construction by and lease to private entities of transportation projects. The Bill mentioned and differentiated between three types of lease: lease of rights-of-way, lease of airspace over or under facility state highways, and lease of the facility (private transportation project). Lease terms would be up to 35 years during which private entities would charge fees for the use of the facilities. Facilities would be state-owned at all times and revert to the state after expiration of the lease term at no charge. Caltrans made available its power of eminent domain to be used in right-of-way acquisitions if requested by CPTC. Acquisitions would be made at all times at CPTC's cost.

Several grants and rights were identified in the SR agreement. A 1.5-mile Absolute Protection Zone was defined to protect CPTC's franchise rights and economic viability. Under this provision, Caltrans would not finance, grant, or convey any franchise to any party other than CPTC for the development or operation of a public transportation project within the protection zone, unless the proposed facility did not represent economic competition to the project. CPTC was given the right of first offer and first refusal with respect to the development and operation of any commercial airspace improvement, over, under, on, or within the State Transportation Facility, State Route 91 right-of-way, in Orange County, California. Such airspace rights could run up to 99 years. CPTC was granted an option for the development of three phased extensions to the current facility to be exercised during the term of the agreement.

**3.3. Rights dimension: revenue attribute**

The revenue attribute is the second right assigned by governments to developers. The investigation emphasized the requirements in connection with toll and revenue arrangements along with other rights given to developers of the selected projects and acts set out in Table 2. Typically, BTO and BOOT modes as implemented in the U.S. projects and acts provide for freedom in toll setting and application of congestion pricing (except for the Virginia act, Table 2) while setting caps on the rates of return. Governments, in general, tend to control the term of agreement through statements directed at early termination if debt or revenues are satisfied (Western Alignment, Severn Bridge) and with an indirect statement if rates of return are met (SR 91 and U.S. acts). Generally, government seems to have two objectives: (*i*) control the amount of revenue generated by the project and (*ii*) control the amount of revenue the developer is entitled to earn. Both work to achieve the equity principle used in evaluating finance methods for public projects (Blackburn and Dowall 1991; Robinson and Leithe 1990).

*3.3.1. Channel Tunnel*

Governments through the Channel Invitation and Concession Agreement offered political guarantees not to intervene in the conduct and operation of the Link and not to terminate the promoters' right to construct or operate a Link provided that the concession terms are adhered to.

The developer was given commercial freedom in setting tunnel tariffs. Both the invitation and the agreement stated "the Concessionaires will be free to determine their tariffs and commercial policy and the type of service to be offered." Earlier in the Channel Invitation (U.K. DOT 1985), the government explained that the duration of the concession would consider the type of project selected and would be sufficient to allow repayment of debt and permit a reasonable return on equity. The concession period was initially set by the agreement as 55 years. Because of delays and cost increases concession was extended 10 years by the governments involved (Huot 1995).

*3.3.2. Second Severn Bridge*

The S-B Act provided the authority to levy tolls for both bridges, to be exercised by the concessionaire. The government in the tender invitation required promoters to state the initial tolls required by each class of traffic proposed. Further, the invitation required a statement as to the basis for any subsequent adjustment of tolls due to inflation, the index of inflation to be used and its weighting in the adjustment formula, components of cost to which it would be applied, minimum toll increases, and the time period between adjustments. The tender invitation allowed for differential tolls by day or date provided road safety was not impacted.

The government allowed for additional proposals for adjusting the toll level (and (or) concession period) in order to take account of actual traffic flows diverging from the bid assumptions. For this case, detailed information was required regarding the mechanism for adjusting toll levels and (or) the concession period, the traffic demand assumptions, and the upper limit for the concession period. In the U.K., specifications for maximum tolls to be levied on new roads have been described in the New Roads Act (U.K. DOT 1991). This act provides for specifying maximum tolls if the road consists of a major crossing for which there is no reasonably convenient alternative. Toll periods in this act may end on a specific date, or be determined by the achievement of specific financial objectives, or passage of specified number of vehicles, or the earlier or later of specified dates. The S-B Act provided the concessionaire with the power to levy tolls for a maximum of 30 years. It provided, however, for early termination of this right if the revenue requirement had been met, i.e., the toll income received is equal to or greater than the amount the concessionaire is entitled to receive by the concession agreement.

*3.3.3. Highway 104 Western Alignment*

The request for proposals provided for initial tolls and any proposed mechanism for increasing the initial tolls during the concession period to be established during negotiation of the Omnibus Agreement. However, the RFP stated that tolls would be sufficient to (*i*) pay the debt incurred to build the facility, (*ii*) establish an operating and maintenance reserve, and (*iii*) provide for required repair and rehabilitation work. The government included with the RFP a study of the current and future traffic volume and revenue forecasts for a range of toll road options. Beck, president of Canadian Highways, explained that tolls were initially set at Cdn \$3 per car, Cdn \$2 per axle for trucks, and Cdn \$4 for recre-

**Table 2.** Rights dimension: revenue attribute characteristics for selected projects and acts.

| Project or act | PPP mode | Revenue characteristics | Toll characteristics |
|---|---|---|---|
| Channel Tunnel | BOT | Term: 55 years extended to 65; "no second facility" guarantee; "no interference in operation" guarantee | Service levels and tariffs at promoters' discretion |
| Second Severn Bridge | BOOT | Term: 30 years; may be terminated early if entitled revenues are met, and may be extended to account for traffic levels | Initial setting by developer adjusted to inflation; toll may be adjusted to account for actual traffic flow |
| Highway 104 Western Alignment | BOT | Term: to continue until debt retired; return to developer to come from construction, operation and maintenance, return on debt | Tolls set to $3 per car, $2 per axle for truck, $4 for recreational vehicles; toll adjusted for inflation and debt coverage ratio |
| Northumberland Strait Crossing | BOOT | Term: 35 years; revenue floor established; no cap on revenues; revenue distribution mechanism established; subsidy Cdn $42 million per year indexed to inflation | Pre-established tolls adjusted to 75% of consumer price index and adjusted to reflect changes in taxes and insurance premiums |
| SR 91 and AB 680 California | BTO | Term: 35 years; reasonable return on investment with base return of 17% adjusted to T bonds; incentive return, an additional 6% maximum; excess revenues to State Fund | Freedom in establishing and changing tolls; congestion pricing |
| PPTA Virginia 93 | BOOT | A reasonable maximum rate of return; excess revenues to State Fund or developer to reduce debt | User fees to be established by the parties at negotiation; tolls to achieve a reasonable rate of return |
| TREL Minnesota 95 | BTO/BOOT | A reasonable rate of return to be established; residual revenues to developer | Variable tolls are allowed based on time of day (congestion pricing) |

ational vehicles (Beck 1997). Further, he explained that if debt service coverage was not met, tolls were to be adjusted automatically; and that tolls would be adjusted for inflation.

Government required that the Omnibus Agreement term be limited to the length of time toll revenues were needed to repay all the money borrowed or made available to pay for construction as well as to pay for any reserve requirements as mentioned previously. The government reinforced through the first addendum that the selected developer must earn its return from the construction contract, operating contract, and a return on any debt, which the respondent chooses to hold. In the addendum to the RFP, the government stated further that "DOTC will give no assurance or guarantee that a fair market rate of compensation will be achieved by the Selected Respondent within the Concession Period to be fixed in the Omnibus Agreement."

*3.3.4. Northumberland Strait Crossing Project*

The NSC Act allowed the government to make regulations prescribing tolls for the use of the crossing. Toll collection was the responsibility of the developer and tolls were to be adjusted annually by 75% of the consumer price index. As explained in the proposal call and its first and fifth addenda, a toll revenue floor was established to be the greater of either $8 million in 1988 dollars or the actual toll revenues experienced by the ferry service in the full year preceding the date of substantial completion of the facility. It was also explained that toll rates may be increased by more than the permitted 75% of the consumer price index should toll revenues be lower than the established floor, indexed to 100% of any increase in the consumer price index, or if tax changes or insurance premiums result in cost increases. Shortfalls in toll revenues were to be recouped in the succeeding year. With no explicit cap on toll revenues, the government required a separate account for toll revenues where the distribution of revenues would follow certain priorities. The toll distribution priorities included (*i*) payment of all operating costs, including insurance premiums on an insurance program specified by the government, (*ii*) payment of interest and capital for the financing secured against toll revenues, (*iii*) payments into a facility repair and maintenance fund, and (*iv*) payment of the balance to the developer.

*3.3.5. State Route 91*

Caltrans entitled CPTC to establish, levy, and collect tolls, fees, and charges for the use of the facility. Toll adjustments and arrangements were at the discretion of CPTC without prior approval or evaluation of Caltrans. Further, CPTC was authorized by the SR 91 agreement to implement a congestion pricing arrangement to respond to dynamic traffic flows and to maintain the highest levels of service. According to the daily demand patterns, toll rates move from $0.5, $1.0, $1.5, and $2.0 in four time zones with the rate being $0.25 for off-peak hours. Rates for Monday to Thursday differ from those for Friday and the weekend (PWF 1995). High-occupancy vehicles with three or more passengers pay no tolls. However, the SR 91 agreement provides for tolling high-occupancy vehicles after 2 years of operation if the debt coverage ratio is not met.

While Caltrans established no cap or control on toll rates, it established a 17% base return rate for use in discounting calculations; this rate is to be adjusted annually, and upward only, according to the average yield on 5-year U.S. Treasury Bonds. CPTC is entitled to a reasonable return on investment, comprised of a base return on investment and an incentive return on investment for any fiscal year. CPTC is entitled to retain the available cash in any fiscal year as a base return on investment whenever the base NPV calculated using base return rate is less than zero. The incentive return on investment is implemented to encourage CPTC to modify and improve the facility to maximize the number of vehicle occupants travelling during peak demand periods on the combined facility, SR 91. An incentive return rate gives 20 basis points (0.2%) increase on the base return rate for each 1% increase in the annual peak hour vehicle occupant volume; however, incremental increases may not exceed 600 basis points for any fiscal year. If the base NPV is equal to or greater than zero, CPTC will share available cash for the fiscal year with Caltrans only if the total NPV calculated at the incentive return rate is less than zero; otherwise, excess revenues will be directed to a State Highway Fund.

### 3.4. Obligations dimension: development, operation, and environment attributes

This section deals with government requirements under the first three obligation attributes. For all projects, emphasis was placed on the spectrum of functions that government requires developers to be responsible for (planning, design, construction, environment, operation, and maintenance), and the power governments have in project review, inspection, and approvals.

Generally, the projects studied showed that all project functions are the responsibility of the developer unless government assigned certain functions to be its responsibility such as maintenance, traffic management, and police services. For example, maintenance was encouraged to be provided by or contracted to government for the SR 91 (BTO), Western Alignment (BOT), and the TREL Minnesota act (BOOT/BTO). Bylaws requested by developers (e.g., for traffic management) were generally subject to government approvals and could not compromise safety.

Under traditional procurement arrangements, government has an active involvement in all project functions. For public–private partnership, government seeks to maintain a role in those functions for which it has a responsibility for the public at large. The investigation showed that government would provide for (*i*) the appointment of a representative or agent and consultants or independent engineers, (*ii*) the default and substituted entity clauses in case of default by the proponent, and (*iii*) the monitoring functions during development and operation.

Supervision and approval duties may undergo more scrutiny in public–private partnerships. Supervision provides for checking compliance with standards and specifications and takes place while work progresses. Approval provides for accepting the work after it has been reviewed or checked. Approval may hinder the progress of work if it takes time to be done. Government will generally carry out both processes, and promoters will seek strategies to speed them up, for example, by having an independent engineer perform such functions, as in the NSCP case. (It is noted that government often has difficulty ceding the kind of control over design and construction that it exercises under traditional procurement modes. This can create significant tension between government and the developer, especially when government attempts to exercise control through the guise of maintaining standards.)

Generally, the approval process has been substituted or replaced by one or more processes dealing with inspection/monitoring, quality control and quality assurance, with the possible role of an independent engineer who may provide (*i*) concurrence with design and construction as in the Northumberland NSCP project, (*ii*) quality control services during construction as in the Western Alignment project, and (*iii*) review of performance during design and construction as in the Channel Tunnel and Severn Bridge (BOOT) projects. The SR 91 project provided for government approval of design and inspection of construction and operation. Generally, however, government provides for final inspection of completed work, before it accepts the work or authorizes operation such as in the Channel Tunnel, Western Alignment, and SR 91 projects. Table 3 summarizes the major characteristics of the obligation dimension.

The projects examined demonstrate that government may direct or authorize changes to the work at its discretion as in the Western Alignment project or based on pre-agreed reasons such as in the Channel Tunnel and Northumberland Crossing projects where reasons included safety, defense, security, the environment, errors and omissions, or nonconformity. Time and cost adjustments as a consequence of changes may be subject to negotiations as with the Severn Bridge project, or added to the capital or operational costs as with the SR 91 project.

#### *3.4.1. Channel Tunnel*

The Agreement explained the developer's obligations to develop the Link in terms of design, construction, operation, and maintenance. The Channel Tunnel Act provided for the concessionaires to make bylaws regulating the operation and use of the tunnel system, which were the subject of approval by the two national governments involved.

Promoters were required to carry out an environmental impact assessment in both the U.K. and France. Promoters were required to be aware of the procedures of the International Maritime Organization before starting the development such that no permanent structure (e.g., ventilation shafts, artificial islands) would hamper the freedom and safety of navigation. Other requirements included provisions for facilities and installations for policing the tunnel and for frontier controls (customs, immigration, and animal health checks) that the Concessionaires would pay for but which would be organized and performed by the two governments.

For the supervision of construction and operation, the governments authorized an intergovernmental commission and safety authority for the performance of these functions and required the concessionaire to comply with their directions. However, no strict approval process was mentioned in the agreement. The governments provided for their inspection of the completed work before they would authorize operation. An independent project manager, Maitre d'Oeuvre, was appointed to review the performance during design and construction. The agreement explained that the concessionaire could proceed with the works relating to the "Avant Projet" (project outline drawings and documentation list) unless the governments raised an objection to such Avant Projet. Huot (1995) noted that government imposition of the latest innovations, safety or other regulations, after the start of construction led to severe design changes and increased costs.

#### *3.4.2. Second Severn Bridge*

Through the Severn Bridge tender invitation and the S-B Act, government required the promoter to take responsibility

**Table 3.** Obligation dimension for the selected public–private partnership projects and related acts.

| | | Development and operation attributes characteristics | | Financing characteristics | |
|---|---|---|---|---|---|
| Project or act | PPP mode | Proponent responsibility | Government responsibility and power | Proponent responsibility | Government support |
| Channel Tunnel | BOT | All development, operation, and maintenance functions; bylaws* subject to approval | Supervision and right to change; PM reviews compliance; government to inspect completed work before operation is authorized | Financing all phases, and raised based on rights conferred by agreement | No support; no financial guarantees |
| Second Severn Bridge | BOOT | All development, operation, and maintenance functions; bylaws* subject to approval | Right to change; agent monitors design, construction, and operation and maintenance | Financing all phases, inherit debt on existing crossing | Promoter to operate 2nd facility |
| Highway 104 Western Alignment | BOT | All functions; quality control/ quality assurance program; maintenance management plan | Right to change; monitoring and quality assurance; provide regular maintenance services at cost | Financing all phases; no lien to be made on the Western Alignment | $62 million; heavy truck to use Western Alignment |
| Northumberland Strait Crossing | BOOT | All development and operation and maintenance; environmental compliance; regional industrial benefits | Monitors and right to change; independent engineer concurs in design, and approves construction and progress payments | No mortgage of land and facility; equity 10% or $73 million; $10 million prime cost for fisheries | Cdn $42 million annual subsidy indexed to inflation; floor revenue indexed 100% to consumer price index |
| SR 91 and AB 680 California | BTO | All development and operation and maintenance; bylaws* subject to approval | Approval of design; right to change; monitoring all phases; may provide at cost traffic management, maintenance, and police | Financing all phases and based on rights in tolls, agreement, lease, project | No support at all; reimbursed for any service |
| PPTA Virginia 93 | BOOT | All development, operation, and maintenance functions; bylaws* subject to approval | Review and approve plans and specifications; inspections of construction | May pledge property interest in the project | May make grants or loans |
| TREL Minnesota 95 | BTO/BOOT | All development, operation, and maintenance functions | Provide maintenance and police services at cost; regular inspections | May pledge interest in the facility, agreement, income | May issue bonds for toll facility |

*Bylaws required by proponents.
†Proposed based on TREL legislation (State of Minnesota 1993).

for the design, construction, maintenance, and operation of the second crossing as well as for the maintenance and operation of the existing crossing. Other specific requirements included quality assurance, navigational requirements, and environmental aspects.

The S-B Act gave a power of temporary prohibition or restriction of traffic to be exercisable by the concessionaire. The New Roads Act (U.K. DOT 1991) provided for similar power and for all highway functions to be exercisable by the concessionaire except for the power to make schemes, regulations, orders, or give directions under the Road Traffic Regulations Act of 1984, U.K.

The government explained in the tender invitation for this project that special procedures would replace the normal technical approval arrangements. The invitation explained the appointment of a consulting engineer to work as a government agent to monitor design and construction, audit the promoter's quality assurance system, and possibly the maintenance and operation of the works. Further requirements explained that the promoter was required to employ the services of a designer under a formal contractual relationship such that the contract would ensure the designer was sufficiently independent from the promoter. This was required to enable the designer to comply with government requirements, check the promoter's proposed construction methods, materials, and each element of work. Along with that, the detailed design was required to be checked by an independent checker. The government agent was to receive certificates of satisfactory completion from the designer and the checker.

Design changes were allowed and it was explained that if the government issued a change, then the implications for the promoter's program and financial adjustment would be subject to negotiation. If the promoter issued a change, then it would be subject to the agent's approval with no financial adjustment to the promoter, who would also bear the consequences of any delay.

*3.4.3. Highway 104 Western Alignment*

The developer's obligations as set in the request for proposals included design, construction, operation and maintenance, repair, and rehabilitation. The government required an environmental management plan for the facility. The government set a 20-month objective for completion and a guaranteed maximum price for design and construction. Also, it required a marketing plan to maximize the use of the facility. Approvals and permits were the developer's responsibility. The government was prepared to provide maintenance, repair, and rehabilitation services. Beck (1997), president of Canadian Highway, the developer, explained that an annual maintenance agreement was signed with the government for regular maintenance services.

The request for proposals explained that the government at any time might direct or authorize changes in the work to be performed. The government reserved the right to undertake its own quality assurance activities. However, it was stressed that quality control and quality assurance for the development, design, and construction were the developer's responsibility. The first addendum explained that members of the developer could perform quality control; however, quality assurance had to be performed by an independent material testing firm and laboratory.

For the operation and maintenance of the road, the government required the preparation of a road maintenance management plan explaining performance specifications, maintenance functions, and how the developer would perform such functions. The intent of government was to evaluate periodically the performance of the respondent according to this plan.

*3.4.4. Northumberland Strait Crossing Project*

The developer's obligations included all the development and operation functions, including design, construction, operation, and maintenance. A service life of 100 years was a design requirement. Extensive environmental reviews and assessments of the biophysical and socioeconomic consequences of the crossing were required for the project and the developer was required to comply with all the requirements. A fixed crossing was considered to pose a threat of delaying the clearance of ice from the Strait. It was thought that such an "ice-out" could delay the start of the fishing season and could reduce the local temperature, which in turn could delay the spring planting of crops (FHWA 1996). All designs were assessed against a 2-day delay in ice-out in any year over a period of 100 years. Developers were required to comply with this maximum ice-out delay among other requirements, which were addressed by the developer in its commitment to develop an environmental management plan for the management of all environmental aspects of the project (Straits Crossing Inc. 1993).

Among the other obligations, the developer was required to maximize the economic and industrial benefits to the Atlantic region regarding businesses, employment, purchasing (material, equipment, supplies, and services), and technology amongst others. The regional benefit agreement signed for the project included several covenants on the developer such that 70% of all materials, 96% of labor, at least Cdn $20 million of engineering work after closing, and 75% of all marine workers had to be procured from the Atlantic Provinces region (FHWA 1996).

Monitoring performance during design, construction, commissioning, operation, and maintenance was one of government's roles for the project. The government at no cost to itself could request changes to the work if the reason of change was due to errors, omissions, or non-compliance on the part of the developer. Time for additional work resulting from changes authorized by the government would be negotiated. An independent engineer was appointed for the review of design, construction, operation, and maintenance procedures. Work approvals were the subject of negotiation. The government wished to retain the right to approve construction work and progress payments. A compromise was reached where the independent engineer would approve construction work and monitor the cost to complete of major work items (Pirie 1996).

*3.4.5. State Route 91*

Caltrans through the SR 91 agreement required CPTC to design, develop, acquire, construct, install, and operate the project transportation facility. Along with allocating such responsibilities to CPTC, Caltrans offered to assist CPTC in preparing and presenting documents required to obtain any permits and approvals needed for the project. For the operation of the project, CPTC was responsible for performing the administrative, toll collection, and traffic management activities. The Bill and the SR 91 agreement encouraged CPTC to pursue possible contracts with Caltrans to perform traffic management activities and maintenance, and with the California Highway Patrol for police services.

Environmental studies for the facility were CPTC's responsibility. Final approval of the project and commencement of construction were contingent on meeting requirements of the California Environmental Quality Act (CEQA).

The SR 91 agreement explained that Caltrans had the right to review and approve the design prior to commencement of construction. The approval process was limited to validating that the design was in accordance with the Caltrans design standards cited in the agreement, and provided for Caltrans objections or approvals within 21 days. Construction of the facility was required to be in accordance with standards and specifications described in the agreement.

### 3.5. Obligations dimension: financing attribute

For all of the projects studied, emphasis was placed on the developer's financing responsibilities, the security used in raising finance, and the form of government support to the project. Generally, for the projects and acts examined, government provided for all financing risks to be carried by the developer. Further, no financial guarantees were provided. However, support was provided in terms of (*i*) a direct subsidy as in the NSCP project, (*ii*) operation of existing facilities as in the Severn Bridge, and (*iii*) establishing a policy in favor of the facility such as in the Western Alignment. For purposes of calculating capital, operating, and maintenance costs, government generally required developers to maintain reserve funds such as a working capital reserve fund, maintenance and capital improvement reserve funds, and a debt service reserve fund.

To enable lenders to provide finance or credit support, government generally allowed the developer to use an umbrella of security instruments that cover the developer's interests in and rights under development, lease, and any project-related agreements; tolls, income, and project revenues; and all developer's shares. However, as explained below for BOT and BOOT projects and as shown in Table 3, government restricts the use of the project land and facility (i.e., improvements) as security. This restriction is imposed as a government requirement even for a project for which the developer has private possession/ownership, i.e., BOOT, such as the Northumberland NSCP project, and the Severn Bridge project.

However, there are cases where such restrictions may be relaxed until the occurrence of a stated condition or phase such as in BTO procurements. The SR 125 franchise agreement (California DOT 1991*a*) explained that the financing assignment used as debt security might cover the developer's interests in all or any portion of "(*i*) the franchise documents, (*ii*) the project [toll highway, real property on which such toll highway will be located, personal property and intangible property], (*iii*) project revenues and/or (*iv*) any other property or rights (including operating rights) of developer." It was explained that such a financing assignment should not be made in a manner that precludes passing of the project title to Caltrans on the title transfer date before the start of operation. A similar assignment was made for the AB680 — Mid State Tollway project (California DOT 1991*b*); however, it covered only the real property of the project.

The Virginia Public–Private Transportation Act (Virginia DOT 1995) provided the power necessary to the project developer/operator such that it could acquire, construct, improve, or operate the facility. The act stated that the operator may "... secure any financing with a pledge of, security interest in, or lien on, any or all of its property, including all of its property interest in the qualifying transportation facility." Similar provisions for the use of facility as security were included in the cancelled Texas High Speed Rail franchise agreement (State of Texas 1991).

#### *3.5.1. Channel Tunnel*

Governments through the terms of the Channel invitation and the concession agreement ruled out all support from public funds or government guarantees and required financing to meet all construction and likely cost overruns and delays. In its White Paper (HMSO 1986*b*), the U.K. government explained that for the evaluation of proposals, solid financing commitments coupled with the ability to attract financing were the final test for the evaluation, which was best met by Eurotunnel's proposal. Financing was entirely the responsibility of the promoters and was to be raised based on the rights conferred in the agreement to the promoter. The amount of equity capital was left to the determination of the promoters; however, it was expected to be substantial.

The Channel Invitation explained that full information on the promoter's anticipated capital structure, proposed time for calls on the various markets, and expected amounts to be raised on each of these markets were required by government. Further, as evidence of the robustness and viability of proposals, a detailed financial plan and a cash flow forecast along with related assumptions were required from the promoters. Detailed annual financial forecasts up to 10 years after repayment of debt were also required, including assessment of costs, traffic, measures of profitability, and related assumptions. Promoters were required to show the sensitivity of the project's economics to variations in traffic flow, cost overruns, delays in completion, and changes in interest and exchange rates.

#### *3.5.2. Second Severn Bridge*

The tender invitation required the promoter to finance both the existing and new crossings and inherit an estimated debt of £122 million for the existing bridge. The government required that "proposals involve no material risk on financial grounds regarding the completion of the second crossing to time and specification, the acquisition of the concession and existing crossing, and the operation and maintenance of both crossings."

#### *3.5.3. Highway 104 Western Alignment*

The government required the project to be entirely self-financing apart from Cdn $29 million under the SHIP

Agreement (Canada–Nova Scotia Strategic Highways Improvement Program), which was raised to Cdn $55 million by the second addendum. The corporation was to borrow money without recourse to the government. The government explained, "it will not guarantee any debt incurred by the selected respondent or corporation." The government established a policy whereby all heavy trucks, except for local traffic, would use the Western Alignment.

The Western Alignment Act explained that the corporation could borrow money based on its own credits, and could secure its borrowings against any or all of its assets and undertakings and the revenue arising from the collection of tolls. Beck (1997) explained that Cdn $62 million toll revenue bonds were used to finance the project.

A detailed project cash flow model and pro-forma financial statements were required reflecting forecasts and estimates for each year of the concession period. For evaluation purposes, government required the preparation of two sets of financial statements with accompanying cash flow models for two sets of toll revenue forecasts provided with the RFP. Assumptions for both sets included a 2.35% inflation rate, a 20-month completion period, a 35-year concession period, a Cdn $650 000 annual maintenance cost, and an 8.25% yield on 30-year Canada Bonds.

#### *3.5.4. Northumberland Strait Crossing Project*

The government explained in the proposal call and the NSC Act that its annual subsidy to the existing ferry service would be Cdn $42 million (1992 dollars). This subsidy was provided to reduce the government's cost to maintain its obligation for continuous communication with P.E.I. The annual subsidy was to continue for 35 years commencing with the operation of crossing and indexed 100% to the consumer price index.

The government in the sixth addendum insisted that investors should be aware that the project was a private sector venture and the subsidy should be considered as income to support toll revenues. The goal of the federal government was to have its participation "off book." However, the auditor general of Canada subsequently ruled that the NSCP project financing had to be considered a debt obligation "on balance sheet" of the federal government. This subsidy, as determined by the government, was used by the developer to raise about Cdn $660 million. Pirie explained that based on the subsidy, real-rate bonds paying a yield of 4.5% plus the annual inflation rate were issued and were taken up mainly by pension funds (Pirie 1996). Later the developer negotiated a reinvestment strategy of the bond proceeds to maximize the use of the loan considering the project's anticipated drawdown schedule.

Equity for the project, as explained by the fifth addendum, was required to be the lesser of 10% of total project cost (including direct and indirect costs, interest during construction, contingencies, start-up costs, and working capital) or Cdn $75 million. Instead of requiring the deposit of equity up-front in a trust account, the government allowed the developer to pay in equity pro-rata (supported by a letter of credit) with debt proceeds during the course of the project. The developer was also required to designate a "prime cost sum" of Cdn $30 million (reduced to Cdn $10 million) for disbursement at the government's discretion for fisheries compensation.

The government emphasized in the request for proposals and the first addendum that neither the crossing nor the lands could be mortgaged or pledged as collateral by the developer in any way and were incapable of seizure by the developer's creditors. By the third addendum the government explained that it would permit some form of mortgage or pledge to the extent necessary to permit the placement of the required mezzanine financing (subordinated loan). However, by the fifth addendum the government emphasized its earlier restriction and added that "lenders will have available an assignment of cash flow security through the trust accounts and certain insurance proceeds."

#### *3.5.5. State Route 91*

Financing was the responsibility of California Private Transportation Corporation (CPTC). Caltrans explained in the proposal guidelines (California DOT 1990) that the development had to be performed and completed at no cost to the State. All services provided by Caltrans were to be reimbursed by the developers. This included reimbursement for optional services requested by the developer (e.g., traffic projection, maintenance, police services) and reimbursement for non-optional services performed to protect the State's interest (e.g., costs associated with proposal selection, review right-of-way acquisition, design and construction oversight and technical activities). CPTC was required to maintain a number of reserve funds for working capital, major maintenance, capital improvements, and debt service.

Financing and debt security instruments referred to in the SR 91 agreement as leasehold mortgages were made based on CPTC's interest in the agreement, the lease, the project facility, and the tolls and profits of CPTC. Rights of leasehold mortgagees were subject to the provisions of the SR 91 agreement. Equity paid by the CPTC was $19 million. Taxable finance raised by CPTC included $35 million 17-year institutional debt, $65 million 14.5-year variable rate term loans, and a $7 million subordinated loan from the Orange County Transportation Authority (PWF 1995).

### 3.6. Liabilities dimension: general liability attribute

The general liability attribute is the first attribute in the liability dimension. Table 4 summarizes the general characteristics of the general liability, risk, and tax attributes of this dimension for the projects examined. Governments generally require developers to maintain liability insurance policies sufficient to (*i*) insure coverage of tort liability (claims arising on account of personal injury or death or damage to real or personal property) to third parties, users, and employees; (*ii*) protect against physical loss or damage to the facility in order to ensure continued use of the facility; and (*iii*) provide protection against business interruption (loss of income or earnings due to an insured peril such as delay in start-up and (or) completion). Other policies may be required for other reasons, particularly if government provides support or will carry risk if the project is not completed, such as in the Northumberland Strait crossing project. Exceptions, however, can be made to relieve a developer from part of the liability coverage requirement as in the SR 91 project. It

**Table 4.** Liabilities dimension for the selected projects and acts.

| Project or act | PPP mode | Liability attribute | Risk attribute | Tax attribute |
|---|---|---|---|---|
| Channel Tunnel | BOT | By developer for all phases; insurance: third parties, facility damage, start-up delay and business interruption | All by developer; time extension for FM*; government compensation for defense interruption | All taxes by developer |
| Second Severn Bridge | BOOT | By developer for all phases; insurance: third parties and facility damage | All by developer; performance bond; time extension for FM; government retains war repairs | Capital allowance for corporation tax; value added taxes on construction |
| Highway 104 Western Alignment | BOT | By developer for all phases; insurance: third parties, facility damage, and business interruption | All by developer; performance and ML[†] bonds; time extension for FM | All taxes by developer; the non-public corporation is exempted |
| Northumberland Strait Crossing | BOOT | By developer for all phases. insurance: third parties, facility damage, and business interruption | All by developer; performance, ML bonds, and others; time extension for FM*; government retained certain FM repairs | All taxes by developer; provinces to give municipal and provincial property tax exemption |
| SR 91 and AB 680 California | BTO | By developer before acceptance date, and shared thereafter; insurance to third parties and facility damage | All by developer; performance and ML bonds; time extension for FM; government retained certain FM repairs | All taxes by developer; developer may depreciate the improvements; franchise fees to be reduced by taxes |
| PPTA Virginia 93 | BOOT | By developer for all phases; insurance: third parties and facility damage | All by developer; delivery of performance and ML bonds | na |
| TREL Minnesota 95 | BTO/BOOT | na; in TH 212[‡] (BTO) the developer was to carry all liabilities and government to carry liabilities from developer's compliance with design and construction standards defined in the agreement | All by developer; in TH 212, included performance and ML bonds acceptable to lender or completion guarantees; time extension for FM | na; in the TH 212, developer pays all types of taxes |

**Note:** na, not applicable.
*FM, force majeure.
[†]ML, material and labor bond.
[‡]Proposed based on TREL legislation.

should be noted that in general, it is not possible to insure against all liabilities.

*3.6.1. Channel Tunnel*

The two governments in the invitation and the agreement required the promoters to be liable for damage caused to users of the Link and third parties. Two insurance programs were required, one during construction and one at start of operation which had to be renewable on a one-, two-, or three-year basis. The risks to be insured included (*i*) physical damage to the Fixed Link, (*ii*) tort liability to third parties, and (*iii*) delay in start-up and interruption of operations resulting from facility physical loss or damage. Such requirements proved to be invaluable when in November 1996 a fire erupted in the freight shuttle train and caused serious damage to the concrete lining. As a consequence, the tunnel was closed for 16 days with revenue losses per day of the order of £1 million. The damage cost was approximately £230 million and insurance coverage repaid about 98% of the cost (Bennette 1997).

*3.6.2. Second Severn Bridge*

During construction, the government required full contractor's all risk, third party, and employer's liability coverage. During operation, the invitation required insuring both crossings against all loss or damage. No explicit coverage was mentioned for liabilities of third parties during operation. However, the tender invitation required the promoter to indemnify the government against liabilities to third parties arising out of development and operation of the two crossings.

*3.6.3. Highway 104 Western Alignment*

The request for proposals required the corporation to indemnify and hold harmless the government against any and all claims, damages, losses, liabilities, costs, and expenses arising out of the performance or non-performance by the corporation in relation to the design, construction, maintenance, and operation of the facility. The request for proposals required the respondent to maintain throughout the concession period a liability insurance coverage acceptable to the government. The fourth addendum described the insurance and bonding requirements during construction and operation to include coverage for all risks of property damage to the facility and coverage to protect against all claims of liability arising out of property damage, bodily injury including death and personal injury.

*3.6.4. Northumberland Strait Crossing Project*

To protect itself from being required to pay the subsidy payments and operate the ferry service or complete or repair the work (i.e., double payments), the government took certain precautions. A very expensive insurance coverage before and after completion was required in the sixth addendum (*i*) to preserve the work (property) against all risks of physical damage, (*ii*) to pay damages arising from claims from third parties for injury, death, or loss of property, and (*iii*) to reimburse the government the cost of the subsidy or of providing ferry service if the completion date was not met. Pirie (1996) explained that Strait Crossing Development Inc. managed during negotiations to change the insurance limits so that they were based on the maximum foreseeable loss rather than the full replacement cost/value required by the government.

*3.6.5. State Route 91*

Caltrans through the AB 680 and the SR 91 agreement provided for CPTC, the developer, to be protected and indemnified by the Tort Claim Act. Reasons and explanations for this protection included (*i*) Caltrans authority and obligation to supervise and provide specifications and operational requirements for the design, construction, and maintenance of the project, (*ii*) Caltrans to hold title to the real property and facility, and (*iii*) the designation of the facility to be deemed part of the state highway system. This enabled savings to CPTC which otherwise would have been reflected in the toll rates.

Before the transfer of title to Caltrans, the agreement provided for CPTC to bear the risk of injury, loss, or damage to the facility. Third-party claims, except those that arise out of CPTC fault, were carried by Caltrans. These included claims that arise out of fault of Caltrans, any non-negligent actions taken or omitted by CPTC in compliance with any Caltrans permits or regulations, or design and construction that conforms to the standards in the agreement. The same also applied after the acceptance date. However, Caltrans also assumed the tort claims arising out of any act or omission in connection with traffic management and maintenance activities for which it was responsible. CPTC was required to maintain throughout construction and operation, bodily injury and property damage liability coverage of at least $50 million general aggregate per year.

**3.7. Liabilities dimension: risk attribute**

Governments in general seek procurement by public–private partnership in order to transfer more risks to the private sector than can be done using conventional procurement arrangements (U.K. Secretary of State for Transport 1993). In general, three categories of requirements can be distinguished from the requests for proposals and agreements for the projects studied: (*i*) risks related to the developer's obligations in the project; (*ii*) risks related to the developer's rights, particularly those related to revenues; and (*iii*) force majeure risks. An overview of how the risk attribute was handled for the selected projects is outlined in Table 4.

For the first category of risks, governments generally allocate all development and operation risks to the developer in clear wording in the requests for proposals and agreements. Emphasis was placed on explaining that government monitoring, inspection, and quality assurance processes did not relieve the developer from his responsibility for the work. This is different from government-directed changes to the work for which time and cost consequences may be negotiated as explained earlier. Further, as part of the allocation of risk, governments usually require completion guarantees, performance bonds, and labor and material payment bonds with amounts that vary according to each project's circumstances. This approach strengthens the allocation of development and operation risks to project developers.

The second category under the risk attribute deals with financing, economic, and revenue risks. The general requirement is for developers to carry all such risks with no guarantees. Governments may provide (*i*) adjustments for facility rate and (or) term of agreement to account for some risks such as inflation, and actual traffic growth rates as in the Severn Bridge, and (*ii*) policies to protect the developer's revenues from competing facilities through a "no second facility" guarantee as in the Channel Tunnel, or "absolute protection zone" for the SR 91 project.

The third risk category deals with force majeure risks. The definition of force majeure varied among the projects studied. It is helpful to categorize force majeure risks in general to include (*i*) war actions, including war, invasion, act of foreign enemy, and nuclear events; (*ii*) civil actions, including riots, insurrection, acts of terrorism, sabotage, and strikes; (*iii*) government actions, including expropriation, changes in law, interference by civil or military authorities; and (*iv*) natural catastrophes, including floods, earthquakes, unforeseeable geological conditions, chemical contamination, and epidemics.

When force majeure risks are realized, governments in general provide developers with a time extension for the performance of their obligations. Cost consequences, however, vary among projects and may more usefully be considered along with the insurance coverage for facility physical damage and loss generally required from developers. Governments in general provide no financial compensation for force majeure risks except for war actions, as defined above, for which the government provides compensation or retains the risk and carries the cost of repairs, such as in the Severn Bridge (BOOT), Channel Tunnel (BOT), and Northumberland Crossing (war and extreme catastrophes) (BOOT). In SR 91 (BTO), for all force majeure risks government will restore land and reinforcements to restore the weight-bearing capacity of the real property.

*3.7.1. Channel Tunnel*

Both the Channel invitation and concession agreement emphasized that the Link would be constructed and operated at the promoter's own risk without recourse to the governments. For force majeure risks or exceptional circumstances, the agreement explained that the time allowed for the performance of obligation would be extended accordingly. However, no compensation would be made to the concessionaires due to interruption of construction or operation based on such risks. However, if interruption occurred based on national defense, the concessionaires would be compensated. If these conditions/risks lead to the termination of the concession, "no compensation will be made to the concessionaires but the Principals may pay to the Concessionaires such amount which takes account of the net financial benefits, if any, to the Principals resulting therefrom." As mentioned earlier, insurance coverage was required for physical loss or damage to the facility arising from civil actions and natural catastrophes.

For financial and revenue risk, along with the requirement for no-recourse to government funds, governments gave concessionaires the freedom to determine their tariffs and commercial policy. Further, the government undertook not to facilitate the construction of another fixed link whose operation would commence before the end of 2020.

*3.7.2. Second Severn Bridge*

Through the tender invitation, the government required all design and construction risks to be allocated to the developer. The government transferred all geotechnical risks arising from physical conditions and artificial obstructions to the developer. A substantial on-default performance bond and (or) parent company guarantee was required from the developer.

Basically, the developer was responsible for the care of works including cost of repairs from any causes except for force majeure risks for which compensation and time extension would be allowed. These force majeure risks did not include natural catastrophes. Insurance for physical loss or damage of the crossing was required as mentioned earlier.

Revenue risks related to changes from initial traffic volume and traffic growth forecasts were transferred to the developer. The government provided traffic records on the existing crossing and projections for future levels of traffic. However, it assumed no liability from the use of such projections (U.K. DOT 1988, 1989). Given the provisions dealing with toll adjustment and the variable concession period that account for the actual traffic flows, the cost of such risks to the developer was reduced.

*3.7.3. Highway 104 Western Alignment*

The government stated in the request for proposals that the developer must assume all project risks and for that it was entitled to earn a fair market rate of return commensurate with the risks assumed. Performance and labor and material bonds in the amount of 50% of the maximum price were required for the construction phase. A performance bond was also required for the operation phase in an amount of 50% of the annualized contract for operation and maintenance.

For force majeure risks, the request for proposals explained that an extension of time for completion of the road would only be allowed for the affected activities on the critical path of the project. No time extension for force majeure would be made unless it was filed within seven days of its first occurrence. An "all risk" property insurance policy was required from the developer.

For financing and revenue risks, the government stated that it would not guarantee any debt incurred by the respondent nor the corporation, forecasted traffic levels, and any factors that might impact revenues or costs. However, it covenanted the use of the highway by all heavy trucks, except for local traffic.

*3.7.4. Northumberland Strait Crossing Project*

The government explained in the request for proposals that the developer must bear all project risks during both the construction and operation periods with the exception of legal challenges and regulatory impediments risk (delays and cost increases directly attributable to government actions). The government explained that its inspection and independent check of the work did not relieve the developer of his responsibility for the work.

The government through the NSCP proposal call and its addenda required the developer to provide a security package that assured the completion of the facility, assured the specified level of operating performance, assured the specified condition at the time of turnover, and assured the interim funding of the ferry service. Pirie (1994, 1996) explained that the security package against completion risk and cost overrun included along with parent company guarantees, a cover of Cdn $200 million performance bond and a Cdn $20 million labor and material bond along with a Cdn $73 million letter of credit for cost overrun risk. Further, the developer agreed to pay the operating cost of the ferry in case of completion delay.

Through the terms of the NSCP proposal call and the first addendum, the government relieved the developer from its responsibilities for the normal operation of the facility and completion of the facility in four force majeure cases: (*i*) acts of the Queen's enemies, (*ii*) government retroactive legislation, (*iii*) earthquakes in excess of design criteria, and (*iv*) a catastrophic event. A catastrophic event was defined as an event that damages the facility and renders it inoperable. Under such circumstances and where the government was bound by its constitutional obligation for "continuous communication," the government required the developer to provide as part of the security package reimbursement of an amount equivalent to the total subsidy paid during the period of time the government assumed responsibility and operated the crossing service.

Pirie (1996) explained that during negotiations with the government, force majeure risks were replaced by what was defined as project risk event and project delay event. Project risk events were retained by the government. Project risk events covered acts of war, acts of government, extreme weather conditions, earthquakes beyond certain standards, and a nuclear event. Project delay events described events beyond the developer's reasonable control such as contaminated material, third party strike or walkout. Their realization could, subject to negotiations, provide the developer with time extension and toll adjustments. Geotechnical risks and labor strikes and lockouts were among the risks the developer was required to carry.

#### *3.7.5. State Route 91*

In addition to liability requirements for facility damage and tort, Caltrans required CPTC in the SR 91 agreement to furnish payment and performance bonds or completion guarantees. For events of force majeure, CPTC's time to perform its obligations would be extended by an equal amount. Where the force majeure event damaged or destroyed all or any part of the real property, Caltrans would be obligated to restore the land, grading and reinforcements necessary to restore the weight-bearing capacity of the real property immediately prior to such event. However, the agreement explained that failing to restore the land should not be considered default if Caltrans had also declined to restore the land on the state transportation facility (SR 91 is a median improvement to State Route 91 that includes an adjacent SR 91 free highway).

Strong protections were provided by the SR 91 agreement for CPTC against Caltrans' default, event of loss, and change in law. In the agreement Caltrans stated that it would not grant, nor convey to any other party other than CPTC, and would not finance with public funds, the development of a transportation facility that might present economic competition to the project within the absolute protection zone. Failure of the application or performance of representations, warrants, and obligations would constitute a default by Caltrans, while failure to comply with covenants or requisition of title or requisition of use would constitute an event of loss. Both entitled CPTC to remedies, compensation, and (or) termination of the agreement and the lease.

The agreement explained that under a "change in law" that adversely impairs CPTC's exercise of its property, franchise, and other contract rights, CPTC could elect to close the project and seek payment by Caltrans of all unrecovered costs at the date of calculation (capital and operating costs, interest on debt, distribution to equity investors minus total revenues at that date). Caltrans stated in the agreement that it would protect and defend CPTC against any challenges to the validity or enforceability of the acts and challenges to the enforceability of the agreement.

### 3.8. Liabilities dimension: tax attribute

The treatment of taxes is the third attribute under the liabilities dimension. Generally, for public–private partnership projects, governments require developers to be familiar with all tax rulings (e.g., corporate, income, and property taxes) that might apply to their proposed business structure. Further, governments make no representations or warrants to the tax consequences or accuracy of the developers' proposed business structure. Summarized in Table 4 are the tax attributes of the projects examined.

Governments, according to the circumstances for each project, may provide for certain vehicles to support project development. These vehicles may include exemptions for certain types of taxes such as the exemption of property tax in the Northumberland Strait crossing project (BOOT), capital allowance such as in the Severn Bridge (BOOT), or creation of a corporate body with special characteristics such as in the Western Alignment (BOT).

#### *3.8.1. Channel Tunnel*

The Channel invitation (U.K. DOT 1985) explained that the principle of territoriality of taxation would be applied where each country will apply its normal laws to the construction, maintenance, and operation of that part of the project falling within its jurisdiction. The requirement for the levying of taxes was set also in the Concession Agreement (HMSO 1986*a*) requiring that "all duties and taxes levied or to be levied, including taxes on immovable property, will be liabilities of the Concessionaires and will be applied according to the provisions of national law."

#### *3.8.2. Second Severn Bridge*

The promoter as mentioned in the tender invitation was to be treated as "trading" for corporation tax purposes and would be able to claim capital allowance for construction expenditure. The invitation explained that value added taxes were payable on construction and exempted for project tolls. The invitation mentioned that local authority rates would be excluded.

#### *3.8.3. Highway 104 Western Alignment*

The request for proposals (RFP) explained that the government made no representation or warrants concerning the tax or legislative consequences of any structure used by the respondent. Further, it explained that the respondents must satisfy themselves about the consequences of the provisions of Canadian and Provincial tax laws. The government did not entertain special tax concessions.

The Western Alignment Corporation, not a public authority or crown corporation, was created by the W-A Act to assist the RFP respondent in the realization of the project (development and finance). The W-A Act, enacted in July 1995, stated that neither the corporation nor its property was liable to taxation, including income tax under any enactment. The government required the RFP respondents to satisfy themselves as to the tax status of the corporation. In the first addendum to the RFP, the government emphasized that "each respondent is responsible for obtaining its own advice as to all tax matters" and added "if necessary the corporation will be declared an agent of the Crown in relation to its toll collection activities."

*3.8.4. Northumberland Strait Crossing Project*

The government explained that the development was designed as a private sector venture and the developer's corporate structure was required to comply fully with both the letter and the spirit of the Income Tax Act of Canada in order to be accepted. The developer was required to satisfy itself and make appropriate allowances in regard to all taxes of every nature and kind that may be imposed on the facility, improvements, equipment, or any property brought on lands. The government explained that special tax concessions would not be entertained. A potential increase in sales tax liability was considered a business risk, which must be assumed by the developer. The provinces of New Brunswick and Prince Edward Island were considering exempting the crossing facility from municipal and provincial property taxes.

*3.8.5. State Route 91*

The SR 91 agreement explained that all taxes imposed on the real property and the project were the sole responsibility of CPTC as part of its capital and operating costs despite the fact that the real property and the project were to be considered property of Caltrans at all times. The agreement, however, provided for franchise fees (base, variable, and excess) to be reduced by the amount of taxes after title transfer to Caltrans. CPTC was concerned about depreciating the project, after title transfer to Caltrans, and was advised it could depreciate the improvements.

## 4. Recommendations

The above investigation explains how government requirements have been realized for each of the nine attributes of the requirement structure in the projects and acts examined. Each attribute had a range of terms or conditions attached to it and the investigation emphasized important aspects of each attribute. The following recommendations relate to the attributes of the three dimensions that need to be treated in public–private partnership documents. Emphasized is the need for clear articulation of government requirements in such documents and public–private partnership agreements in order to reduce the amount of supplemental materials issued to request for proposals, help consortiums in responding with proposals that can fit the requirements, and reduce the amount of time spent in negotiations and (or) the need for contract amendments to reflect marketplace realities missed earlier.

### 4.1. Rights dimension

A clear statement of possession requirements in general and with each property type is needed. Items that should be addressed include the following:

(a) types of project properties (land, improvements, airspace, intangible property);
(b) type of possession permitted for each type (e.g., public, private, lease);
(c) properties, if any, that can be taken as a security instrument;
(d) clear title statement during the different phases and terms of agreement;
(e) who will carry the responsibility for the acquisition of land and right-of-way and its related costs (e.g., government, developer, or both); and
(f) properties that are the subject matter of reversion, transfer, or dedication at the expiration of the agreement or at default.

While many of the revenue terms are kept for the negotiation phase, explicit statements regarding project revenues are needed for the following:

(a) term of agreement: type (e.g., fixed, variable);
(b) term of agreement: measure (e.g., NPV, IRR before and after tax, specified amount of revenues, specified number of vehicles);
(c) types of revenues permitted to the developer (tolls, charges);
(d) treatment of collateral revenues (e.g., revenues from airspace improvements);
(e) toll types allowed (e.g., direct, shadow, congestion, or at developer's discretion);
(f) toll setting authority (e.g., developer, government, or both);
(g) toll adjustment mechanism (e.g., formula for inflation, traffic demand, debt ratios);
(h) toll caps (e.g., maximum toll rates allowed);
(i) base returns allowed: measure and value (e.g., NPV, IRR, specified revenues);
(j) incentive returns allowed and related performance measure (e.g., achieving specified use of the facility, vehicle occupants, number of cars); and
(k) excess revenues, their measures and their distribution (e.g., shared, or allocated).

### 4.2. Obligations dimension

The obligation dimension represents the purpose of the public–private partnership venture and the core of the requirement structure. Explicit requirements have to be set for two issues. The first is the developer's extent of obligations and responsibilities. The second relates to the extent and terms of the government's power in performing inspection/supervision, approval, and the right to request changes. Public–private partnership acts, request for proposals, and agreements have to consider details for the obligation requirements, some of which include the following:

(a) description of project functions for which the developer is responsible (e.g., planning, permits, acquisitions, design, construction, operation, maintenance, environmental assessments and compliance);

(b) project functions the government prefers, or is required, to perform (e.g., traffic management, maintenance, police services);
(c) statement of the applicable standards and specifications;
(d) extent of government monitoring, inspection, and approval processes, and right to make changes;
(e) statement of quality control and quality assurance systems and the responsibility for performing such activities (e.g., developer, independent consultant, government); and
(f) processes for addressing time and cost effects resulting from changes made by government (e.g., allocated to capital/operating costs, to be negotiated).

While general statements are provided by government regarding project financing, it is important that call for expressions of interest and request for proposals treat the following:
(a) financial risks, if any, that may be absorbed by the government, (e.g., interest rate);
(b) type of financial support or guarantees that might be provided; and
(c) type of security instruments permitted (e.g., project revenues and rights).

### 4.3. Liabilities dimension

Explicit statements are needed by government to explain its requirements regarding project general liabilities, risks and taxes. They should cover the following:
(a) types of liability coverage (e.g., facility damage, tort and business interruption);
(b) responsible party for each liability during project development and operation;
(c) amounts of each insurance coverage required during construction and operation;
(d) types and amounts of project bonds needed for construction and operation;
(e) extent and conditions, if any, of government liability (e.g., due to developers compliance with government specifications and standards);
(f) statement regarding the allocation of risks in relation to the developer's obligations;
(g) explicit definition of force majeure risks;
(h) time and cost consequences of force majeure risks; and
(i) statements about tax policies, exemptions, or allowances for the project.

## 5. Conclusions

Rights, obligations, and liabilities are three dimensions of a structure used to explain government requirements in public-private partnerships. These dimensions in turn consist of nine attributes: possession and revenues for the rights dimension; development, environment, operation, and financing for the obligations dimension; and general liabilities, risks, and taxes for the liabilities dimension. The structure was used to demonstrate the requirements government has regarding the rights, obligations, and liabilities of private developers in a number of public–private partnership (PPP) projects and acts. Generally, the structure can be used as a starting point for government to organize its requirement for PPP and formulating project documents such as call for expressions of interest, request for proposals, and agreements.

The requirement structure and its nine attributes was useful in explaining how governments implemented BOT, BOOT, DBFO, and BTO modes for the procurement for a number of PPP projects. Alternatively, the structure can be used to identify the basic arrangements under the several PPP modes and in formulating other modes. Government can decide on the contents (e.g., conditions or requirements) and the allocation for each of the attributes, which in turn will provide for a number of arrangements or modes for implementation. The structure, as such, can be used to show that under the traditional public procurement all nine attributes are the responsibility of the government, while under build–own–operate or full privatization, all attributes are the responsibility of the private developer. Between these two extremes come all other PPP procurement modes.

Further, the structure can be used by government in negotiation such that it can manipulate the nine attributes to achieve a balance between the rights, obligations, and liabilities of the private developer. More importantly, governments can use the structure to develop an analysis framework, preferably a quantitative one, to assist in making decisions about the nine attributes and on which allocation of the attributes will attain the best value for the public at large or which will best suit the social and political environment. For example, what would be the benefits (e.g., reduction in facility rates as a requirement in the revenue attribute) if ownership of the facility (possession attribute) would be in the hands of the private sector instead of the government during the term of the agreement? Comprehensive economic models (Abdel-Aziz and Russell 1999) can further be formulated to assess how each of the attributes is best handled.

## References

Abdel-Aziz, A.M., and Russell, A.D. 1999. Decision support system for infrastructure project appraisal and risk analysis. Proceedings of the 27th Annual Conference of the Canadian Society for Civil Engineering, June 2–5, Regina, Sask.

Assembly Bill. 1989. No. 680. Chap. 107: State transportation facilities. July 10, Calif.

Augenblick, M., and Custer, B.S. 1990. The build, operate, and transfer (BOT) approach to infrastructure projects in developing countries. World Bank, Working Papers, WPS 498.

Beck, J.M. 1997. Highway 407ETR — express toll route, Highway 104 Western Alignment: innovative highway development through public private partnerships. Proceedings of the Annual Conference of the Canadian Society for Civil Engineering, pp. 89–96.

Bennette, S. 1997. Traffic returns as fire probe continues. International Railway Journal, 37(3): 21–30.

Blackburn, S.J., and Dowall, D.E. 1991. The tools for financing infrastructure. Paper presented on financing public infrastructure in Mexico City: problems and solutions. Lincoln Institute of Land Policy, Cambridge, Mass.

California DOT. 1990. Guidelines for conceptual project proposals for toll revenue transportation projects. California Department of Transportation, Office of Privatization, Calif.

California DOT. 1991*a*. Development franchise agreement for a privatized transportation project by and between California Transportation Venture Inc. and the State of California Depart-

ment of Transportation (SR 125). California Department of Transportation, Calif.
California DOT. 1991*b*. Development franchise agreement for a privatized transportation project by and between California Toll Road Company, and the State of California Department of Transportation (Mid State Toll Way). California Department of Transportation, Calif.
California DOT. 1993. Amended and restated development franchise agreement: State Route 91 median improvements, Orange and Riverside Counties, California. California Department of Transportation, Calif.
FHWA. 1996. FHWA study tour of Northumberland Strait crossing. Project NSCP, Federal Highway Administration, U.S. Department of Transportation, Washington, D.C.
Government of Canada. 1993. An act respecting the Northumberland Strait crossing. Chap. 43. Government of Canada, Ottawa, Ont.
HMSO. 1986*a*. Concession agreement — the Channel Fixed Link. HMSO Cmnd 9769, Her Majesty's Stationery Office, London, U.K.
HMSO. 1986*b*. The Channel Fixed Link. White Paper. HMSO Cmnd 9735, Her Majesty's Stationery Office, London, U.K.
Huot, J. 1995. The Eurotunnel financial black hole. AACE Transactions, pp. D&RM.5.1–D&RM.E.5.
Lawson, G. 1994. Will the private sector fund roads. *In* Transport financing. Proceedings of Seminar L held at the PTRC European Transport Forum, University of Warwick, England.
Minnesota DOT. 1995. Request for proposals for TRANSMART: Minnesota's toll facilities public–private partnership initiatives program. Minnesota Department of Transportation, Minn.
Minnesota DOT. 1996. TH 212 development agreement: a public-private partnership between the Minnesota Department of Transportation, TH 212 Community Highway Association, and Interwest/DLR Infrastructure Group, LLC. Minnesota Department of Transportation, Minn.
N.S. DOTC. 1995. Highway 104 Western Alignment request for proposals. Department of Transportation and Communication, Nova Scotia.
Pirie, J.D. 1994. Overview of infrastructure projects in North America and a specific review of the Northumberland Strait crossing project. Technical paper prepared by Straits Crossing Inc., April 29, 1994.
Pirie, J.D. 1996. Public private partnering — project financing and development. Proceedings of the 1st Structural Specialty Conference of the Canadian Society for Civil Engineering, pp. 17–31.
Price Waterhouse. 1993. A public guide to public–private partnerships in infrastructure: bridging the gap between infrastructure needs and public resources. Public–Private Partnership Services, Price Waterhouse, Ont.
Province of Nova Scotia. 1995. An act to provide for the financing, construction and operation of the Western Alignment of Highway 104 — Bill No. 10. Nova Scotia.
Public Works Canada. 1987. Northumberland Strait crossing project — call for expression of interest. Public Works Canada, Ottawa, Ont.
Public Works Canada. 1988. Northumberland Strait crossing project — proposal call. Public Works Canada, Ottawa, Ont.
PWF. 1995. 91 express lanes opened. Public Works Financing, Vol. 91, December.
Robinson, S.G., and Leithe, J.L. 1990. Building together: investing in community infrastructure. The National Association of Counties of the United States (NACo) and the National Association of Home Builders (NAHB), Washington, D.C.
State of Minnesota. 1993. An act: toll road enabling legislation. Chap. 211. State of Minnesota.
State of Texas. 1991. Franchise agreement between the Texas High-Speed Rail Authority and the Texas High Speed Rail Corporation. State of Texas.
Straits Crossing Inc. 1993. Northumberland Strait crossing project — final registration. Prepared for the New Brunswick Department of the Environment, Fredericton, N.B.
U.K. DOT. 1985. Invitation to promoters for the development, financing, construction, and operation of a channel fixed link between France and the United Kingdom. Department of Transport, U.K.
U.K. DOT. 1987. Channel Tunnel Act 1987. Chap. 53. Department of Transport, U.K.
U.K. DOT. 1988. Information for prospective tenderers — Second Severn Crossing. Department of Transport, U.K.
U.K. DOT. 1989. Tender invitation — Second Severn crossing. Vol. I: Administration, contractual and financial aspects. Department of Transport, U.K.
U.K. DOT. 1991. New Roads and Street Works Act 1991. Department of Transport, U.K.
U.K. DOT. 1992. Severn Bridges Act 1992. Chap. 3. Department of Transport, U.K.
U.K. Secretary of State for Transport. 1989. New roads by new means: bringing in private finance — a consultation paper. Presented to Parliament by the Secretary of State for Transport by Command of Her Majesty, London, U.K.
U.K. Secretary of State for Transport. 1993. Paying for better motorways: issues for discussion — Green Paper. Presented to Parliament by the Secretary of State for Transport, for Scotland and for Wales, Cmnd 2200.
Virginia DOT. 1988. Virginia Highway Corporation Act of 1988. Virginia Department of Transportation, Va.
Virginia DOT. 1994. Qualifying Transportation Facilities Act of 1994. Virginia Department of Transportation, Va.
Virginia DOT. 1995. Public–Private Transportation Act of 1995 — implementation guidelines. Virginia Department of Transportation, Va.
Washington State DOT. 1994. Public–private initiatives in transportation. New partners. Request for proposals. Washington State Department of Transportation, Washington, D.C.
World Bank. 1994. World development report 1994: infrastructure for development. Oxford University Press, New York.

# [17]

*The Economic Journal*, **113** (*March*), C69–C76. © Royal Economic Society 2003. Published by Blackwell Publishing, 9600 Garsington Road, Oxford OX4 2DQ, UK and 350 Main Street, Malden, MA 02148, USA.

# INCOMPLETE CONTRACTS AND PUBLIC OWNERSHIP: REMARKS, AND AN APPLICATION TO PUBLIC-PRIVATE PARTNERSHIPS*

*Oliver Hart*

The question of what should determine the boundaries between public and private firms in an advanced capitalist economy is a highly topical one. In this paper I discuss some recent theoretical thinking on this issue. I divide the paper into two parts. First, I make some general remarks about the relationship between the theoretical literature on privatisation and incomplete contracting theories of the firm. Second, I use some of the ideas from this literature to develop a very preliminary model of public-private partnerships.

The question of what should determine the boundaries between public and private firms in an advanced capitalist economy is a highly topical one. In this paper I will discuss some recent theoretical thinking on this issue. I will divide the paper into two parts. First, I will make some general remarks about the relationship between the theoretical literature on privatisation and incomplete contracting theories of the firm. Second, I will use some of the ideas from this literature to develop a very preliminary model of public-private partnerships.

## 1. Parallels Between Theories of the Firm and of Privatisation

Let me begin by discussing the very close parallel between the theory of the firm and the theory of privatisation.[1] In the vertical integration literature one considers two firms, *A* and *B*. *A* might be a car manufacturer and *B* might supply car-body parts. Suppose that there is some reason for *A* and *B* to have a long-term relationship (e.g., *A* or *B* must make a relationship-specific investment). Then there are two principal ways in which this relationship can be conducted. *A* and *B* can have an arms-length contract, but remain as independent firms; or *A* and *B* can merge and carry out the transaction within a single firm. The analogous question in the privatisation literature is the following. Suppose *A* represents the government and *B* represents a firm supplying the government or society with some service. *B* could be an electricity company (supplying consumers) or a prison (incarcerating criminals). Then again, there are two principal ways in which this relationship can be conducted. *A* and *B* can have a contract, with *B* remaining as a private firm, or the government can buy (nationalise) *B*.

There are, of course, some important differences between the two situations. First, if *B* is an electricity company, it is likely to have direct dealings with consumers, independent of its relationship with the government. In this case the

* I am grateful to the National Science Foundation through the National Bureau of Economic Research for financial support, and to Donald Franklin, Paul Grout, Rohan Pitchford, and Andrei Shleifer for helpful comments.

[1] For an excellent recent summary of thinking about privatisation, see Shleifer (1998).

contract the government has with a private electricity company can be thought of as an attempt to *regulate* the company's dealings with consumers. There is no obvious analogy in the case of vertical integration. Second, decisions to privatise or nationalise are often highly political, presumably because of the government's unique position in society, whereas vertical integration decisions are usually strictly economic. Third, the government is often thought of as a very different agent from a private firm: it is concerned with social welfare rather than just profit. Here, however, the distinction is less sharp than it might seem at first sight since there are a number of firms (particularly nonprofits or cooperatives) that have broader concerns than just profits.

In spite of these differences, the issues of vertical integration and privatisation have much more in common than not. Both are concerned with whether it is better to regulate a relationship via an arms-length contract or via a transfer of ownership. Given this, one might have expected the literatures to have developed along similar lines. However, this is not so. Whereas much of the recent literature on the theory of the firm takes an 'incomplete' contracting perspective, in which inefficiencies arise because it is hard to foresee and contract about the uncertain future, much of the privatisation literature has taken a 'complete' contracting perspective, in which imperfections arise solely because of moral hazard or asymmetric information.

My own view is that this is unfortunate. One of the insights of the recent literature on the firm is that, if the only imperfections are those arising from moral hazard or asymmetric information, organisational form – including ownership and firm boundaries – does not matter: an owner has no special power or rights since everything is specified in an initial contract (at least among the things that can ever be specified). In contrast, ownership does matter when contracts are incomplete: the owner of an asset or firm can then make all decisions concerning the asset or firm that are not included in an initial contract (the owner has 'residual control rights').

Applying this insight to the privatisation context yields the conclusion that in a complete contracting world the government does not need to own a firm to control its behaviour: any goals – economic or otherwise – can be achieved via a detailed initial contract. However, if contracts are incomplete, as they are in practice, there is a case for the government to own an electricity company or prison since ownership gives the government special powers in the form of residual control rights.

Even if this position is accepted, it does not follow that one can take an 'off the shelf' model from the theory of the firm literature and apply it to privatisation. In the standard 'property rights' model found in that literature, ownership serves to elicit appropriate *ex ante* investments, particularly those in human capital.[2] If firm *A* acquires firm *B*, then *A*, having more residual control rights, has greater bargaining power when uncontracted-for contingencies arise; *A* earns a greater return on her investment and therefore invests more. Conversely, *B*'s incentive to invest

[2] For a summary of the property rights literature, see Hart (1995).

falls since *B*'s bargaining power is lower. The optimal allocation of ownership trades off these two effects.

Applying this logic to the privatisation context, one concludes that, if the government buys an electricity company or prison, the benefit is that some government bureaucrat who is in charge of the prison will invest more (have more ideas, be more entrepreneurial); but the cost is that the manager of the prison – who used to be an owner but is now an employee – will invest less. The latter effect – that a government employee will be less entrepreneurial than an owner-manager – seems very plausible, but the idea that government ownership leads to more entrepreneurship by bureaucrats seems less so.

For this reason the literature has explored other trade-offs.[3] Consider, for example, the model in Hart *et al.* (1997) (HSV). HSV compare two cases. (1) The government can own a facility, a prison, say, and employ a manager to run it; or (2) the government can contract with a company owned by the prison manager to run the prison for a period of time. HSV ignore investments on the government side, but suppose that the prison manager can make two kinds of investment. He can invest in efficiency-enhancing ideas that raise the quality of prison services, e.g., develop new rehabilitation programmes; he can also spend time figuring out how to cut costs and quality, while staying within the letter of the contract. A government employee has little incentive to engage in either activity since it is easy for the government (as owner) to 'hold up' the employee without rewarding him appropriately. In contrast, a private prison owner-manager is less subject to hold up. The good news about this is that private ownership encourages the first, innovative type of investment. The bad news is that private ownership also encourages the second, quality-shading kind of investment. The choice between public and private ownership depends on which of these effects is more important.

In summary, the HSV model differs from the standard property rights model of the firm in two ways. First, only one party (the prison manager) invests, but he makes two kinds of investments (as in the multi-tasking model of Holmstrom and Milgrom (1991)). Second, the contract between the government and the prison provider plays a crucial role – it defines the extent to which quality shading can occur. In contrast, in the standard property rights model, long-term contracts are assumed to be sufficiently incomplete to be useless.

## 2. Public-private Partnerships (PPPs)

In this Section, I use an HSV-type model to understand the costs and benefits of public-private partnerships.[4] To repeat what I said in the introduction, this model is extremely preliminary. For simplicity, I will now ignore the choice between public and private ownership and assume that all provision is private. I will take a key property of a PPP to be that facility construction and service provision are

[3] For some representative contributions, see Schmidt (1996), Laffont and Tirole (1993), Besley and Ghatak (2001), and King and Pitchford (2001).

[4] For related work, see Bentz *et al.* (2002) and Bennett and Iossa (2002). Bennett and Iossa's model is based on incomplete contracts and is similar in a number of ways to the model presented here (it was developed independently). In contrast, Bentz *et al.*'s model emphasises asymmetric information.

bundled, i.e., in the case of a prison the government contracts with a private party – henceforth known as the 'builder' – to build *and* run the prison (the builder may then subcontract with someone else to run the prison).[5] In contrast, under 'conventional' provision, the government contracts with the builder to build the prison and then later on with another (private) party to run it.

There are three dates, 0, 1, 2, as in Figure 1.

The government and builder contract at date 0, the prison is built between dates 0 and 1, and the prison is operated between dates 1 and 2. (There is no discounting.) The contract specifies either the basic characteristics of the prison that should be delivered at date 1 (in the case of conventional provision) or the basic prison services that should be provided between dates 1 and 2 (in the case of a PPP).[6] In each case the contract is assumed to be incomplete in the sense that the builder can modify the nature of the prison or the nature of prison services in various ways, without violating the contract. Specifically, the builder can make two investments, $i$, $e$, that have consequences for the costs and benefits of running the prison between dates 1 and 2. We write

$$B = B_0 + \beta(i) - b(e),$$

$$C = C_0 - \gamma(i) - c(e),$$

where $\beta, b, \gamma, c > 0$, $\beta' > 0$, $b' > 0$, $\gamma' > 0$, $c' > 0$, $\beta'' < 0$, $b'' > 0$, $\gamma'' < 0$, $c'' < 0$. Here $B$ represents the (unverifiable) benefit to society (measured in money) from running the prison and $C$ represents the (unverifiable) costs from doing so (borne by the prison operator). The builder's total investment costs equal $i + e$.

We can interpret these investments as follows. Investment $i$ is a productive investment that makes the prison more attractive and easier to run (it raises $B$ and reduces $C$) – it could correspond to a higher quality/more pleasant/airier building. In contrast, $e$ is an unproductive investment that reduces total costs and quality. It corresponds to the quality-shading investment in HSV. For example, in the process of building the prison, the builder might realise that he can install an electric fence that reduces the likelihood of escapes. This reduces prison operating costs since fewer guards have to be hired, but may not be what the government had in mind (it reduces quality).

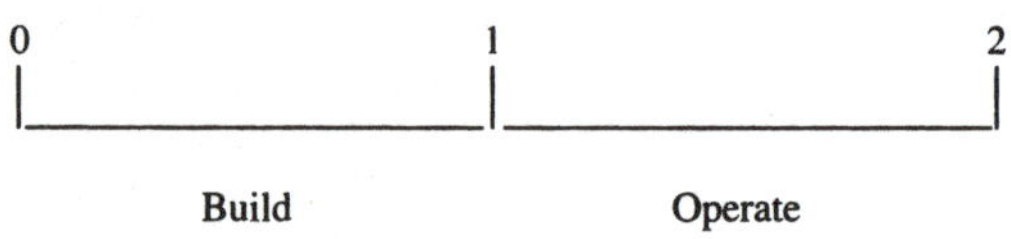


Fig. 1. *Time Line*

[5] It is worth stressing the symmetry of the situation: it could just as well be that the government contracts with the provider of prison services, who then subcontracts with someone to build the prison.

[6] In the case of a PPP, the contract can also say something about the characteristics of the prison. We discuss this point further below.

In the first-best, $i$ and $e$ are chosen to maximise net benefit, $B - C - i - e$, i.e.,

$$B_0 + \beta(i) - b(e) - C_0 + \gamma(i) + c(e) - i - e.$$

The first-order conditions are

$$\beta'(i^*) + \gamma'(i^*) = 1,$$
$$c'(e^*) - b'(e^*) \leq 1 \text{ with equality if } e^* > 0.$$

We will assume that $c'(0) - b'(0) \leq 1$, i.e., $e$ is socially unproductive. This means that we get a corner solution in the first-best: $e^* = 0$. (In contrast, all other first-order conditions are supposed to have interior solutions.)

We now consider the second-best, where the builder's investments are nonverifiable and hence cannot be contracted on. We assume, however, that the provider of prison services observes $i$, $e$; in particular, he knows what his costs will be. We compare two cases.

*Case 1: Separate contracts to build and operate, or 'unbundling'*

In this case, the government contracts with a builder at date 0 to build a basic prison for price $P_0$. At date 1 the government auctions off the contract to operate the prison. If there is a competitive supply of contractors, the government will pay the prison operator a price equal to his operating cost $C = C_0 - \gamma(\hat{\imath}) - c(\hat{e})$, where $\hat{\imath}$, $\hat{e}$ are the builder's equilibrium choices of $i$, $e$. At date 0, the builder chooses $i$, $e$ to solve:

$$\text{Max}(P_0 - i - e).$$

The solution is extremely simple: $\hat{\imath} = \hat{e} = 0$. That is, the builder builds the cheapest prison possible (while staying within the contract). Note that, although $i$, $e$ affect the operating contract price the government has to pay, the builder does not internalise this externality.[7]

If there is a competitive supply of builders, $P_0 = \hat{\imath} + \hat{e} = 0$, and so the government's net payoff is

$$B - C - P_0 = B - C - i - e, \text{ evaluated at } \hat{\imath} = \hat{e} = 0.$$

*Case 2: PPP, or 'bundling'*

In this case, the government offers a contract at date 0 that specifies the basic quality of the service to be provided between dates 1 and 2 and a price $P$. Now the builder internalises the cost of service provision since either he provides the service himself or he subcontracts the service. In the latter case, given competition, he will pay the subcontractor a price equal to the subcontractor's cost, $C = C_0 - \gamma(i) - c(e)$.

[7] One can imagine that one way for the externality to be internalised is for the builder's payment $P_0$ to be made contingent on the price the government pays to the prison operator at date 1. One problem with such an arrangement is that this price may not be verifiable. In any event, we will see shortly that a PPP achieves a similar outcome.

At date 0 the builder chooses $i$, $e$ to solve:

$$\text{Max } P - C - i - e = P - C_0 + \gamma(i) + c(e) - i - e.$$

The first-order conditions are

$$\gamma'(\hat{\hat{i}}) = 1,$$

$$c'(\hat{\hat{e}}) = 1.$$

If there is a competitive supply of builders, $P = C + i + e$, and so the government's net payoff is

$$B - P = B - C - i - e, \text{ now evaluated at } i = \hat{\hat{i}}, \; e = \hat{\hat{e}}.$$

The PPP equilibrium is illustrated in Figure 2 along with the first-best and the unbundling equilibrium.

The trade-off between unbundling and bundling is simple. Under unbundling, the builder internalises neither the social benefit $B$ nor the operating cost $C$. By setting $i = e = 0$, he does too little of the productive investment, $i$, but the right amount of the unproductive investment, $e$. In contrast, under bundling or PPP, the builder again does not internalise $B$, but does internalise $C$. As a result, he does more of the productive investment, although still too little, but also more of the unproductive investment.[8]

The model yields a simple conclusion. Conventional provision ('unbundling') is good if the quality of the building can be well specified, whereas the quality of the service cannot be. Under these conditions, underinvestment in $i$ under conventional provision is not a serious issue, whereas overinvestment in $e$ under PPP may be. In contrast, PPP is good if the quality of the service can be well specified in the initial contract (or, more generally, there are good performance measures which can be used to reward or penalise the service provider), whereas the quality of the building cannot be. Under these conditions, underinvestment in $i$ under conventional provision may be a serious issue, while overinvestment in $e$ under PPP is not.[9]

It is worth being a little speculative. Arguably, prisons and schools fall into the first category: contracting on the building is relatively simple, while contracting on the service may not be. On the other hand, hospitals may fall into the second category: although specifying service quality is far from straightforward, it may be easier to come up with reasonable performance measures concerning how patients are treated than it is to specify what may be a very complex building.

[8] Note that we have implicitly assumed that the builder has the same freedom to shade on the productive investment $i$ under a PPP as under conventional provision. This makes sense if the PPP contract places the same constraints on the nature of the building as under conventional provision, along with constraints on service quality (see footnote 6). However, an often-mentioned benefit of a PPP is that one can reduce contracting costs by omitting details of the building, and focusing on service provision. The problem with this is that it may give the builder the flexibility to choose a *lower* $i$ under PPP than under conventional provision (i.e., there is a change in the constraint set that may dominate the incentive effect discussed in the text). Thus PPPs that omit details of the building may have costs in addition to those emphasised here.

[9] These conclusions about the relative desirability of PPPs mirror those in Grout (1997).

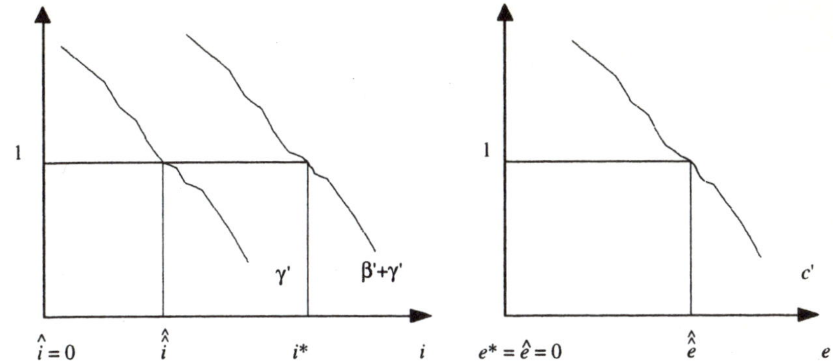


Fig. 2. *Illustration of Equilibria*

## 3. Final Comments

In this paper I have discussed some recent theoretical thinking on public versus private ownership, and I have developed a simple incomplete contracting model to analyse PPPs. The model suggests that the choice between PPPs and conventional provision turns on whether it is easier to write contracts on service provision than on building provision.

Note that, although perhaps not surprising, this conclusion is at odds with much current thinking by policy makers. Policy makers frequently argue that PPPs are good because the private sector is a cheaper source of financing or insurance than the public sector. This thinking is strange for an economist since it is hard to imagine an agent that is more able to borrow or to provide insurance than the government (with its enormous powers of taxation). One of the (modest) benefits of the current paper is that it may shift attention from what seem to be secondary financing issues to what seems to be the central issue: (relative) contracting costs.

Our model could be usefully extended in various ways. The model takes the length of contract as given – implicitly it is assumed that the world ends at date 2. As a result, it does not matter who owns the asset (prison) at the end of the contract. With more periods, both contract length and who owns the asset after the contract ends become interesting choice variables.

The model could also be applied outside the public-private context. For example, it may throw light on the choice a purchaser in the private sector faces between hiring a general contractor to do a job and contracting separately with specialists. It may also provide ingredients for a general analysis of optimal contract length between (private) firms – an issue about which economists have had remarkably little to say.[10]

*Harvard University*

[10] For some progress on this topic, however, see Ellman (1999).

## References

Bennett, J. and Iossa, E. (2002). 'Building and managing facilities for public services', (January) Brunel University, mimeo.

Bentz, A., Grout, P.A. and Halonen, M. (2002). 'Public private partnerships: what should the state buy?', (March) Dartmouth College, mimeo.

Besley, T. and Ghatak, M. (2001). 'Government versus private ownership of public goods', *Quarterly Journal of Economics*, vol. 116 (4), pp. 1343–72.

Ellman, M. (1999). 'Essays on the economics of organisations', Ph.D. dissertation, Harvard University.

Grout, P. A. (1997). 'The economics of the private finance initiative', *Oxford Review of Economic Policy*, vol. 13 (4), pp. 53–66.

Hart, O. (1995). *Firms, Contracts, and Financial Structure.* Oxford: Oxford University Press.

Hart, O., Shleifer, A. and Vishny, R.W. (1997). 'The proper scope of government: theory and an application to prisons', *Quarterly Journal of Economics*, vol. 112 (4), pp. 1126–61.

Holmstrom, B. and Milgrom, P. (1991). 'Multi-task principal-agent analyses: incentive contracts, asset ownership and job design', *Journal of Law, Economics and Organization*, vol. 7, pp. 24–52.

King, S. and Pitchford, R. (2001). 'Private or public? A taxonomy of optimal ownership and management regimes', (July), Australian National University, mimeo.

Laffont, J.-J. and Tirole, J. (1993). *A Theory of Incentives in Regulation and Procurement*, Cambridge: MIT Press.

Schmidt, K. (1996). 'The costs and benefits of privatization: an incomplete contracts approach', *Journal of Law, Economics and Organization*, vol. 12, pp. 1–24.

Shleifer, A. (1998). 'State versus private ownership', *Journal of Economic Perspectives*, vol. 12 (4) (Fall) pp. 133–50.

# [18]

Available online at www.sciencedirect.com
SCIENCE @ DIRECT®

PERGAMON

Journal of Purchasing & Supply Management 9 (2003) 97–108

JOURNAL OF PURCHASING AND SUPPLY MANAGEMENT
www.elsevier.com/locate/pursup

# Transaction costs, relational contracting and public private partnerships: a case study of UK defence

David Parker[a,*], Keith Hartley[b]

[a] Centre for Innovation Research, Aston Business School, Aston University, Aston Triangle, Birmingham B4 7ET, UK
[b] Centre for Defence Economics, University of York, Heslington, York YO1 5DD, UK

Received 25 April 2001; received in revised form 16 October 2002; accepted 31 October 2002

**Abstract**

This paper is concerned with the economics of public private partnerships (PPPs)/private finance initiative (PFIs) and in particular the role of transaction costs and the importance of trust in relational contracting. The discussion is illustrated by reference to the UK defence sector. The paper begins by discussing the nature of PPPs/PFIs before moving on to consider how the economics of contracting literature can shed light on their strengths and weaknesses. The transaction cost literature is reviewed alongside a resource-based perspective of procurement decisions. The concepts of trust and reputation are then considered in the context of minimising procurement transaction costs. The theoretical framework developed is then applied and illustrated through a case study of UK defence contracting, in an attempt to assess whether the use of PPPs will necessarily lead to improved economic efficiency. The case study highlights both the scope of PPPs/PFIs and their potential transaction costs in defence procurement, with the normal perils in terms of contracting given information asymmetry, asset specificity and the resulting scope for opportunistic behaviour.


*JEL:* D23; H54; H57; L14; L33

*Keywords:* Public private partnerships; Private finance initiative; Procurement; Trust; Supply chain; Defence contracting

## 1. Introduction

Public private partnerships (PPPs) are intended to harness the incentives of private markets to the public interest criteria of the state. Private capital and private sector companies finance and operate infrastructure that previously was publicly funded and managed. In recent years, PPPs have become popular in a number of countries. Governments keen to reduce government spending and borrowing and aware that private enterprise can provide services at lower cost, have introduced PPP programmes in place of or to supplement direct state investment. This paper considers the economics of public private partnerships and more specifically the roles of transaction costs, trust and relational contracting in the achievement of successful PPPs. The discussion is illustrated with reference to the UK defence sector, which has a long track record of partnerships with the private sector.

PPPs including in the UK 'private finance initiative' (PFIs) are part of a wider policy of 'privatisation' based on the expectation that the private sector provides services more efficiently and more effectively than the public sector. PPPs/PFIs permit an expansion of infrastructure provision; an expansion beyond what the state on its own could achieve given budgetary constraints and a lack of project management skills (Roger, 1999). At the same time, however, concerns have been raised about their true long-term costs and therefore on their ability to provide public investments more cheaply on a life-time cost basis. The purpose of the paper is to set out a framework for assessing PPPs drawn from economics to assess the use of PPPs in the UK defence sector. The main research question is, will the use of PPPs necessarily lead to improved economic efficiency in defence procurement?

The structure of the paper is as follows. First there is a general discussion of the rationale for PPPs. Then the theory of transaction costs from economics is reviewed,

*Corresponding author. Tel.: +44-121-359-3622; fax: +44-121-333-3474.
*E-mail addresses:* d.parker1@aston.ac.uk (D. Parker), kh2@yorkyork.ac.uk (K. Hartley).

1478-4092/03/$ - see front matter 
doi:10.1016/S0969-7012(02)00035-7

followed by a discussion of the roles of reputation and trust in relational contracting and joint ventures. The theoretical framework developed is then applied to UK defence contracting, where many difficult issues relating PPP deals feature. Finally, the main conclusions for defence procurement are summarised.

## 2. Public private partnerships

Under the title of the PFI, in the UK a Conservative Government began from 1992 to tap the private sector to manage the building and sometimes the operation of investments previously undertaken within the public sector (Terry, 1996). The Labour Government elected in May 1997, although previously critical of the PFI, re-launched the programme under the banner of PPP and acted to speed up the process by which public–private contracts are awarded (HM Treasury, 1998a).[1] The latest initiative is the establishment of Partnerships UK.[2] The objective of Partnerships UK is to accelerate the process by which PPP contracts are agreed, in part by taking equity stakes in projects and in part by providing loans to public bodies. Another recent initiative by government is the proposal to publish model contracts so as to reduce the costs to private firms of tendering for public sector work.

To date the UK has dominated in Europe in terms of both the number and value of PPPs. For example, in 1999 around 40% of all PPPs in Europe by value occurred in the UK, compared with 8% in Germany, 4% in Spain and 9% in Italy, France and the Netherlands combined (Privatisation International, 2000, pp. 4–5). PFIs and now PPPs have been adopted in the UK in such areas as new government IT programmes, education, hospital building, waterways, road schemes, prison management, re-development of the London Underground, estate transfers by government departments and Ministry of Defence projects. The total value of capital projects is estimated at around £22.5bn (The Business, 6/7 October 2002, p. 16). Concerns have been raised in the UK, however, about the resulting costs and benefits. For example, the National Audit Office (NAO) that supervises probity and efficiency in public spending in the UK, criticised the first big hospital development project. The NAO found that savings from the contract were greatly over-estimated by the NHS Trust that awarded it. Instead of achieving cost savings of £17m, the NAO estimated the likely savings to be around only £5m (Financial Times, 1999, p. 13). The NAO has also criticised the profits made by private companies on certain deals (NAO, 1997a, b).

In principle, PPPs involve clarity in specification and requirement, clear and enforceable contracts with proper cost efficiency incentives, and transparency in the bidding process. The intention is that government sets either the general objectives or specific outputs and leaves the private sector to design and manage the project, including the input mix. Typically, the private sector becomes responsible for the initial design and construction and operation and maintenance, thereby aligning incentives for low-cost construction with minimising life-time costs of operation. By contrast, capital constrained governments are tempted to lower the construction costs of a publicly financed project at the expense of much higher long-term costs of maintenance and operation. Other expected advantages of PPPs include risk allocation, e.g. cost over-runs managed more effectively through incentive-based contracts; greater transparency when political meddling in project specification occurs; and encouragement of innovation in project design, construction and operation and maintenance. Another reason for PPPs, however, is much weaker, the desire by governments to transfer expenditures from the public budget (and hence the public sector borrowing requirement) to the private sector. The opportunity costs of resources used in projects, and therefore the impact on economic welfare, is only lower by using PPPs rather than other methods of public procurement, including direct state provision, if there are real cost savings. Simply transferring expenditures between the public sector and private sector budgets has no effect on efficient resource allocation if identical resources are used. Also, PPPs can be a mechanism for inter-generational welfare shifting. Public sector financing costs are reduced in the short term at the expense of eventual higher tax burdens, triggered by future leasing costs or similar payments. Heald and Geaughan write (1997, p. 15): 'The present generation of voter/taxpayers benefits from the assets (for example prisons, roads and hospitals) inherited from earlier generations but in turn bequeaths to the next generation a run-down public asset base and an extensive web of contractual obligations to buy the output from PFI assets.'

Governments can always borrow more cheaply than the private sector. For PPPs to produce overall cost savings, therefore, the extra financing cost (estimated at between one and three percentage points in the UK) needs to be offset by savings in other aspects of the

[1] '...... through which the public sector can secure improved value for money in partnership with the private sector' (HM Treasury, 1998b). In the UK the terms PFI and PPP are both used and often interchangeably. However, correctly PFIs involve the provision of an asset and possibly a full-service package under a long-term contract. PPPs integrate the private and public sectors, with assets not returning to government. The Government has identified partial asset sales, concessions and joint ventures and partnerships as comprising PPPs. In this paper for brevity we often refer simply to PPPs, but the comments apply to PFIs too.

[2] Another recent initiative is the creation of the Office of Government Commerce to issue guidance on government procurement matters.

project achieved by the private sector. Calculations of cost saving are, however, sensitive to the assumptions made. A study of PFIs in the NHS concluded that: 'The PFI has had the effect of raising the costs of infrastructure development in the health service. The assumption that higher capital costs would be offset by savings resulting from the involvement of the private sector has proved incorrect' (Gaffney and Pollock, 1999). Another recent report, by The Institute for Public Policy Research in London, is also critical, arguing that savings from the PFI are likely to amount only to between £360 m to £720 m a year by the middle of the next decade (Financial Times, 2000a, p. 2). A detailed study of an education PFI in the UK has questioned whether the expected innovation in project design and execution on the part of private companies will actually occur (Ball et al., 2000). PPPs hide the true value of the government's future liabilities when not included in public sector debt and therefore government has been criticised for 'using techniques of which WorldCom and Enron would be proud' (Financial Times, 2002, p. 21). Nevertheless, the Labour Government appears to remain firmly wedded to the advantages of PPPs.

## 3. The economics of contracting

PPPs involve contracting between government and the private sector under conditions of imperfect information. The last 20 years or so have seen a growth in the 'economics of contracting' literature and its main findings are very relevant to an understanding of the strengths and weaknesses of any PPP deal. The economics of contracting literature is based on transaction costs. Transaction costs 'arise from the costs of seeking out buyers and sellers and arranging, policing and enforcing agreements or contracts in a world of imperfect information' (Cowen and Parker, 1997, p. 37). The idea has been popularised by Oliver Williamson since the 1960s (Williamson, 1975, 1985; Williamson and Winters, 1993). Williamson's early development of transaction costs was based on the idea of 'small numbers contracting' under conditions of imperfect and asymmetrically distributed information (Williamson, 1975). Three related concepts resulted, namely *bounded rationality*, *opportunism* and *asset specificity*. Bounded rationality implies rational decision making by buyers and sellers but under conditions of incomplete information. Opportunism refers to 'the incomplete or distorted disclosure of information, especially to calculated efforts to mislead, distort, disguise, obfuscate or otherwise confuse' (Williamson, 1985, pp. 47–48). The result of bounded rationality and opportunism is the risk that one or other of the parties to a transaction or series of related transactions will exploit his or her information advantage. Williamson has described this as 'self-interest seeking with guile' (Williamson, 1983, p. 26). Akerlof's concept of the 'lemon' is an extension of this argument. In an influential paper, Akerlof pointed out that buyers in one-off exchanges were especially at risk of buying something that would disappoint (Akerlof, 1970).

Where buyers and suppliers have imperfect and asymmetric information when contracting, contracts cannot be optimal in a full information sense. It is difficult to write complete contingent claims contracts (allowing for uncertain events) especially where contracts cover a lengthy period of time, technologies and costs are inherently uncertain or the economic environment is in a state of flux. Imperfect information enables parties to a contract to operate opportunistically exploiting any information asymmetry (e.g. about the true costs or quality of supply). Opportunism in a transaction becomes a threat particularly where there is 'asset specificity'. Asset specificity is emphasised by Williamson, and others, as a prime condition for 'hold-up' in contracting (Williamson, 1985, 1993a; Hart and Moore, 1988). Investment in an asset to fulfil the contract may lead one of the contracting parties to behave opportunistically when the contract is renegotiated. Often the investing party will not be able to recover the full costs of the investment (the costs are sunk) except through continuation or renewal of the contract. The asset may be tangible (e.g. buildings or machinery) or intangible (e.g. workforce training). Where a party decides not to invest in assets because of the risk of post-contract exploitation, this can lead to a sub-optimal supply of goods and services in social welfare terms.

One possible outcome is that what was ex ante competitive contracting becomes, ex post the contract negotiation, an imperfectly competitive or a monopsony market or a bilateral monopoly. Here the small numbers condition is important. In its absence, a victim of hold-up would have a higher probability of finding an alternative party with whom to contract and thereby recover the sunk costs. 'Hold-up' requires that there is no alternative party with whom to contract without net costs that equal or exceed those resulting from acceding to the opportunistic contractor's demands. A recent example of 'hold-up' in UK government contracting was Railtrack's threat that it would only be able to complete Phase Two of the Channel Tunnel Rail Link if there was a relaxation of the regulatory régime in its favour (Glaister, 1999, p. 32).[3]

The result of opportunistic behaviour may be *adverse selection*, the ex ante choice of an inferior option, or *moral hazard*, increasing the ex post risk that one party

[3] Railtrack plc is the private sector company that owned the rail infrastructure in Britain until its financial failure in 2001/2002.

100 D. Parker, K. Hartley / Journal of Purchasing & Supply Management 9 (2003) 97–108

will exploit the terms of the contract to the disadvantage of the other party. For example, changes in specification have been used by contractors as an excuse for raising prices and profits under government contracts. One obvious way of reducing the risk of opportunistic and related behaviour is to integrate vertically, but direct ownership and control, or what Williamson calls 'hierarchies', also involves costs in terms of the direct management and administration of resources. While in-house production is one possible way of reducing the hold-up threat, it can raise costs as a result of diseconomies of scale in procurement and a lack of competition for supplies that in turn reduces efficiency incentives (Grossman and Hart, 1986; Hart and Tirole, 1990). It is unlikely that government will achieve superior economies of scale and scope in infrastructure provision than private sector firms; indeed the opposite may well be true, private sector contractors are able to pool orders.

Transaction cost analysis supplemented by consideration of economies of scale and scope provides a powerful framework for analysing government procurement policy. This is not to suggest, however, that this approach to transacting is necessarily a *sufficient* explanation of procurement arrangements (Pitelis, 1993; Dietrich, 1994). Sourcing decisions are driven by internal resource capabilities or competences as well transaction cost and scale considerations (Walker and Weber, 1984). Ebers (1997) refers to increased responsiveness and flexibility, enhanced learning and capabilities, as well as economies of scale and scope, as the motivation for collaboration. The goal is to minimise a cost function while endeavouring to maximise organisational benefits. In other words, sourcing decisions should be seen not as the product of some deterministic relationship based on transaction costs and scale issues alone, but rather the consequences of strategic choices taking account of both costs and firms' internal capabilities and strategic goals (Parker and Vaidya, 2000).

Fig. 1 summarises the argument using a 'make or buy' matrix, with transaction costs on the vertical axis and internal capability on the horizontal axis. This figure combines both the transaction cost perspective with the resource-based perspective. Where transaction costs and internal capability are low, the case for outsourcing ('buy') based on market contracts is high. Whereas, where transaction costs are high (perhaps because of the strategic importance of the activity or because of the threat of hold-up resulting from power asymmetries in the supply chain) and internal capabilities to supply the activity efficiently exist, the case for outsourcing is much reduced ('make'). In the other two cases, where pressures to outsource or insource from transaction costs and internal capabilities conflict, the decision is less obvious. It will depend on careful calculation of the relative transaction costs and internal capabilities or benefits. In some cases, the optimal sourcing decision on cost–benefit grounds may be to enter into some kind of 'joint venture' or 'partnership' to procure the good or service. Joint ventures or partnerships are a compromise between pure market contracting and vertical integration (Parker and Hartley, 1997). Where outsourcing occurs, opportunistic behaviour and hold-up are protected against through long-term collaborative arrangements.

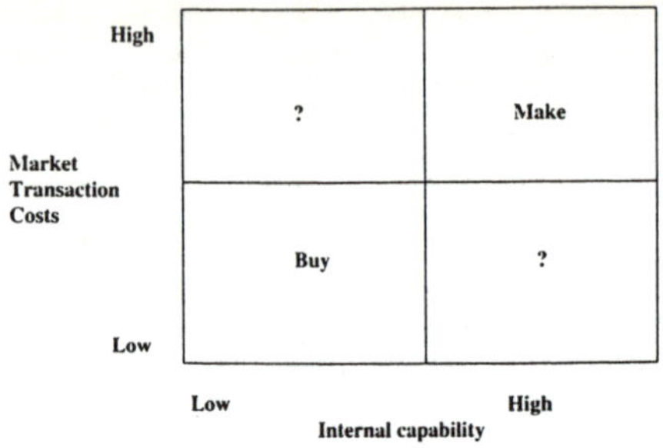


Fig. 1. Transaction costs versus internal capabilities in the 'make or buy' decision.

## 4. Reputation, trust and motivation

Risk management of private participation in infrastructure projects (PPIs) has been found to have both technical and political dimensions (IFC/World Bank, 1996, p. 2). The early history of PFI in the UK was clouded by private sector complaints of over-protracted and wasteful project bidding and aborted projects. The cost of taking part in a PFI bidding process was estimated at between £0.5 m and £2.5 m (NAO, 1997a). The Treasury PFI Taskforce and now Partnerships UK and model contracts are responses aimed at reducing these transaction costs.

One approach to controlling the behaviour of agents is to set down agreed rules usually in the form of written contracts. But writing long-term complete contracts is very problematic, as already discussed. The transaction cost literature emphasises that transaction costs will be lower the more 'good information' is available to the contracting parties before and during the performance of the contract. Therefore, it is rational for parties to seek out information that will improve their contracting ability. In this respect reputation (based on past behaviour) and trust (based on expectations of future behaviour) are central to the economics of contracting (e.g. Kramer and Tyler, 1996; Lane and Bachmann, 1998). Williamson has acknowledged that institutions such as trust reduce transaction costs and therefore help determine the comparative costs of governance (Williamson, 1993b).

PPPs have been likened to a form of 'network' between government and the private sector (Jackson and Stainsby, 2000). Casson has linked transaction costs and trust to provide insights into the formation of intra- and inter-firm networks (Casson, 1991, 1997, 1998). Networks, partnerships and alliances depend on co-operation and inter-dependency, leading, ideally, to mutual interest, shared goals and shared norms (Klijn and Koppenjan, 2000, p. 143). In these forms of contracting, which lie between pure markets and hierarchies, information is expected to flow more freely leading to reduced transaction costs because of mutual dependency. Shifting patterns of relationships over time can then be viewed as resulting from changes in mutual interest and shared goals and norms.

In the procurement of supplies, agents gain experience and learn so that the scope for opportunism is reduced. A reputation for 'fair dealing' becomes a business asset and can substitute for detailed contractual controls (Powell, 1990; Klein, 1997; Gulati, 1998, p. 303),[4] and it is to be expected that the smaller and more stable the supply base used the more quickly reputation and trust building occur. Other related issues are contract frequency and the social and economic context of transacting: some markets are more conducive to trust building (Lane, 1997). Similarly, the expectation is that in response to greater costs of opportunism, there will be greater incentives to invest in solidifying relations (e.g. more personal visits and face-to-face contact). From this perspective, reputation and trust serve as a form of 'social capital' increasing with use. 'Partnership sourcing' implies the use of one or a few preferred long-term suppliers based on trust and reputation in place of competitive contracting.

Reputation and trust may not, however, be sufficient for effective 'partnerships'. Partnerships may need to be supported by sanctions for 'deviant' behaviour (Grabher, 1993). In other words, reputation and trust are supplemented by mechanisms that contain the risk of misplaced trust in small numbers bargaining. The contract is one such mechanism supported by legal redress (Luhmann, 1979, p. 34; Deakin and Wilkinson, 1998); although where there is trust there should be less need for detailed and formal contracting.[5]

In summary, markets tend to be associated with frequent recontracting and therefore scope for opportunistic behaviour at recontracting, especially in the presence of asset specificity. 'Relational contracting', by contrast, is associated with forms of procurement that place more reliance on reputation and trust in small numbers contracting; although the threat of opportunistic behaviour ex ante and ex post contracting remains. In particular, where there are very few contractors, as is usually the case in the defence sector, the risks from collusion and small numbers bargaining increases.

Finally, the efficient negotiation of PPPs requires that those negotiating the contracts act in 'good faith'. More specifically, government officials pursue economic efficiency in contracting even when it adversely affects their own status, power and income. But as the 'public choice' literature from economics demonstrates (Buchanan, 1972; Tullock, 1965), motivation in the public sector is likely to involve at least some element of self-interest. Will government personnel pursue efficiency in PPPs even though they are unable to share in any cost savings to government, or will they pursue their own utility leading to a disfavouring of schemes that adversely affect their position, status and income? Efficient PPP contracting appears to be premised on having government in which pursuit of the 'public interest' dominates.

These arguments are now applied and illustrated using a case study of the UK defence sector. The defence sector was chosen because it has been a leading user of PPP/PFI initiatives in recent years and, prima facie, involves a number of significant problems for long-term contracting given the uncertainties surrounding defence from both supply and demand perspectives. Uncertainties arise on the supply side in terms of the high-technology and speedy obsolescence of defence systems and the multi-faceted nature of defence provision, and on the demand side because of the uncertainties surrounding when and in what ways the defence forces will be called upon to act. In other words, the defence sector appears to be acutely prone to information imperfections and asymmetries when PPP contracts are negotiated.

## 5. A case study: UK defence

Defence is a sector that is dominated by 'national security' concerns and so might be expected to be resistant to PPP/PFI initiatives (e.g. 'national security

[4] Dollinger et al. (1997) find in their experimental study that the better a firm's reputation the more likely it is to be targeted as an alliance partner.

[5] Maher (1997) undertook detailed interviews in a number of industries and found that in automobile manufacturing transactions were governed by bilateral, long-term relationships with buyers and suppliers. Not all of these relationships were governed by written contracts. Arrighetti, Bachmann and Deakin, by contrast, in empirical work involving firms in Germany, Britain and Italy, found that

(*footnote continued*)
'relational' contracting, involving higher frequency of contracting as well as asset specificity, may also be associated with a formal agreement and with the use of legal enforceability as a form of security. The role of the legal system in underpinning relational contracting is arguably greater than was previously recognised (Arrighetti et al., 1997, p. 192).

cannot be left to partnerships with private industry'). It is a classic example of a public good that traditionally has involved both *public finance and public provision*. In fact, defence has adopted PPP/PFI initiatives as a major part of its efficiency programme and has been innovative in some of its partnering with private industry, so demonstrating opportunities for the private finance and private provision of some defence activities. PPP/PFI has resulted in MoD and the Armed Forces shifting from 'make to buy' in Fig. 1.

By 1996, PFI was announced as a recognised part of MoD's drive for increased efficiency and value for money. The Ministry identified six areas for PFI, comprising training, equipment, property and accommodation, support services, utilities and information technology. The Labour Government's 1998 Strategic Defence Review, which announced UK defence policy to the year 2015, made specific reference to the importance of private finance and PPPs as part of the continuing pursuit of improved efficiency in the defence sector. These efficiency savings are central to ensuring that MoD can adequately fund its new equipment programme. By early 2002, MoD had signed 42 PFI contracts with a capital value of over £2 billion with a further 40+ projects to a capital value of £12 billion under consideration (MoD, 2001a; HCDC, 2002).

PPPs/PFIs are, therefore, a central feature of the MoD's new procurement policy. They differ from complete privatisation in that the MoD retains the responsibility for ensuring service delivery, with the private sector investing in, managing and operating any capital assets needed for delivering the service. As the customer, the MoD pays directly for services or output, usually through a long-term contract, typically in excess of 10 years, with MoD payments covering the whole or the majority of the project cost. Policy requires that for all projects, MoD will only consider using its own capital funding resources if PFI and other forms of PPP have been demonstrated to be 'unworkable, inappropriate or uneconomic' (MoD, 2000a).

Examples of PFI/PPP contracts signed by MoD are shown in Table 1.

The selection of Lex Defence Management to supply MoD's commercial vehicle requirements over the next 10 years was claimed by MoD to be an 'innovative, cost-effective solution, offering significant cost savings.' The company will buy MoD's existing fleet of commercial vehicles and then provide MoD with vehicles as and when required, with the firm being responsible for repair and maintenance. Strategic sealift is another novel PFI contract. Six vessels will be available to move UK military forces world-wide and at short notice. Since the six ship service will only be required for major operations, the contractor can make the ships available for the generation of commercial revenues when they are not needed by MoD; hence, potentially offering the taxpayer better value for money. Also, since the ships are equipped and classed as merchant ships (non-warlike), the competition was conducted under the EC Treaty and public procurement rules. There were four competing bidders (NOVOMAR; Maersk; AWSR Shipping; Sealion) and the contract was awarded to AWSR Shipping on the basis of price, quality and delivery. The contractor will provide British officers and crews for the ships while in MoD use and the seafarers will be eligible for call-out as Sponsored Reserves for operational requirements (MoD, 2001b).

The proposed PFI for the RAF's Future Strategic Tanker Aircraft is especially innovatory and is currently the largest of MoD's PFI contracts. It involves MoD paying for the availability and usage of air tanker capability and services, with a leasing contract for services replacing the traditional solution whereby the RAF owns, operates and services its fleet of tanker aircraft. Total procurement and support costs are estimated at some £13 billion for a 27 year fixed price contract with variation of price (VOP) based on output indices, but including a substantial firm element and opportunities for gain sharing. This contract is also different in that it involves the provision of a complete military capability that is closer to the front line than many other PPP/PFI contracts. As with strategic sealift, the number of tanker aircraft required for large-scale operations is greater than the peace-time needs; hence, there is the potential for the private sector partner to use tanker aircraft to carry commercial cargo when they are not required by the MoD.

MoD believes that it benefits from PPPs/PFIs by obtaining better value for money from existing budgets; from improved quality of services through opportunities for innovation and the application of the latest commercial techniques; from reduced risk to MoD by transferring risk to the private sector and through the use of appropriate incentive contracts; and by exposing its staff to private sector management, commercial and financial skills. Similarly, PFI and PPP offer benefits to private industry. There are more opportunities for business with MoD, including opportunities to use spare capacity, to share overheads and to undertake long-term investment against the security of income from a long-term contract. These market opportunities provide further support for the UK defence industrial base.

MoD's requirement in the future for any PFI project will be determined by the obligation for services linked to the need for current or future capital investment and will be associated with an asset that needs management, maintenance or replacement. Typically, PFI projects are characterised by a requirement for capital investment, a significant service element that can be expressed in a long-term contract, and the possibility of a competitive market where risks are better managed by the private

Table 1
Examples of PPP/PFI Contracts

| Project | Description | Value of contract (£m) | Duration (years) |
|---|---|---|---|
| Allenby/Connaught | Re-development of garrisons around Salisbury plain and Aldershot | 845 | 30 |
| Skynet 5 | Range of satellite services | 682 | n.a. |
| Tri-Service White Fleet | Lex defence management to supply MoD's commercial vehicles | 500 | 10 |
| Main building re-development | Re-development of MoD main building, London | 208.6 | 30 |
| Roll-on/Roll-off strategic sealift | Provision of strategic sealift services: six vessels | 950 | 25 |
| Tank transporters | Heavy equipment transporters for army | 290 | 20 |
| Armoured vehicle training Services | Provision of gunnery and specialist driving AFV training services | 102.4 | 30 |
| Tri-service airfield support services | Fire/crash cover; fuelling; movements; airfield clearance; air traffic control | 350 | 25 |
| Medium support helicopter aircrew training facility | Training for Chinook, Merlin Mk3 and Puma | 105 | 40 |
| Attack helicopter training service | Training to support apache attack helicopter | 165 | 30 |
| Defence fixed telecommunications Service | Telecommunications services consisting of six services | 70 | 10 |
| Joint service command & staff college | Construction, IT, Furnishing and support, including some academic support | 80 | 30 |
| RAF Lossiemouth Family Quarters | Re-development of 279 married quarters | 38.3 | 21 |

*Source*: MoD (2002).

sector. Ultimately, PFI is preferred if it offers better value for money than the public sector comparator (PSC). A distinctive feature of MoD's business is the requirement to provide an operational capability in peace, crisis and war and PFI/PPP projects have to meet this criterion. This increases the difficulty of writing a long-term contract dealing with all contingencies. As a result, MoD is relying more on partnership arrangements based on trust and reputation rather than using detailed contractual controls, as the earlier theoretical framework predicts. Thus, MoD states that "much of Defence PPP is about closer, long-term relationships with private sector partners which require commitment and effort on both sides in order to achieve common goals, etc. Such relationships are based on open, co-operative means of doing business with shared risks and rewards" (MoD, 2001a, p. 13). Although the language and aspirations are attractive, it has to be recognised, however, that both parties to a defence contract have different objectives and different principals. Private firms have to satisfy shareholders and, ultimately, MoD has to satisfy its political masters and voters.

The long-term nature of PFP contracts requires a clear procurement policy with provision for changes, resolving disputes, risk management, contract pricing, performance incentives and exit strategies. Typically, contracts involve at least five features and associated choices under uncertainty. First, a PSC. The key value for money test requires that the net present value of the PFI agreement, including an assessment of its risks, should be lower than the PSC. Where there is competition, MoD releases figures for the PSC as early in the process as possible: this is designed to promote competitive bidding and to save on private sector tendering costs where the PSC is likely to be below the private sector bids. Competition and rivalry is expected to lead to the best PFI option. Competition requires at least two bidders and, ideally, MoD prefers three.

Second, project funding. With PPP/PFI contracts, the contractor is only paid on successful delivery of the service. Usually, a medium risk PFI contract is expected to be funded with a ratio of debt to equity of 90:10, but the ratio could be 80:20 for higher risk contracts. There are also accounting rules that determine whether PFI projects are 'on' or 'off' balance sheet. Most PFI projects are regarded as contracts for services, which means that they do not appear on the MoD balance sheet for Resource Accounting and Budgeting requirements. By 1999 there had been two exceptions, namely a utilities contract for RAF Fylingdales power station and family quarters at RAF Lossiemouth, neither of which were accepted as off-balance sheet.

Third, in common with other types of PPP contracts, those in the defence sector involve long durations. For example, PFI contracts of up to 40 years on aircrew training simulators; up to 30 years for housing; and over 20 years for water and sewerage have been signed by MOD. Long-term contracts encourage suppliers to undertake costly investment projects, but also create a long-term monopoly and scope for 'hold-up'. The problem of specifying completely such long-term contracts means that both principal and agent have to rely more on partnership, trust and reputation. Reliance on these means of contract bonding makes it more difficult, however, to monitor and legally enforce contracts because of inherent uncertainties as to partners' future commitments.

Fourth, pricing mechanisms vary between firm price, fixed price with VOP, and target cost incentive fee contracts (TCIF) where payments are related to delivery of the contracted service at the required quality (e.g. payment per flying hour, per occupied bed, per available house). Penalties for late delivery or poor performance can take the form of liquidated damages or a service credit regime (i.e. a points system reflecting poor performance). There are also possible index payments to reflect inflation, especially for long-term contracts (VOP clauses). As part of its Smart Procurement Initiative (now Smart Acquisition) aiming to 'bear down on defence inflation,' MoD prefers appropriate output (e.g. the GDP deflator) rather than input indices (Hartley and Martin, 1999).

Fifth, there are choices about whether MoD needs to retain ownership of the asset for defence purposes or whether it retains the right to control of the asset at the end of the contract. Procedures are needed for settling disputes, step-in rights for MoD and exit strategies. Long-term contracts involve unforeseen events that require a procedure for settling disputes and/or MoD rights to intervene temporarily in the provision of the service. Alternatively, MoD may opt for early termination of the contract, which might require compensation to be paid to the supplier; but no compensation should be paid to the contractor where termination is due to contractor default. Decisions are also needed about follow-on contracts. Once a contract has expired, MoD has to consider the following in deciding the new contract—the time scale and costs involved in running a new competition and the ownership of assets and the arrangements for the transfer of assets, including intellectual property rights (e.g. management records and information needed for a new competition). Such factors could lead to a tendency to renew with the existing supplier, thus reducing the scope for competition to minimise long-term supply costs.

### 5.1. *A critique of MoD policy*

PPP is highly flexible, embracing elements of PFI, contracting out and commercial exploitation applied to MoD services, activities and physical assets. MoD views PPP as representing 'a new way of identifying cost-effective solutions to requirements, and even to take advantage of opportunities for maximising the utilisation of MoD assets, whether irreducible spare capacity or intellectual property rights' (MoD, 1999, p. 7). The emphasis of MoD is on innovation by encouraging industry to offer innovative solutions that meet the output requirements faster and at lower costs, with a sharing of risks and rewards resulting in 'win-win' solutions. These aims and the accompanying rhetoric are attractive and persuasive; but appearances can be deceptive and need to be subject to critical scrutiny—carefully distinguishing myths, emotion and special pleading from statements which can be supported with reliable empirical evidence.

MoD and its Armed Forces are vertically integrated organisations forming 'in-house' or publicly owned monopolies (e.g. typically undertaking training, repair and maintenance activities 'in-house'). Such 'hierarchies' are likely to be inefficient and are unlikely to be innovative (e.g. preferring a 'quiet life'). Opening up such public monopolies to competition from private contractors provides a check on their efficiency. However, the extent of efficiency savings depends upon the methods used to 'open-up' defence markets. Economists define efficiency to embrace two components, technical and allocative efficiency. *Technical efficiency* seeks the lowest-cost solution to providing a given level of output or service: this is the standard public procurement approach, seeking rival bids for a *MoD-specified level of output or service*. But, problems arise in determining whether the MoD-specified level of output/service is the 'best' level. The second component of efficiency addresses this issue by seeking competitions for *different levels of output or service*. Such competitions enable MoD policy makers to assess the costs and benefits of various output levels so that they can select the 'best' output (where at the margin benefits and costs are equal) in the pursuit of *allocative efficiency*. The challenge in PPP projects is to formulate contracts which allow competition to achieve both elements of efficiency, namely technical and allocative, while taking account of the impact in terms of both transaction costs and internal capabilities. Transaction costs arise in organising a competition and in writing, policing and enforcing contracts. Here, both MoD and the contractor can incur substantial legal and associated costs (Arrowsmith and Hartley, 2002).

Nor should efficiency be seen as a static concept: competition also promotes innovation that requires MoD to formulate its requirements so as to encourage rival bidders to offer innovatory solutions. For example, if the RAF introduces a competition for flying training, which specifies a minimum number of actual aircraft flying hours, it could exclude the possibility of innovatory solutions using flight simulators, which might produce trained pilots faster and at lower cost. Currently, MoD is considering a PPP solution for all UK military flying training. In principle, all military flying training could be completely privatised with private companies providing all assets, including aircraft, bases and simulators, as well as air and ground crew for flying operations. Companies would be responsible for maintenance and repair of aircraft and facilities. With such a solution, MoD would no longer own its training aircraft and bases and would pay the contractor for services either per flying hour or per trained pilot (i.e. reaching a certified level of competence). Contracts would be for, say, up to 30 years, with companies able to determine the most efficient mix of simulators and flying training as well as the best locations for training (e.g. good weather climates for initial pilot training) and the possibility of third party use and revenue from training activities. However, MoD would lose its internal capability for flying training, including its ability and freedom to re-allocate training resources to the 'front-line' in emergencies and conflict.

Some PPP/PFI contracts involve highly specific assets, such as air-crew training facilities (e.g. simulators) located on UK air force bases (asset and locational specificity). As discussed earlier, long-term contracts are required to induce firms to invest in specific assets, but these contractual features create the conditions for opportunistic behaviour (the 'hold-up' problem again). Also, MoD risks a long-term decline in internal capability to provide particular services, in effect involving a movement from right to left in Fig. 1; and thereby raising the costs of a future switch to in-house provision. Moreover, once a contract has been awarded, firms can be expected to seek to exploit their monopoly power; for example, by charging highly for extra services beyond the original contractual requirement, or by insisting upon an extension to the original contract. But, MoD, as a major buyer, can also behave opportunistically, especially at the contract renewal stage, because of the contractor's sunk costs. At this stage, however, the incumbent should have an advantage over its rivals in any new competition.

MoD claims that PPP/PFI enables it to transfer risk to the private sector using 'appropriate incentive contracts', with penalties for poor performance and late delivery. 'Appropriate contracts' are firm or fixed price or TCIF contracts. These contracts reflect choices between efficiency incentives, risk sharing (insurance) and contractor profitability. Firm or fixed price contracts for periods of up to 30 years provide maximum efficiency incentives; but the risks borne by firms over such lengthy contracts can result in 'excessive profits' or losses and possibly bankruptcy. In turn, bankruptcy might require MoD to 'bail-out' the firm leading to moral hazard in contracting. The alternative of target cost, incentive fee contracts involves risk sharing between the MoD and the contractor with both parties sharing in 'excessive' profits or losses. However, MoD still has to determine the *appropriate* sharing of profits and losses with the contractor. Moreover, in recent years, MoD has made relatively little use of such incentive contracts in procurement. For example, between 1995 and 2000, incentive fee contracts accounted for between only 1% and 5% of the total annual value of MoD contracts (MoD, 2000b). MoD can also impose penalties for poor performance and late delivery; but the imposition of penalties could destroy trust, something, as explained earlier, which is a requirement for successful long-term procurement partnerships in the face of information asymmetries. It is by no means self-evident that through PPPs trust is being successfully developed between MoD and key suppliers to any greater degree than existed previously. Moreover, while a sound reputation as a reliable supplier is important in winning PPP contracts, this was also true under more traditional forms of MoD contracting.

Nor are savings to taxpayers guaranteed. The MoD claims that PPPs/PFIs have resulted in savings, but the supporting evidence has been sparse (this is consistent with the findings for other PPP/PPI initiatives in the UK, reviewed earlier). There is much evidence on the capital value of PFI projects and a general claim that PPP contracts result in cost savings of between 5% and 40% compared with the public sector comparator (MoD, 1999, p. 7). However, no indication is given of the cost base and time period over which these savings apply. For example, is the 40% saving on a sum of £10 million or £100 million, each over 30 years; and what is the contribution of such savings to assisting the new equipment programme? Also, the savings are estimates expected over a long contract period, where events can change so that the estimated savings might not be realised; and, of course, over such time periods, governments and policies change![6] Moreover, the economic basis of any cost savings from PFI needs careful scrutiny, distinguishing genuine efficiency improvements from ideological arguments and MoD's enthusiasm for the initiative. Further lobbying pressures and support for PPP come from interest groups likely to benefit from the policy, including banks, lawyers and contractors.

If PPPs are to lead to genuine economic efficiency improvements, they have to result in lower costs over the project's life cycle for a given quantity and quality of service. Since the government can borrow at lower interest rates than the private sector, the economic advantages of PFI have to be in more efficient management during construction of the project and/or in lower operating costs. Here, there are concerns that unless contracts are tightly specified, private firms might economise on the quality of output. In defence, quality of output can determine the difference between success

[6] For an example of where political changes undermined a contracting out programme in UK local government see Kavanagh and Parker (2000).

and failure in conflict. Moreover, PFI contracts are for long periods over which events can change and, however careful the MoD is to specify the contract, industry will always seek to protect itself from income losses (e.g. by seeking cancellation payments; or renegotiating the contract; or through litigation) even where there is a supposed 'trust' and 'partnership' relation.

Further problems arise from the incentives given to Top Level Budget Holders in the Armed Forces to implement PPP/PFI policies. MoD assumes that military personnel will behave efficiently and that best practice from the private sector can be easily applied to defence. There are, though, major differences between defence and the private sector. Private markets are characterised by competition, by profit incentives and by the capital market which provides a threat of take-over and bankruptcy. Military commanders and their personnel are not subject to competition, nor do they share in any profits from efficient behaviour or experience losses from poor performance, and they cannot be made bankrupt or taken-over. Military personnel can be expected to use arguments about 'operational disadvantages' to oppose unwelcome PPPs and PFIs (e.g. those policies which will make them worse-off because of job losses and loss of 'perks'). In other words, they can be expected to act opportunistically, leading to costs associated with both moral hazard and adverse selection. They can be expected to pursue enthusiastically those PPPs that do not threaten their traditional interests and favour projects that make them 'better-off' (e.g. property and accommodation). Similarly, PPP projects that involve front-line units and equipment may be opposed for 'operational reasons' or the terms of the contract and the public sector comparator might be used to deter private sector bidders.

Challenges arise in ensuring genuine competition and contestability for PPP contracts. Costly and long period contracts might require large firms to bear the risks and industry re-structuring has led to a smaller number of large defence firms in each national market. Small numbers contracting provides opportunities for cartels and collusive tendering; and even where there is competition, a major loser could take over the winning firm. The competition issue also raises the question of whether the public sector comparison should be released to industry during the bidding process. Genuine competition and a 'level playing field' requires that all bidders submit on a 'sealed envelope' basis and that the range of bids should be published after the contract award. In some instances, competition might not be possible. Where contracts are non-competitive, MoD guarantees firms a rate of return on capital equal on average to that earned by British industry (i.e. a target rate of return of almost 22% on capital on an historic cost basis in 1999). Critics claim that defence profit rates on non-competitive contracts are too high; that non-competitive defence work is less risky; and that the arrangements do not provide contractors with sufficient efficiency incentives (Hartley, 2001; Arrowsmith and Hartley, 2002).

To date, PPP/PFI in defence has been restricted to support activities. There remains, however, the option of applying the policy to front-line units and equipment. For example, equipment might be leased from defence firms rather than purchased for ownership by the Armed Forces. Defence firms would enter into long-term contracts offering to provide a guaranteed number of operationally available front-line equipment on a daily basis (e.g. combat aircraft, tanks, warships) with the contractor assuming responsibility for maintenance and repair over the life of the contract and eventually disposal of the equipment (e.g. nuclear-powered submarines). As with all PPP projects, such a proposal would be subject to the public sector comparator test. However, risk assessment would be a major challenge when writing such contracts, with the need to allow for the use, destruction and re-supply of equipment in conflicts and wars (currently, the Armed Forces bear such risks). Defence firms would also need guaranteed contracts with cancellation provisions before they would be willing to invest private funds in developing and producing highly specialised equipment where there might be only one buyer, for asset specificity reasons. For both MoD and defence contractors, writing such contracts appears to be a challenge, although these are all problems the Ministry 'solves' whenever it buys equipment for the Armed Forces. The interesting question is whether a PPP solution would be more efficient than the current arrangements, where the Armed Forces purchase and own their equipment and assume responsibility for its operational availability, maintenance and repair throughout its life cycle (none of which is costless). There is at least one published example where PFI was rejected in favour of a conventional approach. This occurred with combat support vehicles, where an investment appraisal showed that a PFI solution would not offer better value for money than buying vehicles and using military personnel (HCDC, 2002).

## 6. Conclusions

Organisational boundaries are becoming much more fluid, involving networking, joint ventures, strategic alliances, partnership sourcing, and the like (Van Tulder, 1999). PPPs including in the UK PFIs are part of this new 'relational contracting' environment aimed at reducing costs, speeding up time to market, and promoting innovation. They involve a change in the boundary of government, blurring the distinction between public and private provision. Not surprisingly, the early entrants to PPP contracts in the UK 'tendered on the basis that the political risks were high and construction costs were likely to overrun……' (Financial Times, 2000b, p. 28).

PPP is a new policy initiative in need of economic analysis and evaluation. The paper has developed a framework for assessing PPPs drawing on transaction cost theory, supplemented by resource-based theory and an understanding of the roles of reputation and trust in contracting. The implications from this framework have been considered using a case study of the UK defence sector. The defence sector was chosen because it has been a leading user of PPP/PFI initiatives in recent years and, prima facie, involves a number of significant problems for long-term contracting given the uncertainties surrounding defence from both supply and demand perspectives.

PPPs involve agreeing long-term contracts characterised by incompleteness in their specification, asset specificity and scope for opportunism because of asymmetric information. The case study has highlighted a number of major potential transaction costs in defence procurement, arising from incomplete information, asset specificity and the resulting scope for opportunistic behaviour, which cannot be obviously offset by developing trust relationships. It has particularly illustrated the tensions between competition to reduce costs, the need for contractors to generate profits, and the building of partnerships and trust. The study has also drawn attention to motivation in the public sector. PPPs can be distorted by the incentives within the Armed Forces; it does not necessarily follow that military personnel will behave efficiently. They neither share in any profits from efficient behaviour or experience losses from poor performance. Military personnel may pursue their own utility, shunning those schemes that adversely affect their own status.

The conclusion of the analysis is that the use of PPPs will not necessarily lead to improved economic efficiency in defence procurement and that considerable care will need to be taken both in terms of negotiating PPPs, monitoring their performance, and in their renewal. The UK defence sector illustrates that PPPs involve significant transaction costs which must be set against any benefits in terms of economic efficiency incentives. This conclusion has significance going beyond the defence sector to other forms of PPPs sharing the same sort of uncertainties, both in the UK and internationally. The study suggests that the costs and benefits of PPPs must be carefully balanced against the costs and benefits of more traditional forms of public sector procurement. Future research could usefully focus on better quantification of PPP costs and benefits and identification of the circumstances in which information asymmetry problems can be overcome by developing true partnership relationships.

## References


Akerlof, G., 1970. The market for lemons: qualitative uncertainty and the market mechanism. Quarterly Journal of Economics 84, 488–500.

Arrighetti, A., Bachmann, R., Simon, D., 1997. Contract law social norms and inter-firm cooperation. Cambridge Journal of Economics 21 (2), 172–195.

Arrowsmith, S., Hartley, K., 2002. Public Procurement, Vol.2, International Library of Critical Writings in Economics 144, Edward Elgar, Cheltenham.

Ball, R., Heafey, M., King, D., 2000. Managing and concluding the PFI process for a new high school: room for improvement? Public Management 2 (2), 159–179.

Buchanan, J.M., 1972. Theory of Public Choice. University of Michigan Press, Michigan.

Casson, M., 1991. Economics of Business Culture: Game Theory Transaction Costs and Economic Performance. Clarendon Press, Oxford.

Casson, M., 1997. Information and Organization: A New Perspective on the Theory of the Firm. Clarendon Press, Oxford.

Casson, M., 1998. Institutional economics and business history: a way forward? In: Casson, M., Rose, M.B. (Eds.), Institutions and the Evolution of Modern Business. Frank Cass, London, pp. 12.

Cowen, T., Parker, D., 1997. Markets in the Firm: A Market-Process Approach to Management, Hobart Paper No. 134. Institute of Economic Affairs, London.

Deakin, S., Wilkinson, F., 1998. Contract law and the economics of interorganisational trust. In: Lane, C., Bachmann, R. (Eds.), Trust Within and Between Organisations: Conceptual Issues and Applications. Oxford University Press, Oxford.

Dietrich, M., 1994. Transaction Cost Economics and Beyond: Towards a New Economics of the Firm. Routledge, London.

Dollinger, M.J., Golden, P.A., Saxton, T., 1997. The effect of reputation on the decision to joint venture. Strategic Management Journal 18 (2).

Ebers, M. (Ed.), 1997. The Formation of Inter-organizational Networks. Oxford University Press, Oxford.

Financial Times, 1999. PFI deal may prove more costly than public financing, 19 May, p. 13.

Financial Times, 2000a. Ditching PFI would not have broken the rules, 13 March, p. 2.

Financial Times, 2000b. Contractors suffer as City thinks it's PFI in the sky, 6 April, p. 28.

Financial Times, 2002, What Whitehall has learnt from Enron, 22 July, p. 2.

Gaffney, D., Pollock, A.M., 1999. Pump-priming the PFI: why are privately financed hospital schemes being subsidized. Public Money & Management 19 (1), 55–62.

Glaister, S., 1999. Past abuses and future uses of private finance and public private partnerships in transport. Public Money & Management 19 (3), 29–36.

Grabher, G. (Ed.), 1993. The Embedded Firm: On the Socio-Economics of Industrial Networks. Routledge, London.

Grossman, S., Hart, O., 1986. The costs and benefits of ownership: a theory of vertical and lateral integration. Journal of Political Economy 94, 601–719.

Gulati, R., 1998. Alliances and networks. Strategic Management Journal 19, 293–317.

Hart, O., Moore, J., 1988. Incomplete contracting and renegotiation. Economica 56, 755–785.

Hart, O., Tirole, J., 1990. Vertical integration and market foreclosure. Brookings Papers: Microeconomics, 205–286.

Hartley, K., 2001. The UK submarine industrial base: an economic perspective. In: Edmonds, M. (Ed.), One Hundred Years of the

Trade: Royal Navy Submarines: Past, Present and the Future. CDISS, University of Lancaster, Lancaster.

Hartley, K., Martin, S., 1999. Study into Problems Related to Inflation and VOP Clauses in Ministry of Defence Procurement Contracts, Research Monograph Series 12. Centre for Defence Economics, University of York.

HCDC, 2002. Defence: Fourth Report, House of Commons Defence Committee. The Stationery Office, London, July.

Heald, D., Geaughan, N., 1997. Accounting for the private finance initiative. Public Money & Management 17 (3), 11–16.

HM Treasury, 1998a. Step by Step Guide to the PFI Procurement Process. HM Treasury, London.

HM Treasury, 1998b. Partnerships for Prosperity: The Private Finance Initiative. HM Treasury, London.

IFC/World Bank, 1996. Financing Private Infrastructure. International Finance Corporation, World Bank, Washington, DC.

Jackson, P.M., Stainsby, L., 2000. Managing public sector networked organizations. Public Money & Management 20 (1), 11–16.

Kavanagh, I., Parker, D., 2000. Managing the contract: a transaction cost analysis of externalisation. Local Government Studies 26 (4), 1–22.

Klein, B. (Ed.), 1997. Reputation: Studies in the Voluntary Elicitation of Good Conduct. Michigan University Press, Michigan.

Klijn, E-H., Koppenjan, J.F.M., 2000. Public management and public networks: foundations of a network approach to governance. Public Management 2 (2), 135–158.

Kramer, R.M., Tyler, T.R. (Eds.), 1996. Trust in Organisations. London: Sage.

Lane, C., 1997. The social regulation of inter-firm relations in britain and germany: market rules, legal norms and technical standards. Cambridge Journal of Economics 21 (2), 197–215.

Lane, C., Bachmann, R. (Eds.), 1998. Trust Within and Between Organisations: Conceptual Issues and Applications. Oxford University Press, Oxford.

Luhmann, N., 1979. Trust and Power. Wiley, Chichester.

Maher, M., 1997. Transaction cost economics and contractural relations. Cambridge Journal of Economics. 21 (2), 147–170.

MoD, 1999. Investment Strategy, Ministry of Defence. The Stationery Office, London.

MoD, 2000a. PFI Guidelines, www.mod.uk/index, para 1.14. Ministry of Defence, London.

MoD, 2000b. UK Defence Statistics, DASA. Stationery Office, London.

MoD, 2001a. Defence Acquisition, Policy Papers, No. 4. Ministry of Defence, London.

MoD, 2001b. Strategic Sealift, www.mod.uk/business/ro-ro.htm.

MoD, 2002. Ministry of Defence: PFI Projects, MoD web page, 11/6/02.

NAO [National Audit Office], 1997a. The PFI Contracts for Bridgend and Fazakerley Prisons, HC 253, Session 1997–98, London.

NAO, 1997b. The Skye Bridge. London: HMSO.

Parker, D., Hartley, K., 1997. The economics of partnership sourcing versus adversarial competition: a critique. European Journal of Purchasing and Supply Management 3 (2), 115–125 (reprinted in Arrowsmith, S., Hartley, K. (Eds.), 2000. Public Procurement. Edward Elgar, Aldershot).

Parker, D., Vaidya, K., 2000. An economic perspective on innovation networks. In: Conway, S., Jones, O. (Eds.), Social Interaction and Organisational Change. Imperial College Press, London.

Pitelis, C. (Ed.), 1993. Transaction Costs, Markets and Hierarchies. Blackwell, Oxford.

Powell, W.W., 1990. Neither market nor hierarchy: network forms of organisation. Research in Organizational Behaviour 12, 295–336.

Privatisation International, 2000. Building the infrastructure of a new world, June, pp. 4–5.

Roger, N., 1999. Recent trends in private participation in infrastructure, Private Sector, World Bank, December, pp. 5–8.

Terry, F., 1996. The private finance initiative—overdue reform or policy breakthrough? Public Money & Management 16 (1), 9–16.

The Business, 6/7 October 2002: Labour at pains over PFI.

Tullock, G., 1965. The Politics of Bureaucracy. Public Affairs Press, Washington DC.

van Tulder, R. (Ed.), 1999. Redrawing Organizational Boundaries. Sviib/Department of Public Management, Rotterdam School of Management, Erasmus University, Rotterdam.

Walker, G., Weber, D., 1984. A transaction cost approach to make or buy decisions. Administrative Science Quarterly 29, 373–391.

Williamson, O.E., 1975. Markets and HierarchiesAnalysis and Antitrust Implications: A Study in the Economics of Internal Organization. Free Press, New York.

Williamson, O.E., 1983. Markets and Hierarchies: Analysis and Antitrust Implications. Free Press/Collier Macmillan, London.

Williamson, O.E., 1985. The Economic Institutions of Capitalism. Free Press, Cambridge, New York.

Williamson, O.E., 1993a. Transaction cost economics and organization theory. Journal of Industrial and Corporate Change 2, 107–156.

Williamson, O.E., 1993b. Calculativeness, trust and economic organisation. Journal of Law and Economics 36, 453–486.

Williamson, O.E., Winters, S.G. (Eds.), 1993. The Nature of the Firm: Origins, Evolution and Development. Oxford University Press, Oxford.

# Part IV
# The UK Experience

# [19]

*Engineering, Construction and Architectural Management* 1997 4 | **3,** 163–177

# The Private Finance Initiative

G. OWEN & A. MERNA
*Oriel Group Practice, c/o Mrs J Carey, Department of Civil Engineering, UMIST, PO Box 88, Manchester M60 1QD, UK*

**Abstract** This paper outlines the concept of the Private Finance Initiative. It covers some of the basic PFI mechanisms and provides the reader with a general understanding of PFI and the purpose it serves. The paper will look at how the policy has been received specifically within the construction industry and the problems highlighted to date.

**Keywords** *bidding projects, bodies of influence, financial structures, health care, prisons*

## INTRODUCTION

The Private Finance Initiative (PFI) was introduced in November 1992 by the Chancellor of the Exchequer, Normal Lamont. It came against the backdrop of a major programme of privatisation during the 1980s under the leadership of the Prime Minister, Margaret Thatcher. Over this period many state owned and operated organisations were sold off to the public sector, in many cases floated on the Stock Exchange, such as British Telecom and British Gas. This was in the drive to 'free up' the economy, allowing market forces to dictate and reduce public sector inefficiencies and overspending.

## CONCEPTUAL STANDPOINT

The selection of a procurement strategy was driven originally by the need to acquire an asset; the emphasis of PFI is not acquisition of an asset but to procure a service (Private Finance Panel 1995). The route to achieve this is infinitely variable but the concept is broadly unchanged. The private sector will provide funding for the capital projects and operate a facility to provide a public service. Revenue will be achieved from this, either directly from the user or through a payment mechanism negotiated with the public sector.

Historically government has only procured assets in order to supply a service from them. Current political thinking places greater emphasis on the service rather than the asset.

'The only reason why governments ... occupy buildings ... is to help them deliver services or achieve policy objectives.' (RICS 1996)
'What counts is the quality of the service provided from those buildings.' (Jack 1996)

Having a private provider of a capital asset can enable public bodies to purchase services without the need for the initial capital investment. Therefore the PFI seeks to obtain the service and how this is achieved is dictated by the ingenuity of the private sector.

## THE PRIVATE FINANCE INITIATIVE

### What is PFI?

The Private Finance Initiative was a policy born out of a series of privately financed projects beginning with the Channel Tunnel project in 1987 (ICE 1996). Other transport orientated projects followed swiftly: Second Severn Crossing, Dartford Bridge, Skye Bridge, Manchester Metrolink and London City Airport.

PFI is an alternative method of procuring services for the public sector. Historically the public sector has procured capital assets from which they base their service. The selection of a strategy was driven originally by the need to acquire an asset (Private Finance Panel 1996a). The emphasis of the PFI is not acquisition of an asset but procurement of a service (Private Finance Panel 1995). The private sector will provide the funding for the capital projects and operate a facility for the public benefit. They will receive revenue from operating this service and hence make a profit. Having a private provider of a capital asset can enable public bodies to purchase services without the need for the initial capital investment.

### PFI – Why?

The underlying principle behind the introduction of the private sector has many dimensions. The obvious one is in the pure PFI case where a facility and service is provided at minimal cost to the public sector. An example of this is the Second Severn Bridge, held up as the perfect PFI project (Smith 1996). Secondly, it is the public sector's exploitation of the private sector's ability to design and manage more effciently (Private Finance Panel 1995). The public sector is characterized by substantial cost overruns and poor management skills; utilizing PFI and passing over control may eliminate these inefficiencies. Many public sector projects have been unsuccessful in the integration of design, build and operation of assets which are used to deliver public services.

The role of PFI has been debated. Is it a substitute for government spending, or a complement? This will be looked at in a later section. Whatever its role, capital expenditure reductions need to be made up by PFI schemes, but spending cuts announced in November 1996 of £2.6bn were compensated for by £2.1bn in PFI provision (Jones 1996). Warnings were made by the construction industry that the government must not become 'over dependent' on the PFI. There is a pan-European downward pressure on public capital budgets. This has forced governments to rethink their procurement strategies, with PFI type schemes becoming more popular throughout Europe.

A privately financed public sector is not a new concept, with French canals and bridges privately financed in the seventeenth century and the railways in the UK in the nineteenth century. Currently other projects throughout Europe have included toll roads in France and Spain, and power stations in Italy, Spain and Portugal. There is particular emphasis on reducing public expenditure with regard to satisfying the criteria for monetary union under the Maastrict agreement. However, it must be noted that the targets set under Maastrict are subject to the European Union's standard measures. Therefore reducing the Public Sector Borrowing Requirement (PSBR) will only go towards meeting this target if the PFI project ' adds value'. The pressure on public finance is not restricted to Europe. There is growing interest in the use of private finance all over the world, especially in the emerging economies in Asia.

## PFI – How?

There are different types of projects that qualify within PFI. With the emphasis on 'deals not rules', the Treasury has described three strategies:

### *Financially free standing projects*

In these circumstances the project is entirely financed and managed by the private sector. The project is financed by the payment by the end users. This type of project does not require a value-for-money (VFM) test and requires government approval. Examples are the Second Severn Crossing and the Skye bridge. It is envisaged that some road schemes will fall into this category in the future.

### *Joint ventures*

A public and private sector partnership where the private sector retains control. The public sector is involved as it perceives some public benefit that cannot be accounted for in strict monetary ways, such as the reduction of traffic congestion in certain areas. This type of project does require a VFM and will conform to these criteria:

- Private sector partner chosen in competition
- JV control held by private sector
- A clear definition of the government contribution and its limitations
- Clear agreement of risk and reward allocation, defined and agreed in advance, ensuring that the private sector returns are genuinely running some risk

Government contributions can take various forms and include equity, concession loans and asset transfer. However, equity stakes are not controlling.

Typically governments contribute through aiding initial planning or grant subsidy. Local authorities can also contribute and this is aided by the relaxation of the capital receipt regulations placed on them.

*Services sold*

This can take various forms but examples include a private firm supplying an NHS Trust with kidney dialysis services, clinical waste incinerator or a hospital information support system. Prison provision is a particularly good example of this with consortia providing accommodation and prisdoners' services for Her Majesty's Prison Service (HMPS). There is an element of 'leaseback' in some projects but to avoid this showing on public bodies' spending allocation it is necessary to include a service incorporated with the facility lease, i.e. HMPS does not lease the prison accommodation, rather it pays for a complete service provided to the inmates. This is an extremely important distinction.

## MAIN BODIES OF INFLUENCE

### Private Finance Panel

The Private Finance Panel (PFP) was an independent body set up by the Treasury. It was convened in 1993, a year after Norman Lamont announced the Private Finance Initiative (PFI). Its initial chairman, Sir Alastair Morton, was charged with the responsibility of initiating projects whereby private finance could be introduced for the provision of public services. The chairman headed the panel of eight unpaid nonexecutives who shared the common ground of interest and commitment to making PFI work. The panel was advised by 24 executive members (from January 1996); these acted as the problem solvers and prompters of action. These executives were from the private and public sector and were appointed by the Chancellor. The executive panel should have been the focus for the participants in PFI to discuss problems and seek advice and solutions.

The PFP offered an advisory and guidance facility for those involved or wanting to become involved in PFI schemes. The PFP was originally used as an intermediary to move the policy forward and try to unblock the failure of communication coupled with failures in attitude.

The PFP acted as a broker on two fronts: addressing private sector concerns that it is not getting the response it wants, and the public sector if it does not understand how to apply PFI to its particular set of circumstances. The PFP attempted to overcome problems and misconceptions with PFI. The PFP hoped to avoid increased costs, delays and the provision of suboptimal service, all of which will damage the credibility of PFI.

The role of the PFP was constantly evolving and in April 1996 new roles were defined in the attempt to smooth the procurement process (Private Finance Panel 1996b). These were:

- To act as a central repository of information about people offering advisory roles in PFI
- To produce case studies of previous PFI projects to improve the learning curve and prevent similar mistakes from being repeated
- To provide a training course at the Civil Service college in association with Price Waterhouse, allowing for specific training of civil servants and enrolment of the private sector

## Criticisms of the PFP

There was a lack of confidence in the PFP, originating from both financiers and clients. They believe that the PFP is not an effective vehicle for driving the PFI forward, although there is a great need for such a drive, in order to capitalize on and pursue the tentative interests of leading industrial and commercial groups.

Lovell *et al.* (1996) criticized the efforts of the PFP in trying to streamline and speed up the PFI. They indicated that the guidance documents produced by the PFP were too basic and did not cover the issues in sufficient detail, with specific reference to the attempts to develop a standard form of contract. The PFP was eventually disbanded early in the administration of the Labour government.

## Public Private Partnership Programme Ltd (4Ps)

The 4Ps was set up in April 1996 enjoying all party support, with an initial edstimated life of 3 years. Essentially the 4Ps is modelled on the Private Finance Panel Executive (PFPE) and Private Finance Units (PFU) in government departments, but with specific emphasis to aiding local authorities. It came into effect on the back of local authorities continually faced with increased constraints on infrastructure provision, with the aim of helping by encouraging '... greater investment in local services through partnerships between the public and private sectors (Private Finance Panel 1997a).

Its stated objectives are outlined below:

- Lobby government to improve the process of implementing PFI when regulation proves restrictive
- Assist the Audit Commission in providing clear guidance on PFI and partnership schemes to district auditors
- Assist in delivering Pathfinder projects in housing, education, transport
- Compile a database of proposed and recently completed projects for future reference, thus preventing continual reinvention of the wheel

Both the 4Ps and the PFP have opened databases which allow public and private sector organisations to register their details. This facilitates interested parties to interrogate the information and gain information including project prograss and company experience.

## IMPACTS OF THE PRIVATE FINANCE INITIATIVE

### Teething problems–risk

Risk allocation has been a major source of problems for the early PFI projects. Risk can be allocated in two ways: payment mechanism and specific contract terms. As the public sector has no need to own the facilities it uses it has to become the specifier of services, which is a great change from the past. Many private operators have felt that they have been expected to shoulder too much risk. This prompted a publication by the Private Finance Panel, *Risk and Reward in PFI contracts.* Some further problems are identified and discussed below;

### Inequitable allocation of risk

Some concessionaires are concerned that risk transfer from public sector to private sector is too great. Some consortia feel that local authorities do not properly understand the spirit of PFI and try to transfer all the risks to the private sector in order to fulfil their 'off balance sheet' accounting objectives. In some cases consortia have felt they have to run risks that are beyond their control, i.e. legislative risks which may be influenced by the public partner. However, the counter argument to this is, what kind of protection do wholly private sector companies receive in the normal business environment? In most cases this is a common business risk borne by most of industry. The question arises as to whether the PFI special project vehicles (SPVs) should lay claim to protection from this aspect of risk.

### Inflexibility

With PFI sanctioned projects there appear to be little scope to deal with work redefinition. There does not appear to be provision for this within the contract, hence greater risk run by consortia. This is different to other foreign countries, particularly in France where public/private works contracts have clauses which allow for rescoping the work. Built-in mechanisms allow for the contractor/operator to be fairly compensated for this change.

### Legality of underwriting?

Even when local authorities are willing to shoulder greater risk through underwriting projects, it appears that recent judgements could prevent this occurring. *Credit Suisse. Borough Council of Allerdale* 1996 4 All ER 129 and Waltham Forest London Borough Council 1996 4 All ER 176 saw the Court of Appeal rule that the local authority in question was not legally able to provide such a guarantee on the project. The piece of legislation in question is section 111 of the Local Government Act 1972. In its interpretation the Appeal Court decided that the local authority had acted outside its statutory function and therefore was not obliged to honour any guarantees it had made to the banks.

This has implications on other areas of PFI where government bodies may not have the power to form their own development companies. To finance the development the company would have to guarantee any loans it sought to acquire. Assurances were sought by potential consortia regarding the impact of a Trust becoming insolvent and the implications on the service contract between the two parties.

## BIDDING PROJECTS

If a PFI project requires some investment from the public sector, i.e. it is a private/ public partnership, then the project has to satisfy a value-for-money test (VFM). The VFM has three possible outcomes:

1 Decides whether the project proceed at all
2 If it proceeds, PFI or traditional?
3 Which PFI supplier chosen to provide service?

A secondary application for the VFM test is to achieve the proposed benefits of PFI. In addition to this some sources of improved VFM are:

- Ensure fitness for purpose, i.e. avoid overdesign
- Integration of operational needs to achieve optimum efficiency
- Increasing efficiency of construction and operation by allocating expertise
- Using new technology or more effective business processes
- Identification of potential economies of scale, using the asset to service a third party client, i.e. extend customer base
- Design the asset to maximize residual vfalue or allow for a change of use at end of concession period

This VFM process impacts on the procurement process and the time taken to begin the construction phase. Hence common stated problems with PFI procurement are the time and costs of tendering, the resources, the number and types of organisations involved, and the VFM process itself. Many bidding organizations complain that in addition to the time problemthere is a significant cost element involved. This is due to the way the competition is administered with the awarding body allowing perhaps four consortia to bid, then selecting two for the final stage. This involves a great deal of expense on behalf of the bidders, with one ultimately losing. Many organisations are for the first time tendering PFI projects which often involve not only the design and construction but also the operating phases, with each phase requring a high level of familiarity.

However, under current rules this is how the competition must be run. These problems have been quoted as the reason behind several high profile withdrawals, with Bovis deciding against any further DBFO road bids and Laing pulling out of several hospital projects, and some preferred bidders being selected by defaults as the competition withdrew. Critics argue that this signals the demise of the PFI and that the industry is turning its back on the initiative. This would appear not to be the case, as consortia are pulling out to bid alternative PFI schemes rather than abandoning the idea altogether. Many companies found themselves bidding in unfamiliar business environments and decided to concentrate on their specialist activities rather than diversifying into completely new areas. This makes a great deal of sense when considering the cost and resources needed to submit a good bid. The Pathfinder prison report (Private Finance Panel 1996) states that the total time from advertising in the Official Journal of the European Community (OJEC) to closure was 25 months, with 17 months from the invitation to tender (ITT) to commencement. The aim is to reduce the time from ITT to contract award to 9 months.

Industry commentators warn that the variety and number of PFI schemes in the pipeline could be so great that there is an implication that competition could be eroded, with projects chasing consortia. This has the potential to allow the private sector to dictate terms that it would bid for, hence allowing the private sector to pick and choose profitable projects. There is evidence that the market is becoming increasingly selective (cherry picking) and only bidding for good projects. This may be good news for the taxpayer as ill conceived schemes or those that are not financially viable should be weeded out by market selection. In this case service provision would be made on the basis of economic viability rather than need. This problem could be diminished if there was an influx of overseas private operators into the PFI market. At present this threat of increased competition has not materialised but would surely benefit the public sector. Such companies are experienced in operations and have a track record in service provision, thus may stimulate greater competition.

### Contractors' reaction

It is basically assumed that contractors will be the main bodies behind PFI consortia, but there is a problem of whether they are the best people to operate a facility once it has been built. Generally, large contracting organisations have the operational and maintenance expertise to run a PFI facility. The motives for entry into the PFI have to be looked at. Some would argue that in a time of limited conventional project opportunities, contractors are merely chasing work, but with conventional margins running at 0–3% PFI offers a good opportunity to diversify their work and realise greater margins.

A major failing with UK contractors is there inability to contribute equity into the finance package; however, equity maybe in the form of 'in kind' or cash injection and may be transferable during the contracts. This could change with the acquisition of large UK contractors by financially strong overseas counterparts. At present UK contractors' balance sheets are not as helathy as, say, their French counterparts. This restricts their involvement in PFI schemes as they have less capital to invest. However, with the influx of foreign investment in the form of large stock acquisitions of major UK construction companies (e.g. Malaysia's

Intria Berhad into Costain and Kvaerner into Trafalgar House and Bouygues into Tarmac), it seems that Middle Eastern and Asian firms are waiting to tap into the UK's civil engineering expertise.

The contractor involvement in PFI is somewhat dependent on the type of project in question. It is generally accepted that financially free-standing static infrastructure projects such as toll bridges and tunnels are ideally undertaken by contractor-led consortia, as this does not represent a shift away from their traditional work, with the exception of managing the revenue stream. But when considering nopnclinical health care provision, it can be argued that a contractor is not the best person to manage that service.

The Construdtion Research and Innovation Strategy Panel (CRISP) is concerned with the impact of PFI on the construction industry. Confusion and ignorance are cited as early reactions to this procurement strategy. PFI is described as the biggest challenge to the construction industry and CRISP predict 20% of all new building being PFI procured prior to 2000.

This poses an obvious threat to UK contractors as limited experience and knowledge will not improve chances of gaining work, although many contractors are perfectly happy with BOOT (Build Own Operate Transfer) strategies which share some common ground with PFI. Unless these problems are modified, the industry may expect competitors from the US and Europe to enter the market. This has not yet happened to any signifiant degree, giving UK industry the opportunity to expend into this market.

Obvious opportunities to the industry are the healthier margins achieved in PFI than in more traditional strategies. Looking at 1995 figures CRISP (1996) industry performance, with a profit of £7m achieved from a turnover of £4.5bn (from the top 10 companies).

## CONSULTANTS' REACTION

Some consultants are particularly worried about the growth of PFI funding as it is a radical departure from traditional public works procurement. In some public contracts little incentive to ensure cost and schedule overruns has been considered. The potential is that if the bidding consortia are led by the large contracting organisations, then they will possibly already encompass a good design capability. This could signal a reduced requirement for consultancy services. Consultancies can counter this by joining the consortia themselves, but this would require capital which many cannot provide. Consultants could, however, invest their time, charging at their marginal rate, and recoup an equity return downstream. This would require acceptance of design and performance risk. Increasingly consultants are modifying their services, with a plethora of PFI technical advisors now appearing. They join the ranks of the public bodies' advisory team, incorporating financial, legal and technical disciplines. Although consultants appear to be able to command premium fees for this advisory work, there are two major disadvantages:

- Many public clients demand bidding in the form of fees incorporating a success element. This is troublesome as many hours of work are undertaken, in some cases for little or no payment. Consultants are running this risk, particularly on hospital projects, as the success element would be considerable, but to date elusive.
- The advisory team is relatively small in comparison to a design team and possibly retained for a shorter period.

The advantage of acting in an advisory role is that there is scope to secure downstream design business. Hence gaining entry into the client's team at the point of facility/service definition is extremely important. It is important that there is no conflict of interest between the consultant and the public sector. Consultants face a similar problem of inexperience as contractors, which hampers their chances of gaining advisory positions. With many projects stalled or cancelled it is difficult for public clients to separate good from bad, making them suspicious of anyone offering 'advisory' capabilities.

The nature of PFI changes the way consultants respond to clients. Instead of a design to meet a technical specification they have to react to an output or service specification. To many firms this is unfamiliar territory and one which requires a careful approach. It is simpler to work with input terms than output terms. Clients are asking whether design consultants have the strength and depth of skill base to cope with this change in demand.

### VFM paradox?

A paradox that may occur in PFI projects is that in trying to achieve VFM through the transference of risks to consortia, the actual VFM may deteriorate. This is of particular concern as one of the cornerstones behind PFI is achieving value for money. It is an important fact to bear in mind that the private sector borrows at 6–9 points above gilt rates , hence the private sector must more than make up for this in efficiency gains if VFM and profitability are to be achieved. It is because of the high cost of financing that some critics argue that PFI is fundamentally flawed. Chris Waites (1996) proposes an interesting analysis, illustrated in Fig. 1.

This diagram shows that as the risk transfer increases, the greater level of risk is borne by the consortium. This means that a greater amount of equity is required as banks would be less willing to finance such deals. Hence greater equity means greater financing costs, as demonstrated by the curve. As the project will be in the long run paid for by the tax payers, there is an argument that VFM may not be achieved and the public sector will pick up the burden. The relationship between VFM and risk transfer is shown in Fig. 2, from the same source. In large risk transfer projects the private sector will not be reluctant to bid the project as was the case in early PFI projects,. but will price the risk. This means that project costs grow and possibly violate the VFM criteria, hence it is vitally important that risk transfer is not excessive.

In addition to this paradox there are inefficiencies which must be addressed.

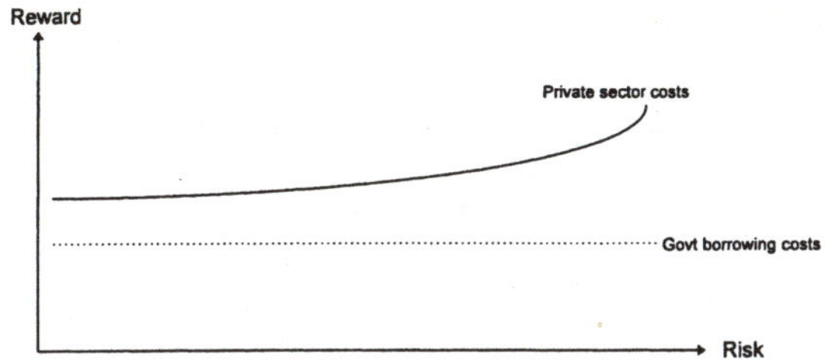


**Figure 1** Cost of borrowing and risk.

These include the cost of compulsory evaluation of projects to see if PFI suitability could be established, and the cost of assessing if they do meet the VFM criteria. These costs are due in part to the team of PFI advisers, consisting of technical, financial and legal experts. In addition to this there is the large cost to industry of bidding PFI projects, especially when the scheme is cancelled late on.

## Facilities provided – sectors

The PFP have identified many sectors of the public sector which they believe are suitable for PFI. The Treasury categorises them:

- Defence
- Agriculture
- Education and employment
- Environment
- Legal departments
- Health
- Scotland
- Northern Ireland
- ODA
- Trace and industry
- Transport
- Home Office
- National heritage
- Social security
- Wales
- Chancellor's departments

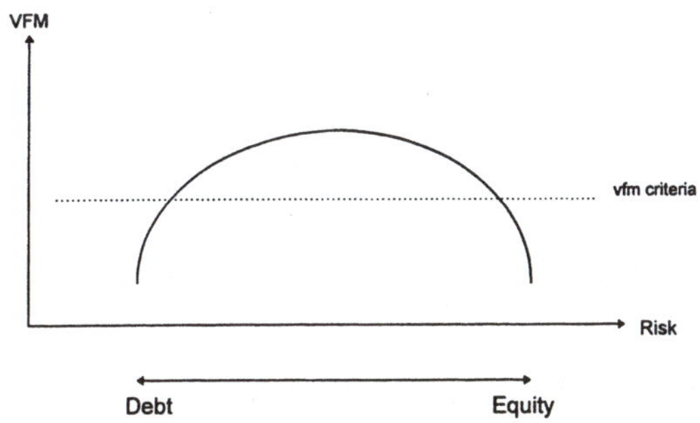


**Figure 2** VFM and risk.

### Healthcare

There has been massive interest in the provision of services for the health sector, which has attracted much negative publicity (Tolford 1996) and the conspincuous absence of signed deals. According to the Private Finance Panel (1997b) there have been 47 signed contracts for PFI service provision for the Department of Health. These range from clinical waste incineration to information systems or office asccommodation. Those looking for new hospital provision will be disappointed; only two deals have been signed – Norwich and Norfolk and Dartford and Gravesend – being valued at £ñ70m and £115m, respectively. Both are subject to financing, indicating that the banks are less than confident about the projects.

The figures quoted in the Autumn 1996 ediction of *Private Finance Quarterly* outline some £2600m of proposed health service expenditure. This demonstrates the level of interest by Trusts to see new PFI hospitals, but the process appears to fall down at the financing stage. KPMG (1997) suggest that a detailed contractual framework which was drawn up prior to inviting bids improved the process. Former chair of the Private Finance Panel, Douglas Hogg, suggested that possible early involvement in the project by financiers could ease the process (Hogg 1997). Although this may possibly restrict competition, it would define 'minimum requirements', hence preventing the progression of unfinancable projects.

A sticking point with high value PFI hospitals is that Trusts do not appear to be realistic in their requirements. Consortia responding to output specification spend large sums of money preparing bids which ultimately are not affordable. This problem arises because of the intensive level of borrowing required by the consortium at the early stages of a project, and subsequent debt servicing. These costs are passed on to the Trust who find them too high. To rectify this problem there is a mechanism proposed for the Swindon and Marlborough Trust. This will allow for the transfer of money from the NHS capital budget to the PFI project, helping to overcome the initial high costs, and it will be repaid at the end of the concession period at an interest rate of 6%.

### Prisons

The prison sector has been the beneficiary of modest PFI success, with two privately financed prisons currently under construction and several others in the pipeline. Design Construct Manage and Finance (DCMF) prisons were a progression from privately operated facilities which existed in three prisons across the UK, including HMP Doncaster and Wolds Remand Prison. These prisons are still operating successfully showing 'significant cost benefits' over comparisons with existing public sector best performers. Alongside this was the contracting out of prisoner escort services, provided by Group 4. This initiative was to eliminate inefficiencies apparent in current facilities. The natural course of action follows that, when expanding the prison number capacity through building more prisons, the potential private sector operators should input into the design, construction and finance of the asset. The existing links within HMPS and experience with private operators meant that it was well suited to PFI treatment. There was an existing culture within HMPS to work alongside private organisations.

In addition to 'contractors turned operators' bidding the project, there was the arrival of the US operator Wackenhut Correction Facilities, who joined the bid as consortium members. This existing track record and the existing privately operated prisons in the UK meant there was already in place a valuable benchmark on which to evaluate the bids. The success of the Pathfinder projects was aided by the government's desire to see PFI realised, and the help they provided reflected this. In the Fazakerley and Bridgend prisons the government acted as insurers as a last resort if the operators could not obtain commercial insurance. The follow-up projects, particularly in Lowdham Grange, have hit problems due to the government's refusal to repeat this. This potentially terminates the concession agreement with Premier prisons unless their record in Doncaster can reassure the insurers as to their record on riot and disturbances. It was felt by HMPS that the success of Fazakerley and Bridgend meant they could transfer greater risks in forthcoming projects. They felt that commercial insurance would give operators the incentive to maintain an exemplary record when it came to discipline, as no-claims bonuses could be earned.

## STRUCTURE OF PROJECT FINANCE

### Banks or bonds?

Over the last few years banks have become more accustomed to lend on a 'non-recourse' basis. This means that the loan is secured purely on the revenues generated by a facility. Conversely this is faced with a move by developers away from syndicated loan sources, as they try to achieve a more broad portfolio of funding solutions. It is hoped that because of the globally low interest rates, investors will achieve higher returns on bond issues. These issues are becoming more popular, with two examples highlighted: Docklands Light Railway link to Lewisham and the Road Management Group (RMG). The RMG issue was used to fund the Amec and Alfred McAlpine led consortium to undertake the DBFO A1(M) and A419/A417 road projects. This was undertaken using a 25 year bond issue. Under the circumstances it was felt that due to the low levels of risk borne by the consortium it would be straightforward to market the bonds. The Lewisham scheme was managed by BZW and the issue was based upon the well-received issue by RMG. This issue was for 24 years. Each of these schemes has raised £165m from issuing bonds. The *Financial Times* reports (1996) that there is the emergence of dedicated holding companies whose specialisation is the private financing of previous public projects. These companies can then be floated on the stock exchange. Examples of these are Consolidated Electric

Power Asia (CEPA), Southern Company, and Central South West Corporation (CSW) from the USA.

The use of bonds has an upside and a downside. With banks reluctant to back a loan period longer than 10 years, it suits infrastructure projects particularly well. It also gives the investors the flexibility to buy and sell publicly listed bonds as and when they desire. Bond financing proves attractive to certain types of institutional investors; pension fund managers sometimes look toward investments that match their long term liabilities, with bonds maturing after 30 years.

With bond financing there is a problem for the consortium on the level of funding to seek, and the inflexibility thereafter. The problem arises when a cost overrun occurs, and how these extra costs are met. Also the consortium does not require all the finance upfront, which is a disadvantage of a bond issue. Coupled with this is the problem that projects which come in under budget are liable to pay dividends on unused capital. Unpredictable markets can slam shut an opportunity to raise finance purely on the basis of a change in attitude, totally unrelated to the project' viability. For these reasons it is advocated that bond financing should be complementary rather than as a replacement.

## CONCLUSIONS

It is clear that a privately financed public sector is here to stay. With the general principals enjoying all party support, it is necessary for the construction, and related, industries to adapt. However, it would appear that the most successful projects to date have been of the financially free-standing variety. This questions whether the lack of PFI development in certain sectors is due to industrial inertia or a failure at government level. Certainly it would appear that there is widespread frustration at the lack of progress and the below target number of projects financially closed. Perhaps there has not been enough time for dedicated service providers to develop and establish their skills, with an over-reluctance by construction orientated organisations to progress the initiative. At governmental level, gains could possibly be achieved through a more prescriptive approach, especially with regard to local authority PFI development. Local authorities in particular have a generally ambivalent attitude towards the initiative, with many ignorant about the whole concept. Those wanting to tap into the benefits are finding that they do not have the knowledge and experience to develop their plans alone, hence advisory teams abound. Some councils are deeply suspicious of PFI and are not in-line conceptually with such issues as asset transfer.

Industry spectators are asking whether the construction depression is the only reason why current PFI operators are in the market. It has been suggested that once the construction industry becomes stronger companies will turn their back on costly PFI bidding to return to their traditional work. The answer to this will only be revealed in time. Whatever the cause of the current lack of progress, greater effort needs to be made on both sides if the true benefit of private finance is to be achieved.

The recently elected government has backed the concept of private finance and released a twelve point plan to shake up the PFI; this plan is not essentially radical.

## References

CRISP (1996) *Risk and Reward: Construction and the Private Finance Initiative.* Report of the CRISP PFI Focus Group including Technology Foresight.
Hogg, D. (1997) *Building*, 7 February.
ICE (1996) PFI. *Ice briefing*, May. ICE website.
Jack, M. (1996) Editorial. *Private Finance Quarterly*, autumn.
KPMG (1997) PFI. *New Civil Engineer*, 13 February.
Lovell, White, & Durrant (1996) PFI. *Building*, 29 November.
Private Finance Panel (1995) *Private Opportunity, Public Benefit.* HMSO, London.
Private Finance Panel (1996a) *Risk and Reward in PFI.* HMSO, London.
Private Finance Panel (1996b) *Guidelines for Smoothing the Procurement Process.* HMSO, London.
Private Finance Panel (1997a) *Objectives.* Private Finance Panel website, 11 February.
Private Finance Panel (1997b) *Bi-monthly report*, Jan/Feb. HMSO, London.
Private Finance Panel (1996) *Report on DCMF Fazarkerley and Bridgend Prisons.* HMSO, London.
RICS (1996) *The Private Finance Initiative (the essential guide).* The Royal Institute of Chartered Surveyors, London.
Tolford, N. (1996) The symptoms of slow progress. *Private Finance Quarterly*, autumn.
Tolford, N. (1996) Commentary: Bonds or borrowing? *Private Finance Quarterly*, autumn.
Waites, W. (1996) Risk and capital structure of successful deals. *PFI Intelligence Bulletin.* November.

[20]

OXFORD REVIEW OF ECONOMIC POLICY, VOL. 13, NO. 4

# THE ECONOMICS OF THE PRIVATE FINANCE INITIATIVE

PAUL A. GROUT
*University of Bristol*[1]

*This article outlines and assesses the private finance initiative in the UK. The initiative has been slow to develop despite pressure from governments (anxious to limit the PSBR) and several revamps to facilitate the PFI approach. Within a PFI project there are beneficial incentives to avoid cost over-runs but not to reduce costs where they affect long-run services. These incentives and the limits to their effectiveness are explored. Such contracts require the transfer of risk from the public to the private sector. The role and pricing of risk in the PFI is analysed. It is argued that the PFI does not value risk correctly and that the value for money test is biased against private-sector provision. Policy implications are discussed, including a revamp of the value for money test and the introduction of explicit assessment of the impact of potential renegotiation and other contractual difficulties.*

## I. INTRODUCTION

The direct role of the public sector has been rolled back significantly in the last 15 years as part of a worldwide drive to introduce incentives into traditionally publicly provided activities. The UK has been one of the leaders, particularly with the large-scale privatization of the telecommunications, energy, water, and transport sectors. These privatizations have led to a modernization of infrastructure which had deteriorated under the strict financial controls of the public sector. There are many activities, however, that are capital-intensive and have poor infrastructure but may not suitable to be fully privatized. They can be characterized as activities where the final customer remains chiefly, and often in its entirety, the public sector, and where the public sector retains a very close interest in the quality and nature of the service, e.g. the health service, penal service, defence, roads, education, etc. These institutions, whether on the boundary of the state or well within the public sector, face a common problem of how to modernize infrastructure and incentive structures in the presence of the strict public-sector spending controls which seek to limit the public-sector borrowing requirement (PSBR).

[1] I am grateful to Helene Turon Lacarrieu for excellent research assistance.

OXFORD REVIEW OF ECONOMIC POLICY, VOL. 13, NO. 4

The main attraction for a politician of the Private Finance Initiative (PFI) is that it is an attempt to resolve this problem by changing the basic model of public provision. The traditional public-sector model is one of the public sector contracting with the private sector to build an asset which will be owned and controlled, directly or indirectly, by the public sector to provide a flow of services. Such investment must be funded 'up front' and as a result increases the PSBR. The PFI model is one where the private sector funds, builds, and owns the asset and the public sector only purchases the flow of services as they occur, albeit through a long-term commitment made at the time of construction. Since the asset is funded and owned by the private sector, the investment may be provided without affecting the PSBR, even though the present value of the financial commitment by the government may be very similar whether the public sector owns the asset or not.

The aim of this paper is to provide an economic assessment of the PFI. The structure is as follows. Section II outlines the PFI and summarizes the UK experience. Two common themes appear. One is that governments (both Conservative and New Labour) have been extremely anxious to promote the programme since it enables them to restrict the PSBR while improving the infrastructure in key areas. The full weight of the Treasury and ministries have been thrown behind this form of funding and at times it has been made extremely difficult to proceed with projects using conventional public-sector funding. The second common theme is that, despite all this pressure, the take-up has been persistently lukewarm. New initiatives to speed up the system and revamps of the government machinery have been frequent in the attempt to accelerate the take-up.

Section III of the paper discusses the economics of the programme. Subsection III(i) considers the issue of risk shifting and the pricing of risk. The treatment of risk is central to the initiative, and this subsection contains the main theme of the paper, which is that the test for the viability of the PFI approach is flawed in its treatment of risk in a manner that is biased against private-sector provision. The 'value for money' (VFM) test does not compare like with like when it tests for the viability of private provision, since the risk that is passed from the public to the private sector is incorrectly priced in the test. For a project that is identical in every respect, whether conducted in the private sector or the public sector, it should be a matter of indifference, if public-sector money is available, whether a project is publicly provided or a PFI project. However, the VFM test will suggest that public provision is superior. The implication is that PFI projects may be difficult to promote and this may be particularly so when one takes account of the tendering, legal, and contractual complications. This raises the question of why PFI projects survive. One reason is that with very limited public funding PFI projects are the only option in many cases. Another major reason is that in many instances there may be good reasons why PFI is the most efficient form of provision and these efficiencies can offset the inherent bias in the VFM test. The latter point is discussed in subsection III(iii). Finally, section IV summarizes the policy implications.

## II. STRUCTURE AND THE UK EXPERIENCE

### (i) What is the PFI?

The PFI concerns the transfer to the private sector of infrastructure projects which have traditionally been directly or indirectly delivered by the public sector. The traditional public-sector model is one where the public sector employs private-sector companies to construct infrastructure assets which are funded by government borrowing. The central feature of PFI projects is that the private sector funds and builds the asset and it is the flow of services from the asset that is sold to the public sector; that is, the obligation on the part of the government is to purchase, directly or indirectly, a flow of services over time rather than the capital asset that provides the services. In effect it is a form of leasing rather than purchase of assets. A common characteristic of PFI projects is that they are concerned with core public services which are often politically sensitive (e.g. health care, custodial services, etc.).

There are three main criteria that schemes should satisfy to fall under the PFI umbrella:

(i) funding is to be predominantly (usually fully) from the private sector and the contractual structure relates to the consumption of services not the asset itself;

(ii) a 'substantial' amount of risk must be transferred into the private sector; and

(iii) the project must be shown to offer value for money to the taxpayer.

Projects differ in the degree of private funding and the degree of direct involvement of the public sector in the purchase of the services. Joint ventures, less common than full private-sector funding, occur when the private sector's costs are met partly from public funds and partly from private sources. Control of the asset even with a joint venture, however, must remain with the private-sector participants.

The involvement of the public sector in the purchase of these services may be direct, fixed, public-sector purchase or, at the other extreme, the project may be self-standing, i.e. funded through fees charged directly to the public where the public-sector involvement is limited to one of monitoring adherence to the contract and renegotiating any changes to the service supplied. A good example of the former is the purchase of prison services. The first three prisons built this way will come into operation in late 1997 and early 1998, and two more contracts are about to be signed. Examples of self-standing projects are most common in transport. Indeed, the initiative has found most success in the transport sector, which accounts for approximately 80 per cent of the total value of all current PFI projects. There are £4.4 billion worth of projects that are at the stage of having identified the preferred bidder, although this can create a slightly false picture since £2.7 billion of this rests with a single project, the Channel Tunnel Rail Link. There are, however, a reasonable number of transport projects—the typical size being about £150m. Examples include the Skye Bridge, the Second Severn Crossing, and several DBFO (design, build, finance, and operate) roads, such as the M6 extension from Carlisle to Glasgow.

The standard approach to the use of private finance in the provision of roads provides a good example of the role of the PFI. The asset is provided by the private sector, the provider retains ownership and contracts to supply free entry to traffic for a prespecified period. The provider is remunerated directly from the government, not the user, in the form of a fixed fee per vehicle, which is monitored at various points on the road. The public sector is thus paying directly for the consumption of the service by the public, rather than for the provision of road services. Consequently, at the time of contract negotiation, neither the government nor the provider is sure of the level or time profile of the future flow of funds. Such PFI partnerships between the public and private sector do not fall into the conventional categories of privatization, contracting out, or asset procurement, although some PFI projects in transport, such as self-funding bridge contracts met by direct toll charges, come quite close to the conventional regulated privatization model.

Other sectors affected by PFI projects include health, defence, and education. The basic model is more complex in the health sector in that, although there is a clear government policy (HM Treasury, 1996) to allow provision of hospital buildings by the PFI, the final service, i.e. clinical services, remains with the National Health Service (NHS). The defence sector has started to take advantage of the PFI and has approximately £1.4 billion of projects at the preferred-bidder stage, the biggest of which is the 20-year contract involving the Services Defence Helicopter Flying School. Schools have limited involvement in the PFI, but many universities have taken advantage to fund expansion in student accommodation.

The PFI arrangements usually involve three groups—the public-sector agency, the private consortium that builds and supplies the services, and the bank or other financial agency that funds the programme. The typical steps involve: (i) the establishment of a business need and the test of PFI nature by the public agency, (ii) a tendering and negotiation process involving short-listing and detailed negotiation with short-listed firms, (iii) negotiation of a contract with the preferred bidder, (iv) building, and (v) supply of service and renegotiation as required. The contractual agreements are lengthy, typically 25–30 years, but the chain between agents is limited in that, although the public-sector agency will be bound to an agreement with the consortium and the consortium will be bound to the bank, there will be no link in general between the bank and the public agency.

OXFORD REVIEW OF ECONOMIC POLICY, VOL. 13, NO. 4

The distance between the lender and the state agency, and agreement to pay for services only upon satisfactory delivery, enables the projects to be treated differently for accounting purposes from a public-funded activity and affects the structure of cash flows and the location of risk and incentives to deliver. In a world of efficient capital markets, full information, and complete contracts, the ownership transfer between the public and private sectors should have no economic effect. In practice, contracts cannot be complete and capital markets may not be perfect, so there is considerable scope for economic impact to arise as a result of the specific ownership and contractual structure.

As indicated in the introduction, the big attraction for the government of the PFI is that it enables infrastructure to be built without it appearing as an increase in the PSBR. Because the assets remain within the private sector, they count as private-sector investment for national accounting purposes. However, since the building of the asset is accompanied with a public-sector commitment to purchase a flow of services, then the impact on underlying government finance may be the same. If the public sector owns the asset, there is a commitment to fund the debt, while if the private sector owns the asset there is a similar commitment, but now in the form of a service contract.

Formally, there is a clear distinction in that, in the case of public provision, debt has been funded regardless of the outcome, whereas in the case of private provision, the public sector only pays for services it receives. In addition, where agencies are at arm's length from the government, e.g. universities, NHS trusts, etc., the government retains a degree of control over the funding, in that the agency is forced to meet the contract but the government is not contractually bound to the agency. The chain is often complex. For example, the Department of Health funds health authorities which buy from NHS trusts which sign long-term contracts with PFI consortiums which own and operate the hospitals. The government can claw back part of the cost to the exchequer of PFI projects by reducing financial flows to the agencies along the chain. Thus the government is able to take advantage of the structure to reduce quality when finance is tight. In this sense it enables governments to retain control over agencies in the future. On the other hand, to the extent that it is easier for agencies to obtain PFI projects rather than direct funding, the government loses control over aspects of future expenditure. The fact that the governments set the rules rather than the number of projects makes it harder to retain tight control on infrastructure investment.

The central feature in the accounting treatment of a PFI project is the extent to which risk is transferred to the private sector. If insufficient risk is transferred, then the project should still count against the PSBR. That is, the contractual obligation counts against the PSBR as if the asset itself had been purchased by the public sector itself. Clearly, the accounting treatment of the PFI brings the role of the pricing of risk to the fore. If the driver is to keep projects off the PSBR, and this requires persuading the private sector to take such risks on board, it is essential that such risks are correctly priced in a PFI assessment. A major difficulty is that the rules for accounting of PFI projects are not clear and still evolving. It is quite possible that they may be formalized and tightened significantly. Clearly, the stronger the rules the more significant the issue of risk pricing.

### (ii) The Experience in the UK

The PFI began life formally in 1992, when rules relating to the use of private funds by the public sector were revised. The original 'Ryrie rules' set in 1981 had two principal themes: a privately financed solution must be tested against a publicly financed alternative and shown to be more cost-effective, and privately financed expenditure by the nationalized industries could not be additional to public expenditure provision—i.e. the public-expenditure provision would be reduced by the amount borrowed from the private markets. Later, John Major relaxed this non-additionality rule, but other aspects of the old rules remained largely in place until 1992.

In autumn 1992, the Chancellor announced significant changes in the role of privately raised finance. The two main changes were that self-standing privately financed projects would be allowed to go ahead without any need to compare them with a similar project in the public sector, and there would be use of leasing which would not have to count against public expenditure limits. The detailed structure that emerged became the PFI as described in section II(i) above. Hancock (1995) gives some indication of the expected effect when quoting an unnamed public corporation—'We confidently expected to be flooded by an innovative and hungry private sector, straining at the leash to do all sorts of deals.' The reality was very different.

After a year the new Chancellor, Kenneth Clarke, described the progress of PFI as disappointingly slow. In an effort to promote projects, the Private Finance Panel Executive, the Private Finance Office within the Treasury, and Private Finance Units within Departments were created. The Private Finance Panel Executive issued guidance notes on the process and on how to write suitable contracts between the public client and the private-sector provider. Yet, again, the net effect was limited. For example, the Treasury Committee commenting on the November 1994 budget 'noted that the scheme had failed to attract significant private interest' (HM Treasury, 1996).

To enhance the scheme the decision was taken in November 1994 that the PFI should be the preferred option for capital projects. That is, the Treasury would not approve any public-sector funding for a capital project unless private-finance options for the project had been explored and found uneconomic. This test remained in place throughout the Conservative administration. Although difficult to measure, it is frequently suggested that the practice of universal testing for private finance had the opposite effect to that intended in some areas. For example, in the health sector the initial rush to test all projects as suitable for PFI appears to have clogged the system, added delay to conventional projects and actually slowed the development of investment in infrastructure.

There were some advances following the 1994 changes. In 1995 there was £400m fixed investment arising from PFI projects which had doubled by the following year. However, this figure compares with £15.2 billion and £12 billion of public investment in the same years and £102 billion and £104 billion respectively of total investment. It was hoped that the PFI would reach £14 billion by the end of the fiscal year 1997/98 and the Private Finance Panel identified with government departments in excess of 1,000 potential PFI projects with a capital value of around £25 billion. On the other hand, these figures were judged by the OECD to be far too optimistic. Considering UK public investment at the time, they remarked that capital expenditure under the PFI might be in excess of £7 billion over the 3 years to financial year 1997/98, although this will not be counted as public investment (OECD, 1996). In practice, the total amount of signed deals met this figure rather than actual investment (total value of signed deals was £7.5 billion by October 1997). By early 1997 about a hundred PFI projects had reached the stage of the preferred partner, while about another hundred of projects had reached the short-list stage. The Red Book shows that by 1998/99, more than 12 per cent of 'publicly sponsored' capital investment should be derived from the PFI (HM Treasury, 1996). However, these figures do not fully reveal how few PFI significant projects are actually signed. What constitutes a separate contract is difficult to define, but it appears that in the first half of 1996, only four largish contracts were signed, representing £673m; in the second half of 1996, 10 were signed, representing £3.3 billion which includes the £2.7 billion Channel Tunnel Rail Link. In the first half of 1997, 11 were signed, representing £1.9 billion, and £1.1 billion are to be signed in the near future. Furthermore, it is clear that much of this activity is substitutional not additional. The Treasury Committee (HM Treasury, 1996) points out that it has become increasingly apparent that the sums of money projected under the PFI are, in practice, replacing orthodox public capital spending and allowing cuts in expenditure to be made.

Against this background the New Labour government ordered a speedy review of the PFI process conducted by Malcolm Bates, a former member of the Private Finance Panel. The review's aim was to identify the fundamental obstacles to progress and make recommendations for their removal while retaining VFM as the critical test. The review was delivered to the Treasury in June 1997 and accepted in full.

The Bates review argued that there were too many institutions involved on the public-sector side and that the structure should be simplified. The main recommendations represent changes in the institutional structure, practical procedures, and expertise within the public sector:

(*a*) The institutional structure has been completely revamped by scrapping the Private Finance Panel and the Private Finance Panel Executive to be replaced by a new Task Force in the Treasury. The new Task Force is to sign off the commercial viability of all significant projects before the procurement process in an aim to minimize procurement costs and to speed up the procurement process. There is an explicit recognition that expertise in structuring deals and project management needs to be increased through hiring from the private sector.

(*b*) On a practical level procedures are to be standardized, small projects should be grouped and the Treasury will explicitly confirm that after signature of VFM contracts a Department's expenditure allocation for such contractual commitments will not subsequently be cut. Significantly, the concept of universal testing of projects for private finance has been rejected completely. Indeed, the rule that all projects have to be tested initially for private finance potential before being given permission for public provision was not merely dropped but replaced with a deliberately concentrated approach. A list of priority areas that may be suitable for private finance is to be drawn up with no requirement for other projects to test against privately financed options. Furthermore, costs will now be refunded to the private sector when a project is withdrawn for reasons other than the viability of tenders received and the information required from short-listed bidders is reduced along with a reduction in the number of bidders.

(*c*) Within the civil service training is to be refocused, there will be further guidance manuals, a dedicated library will be established, active liaison with the private sector increased and specific guidance on the VFM exercise will be provided (HM Treasury, 1997).

At the time of accepting these proposals, the government expressed its enthusiasm and pledged that the recommendations in the review would at last 'make a reality of the PFI idea'.

The PFI has also encountered legal difficulties. This is a particularly prominent problem in the health sector, where there has been real fear that PFI projects may be *ultra vires* with regard to NHS hospital trusts. The case that worried potential investors is not one in the health sector but the Allerdale Borough Council versus Crédit Suisse case. Since a local authority is not a sovereign body but a statutory corporation, if it acts outside its powers its contracts are void and unenforceable (Causer, 1997). This arose with the contract between Allerdale and Crédit Suisse, where the former was not liable to repay Crédit Suisse. There are £2.5 billion PFI projects in the health sector having at least reached the stage of choice of preferred bidder, but by early 1997 few of them had been signed because of the legal uncertainty surrounding NHS trusts. At the same time as the Bates Review, steps were initiated to avoid the legal problems in the health sector and in schemes involving local authorities. The NHS (Private Finance) Bill 1997 will provide specific powers to NHS trusts allowing them to enter into externally financed developments agreements and the Local Government (Contract) Bill 1997 is aimed at preventing a recurrence of the Allerdale case in this context.

### (iii) Summary of the Experience

The history is one of governments, both Conservative and Labour, wishing to use private finance as a replacement for public-sector investment. A considerable amount of effort has been devoted by ministers and civil servants to promoting the scheme, even to the extent of insisting, between late 1994 and mid-1997, that all public-sector capital projects must give prior consideration to funding under the initiative and can only avoid private finance if it is shown to be inferior. The disappointing lack of interest has led to persistent revisions of the structure. Furthermore, the process of moving initial interest to final conclusion has been slow, which has further added to the limited effect of the initiative. Together with the universal testing of all projects for private finance, this may have reduced rather than increased the aggregate level of investment in the economy. As with earlier changes, the latest proposals by the new government have focused on the practical aspects of promoting the scheme and increasing the efficiency of the process. Throughout there have been no fundamental changes in the concept itself.

## III. ECONOMIC ASSESSMENT

Given the long-run nature of the projects and the slow development of the programme, empirical evidence is emerging too slowly to measure at present the success or otherwise of PFI projects against the public equivalent. Of course, the acceptability of a PFI in a VFM test indicates that the providers believe that they will be able to provide the service profitably at a lower price than the public sector. The shortage of projects in the time since the scheme was introduced could be taken as an indication that privately funded activities do not provide VFM, that the test is not appropriate, or that the contractual structure is flawed in some way. The purpose of this section is to provide an economic evaluation of the policy which may help to throw light on these issues. At the core of the notion is the transfer of risk and the pricing of and compensation for holding risk. Although this is intertwined with broader contracting and accounting issues, we will try to separate these as much as possible. This section begins by dealing with the risk issue and then moves on to a brief consideration of broader contracting issues.

### (i) Risk and Compensation for Risk within the PFI

This section discusses the price for holding risk, then considers where this price appears in public-sector and private-sector projects, and relates this to the PFI VFM test in a third subsection, which also broadens the discussion to incorporate some complications to the simple picture.

*The price of risk*

In order to identify what one means by risk and how those holding risk should be compensated, it is necessary to provide an intuitive discussion of the various forms of risk and how they are priced in a capital market. At the simplest level, a risky outcome is one that is not certain. However, such a simple notion of risk is inadequate for our purposes since it is necessary to identify for each specific investment the competitive market price that will need to be paid to persuade individuals to bear that risk. If risks are to be passed from the public to the private sector, then there will be a competitive price for that risk, just as there will be a price for any other cost of the project that is passed on to the private sector.

To see how this price is determined in a market, it is useful to consider an investor with a significant amount of wealth to invest. The law of large numbers indicates that risk is reduced when the portfolio is diversified across all investments, i.e. the investor holds the market portfolio. With such a portfolio the investor has not removed all risk, however, since there is still exposure to shifts in the whole market of risky assets, so-called market risk. How valuable any individual asset is to this investor will depend on how much it reduces or increases the exposure to the market risk. Suppose the return on a specific asset is perfectly correlated with the market. Adding a little more or less of this asset to the investor's portfolio will neither increase nor reduce the risk of the portfolio, so if the asset pays a higher return than the average in the market the investor would like to buy a little more (since expected return is then increased without any increase in risk) and, conversely, if it pays less than the average in the market the investor will try to sell some of it. In equilibrium the return on the asset that is perfectly correlated with the market must offer an expected return equal to the average in the market, i.e. the risk-free rate plus the market risk premium. Assets that are more highly correlated with the market (and thus contribute disproportionately to overall risk) must earn a higher expected return, otherwise investors will try to sell, and those that are less correlated must earn a lower expected return, otherwise they will try to buy. Thus it is the correlation of (or covariance between) returns from the asset with the returns on the overall market portfolio that determines the equilibrium return on an asset. This is the price of risk in a competitive market.

The capital asset pricing model (CAPM) formalizes this idea.[2] It states that the equilibrium expected rate of return for asset $i$ is given by

Expected return on asset $i$ = risk-free rate of return + beta of asset $i$ × the market risk premium,

where beta is the (weighted) covariance between the return on the asset and the return on the market

[2] See Brealey and Myers (1996) for an introduction to the CAPM and Grout (1995) for a discussion in the context of regulation.

OXFORD REVIEW OF ECONOMIC POLICY, VOL. 13, NO. 4

portfolio. If the beta is one (as would be the case if the asset is perfectly correlated with the market), then the equilibrium return on the asset is the return on the market portfolio, and if the beta is zero (as is the case if there is no correlation between the asset and the market), then the equilibrium return is the risk-free rate of return. Once one knows the beta of an asset or cash flow it is possible to predict what is the appropriate expected rate of return. This can be thought of as the price of risk, since the equilibrium expected return is the return that is necessary to compensate investors for the risk of the investment they are undertaking. It is the price that must be paid to investors to persuade them to hold the risk.

The CAPM provides a measure of the risk that can be used to assess the implications of the risk transfer involved with the PFI. The official documentation refers to delay risk, construction risk, cost overruns, real interest rate risk, etc. Each part of the financial transaction has a risk and hence a competitive price associated with it. The contract to purchase the services and not the asset itself immunizes the public sector from some of the risks and passes them on to the private sector. Just as the benefit of passing on of any other part of the cost of building the asset, say labour costs, is calculated in the VFM test comparison, then so should the benefit of passing on particular risks. It is possible using the CAPM to assess this price. Note that the cash-flow components of the investment will have different risk characteristics. For example, revenues will have a positive risk if they depend on the state of the economy. At the other extreme, the cash flow associated with fixed costs will have a zero risk in the CAPM sense since, by definition, the cash flow is fixed and cannot have a positive correlation with the market.

*Risk and private- versus public-sector provision*

The first point to consider when pricing the risk transfer is to ask whether the actual aggregate risk is constant as it is transferred from public to private sector. Does the amount of additional risk taken on by the private sector exactly equal the amount of risk reduced from the public sector? If so, then the public sector should be willing to and will have to pay the market price for all risks transferred to the private sector.

There are two arguments that are sometimes made in this context. One is that public-sector provision may indeed involve less risk, i.e. there is something inherent in public-sector provision that reduces risk, usually because the public sector is very large. The other is that the public sector can fund projects more cheaply than the private sector. This is often used as the proof of the former. At a general level, neither view is correct. The most useful way to think of this is in an economy where the population consists of $n$ identical individuals.

If the public-sector agency provides the asset then it must borrow the cost of the project, say $C$, from the private sector, each person reducing consumption by $C/n$. The government promises to pay the risk-free rate $r$ on the debt and people are happy to lend at this rate since they will indeed receive $(1 + r)C/n$ with certainty. Services flow to the public, who also service the debt through taxation. That is, each person pays $(1 + r)C/n$ in tax and receives an equal amount back on their loan. The net effect is that each individual consumes a flow of services in the future and pays $C/n$ in the first period. The increment in risk rests with the consumers, in that they are provided with a service of risky value in the second period and contribute $C/n$ in the first period.

If the private sector provides the project, then the shareholders, everyone in the economy in this example, provide $C/n$ to a private contractor instead of the government. This provides a return based on the service contract. If the value of the service to the economy is risky, such as in the roads examples, where revenue depends on usage which depends on the economy, then the flow of funds to the contractor will have positive beta and the rate of interest will be higher, say $i > r$. Each shareholder will only supply funds at the rate of interest $i$ or above, since this is the price of the risk they are adding to their financial portfolio. In the second period each person pays $(1 + i)C/n$ in tax and receives an identical amount via the contractor back on the loan. Again the net effect is that each individual consumes a flow of risky services in the future and pays $C/n$ in the first period.

The consumers have identical utility in this example, whether there is public or private provision, and the consumers in the economy bear the same amount of risk. That is, the aggregated risk remains constant when the project is transferred to the private sector from the public sector. This is true regardless of the level of risk of the project, regardless of the scale of the public sector, and regardless of the risk written into the private-sector contract. It may appear that there has been an increase in risk, but this is merely because the price of the risk of the project (built into $i$) is made explicit in the private-provision context but is not priced in the public sector. The fact that the government can fund the project at the risk-free rate, $r$, is totally independent of the true risk of the project and tells us nothing of that risk since the direct cost of raising debt is not the price of risk to the public sector (i.e. the consumers in aggregate). The cost of raising funds for this project is set at $r$ simply because the government can always tax everyone to meet the obligation. The debt is risk free to the lender, but that is because the risk is passed on to the general public, who bear the risk through riskier future tax payments and consumption. The impact of one small risky project is so small on the overall riskiness of the public sector that it may be barely noticeable, but it is still there. Aggregating this almost negligible risk across millions of consumers brings us back to the same risk as is borne by the private provider.

Of course, this is an abstract example, but it shows clearly, that there is nothing in public-sector provision *per se* that implies lower risk and that the cost of government funding is not an indication that risk is lower with public provision. The example also makes clear that if it is the case that the public-sector project is less risky than the private sector, then this must arise because of heterogeneity in the population, contractual problems, or because financial markets do not work efficiently. It can be argued that the private sector only borrows from a subset of the population whereas the public sector can force everyone to invest because of its control of the tax system. An alternative argument is that the private sector can focus borrowing more accurately. At a first approximation it is not clear that there are dominating benefits either way and it seems reasonable to assume that risk neither increases nor decreases as projects are passed between the sectors. Brealey, Cooper, and Habib, in this issue, provide a good discussion of public- versus private-sector risk (see also Lind, 1982).

*Risk and the value-for-money test*

We outlined above how one prices risk and pointed out that different cash flows will have different risks attached to them. At a simple level, the cost of a project can be broken down into several categories, each of which will have different risk characteristics. The building element of a project is usually low risk in the CAPM sense. Fixed costs, as pointed out above, have no associated risk since the money flow is known with certainty. Many of the other build costs, although uncertain, are also low-beta or zero-beta activities. For example, the outcome of deep drilling work necessary for a construction project may be very 'risky', but is unlikely to be correlated with the market. Supply costs are much more variable, since they tend to have a large element of variable costs which are usually driven by the use of the entity. In contrast, revenues for projects tend to be volume-related in some way. In this case, the cash flow depends on the take-up. This is true for PFI projects, although perhaps not as much as other projects in the private sector. As we will discuss in the next section, it is essential that revenue streams reflect real risk of this type since one wishes to provide incentives to the private sector to build the right type of activity.

The price of risk associated with a cost stream of a typical PFI project will be low, and so to obtain the present value of the cash flow associated with the cost stream it should be discounted at a rate close to the risk-free rate (adjusted for taxes, etc., which we ignore in this discussion). In contrast, the revenue stream may be far more risky. The rate of return required to persuade an investor to exchange money today for the uncertain risky cash flow is higher, and thus the present value is found by discounting at a higher rate appropriate for the risk built into the revenue streams. In a competitive market, these rates of return will determine the expected output price of the project. If the revenue stream discounted by the appropriate rate of interest to reflect risk of that stream is less than the present value of the cost stream discounted at the rate of interest appropriate for the cost stream, then firms will cease to supply the product and the price of output in the market will be bid up until the present value of the revenue stream is equal to the present value of costs. These prices will reflect the economist's notion of normal profit.

Breaking a project down in this way shows the difficulty with the existing VFM test. This test compares the cost to the public sector of conducting the project with the cost of buying in the service from the private sector. When the public provision side is considered, the project is being valued from the cost side. That is, the Treasury is calculating the present value of the cash flows of the costs of the project. When private provision is considered, the project is valued from the revenue side. That is, the Treasury calculates the present value of the cash flows of the revenues of the project. Providing the correct price of risk is used for each calculation, then these two valuations are exactly the correct ones and the route with the lowest present value should be chosen. The problem with the VFM test in the present form is that it has used the same rate of interest, normally 6 per cent, to find the present value of both streams. This is only appropriate if the risks of the cost stream and the revenue stream are the same, which is most unlikely. Furthermore, the difference in risk is generally in the same direction, i.e. costs are less risky than revenues. The cost stream should use a lower discount rate than the revenue stream. Using the same number favours public provision—the very thing the government is trying to prevent. Since money is not available for public provision we have the worst of all worlds. There is insufficient being paid for the private projects to implement the government's desire to make the whole thing a huge success, but insufficient money in the public sector to deal with the bias in favour of public-sector provision.

The critics of the PFI have often pointed to the low cost of borrowing for the government, relative to the privately funded projects, to argue that the PFI is an expensive method of provision. It is clear from the above that this is the wrong comparison. It is simply that the PFI route explicitly builds in the price of risk whereas the public-provision route masks it. The situation is complicated by the fact that there are two separate representatives of the public sector involved, the representative of public sector in total (the Treasury in most practical cases) and the specific public-sector agency (such as the Department or a NHS trust). There is an inherent conflict between these. The public-sector agency has no incentive to correct the distortion in a VFM exercise. The preference for public provision within the existing VFM exercise is indeed a sensible one for the public-sector agency if it acts as a separate decision-making unit. The agency is forced to face the full risk of the project if it purchases the project through the PFI, since the price of the risk is built into the price for the services. The cost of risk cannot be avoided. In contrast, with public provision the agency is able to borrow at the public-sector risk-free rate, or near to this rate, even if the capital project provides an output with a high beta. Providing the agency is small relative to the public sector, the agency is able to side-step the cost of the risk if the public sector provides, since the risk is transferred from the specific agency to the rest of the public sector which now has one more positive beta project than before. As long as the agency is small, the impact on the cost of finance for the agency is unaffected.

An additional problem is that the risk written in a contract for services from the private sector need not reflect the riskiness of the underlying project. The contract can be more or less risky than the underlying investment. As we have argued, the individual agency has an incentive to distort provision in favour of the public sector. However, the agency may not have resources to conduct the project, and the final outcome may be private provision with an inefficient set of risks passed on to the private sector. That is, the scheme that arises in negotiation is likely to shift zero beta risks off to the private sector and may tend to preserve positive beta risks within the public sector. There is some evidence that this may be the case, since the impact of volume risk is often borne by the public sector. Of course, this may be a feature of an optimal incentive contract anyway, but it is more likely to be the other way round since the scheme should provide the private sector with the incentive to build the best possible asset. Usage is often an observable variable which is a function of quality and associated risks ought to be borne by the builder and owner. If the agency is anxious for the project to succeed but faces a financial allocation problem, then it may wish to pass a larger amount of certain types of risks to the private sector than is optimal in order to compensate for those that must be withheld. Furthermore, it is unlikely that the type of risk allocation identified above will arise by formal mathematical models of the incentive to distort risk allocation, but will arise through the negotiation between parties concerning the relationship between the cost of providing the service and the type of risks that are being carried. This suggests that there may be good reasons why the negotiation is long and complex—another common complaint of PFI projects.

The extent of the problems identified here depends on the risk characteristics of the projects and the extent to which differences in risks are appreciated by the VFM process. The experience of the regulated water companies may be useful here. These companies provide a service involving high capital expenditure and low-risk cost structures, implying cost betas will be quite small. There is some, albeit limited, volume risk. In some respects because the regulated prices are renegotiated at least once every 5 years one might expect these companies' revenues to have lower betas than many PFI contracts. The typical beta for a water and sewerage company is around 1.1 at the moment, which implies that there may be significant differences in risk between revenues and costs of a typical PFI project.[3] Clearly, a far more thorough approach to the VFM exercise would benefit the PFI exercise.

### (ii) Incentives

As section II(i) makes clear, the identifying feature of the PFI is that assets are owned by the private sector and services are provided. Thus the test of the appropriateness of the PFI structure is not simply one of public versus private provision.[4] Assets could be built by the private sector for the public sector and then the management of the public assets contracted out to the private sector. Indeed, this is a common model. The justification for the PFI must be that the model where assets are owned by the private sector even when the public sector is the client is superior in some way to others.

At a simple abstract level there would appear to be little difference between the two models described in the previous paragraph. If contracts can always be written to replicate any reward scheme, then it should not matter whether we have the same entity building, owning, and providing services, or have different entities with public ownership. The difficulty with this argument is that it assumes that contracts can always be complete in the sense that every eventuality can be covered and, therefore, incentives are not a problem. In practice, building contracts are notoriously problematic and there are large information problems.[5] Design changes, resolutions of uncertainty, unexpected events, etc., all lead to disputes such as whether this is a fresh specification, hence falling on the purchaser, or a response to a reasonably foreseeable event that the contractor should have built into the price. Responsibility for cost over-runs is a major source of conflict in large projects. In addition, monitoring can be difficult, so there are incentives for the builder to cut on quality where the consequences are not immediately obvious. The result is that build contracts need to include service specifications to ensure that they have been properly conducted.

The argument for the PFI route is that many of these problems disappear if the contract is written over the flow of services rather than the build process. If the same entity builds and sells the services but is only remunerated for successful supply of services, then there are no incentives to reduce quality even if the consequences do not appear for many years. Similarly, without any possibility of pushing the cost over-run on to the client, there are strong incentives to reduce costs but not to jeopardize quality. Where there is choice of technology, there are strong incentives to build the right type of asset when revenues purely depend on a flow of suitable quality services from the asset. As indicated earlier, this implies that the revenue streams of PFI projects should be inherently risky for the supplier.

This is a powerful argument for private ownership but there are offsetting problems. Reducing the need to elicit information at the build stage and

[3] London Business School Risk Management Service. Note that this figure relates to an equity beta.

[4] This excludes the small number of projects that are fully funded directly from the public. Here the model is the basic privatization one.

[5] See, for example, Grout (1984), Hart and Holmstrom (1987), and Hart (1995) for a discussion of the consequences of incomplete contracts.

OXFORD REVIEW OF ECONOMIC POLICY, VOL. 13, NO. 4

reducing the dead-weight loss of the revelation problem at this stage will not be obtained without cost. It will probably lead to greater incentive problems at the service provision stage. For example, public- and private-sector suppliers may have different incentives at this stage. Furthermore, the dead-weight loss of ensuring a correct build cannot be totally avoided with PFI-type provision, since the incentives to build correctly with private ownership will still depend on the nature of the service contract, and these are signed before the asset is built. This will limit the type of service contract that can be written. For this reason PFI projects may still include monitoring of the build process, particularly if it is a joint venture. For example, in the case of Channel Tunnel Rail Link, the 'client has employed professional advisers to monitor the achievement of required project milestones during the preparation and construction of the Link, and to record when payments of tranches of the Government contribution become due' (Private Finance Panel, 1997).

Probably the biggest problem of the service-based approach is that the service structure needs specification in advance, which may not always be optimal. For example, it is difficult to get a good idea of what reasonable standards of quality will be like in 20 or 30 years time. In many university accommodation contracts, the quality standards mention microwave cookers which could not have been written into a contract 20 years ago (McWilliam, 1997). Furthermore, contracts need to be extremely long (to limit expropriation), but this reduces flexibility. Renegotiation of contracts avoids this problem but generates inefficiencies. If there is likely to be renegotiation, then residual rights (which follow ownership) will have a significant impact on the outcome and drive the ownership decision. Hart *et al.* (1997) show that if assets are owned by the private sector, then cost-reducing changes can be introduced without renegotiation, since the sole contract with the public sector is on services. Thus the full benefit of such changes flows to the private owner and encourages efficiency. In contrast, benefits that improve service quality require renegotiation and the public body may be in a position to extract part of the benefit by offering a lower price per unit of service since the private owner has no alternative purchaser for the incremental gain. The effect is that the private owner receives less of the benefit of such changes and the incentives are weakened. The implication is that PFI-type projects may lead to inefficient development over time even with renegotiation. Furthermore, the owners have incentives to concentrate on cost-cutting rather than service-enhancing activities.[6]

Another difficulty is that pricing directly for the service, rather than owning and dictating use of the asset, causes the usual problems of the divergence between social and private costs to arise even when the customer is the public sector. For example, once prices have been set for road usage, a contractor may have incentives to encourage incremental road usage and to divert location of other construction, e.g. out-of-town shopping centres, away from socially optimal locations. This introduces yet another set of events that should, in an ideal world, be included in a contract.

In general terms, where build contracts are easy to specify but service contracts are not, then it is useful to have the public sector closely involved in the build process. This does not imply that the public sector need own the asset, since it may be helpful in renegotiation for the asset to be in private-sector hands, but the incentives for it to remain in the private sector are less obvious. At the other extreme, where service contracts are easy to write and build contracts are difficult, the PFI approach may be particularly sensible. Sectors, and projects within sectors, will have different characteristics, and for some the PFI model will bring large efficiency gains and for others the approach of less control at the build stage may be positively harmful. This suggests that the policy of looking to private funding first for all public-sector infrastructure projects is an inefficient use of resources. Identifying in advance sectors and project types within sector for careful analysis is a far better strategy.

## IV. SUMMARY AND CONCLUSION

The PFI is designed to bring the positive efficiencies associated with private provision to those invest-

[6] The Hart *et al.* (1997) paper provides a detailed analysis of this problem in the context of prisons.

ments where the public sector remains the main or only customer. The essential feature is that the infrastructure is built and owned by the private sector, the public sector purchasing the flow of services from the asset rather than the asset itself. Such a contract transfers risks from the public to the private sector, thus preventing the investment cost from appearing in the PSBR. Despite the considerable effort devoted to the promotion of the initiative by ministers and civil servants, the outcome has been disappointing. Even the rule that all public-sector capital projects must give prior consideration to private funding failed to get the ball rolling in a major way. The lack of interest has led to persistent revisions of the structure culminating in the recent overhaul by the new government.

The VFM test appears to be a major problem, since it is generally biased against private-sector finance. This is likely to result in good private-sector projects being rejected and a distortion in contractual structures. The problem stems from the use of the same rate of discount for assessment of the public (which is a cost-based test) and private (which is a revenue-based test) alternatives. The public alternative does not price the risk of the project but the price of risk is explicitly built into the private alternative. There is a clear need to improve the VFM test and to remove the bias. Without this, there is no guarantee that the right projects are funded or that the initiative will succeed.

The view that optimal incentive structure rests with the private sector owning the asset and the government contracting for the service has been considered in section III(ii). A major justification depends on the inability to write complete contracts that cover all contingencies. Since this is clearly a feature of construction and long-life service contracts, this effect is likely to be strong. Generally, where service contracts are easy to write, where there are good possibilities to reduce costs, and where build contracts are difficult, the PFI approach can be particularly useful and should improve incentives and increase efficiency. Thus there is a clear role for this initiative. However, where build contracts and service contracts are not, then the incentives for assets to be built by and remain in the private sector appear less strong, although private ownership may still be the best option. Sectors and projects within sectors will have different characteristics and it ought to be possible to identify areas that are ripe for PFI and areas that are unlikely to bring benefits. Selective advance screening of project types is essential if resources are not be wasted. In particular, the policy of looking to private funding first for all public-sector infrastructure projects was clearly inefficient.

Finally, most PFI projects do not affect the PSBR but clearly involve some commitment by the government. Funding future debt repayments is little different from meeting future service contracts. There are technical differences in that with private provision the failure to supply services frees the government from its payment obligations and long service contracts affect the future relationships between the central government and public-sector agencies. However, these are second-order and the impact of future commitments ought to be published in an accurate aggregate form, indicating the extent of the commitments over time. Unfortunately, unlike a PSBR count, the true figure for future obligations would require a detailed analysis of each contract and a specification of payments in expected-value terms.

Overall, there is clearly a role for the PFI and there is every reason to encourage the policy. This should be focused tightly on areas where contractual characteristics suggest the scheme has most to contribute, and other areas should be put on the back burner in the near future. Given that a significant part of the benefit comes from the difficulty in writing complete contracts, this suggests a simple financial test is inappropriate, since it may mask the central issue. Less objective aspects, such as assessment of the scale and consequences of events occurring that are outside of contract specifications, the impact of ownership on renegotiation, etc., should be addressed on a project-by-project basis. Similarly, consideration of the pricing of risk, again on a project-by-project basis, needs to be included. These suggestions may introduce a degree of arbitrariness into the process, but it is hard to see how this could be worse that the present system.

OXFORD REVIEW OF ECONOMIC POLICY, VOL. 13, NO. 4

## REFERENCES

Brealey, R. A., and Myers, S. C. (1996), *Principles of Corporate Finance*, McGraw Hill.

Causer, C. (1997), 'How not to be *ultra vires*', *The PFI Report*, May.

Grout P. A. (1984), 'Investment and Wages in the Absence of Binding Contracts: A Nash Bargaining Approach', *Econometrica*.

— (1995), 'The Cost of Capital in Regulated Industries', in M. Bishop, J. Kay, and C. P. Mayer (eds), *The Regulatory Challenge*, Oxford, Oxford University Press.

Hancock, D. (1995), 'The Private Finance Initiative', *Proceedings of the Institution of Civil Engineers—Municipal Engineer*.

Hart O. D. (1995) *Firms Contracts and Financial Structure*, Oxford, Oxford University Press.

— Holmstrom, B. (1987) 'The Theory of Contracts' in T. F. Bewley (ed.) *Advances in Economic Theory*, Cambridge, Cambridge University Press.

— Schleifer, A., and Vishny, R. W. (1997), 'The Proper Scope of Government: Theory and an Application to Prisons', *Quarterly Journal of Economics* (forthcoming).

HM Treasury (1996), *Treasury Committee, Sixth Report, The Private Finance Initiative*.

— (1997), *News Release*, 23 June.

Lind, R. C. (ed.) (1982), *Discounting for Time and Risk in Energy Policy*, Resources for the Future.

McWilliam, J. (1997), 'A Commissioner's Tale: Avery Hill Student Village, University of Greenwich', *Public Money and Management*.

OECD (1996), *Economic Survey: UK*, Paris, Organization for Economic Cooperation and Development.

Private Finance Panel (1997), *Further Contractual Issues*, HM Treasury.

# [21]

OXFORD REVIEW OF ECONOMIC POLICY, VOL. 13, NO. 4

# THE RISK PREMIUM FOR EVALUATING PUBLIC PROJECTS

MICHAEL KLEIN
*Shell International*[1]

*Governments face a lower apparent cost of capital than private firms. However, the low cost of borrowing by governments does not reflect superior capabilities to choose or manage projects. Instead, it reflects the fact that governments have recourse to taxpayers, who* de facto *provide a fairly open-ended credit insurance to the government. If taxpayers were remunerated for the risk they assume in the case of tax-financed projects, then* ex ante *there would be no capital cost advantage to government finance. The risk premium on government finance would, in principle, be no different from that of private investors. There is thus no justification on the basis of capital cost advantages for government funding or guaranteeing the provision of private goods or services. Privatization is, therefore, valuable, if it improves business efficiency when evaluated at the risk-adjusted private cost of capital. No more need be demonstrated in a value-for-money test.*

## I. INTRODUCTION

> The other solution [to highway finance] is to finance the project wholly in the public sector, either with government or multilateral funds. It is, after all, more expensive to raise debt on a project finance basis. When considered alongside the guarantees and commitments which have to be provided to attract commercial finance, the best approach would be to borrow on a sovereign basis. (*Euromoney*, 1995)

> The view that 'private-sector capital costs more' is naïve, because the cost of debt both to governments and to private firms is influenced predominantly by the perceived risk of default rather than an assessment of the quality of returns from the specific investment. We would lend to government even if we thought it would burn the money or fire it off into space, and we do lend to it for both these purposes. (John Kay, 1993)

These two quotations provide a flavour of the opposite positions that are being advocated for the finance of infrastructure projects. In an ironic twist, a trade magazine for the private sector advocates

[1] The author, now Chief Economist at Shell International, was until recently Manager, Private Participation in Infrastructure at the World Bank. The views presented in the paper do not necessarily reflect the views of Shell International or the World Bank.

Basing this on a previous working paper, I received very insightful comments from Jean-Jacques Laffont and Tyler Cowen, as well as from Chris Lewis, Colin Mayer, Ignacio Mas, and Sweder van Wijnbergen. My colleagues Phil Gray, Tim Irwin, and Neil Roger at the World Bank helped clarify many points in tireless discussions, as did other colleagues, including Pedro Belli, Mansoor Dailami, Dale Gray, Ulrike Hoffman-Burchardi, Ashok Mody, Shanta Devarajan, and Sethaput Suthiwart-Narueput.

 

government solutions, whereas a prominent advisor to the current leader of the Labour Party in the United Kingdom, takes the opposite view.

One may look at the issue as follows. For example, when a toll-road is financed on the basis of sovereign borrowing, the tolls will be lower than if the road had been funded by private investors. But the taxpayers will have assumed a contingent liability for which they are not remunerated, i.e. there is no risk premium in the sovereign borrowing rate. In fact, the taxpayers play the role of investors bearing the risk of failure. The question is, who is better placed to *bear* (as opposed to 'manage') the risk—taxpayers or investors? If taxpayers are just as good or bad at bearing risk as investors, then they should ideally receive a remuneration equivalent to the risk premium demanded by investors. If they are better at bearing risk, then project finance by way of sovereign borrowing is 'truly' cheaper than private funding, because the cost of risk-bearing is lower, i.e. taxpayers would be less interested in buying insurance—via charging risk premiums—than investors.

Obviously, the view one takes on the 'true' cost of sovereign funds affects one's attitude toward the role of government in financing projects. If government funding is really cheaper than private finance, then the government should have a greater role. At the same time, it is clear that the cost of funds is only one argument among others that determines what governments should or should not do.

This paper takes the view that the apparent cheapness of sovereign funds reflects the fact that the taxpayers,[2] who effectively provide credit insurance to the sovereign, are not remunerated for the contingent liability they assume. If they were to be remunerated properly, then the advantage of sovereign finance would—almost by definition—disappear.

If one takes that view, then the government should, in principle, not participate in the financing of projects, either with debt or with (quasi) equity. There are other useful roles for the government (see Annex 1), but there is no argument for government funding of projects based on the cheapness of government funds.

Also, there is then no argument for the typical 'lobbyist' position on private finance, which argues for privatization of some sort (because the private sector is more efficient), but then requests financial support from the government or an agency underwritten by government (because government funds are cheaper).

The implication of the argumentation that government funding is not cheaper than private funding runs counter to the worldwide practice of using risk-free rates to discount cashflows in public-sector project appraisal (cost–benefit analysis), whereas risk-adjusted discount rates are used in private appraisals. Current practices of cost–benefit analysis introduce a bias against private solutions in decisions about projects.[3]

The paper starts with a review of both basic positions and some of their implications, followed by an analysis of the rationales for each view. The policy implications of this view are drawn out. Annex 1 sketches some other arguments affecting the role of government in project finance, using, in particular, examples from highway finance.

The arguments are crucial for many current policy debates. The governments of various Australian states, Canada, New Zealand, and the United Kingdom are grappling with them in the context of promoting all sorts of private investment, for example, under the British private finance initiative. In France and Brazil, the arguments are currently debated because they would imply that politically favoured nuclear and hydro plants would become uneconomic. In Britain, the non-governmental organization, Friends of the Earth, has drawn the conclusion that advocacy of privatization is the way to go for groups opposed to nuclear plants—thus implicitly supporting the arguments presented here. In Colombia, the arguments pop up as the government is introducing a system to value contingent

[2] Taking into account that one form of taxation is inflation.

[3] Standard arguments in cost–benefit analysis on the relative discount rates to be used for public versus private investments are surveyed in Spackman (no date). He concludes for the case of the United Kingdom that public and private discount rates are similar essentially because the risk premium of private rates happens to correspond to the adjustment to public rates required to correct for taxation of private investment. He believes the tax system can almost completely diversify risk for public investment.

fiscal liabilities. To value them, one needs to discount cashflows and doing so at the risk-free rate would favour public over private investment. Some implications for the role of development finance institutions are sketched in the conclusion.

## II. THE BASIC POSITIONS STAKED OUT

### (i) 'Private-sector Capital Costs More'

The view that private-sector capital costs more starts from the observation that, in general, sovereign borrowing is cheaper than borrowing by private firms.[4] This reflects the lower default risk of the sovereign, which tends to be able to raise money by way of taxation including the inflation tax. As a result, the interest rate on sovereign debt is commonly called 'risk-free.'

To put this in the context of the example of an independent power generation project, a privately funded project would have to charge higher tariffs than a publicly funded project—everything else being equal. Why then is anyone advocating private power projects?

*'The public sector cannot fund all the project needs'*
One commonly heard answer is that the government cannot be expected to fund the enormous projected requirements for new projects. But somehow the private sector is expected to be able to do so. This answer is not convincing *per se*. Total saving (domestic and foreign) available to fund investment is unlikely to be affected by the shift from public to private projects. Why should the private sector be better able to tap these savings than the public sector—for the very same projects? For there to be substance to the argument the government must be credit-rationed, while the private sector is not. In other words, government debt would need to be more risky than private debt. This is conceivable when government default is a possibility, i.e. when the government is not able to print the means of payment itself.[5] In a sense government is, then, like a firm that is not able to borrow for the great new project it has identified but has to let others invest in it, because it is already overextended. Overextension means the government (the firm) has financial obligations owing to other projects, which may render service of new financing difficult. So the new project needs to be incorporated separately and independently—the definition of project finance. Alternatively, a creditworthy firm could fund the project on-balance-sheet. In any case, the government is a riskier, i.e. more expensive borrower—contrary to the basic assumption that 'private-sector capital costs more.'

*'Government funding is cheaper, but private management is better'*
When governments are not credit-rationed, they tend to be able to raise funds at lower rates than private firms. Still, to advocate private projects in this situation one would need to assume that the government's funding advantage is more than offset by the private sector's management efficiency.

An example of this argument can be found in the World Bank's *World Development Report 1994*:[6] 'In infrastructure projects, the cheaper credit available to governments needs to be weighed against possible inefficiencies in channelling funds through government.' The report cites an example where a 3 per cent interest-rate advantage of government funding would need to be offset by cost savings of more than 20 per cent for private ownership to be advantageous.

[4] In fairly stable economies with well-functioning capital markets (e.g. the United Kingdom, the United States, and other major OECD economies), 'risk-free' interest rates on sovereign debt are currently about 3–4 per cent in real terms. Private corporate debt may be priced one percentage point higher, and structured project debt yet another one or two percentage points above this. On average, private equity tends to trade at some 2–4 per cent above the risk-free rate on sovereign debt, the so-called equity premium. Rates tend to be higher in other economies owing to higher country risk, which affects all rates, or higher policy risk in a particular sector, which affects firms and projects in that sector (Blanchard, 1993; Spackman, no date).

[5] Government is unable to print the means of payment when a project contract is, for example, denominated in foreign currency. In some extreme cases governments may have been so abusive that their own citizens are unwilling to pay taxes and to hold domestic currency. That, first of all, reduces the scope for viable contracts drastically and, second, means that new contracts may often be concluded in 'foreign currency', which government cannot debase, e.g. payment in commodities such as gold or cigarettes.

[6] World Bank, 1994, Box 5.1, p. 91.

OXFORD REVIEW OF ECONOMIC POLICY, VOL. 13, NO. 4

There are a number of cases where efficiency gains of 20 or more per cent have, indeed, been achieved by transferring management to the private sector.[7] But efficiency gains vary widely. They may amount to only a few per cent and, in some important cases, it is not clear whether private is really more effective than public management, particularly when private enterprise is subject to monopoly regulation. For example, the most thorough study of the relative efficiency of private- versus public-sector power utilities in the United States suggests that—controlling for differences in cost of capital, tax treatment, and other factors—public utilities are more efficient than investor-owned ones (Kwoka, 1996). Should the United States, therefore, nationalize all power utilities? If we believe in the basic arguments about the cost of government borrowing, the case would seem strong, because public-sector utilities deliver slightly cheaper service, even when one does not add in the borrowing cost advantage.

If one believes that a trade-off between low-cost government finance and greater private-sector efficiency exists, then one needs to be careful with privatization unless it is reasonably clear that private management will yield sufficient benefits to offset the lower cost of sovereign funds. By the same token, private management is then justified in clamouring for government financial support up to the point where its own incentives to perform efficiently are undermined.

This line of argument also lies behind calls for government or multilateral financial participation in private projects. Such calls are, for example, made by the Institute for International Finance (IIF),[8] which suggests World Bank lending to the private sector. As is well known, a number of infrastructure projects benefit from some type of government financial participation (beyond guarantees for policy failures), for example, Hungary's M5 motorway project.

Extending this argument, then, means that privatization of infrastructure should often be reserved for countries with highly inefficient government enterprises. But countries with good public enterprises could gain relatively little from privatization. Given the cost advantage of public borrowing, they should then not privatize. In particular, the cost of government funds would appear cheaper than private equity.

### (ii) 'There is No Real Cost Advantage to Public Borrowing'

How can one deny that sovereign borrowing is not cheaper than private finance? A task force of the Australian government on private infrastructure has formulated the position thus:

> [The task force] rejected the argument that the cost of government debt is necessarily cheaper than the private-sector cost of capital (which would have implied that government should finance most infrastructure investment). The task force argued that governments' lower cost of funds largely reflects the fact that taxpayers are providing an implicit guarantee for project risks under public ownership. Thus, it concluded that much of the difference in the private and public cost of capital is apparent rather than real. (Economic Planning Advisory Commission, 1995, p. 37)

In other words, if the taxpayers were to receive appropriate remuneration for the insurance they provide, the apparent cost advantage of government finance would disappear. If this were so, there would be no trade-off between the cost of sovereign funds and efficiency gains from private management. It would still be true that in countries with good public enterprises the benefits from privatization may be lower than in countries with bad ones—assuming equally good private firms. Yet, privatization could still be advocated, even if it brought only very small improvements. By the same token, there would be no rationale for private firms to ask for government financial support in the form of debt or equity or guarantees of credit obligations. To take the example of World Bank instruments, there would be no rationale to use straightforward loans or credit guarantees—only policy guarantees and like instruments would be justified.[9]

[7] See, for example, Carnaghan and Bracewell-Milnes (1993) and Domberger *et al.* (1994).

[8] Institute of International Finance (1995, p. 6). The IIF suggested World Bank lending to the private sector without a host government counter-guarantee. Private companies would thus benefit from the low-cost funds the World Bank can raise owing to its backing from the best credit risks of the world, i.e. the major governments of this world.

[9] In the case of World Bank credit, taxpayers in industrial countries underwrite risks. When loans or guarantees are counter-guaranteed by the host government, then taxpayers of that country also underwrite, leaving taxpayers in developing countries to assume risks as a last resort.

Government efforts should be directed to improving macroeconomic stability, improving the policy environment for private projects, and deregulating and liberalizing the financial sector to allow private entrepreneurs to put together the best possible deals. Multilaterals should support governments in these efforts but stay away from taking on commercial risk. This position has, for example, been forcefully expressed by Charles Frank of GE-Capital (Frank, 1995) and underlies the philosophy of the World Bank's new policy guarantee programme.[10]

## III. THE UNDERPINNINGS OF THE BASIC POSITIONS EXPLORED

Is one of the basic positions the right one or is there some middle ground? In the following discussion the analytical underpinnings for a possible answer will be explored. To do so, a central position will be taken, namely that—from a normative point of view—the government has no interests apart from those of the individuals it represents. Government policy should thus express and represent the interests of individual citizens. It may not do so in practice, but such deviations from the will of the citizens would be illegitimate and could not be adduced to justify policy.

### (i) The Cost of Risk-bearing and the Choice of Discount Rates

The core issue can then be recast as follows. Differences in the cost of finance or capital reflect differing abilities to bear risk or cope with it. In a seminal article written by Nobel prize winners, K. Arrow and R. C. Lind (1970), the essence of the controversy is introduced as follows:

> It is widely accepted that individuals are not indifferent to uncertainty and will not, in general, value assets with uncertain returns at their expected value. For example, risk aversion implies that an individual would be interested in trading a gamble with a 50–50 chance of winning or losing US$5,000 for the certainty of neither gaining nor losing anything and would be willing to pay some positive sum—not choose investments to maximize the present value of expected returns, but to maximize the present value of returns properly adjusted for risk. The issue is whether it is appropriate to discount public investments in the same way as private investments.

This issue is equivalent to the basic question here of whether the cost of sovereign borrowing is cheaper than that of private finance, because the cost of capital determines the discount rate for projects.[11] Projects have to earn at least the cost of capital to be acceptable to investors. Discounting project cashflows by the cost of capital, therefore, is an appropriate method to identify viable projects. If the cost of risk-bearing in the public sector, i.e. of the taxpayers, were the same as in the private sector, then the discount rates would be the same. The lower cost of sovereign borrowing would simply be due to the fact that government forces taxpayers to provide funds without remunerating them for the risks they take. If the cost of risk-bearing of the taxpayers were, however, lower than that of private parties, then the lower cost of sovereign borrowing would be due to a 'real' advantage, i.e. a lower cost of risk. Note that each individual, whether in the role of taxpayer or investor, has identical attitudes to risk, although such attitudes will vary among individuals.

Arrow and Lind argued that government finance was indeed cheaper than private finance. They claimed that the government discount rate should be a risk-free rate reflecting risk-neutrality on the government's part. Private discount rates, however, should reflect risk-aversion and therefore contain a risk premium rendering private finance more expensive than public finance.[12]

Before looking at the arguments in detail, it may be worth mentioning that the Arrow–Lind view of government discounting has in fact dominated the debate for years. Recently, a new World Bank handbook (World Bank, 1996) states that 'the accepted view is that, save for very special cases, governments should not be concerned with the probability of failure or with the variance of outcomes [of projects]. . . . Government decision-makers should be "risk-neutral".'

[10] The policy risk guarantees are also called partial risk guarantees by the World Bank—as opposed to partial credit guarantees, which guarantee full loan obligations.

[11] For a standard exposition see Brealey and Myers (1991).

[12] A higher private discount rate would also imply that the private sector would tend to choose projects and technologies with quicker pay-back or shorter gestation periods than the government.

In other words, governments should care only about expected values, not variances of outcomes. That is, they should be indifferent between a project with a certain value of US$100, and a project, with an expected value of US$100, which is based on a 50–50 chance of losing US$100 or winning US$300.

### (ii) Risk-pooling and Risk-spreading

As stated by the World Bank (1996), the position of Arrow and Lind

> is based on the concepts of 'risk pooling' and 'risk spreading.' If a country's portfolio has many projects whose outcomes are mutually independent, the country need not be concerned with the variability of the net present value (NPV) of a project around its expected values, as measured, for example, by the 'variance' of the probability distribution of the NPV. The reason for this is that while many projects will result in lower-than-expected NPVs, others will result in higher-than-expected NPVs; if the projects are small and do not systematically reinforce each other's outcomes, then the negative and positive effects will tend to cancel out to a large extent.

In the case of zero correlation between all projects the variance of the portfolio is reduced towards zero by diversification.[13] If project risks are correlated, risk-pooling will not eliminate all risk. The size and sign of the covariance of returns on prospective projects is an empirical question. It seems, though, that a large number of projects undertaken by the state have outcomes correlated with national income. Electric power, highways, waterways, airports, and postal services, for example, all facilitate ordinary commerce and will thus be positively correlated with national income, allowing for a lower degree of risk reduction.

Arrow and Lind had mentioned the risk-pooling concept in their article, but did not present it as crucial. The private sector, too, can pool risks. Any advantage the state may have in pooling diverse risks can be transferred to the private sector by privatizing the projects in question.

The crucial argument by Arrow and Lind is about risk-spreading. They suggest that any financing system that is able to spread risks in tiny amounts over very large numbers of investors can tap funds at the risk-free rate. Increasing the number of investors will diminish the overall costs of risk-bearing at a faster rate than the summation of the individual costs will increase the overall costs. With an infinite number of investors the costs of risk-bearing will therefore converge to zero. Figure 1 illustrates the main point of Arrow and Lind. Investors with declining marginal utility of income will value losses more highly than gains. The utility of a project with uncertain outcome will thus be lower than the utility of a certain outcome equal to the expected value of the project. By subdividing the same project in equal shares among two parties the cost of risk-bearing will be reduced by more than half, because the slope of the marginal utility curve is steeper for smaller amounts. Consequently, when the number of investors bearing the risk becomes very large the total cost of risk-bearing approaches zero. Thus, the total cost of risk-bearing of a project which is independent of all other projects in the economy[14] is made negligible by the spreading of the risk over a large number of individuals.

Figure 1 illustrates the basic Arrow–Lind argument. The curve implies that the utility of income grows at a slower rate, the higher the income. Losses thus count more than gains of equal risk, a definition of risk aversion. The diagram depicts a gamble which yields income of $Y_1 = 6$ or $Y_2 = 10$ units with equal probability for an expected income of $\bar{Y} = 8$. Subdividing the gamble among two persons with identical utility functions would yield two gambles yielding incomes of $Y'_1 = 3$ or $Y'_2 = 5$ with equal probability for an expected income of $\bar{Y}' = 4$. The expected utility of the gambles $EU(Y)$ is smaller than the utility from

[13] Paul Samuelson (1966) clarified the debate about the benefits from pooling by pointing out that pooling *per se* may not help to make a gamble more attractive. Pooling of uncorrelated risks does create a new gamble with a larger mean and reduced relative variance. But, to paraphrase the argument, flying with a dangerous airline many times does not help reduce risk. It may just increase the chance that very big losses will occur. But pooling combined with subdivision of risk would definitively help. Thus, for an investor with a given budget, risk is reduced by buying a share in a pool of uncorrelated projects, rather than buying a single one of the projects with the same expected value.

[14] Risk-spreading crucially depends on the returns from the project being independent of other components of national income. As discussed in the case of risk-pooling, this is not necessarily the case for infrastructure projects since (*a*) they are often correlated with other components through the business cycle, or (*b*) they constitute a large fraction of national income.

M. Klein

**Figure 1**

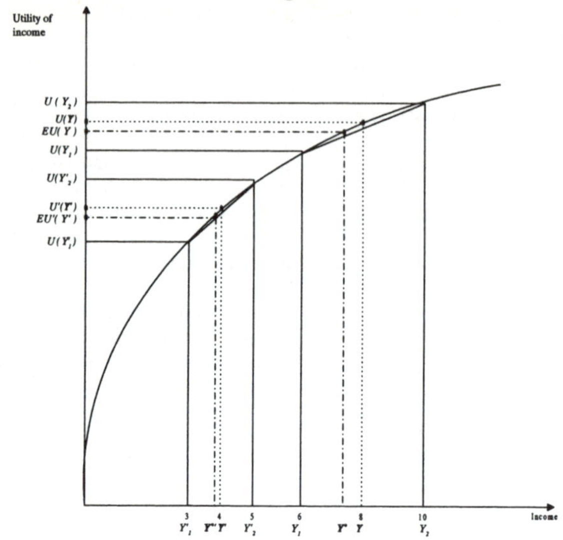


a certain income equal to the expected value of the gamble. The expected utility of the gamble may be set equal to that of a certain outcome, $Y^*$, the certainty equivalent, i.e. a sure return of $Y^*$. The difference between the expected income from the gamble and the certainty equivalent is the cost of risk-bearing. The cost of risk-bearing is the price the individuals in question would be willing to pay to exchange the gamble for the certainty equivalent. The cost of risk-bearing declines faster than the number of individuals sharing in the risk and approaches zero as the number of individuals increases.

Arrow and Lind argue that the government is actually able to spread risks in tiny amounts over millions of taxpayers, thus exploiting their 'near-zero' cost of risk-bearing. Thus, the government could help the economy exploit the willingness of taxpayers to insure projects with non-negative NPVs without asking for remuneration, given that the cost of risk-bearing is zero. In this way the government provides a good substitute for missing insurance markets.[15] By relying on taxpayer guaranteed finance, the economy could reach the level of investments that is technically possible.

The government would thus be able to tap the low cost of risk-bearing of individuals carrying small amounts of risk efficiently. But then why could large corporations not achieve the same result? Arrow and Lind argue

> that in order to control the firm, some shareholder may hold a large block of stock, which is a significant component of his wealth. If this were true, then, from his point of view, the costs of risk-bearing would not be negligible and the firm should behave as a risk averter . . . even though from the stockholder's point of view, risk should be ignored, it may not be in the interest of the corporate managers to neglect risk. Their careers and income are intimately related to the firm's performance. From their point of view, variations in the outcome of some corporate action impose very real costs. In this case, given a degree of autonomy, the corporate managers, in considering

[15] Imagine a hypothetical bench-mark case in which insurance markets exist for every conceivable risk and circumstance. If such a complete set of insurance products existed, everybody could lock in riskless values of investment (Arrow and Hahn, 1971). Financing such investment would then be possible at the risk-free rate, which would also be the appropriate discount rate. A complete set of insurance markets does not, however, exist, a major reason being that the existence of insurance would make people behave more recklessly (moral hazard) and thus change the underlying risk profile of the projects. Owing to moral hazard, total investments in the country will be lower than they ideally could be if people were to 'restrain themselves better'.

prospective investments, may discount for risk when it is not in the interest of the stockholders to do so.'

If one accepts the Arrow and Lind arguments, then decisions on projects will be biased against private participation. This is not based on considerations of fairness and equity in the economy or arguments about so-called public goods, such as the rule of law or defence, where some form of government may be required. The argument is valid even for pure private goods, i.e. those where benefits and costs can be fully appropriated by individuals.

### (iii) Risk Allocation and Incentives of Intermediaries

What are possible counter-arguments? First, the Arrow–Lind argument as originally presented is overstating its case. There are cases where large projects are highly correlated with national income. Dixit and Williamson (1989) highlight some of these, for example, oil production projects in Nigeria. More fundamentally, later advances in theory have shown that the theorem at best holds under rather restrictive conditions. Gardner (1979) shows that the theorem only holds for government projects, which are insignificant in relation to overall income in the economy. The capital-asset pricing model as presented, for example, in Brealey and Myers (1991) implies that there remains a remnant of undiversifiable or systemic risk, which requires discount rates to be risk-adjusted.

Spackman (no date) of the UK Treasury tried estimating the undiversifiable risk after optimal pooling of projects, which is correlated with incomes or wealth of taxpayers and thus imposes some positive cost of risk-bearing on taxpayers.[16] When estimating the cost of risk-bearing for taxpayers, he finds that it affects the discount rate—estimated at some 6 per cent annually in real terms—only marginally, adding 0.1 per cent.[17] The discount rate of small countries or countries with a small tax base would, of course, be affected more dramatically. Dixit and Williamson (1989) find that, in small economies, risk-adjustment to discount rates may often require more substantial adjustments for risk, but normally not more than 1 percentage point.

The Arrow–Lind argument may thus hold only in a small number of cases. Yet, more often than not, the risk-adjustment to discount rates that is required may not be large when based on calculations of the covariance of project income with general income. Applying private-sector discount rates as derived, for example, in a capital-asset pricing framework, would appear to result in larger risk premiums. Thus the bias in favour of public financing still appears to obtain.

Any remaining bias in favour of public financing tends to become questionable when one considers explicitly not only risk-diversification issues, but also associated agency costs. To begin with, one may note that one large shareholder may not be necessary for reasons of corporate control. If there are private benefits of control, the threat of exit to the manager (with a concurrent drop in share prices) may serve for control purposes. Moreover, the major shareholder could be an equity fund consisting itself of a large number of shareholders, thus spreading the costs of risk-bearing over an even greater number of shareholders, given that the internal incentives mechanism of the fund manager are appropriately designed. Furthermore, bureaucratic managers might be just as risk averse and reluctant to undertake risky projects as corporate managers are. The rationale for the better risk-spreading capabilities of the government is thus rather doubtful.

More fundamentally, one may ask what it is about the tax system that allows it to tap lots of 'investors' with low costs of risk-bearing. Is it the unique 'technology' of the tax system, or the fact of coercion, or maybe both? If individuals are willing to part with small amounts of money in return for no more than the risk-free rate of return, why are private players not able to exploit this?

[16] Analysing the correlation of project cash-flow with national income is similar to the analysis underlying the standard capital-asset pricing model in finance theory. However, society is treated as if it were an individual, which would require strong assumptions about comparability of utility or compensation schemes among individuals.

[17] The social cost of the risk that taxpayers bear would be higher if one accounted for the distortions that are typically associated with taxation. The full cost of raising a dollar of tax revenues may well be much higher. Studies suggest ranges from 20 to over 100 per cent higher. However, accepting Spackman's calculations, that would still leave the discount rate essentially unchanged, perhaps rising to 6.2 per cent.

M. Klein

Many financial systems have large banks, which raise small deposits from a large number of people. However, when investing in projects, the first-in-line risk-takers are the equity investors, for many of whom the project risks are not negligible. They therefore require risk-adjusted rates of return.

If large banks could collect 'deposits' from their customers and invest them without exposing the bank's equity holders, then they should be able to mimic the tax system's ability to tap low-cost funds. Indeed, 'trust' accounts would be the equivalent of such a transaction being mere pass-throughs. But we observe no project finance based on such pass-through mechanisms. Apparently, depositors will want to be reasonably sure that their money will not be abused. If the trustee is not exposed and small depositors cannot directly assess and monitor project performance, it is not likely that people will provide money. Almost by definition, small depositors will not be able to monitor projects. An exposed agent is thus necessary to gain confidence. As a result, depositors in banks are willing to provide money at low interest rates, but the bank will require risk-adjusted rates when investing in projects or portfolios of assets.[18]

One could easily test the hypothesis that providers of small amounts of money would require an exposed agent. On income tax returns a field could be created where taxpayers could voluntarily indicate the amount of money they would be willing to invest in projects via the government. The money could be collected with the tax bill and returns from such voluntary investment could be automatically credited to future tax bills.

Somehow we might expect that not too much money would be raised that way. If so, this would support the view that the financial advantages of government finance are based on coercive powers and not on a superior system of exploiting the low-cost of risk-bearing of tiny investors. In fact, it would become clear that the low cost funds cannot be tapped unless the intermediaries have good incentives to use the money well, which by necessity gives rise to significant costs of risk-bearing on the part of the exposed intermediary. In turn, this requires risk-adjusted rates of return on financial instruments. Crucially, we cannot consider the cost of funds independently of the incentive system, under which intermediaries collect them. This is similar to modern theories of intermediation, which emphasize the monitoring problem of small investors in intermediaries and not only optimal risk-diversification issues (Hellwig, 1990).[19]

### (iv) Incentives of the Government as Intermediary

For the Arrow and Lind argument to hold, the government as intermediary would need to have better incentives to invest well than private parties. Arrow and Lind state that

> many of the uncertainties which arise in private capital markets are related to what may be called moral hazards. Individuals involved in a given transaction may hedge against the possibility of fraudulent behaviour on the part of their associates. Many such risks are not present in the case of public investments and, therefore, it can be argued that it is not appropriate for the government to take these risks into account when choosing among public investments.

It seems Arrow and Lind assume that the government will, in fact, do what it ought to do, namely act benevolently and efficiently. Clearly, that is not the case in practice for many governments throughout history. So Arrow and Lind may be right that there are low-cost funds out there, but they may err in

[18] Because depositors cannot monitor intermediaries easily, they like contracts with specified interest rates, so that they can easily recognize default (Diamond, 1984).

[19] It might be argued that the attitude of individuals to risk may, in practice, not be rational in the sense of standard economic theory. Prospect theory is an attempt to come to grips with observed departures from 'rational' behaviour (Thaler, 1992). To some extent, the rules of thumb and habits that people use to deal with risk may still be rational in the sense that they make life more easily manageable in the face of overwhelming complexity. However, whatever the reason, small departures from rational behaviour can, in principle, have large aggregate effects (Akerlof and Yellen, 1985). If individuals are dealing with risk 'irrationally' there might be a role for government, if only the wise and benevolent were in charge. But if politicians are 'just human' there is no a priori reason to believe they would deal with risk better than capital markets. Even if policy-makers are benevolent and wise to the ways of risk, it is unclear whether they can accurately predict the distortions arising from 'irrational' behaviour and whether they can, in practice, design interventions to offset them.

OXFORD REVIEW OF ECONOMIC POLICY, VOL. 13, NO. 4

jumping to the conclusion that the tax system is a good way of tapping them.[20]

But maybe one could argue that government should collect 'cheap' money and pass it on to projects which have private sponsors, who have first-risk-of-loss and will want to invest well. This line of argument may be seductive at first sight. However, any such rule 'invest only when there is serious private equity' or 'invest only *pari passu* in senior debt and not more than 5 per cent of total project costs' can be adopted by private pass-through trusts, the trustees of which may have quite reasonable incentives to maintain a decent reputation, arguably better than government officials, whose reputation is much less dependent on any particular project than a trustee's reputation. But we know that in practice investors are wary of trustees who are allowed considerable discretion in interpreting rules of a trust.[21]

Full government funding combined with private service provision weakens incentives for project selection. When the government selects projects, privatization may amount to managing the wrong thing efficiently. Yet, to paraphrase Peter Drucker, it is much more important to do the right thing in the first place—the fundamental argument behind using financial markets rather than central planning to guide investment decisions.

The preceding arguments apply to all sectors. It has been argued that the case of infrastructure is different, to the extent that there are elements of natural monopoly requiring price regulation. Regulation, by definition, implies the exercise of discretion by some form of governmental authority. The regulatory agency may then create 'artificial' risks leading to high private-sector risk premia. The argument continues that public funding or ownership would reduce artificial risk and thus be preferable. However, the argument neglects to recognize that regulatory discretion of some sort will also be exercised in the case of public enterprises. In fact, complaints about political interference in state-owned utilities are rampant. So we are once again left with the question whether risk—in this case regulatory risk—can better be diversified by financial markets or the tax system. The arguments presented above thus apply. In addition, the best way for governments to commit themselves to certain policies may often be to limit the tax powers of government, because this reduces options on the government side for alternative solutions.

So far, the argument is that there is no a priori reason to believe that taxpayers can better diversify risk than capital markets. In a world where taxes are imposed by small states in a large world economy with liberalized cross-border capital markets, it would seem that all sorts of risks can actually be better diversified by capital markets than taxpayers. This would also apply to regulatory risk, which varies among countries and jurisdictions. More broadly, policy risks, such as foreign-exchange-related ones, should not be imposed on taxpayers of—often small—countries, but left for investors. This goes against widespread practice in project finance, where governments and investors often agree to impose, for example, the risk of currency convertibility on taxpayers.

Finally, the argument that government has a lower cost of risk-bearing than private investors would appear to entail absurd consequences, for example that government should invest in projects and funds with high expected values, such as venture capital, or that companies such as General Motors should benefit from free government credit guarantees on all their borrowings.[22]

The preceding points suggest that the apparent benefits of sovereign finance are all due to coercive powers with no social value. To construct an argument in favour of socially useful coercion, one would need to find some market failure that can be rem-

[20] We know that, in some cases, people are willing to invest in opportunities with negative expected values, for example lotteries. If one could create a lottery for project finance this should lower the cost of funds. After investment in a project, investors' lots could be drawn, assigning very high proportions of the project return to some investors and nothing to others. The fact that we do not see such mechanisms may have to do with the fact that abuse under normal lotteries is easier to monitor. But perhaps there are unexploited ways of setting up mutual funds here. The equity contributors to projects such as Eurotunnel may, in fact, have been driven by a lottery spirit. In earlier days lottery bonds were issued, for example, to finance the Panama Canal.

[21] See, for example, Millman (1995).

[22] Note that modern tax theory assumes that governments are not risk-neutral, with important implications for optimal asset-liability management (Kaplow, 1994).

edied by coercion. One such argument derives from adverse-selection problems in private financial markets. Very large projects may require sponsors to tap a large set of investors, many of whom may not be very informed investors. Such badly informed investors may be afraid of being systematically at a disadvantage compared to others, and thus shy away from investing. In a sense, they may think that any project seeking funds from them must be of inferior quality. Otherwise the well informed investors would have snapped it up. If the government were to recognize correctly those projects which would not be funded owing to adverse selection, then coercive financing via the tax system could get investors to put up money without being afraid of being saddled with a project nobody else wanted.[23] Of course, the problem remains that the government may neither be capable nor interested in correctly judging project quality and identifying when a serious adverse selection issue exists.

## IV. CONCLUSION

The discussion suggests that government through the tax system cannot be expected to do better than private financial markets—unless government policy places constraints on financial markets such as restrictions on capital movements or interest-rate controls. As a result, all the financial advantages of sovereign finance are purely due to coercive powers. Because very often there is no free-rider issue here, which can be remedied, such coercion rarely has social value.[24] As argued by the Australian task force cited earlier, under government finance the taxpayers would bear a contingent liability, which if properly remunerated would wipe out any cost advantage of sovereign borrowing. Governments should then refrain from investing in projects or firms, whether with equity or with debt. They should not cover commercial risks.

In particular, one cannot argue that there is a trade-off between the lower cost of government finance and higher private efficiency. Private markets will do the best they can to tap low-cost funds while maintaining project discipline. They solve whatever trade-off there is. The government cannot do better by raising funds. A corollary is that discount rates for private- and public-sector projects would not be expected to differ—contrary to standard practice.

Arguing that the government cannot be expected to improve on the outcome of free financial markets is not to argue that all is for the best in the best of all possible worlds and that there is no role for government. Private markets may not always find the best solution. Market participants constantly search for better ways of trading risks.[25] But on average we could not expect governments to do better.[26]

More importantly, governments can significantly reduce the cost of risk-bearing by conducting prudent macroeconomic policies, supporting secure property rights, and deregulating and liberalizing the financial markets, so that private players can do their best to take advantage of low-cost funding opportunities. But it is not efficient to offset the risks created through bad policy by taxpayer-supported funding. That would amount to stealing from investors and compensating them by taking away from taxpayers.

In principle, multilateral finance institutions should apply their instruments to support the development of better government policies, for example by granting

[23] I am indebted to Colin Mayer for this argument.

[24] The real issue is not whether governments should be treated as risk-neutral or not, but whether there is a problem of collective action and whether it requires tax powers to solve it. In this sense, the real debate is simply about whether privatization makes sense or not. The cost of capital is determined simultaneously by the decision about the appropriate form of governance for an activity, i.e. the best possible allocation of risks and incentives among various parties. There is no separate trade-off between the cost of capital and efficiency of an arrangement.

[25] In fact, if financial markets were fully efficient, i.e. all arbitrage opportunities (profitable trades) had been exhausted, there would be no incentive left to look for better deals. That, in turn, would imply that arbitrage stops and we could not assume that markets would really be efficient.

[26] The argument is not simply tautological. It just says that we do not know whether governments have discount rates that are systematically different from those of private investors. One reason why they might be systematically different is that private entrepreneurs may be protected by limited liability provisions, which limit the feasible set of risk diversification and incentive schemes. Governments, on the other hand, can to some degree circumvent this constraint by imposing and adjusting taxes. However, we currently do not know how to weigh these considerations.

insurance against policy failures, where new policy regimes are not yet credible, but not by investing in projects or by guaranteeing the full credit risk of loans.

In this paper examples have been drawn from infrastructure projects, but none of the arguments about risk allocation and management is specific to infrastructure. In competitive markets it is by now fairly widely accepted that there is no clear role for government finance. The debate is, however, still alive for services, which are provided by monopolies or exclusive providers, such as many infrastructure services.

As sketched in Annex 1, there may be cases where subsidies are advisable, for example, to enable prices to be set at efficient levels, i.e. marginal cost. For example, on uncongested toll-roads the government may choose to pay subsidies in the form of shadow tolls, so as not to push drivers off the toll-road by high average cost-covering tolls. However, the policy-maker should not offer to fund construction of the road with either debt or equity.

## ANNEX 1: SPECIAL POLICY ISSUES FOR NATURAL MONOPOLIES

In this section, some special issues relating to infrastructure projects are sketched, which are sometimes used to argue for government funding of infrastructure projects. In sectors such as gas and water pipelines, power transmission and distribution, or road networks, competitive markets do not exist. First, consumers may be 'taxed' through regulation or by monopolists. Second, governments might need to pay subsidies[27] to ensure efficient pricing of infrastructure services.

### (i) Risk-sharing between Investors and Consumers

In infrastructure sectors, private incentives to operate efficiently may be weakened, because all forms of regulation or contracting tend to contain elements of cost-plus pricing. Wherever cost-plus pricing methodologies are pronounced, risks are shifted from investors to consumers. The cost of capital for investors and their projects is accordingly reduced. A number of US investor-owned utilities are effectively able to raise finance at little more than the risk-free rate of return (Alexander, 1995). Shifting risks to consumers may yield similar implications for the cost of capital as shifting it to taxpayers. But at least consumers have the option of not buying the service. Their effective willingness-to-pay places a limit on the scope for exploitation, which does not exist in the same way for taxpayers. Even if one interpreted the high cost to consumers as a tax, it would be a tax with some optimality features as it is imposed on price-inelastic consumption.

### (ii) Subsidies to Support Efficient Pricing

Those elements of infrastructure that contain strong elements of natural monopoly have by definition low variable and high fixed costs, such that average cost will generally be above marginal cost. For investors to amortize their investment they need to receive prices that are at least equal to average cost. However, optimal pricing should be marginal-cost-based. For example, in the case of a toll-road, if the road is uncongested, the cost an additional passenger car imposes on the road is minimal. Ideally, all cars should be allowed to drive on an uncongested road as long as they pay for marginal cost. Tolls would thus collect prices corresponding to marginal cost and uncongested roads would not recover

[27] Traditionally, it has been argued that there are cases where financial subsidies from the state are justified on other grounds than the taxpayer's low cost of risk-bearing. Social justice may argue for supporting the poor. Environmental concerns may argue for subsidies for clean production processes. In all these cases, economic reasoning suggests that the best possible outcomes for society cannot be expected to result from the free interplay of private parties. Instead, properly designed 'subsidies' should improve the outcome. In this respect the arguments are similar to the Arrow–Lind argument. However, the Arrow–Lind thesis assumed that taxpayers were willing to provide small amounts of insurance for 'nearly' free. As argued, intermediaries would have the option of attracting many mini-investors into an insurance scheme. Subsidies, on the other hand, are unlikely to be paid voluntarily, because individuals might not directly gain from them and/or are likely to hope that others will pay and try to free-ride on them.

sufficient funds to service debt and equity.[28] The difference between marginal and average cost should be paid as a 'subsidy' or shadow toll to the operator of the toll-road.

The problem is, of course, that demands for subsidies may well get out of hand. In the case of toll-roads it might well be that all sorts of uneconomic roads would get built if taxpayers were to foot the bill, the Mexican toll-road programme being a recent example. While no perfect solution exists, a number of methods are available to limit undue discretion of government authorities while trying to retain as many optimality features as possible.

*Balanced budgets*
The first may be called the 'balanced budget rule.'[29] Adam Smith (1776) noted that marginal cost pricing for roads and bridges might tempt the monarch into excessive construction. This is a reason why we may see infrastructure funded fully by consumers, for example, water in France or power in the United States. Utilities do not receive government transfers and are thus subject to a tighter budget constraint. As mentioned before, 'taxation' via high consumer prices may also have certain optimality properties.

A further rationale for a balanced budget pricing rule hinges on different incentives to monitor the government. When the firm overstates its true fixed costs under marginal cost pricing, taxpayers will bear the costs in the form of subsidies. Under average-cost pricing, an over-report of fixed costs is passed to consumers in the forms of higher prices. If consumers are better organized than taxpayers, average-cost pricing might induce better monitoring of the firm's activities and prove superior to otherwise first-best marginal-cost pricing.[30]

*Transparency*
Greater transparency is another method to limit governmental discretion by exposing decisions to greater scrutiny by interest groups. Cross-subsidies are often criticized for not being transparent and for being open to abuse. In many countries, cross-subsidies benefit the middle classes, while the poor do not get any service at all.

*Elements of competition*
Finally, multiple players with conflicting objectives might be introduced to limit abuse. Auctions among competing bidders may, for example, be used to obtain a quotation for the lowest possible subsidy.

## REFERENCES


Akerlof, J., and Yellen, J. L. (1985). 'Can Small Deviations from Rationality Make Significant Differences to Economic Equilibria?', *American Economic Review*.

Alexander, I. (1995), 'Regulatory Structure and Risk: An International Comparison', Washington, DC, World Bank, mimeo.

Anderson, J. R., and Quiggin, J. C. (1990), 'Uncertainty in Project Appraisal', paper presented at the World Bank Annual Conference on Development Economics, Washington, DC.

Arrow, K. J., and Lind, R. C. (1970), 'Uncertainty and the Evaluation of Public Investment Decisions', *American Economic Review*.

Bishop. M., Kay, J., and Mayer, C. (1994), *Privatization and Economic Performance*, Oxford, Oxford University Press.

Blanchard, O. J. (1993), 'The Vanishing Equity Premium', in *Finance and the International Economy 7*, Oxford, Oxford University Press.

Brealey, R. A., and Myers, S. C. (1991), *Principles of Corporate Finance*, 4th edn, McGraw Hill.

Carnaghan, R., and Bracewell-Milnes, B. (1993), 'Testing the Market: Competitive Tendering for Government Services in Britain and Abroad', London, Institute of Economic Affairs.

Diamond, D. (1984), 'Financial Intermediation and Delegated Monitoring', *Review of Economic Studies*.


[28] The development of transport infrastructure may have positive effects on adjacent land development, i.e. benefits owing to the infrastructure but not captured by its builders. Therefore, the infrastructure developers should be able to obtain land at its value prior to their investment so as to provide optimum incentives to them for the expansion of infrastructure. Alternatively, they might benefit from the rise in property taxes owing to appreciation of property consequent to infrastructure development.

[29] See Laffont and Tirole (1993, chs 15 and 16) for a discussion.

[30] Laffont and Tirole (1993, pp. 591–613).

Dixit, A., and Williamson, A. (1989), 'Risk-adjusted Rates of Return for Project Appraisal', Policy, Planning and Research Working Paper 290, Washington, DC, World Bank.

Domberger, S., Meadowcroft, S., and Thompson, D. (1994), chapter in M. Bishop *et al.* (eds) (1994).

Economic Planning Advisory Commission (1995), 'Private Infrastructure Task Force Report', Canberra.

*Euromoney* (1995), 'Where, When—and How Much?', March.

Frank, C. R., Jr (1995), 'The Role of the World Bank in Infrastructure Investment', paper presented at Forbes Infrastructure Conference, New York, 18 January.

Gardner, R. (1979), 'The Arrow–Lind Theorem in a Continuum Economy', *American Economic Review*, June.

Hellwig, M. (1990), 'Banking, Financing Intermediation, and Corporate Finance', Discussion Paper 9015, University of Basel.

Institute of International Finance (1995), 'Increasing the Supply of Bankable Infrastructure Projects in Developing Countries', Washington, DC.

Kaplow (1994), 'Taxation and Risk-taking', *National Tax Journal*, **47**, 789.

Kay, J. (1993), 'Efficiency and Private Capital in the Provision of Infrastructure', in *Infrastructure Policies for the 1990s*, Paris, OECD.

Kwoka, J. E., Jr (1996), 'Privatization, Deregulation, and Competition: A Survey of Effects on Economic Performance', World Bank, Washington, DC, mimeo.

Laffont, J.-J., and Tirole, J. (1993), 'A Theory of Incentives in Procurement and Regulations', Cambridge, MA.

Millman, G. (1995), 'In Whom Should Projects Trust?', *Infrastructure Finance*, June/July.

Samuelson, P. A. (1966), 'Risk and Uncertainty: A Fallacy of Large Numbers', in J. Stiglitz (ed.), *The Collected Scientific Papers of Paul A. Samuelson*, Cambridge, MA, MIT Press.

Smith, A. (1776), *The Wealth of Nations*.

Spackman, M. (no date), 'Discount Rates and Rates of Return in the Public Sector', Government Economic Service Working Paper 113, London, HM Treasury.

Thaler, R. H. (1992), 'The Winner's Curse—Paradoxes and Anomalies of Economic Life', Princeton, NJ.

World Bank (1994), *World Development Report 1994*, Washington, DC, World Bank.

— (1996), *Handbook on Economic Analysis of Investment Operations*, Washington, DC, World Bank.

# [22]

*Fiscal Studies* (1998) vol. 19, no. 2, pp. 121–140

# *Private Opportunity, Public Benefit?*

JOHN HALL*

***Abstract***

The newly elected Labour government has pledged to 'reinvigorate the Private Finance Initiative', as part of the new emphasis on 'public/private partnerships' in the delivery of core public services. This article assesses the merits of using private finance to deliver public services against three criteria: whether it will lead to additional investment in social infrastructure, whether it represents good value for the taxpayer's money and whether the use of private finance will reduce the public sector's flexibility to pursue its public service objectives.

*JEL classification:* H54, H11.

## I. INTRODUCTION

In recent years, governments world-wide have sought to increase the involvement of the private sector in the delivery of public services. These initiatives have taken many forms such as outright privatisation of previously state-owned industries, contracting out of services such as refuse collection or cleaning to private firms, and the use of private finance in the provision of social infrastructure. Privatisation has occurred in over 100 countries, most notably in the former Communist countries of central and eastern Europe. Contracting out of labour-intensive services has also been widespread.[1] Concessions to build and operate large-scale infrastructure networks such as roads have been of particular

---

*Senior Research Economist at the Institute for Fiscal Studies.

This research was financed as part of the programme of the ESRC Research Centre for the Microeconomic Analysis of Fiscal Policy at IFS. The author is grateful for comments from Tom Clark, Andrew Dilnot, Ian Preston and two anonymous referees.

[1]Refuse collection, for example, has been contracted out in the US and Canada amongst others (McDavid, 1985).

interest to rapidly developing countries in South America and South-East Asia (Desai and Brooks, 1997).

Within the UK, interest in introducing 'private capital and expertise in to the provision of public infrastructure'[2] appears to have survived last year's general election, with the Labour Party's election manifesto pledging to 'reinvigorate the Private Finance Initiative' (PFI). Once in office, the government-commissioned Bates Review recommended 29 legislative and procedural changes intended 'to identify any obstacles in the way of bringing PFI projects to fruition'.[3] More recently, the terms of reference for the Comprehensive Spending Review called for departments to examine the scope for greater use of public–private partnerships in the delivery of public services. This paper provides a preliminary assessment of the effects on social welfare of using private finance in the delivery of public services on the basis of three criteria:

- *Additionality.* Does the PFI allow the creation of additional social infrastructure?
- *Value for money.* Does the PFI provide value for money?
- *Public objectives.* Does the use of private finance reduce the public sector's flexibility to pursue its public service objectives?

Section II traces the development of the Private Finance Initiative in the UK. Section III considers whether the PFI is likely to result in the provision of more social infrastructure than would have gone ahead under traditional procurement routes. Section IV looks at the arguments and initial evidence on whether the PFI is likely to prove good value for taxpayers' money. Section V assesses the impact of using private finance on the public sector's ability to deliver its public service objectives. Section VI concludes.

## II. THE DEVELOPMENT OF THE PRIVATE FINANCE INITIATIVE

The launch of the PFI in the UK marks a dramatic shift from the general presumption against the use of private finance in social infrastructure projects which had previously existed in the UK. This presumption against private finance was embodied in the Treasury's Ryrie rules which operated during the 1980s. These rules insisted that privately financed projects could only proceed if they offered better value for money than a hypothetical public sector 'comparator', even if budget constraints meant that the public sector alternative would not go ahead. As Willetts (1993) argued, 'the notorious Ryrie rules were a tease — the conditions they set for privately financed projects were never likely to be met in practice'.

[2] HM Treasury, 1997.
[3] HM Treasury Press Release 69/97.

The Ryrie rules were relaxed in two stages (in 1989 and 1992) so that a public sector comparator would no longer be required if either the project could be financed through user charges or there was no reasonable possibility of the project going ahead within the public sector (Heald and Geaughan, 1995; HM Treasury, 1992).[4] HM Treasury (1993) distinguished three types of PFI project:

- *Financially free-standing projects* where the outlay can be recouped through user charges such as the Skye Bridge.
- *Joint ventures* where the public sector provides the PFI contractor with a subsidy to reflect the social benefits of a project not reflected in cash flow, such as the Docklands Light Railway extension to Lewisham, the Manchester Metrolink and the Channel Tunnel Rail Link.
- *Services sold to the public sector* such as those provided by Bridgend Prison, Design, Build, Finance and Operate (DBFO) road schemes and new trains for London Underground's Northern Line.

Under traditional procurement practices, the construction of publicly owned assets such as roads or prisons is typically undertaken to detailed specifications by private contractors following a competitive tender. Once completed, the public sector is responsible for providing public services using publicly owned infrastructure. Under PFI service contracts, the public sector purchases services such as the availability of prison places or office accommodation from the private sector which owns and manages the underlying infrastructure. This affects how public services are financed and delivered but not who ultimately pays for them. Instead of capital spending having a one-off impact on the public accounts when the investment occurs, there is a stream of future revenue commitments over the lifetime of the service contract, pushing the date at which capital investment scores against public spending totals and the public sector borrowing requirement (PSBR) into the future. Even when a private contractor recoups its costs via user charges, such as with the Skye Bridge or the Second Severn Crossing, this represents income that would otherwise have accrued to the state.

Despite some concern over delays in the process of tendering and signing PFI contracts (Treasury Select Committee, 1996), deals with a capital value of over £7.5 billion had been signed by November 1997.[5] Whilst the fact that PFI deals are actually going ahead is welcome evidence that the initial hurdles involved in getting the PFI off the ground are being overcome, the value of contracts signed

[4]In 1989, the requirement of public sector comparators was dropped when 'the private sector takes full responsibility for the success or failure of a project'. In 1992, the need for a comparator was dropped 'if the private sector is wholly responsible for a project which needs government approval and can recoup all of its costs by charges at the point of use' or where public finance would not be considered affordable 'in the foreseeable future'. See Dilnot and Giles (1995) for a fuller discussion.

[5]Source: HM Treasury, 1997.

is at best a partial measure of policy success. In the following sections, we present a broader assessment of the merits of the PFI based on whether desirable projects would not have gone ahead in the absence of the PFI and whether the use of private finance represents value for money for the taxpayer or a suitable basis for realising public service objectives.

## III. HAS THE PFI LED TO ADDITIONAL INVESTMENT IN SOCIAL INFRASTRUCTURE?

During the early stages of developing the PFI, the Treasury implied that the PFI would allow additional investment in social infrastructure compared with what would be possible using conventional public finance alone. The November 1994 Financial Statement and Budget Report stated that the 'private sector's contribution is additional to public provision. This means that, for a given amount of public expenditure, new and better quality capital investment will be secured by the nation'. For the use of private finance to allow *desirable additional* investment in social infrastructure implies that there is some artificial constraint on public sector borrowing which would otherwise prevent investment in social infrastructure with positive net benefits from proceeding. This appears to depend on an argument that the public investment programme is constrained because it scores against the current year's PSBR, used by many commentators as an indicator of the government's fiscal competence, whilst PFI spending is not constrained in the same way because it involves a string of (perhaps uncertain) commitments which will affect the PSBR at some stage in the future. In such a case, additional investment might enhance social welfare, whether or not private finance were more efficient.

Of course, if the public and private sectors are equally efficient, the present discounted value of the government's liabilities should be the same under traditional procurement and under the PFI. Therefore, if the PSBR is seen as a useful measure of the government's impact on the macroeconomy, then attempts to get around the precise definition of the PSBR will simply distort its usefulness as a measure or lead to the measure being redefined to include all 'government-sponsored capital investment'. In any case, central government departments plan to produce budgets using resource accounting methods by April 1999 (HM Treasury, 1995a). Rather than public sector investment scoring against public spending totals in the year the investment occurs, it will be depreciated over the lifetime of the asset in a similar fashion to PFI spending, reducing any incentives for public sector managers to choose PFI rather than traditional procurement for reasons other than value for money.

Since the use of private finance pushes forward the time when capital investment scores against public expenditure, there is a danger that public sector managers used to the traditional three-year public expenditure planning horizon

TABLE 1

**Forecast Publicly Sponsored Capital Expenditure for 1997–98**

*£ billion*

| | *Nov. 1994* | *Nov. 1995* | *Nov. 1996* | *March 1998* |
|---|---|---|---|---|
| Public sector investment | 21.8 | 19.8 | 18.0 | 17.0 |
| PFI investment | *** | 2.6 | 2.5 | 1.5 |
| Publicly sponsored investment | 21.8 | 22.4 | 20.5 | 18.5 |

might pay insufficient attention to the growth of contractual commitments in the future.[6] The Treasury decision to publish information on such future commitments alongside the Budget documentation is to be welcomed in this respect. In practice, however, the planned expansion of the PFI in recent years has been accompanied, in successive Budgets, by cuts to the public sector capital programme, suggesting that private finance has been used as a *substitute* for rather than as an *addition* to public sector investment.

Table 1 shows that, since the November 1994 Budget, public sector investment plans for 1997–98 have been cut three times — by £2 billion in November 1995 (representing a 9 per cent cut), £1.8 billion in November 1996 (9 per cent) and £1 billion in March 1998 (5.5 per cent).[7] In the November 1995 Budget, planned spending of £2.6 billion under the PFI more than compensated for reductions in public sector investment, leaving total publicly sponsored investment £0.6 billion higher overall. However, subsequent reductions in public sector investment plans, combined with delays in taking PFI projects forward, have resulted in an estimated out-turn for total publicly sponsored investment in 1997–98 that is some £3.3 billion lower than originally planned within the public sector alone. Forecasts of publicly sponsored investment for 1996–97 and 1998–99 have evolved in a similar manner.

Far from generating additional investment, this evidence might be taken to suggest that PFI spending has not even compensated for cuts to public spending plans. We cannot draw any definite inferences from such evidence since we cannot determine whether public sector capital investment plans would have been cut even in the absence of the PFI. Since it is often politically more expedient to delay capital projects than to rein in current spending in times of fiscal restraint, capital budgets have traditionally been targeted (Sentance, Hall and O'Sullivan, 1998).

[6]See, for example, Treasury Select Committee (1996).

[7]The out-turn GDP deflator for 1997–98 was forecast to be 2.75 per cent in the March 1998 Budget compared with forecasts of 2.5 per cent in the 1994 and 1995 Budgets and 2 per cent in the 1996 Budget. The cuts in cash plans between Budgets therefore represent substantial real-terms cuts.

Even if the existence of the PFI had driven the cuts to public budgets in recent years, this is compatible with a strategy of overcoming institutional inertia by placing more pressure on public sector managers to give serious consideration to the use of private finance. This does not necessarily mean that PFI spending will not be 'additional' in the longer run since such incentives may no longer be required once the initiative has developed.

In other cases, the observed shortfall between forecast and realised levels of PFI expenditure to date may reflect one-off delays associated with developing a new method of public procurement or the need for legislative reform.[8] The third PFI prison contract was let six months after the invitation to tender was issued, roughly 65 per cent more quickly than the first two deals (National Audit Office, 1997c). In health-care and local authority services, legislative clarification of the powers of NHS Trusts and local authorities to enter into PFI contracts was required. This might mean that concerns over delays to investment as a result of using the PFI may soon be of mainly historical interest.

## IV. DOES THE PFI REPRESENT GOOD VALUE FOR MONEY?

This section considers whether the use of private finance is likely to provide value for money in the delivery of public services. One reason for expecting public finance to provide better value is that governments, as large-scale low-risk borrowers, can usually borrow money more cheaply than private sector bodies. Of course, the government borrowing rate does not reflect the risks of individual projects whereas private borrowing rates may do, and it would be wrong to discriminate against private financing because it made explicit costs that, with public financing, are hidden but no less real. However, it is reasonable to expect that costs of uncertainty around the expected return from the project will be greater when they are concentrated on the providers of private finance. The loan stock for the Skye Bridge had a 2 per cent risk margin over comparable gilts.[9] The use of the PFI will incur additional financing costs due to the need for some element of equity finance. The projected real rates of return on equity invested in the Fazakerley and Bridgend prison contracts were 12.8 per cent and 19.4 per cent respectively. Whilst the use of private finance on the Skye Bridge led to £4 million additional financing costs compared with the 6 per cent real cost of capital used by the public sector, 73 per cent of this represents the return to the providers of equity capital.[10]

Value for money in PFI schemes depends on any gains in efficiency through private sector involvement more than compensating for higher finance costs

[8]The National Audit Office (1997b) found that using the PFI route delayed progress on the contract for a replacement National Insurance recording system (NIRS2) by six months.

[9]The real rate of return in gilts at the contract date was 4.5 per cent.

[10]National Audit Office (1997a) estimate based on central forecasts of traffic, inflation and interest rates.

(Heald, 1997). It is difficult to obtain clear evidence on this, since many PFI projects are large-scale one-off projects for which it is very difficult to calculate an *accurate* and *uncontroversial* public sector comparator. Given the paucity of reliable empirical evidence available at present, we examine three arguments that have been advanced to suggest that the use of private finance can indeed represent value for money. First, the private sector might be inherently more efficient or more innovative than the public sector. Second, private finance might extend competitive pressures to more of the processes involved in the delivery of public services. Third, the private sector may be able to manage some types of risks more effectively than the public sector. We examine each of these arguments in turn.

*1. Public versus Private Provision*

Whilst capital market disciplines and different managerial incentive structures are often claimed to make the private sector inherently more efficient than the public sector, there is little empirical evidence to support this view (Kay, 1993) since there are relatively few examples of public and private firms competing against each other in the same markets and under the same competitive pressures. Recent experience in contracting out refuse collection services in the UK did, however, suggest that public sector organisations winning contracts achieved less than half the cost reductions made by private firms (Szymanski, 1996).

Public sector managers may not face incentives to take risks through innovation (Dixit, 1997). This is one reason why third-party income (revenue from users of the asset in addition to the government) may be an important source of value for money on PFI contracts where spare capacity is created. The provision of computer systems for the National Insurance system (NIRS2) was found by a recent National Audit Office report (1997a) to represent 'strikingly good value provided the service contracted for is delivered'. The contractor, who retained intellectual property rights to the system, made a final bid well below the level of its original bid since it hoped to spread the substantial fixed costs of the project by making further sales to other organisations. The generation of additional receipts through more intensive exploitation of assets in this way may allow lower costs for other public sector programmes such as school sports facilities.

*2. The Role of Competition*

Even if private firms are not inherently more efficient than public sector organisations, PFI could bring efficiency gains by exposing more of the stages involved in the delivery of public services to the process of competition. Under traditional public procurement, private sector firms competed in how to deliver detailed project specifications at lowest cost. Under the PFI, private firms compete to provide specified services to the public sector, being left free to innovate in project design, the balance between construction and maintenance costs and the transfer of risks from the public sector. This is not the traditional notion of competition within the market, of course, since many public services have a significant monopoly component, but rather a process of competition for the market (Chadwick, 1859). Baumol, Bailey and Willig (1982) argue that the process of competition for a market could still deliver welfare gains for society as a whole, even if there were no process of competition within the market. Limited availability of data and non-homogeneous contracts have resulted in few empirical studies of this issue, other than for refuse collection.[11] Szymanski (1996) found that the introduction of compulsory competitive tendering (CCT) in refuse collection in the UK in the late 1980s had led to average savings in net spending of 18 per cent, even though 75 per cent of the contracts were awarded to public sector organisations. In each case, cost reductions appeared to be linked to changing the input mix and reducing wage costs towards market levels.

Value-for-money gains depend on the existence of a competitive bidding process. Gómez-Lobo and Szymanski (1997) found that a higher number of bids in the process of contracting out local authority refuse services was associated with a lower cost of service. The National Audit Office (1997b) has therefore expressed concern that some important financing costs in the Skye Bridge contract were determined through negotiation with the preferred bidder rather than through competition.

The number of consortia interested in large-scale PFI contracts is likely to be influenced by the likelihood of incurring significant bidding costs, varying from £0.5 million to £2.5 million in the NIRS2 contract, for example (National Audit Office, 1997b). The deterrent effect of these costs will be greater if there is any uncertainty over whether departments will take projects forward through the PFI, leading to the Bates Review recommendation for departments to 'road-test' projects for commercial viability before issuing formal invitations to tender. One feature of contract design that is likely to influence the number of potential bidders, as well as the amount of risk that private bidders are willing to bear, is the liquidity of their investment. The public sector needs to achieve an appropriate balance between allowing the transfer of equity stakes and the importance of having a clearly defined private sector partner. This is particularly important for public–private partnerships or where the public sector provides either upfront subsidy or assets such as land with development potential as part of the deal (HM Treasury, 1996a). Whilst too few bidders in large-scale capital projects may lead to insufficient competition, inviting too many firms to submit

[11]The main exceptions to this being oil drilling rights in the US and timber in the US and Canada. See Laffont (1997) for a survey.

formal bids may reduce effective competition due to the lower probability of each bidder winning the contract.

*3. Risk Transfer*

A central issue in PFI is a more efficient allocation of risk between the public and private sectors (HM Treasury, 1995b). This is not simply a question of how much risk is transferred but what types of risk are transferred, since the private sector will only be able to reduce the cost of risk if firms can either reduce the overall level of risk or manage those risks more effectively. This is explicitly recognised in the HM Prison Service study (1996) of the first two Design, Construct, Manage and Finance (DCMF) prison contracts, in which it was felt that 'the proposed allocation of risk to be transferred under the DCMF package maximises the chance that such risks *do not materialise*' (italics added).

The allocation of risks and incentives faced by the private sector in PFI projects is largely determined by the choice of payment mechanism under the PFI contract. Long-term service contracts based on service availability, such as the DCMF prison contracts or the DBFO road contracts, encourage private firms to minimise the 'lifetime costs' of projects by balancing higher construction costs against lower maintenance costs in the future. Payment mechanisms that are not triggered until a service is being supplied, such as the NIRS2 contract, provide strong incentives to avoid delays in design and construction, especially where the contract termination date is independent of when service delivery actually commences.[12] Similarly, payment mechanisms based on the availability of prison cells or Underground trains give incentives for adequate maintenance. The potential for efficiency gains may be considerable, especially where construction risks, which have sometimes led to large cost overruns under traditional public procurement, can be reduced or simply better managed by the private sector. HM Prison Service (1996) reports that out-turn costs averaged 18 per cent higher than tender price under traditional procurement.

In principle, the gains resulting from minimising 'lifetime costs' rather than construction costs could be realised within the public sector. Public sector managers faced with pressures to control annual departmental budgets may be tempted to economise on short-term construction costs, and construction companies may face few incentives to look for design or construction changes that would give long-term economies. The introduction of resource accounting will improve these incentives, at least for public sector managers, but only to the extent that it is annual resource costs rather than cash costs that limit their spending.

[12]Whilst the contractor has borne the risk of lost service charges as a result of delayed implementation, the Contributions Agency was not compensated for the loss of efficiency savings resulting from relying on the original National Insurance recording system for longer than anticipated.

The degree of price and cost indexation built into service contracts will be more important to the overall allocation of risk in contracts where complementary inputs are purchased alongside the core service. In the Skye Bridge contract, where complementary inputs are negligible, the real value of total payments is fixed, effectively transferring all cost risks to the private sector.[13] For prison contracts, by contrast, cleaning, catering and security services are packaged together with the core service of cell availability. In such cases, periodic pricing reviews or the specification of circumstances that can trigger price revisions, such as changes in costs outside the contractor's control, may need to be written into contracts. In the DCMF prison contracts, provisions allow both parties to demand a variation in the price of services if there is a change in the consortium's costs outside its control. Price variations should always be related to published price indices which reflect input costs but are outside the control of the contractor concerned.

Whilst a more efficient allocation of risk between the public and private sectors carries considerable scope for improving value for money in public service provision, the precise allocation of risk is a complex and difficult process. Poor value for money is likely to result from the transfer of either *too little* risk to the private sector (which may dull efficiency incentives) or *too much* risk or the wrong types of risk, leading to higher costs. The latter may occur where the private sector is asked to bear risks that it cannot control, such as *volume risk* and some types of *residual value risk*. There is also a question of whether transfers of risk to the private sector will turn out to be more apparent than real. We consider each of these issues below.

(a) Volume Risk

Transferring risks associated with public policy decisions, such as the public sector's demand for a service, over which a private contractor has little control, is more akin to the public sector purchasing an insurance contract. This is unlikely to be a cost-effective strategy. There should be cause for concern where the principal payment mechanism under PFI contracts is related to volume of usage rather than availability of a service, since the former is largely outside the control of the private operator.

PFI deals signed to date have experimented with alternative allocations of volume risk. In the tenders for the first two DCMF prison contracts, private firms were unwilling to accept volume risks associated with sentencing policies, which were seen as outside their control. In the Skye Bridge contract, which is similar to the Least Present Value Auctions proposed by Engel, Fischer and Galetovic (1997), the contract length is variable, ending when a predetermined volume of toll revenue has been collected. By contrast, the first eight DBFO road contracts

[13]One risk that could obviously not be transferred to the private sector was the policy risk that the government would succumb to local political pressures and subsidise bridge tolls.

involve the use of 'shadow tolls' where payments depend on the volume of traffic (subject to a volume 'cap') but are paid by the government, not by service users. Unlike lane closures resulting from poor maintenance, risks arising from traffic volumes are largely outside the control of road operators and hence risk transfer is unlikely to lead to value for money. The National Audit Office (1998) recently concluded that the 'use of shadow tolls as the primary means of payments to operators may have reduced the net savings generated by the contracts'.

Payment mechanisms based on traffic volumes raise two additional sets of dangers. First, the winning bid comes from the consortium with the most optimistic forecast of general traffic growth, not the most efficient. Such a 'winner's curse' may generate considerable pressure for the government to extend the length of the original concession, effectively returning the demand risk to the public sector. Second, tender prices may be highly sensitive to policy decisions by the public sector over the availability of competing services such as the withdrawal of the public sector Caledonian MacBrayne ferry service upon completion of the Skye Bridge and upgrades to roads competing with DBFO schemes. Whilst contracts that terminate once an agreed present value of tolls has been collected avoid some of these problems, consideration needs to be given to providing incentives to avoid delays in construction and ensure adequate maintenance.

(b) Residual Value Risk

The assets created under PFI deals typically have an expected useful life beyond the formal contract period.[14] Risks associated with how much the assets will be worth at the end of the service contract will have an important influence on the value of initial bids and the incentives facing contractors. The (now defunct) Private Finance Panel (1996) argued that 'there is no need for the public sector to concern itself with the residual value of an asset in a carefully structured PFI contract'. Whether such an approach is desirable depends on whether the residual value of an asset is largely subject to decisions taken by the contractor, as occurs when competitive markets already exist for the supply of assets, or may reasonably be expected to develop in the future. In office accommodation contracts (see HM Treasury (1996b)), for example, competitive markets already exist and private contractors can control some of the risks associated with residual value, such as maintaining the accommodation to a good standard.

Many PFI contracts involve highly specific assets for which competitive markets are unlikely to develop and where contract renewal will largely depend on decisions by public sector managers. This may lead private contractors, fearful of the residual value of assets being close to zero, to attempt to recover

[14]The major exception to this is Information Technology contracts which typically have both a shorter contract length and a requirement for a 'technology refresh' mid-contract.

their full costs over the service contract and yet retain ownership of the assets. Where contracts involve significant investments in relationship-specific capital, contracts that rely on repeated bargaining at a later date are likely to be unattractive (Joskow, 1987). This is a familiar issue in the literature on franchising in the presence of specific capital assets (Williamson, 1976). The general result is that this degree of uncertainty over the residual value of the asset at the end of a contract whose length is shorter than the expected useful life of the asset leads to private firms being less willing to invest in such capital assets or demanding a higher price for doing so.

In some PFI deals, such as the DCMF prison contracts, residual value risk has been largely retained by the public sector, which takes ownership of the prisons at the end of the formal service contract, with the assets maintained to pre-arranged quality standards.[15] This seems sensible since difficulties associated with obtaining planning permission for new prisons may render the supply of such assets relatively inelastic, even in the longer run. Private operators can be expected to recover the full value of their investment during the 30-year contract period.

PFI deals where ownership of the underlying assets remains in private hands at the end of the PFI service contract are of more concern. In the Northern Line trains contract, the expected train life of 36 years exceeds the initial service contract length of 20 years. Whilst such contracts may give private operators incentives for adequate maintenance in order to improve their prospects for extending the original contract, reversion to public ownership at a fixed quality standard would provide similar incentives. Indeed, a second auction for the operation of the trains after 20 years could plausibly yield lower costs than negotiation with a single asset-owner in a quasi-monopoly position *vis-à-vis* the public sector. The transfer of residual value risk may, however, be appropriate for Information Technology contracts, where the speed of technological progress makes contracting future quality standards very difficult and private management of system upgrades may have a significant bearing on contract renewal and hence residual value.

(c) Risk Transfer More Apparent than Real

Value for money in PFI deals will clearly be compromised if the public sector ends up bearing risks that have supposedly been transferred to the private sector. The National Audit Office study (1997c) of the Bridgend and Fazakerley prison contracts, recognising such concerns, recommended that future contracts should unambiguously reflect the department's understanding of how the risks are to be allocated between the signatories. Most of the risk transfer in PFI contracts

[15]To ensure this risk is transferred to the private sector in practice, it may be necessary for operators to post a 'maintenance bond' with the department which is released once transfer has occurred. This was built into the Skye Bridge contract, amongst others.

signed to date does, however, appear to have been real. PFI deals are contracts for the delivery of a public service at an agreed price, not for the supply of an asset. As a result, PFI service contracts typically specify payment mechanisms that are not triggered until service delivery commences, that are not responsive to realised construction or maintenance costs and that apply financial penalties for delivery failure. Payments in the first two prison contracts depend on the availability of both cells and complementary inputs such as staffing, food and health-care services. Controllable risks, such as non-availability of cells due to inmate damage, will also result in penalties (HM Prison Service, 1996). Similarly, payments to the contractor for the NIRS2 contract will not commence until the system is operating satisfactorily, and £3.1 million of the £3.8 million additional costs incurred through unforeseen delays are to be borne by the private sector (National Audit Office, 1997b).

Whilst a clear allocation of risk in PFI contracts should minimise such concerns, this may be imperilled if private operators get into financial difficulties.[16] In cases of default, the government can contract for 'step-in' rights to take over the service and can cap its liability. In the first two prison contracts, for example, the public sector's liability is the minimum of outstanding borrowings[17] or the net present value of the unexpired part of the service contract. Whilst the risks of default could be fully transferred to the private sector if adequate insurance were available, this is unlikely to be cost-effective. In the Bridgend and Fazakerley prison contracts, for example, the government agreed to act as 'insurer of last resort', effectively transferring the risk back to the public sector.

The greatest potential risks for the public sector may occur where a contractor goes bankrupt before the construction of the infrastructure is complete. This risk will typically be minimal unless the cost of rectifying the problem that caused default exceeds the value of the work undertaken. In cases where this is likely, it may be necessary to write contracts that include the posting of performance bonds that can be released once certain milestones in the construction process are passed, as in the DBFO road contracts. The problem is far more worrying where the government has already made a capital contribution as part of a public–private partnership, such as the Docklands Light Railway extension or Channel Tunnel Rail Link. Even if the government is willing to contemplate the bankruptcy of a high-profile project, it may be unable to recover the value of its original contribution, even though the level of compensation payable to the defaulting contractors may be zero. In addition, projects involving infrastructure required as part of a network will have to be re-tendered, effectively transferring

[16]In some cases, lenders have been given 'step-in' rights so that they can replace an operator without contract termination, thus reducing their risks and ensuring service continuity.

[17]Obviously, equity investors would not be compensated. Equity covered 2 per cent of the capital raised for the Skye Bridge, for example.

the realised construction risk back to the public sector. In practice, the government might be tempted to alleviate pressure on private consortia by agreeing to additional public contributions, as demanded by the contractors for the Channel Tunnel Rail Link, or to extending the term of the concession on the asset, as occurred in the case of the Channel Tunnel. Both of these represent hidden subsidies and should be borne in mind when assessing the efficiency of the PFI. Similar demands have arisen in many other countries (Engel, Fischer and Galetovic, 1997).

*4. Initial Evidence*

An accurate assessment of the cost savings that have been realised through the use of PFI deals is difficult, both because a public sector comparator was not made in many cases and because those that were used can be highly sensitive to the assumptions on which they are based. Indeed, the practice of cutting public sector spending *in anticipation* of PFI deals going ahead led to some criticism that the initial tranche of PFI contracts would represent 'best available value' (since public sector alternatives may not be available, even if better value) rather than 'best value' since public sector managers may have faced considerable pressure to go ahead with PFI projects as the only practical method of proceeding (Treasury Select Committee, 1996; Heald and Geaughan, 1997).

The initial evidence from the first tranche of DBFO road schemes suggests that, whilst significant cost savings have been achieved overall, estimated savings vary considerably between different projects and according to the assumptions on which the estimates are based. The Highways Agency case study (1997) of the contracts claimed total quantifiable financial savings of £168 million compared with previous public sector procurement, using the 8 per cent discount rate applied by the Treasury to publicly financed road and rail projects. When the National Audit Office (1998) used a 6 per cent discount rate, which gives more weighting to future payments, this saving was reduced to £100 million. In addition, the second study suggested two of the four projects would have provided better value for money under traditional procurement methods.

Whilst the two DCMF prison contracts at Bridgend and Fazakerley generated estimated total savings of 10 per cent compared with prisons that were publicly financed and had operations contracted out to the private sector, all of these savings came from Bridgend. Fazakerley cost roughly the same as the public sector comparator (National Audit Office, 1997c). By contrast, the NIRS2 contract cost an estimated 60 per cent less than an equivalent public sector development (HM Treasury, 1997).

It may well be that estimates of the cost savings achieved in the first batch of privately financed projects are not particularly informative as to the cost savings that can be achieved as the initiative develops, especially when departments have had objectives additional to simply achieving value for money from their first few PFI contracts. The first tranche of road contracts were partially driven by the Highways Agency's interests in examining how PFI would work for different types of contract and in developing a competitive road-operating industry. In other cases, experiences gained in writing the first PFI contracts may lead to significant additional savings in future contracts. The Lowdham Grange prison contract was signed more quickly and at a lower cost than the first two prison contracts.[18] Estimates of cost savings on the basis of contracts already signed may not, of course, prove to be reliable indicators of whether these contracts turn out to be good value for money in the longer term.

## V. IMPACT OF PRIVATE CONTRACTS ON PUBLIC OBJECTIVES

Whilst the initial evidence on value for money from the use of private finance provides some grounds for optimism, doubts exist over the welfare effects of allowing 'PFIability' to determine which projects go ahead and whether long-term contractual commitments will reduce the flexibility with which the public sector can respond to changing circumstances.

### *1. Project Mix*

Ideally, to maximise social welfare, both the public sector overall and individual departments would prioritise projects according to a strict cost–benefit analysis of the relative merits of each competing demand on the public purse — those projects offering the highest expected social returns would go ahead. If private finance partially substitutes for public finance, however, the PFIability of projects may have a crucial influence on the composition of publicly sponsored investment. Heald (1997) reports that a public sector alternative to the Skye Bridge would not have gone ahead for at least 20 years. However, maximising social welfare would suggest that projects should be given the same priority, however they are financed. Otherwise, the bridge has replaced an alternative project, which presumably generated higher expected social returns when the public sector's priorities were drawn up.

The projects with the highest PFIability are typically those where the quantity and quality of outputs can be accurately measured (so real or shadow revenue streams can be used as a payment mechanism), that have the lowest element of risk and complexity and that are sufficiently large (or can be bundled together with similar projects). These characteristics are common amongst many transport projects, which might explain why these projects accounted for 71 per cent by value of the PFI contracts signed by October 1997.[19] These typically either produce marketable services that can be financed largely through user charges or

[18]The contract was 21 per cent cheaper than Bridgend and 36 per cent cheaper than Fazakerley.
[19]Source: HM Treasury, 1997.

have easily measurable outputs such as traffic volumes. Even for specific projects such as hospital developments, PFIability concerns may lead to a bias in favour of rebuilding over refurbishment. This raises a danger that projects may be given the go-ahead because of the practicality of the payment mechanism, and tolling schemes may be chosen even if other methods of finance would yield greater social or environmental benefits.[20]

It is probably too early to draw any long-run conclusions as to the impact of the PFI on the mix of projects commissioned by the public sector. If cuts to public budgets in the early years of the initiative were primarily used to put pressure on public sector managers to give serious consideration to the use of private finance, a temporary imbalance in the composition of the overall publicly sponsored capital programme is inevitable, with few longer-term consequences.

In some cases, the early bias towards transport projects may simply reflect short-run delays in other departments due to greater complexity, the testing of alternative models and the need for legislative reform. The Highways Agency chose the first four roads contracts to experiment with different types of scheme rather than to take forward its top-priority projects. Recent legislative reforms, such as the NHS (Capital Finance) Act and the Local Government (Contracts) Bill, which have clarified the powers of NHS trusts and local authorities, have helped to remove obstacles to many health and education projects. Once such initial delays are overcome, however, it would be regrettable if recourse to private finance resulted in PFIability considerations supplementing net social benefits as the principal criteria driving social investment decisions.

*2. Impact on Public Sector Flexibility*

PFI service contracts typically span 20 or 30 years to allow private contractors to recover their capital costs over a reasonable period, raising concerns that the public sector may end up contractually committed to paying for a service it no longer requires or can obtain more cheaply elsewhere. This inflexibility could result in a significant loss in operational efficiency. In practice, such dangers can be exaggerated, in so far as there is a resource cost to ceasing to use or under-utilising publicly owned assets, despite cash-based public accounting effectively treating the use of assets as having zero cost once constructed.

The cost to the public sector of terminating a PFI contract is likely to depend on how competitive the market for the service provided is. Contracts that share demand risk either continuously or through 'break clauses' at pre-specified dates may provide good value for money where private contractors can manage what is

[20]Heald (1997) quotes Department of Transport figures to suggest that the discounted benefits of an untolled public sector Birmingham Northern Relief Road would be considerably larger than the PFI tolled project that has gone ahead.

effectively a residual value risk at an uncertain future date by supplying the service to alternative customers. Contract flexibility has been built into the Longbenton DSS office accommodation contract via sharing demand risk in this way.

The costs to the public sector of terminating a contract, either because the service is no longer required or because a lower level of provision is desired, are likely to be considerably higher in the case of specific assets. In such cases, risk-averse contractors may be inclined to try to recover their costs before the date at which a break clause can be activated, rather than over the whole lifetime of the contract. Some PFI deals, such as the Bridgend and Fazakerley prison contracts, effectively allow the public sector to 'buy out' the private provider at certain pre-specified dates during the contract. After five years, the prison may step in and terminate the contract voluntarily by paying the consortium its outstanding debt plus fair market value for its equity. In any case, the public sector's maximum liability for a service it no longer requires is capped at the remaining value of the contract, which leaves open the possibility of renegotiations, especially over contractual commitments for complementary inputs. It is not obvious that this leaves the public sector with less flexibility than if it had obtained the assets through traditional public procurement.

At present, the risks associated with reducing the flexibility of the overall £300 billion public expenditure programme appear negligible, largely because of the relatively small scale of PFI activity that has happened to date. Estimated payments under PFI contracts in 1998–99 total £1.03 billion, representing only 0.3 per cent of general government expenditure (HM Treasury, 1998). On the basis of PFI contracts signed to date, annual commitments will peak at about £3 billion around the year 2010. Obviously, the potential dangers of reduced flexibility will be greater for departments such as Transport where the most substantial PFI commitments exist, representing over 8.5 per cent of the department's annual budget by 2000–01.[21]

## VI. CONCLUSION

I have assessed the Private Finance Initiative against three criteria — whether it will release resources for *additional* investment in social infrastructure, whether it will provide *value for money* for the taxpayer and whether the use of private finance will reduce the *public sector's flexibility* to pursue its public service objectives.

[21] John Watts, Minister of State, in evidence to the Treasury Select Committee, 11 July 1996.

The PFI has been accompanied by more-than-offsetting cuts in publicly financed investment. It is likely that these cuts were partly to put pressures on departments to examine PFI options and establish a new PFI culture. They also partly reflect the delays sometimes imposed by the development of new procedures. It is also possible that the cuts in publicly financed investment would have been substantial even in the absence of the PFI. However, it appears that, so far, the PFI has been a *substitute* for rather than a complement to publicly financed investment.

Assessments of *value for money* from individual PFI projects are highly sensitive to the assumptions made about the cost of the public sector comparator. The evidence suggests that the out-turns have been variable but that some PFI contracts have delivered good value.

The effects of the PFI on the *public sector's flexibility* to pursue its social objectives have yet to be established. The PFI tends to distort priorities in favour of PFIable projects, and can discourage activities that would prejudice the commercial interests of the PFI sponsor. On the other hand, the PFI may help the development of competitive markets which should enhance flexibility.

The gains realised through the PFI may increase with time as public sector managers gain experience in how risks and responsibilities can be optimally shared between the public and private sectors in a cost-effective manner. Competitive markets in the provision of many public services may also develop, significantly reducing the residual value risk associated with some PFI contracts, and reforms to overcome initial problems in sectors such as the NHS and local authorities may lead to a better-balanced mix of projects.

Overall, the initial empirical evidence that has emerged suggests that the PFI has the potential to increase the efficiency with which public services are delivered in the UK but that it cannot be taken for granted that private finance will represent good value for taxpayers' money in every type of capital project.

## REFERENCES

Baumol, W., Bailey, E. and Willig, R. (1982), *Contestable Markets and the Theory of Industry Structure*, New York: Harcourt Brace Jovanovich.

Chadwick, E. (1859), 'Results of different principles of legislation in Europe', *Journal of the Royal Statistical Society*, Series A, vol. 22.

Desai, V. and Brooks, D. (1997), 'Implications of private infrastructure investment on public investment and finance in growing Asian economies', paper presented at the conference of the International Institute of Public Finance, Osaka, August.

Dilnot, A. and Giles, C. (1995), *Options for 1996: The Green Budget*, Commentary no. 50, London: Institute for Fiscal Studies.

Dixit, A. (1997), 'Power of incentives in private versus public organisations', *American Economic Review*, Papers and Proceedings, vol. 87, no. 2, pp. 378–82.

Engel, E., Fischer, R. and Galetovic, A. (1997), 'Highway franchising: pitfalls and opportunities', *American Economic Review*, Papers and Proceedings, vol. 87, no. 2, pp. 68–72.

Gómez-Lobo, A. and Szymanski, S. (1997), 'A law of large numbers: bidding and compulsory competitive tendering for refuse collection contracts', mimeo, Imperial College Management School.

Heald, D. (1997), 'Privately financed capital in public services', *Manchester School*, vol. 65, no. 4.

— and Geaughan, N. (1995), 'Concessions, private finance and local governance', paper presented at the ESRC Local Governance Conference, Exeter, September.

— and — (1997), 'Good versus bad arguments for the private financing of public infrastructure', mimeo, University of Aberdeen.

Highways Agency (1997), *DBFO — Value in Roads: A Case Study on the First Eight DBFO Road Contracts and their Development*, London: Central Office of Information.

HM Prison Service (1996), *Report on the Procurement of Custodial Services for the DCMF Prisons at Bridgend and Fazakerley*, London.

HM Treasury (1992), *Private Finance: Guidance for Departments*, London.

— (1993), *Breaking New Ground: Towards a New Partnership between the Public and Private Sectors*, London.

— (1995a), *Better Accounting for the Taxpayer's Money: The Government Proposals. Resource Accounting and Budgeting in Government*, London.

— (1995b), *Private Opportunity, Public Benefit: Progressing the Private Finance Initiative*, London.

— (1996a), *Transferability of Equity*, London.

— (1996b), *PFI in Government Accommodation*, London.

— (1997), *Partnerships for Prosperity: The Private Finance Initiative*, Treasury Task Force on Private Finance, London.

— (1998), *Financial Statement and Budget Report*, London: Stationery Office.

Joskow, P. L. (1987), 'Contract duration and relationship specific investments', *American Economic Review*, vol. 77, pp. 168–85.

Kay, J. (1993), 'Efficiency and private capital in the provision of infrastructure', paper presented at the OECD Forum for the Future conference on 'Infrastructure policies for the 1990s', January.

Laffont, J. (1997), 'Game theory and empirical economics: the case of auction data', *European Economic Review*, vol. 41, pp. 1–35.

McDavid, J. (1985), 'The Canadian experience with privatising residential solid waste collection services', *Public Administration Review*, pp. 191–210.

National Audit Office (1997a), *The Skye Bridge*, London: Stationery Office.

— (1997b), *The Contributions Agency: The Contract to Develop and Operate the Replacement National Insurance Recording System*, London: Stationery Office.

— (1997c), *The PFI Contracts for Bridgend and Fazakerley Prisons*, London: Stationery Office.

— (1998), *The Private Finance Initiative: The First Four Design, Build, Finance and Operate Road Contracts*, London: Stationery Office.

Private Finance Panel (1996), *Risk and Reward in PFI Contracts: Practical Guidance on the Sharing of Risk and the Structuring of PFI Contracts*, London.

Sentance, A., Hall, S. and O'Sullivan, J. (1998), 'Modelling and forecasting UK public finances', *Fiscal Studies*, vol. 19, pp. 63–81.

Szymanski, S. (1996), 'The impact of compulsory competitive tendering on refuse collection services', *Fiscal Studies*, vol. 17, no. 3, pp. 1–19.

Treasury Select Committee (1996), *Sixth Report: The Private Finance Initiative*, London: HMSO.

Willetts, D. (1993), 'The opportunities for private funding in the NHS', Occasional Paper, London: Social Market Foundation.

Williamson, O. (1976), 'Franchise bidding for natural monopoly — in general and with respect to CATV', *Bell Journal of Economics*, vol. 7, pp. 73–107.

# [23]

*Financial Accountability & Management*, 15 (3) & (4), August/November 1999, 0267-4424

# THE PRIVATE FINANCE INITIATIVE IN THE NATIONAL HEALTH SERVICE: AN UNHEALTHY DEVELOPMENT IN NEW PUBLIC MANAGEMENT?

DAVID J. MAYSTON*

## INTRODUCTION

Two of the main objectives of New Public Management (NPM) (see Hood, 1991; Humphrey, Miller and Scapens, 1993; and Gray and Jenkins, 1993) have been those of increasing the efficiency and the accountability of public services, such as health care. This process has involved in many cases seeking to move public sector practice closer to private sector practice, as with the introduction of accruals accounting into the public sector (e.g. CIPFA, 1989; DoH, 1989a; and HM Treasury, 1995). It has also involved reducing the size of the public sector by assets sales and privatisation, and increasing the role of the private sector through 'contracting out' many inputs into the provision of public services. In this paper, we examine what is in many ways a further step along the path of what Rhodes (1994) has described as the 'hollowing out the role of the State', that of the Private Finance Initiative (PFI). While this initiative was first announced by a Conservative Chancellor of the Exchequer in 1992 (see e.g. Broadbent and Laughlin, 1999), it has been continued after 1997 under the umbrella of Public-Private Partnerships of the new Labour Government. NPM's 'contracting out' of the inputs into public services has thereby been extended to include the input of major capital assets, such as hospital buildings, whose ownership and management will now be in private hands under PFI schemes. This paper identifies a number of areas for concern over whether this process is likely to increase efficiency and accountability, and over the role of accounting in meeting the new demands being placed upon it, in the context of one of the most sensitive public services, that of health care.

## THE PRIVATE FINANCE INITIATIVE AND EFFICIENCY

There are a number of potential sources of efficiency gain associated with the introduction of the PFI into the NHS. These may include:

* The author is Professor of Public Sector Economics, Finance and Accountancy, and Director of the Centre for Performance Evaluation and Resource Management, at the University of York. He gratefully acknowledges the valuable comments made by the two anonymous referees on an earlier draft of this paper.

**Address for correspondence:** David Mayston, Professor of Public Sector Economics, Finance and Accountancy, Department of Economics and Related Studies, University of York, York YO10 5DD, UK.

(a) lower levels of expected cost from the private sector (rather than the public sector) managing the design and construction of the key assets, such as hospital buildings;
(b) lower levels of expected costs from the private sector (rather than the public sector) managing the operation of these assets;
(c) a greater capacity of the private sector to mimimise the risks of cost escalation in the costs of constructing and operating the assets;
(d) a superior ability of the private sector to bear the above risks, compared to the public sector;
(e) greater levels of much-needed investment in new capital assets for use by the NHS being available under the PFI rather than from direct capital expenditure in the NHS.

In the context of the above arguments for the use of PFI in the NHS, it is important to note that PFI schemes typically involve *Design, Build, Finance and Operate (DBFO)* contracts (see e.g. NAO, 1998). Given the difficulties of cost escalation which the privately financed, and privately managed, Channel Tunnel project has encountered, there can be no general presumption that points (a)–(c) will necessarily be valid. Private sector involvement is itself no guarantee of satisfactory outcomes from major investment expenditures, as the experience of private sector involvement in the design and implementation of many public sector computer projects in the NHS and elsewhere (see, e.g. PAC, 1993) illustrates. Equally, public sector project management skills have often been sadly deficient, as in the case of the New British Library (NAO, 1996). Mechanisms are therefore required which ensure that maximum value for money and an optimal use of the available skills is obtained in each individual case. Such an outcome can be achieved through ensuring: (i) that the original decision-making mechanism on the individual schemes encourages an optimal mix of public and private sector involvement in the provision of the capital asset, and (ii) that the subsequent monitoring of these schemes involves an adequate control mechanism which will highlight any failure to achieve such maximum value for money.

There are a number of reasons for doubting whether the first of these mechanisms has been in place. One reason relates to the lack of freedom which NHS decision-makers have had to choose freely between publicly and privately provided new capital assets, or between different forms of private sector involvement, following the introduction of the PFI. The available funds for direct capital expenditure in the NHS were reduced from £1.84bn in 1994–5 to £1.19bn in 1997–8, with PFI schemes being the only permitted way of funding the short-fall. Since PFI schemes necessarily involve the use of private sector finance, their use pre-empts a more direct way of obtaining whatever benefits are available from the potential efficiency gains in (a)–(c) above. This is through the use of fixed price contracts for whatever combination of Design, Build, and Facilities Management services offers the greatest value for money in each individual case. Fixed price contracts for simply Design and Build would themselves enable the risks of construction cost escalation, building completion delay, design faults and latent defects to be transferred to private sector contractors, without any necessary presumption that the same contractor will be the most appropriate one for a long-term Facilities Management contract or for providing finance to the project. If the private sector contractor has less experience of hospital design and health care needs than the accumulated experience of the NHS itself (see e.g. DHSS, 1985), there arises the possibility that the total risk of design faults may be *increased*, rather than simply transferred, by greater private sector involvement. The earlier use of well-tested Nucleus designs and the NHS Capricode building code for NHS direct investment in hospital projects resulted in both economies of scale in hospital design and a consistent building code, though this may have resulted in over-specified provision in some cases. Where private sector contractors can provide superior design and project management services, again flexibility of choice is needed in each individual case, without any necessary presumption that private finance will also be more efficient than the use of public sector financing.

A second reason for doubting whether adequate mechanisms have been in place relates to the relaxation of the earlier Treasury-imposed Ryrie rules that required the use of more expensive private finance for public projects to pass a value for money test against a public sector comparator. After very few PFI schemes in the NHS or elsewhere passed this test, the associated value for money criteria have been 'significantly weakened' (Heald, 1997, p. 13), casting doubt on whether the use of private finance has really been justified on value for money grounds. If alternative public sources of funds are not readily available, value for money tests against a Public Sector Comparator become less than real, with public sector managers being pushed towards seeking PFI funding as the 'best and only' alternative in a restricted range of choice (see Gaffney and Pollock, 1997; and Heald and Geaughan, 1997).

A third reason for doubting whether adequate mechanisms have been in place to ensure that value for money is obtained from PFI schemes is the high degree of secrecy and commercial confidentiality which has been claimed concerning these details (see Boyle, 1997), and which has hindered the process of public accountability and accounting for the details of PFI contracts in the NHS and elsewhere. Those existing PFI schemes in the NHS which have been subject to detailed analysis (see Pollock et al., 1997) have been found to imply *major reductions in bed availability*, of the order of 30 per cent, as a result of the accompanying closure of existing NHS facilities to help finance the schemes. This is despite the £2.35bn of private sector capital spending that PFI schemes in the NHS are incurring between 1998 and 2002 (HM Treasury, 1999a). It is also despite the:

> long term increases in activity and the halt in the decline of acute bed numbers [which] suggest little scope for further reductions in numbers of beds without threatening access to care and quality of care (Pollock et al., 1997; p. 1267).

Similarly, there are reasons for doubting that day case treatment can make up such a short-fall in bed availability (Mayston, 1996a, pp. 108–9).

A fourth reason for doubting whether maximum value for money is being achieved is the involvement in some PFI schemes of major construction companies, whose own financial interests are towards perpetuating an earlier *new-build* bias in the NHS (Mayston, 1990b), rather than the potentially more cost-effective maintenance of existing NHS capital facilities. In the case of the Princess Margaret Hospital in Swindon, an Outline Business Case for a £45m refurbishment of the existing 1970s hospital building was replaced within the PFI process by a Final Business Case for:

> a new build hospital on an out-of-town site, at a cost of £148m. The existing site will be made over to the [PFI] consortium. The rises in estimated capital costs during PFI procurement are thus at least partly attributable to changes in scale which were necessary in order to allow the private sector to show a profit: the PFI system leads to an expansion of projects which would not have occurred under public procurement (Gaffney and Pollock, 1997, p. 10).

Because the PFI contract requires payment of the capital sum of £148m over a shorter period, i.e. 30 years, compared to the standard expected useful life of a hospital building of 60 years, additional 'loans' have been made, out of funds that would otherwise have been available for direct NHS investment, by the NHS Executive to the recipients of PFI schemes to make these annual payments more affordable, with this 'loan' element representing a further £42.6m drain on NHS finances in the above example (ibid., pp. 14–5).

Further doubts concerning the value for money offered by PFI contracts in the NHS are raised by the very high *tendering, negotiation and transaction costs* of PFI schemes in the NHS. The costs imposed upon the private sector by this process, which the private sector will seek in the long run to recover from the NHS through higher contract prices, have been estimated to be *seven times* higher than for conventional public capital projects, with substantial procurement costs also incurred directly by NHS Trusts (Pollock et al., 1997). The PFI consultancy fees charged to the NHS were estimated at £30m (*Independent*, 2 June, 1997), even before a single PFI-financed hospital was completed, with some of these consultancy fees likely to have gone to large accountancy firms.

A final reason for concern over the adequacy of the PFI decision-making mechanism for promoting value for money relates to its focus on decisions being made, and legally binding agreements being entered into, by current NHS managers about long-term PFI contracts, extending over the next 25 or more years, for the delivery of hospital and other asset-based services. In the presence of considerable uncertainty of future detailed trends in health service demand and in health care technology over the next 25 years and beyond, the ability of the NHS to maintain *flexibility* of future use and internal design of the available hospital facilities is of some importance. Entering into formal long-term legal contracts now with a private sector provider who has conflicting financial interests to those of the NHS may limit such later flexibility when the PFI contract involves significant payments that cannot readily be avoided. The economic theorist's notion of state-contingent contracts covering all future possible contingencies is unlikely to be a practical proposition in the face of such uncertainty over future health care technology.

While PFI contracts that permit variations in future service levels can accommodate some degree of flexibility, the associated risk-shifting on to the PFI provider may be reflected in a high *risk premium* being borne by the NHS purchaser of the PFI services. Agreeing to the PFI scheme may itself reduce the alternative local health care facilities that are likely to be readily available to the NHS purchaser in the future. The actual likelihood of the NHS purchaser being readily able to transfer its demand elsewhere in future years may then be small. A high risk premium paid for a small amount of risk that may in practice be transferred itself represents poor value for money.

The difficulties that are involved in drawing up well-formulated long-term plans for health care needs, combined with the greater availability of investment finance via the PFI route, may result in PFI schemes being agreed to which prove to be ill-suited to the long-term health care needs of the NHS. As noted by Meara:

> Regional offices are in danger of being bounced into approving [PFI] schemes simply because of the head of steam that has built up behind them rather than because of a rational prioritisation process (1997).

The future financial commitments that many PFI schemes involve may then *seriously constrain* future planning opportunities and pre-empt potentially more beneficial capital schemes. Moreover, as noted by Boyle:

> [PFI] schemes are generated by individual trusts. It is not clear how effectively trusts take account of the interaction between their schemes and those of other trusts or with other parts of the health service (1997, p. 1215).

There will then be significant *opportunity costs* in terms of the foregone opportunities for potentially more beneficial schemes, as a result of the long-term financial commitments which PFI schemes involve, if they are not carried out in the context of a programme of sound long-term planning for capital provision across the NHS as a whole. The need for a national long-term re-configuration in the pattern of acute hospital provision in the NHS has recently been advocated by the Royal College of Surgeons (1998).

## RISK, PFI AND THE PUBLIC SECTOR

In considering point (d) above, namely whether the public or the private sector is a more efficient bearer of risks, it should be noted that risk in practice is not a simple uni-dimensional commodity that can be costlessly assessed and completely transferred to the private sector. A large part of the risk which PFI contracts may seek to transfer to the private sector relates to *demand risk* (see e.g. HM Treasury, 1997a) concerning the level of demand by the public sector for the services offered by the PFI facility. However, as Brealey and Myers (1996, pp. 491–6) note, the private sector has many ways of shifting risk back to the unwary when it has an incentive to do so. In addition, the consequences of demand falling short of or exceeding the available capacity will differ between the PFI promoter and the NHS, with different decisions on the future availability of services then resulting once risk is transferred, unless all of the associated details are specified in great detail in advance. As noted by Boyle:

> Private consortia will tend to err on the side of caution over the size of a facility, since from a commercial perspective excess demand is less of a problem than excess capacity, whereas lack of capacity may be the most serious problem from a public health viewpoint (1997).

It is important to note here that *both* the private PFI provider and the public sector procuring entity are bearing risks, and that all risk of demand fluctuations is not transferred to the private sector. Similarly even where the PFI contract specifies a fixed price per unit of the service, so that the private PFI provider bears the risk that fluctuations in the volume of a service demanded will affect the profitability of the scheme, the public sector entity is also then bearing risk as to the size of the payments it must make to the PFI provider. This goes against the increasing use of *cash limits* to ensure cost containment in the public sector, such as in GP drugs budgets and the Social Fund in Department of Social Security local offices, rather than earlier open-ended *demand-led* forms of budgeting. Predicting future health care demand over the life of a hospital building may be subject to wide margins of error in the face of unknown future technology and epidemiological trends.

Properly modelling and evaluating the *risk transfer* to the private PFI provider are likely to prove complicated and expensive tasks for NHS purchasers and providers (see Terry, 1996). Yet, as the NAO (1997) emphasises, 'appropriate risk transfer is crucial to obtaining value for money in privately financed projects'. If some of the, possibly large, risks which the NHS seeks to transfer to the PFI company materialise, there is in general no necessary guarantee that the Special Purpose Vehicles (SPVs), which are typically specially created to act as the formal PFI provider, will remain *solvent* under all possible claims against their assets. SPVs are likely to have limited liability, with some financial incentive for their backers not to leave large amounts of surplus assets available within their financial structures. If some of the risks have not been fully evaluated and described in advance, there is the risk that expensive legal disputes may ensue, with again no guarantee of full financial redress even when litigation is successful for the NHS, in situations where the solvency of the PFI provider is limited. Risk transfer to the private sector will then be less than fully effective, unless the NHS negotiates in advance priority claims on the assets involved.

The process of attempted risk transfer itself may lead to long and complicated PFI contracts, adding to the evaluation, transactions, negotiation and monitoring costs involved, which can significantly reduce the attractions of privately-financed projects. Such complexity may also conceal large penalty costs and scope for expensive litigation if either side fails to fulfil its obligations, or wishes later to change the contract specifications.

In the parallel context of PFI roads contracts, the National Audit Office has argued that:

> In the absence of substantial innovation, efficiency improvements, or risk taking by the private sector it is very unlikely that a privately financed road project can ever be better value than the same project financed in the traditional way by the Government (1998, p. 26).

While Brealey, Cooper and Habib (1997, pp. 22–26) argue the need to take into account considerations of the demand and other risks that are still borne by taxpayers if the asset is publicly owned, in assessing the full cost of public capital, they acknowledge that the case for government ownership of the asset is increased in the presence of likely informational asymmetries between the public and private sector over the level of future public sector demand and government policy, and by the risk of private sector owners demanding an inefficiently high price for future contract variations in response to later changes in government policy.

## PFI, CAPITAL CHARGING AND AFFORDABILITY RISK

An important further risk from PFI schemes that falls upon the NHS, rather than being transferred to the private PFI provider, is that of *affordability risk*. Once the PFI contract is signed, the payments due under it are likely to involve significant fixed elements to contribute towards the capital repayment and interest costs of the scheme. As such, they have similarities to a mortgage or other debt repayment charge. These payments will fall to be paid initially by the NHS Trust agreeing to the PFI scheme. They will next fall on the local health authority, which is typically required to sign a 'letter of purchaser commitment' tying it to payments over some 30 years as a condition of the PFI scheme proceeding (Gaffney and Pollock, 1997, p. 5). The introduction of any fixed debt payments into the finances of the local health authority acts like a fixed charge in the finances of equity-holders in a private company: they have the effect of increasing the ('beta') coefficient of systematic risk that is incurred even by shareholders in a fully diversified firm (see e.g. Brealey and Myers, 1996, pp. 223, 457) in a linear way with the debt-equity ratio involved. In the NHS, this means that the affordability risk of a PFI scheme (in terms of the proportionate extent to which other budgetary items may have to be cut) in the face of uncertain future funding will increase with the proportion of fixed debt payments involved.

Thus whilst PFI schemes offer the promise of a greater availability of 'much-needed' additional investment finance for the NHS, as in point (e) above, this is not without its long-term costs. These costs are of a similar form to those of direct public borrowing. If these long-term costs are genuinely affordable, there is equally a case for increasing the total amount of permitted direct capital expenditure by the NHS that can be financed through public borrowing, rather than increasing the amount of permitted PFI funding of capital schemes in the NHS. Again if value for money is genuinely the reason for PFI schemes, then full *virement* should be permitted between the total amounts permitted for PFI schemes and the amounts permitted for direct capital expenditure by the NHS that can be financed out of public borrowing.

Concerns over the affordability risk posed by PFI schemes in the NHS are also raised by the way in which PFI schemes interact with the existing system of *capital charging* in the NHS (see e.g. AHST, 1985; DoH, 1989a; and Heald and Scott, 1995). Under its present 'non-neutral' form (see Mayston, 1996a), NHS health authorities receive a joint annual allocation under the weighted capitation resource allocation process (see NHS Execuive, 1997) that may be spent either on current revenue expenditure, or on capital charges associated with the health care services they receive from capital assets owned by NHS Trusts, or on the annual charges for the use of PFI facilities. In the case of the capital charges associated with the use of capital assets owned by NHS Trusts, there is a corresponding payment back into the circular flow of NHS capital charges around the NHS. However, in the case of annual payments for the use of the privately owned assets created by PFI schemes, there is a *'leakage'* from the circular flow of capital charges around the NHS when this part of the total income of the local NHS health authority is paid into the private sector.

The overall outcome of this process depends on whether or not there is a sufficient offsetting *'injection'* into the circular flow of income by HM Treasury to fully neutralise the total leakage that arises from the use of PFI funding. If there is not, there is a sense in which those health authorities that make use of PFI assets in the NHS are essentially *'free-riding' on all other health authorities* (see Mayston, 1997), since they are making use of a total resource which is fed by the capital charges paid by those NHS health authorities that utilise directly-owned NHS capital assets, but are failing to pay back corresponding capital charges into the NHS circular flow. There is evidence that the income all Trusts receive from the re-circulated capital charges which are levied only on directly-owned NHS assets does influence Trust calculations of the affordability of PFI schemes to them (see Hodges, 1998). On the capital side, NHS Trusts that make use of PFI finance are themselves not using scarce NHS direct investment funds that are constrained by public expenditure control, although these direct funds were themselves originally reduced in size to accompany the introduction of the PFI into the NHS.

If there is a *net* leakage to the system from the use of PFI funding, the total cost to the NHS of entering into PFI agreements can be greater than it appears to the NHS Trust and its client health authorities who seek to implement the PFI scheme, since the latter are failing to take into account the loss of circulating income that it implies for the system as a whole. The long-term affordability of the PFI scheme may then be over-estimated by the NHS Trust that is keen to obtain new capital facilities.

Unless there is an addition to the total NHS funding for all health authorities to compensate for the above annual increases in PFI payments into the private sector, the above process of leakage from the circular flow of NHS capital charges will also set up a *multiplier process* that is similar to the multiplier process from the injection of investment into the circular flow of National Income in macroeconomics (see Dornbusch and Fischer, 1984), but here in reverse. A reduction in the circular flow of capital charges in the NHS due to an initial leakage into PFI schemes in Year 1 means a lower than otherwise baseline in subsequent years of the net capital employed of directly-owned NHS assets, and hence a lower level of the offsetting payment HM Treasury makes in Year 2 and subsequent years to fund the lower level of capital charges it expects to receive from the NHS. This lower level of payment in Year 2 from HM Treasury to offset capital charges for any given level of desired revenue expenditure will be spread out across the whole of the NHS by the NHS weighted capitation system of resource allocation (NHS Executive, 1997).

If, as is presently the case, new NHS capital formation, net of depreciation and indexation, is initially negative (DoH, 1998, p. 115 and 1999, p. 136), all NHS health authorities will be under pressure to reduce the capacity that they utilise from directly-owned NHS assets, in order to economise on their capital charges within the new lower level of their payments to fund capital charges. If they as a result divest themselves of capacity at the end of Year 2, by ward and hospital closures, there will be a lower level of net capital directly employed in the NHS than would otherwise have been the case, causing the directly-owned NHS capital base to decline further and HM Treasury to expect a further reduction in the capital charges it will receive in Year 3.

In Year 3, in order to balance its books, HM Treasury would then have to pay into the NHS a correspondingly lower level of funding to offset the lower level of capital charges it can expect to receive from the NHS. This in turn would place further pressure on all NHS health authorities to dispose of NHS directly-owned capital assets, with subsequent iterations of this multiplier process in future years. As with the multiplier process on National Income from a fall in the level of investment, the associated reduction in the purchasing power of all NHS health authorities to pay capital charges on directly-owned NHS assets can be many times the initial leakage due to the PFI scheme. The extent of the leakage, and its associated recessionary multiplier process if the total net leakage is positive, will be further increased if the PFI scheme is partly financed, as it often is, by the disposal of existing NHS assets, such as land and buildings, on which capital charges would otherwise be paid.

Whether or not there is a positive net leakage from the total NHS circular flow in coming years depends upon whether there are to be sufficient additional injections into the NHS circular flow in the coming years to offset the leakages that arise from the build up of NHS payments for the use of PFI funding and from the disposal of NHS assets to offset the cost of PFI schemes. These additional injections may come both from the additional new direct capital expenditure which the new Labour Government has promised for the NHS, and from any additional funding the NHS receives from HM Treasury to pay for the future additional annual payments which PFI schemes impose on the NHS, net of any operating cost savings that the PFI schemes involve. The precise extent of these future additional injections is at present unclear. As above, it is notable that the Net Book Value of NHS Tangible Fixed Assets (DoH, 1998, p. 115 and 1996, p. 136), on which capital charges are levied, has recently shown negative growth, net of depreciation and indexation. Without sufficiently large additional injections into the NHS, the increased level of leakages to the NHS circular flow of capital charges due to build up of PFI schemes is likely to be an increasing problem for the NHS as a whole. It will impact on the affordability for the NHS of payments for the use of key capital assets, such as hospitals, through capital charges on directly-owned NHS assets and annual payments for the use of PFI-owned assets. Such affordability is likely to directly affect bed availability, in a potentially unstable way.

Since the NHS weighted capitation resource allocation system distributes the loss in purchasing power due to the leakage from PFI schemes across all NHS health authorities, whether or not they make use of PFI schemes themselves, any additional injections must also be so distributed if individual health authorities are not to be disadvantaged by the process. The circular flow of capital charges on NHS directly-owned assets will ensure that this does take place as a result of the promised additional direct capital expenditure in the NHS. Any additional future funding from HM Treasury to offset the additional future annual payments for PFI schemes should also therefore be distributed through the NHS weighted capitation process, if the purchasing power of all NHS health authorities is to be maintained.

## PFI AND MYOPIA

In assessing both the desirability of PFI as a major addition to NPM, and the appropriate response of accounting to the issues involved, there is a need to postulate alternative explanations for this 'next step' along the path of NPM than those of value for money and risk transfer. One such alternative explanation has to do with the behaviour of politicians when faced with financial pressures. Thus, as Mayston notes:

> One frequent behavioural response of central government politicians when faced with a large persistent policy problem is that of structural change in the organisation of the public sector institutions concerned. The 'relative price effect' in public finance (see Baumol, 1967; Mayston 1990a) suggests that the labour-intensive nature of many public services, with often limited opportunities for increases in productivity, will be a systematic source of continued upward pressure on public expenditure, presenting central government politicians with a persistent policy dilemma between containing public expenditure and maintaining the quality of public services... A further typical behavioural response of central government politicians under financial and electoral pressure is to act myopically, concentrating on actions which will have an impact within a fairly short time horizon of five years or less (1993, pp. 86–7).

The new Labour Government in the UK has set about attempting to make its own structural changes (DoH, 1997) to undo many of those introduced into the National Health Service (NHS) by Margaret Thatcher (DoH, 1989b), as well as continuing with the introduction of PFI schemes into the NHS. This is in the context of an electoral commitment not to raise income tax rates, and of continued financial pressure for more current expenditure on the NHS, from nurses' pay demands, from higher than desired waiting lists and from other sources. PFI in many ways then provides an *escape route* for politicians responding to the short-term pressures to maintain or increase current expenditure whilst not raising current tax rates. PFI promises increased capital facilities in the near future in return for a stream of financial obligations over many future years, including many when the current generation of politicians, and their managers within the NHS, can expect to be no longer responsible for meeting these future financial liabilities. Unless they are constrained by an adequate system of accounting and accountability, the current generation of politicians and managers has an incentive to '*mortgage the future*' by incurring large future liabilities in return for more immediate benefits. In doing so, they are benefiting by *externalising the cost* (see e.g. Buchanan and Tullock, 1962) of their actions on future generations. PFI then has some attributes of a 'Ponzi game' (Kotlikoff, 1992, p. 97) in which there is a one-off benefit to the first generation who initiates the game, here from additional new hospitals whose cost is only partly borne by the current generation of taxpayers, but at an ever increasing future cost if each subsequent generation behaves in the same way.

The period of time over which the future financial impact on the NHS of current PFI schemes will accrue, namely the next 30+ years, extends into several decades in which the NHS will be suffering from increasingly adverse demographic trends. As in Figure 1, the ratio between the size of 65 year + age group (who, aside from births, make the largest per capita demands on the NHS), and the 16–29 year age group (from whom new entrants to the NHS labour market will need to be largely drawn) changes very dramatically in the coming decades. Under the latest available population projections (ONS, 1996), this ratio is expected to fall from its current level of 1.21 to 0.63 in 2035, becoming 1.0 in approximately 2015. Dumping future financial

**Figure 1**

UK Population Projections

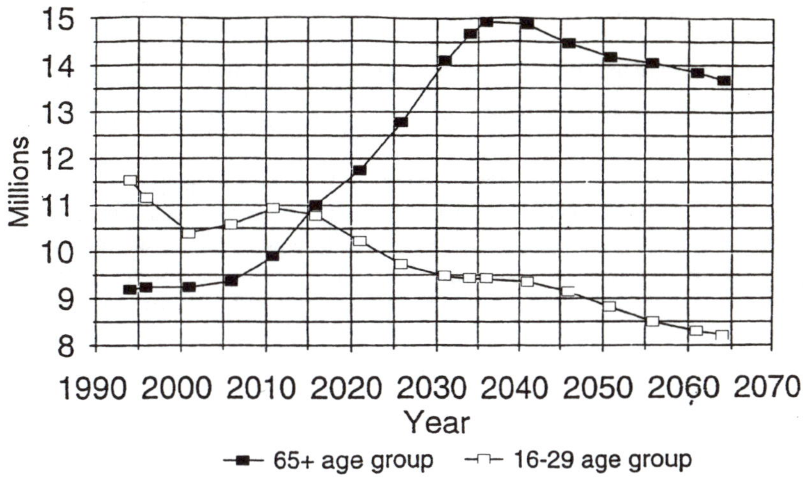


**Source: ONS (1996)**

commitments on the NHS over this next 30+ years in a way which is either not properly planned for or accounted for, or which represents questionable value for money for future NHS service-users, is therefore unwise. Clear plans to finance the long-term revenue consequences of current and future PFI schemes seem noticeable only by their absence.

In the face of earlier large reductions in the funds available for direct NHS capital expenditure, there has been substantial pressure on local managers, and more senior NHS managers and politicians, to agree to PFI schemes and contract terms in order to obtain new capital facilities in the near future, but whose benefit compared to the longer term costs to the NHS is more dubious. The risk of such *moral hazard*, of managers and politicians acting in their own short-term interest but against the longer-term interests of the NHS, is increased by the *financial guarantee* which the former Secretary of State for Health, under the National Health Service (Residual Liabilities) Act 1996, has given for the NHS as a whole to honour whatever PFI financial obligations NHS Trusts undertake. Private PFI providers may then enter into contracts with local NHS Trust managers in the knowledge that the NHS as a whole will pick up the bill for whatever future financial obligations the current managers agree to. A wider moral hazard would have arisen if the PFI had become, in effect, a covert way of privatising the NHS itself, against the wishes of the electorate (see Mayston, 1996b). This process could result from including clinical services within the PFI bid (as in the Stonehaven case discussed in McKendrick and McCabe, 1997) or pressurising more patients (in the face of rising NHS waiting lists from NHS bed losses) into the private health care facilities that may be built on the same site, as part of the overall PFI scheme.

The current generation of politicians and managers also has an incentive to get round, or find loopholes in, whatever mechanisms of accounting and accountability might otherwise stand in their way in this process. Whilst, as Heald notes, criticism of such accounting behaviour is still:

> likely to come from those concerned about 'honest government accounting', [this] group... is neither numerous nor politically weighty (1997, p. 28).

PFI has parallels here with earlier rounds of asset sales in the public sector, which were in the immediate financial interest of politicians attempting to maintain current expenditure on key public services, *whether or not they involve any additional efficiency-improving properties*. Like asset sales counting simply as negative public expenditure under traditional conventions of central government accounting, cash accounting can itself lead to an over-concentration on the short-term interests of those currently in power.

## PFI AND THE ROLE OF ACCOUNTING

Accounting for PFI raises interesting constitutional issues regarding the inter-relationship between accounting, accountability and the benefits and costs that fall upon different generations of taxpayers and consumers of public services, such as health care. As in Mayston (1993), there are important questions as to *who is the principal?*, in the principal-agent relationship that accounting and accountability are designed to foster within New Public Management. In the determination of accounting practice, the UK Accounting Standards Board (ASB) recognises that:

> The prescription of accounting requirements for the public sector in the United Kingdom is a matter for the Government (Wilkins, 1997, p. 18).

Yet this in turn raises the question as to who the Government is itself acting for, in making these prescriptions. In the case of PFI in the NHS and other parts of the public sector, there is a clear potential conflict of interest between the immediate interests of the current generation of politicians, managers and users of health care and those of future generations of taxpayers and NHS consumers upon whom future financial liabilities from current PFI transactions may effectively fall.

One role for explicit on-balance-sheet capital accounting in the NHS and other parts of the public sector is to make clear the extent to which the financial liabilities which are being passed on to future generations are being matched by assets, from which future users can be expected to benefit (see e.g. Perrin, 1984). Such a role can help to meet *user needs* for relevant and reliable accounting information concerning both the *inter-generational equity* of this transfer and the long-term *value for money* which is being obtained from the present PFI transactions. This would require clear information on the extent to which there is likely to be a *matching of the costs and benefits* that each PFI scheme generates across different generations of taxpayers and consumers of health care. Without such detailed accounting information there is a danger that a Government's fiscal policy will result in the accumulation of debt, or liabilities for future PFI payments, without appropriately matching long-term assets.

Adequate accounting for PFI is then best undertaken in conjunction with detailed *Generational Accounts* (c.f. Kotlikoff, 1992) that report on the build up of future financial liabilities and assets for NHS consumers and taxpayers well into the next millennium that result from PFI schemes currently being entered into. Fortunately some initial steps are now being taken in this direction (see Cardarelli, Sefton and Kotlikoff, 1998), supported by HM Treasury (1999a). Adequate accounting for PFI also needs to be complemented by a financial framework that can help to ensure the *affordability* of the costs which current PFI schemes will impose on future generations. As we have seen, major demographic trends are at work which may severely limit the affordability of additional liabilities on the NHS in the coming decades. If additional funds are not available to pay for the additional liabilities which PFI schemes may involve, current PFI schemes will in effect pre-empt the scope for potentially more beneficial capital investment later in the NHS when the current uncertainty over future technological trends and detailed health care needs is reduced by the passage of time. The ability of public sector managers to eat into future capital expenditure, to finance the revenue consequences of current PFI schemes under the proposed financial regime that will accompany PFI, appears to be confirmed by HM Treasury when it states that:

> Departments will be able to channel funds earmarked for capital expenditure into current spending . . . to finance private-public partnerships (1998a, p. 26).

As we note below, the UK central government has appeared at times to have actively encouraged off-balance-sheet finance for the NHS and other parts of the public sector, as part of its own inter-relationship with the EU through the Maastricht criteria, and with financial markets. From the viewpoint of HM Treasury, the off-balance-sheet treatment of PFI assets and liabilities may enable numerical targets related to public sector indebtedness, such as the Maastricht criteria (ONS, 1997), and its own 'strict fiscal rule' that:

> over the economic cycle, the Government will ensure the level of public debt as a proportion of national income is at a stable and prudent level (HM Treasury, 1997b),

to be more easily met without public expenditure cuts or tax increases. Yet, to the extent that these rules are part of a financial control framework aimed at ensuring that excessively high levels of financial liabilities are not passed on to future generations, the use of PFI schemes to side-step their requirements simply serves to undermine their effectiveness as part of an adequate financial framework for ensuring the affordability of the future liabilities incurred.

An off-balance-sheet treatment of PFI liabilities would also seem to run counter to the desire expressed in HM Treasury (1997b)'s own *Code for Fiscal Stability* for 'transparency in the ... presentation of the public accounts'. This *Code* also emphasises the importance of 'stability in ... the way fiscal policy impacts on the economy', 'a disciplined and honest approach to managing the public finances', 'fairness, not least between generations' and 'efficiency in the design and implementation of fiscal policy, and in managing both sides of the public sector balance sheet'. The *Code* recognises that: 'The public sector balance sheet, and the measures of net worth that are derived from the balance sheet, can be important indicators of the sustainability and equity of fiscal policy over time'. Even more recently, HM Treasury (1998a, pp. 6, 10) has stressed that: 'Transparency is an indispensable hallmark of good policy' and that 'Greater transparency and openness are key weapons in avoiding poor policies and bad decision-making'.

While HM Treasury (1999a, Table B17) does provide information on the total future estimated annual commitments, varying from £1.45 billion to £3.71 billion per annum, over the next 30 years across the public sector as a whole that are at present expected, it does not give any detailed breakdown of the long-term commitments for the NHS. Given that some aggregate information is made available on future PFI liabilities, one would nevertheless expect financial markets, and possibly also the EU, over time to 'see through' any off-balance sheet accounting treatments of PFI schemes in assessing the overall fiscal stance of the UK central government.

The desire to keep transactions involving streams of future payments for the use of capital assets off-balance-sheet has led in the past to major financial difficulties building up, both in the private sector from the resultant insolvency of property companies, and in the public sector from 'deferred purchase' and similar arrangements entered into by local authorities, such as the London Borough of Hammersmith and Fulham, and Sheffield City Council. The operational impact of financial difficulties in the NHS is likely to be no less severe than in local authorities, unless sufficient future additional injections are made to NHS funding to pay for the additional liabilities incurred under PFI. Rather than '*Thriving on Chaos*' in the way management gurus, such as Tom Peters (1989), might propose, what evidence there is suggests that financial and other unanticipated pressures can prove dysfunctional in their impact within the NHS (Harrison et al., 1994).

The 'creative accounting' arrangements of local authorities arose as part of their conflict with central government capital controls on local government during the 1980s (see Audit Commission, 1985; and Hale, 1988), but were subsequently effectively outlawed by central government, through measures such as the Department of the Environment's *Local Authorities (Capital Finance) Regulations 1990*.

ACCOUNTING FOR PFI

In the case of PFI transactions, central government has itself been actively involved in promoting the use of this new 'unconventional' form of finance, as well as providing guidelines for its accounting treatment. Rather than simply being the watchdog of financial probity and fiscal rectitude, HM Treasury has therefore been playing in this context a number of potentially conflicting roles. It has done so against the background of a set of accounting standards which were in part developed to counter off-balance-sheet finance, as in the case of *SSAP21* on Accounting for Leases and Hire Purchase Contracts, and to tackle other creative accounting devices in the private sector (see Smith, 1992), as in the case of *FRS5*. The UK Accounting Standards Board was itself set up in 1990, following the Dearing Report (1989), to restore public confidence in the accounting process and to counter creative accounting arrangements. The title of one of its new flagship standards, *FRS5 Reporting the Substance of Transactions*, reflects the ASB's desire to secure the disclosure of the substance, rather than simply the legal form, of financial transactions.

Despite this desire, there remained, however, some uncertainty as to how *FRS5* should be interpreted when it encountered one of its first major challenges, that of accounting for PFI transactions. HM Treasury's Taskforce Private Finance Policy Team sought to fill the temporary vacuum by issuing its own Interim Guidance. This was embodied in its 'PFI Technical Note No. 1: How to Account for PFI Transactions', which 'should be used by all public sector entities to interpret *FRS5* for the purpose of accounting for PFI transactions' (HM Treasury, 1997a, p. 3). *FRS5* was taken here as being 'the element of UK GAAP relevant in the context of PFI', with 'the treatment of PFI transactions in the public expenditure Control Total normally' required to follow UK GAAP.

The Treasury Interim Guidance also indicated when the potentially more stringent requirements of *SSAP21* for capitalising assets and liabilities on balance sheet needed to be applied to PFI schemes. This was when the relative cost of the 'underlying asset' exceeded 90 per cent of the Net Present Value (NPV) of the component of the PFI scheme to which it related. The prescribed 90 per cent borderline for applying *SSAP21* is, however, not the same test as that which defines a 'finance lease' within *SSAP21* itself. The *SSAP21* test for the on-balance-sheet inclusion of leased assets and their associated obligations is that the present value of the minimum lease payments are 'substantially all (normally 90 per cent or more) of the fair value of the leased asset' (Wilkins, 1997, p. 205). The Treasury Interim Guidance requirement for applying *SSAP21* to PFI schemes could be avoided by including within the PFI scheme other cost elements, such as building maintenance, so long as 'the contract . . . is structured so that' it avoids a situation where there are independent payments for these other items or where their different costs 'can be identified'.

The Treasury Interim Guidance required *FRS5* to be applied when the above relative cost of the 'underlying asset' is 90 per cent or less (but not less than 10 per cent) of the relevant NPV of the component of the PFI scheme to which it related. *FRS5* in turn states that:

> Evidence that an entity has rights or other access to benefits (and hence has an asset) is given if the entity is exposed to the risks inherent in the benefits, taking into account the likelihood of those risks having a commercial effect in practice.

As 'indicators of commercial risk' to the private sector PFI provider, the Treasury Interim Guidance included the extent to which demand risk, operating cost risk, availability and performance risk, residual value risk and design risk could affect the return to the shareholders in the private sector entity.

Similar indicators were subsequently proposed also by the ASB (1998) as part of its own Amendment to *FRS5* ('*FRS5A*') on accounting for PFI and similar contracts, in order to resolve the above uncertainty as to how *FRS5* should be applied to PFI schemes by those bodies which are bound to follow the ASB's standards. Even though HM Treasury is not bound to follow the ASB's standards in setting its own requirements for financial reporting by public sector bodies, HM Treasury (1999b) has now incorporated the substance of the ASB's Amendment to *FRS5* into its own revised draft guidelines on Accounting for PFI Transactions. This will be in force for those PFI schemes inviting best and final offers after a date which was to be determined, with the Treasury (1997a) Interim Guidance still to be in force for all other existing PFI schemes. The standard-setting process under the ASB does, therefore, appear to have had a positive influence in securing greater accountability for PFI schemes than might otherwise have occurred. In addition, the proposed introduction of Resource Accounting into central government does make it more likely that there will be a greater recognition of relevant assets and liabilities than would have occurred under the earlier central government accounting regime of focusing on short-term cash transactions.

However, under both the Interim Guidance and the revised rules, transferring 'sufficient' risk to the private sector PFI provider will ensure that the asset is on the private sector PFI provider's balance sheet, and not on the public sector purchaser's balance sheet. The increased expected contract payments, which the private sector PFI operator is likely to require for such a risk transfer, are likely to fall mainly on future generations of public sector taxpayers or consumers, through their impact on future budgets and overall service provision.

Any manager, or politician, who is keen *for other reasons* to keep assets, and their associated liabilities, off-balance-sheet, therefore has an incentive to shift these risks on to the private sector, through entering into PFI contracts that are specifically designed to meet these accounting guidelines. This is the case, moreover, whether or not the terms of such risk transfer are particularly attractive in their own right. These other reasons may include a desire to obtain the use of new facilities in the near future, if approval of additional funds to finance a PFI scheme is more likely if it does remain off-balance-sheet, with the future financial consequences for the NHS then being given implicitly less weight in the minds of current managers and politicians.

It is notable in this context that the Treasury's (1997a) own Interim Guidance involved a relatively wide set of contract elements, including service payments, over which payment variations can be considered as evidence of commercial risk being borne by the private sector PFI provider, making it less likely that PFI assets and liabilities will appear on public sector balance sheets. This was achieved through imposing a more stringent test for separating out service elements from those of the property asset than was involved in the ASB's Exposure Draft (ASB, 1997) of its *FRS5* Amendment on accounting for PFI. In addition, there appeared to be a difference of emphasis between the Treasury and ASB documents, with the Treasury guidance pointing to 'examples of how these risks could, in practice, provide evidence of commercial risk being taken by the [private sector] operator', but with the ASB's (1997) Exposure Draft pointing to 'evidence that the property was an asset of the [public sector] purchaser throughout'.

Similarly it is notable that HM Treasury's Taskforce on Private Finance (1997, p. 15) recommended that:

> where the accounting analysis requires a PFI transaction to be treated in substance as borrowing... the public body should examine the scope for reworking the deal so that it is clearly for the provision of services.

Such massaging of the borderline between capital and current transactions would seem to run counter to HM Treasury (1998a)'s own desire for 'a clear distinction between current and capital spending', and its own recognition that 'the costs to the British economy if fiscal policy were to become unsustainable would be substantial'.

As noted above, the effective date for the implementation of the revised Treasury (1999b) guidelines incorporating the substance of the ASB (1998)'s Amendment to *FRS5* was initially unclear. Their application to the NHS depends also upon their approval by the NHS Executive. Whilst appearing to accept the new ASB (1998) rules, the then Paymaster General, Geoffrey Robinson, announced that the new rules would not apply to schemes that had been agreed before the end of 1998 (*Times*, 10 September, 1998). In such a case, many existing PFI schemes would have escaped its ambit, with a risk that other PFI schemes in the NHS and elsewhere would be hastily implemented to avoid the new accounting requirements. This risk appeared to be confirmed by the Head of PFI at a Big Six firm, who, following the appearance of the ASB (1997) Exposure Draft, was quoted as saying:

> PFI has never moved quicker than it is now... The government has turned up the Bunsen burner and it's going like a train ... we have 140 people working on these schemes around the country... The number of schemes will just keep rising (Bloom, 1998, p. 14).

Following the recommendations of its Financial Reporting Advisory Board (FRAB, 1999, p. 2), HM Treasury has fortunately now agreed in principle to the requirement for retrospection in the reporting of earlier PFI schemes within the above guidelines.

## PFI AND DISCLOSURE

A notable omission from *FRS5A* is any detailed requirements for Disclosures of the detailed financial Commitments on individual purchasing entities (whether in the public sector, as with an NHS Trust, or in the private sector) over future periods of time. *FRS5A* itself enables the disclosure requirements of *SSAP 21* for such commitments to be avoided by including non-separable elements, such as maintenance payments, within the PFI contract. If the risk analysis results in the conclusion that the purchaser 'does not have an asset of the property', *FRS5A* appears to imply by default that no future annual PFI commitments need to be disclosed by the purchasing NHS Trust or other such body.

This omission is despite the general desire of Paragraph 30 of *FRS 5* that:

> Disclosure of a transaction in the financial statements, whether or nor it has resulted in assets or liabilities being recognised or ceasing to be recognised, should be sufficient to enable the user of the financial statements to understand its commercial effect.

Future financial obligations accruing to the NHS are clearly part of the commercial effect of current PFI transactions. Fortunately, paragraph 4.8.4 of HM Treasury's (1998b) *Resource Accounting Manual* asserts that:

> Commitments under PFI contracts will generally need to be disclosed. The appropriate form of disclosure will be similar to that for leases under SSAP 21.

These disclosure requirements are now made more explicit in the revised Treasury (1999b and 1999c) rules for those PFI schemes to which these will apply, and include both disclosure of annual commitments and, where materially different, the estimated annual payments in future years.

Such disclosure may, to some extent, assist in the monitoring of whether or not the claimed objective (Treasury, 1999b and 1999c) of PFI schemes, that of value for money in the procurement of public services, is achieved. However, such monitoring will require detailed knowledge also of precisely which services are bundled together in the PFI contract, with this detailed information not necessarily being publicly available. More direct information for assessing whether value for money is achieved would be provided by knowledge of the implicit risk-adjusted rate of return on the capital invested in the PFI scheme, and of the extent of the actual risk which *ex post* has been transferred to the private sector operator. A high rate of return, and little actual variation in the profit level of the PFI operator, might indicate poor value for money to the public sector from the PFI scheme. Such a calculation would require, however, a separation of payments for the use of any underlying capital asset from those for other services. Many PFI schemes are structured to avoid such a separation, as *FRS5A* implicitly recognises, with such a value for money test being made more difficult in such cases. However, it is notable that Table B16 in HM Treasury (1999a) does itself succeed in identifying the estimated capital spending by the private sector on all existing, and soon to be agreed, PFI schemes as a separate element from the other service elements of the contracts. If value for money really is the main objective of PFI, one might have anticipated a rigorous framework to have been in place which facilitated the detailed assessment of value for money from the different elements of the PFI contract, including its often large capital investment, in both the initial decision-making on the PFI scheme and in the subsequent monitoring of whether or not value for money is subsequently achieved for the NHS and other parts of the public sector that support PFI schemes.

## STANDARD SETTING, PFI AND CONCEPTUAL FOUNDATIONS

It can be argued that the attempt to secure adequate accounting for PFI has represented a major test of the accounting standard setting process under the ASB, and of the extent to which central government will adhere to these accounting standards as part of its planned introduction of Resource Accounting. This initiative, as part of New Public Management, was established with an intention to conform to (the largely private sector) UK Generally Accepted Accounting Practice (GAAP), 'adapted where appropriate to take account of the public sector context' (HM Treasury, 1995, p. 17). As noted above, the ASB was itself set up to restore public confidence in accounting standards. The ASB's 'main initiative in discharging [its] commitment' to '... developing principles to guide it in establishing standards and to provide a framework within which others can exercise judgement in resolving accounting issues' (Wilkins, 1997, p. 743) is its Statement of Principles. Yet, despite being issued in 1995, the ASB's Statement of Principles currently still remains in Exposure Draft form, albeit now as a Revised Exposure Draft (ASB, 1999). The Statement of Principles of the ASB clearly identifies the objective of financial statements to be that of providing information that can help to satisfy user needs. There is, however, no reference to, or explicit analysis of, users and their information needs concerning PFI schemes in *FRS5A* or in its earlier Exposure Draft and accompanying commentary, in seeking to resolve issues of the desirable accounting treatment of PFI contracts.

Without a clear identification of user need, supported by a well-defined Statement of Principles and associated conceptual framework, there is a danger that accounting practice will be influenced by more short-term pressures from special interest groups (see Mayston, 1992b). Not least amongst these special interest groups are those with a commercial interest in promoting, or advising on, PFI schemes. The multiple roles now taken on by large accountancy firms could then generate possible conflicts of interest between these commercial interests and whatever influence such firms may have over the accounting treatment of PFI schemes in the NHS and elsewhere. In the recent debate over the future of its Exposure Draft, it is notable that the Chairman of the ASB, Sir David Tweedie, is quoted as saying that:

> Much will depend on the Big Six. The early signs are that they have mixed feelings. Accountants in PFI departments seem to have sympathy with the ASB, but commercial concerns will weigh heavily on their minds, as they have all invested time and money in this growth sector (Bloom, 1998, p. 15).

Similarly, following the exposure period for the *FRS5A* Exposure Draft, Robert Bruce (*Times*, 12 March, 1998) noted:

> Now all the responses are in. And, by and large, people have stuck to the party line. If you are likely to make money out of the PFI, like members of the CBI for example, you have argued against the ASB's proposed rules.

Some former Big Six firms have nevertheless argued against an off-balance-sheet treatment of PFI transactions (ibid, p. 32).

Without adherence to an adequate conceptual framework, there is also a danger of accounting standard setters adopting a fire-fighting role (Solomons, 1989), rather than 'identifying accounting areas that need improvement before damage is done' (Mayston, 1992a, p. 236). Equally, there is a danger that conceptual frameworks, and Statements of Principle, will be established mainly to boost the perceived legitimacy of the standard-setting body (see Jones, 1992), but without their being the real driving force for the accounting standards adopted. In this context, it is notable that seemingly *all-inclusive* definitions for assets and liabilities are adopted both by the ASB's Statement of Principles (ASB, 1999), and by *FRS5* in its claimed desire to be *Reporting the Substance of Transactions*. Assets are defined as 'Rights or other access to future economic benefits controlled by an entity as a result of past transactions or events', and Liabilities as 'An entity's obligations to transfer economic benefits as a result of past transactions or events'.

## PFI AND CAPITALISATION

However, the assets on which the ASB's *FRS5A* actually concentrates are physical *property* assets. The small print of Paragraph 12 (d) of *FRS 5* excludes from the ambit of *FRS 5* 'expenditure commitments', of which payments for PFI services are implicitly considered part if the application of *FRS5A* results in a conclusion that the 'purchaser does not have an asset of the property'. Nevertheless, it can be argued that what really gives the public sector entity, such as an NHS Trust, a right 'or other access to future economic benefits controlled by an entity as a result of past transactions or events', and associated 'obligations to transfer economic benefits as a result of past transactions or events' is *the PFI contract itself*, rather than necessarily any full or quasi-legal ownership over the underlying *property asset*. In the case of some important PFI contracts, such as for Information Technology services, there may indeed not be a single identifiable property asset, but instead there is a right to services which may be provided by changing physical assets over time, in a way which is not readily identifiable in advance.

The PFI contract itself would seem to involve rights of access to a future flow of services, conferring an Economic Benefit, from using a tangible fixed asset which someone else may legally own. In this context it is notable that Intangible Fixed Assets are defined by *FRS10* as 'Non-financial fixed assets that do not have physical substance but are identifiable and are controlled by the entity through custody or legal rights'. The public sector PFI purchaser acquires legal rights over fulfilment of an identifiable PFI contract, which itself has no more physical substance than a patent. If the PFI contract itself were treated as an intangible fixed asset, the asset would have to be capitalised at cost on the balance sheet under *FRS10*. This would be consistent with the view that:

> a PFI contract is for the provision of a stream of integrated services and the property and service elements are necessarily interrelated to provide the outputs required by the contract (ASB, 1997).

However, maintaining that 'a PFI contract should be viewed as a single contract and not separable into individual elements' (*ibid.*) would not then enable it to be taken off-balance-sheet even if some risk is transferred to the PFI operator.

Such a treatment would also recognise that *both* the public sector procuring entity, such as an NHS Trust, and the private sector PFI provider acquire assets and liabilities as a result of their PFI transaction. In addition, it recognises that both may acquire risks as a result of the transaction. In particular, for the public sector entity, these risks include those fixed obligations under the PFI contract which affect its future affordability. Such a recognition would avoid *the false dichotomy* , which the ASB's concentration upon who 'really owns' the underlying property asset gives rise to, of seeking to place the assets, liabilities and associated risks *either* the purchaser's *or* the operator's balance sheet. Any fixed commitment to make annual payments itself adds to the effective gearing and a*ffordability risk* position which the purchaser faces. Whilst allowance is made by the ASB (1998) for demand risk to the purchaser resulting from such fixed commitments, this is not the only consideration in the ASB's 'all or nothing' classification of whether or not 'the property is an asset of the purchaser', with no clear indication given of how these different risk factors are to be traded-off when they give conflicting indications. Managers keen to avoid the on-balance-sheet recording of PFI assets have an incentive to agree to PFI contracts which have other such risk factors in favour of non-disclosure. If the trade-off depends on 'professional judgement', the result may be increased discretionary power in the hands of accountancy firms and the need for further large consultancy fees.

It can be argued that a non-separable PFI contract should be accounted for instead as an asset in its own right on the balance sheet of the public sector purchaser, irrespective of whether or not the private sector operator is recognised as having ownership of the property asset. There is indeed a case for treating PFI contracts as a distinct recognised category of assets, involving both tangible and intangible elements, and property and service elements, that may prove to be non-separable. If it is impossible to separate the yolk and white of the egg in the PFI contract, this is no reason to fail to recognise and account for the resultant *omelettes* which clearly exist. Since the full legal title of the underlying property is unlikely to be with the public sector body, there is little risk of double counting both the PFI contract and the underlying property on the public sector balance sheet. There should be a *linked presentation* of the asset with the associated financial liability under the PFI contract.

PFI contracts have many aspects which are similar to *operating leases*, which *SSAP21* does not at present require to be capitalised on-balance-sheet. This asymmetric treatment with finance leases has arguably been in part responsible for the escalation of the annual operating lease commitments of UK listed companies to *eighteen times* those of finance leases by 1994 (Beattie, Edwards and Goodacre, 1998). The present lack of on-balance-sheet treatment of operating leases is despite the findings of a report on *Accounting for Leases* by Warren McGregor (1996) published by the UK Accounting Standards Board, the US Financial Accounting Standards Board and other national accounting standard setting bodies, that 'a compelling case can be made that all non-cancelable leases should be capitalised as assets and liabilities by lessees at the present value of their fixed or determinable future lease payments'.

## CONCLUSIONS

As we have noted above, there is no guarantee that the outcome of the process of change in the public sector, such as is involved in the introduction of PFI into the NHS, will be efficient, once there are weaknesses in the associated accounting and accountability procedures. PFI shows the need for positive steps to remedy such weaknesses, including in the longer term a more comprehensive treatment of contracts for PFI schemes, operating leases and similar arrangements.

The potentially damaging impact of PFI in the context of the NHS capital charging system illustrates that great care must be taken to ensure that the interactions between the financial control system, accounting practice and economic pressures do promote economic efficiency. There is indeed a danger that PFI, like some other elements of change within the public sector, proves to serve particular interest groups, such as management consultants, accountants, and current managers and politicians seeking short-term fiscal palliatives, rather than longer-term efficiency goals (see Mayston, 1993 and 1996b). Securing adequate accounting for PFI is then an important step in the principal-agent process of attempting to ensure that current decision-making is properly aligned with the longer-term interests of consumers of key public services, such as health care.

## REFERENCES


Accounting Standards Board (1997), *Amendment to FRS5 'Reporting the Substance of Transactions': The Private Finance Initiative, Exposure Draft- December 1997* (London: ASB).

——— (1998), *Amendment to FRS5 'Reporting the Substance of Transactions': Private Finance Initiative and Similar Contracts - September 1998* (London: ASB).

——— (1999), *Statement of Principles for Financial Reporting: Revised Exposure Draft* (London: ASB).

Association of Health Service Treasurers (1985), *Managing Capital Assets in the National Health Service* (London: CIPFA).

Audit Commission (1985), *Public Expenditure Controls in Local Government in England* (London: HMSO).

Baumol, W. (1967), 'Macroeconomics of Unbalanced Growth', *American Economic Review*, Vol. 67, pp. 415–26.

Beattie, V., K. Edwards and A. Goodacre (1998), 'The Impact of Constructive Operating Lease Capitalisation on Key Accounting Ratios', *Accounting and Business Research*, Vol. 28, pp. 233–54.

Bloom, J. (1998), 'A Battle to the Debt', *Accountancy Age* (15th January), pp. 14–15.

Boyle, S. (1997), 'The Private Finance Initiative', *British Medical Journal*, Vol. 314, pp. 1214–5.

Brealey, R. and S. Myers (1996), *Principles of Corporate Finance* (New York: McGraw-Hill).

———, I. Cooper and M. Habib (1997), 'Investment Appraisal in the Public Sector', *Oxford Review of Economic Policy*, Vol. 13, No. 4, pp. 12–28.

Broadbent, J. and R. Laughlin (1999), 'The Private Finance Initiative: Clarification of a Future Research Agenda', *Financial Accountability and Management*, Vol. 15, No. 2, pp. 95–114.

Buchanan, J. and G. Tullock (1962), *The Calculus of Consent* (Ann Arbor: University of Michigan Press).

Cardarelli, R., J. Sefton, and L. Kotlikoff (1998), *Generational Accounting in the UK (mimeo)*.

Chartered Institute of Public Finance and Accountancy (1989), *Capital Accounting in Local Authorities – The Way Forward* (London: CIPFA).

Dearing, Sir R. (Chairman) (1989), *Report of the Review Committee on the Making of Accounting Standards* (London: DTI).

Department of Health (DoH) (1989a), *Capital Charges*, NHS Review Working Paper 5 (London: HMSO).

——— (1989b), *Working For Patients*, Cm. 555 ( London: HMSO).

——— (1997), *The New NHS – Modern, Dependable*, Cm 3807 (London: Stationery Office).

——— (1998), *The Government's Expenditure Plans 1998–1999, Departmental Report*, Cm 3912 (London: Stationery Office).

——— (1999), *The Government's Expenditure Plans 1999–2000, Departmental Report*, Cm 4203 (London: Stationery Office).

Department of Health and Social Security (1985), *Mereworth 3: Heathbridge* (London: DHSS).

Dornbusch R. and S. Fischer (1984), *Macroeconomics*, 3rd edn. (London: McGraw-Hill).

Financial Reporting Advisory Board (FRAB) (1999), *Second Report – September 1977 to April 1999* (London: HM Treasury).
Gaffney, D. and A. Pollock (1997), *Can the NHS Afford the Private Finance Initiative?* (London: British Medical Association).
Gray, A. and W. Jenkins (1993), 'Codes of Accountability in the New Public Sector', *Accounting, Auditing and Accountability Journal*, Vol. 6, pp. 52–67.
Hale, R. (1988),'Is Creative Accounting Dead?', *Public Money and Management*, Vol. 8, pp. 3–4.
Harrison, S., N. Small and M. Baker (1994), 'The Wrong Kind of Chaos? The Early Days of an NHS Trust', *Public Money and Management*, Vol. 14, pp. 39–46.
Heald, D. (1997), 'Privately Financed Capital in Public Services', *Manchester School*, Vol. 65, pp. 568–98.
______ and N. Geaughan (1997), 'Accounting for the Private Finance Initiative', *Public Money and Management*, Vol. 17, pp. 11–16.
______ and D. Scott (1995), 'Charging for Capital in the National Health Service in Scotland', *Financial Accountability & Management*, Vol. 11, pp. 57–74.
Hodges, R. (1998), 'Learning to Live with the Private Finance Initiative: Case Studies of Three Ambulance Services' (mimeo).
Hood, C. (1991), 'A Public Management for All Seasons?' *Public Administration*, Vol. 69, pp. 3–19.
Humphrey C., P. Miller and R.W. Scapens (1993), 'Accountability and Accountable Management in the UK Public Sector', *Accounting, Auditing and Accountability Journal*, Vol. 6, pp. 7–29.
Jones, R. (1992), 'The Development of Conceptual Frameworks of Accounting for the Public Sector', *Financial Accountability & Management*, Vol. 8, No. 4, pp. 249–64.
Kotlikoff, L. (1992), *Generational Accounting* (New York: Basic Books).
Mayston, D. J. (1990a), 'NHS Resourcing; A Financial and Economic Analysis', in A. J. Culyer, A. Maynard and J. Posnett (eds.), *Competition in Health Care: Reforming the NHS* (London: Macmillan).
______ (1990b), 'Managing Capital Resources in the NHS', in A. J. Culyer, A. Maynard and J. Posnett (eds.), *Competition in Health Care: Reforming the NHS* (London: Macmillan).
______ (1992a), 'Capital Accounting, User Needs and the Foundations of a Conceptual Framework for Public Sector Financial Reporting', *Financial Accountability & Management*, Vol. 8, No. 4, pp. 227–48.
______ (1992b), 'Financial Reporting in the Public Sector and the Demand for Information', *Financial Accountability & Management*, Vol. 8, No. 4, pp. 317–24.
______ (1993), 'Principals, Agents and the Economics of Accountability in the New Public Sector', *Accounting, Auditing and Accountability Journal*, Vol. 6, pp. 68–96.
______ (1996a), 'Capital and Labour Markets for Health', in A. Culyer and A. Wagstaff (eds.) '*Reforming Health Care Systems*' (Cheltenham: Edward Elgar).
______ (1996b), 'Health Care Reform: A Study in Imperfect Information', in N. Lunt and D. Coyle (eds.), '*Welfare and Policy: Research Agendas and Issues*' (London: Taylor and Francis).
______ (1997), *NHS Capital Charging, PFI Contracts and Value for Money in Health Care*, Paper presented to Health Economists' Study Group (July, University of York).
McGregor, W. (1996), *Accounting for Leases: A New Approach* (London: ASB).
McKendrick and B. McCabe (1997), 'An Observer's Tale: Stonehaven Community Hospital', *Public Money and Management*, Vol. 17, pp. 17–20.
Meara, R. (1997), '*Building Services and Servicing Buildings' – The Private Finance Initiative in the NHS* (London: Institute of Health Service Management).
National Audit Office (1996), *Progress in Completing the New British Library*, HC362, Session 1995–6 (London: HMSO).
______ (1997), *The Skye Bridge – Report by the Comptroller and Auditor General*, HC 5, Session 1997–8 (London: Stationery Office).
______ (1998), *The Private Finance Initiative: The First Four Design, Build, Finance and Operate Roads Contracts*, HC476, Session 1997–8 (London: Stationery Office).
NHS Executive (1997), *1998–99 Health Authority Revenue Cash Limits Exposition Booklet* (Leeds: NHS Executive).
Office of National Statistics (1996), National Population Projections (London: Stationery Office).
______ (1997), *Government Deficit and Debt Under the Maastricht Treaty* (London: ONS).
Perrin, J. (1984), 'Accounting for Public Sector Assets', in A. Hopwood and C. Tomkins (eds.), *Issues in Public Sector Accounting* (Oxford: Philip Allan).

Peters, T. (1989), *Thriving on Chaos: Handbook for a Management Revolution* (London: Pan Books).

Pollock, A., M. Dunnigan, D. Gaffney, A. Macfarlane and F. Majeed (1997), 'What Happens When the Private Sector Plans Hospital Services for the NHS: Three Case Studies Under the Private Finance Initiative', *British Medical Journal*, Vol. 314, pp. 1266–71.

Public Accounts Committee (1993), *Wessex Regional Health Authority: Management of the Regional Information Systems Plan, Minutes of Evidence*, HC 658i (London: HMSO).

Rhodes, R. (1994), 'The Hollowing Out of the State: The Changing Nature of the Public Service in Britain', *Political Quarterly*, Vol. 65, pp. 138–51.

Royal College of Surgeons (1998), *Provision of Acute General Hospital Services* (London: RCS).

Smith, T. (1992), *Accounting for Growth: Stripping the Camouflage from Company Accounts* (London: Century).

Solomons, D. (1989), *Guidelines for Financial Reporting Standards* (London: ICAEW).

Terry, F. (1996), 'The Private Finance Initiative – Overdue Reform or Policy Breakthrough?' *Public Money and Management*, Vol. 16, pp. 9–16.

Treasury, HM (1995), *Better Accounting for the Taxpayer's Money: The Government's Proposals – Resource Accounting and Budgeting in Government*, Cm 2929 (London: HMSO).

——— (1997a), *PFI Technical Note No. 1: How to Account for PFI Transactions* (London: HM Treasury).

——— (1997b), *A Code for Fiscal Stability* (London: HM Treasury).

——— (1998a), *Stability and Investment for the Long Term: Economic and Fiscal Strategy Report 1998*, Cm 3978 (London: Stationery Office).

——— (1998b), *Resource Accounting Manual* (London: Stationery Office).

——— (1999a), *Financial Statement and Budget Report* (London: Stationery Office).

——— (1999b), *Accounting for PFI Transactions – Consultation Draft* (London: HM Treasury).

——— (1999c), *Private Finance Technical Note No. 1 (Revised): How to Account for PFI Transactions* (London: HM Treasury).

Treasury Taskforce on Private Finance (1997), *Partnerships for Prosperity* (London: HM Treasury).

Wilkins, R. (ed.) (1997), *Accounting Standards 1997/98* (Milton Keynes: ICAEW).

# [24]

# Public-Private Partnership: An Alternative Institutional Model for Implementing the Private Finance Initiative in the Provision of Transport Infrastructure

AMIRA MUSTAFA

AMIRA MUSTAFA is with Hirequest Consulting.

Provision and financing of infrastructure is of primary concern to governments due to the role that efficient infrastructure plays in economic growth and social activity. In the U.K., infrastructure provision largely has been the responsibility of the public sector since the Second World War. Traditionally, infrastructure procurement was viewed as asset procurement; decisions relating to provision, production, and financing of assets as well as the operation and maintenance of the services were undertaken by the public sector. Assets were procured from private sector contractors whose responsibilities were limited to the construction of the asset, and the risks associated with operation of the facility remained with the public sector. Recently, responsibility for financing, producing, and operating infrastructure facilities has shifted from the public sector to the private sector. This has come about in the U.K. within a wider ideological setting in the 1980s that was manifested in various forms such as privatization, contracting out, and build-operate-transfer (BOT) arrangements.

In 1992, the Government introduced a new policy, the Private Finance Initiative (PFI), to promote the private sector's involvement in infrastructure and public services provision. At the heart of this policy is attracting private sector's funds, management and innovation to the provision of infrastructure services. The policy aims at allocating risk to the party that is best suited to manage it and demonstrating value for money for any expenditure by the public sector.

PFI covers a wide range of infrastructure services such as prisons, roads, light rail systems, health, defense, higher and further education, and the Government's national insurance recording system. The general principles of the policy apply to all sectors alike, however, the implementation varies depending on each sector's characteristics and each client's requirements.

This article addresses the implementation of PFI in the road sector, one of the first sectors to benefit from application of PFI.[1] Over time, this process has improved. However, because many risk allocation issues were not worked out in the earliest stages, financing for the first PFI road projects took longer than expected. Other PFI projects since then have benefited from this learning experience. This article seeks to identify whether the current model of PFI implementation has been successful. It concludes that it has been partially successful and could be improved. The article outlines an alternative model for improving it.

## FACTORS LEADING TO THE DEVELOPMENT OF PFI

Forces interacted at various levels to encourage private sector participation and the development of PFI. Exhibit 1 illustrates the developments that led to the conception of PFI.

Over the past two decades, a steady increase in traffic volume has resulted in congestion and delays. Since the 1980s, the Government has been committed to a budget-control policy in an effort to reduce the public sector borrowing requirement (PSBR). Because continued growth in traffic was forecast and Government expenditure on the national road network was already at record levels, finding an alternative source of funding was mandatory. Due to increasing demand for road networks and dissatisfaction with the existing system of procurement, which was plagued by cost and time overruns, the Department of Transport began to develop an alternative means for provision of services with the objective of creating a road operating industry within the private sector. At the time, the private sector, particularly large civil engineering contractors faced with decline on construction orders during the recession, started to take a proactive role in generating work by participating in the financing, construction, and operation of infrastructure facilities. These combined forces led to the development of PFI and a new procurement system.

**THE IMPLEMENTATION OF PFI**

H.M. Treasury has structured PFI, set the guidelines for the various government departments, and monitored its implementation and development. This article takes a view that one of the main objectives underlying PFI is achieving value for money in infrastructure procurement and public service provision. The main strategies used to implement this objective are: 1) allocating risk to the party that is best able to manage it, and 2) promoting private sector innovation. The method of implementation has a direct impact on achieving the policy objectives. A schematic presentation of the relationships among PFI objectives, strategies, and implementation is shown in Exhibit 2.

The mechanism used for implementing PFI is concession contracting on a project basis, including variants such as design-build-finance-operate (DBFO). Exhibit 3 illustrates the participants and the contractual arrangements of a DBFO road project. Under the umbrella of the concession contract the risks associated with provision and production are transferred to the private sector. Hence, parallel to the concession agreement there is the design and construction contract, on one hand, and the operation and maintenance contract on

**EXHIBIT 1**
**The Developments that Led to the Conception of PFI**

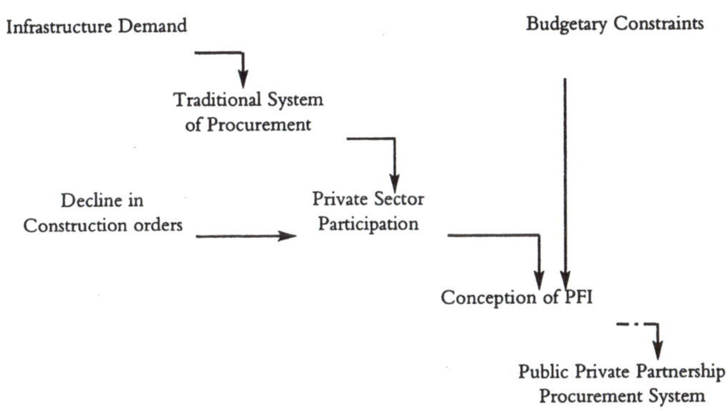


Source: A. Mustafa, 1998.

EXHIBIT 2

**Relationship Between PFI Objectives, Strategies, and Implementation Method**

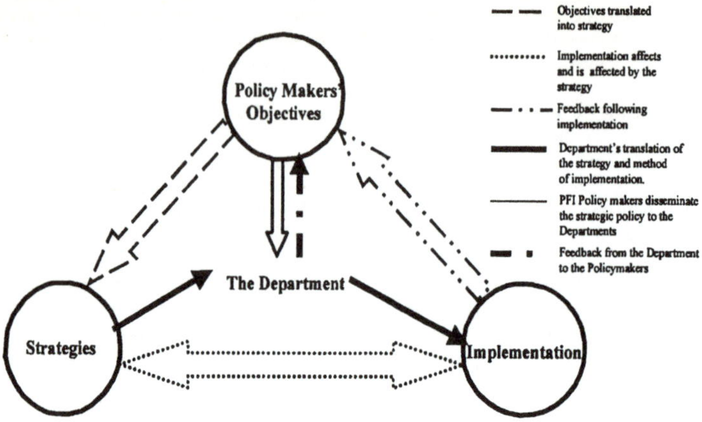


Source: A. Mustafa, 1998.

the other. These "sub-contracts" serve the purpose of allocating risks to the parties best able to manage them. In addition, the roles of the contractor, the operator, and the concessionaire must be separated to prevent role conflict.

A PFI project generally passes through five phases: planning, implementation, construction, operation, and transfer. These phases are shown in Exhibit 4. In the planning phase, the Government department clarifies its objectives; identifies the need for a project; identifies the kinds, quantities, and quality of services and associated assets to be provided; investigates the market; produces an outline plan; decides the procurement route; appoints appropriate advisors; and assembles the project team. Careful project planning by the Government client is crucial to the achievement of public-sector objectives. Only projects of the scale and complexity where private-sector participation could be beneficial should proceed along this route.

In the implementation phase, the client develops the output specifications taking into account the service requirements. A significant part of the implementation phase is the bidding process. Bidding for PFI projects follows negotiated procedure under the European Union Procurement Rules. The choice of the successful bidder is based on the most economically advantageous proposal, the tender that provides most value for money to the client.

Following the award of the contract, detailed engineering, design, and construction work begins under a fixed-price, design-and-build contract. All the risks associated with construction are transferred to the design-and-build contractors. A bidding consortium invariably includes an operator who takes on the responsibility of delivering the service specified by the client and carrying out routine maintenance with minimum disruption to operations. Typically, there are provisions within the contract to ensure effective service delivery with minimum disruption to traffic flow during the routine maintenance operation, in addition to maintaining safety standards. At the end of the specified concession period, the asset reverts to the public sector.

The mechanism by which the DBFO Co. is reimbursed for service delivery is the shadow toll. That is, payment is made by the Client (as opposed to direct road users). It involves payment per vehicle kilometer of the project road in accordance with a banding toll struc-

# EXHIBIT 3
**Participants in a PFI Project and the Contractual Arrangements**

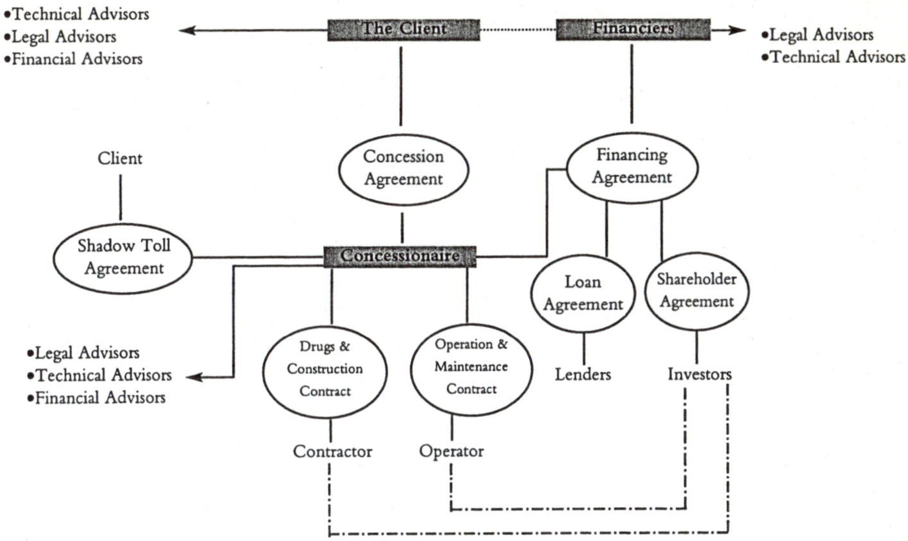


Source: A. Mustafa, 1996. Adapted from McCarthy, 1991, and Merna and Smith, 1993.

ture and type of vehicle using the road, with adjustment made for the lane closure and safety performance. Bands are defined levels of traffic volume. Bidders were asked to bid the parameters of traffic levels for a maximum of four and a minimum of two bands. For traffic exceeding a defined level of vehicle kilometers per year, the toll level was set at zero to ensure that the client's maximum liability under the DBFO contract was capped (Highways Agency and Private Finance Panel [1997]). In shadow toll schemes, road lenders and investors assume the risk of traffic volumes falling below forecast levels.

Financial advisors to the Highways Agency argued that banded shadow tolls allowed bidders to propose their own risk profile and from client's perspective, this was considered a good way of testing the market. It allowed bidders' advisors to develop a wide range of different bidding and funding strategies and provided for a measure of protection for senior lenders (Poulter and Stewart [1996]).

The National Audit Office reports on the first four DBFO projects in England [1998] and Scotland [1999] state:

> that "the private sector cannot manage the traffic risk [therefore] the use of shadow tolls has introduced a new risk which can be expected to have increased the cost of these roads, offsetting to some extent the benefits of placing other substantial risks appropriately."

The only current Highways Agency scheme, the A13, moves significantly towards an availability model. It is expected that around 25% of payments will still be traffic based.

## ISSUES AFFECTING PFI

Public sector procurement has often failed to achieve its expected objectives because of high con-

**EXHIBIT 4**
**The Phases of a PFI Project**

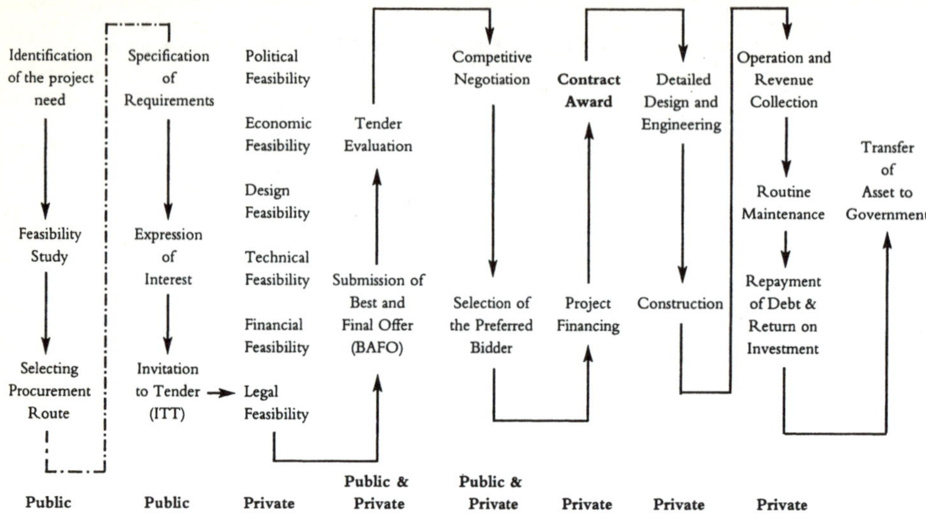


struction costs, time overruns, and operational inefficiencies attributed to poor design (Flynn [1994]). PFI has addressed some of the issues that plagued the traditional system of procurement. The underlying rationale of the PFI is based on the relative efficiency of this procurement method in comparison to the traditional procurement system. However, PFI is not with out its difficulties. Exhibit 5 summarizes some of the problems of the traditional and the PFI systems.

Issues affecting PFI implementation could be divided into generic issues that are commonly experienced in projects as a result of procuring projects by PFI and issues that are characteristic of a particular project.

### Generic Issues

One of the problems encountered in the first group of PFI road projects, and PFI projects in general is high tendering cost, incurred by the client and the bidding consortia alike. The National Audit Office [1998] reported that the Highways Agency incurred cost for external advisors of £8.3 million for the first four DBFO road schemes.

The bidding consortia incur high tendering costs partly because they have to take into account, in their bid preparation, the client's and financiers' objectives as well as their own. Therefore, for a consortium to win the contract, the bidder has to provide value for money to the client; offer lenders and investors a reasonable return; and maintain the consortium's profitability. A consortium needs diverse range of skills and professional services to prepare a competitive bid.

Lengthy negotiations between a consortium, its financiers and the client may increase the cost of tendering even further. The cost of professional services drives up the tender cost significantly for both the client and bidders. Also, there is a need for public sector clients to have a better understanding of risks the private sector is able to manage and the types of projects that can be financed in the bank or capital markets.

**EXHIBIT 5**

**Problems with Traditional and PFI Systems of Provision**

| **Public Provision** | | |
|---|---|---|
| Traditional System → | **Private Provision** | |
| | PFI System → | **Public-Private Partnership System** |
| • Cost and time overruns | • High cost of bidding | Alignment of public and private sectors' objective and appropriate risk allocation to improve the efficiency of the system |
| • Over/under design | • Bidding process is lengthy | |
| • Risks connected construction and operation are not clearly identified | • Risk allocation and value for money definition are ambiguous | |
| • High cost of maintenance | • Scope for innovation is restricted | |

The technical innovative input by the private sector has not fully achieved its potential. There is limited scope for innovative changes in base design because projects are cleared through the statutory approval procedure. The large risk associated with the planning approval procedure limits substantial technical input by the private sector. Hence, under the current arrangement, innovative technical input is limited to detail design and the use of material because the private sector has limited opportunity to participate at the early stages of project design when the parameters shaping the service are developed.

### Project Specific Issues

Each deal is typically tailored to suit the project's characteristics and circumstances. A successful deal hinges on establishing the nature and scope of each project's risks and mitigating them away from the project company to the party best able to manage them. Also, establishing a project team with the strength and integrity which not only contribute to the success of the project but could also add value to the client bidder relationship is essential. Appendixes A and B illustrate three examples of the first DBFO road projects.

These projects are: the A1-M1 link road where the project sponsors are the Yorkshire Link Ltd. (YLL); and the A1 (M) and the A419/A417, where the sponsors for both projects is Road Management Group (RMG). The A1-M1 link road and the A1(M) are reported to show significant savings over both the public sector comparators (NAO [1998]).

***A1-M1 Link Road.*** One of the major issues that faced the project sponsors and had a direct impact on transactions is the change in shareholding structure for YLL. The original consortium comprising Trafalgar House PLC and George Wimpey PLC, both large U.K. contracting companies.[2] The changes took place when Tarmac PLC bid for assets of George Wimpey PLC including the construction division which was involved in the bid for this project. Forshaw [1996] argues that, given that the consortium members are equal shareholders, these changes could affect the project in the following ways:

1. Destabilize project finance transactions;
2. Affect client's assessment of a consortium's ability to achieve financial close;
3. Affect the way bank credit exposures are monitored internally as far as credit exposure exists through

construction and operation contracts on the respective consortium members; and

4. Changes the structure of the transactions because of the need to brief new personnel.

Despite the uncertainties, the senior lenders were able to provide strong letters of support during the bidding process, conditioned upon ultimate resolution of ownership structure. This provided reassurances to the client and dampened the initial effect of the change in ownership. Furthermore, it contributed to the building of trust between the bidding team and the Highways Agency, which added value in the later stages of ownership changes. During the final stages of ownership-change transactions Tarmac PLC withdrew its support for the tender and BICC PLC, in a short time, stepped in and supported the project on the basis agreed in the concession contract. Forshaw [1996] argues that the sponsors' relationship with key bankers and the influence of key personnel of the bidding team of the sponsors downplayed the effect of ownership change.

***A1 (M) and the A419/A417***. Davis [1996] states that the financial advisors to RMG (Lehman Brothers) believed that the most appropriate type of financing for this type of projects would be long-dated with principal redemption throughout most of its life. The problem is that neither the commercial banks nor the capital markets had ever done a project financing with the terms that were required here and the banks were unwilling to commit for more than fifteen years. Repaying the loan within such a period would have been a heavy cash burden for the sponsors, and would not have allowed them any dividends. Another problem is that banks prefer to lend at floating rates but the sponsors wanted fixed-rate financing. After the banks failed to agree on financing terms acceptable to the sponsors, Lehman Brothers decided to try the capital markets. This decision was made against the background that amortizing structures are not the norm in the U.K. bond market, and the U.K. government is more accustomed to seeing bank letter of support as evidence of a project sponsor's financing. Moreover, Bond investors do not provide such commitments.

Hence, the transactions involved accommodating a number of the characteristics of project financing to the requirement s of the bond issue, in particular the level of project risk. Bliss and Stewart [1996] states that in addition, considering that there was no precedence and these projects were the first of their type to be financed by bond issues, RMG was reliant on its advisors to provide guidance on what was likely to be acceptable to bond holders. Furthermore, there was the problem of a single bond issue for two projects. Although a single bond provided greater liquidity and eliminated marketing problems inherent in launching two similar but separate bonds, the client insisted that the projects not be cross-collateralized and failure of one project performance not jeopardize the financing of the other. Hence, considerable efforts were made to ensure that each project was effectively isolated from any poor performance by the other, this was partly achieved by the use of special purpose vehicle company Road Management Consolidated (RMC). More detail is provided in Appendix B.

The M1-A1 provided an interesting contrast to the A1(M) and both projects illustrate the different examples of risk transfer that projects are exposed to. In the case of the M1-A1 the debate about the risk transfer was about the traffic forecast risk and how the risk could be assessed for a greenfield project with no historical traffic data. The A1(M), on the other hand, provided an entirely different risk transfer. In both case protracted negotiations could have been avoided if the risk-transfer structure had been developed in the early stages of the process.

## PROGRESS OF THE PFI

The PFI has become one of the Government's main instruments for delivering public services. In 1997 the Government commissioned a policy review, commonly known as the Bates' review to make recommendations as to how to improve the PFI. The review identified the medium-term answer as highly skilled procurers in departments — without central support, and a small Treasury unit as a guardian of policy principles and promoter of best practice. In the short term, a need was identified for strong central input to help departments and agencies ensure implementation of quality transactions.

The Bates review recommendations fall into four categories:

a. Institutional structure
b. Improving the process
c. Lessons learned
d. Bid costs

## EXHIBIT 6

**The Institutional Structure of PFI Implementation**

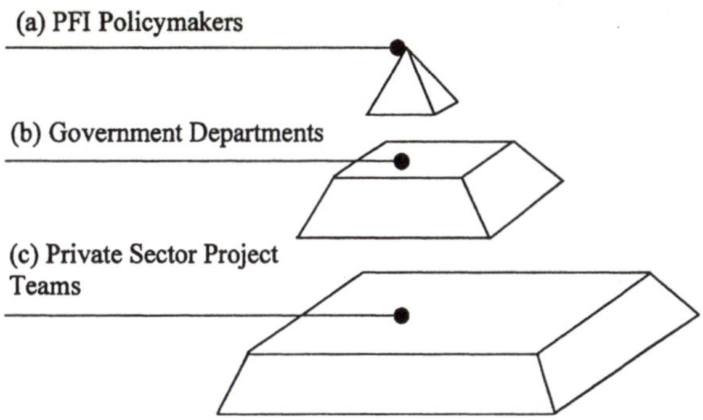


a. *Intra-institutional* — refers to the interaction within institutional boundaries that are governed by the same norms.

b. *Inter-institutional* — refers to the interaction across institutional boundaries with differing norms.

Exhibit 6 shows a schematic presentation of this institutional structure. At the apex of the pyramid (a) are PFI policymakers who develop the policy, objectives, and implementation strategies, and monitor its implementation and development. The Government departments (b) translate the policy guidelines into policy objectives and departmental objectives. The private sector participants (c) enter into a long-term agreement with the particular government department maintaining a balance between their objectives, policy objectives and the department's objectives.

Each organization, at all levels of this structure, has a set of organizational goals and "internalities" that influence its objectives.[5] These objectives vary with institutional characteristics, the nature of each organization, and its role in the implementing PFI. The diversity of objectives results in conflicts of interests among participants within the same institutional level as well as across institutional boundaries. The objectives could be classified into lower objectives, which are short-term objectives related to a particular project, and higher objectives, which are more general, long-term objectives of an organization with regard to PFI.

Forshaw [1996] highlighted, in the example of the A1-M1 road link project, the importance of the common goal shared by the project team and the sound relationship between the project sponsors and their bankers — transversely across the intra-institutional level (c) in Exhibit 6. This has not only helped stabilize the project but also propagated across inter-institutional levels and contributed to "the building up of a level of trust between the bidding team and the Highways Agency" — vertically across to level (b) in Exhibit 6 — and hence contributing to the success of the deal.

The client's short-term objective with regard to a particular project is to contribute value by adding and/or improving infrastructure services. The involve-

As a result, a new Treasury task force was set up. It has a policy arm and a project arm. The project arm has a life span of two years and is composed of a number of executives from the private sector with direct project management, financial, and legal experience. The task force helps government departments and agencies assess the commercial viability of large projects and help departments to close good quality projects.

A second Bates review is due shortly. It is reported that bankers, lawyers and contractors are concerned about the proposals put forward by the Treasury task force that are being considered by the review.[3] These proposals include: a) a creation of a Government investment bank to fund projects which have difficulty attracting private-sector equity, and b) a proposal to transform the task force into a negotiating team which would first establish where the risks lie in construction and then invite banks to fund the deal.

### ISSUES OF SUCCESSFUL IMPLEMENTATION

One of the fundamental issues influencing implementation of PFI is the institutional arrangement and the pattern of interactions within the "PFI Sector."[4] The current structure of interactions between public and private sector organizations is hierarchical in nature; the institutional structure is a pyramid form.

The interactions within this structure occur at two levels:

ment of the private sector in these projects facilitates effective allocation of responsibilities provided that risks and rewards are balanced. The long-term objective of the client is to achieve value for money for any government expenditure. Private sector organizations have long-term interests in sustaining a competitive advantage and increasing their share of the PFI market. The overall objective is to achieve efficient provision of infrastructure services.

A model for analyzing these objectives is developed and is illustrated in Exhibit 7. Given that the overall objective is the efficient provision of infrastructure services, this could be achieved in three phases: 1) by moving away from lower objective intra-institutional level towards an inter-institutional level, to 2) a higher objective intra-institutional level, and the final stage 3) is to move away towards the inter-institutional higher objectives.

Exhibit 7 displays the stages through which participants (public and private sectors) evolve and move towards the shared common objective of procuring/delivering efficient service, the underlying objectives may vary but the desired outcome is the same. This model helps in identifying the organizational goals of the PFI sector and differentiating the parties interested in short-term involvement, from the ones with long-term outlook. A contractor that is interested in PFI solely as a source of construction contracts and intends to "recycle" its equity share would have a different strategy and level of commitment to PFI transactions than a company that sees PFI projects as equity investment opportunities.

Most organizations involved have been concerned with lower objectives in the inter-institutional phase and few have moved toward higher objectives in the intra-institutional phase. The private sector, in particular some large construction firms, has responded to PFI and the development of public-private partnership through internal reorganization and strategic alliances that permit effective and successful involvement.

## AN ALTERNATIVE MODEL FOR IMPLEMENTING PFI

PFI is implemented using the technology of project finance. Given that achieving efficient service provision is the long-term goal of the PFI, the issue remains: How can the strategies be implemented in order to achieve this objective?[6] Given the diverse objectives of the participants, what institutional arrangement would "even out" these diverse objectives, provides a better scope for private sector innovative input, provide the scope for optimum risk allocation and introduce an additional source of finance?

Various institutional options for provision of infrastructure services have been examined. They vary from mainly public sector to mainly private sector (Kessides [1993] and Ostrom, Schroeder, and Wyne [1993]). The objective is to allocate the responsibilities of plan-

**EXHIBIT 7**
**A Model for Analysis of Institutions' Objectives**

| | **Intra-Institutional** | | **Inter-Institutional** |
|---|---|---|---|
| | ***Public*** | ***Private*** | |
| **Lower** | Addition/ Improvement to Infrastructure Services | Winning the project | Allocating Responsibilities and Rewards Effectively |
| **Higher** | Value for Money | Increasing market share in PFI market | **Efficient Service Provision** |

EXHIBIT 8

**An Alternative Institutional Model of Implementing PFI**

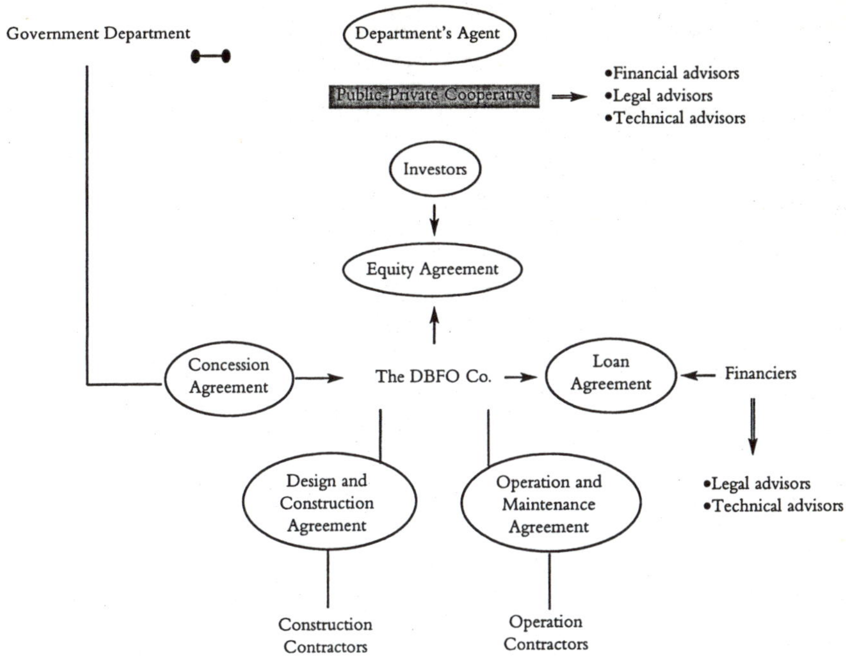


ning, policy making, ownership, regulation, financing, investment, operation and maintenance for a wide range of infrastructure. The general consensus is that implementing adequate institutional arrangements should take into account: the basis of activities, characteristic of infrastructure services, the incentives provided by the various arrangements, and the issues involved in implementing the institutional arrangement to achieve the desired outcome.

A model that takes these issues into account is developed and coined as the Public-Private Cooperative (PPC). This alternative institutional model for implementing PFI is shown in Exhibit 8. The model is aimed at the sector level rather than the project level. PPC is a joint arrangement between public sector client's agent such as the Highways Agency (in the case of roads), and a consortium of long-term investors. The investors are classified in two categories the a) investors solely interested in long-term equity investment, e.g., pension funds, and b) investors that are interested in long-term investment in addition to having the technical skills in construction and/or operation of the facilities. A typical example of the latter is a construction group or a utility company whose investment in PFI projects is separate from its core business.

The investors set up an investment fund to make

equity investments in specified types of projects within a particular sector (for example, Roads Investment Fund). The investors and the department's agent would be jointly involved in the early stages of project identification, planning and feasibility study (refer to Exhibit 4). This is particularly beneficial in the case of road projects where technical innovation is restricted due to the limited involvement of private consortia in the outline design stage of the project. PPC provides an opportunity to assess which projects can and cannot be financed and provides a setting for a more realistic view of the risk apportionment between the public and private sectors at an early stage of a project's life. This allows PPC to facilitate a sound assessment of individual projects based on their business and economic merits. It provides the opportunity of weeding out projects that are not fundable through PFI at an early stage.

PPC brings together public and private sector parties that have a mutual long-term interest in the project helps separate long- and short-term objectives. Moreover, PPC provides the opportunity of increasing equity funds in these projects, hence reducing the high debt-equity ratio.

## CONCLUSION

PFI started as a policy initiative to attract and encourage private sector participation in the provision of infrastructure services. The Labour Government recognized the potential of PFI and set out to move it forward by way of the Bates Review. Despite some criticism dismissing PFI as a tool of Government off-balance-sheet financing strategy, the benefits from the implementation of PFI were evident in a number of successful projects in central as well as local government such as roads, light rail, prisons, defense, and schools.

The scale of the Bates second review — due soon — is proof that PFI is taking public services provision in the U.K. into the Millennium. However, PFI, as such, has surpassed the stage of an initiative. It has served in mobilizing the joint efforts that propel the various forms of public-private partnerships in provision of infrastructure services across virtually all Government departments.

Defining the roles and responsibilities of each party is an integral part to effective implementation of PFI objectives. For this to work efficiently, the framework within which the public and private sectors interact needs to be enhanced and a formula that maximizes the best of public and private sectors skills and minimize the impact of the disparity in institutional objectives and culture needs to be developed. The relationship between the private and public sectors and within the private sector is a significant factor in successful implementation.

This article has outlined several issues that affect the implementation of PFI in the road sector, including the high cost of bidding, protracted negotiations, the restricted innovative input by the private sector, and the differing objectives of public and private sector participants in these long-term projects. There are many ways these issues could be solved.

This article also focuses on the institutional arrangements. The institutional structure for implementing PFI is a pyramid structure, and within each layer there exist differing objectives that increasingly vary as we move down this structure. A model for analyzing the objectives of the public and private sectors against the background of institutional boundaries is introduced. This provides a framework for categorizing and locating public and private sector participants in PFI in relation to their "internalities" and organizational goals.

This article takes the view that the implementation of PFI in a particular sector ought to be addressed at a sector level as opposed to a project level. A joint public-private institutional arrangement is inclined to yield a more efficient outcome provided that the appropriate framework exists and that the analysis takes in to account the characteristics, objectives and norms of interacting parties. An alternative model, the Public-Private Cooperative is introduced; it redresses some of the constraints of the current arrangement. The current model would be more suitable for larger, one-off projects. However, the PPC model would provide a more efficient setting for typical projects albeit new construction or improvement to existing assets.

## APPENDIX A

**M1-A1 Road**
**Excerpt from Article by**
**Anthony Forshaw (See References)**

### DISTINCTIVE FEATURES

- The M1-A1 project was a greenfield road project without historical traffic forecasts, except on three existing sections of the road;
- The financing amount was large compared to other sterling Eurobond offerings;

- Along with the other three tranche 1 road schemes, this was the first time lenders and investors had been introduced to the concept of shadow tolling; and
- This was the first time the Highways Agency had undergone such a process in its history and the first its internal staff, at all levels, had been required to negotiate this type of contract.

The M1-A1 Link Road in Yorkshire was a predominantly greenfield construction project comprising a new road to be built connecting the M1 with A1 South of Leeds. The successful consortium, Yorkshire Link Ltd.. (YLL) was comprised of Trafalgar House PLC (now Kverner PLC) and BICC plc (who replaced George Wimpey PLC following the acquisition of Wimpey Construction by Tarmac PLC).

## PROJECT RISKS

In addition to the construction risks, the lack of historical traffic data increased the traffic risk. In shadow toll roads, lenders and investors assume the risk of traffic volumes falling below forecast levels. The Highways Agency's banding mechanism has resulted in different levels of traffic volume risk being assumed by different financiers. The following diagram illustrates the hypothetical case:

**Traffic Volume**

Band 3
Covers equity upside returns

Band 2
Covers subordinated debt service and equity returns

Band 1
Covers operating costs and senior debt service

In this example, senior lenders would be uncomfortable if revenues were at the Band 1 level, but the project company would be solvent. Early on in the process YLL was provided by its outside consultants with a surprisingly conservative forecast for the scheme — lower than the scheme forecasts provided earlier during the planning process.

This was a concern because a low revenue forecast would reduce the tender's competitiveness. A strategy was developed to convince senior lenders to accept exceptionally low cover ratios at the most likely volume level forecast by the sponsor's consultants using the Highways Agency's proposed banding mechanism. Without their own independent advisors the senior lenders were unable to commit to a specific revenue strategy. Once an advisor had been appointed, the negotiation process was sufficiently advanced that is was in the senior banks' interest to support conservative revenue assumptions as part of negotiations on other aspects of the transaction, such as cover ratio levels.

Ultimately the banding approach enabled the shareholders to compensate for the lenders' conservative approach by accepting lower returns at the lenders base-case volume level than originally intended, but inevitably, given the lack of historic traffic flows, the traffic volume debate continued through our negotiations.

## STRUCTURE OF THE FINANCING

A consortium of commercial banks provided the largest component of the funding structure of approximately £300 million. The senior banks are led by an arranging group comprising Lloyds Bank as agent bank, Da-Ichi Kangyo Bank, Banque Indosuez, Credit Suisse, ABN Amro and National Westminster Bank.

Subordinated debt funding was provided by Deutsche Bank, 3i PLC, and Royal Bank of Scotland. A substantial component of the subordinated debt is guaranteed by the European Investment Fund. The European Investment Bank provided a portion of the senior debt funding; it is guaranteed by the commercial banks for the period of construction and operation. The sources and uses of funds forecast at the beginning of the project follow.

### Cover Ratios

A key driver of a tender's economics is the level of cover ratios that senior lenders will accept to cushion them against poor project performance. As with many projects, cover ratios were an area of contention with the M1-A1.

There are two cover ratios commonly used, the debt service cover ratio and the loan loss cover ratio:

- The *debt service cover ratio* is calculated as follows: Post-tax, pre-debt-service cash flow is the numerator. All debt service principal and interest in the last twelve months is the denominator. The ratio is calculated every six months on a rolling twelve-month basis. It tests for liquidity and historic performance.
- The *loan loss cover ratio* is a look-forward test. It looks forward over the entire life of the concession and discounts the cash flow over the life of the concession at the weighted average cost of debt. (Discounting at the cost of debt in effect deducts interest from the cash flow line.) The discounted future cash flow is divided by the amount of principal outstanding. A project company is a single-company asset and the value of the asset is the discounted value of future cash flows. This ratio is used as a test

**Projected Sources and Uses of Funds**

| Uses | | Sources | |
|---|---|---|---|
| Construction Costs | 81% | Senior Debt | 81% |
| Other Costs | 19% | Subordinated Debt | 11% |
| | | Shareholders Fund | 7% |
| | | Revenue During Construction | 1% |
| Total | 100% | Total | 100% |

to show by how much the discounted value of future cash flows exceeds the principal amount of debt. This ratio shows the effect of a problem in the future. Take, for example, a power project with a fifteen-year power purchase agreement (PPA) and twenty-year financing provided with the assumption that the fifteen-year PPA will be extended. If, for some reason, the lenders learn that the PPA will not be extended, revenues between years 15 and 20 will be eliminated and the loan loss cover ratio will collapse. The lenders will start setting aside shareholders' cash to prepay debt principal.

One component of the cover-ratio debate in the M1-A1 project was the extent to which different types of senior debt with different maturities should attract different cover ratio calculations. The EIB debt for this project had a twenty-five-year final maturity and the commercial bank debt had an eighteen-year final maturity. Competitively structured funding would recognize that the longer maturity EIB debt (or bond debt) should fall outside of the senior commercial bank debt cover ratio at least for the portion of debt maturing after senior commercial bank debt. One argument was that including all the longer maturity EIB debt in the eighteen-year commercial bank debt cover ratio failed to recognize the benefits of long-term debt providers, such as bond investors or the EIB, to a successful tender. But commercial bank lenders argued that default under the EIB facility would result in the acceleration of the longer term debt into a pari passu debt tranche, thereby extending the likely repayment profile of the commercial bank debt. All senior debt sensitivities therefore should have been measured under the shortest loan life cover ratio. This debate continued to the last month before financial close and compromises were required on all sides to achieve a workable solution. The commercial banks had a powerful weapon in their ability to insist on conservative traffic volumes forecasts, which aside from changing the cover ratio calculations, usually means equity or tolls must be increased.

### The European Investment Bank

The EIB's guidelines typically prevent it supporting one bidder over another during the competition selection process and accordingly it does not undertake detailed due diligence until a preferred bidder is selected. Inevitably this delays financial closing if other lenders are already at an advanced stage in negotiations. In this case, the Highways Agency accepted that if the EIB was to participate some delay was likely.

The benefit of the EIB to the economics of the NPV cost to the Highways Agency can justify such a delay. However, pricing the benefit of EIB finance is complex and can be a function of commercial banks' willingness to compromise on cover ratio calculations for their shorter-term debt. A particular benefit of the EIB in this transaction was the assistance they were able to give in introducing the European Investment Fund, which proved to be a helpful and innovative source of support.

## Appendix B

**The A1(M) and the A419/A417 Road Projects**
**Excerpt from Case Study by**
**Henry A. Davis (See References)**

### DISTINCTIVE FEATURES

- First bond offering under U.K. private finance initiative (PFI);
- Large amount compared to other sterling Eurobond offerings;
- First monoline-guaranteed project finance bond in the U.K.;
- Bond financing prior to construction;
- Acceptance of deferred annuity structure by U.K. investors;
- Dual project structure with limited cross-collateralization;

- Shadow tolls as a basis for project revenues; and
- Joint and several guarantees by sponsors with varying credit capacity.

The A1(M) between Alconbury and Peterborough and the A419/A417 between Swindon and Gloucester were part of the the first tranche of DBFO road schemes in the U.K., both these projects involved upgrading of existing road schemes. The four project sponsors and shareholders of RMG are AMEC p.l.c. and Alfred McAlpine PLC, both U.K. contractors, Dragados Limited, the U.K. subsidiary of Dragados y Constructiones SA, a Spanish contractor, and Brown & Root Limited, a subsidiary of Brown & Root, Inc. in the U.S., owned by the Halliburton Company.

## PROJECT RISKS

The principal project risks were that the contractors would not complete the required road upgrades to budget and standard within the contractually committed period and that the margins between shadow toll revenues and capital operating costs would not be sufficient to service the debt. There was also risk in a complex and untested DBFO contract that transferred substantial project risk to the sponsors while the government retained a number of avenues of intervention and control. Other risks include obstruction by environmentalist groups opposed to construction and expansion of the motorway network. This was not an incremental risk. Protesters either appear or not, but if they do they can cause a real problem. There was in indication that RMG's projects had not encountered huge community opposition and that the environmental groups were likely to concentrate their efforts elsewhere.

## STRUCTURE OF THE PROJECT

Two concession companies named Road Management Services (Peterborough) Limited (RMS Peterborough) for the A1(M) and Road Management Services (Gloucester) Limited for the A419/A417, entered into DBFO contracts with the Secretary of State for Transport to widen and improve the roads and to operate and maintain them for 30 years. The RMS companies in turn entered into construction contracts with design-and-build joint ventures comprised of the four companies that own RMG. he concession companies entered into fixed-price, fixed-time, turnkey construction contracts. These contracts were joint and several obligations of each joint venture member to perform design and construction work on schedule within a specified price. To the extent the construction programs were delayed, the joint venture partners were liable for full liquidated damages. These obligations were backed by full guarantees from each entity's ultimate parent company. The fixed-price, fixed-time, turnkey project was a relatively new concept for road construction companies in the U.K. By assuming responsibility for cost overruns, the contractors eliminated construction risk from the project financing, helped the stand-alone credit rating of the project, and facilitated raising the required funds.

During the construction period, the sponsors received partial tolls. These amounts increased as certain construction milestones are met and reached the full level when construction was complete. The toll level was partially indexed with inflation.

## STRUCTURE OF THE FINANCING

Sources of financing for the projects totaled £323 million, excluding cash generated from operations.

## THE SPECIAL PURPOSE FINANCING VEHICLE

The financing for the two road projects was raised through Road Management Consolidated PLC (RMC), a newly created special purpose financing vehicle, 100% controlled by RMG, that provided funds to the individual RMS companies through back-to-back on-loans. This structure allowed cross-application of dividends so each project could support the other. It enabled projected interest coverage levels to be tighter than they could have been otherwise, thus lowering the cost of financing. Combining two different roads diversified the lenders' risks. It eliminated the need for two separate financings, minimized the duplication of documentation and negotiation with financing parties, and created a public bond offering large enough to be liquid and to meet demand at the long end of the sterling bond market.

The financing vehicle raised money and then on-lent it to the project companies. The on-loans for the two projects were separate. Each project company is obligated to service its own on-loan first. And then if there is money left over, and the other project is in trouble, the returns that would have gone to the equity holders are pledged. This could be viewed as a limited cross-collateralization or a mutual pledge of equity returns from one project to the other. A complex agreement spells out what happens when one project, the other, or both are in various degrees of difficulty, and which accounts the funds flow through. Christopher Haga of Lehman Brothers points out that this is hard enough in a single project financing, but a Herculean task when all the combinations of circumstances for two projects are considered. This was the crux of the credit issue for the RMG projects. Internal diversification helped the credit but also made it more complex. AMBAC, EIB, Moody's, Standard & Poor's, and Lehman

Brothers all had to do a lot of work to make sure the legal documentation reflected the concept of pledged dividends and limited cross-collateralization. The greater the complexity of a transaction, the more people will perceive the legal risk of some flaw in the documentation. In this case, as people became more comfortable with the credit they became less comfortable with the legal risks. Haga recalls, "It took a lot of time and brainpower."

The four sponsors contributed equity and subordinated debt to the project, and the joint and several guarantees were backed by the balance sheets of all four of the ultimate parent companies.. In addition to providing cash equity, they agreed to an undisclosed amount of contingent equity, giving lenders comfort that there was an additional cushion if one or both of the projects ran into trouble. They also pledged the dividends from either project to service the debt of the other project if one was in difficulty.

## THE BOND ISSUE

Lehman Brothers and SBC Warburg were co-underwriters for the £165 million bond issue. The bond was structured as a deferred annuity with a four-year principal payment grace period. The amortizing repayment schedule allowed the sponsors to fund level repayments of principal and interest from operating cash flows. Otherwise, they would have suffered negative arbitrage, setting aside funds for the eventual repayment of principal in investment instruments that paid less than their cost of borrowing.

The £165 million secured bonds are guaranteed by AMBAC, a monoline insurance company rated AAA by Standard & Poor's and Aaa by Moody's. As a result of credit enhancement, the RMC bonds are AAA/Aaa-rated, and investors are immunized from the risks of the project. Though costly, credit enhancement was helpful because this project was one of the first financed under the PFI and it had unusual features such as an amortizing repayment structure.

## OTHER CREDIT ENHANCING FEATURES

A number of other features were incorporated into the financing package to permit tighter interest and principal coverage and lower amounts of scheduled equity than otherwise would have been possible. They included contingent equity provided by the four sponsors on a joint and several basis; a twelve-month debt service reserve, with an additional reserve required in certain circumstances; a reserve mechanism for major maintenance; letters of credit for scheduled equity insertions and certain other obligations; a restricted payments covenant; and an operating and maintenance support agreement.

## THE EUROPEAN INVESTMENT BANK (EIB) FACILITY

The £111 million EIB facility helped the overall transaction in several ways. The interest rate was fixed, and at a level lower than most alternative sources of funds. The term was twenty-five years, feasible in the capital markets, but substantially longer than most commercial bank loans. EIB was willing to provide a deferred annuity repayment structure that complemented the bond transaction. Bringing in EIB also had a cost. A lot of time and effort was required to negotiate the facility. EIB invests in only AAA-rated paper. Therefore, for a project such as the Road Management Group, it requires a guarantee or a standby letter of credit from a financial institution rated AA or above. EIB often lends alongside a commercial bank, with the commercial bank providing the standby letter of credit to back the paper EIB holds. The borrower bears the cost of the letter of credit.

## MARKETING AND PRICING

Because the RMG financing had a number of innovative features such as the annuity repayment structure, connection to a PFI project, and the AMBAC guarantee, there were no comparable deals to serve as pricing benchmarks. Recent deals included a £105 million GESB bond due 2018 yielding sixty-eight basis points over the gilt yield curve, a £105 million issue for the North British Housing Association due 2020 that yields seventy-two basis points over, and a £50 million Northern Counties deal due 2025 that offers a seventy-three basis point spread. Bullet maturities are generally preferred by U.K. investors because they make asset and liability management easier. The amortizing structure alone required a premium of three to five basis points.

To market the bond issue Lehman Brothers and SBC Warburg organized road shows in London and Scotland, taking along representatives from RMG and AMBAC. Based on perceived reactions from potential investors, they were able to narrow and refine their initial pricing. Despite turmoil in the Treasury and Gilt markets related to higher-than-expected employment figures announced the previous week in the U.S., the issue was oversubscribed prior to launch.

## ENDNOTES

[1]This article forms part of the author's current research on implementation of PFI in the transport sector. Some of the models and definitions used here were developed within the context of the transport sector, but they generally are applicable to other sectors as well.

[2]Trafalgar House was acquired by Kvaerner Group in October 1996.

[3]*Contracts Journal*, February 17, 1999, and February 24, 1999.

[4]PFI Sector is defined as including both public and private sector organizations that procure services or derives business from engaging in PFI projects.

[5]Wolf [1998] coined the term "internalities" which are analogous to "private" organizational goals. Wolf maintains that public sector organizations have private internal goals that influence the real agenda.

[6]1)Allocating risk to the party that is best able to manage it, and 2) attracting private sector innovation.

## REFERENCES

Bliss, Nicholas, and Bobby Stewart. "Bond Issues and the PFI PLC." Road Management Group, September 1996.

Davis, Henry A. "Road Management Consolidated," in Henry Davis, ed., *Project Finance: Practical Case Studies*. London: Euromoney Books, 1996.

"DBFO — Value In Roads: A Case Study on the First Eight DBFO Road Contracts and Their Development." Highways Agency and Private Finance Panel. Central Office of Information, 1997.

Flynn, Ruth. "The Principal Organization," in Merna and Smith, eds. *Projects Procured by Privately Financed Concession Contracts*. Hong Kong: Asia Law and Practice, pp. 41-58, 1994.

Forshaw, Anthony. "M1-A1 Link Road — A U.K. DBFO Case Study." *Project Finance International*, Autumn 1996.

Kessides, C. "Institutional Options for the Provision of Infrastructure." Discussion paper (212), World Bank, Washington, 1994.

McCarthy, S.C. "BOT & OMT Contracts for Infrastructure Projects in developing Countries." Unpublished Ph.D. thesis, Birmingham University, 1991.

Merna, A., and N. Smith. "The Guide to the Preparation and Evaluation of BOOT Project Tender." Project Management Group, UMIST, 1993.

Mustafa, A. "Provision of Transport Infrastructure in the U.K.: The Private Finance Initiative." The 22nd Australasian Transport Research Forum, Sydney, 1998.

Ostrom, E., L. Schroeder, and S. Wyne. *Institutional Incentives and Sustainable Development: Infrastructure Policies in Perspective*. Boulder, CO: Westview Press Inc., 1993.

Poulter, T., and B. Stewart. "DBFO — Behind the Scenes with Highways Agency's Advisors." *Project Finance International*, Autumn 1996.

"The Private Finance Initiative: The First Four Design, Build, Finance and Operate Roads Contract." National Audit Office, 1998.

Wolf, C. *Markets or Governments: Choosing Between Imperfect Alternative*. MIT Press: Cambridge, MA, 1988.

*The Economic Journal*, **113** (*March*), C62–C68. © Royal Economic Society 2003. Published by Blackwell Publishing, 9600 Garsington Road, Oxford OX4 2DQ, UK and 350 Main Street, Malden, MA 02148, USA.

# PUBLIC AND PRIVATE SECTOR DISCOUNT RATES IN PUBLIC–PRIVATE PARTNERSHIPS*

*Paul A. Grout*

Whether public sector projects should be discounted at a lower rate than private sector projects is highly contentious. This paper assesses the appropriate private and public sector discount rates in the context of public private partnerships. It shows that there are powerful arguments for using a higher rate to discount private projects than public sector projects and that failure to recognise this may lead to excessive reliance on public provision. However, the reason for the divergence is not related to the conventional incomplete market arguments in the literature. The results may have far broader implications for private sector involvement in public services.

In the last 20 years there has been a major increase in the role of the private sector in the delivery of what were once considered public sector services. Outside transition economies, probably the single most significant change has been the international wave of privatisation of utilities. Such privatisations typically involve the complete transfer of ownership to the private sector with the role of the state being reduced to policing prices and conduct. More recently, however, there has been a rapid growth in more complex forms of private involvement. In many cases the public sector or its agencies remain the immediate final purchaser of the services but no longer own or operate the assets necessary for the provision of the service. Such arrangements tend to be referred to as public-private partnerships (PPP). In a typical PPP, the government signs a long-term contract with a private consortium to supply a service to the government and the private consortium designs, builds, owns and runs the physical assets required for the delivery of the service. This contrasts with traditional public sector provision where the government builds or purchases physical assets, retains ownership and uses public sector employees or a private contractor to deliver the required service. A PPP can be characterised as a situation where the government becomes a purchaser of services not physical assets.[1] This type of arrangement is now common in the case of roads, prisons, hospitals and schools both in the UK and elsewhere.[2]

The economic justification for PPPs is that they increase efficiency by aligning the incentives of the parties.[3] As a result the government is able to provide the service at lower cost than would be possible with conventional public sector delivery. Indeed, the standard test criterion for a PPP project is that the cost to the

* This paper has benefited from comments at seminars at the University of Brunel, University of Manchester, HM Treasury and the Projects International Conference, 2001, Paris.

[1] There are many complex forms of PPPs and the characterisation here focuses on the most basic model.

[2] For example, in the US alone there are 151 privately built prisons and the leader in the private management of public 'contract' schools has over 136 schools under contract. In many countries, including Canada and the UK, air traffic control is privately owned and run.

[3] There are several theoretical papers that address the efficiency of PPPs, notably, Bennett and Iossa (2002), Bentz *et al.* (2002) and Hart (2002); see also Hart *et al.* (1997). See Grout (1997) for an assessment of the private finance initiative.

government is less with a PPP than with conventional public provision. Clearly, this assessment is sensitive to the rate used to discount the cost of public provision and PPP. Of particular concern is whether the discount rate used to assess public provision should be the same as that used to assess a PPP. Whether public sector projects should be discounted at a lower rate than private sector projects is a highly contentious issue and one that has spawned an enormous literature. Writing in the 1980s on public sector discount rates and their relation to private sector discount rates Lind pointed out that 'the profession was no closer to agreement on the theory, on a procedure for computing the discount rate, or on the rate itself than it was in 1966'.[4] Despite this lack of unanimity there is a tendency for economists to favour the use of similar discount rates in the idealised situation of complete markets. Similarly, there is tendency for governments to use the same discount rate for a project whether it is publicly provided or is to be provided to the government by the private sector. For example, in the UK the rate of 6% real is used to discount and compare the cost of public provision with a PPP alternative.

The purpose of this paper is to assess the appropriate discount rates for PPP and public projects. It is shown that there are powerful arguments for using a higher rate to discount private projects than public sector projects. It is important to emphasise, however, that the reason for the divergence between private sector and public sector discount rates is not related to the normal arguments given in the literature. Even in a world of complete capital markets and no distortionary taxation it may still appropriate to use a higher discount rate for the PPP than the public sector equivalent.

## 1. Public and Private Discount Rates

### 1.1. *Introduction*

As indicated in the introduction the view that the public sector should discount projects at the same rate as the private sector is not without controversy.[5] A large literature developed on this topic in the 1960s and 1970s and several contributors[6] took the view that public sector rates should be lower because the public sector can pool risks. These views have been criticised, notably by Bailey and Jensen (1972), Diamond (1967) and Hirshleifer (1964), who have pointed out that the arguments that the private sector cannot pool risks are not theoretically sound and that the nature of risks in the public sector are unlikely to satisfy the Arrow and Lind requirement that the outcomes of public projects are independent of each other and of private investments.[7] Putting to one side adjustments that may be necessary because of taxation (see Baumol (1968), Sandmo and Drèze (1971) and Harberger

[4] Lind (1982).

[5] Note, one common argument used is that the public sector can borrow at far lower rates. This, however, clearly relates to the default rate not the nature of differences in risk between public sector and private sector projects and is a obviously a false justification for any difference in discount rates.

[6] See, for example, Arrow (1965, 1966), Arrow and Lind (1970), Samuelson (1964), Solow (1965) and Vickrey (1964).

[7] See Lind (1982) for a detailed discussion of discount rates in the private and public sectors and Brealey *et al.* (1997) for an excellent summary of the issues.

(1968)), if there are complete markets then projects should be spanned by existing securities and so, at least theoretically, individuals should be able to divest themselves of their risks at market prices whether these arise in the public or private sector. This would appear to indicate that arguments for using higher discount rates for private projects must rest with imperfections in markets.

### 1.2. *Finance Tests for PPPs*

A feature of assessment procedures for public private partnerships is that the central test is one of cost minimisation to the public sector for a specified standard of service. In this respect it differs from conventional cost benefit test approaches that have traditionally been advocated and often employed in other areas of public provision. Here we outline when a pure finance test and a cost benefit test provide the same answer. This has important implications for the debate on public versus private sector discount rates.

Consider a public service project that can be conducted fully in the public sector or with a PPP. It is helpful to focus the discussion if one thinks of a specific example of a road that will have zero charges to the public at the point of use. With public provision a public sector agency can either build the road itself directly or can engage a contractor to build the road for the agency. The government will then own the road and undertake its upkeep. Within a PPP the private sector will build, own and maintain the road and the government's role is to enter into a contract to pay for the flow of services to the public. A standard model is one where the government makes a payment to the private owner for each vehicle that uses the road.

In each case the project delivers a flow of benefits, $v_t(g)$ and $v_t(p)$, and costs, $c_t(g)$ and $c_t(p)$, where $p$, $g$ and $t$ denote PPP, public sector and time respectively. A cost benefit test would opt for public provision if

$$\int_0^\infty v_t(g)e^{-r_v(g)t}dt - \int_0^\infty c_t(g)e^{-r_c(g)t}dt > \int_0^\infty v_t(p)e^{-r_v(p)t}dt - \int_0^\infty c_t(p)e^{-r_c(p)t}dt \tag{1}$$

and the PPP if the inequality in (1) is reversed, where $r_v(i)$ and $r_c(i)$ are the discount rates for benefits and costs, $i = p, g$.

In contrast, a pure finance base test compares the cost to the government of public provision with the cost to the public sector of conducting the project as a PPP. The financial cost to the government of public provision is the cost stream that the public sector has to fund:

$$\int_0^\infty c_t(g)e^{-rt}dt \tag{2}$$

where $r$ is the discount rate used by the government in the pure finance test. Within a PPP, the government has to fund the present value of the service specified in the contract. That is, service quantity, $q_t$, is measured and the private sector is funded according to the agreed price, $p_t$ per unit. The financial cost to the government of the PPP is

$$\int_0^\infty p_t q_t e^{-rt} dt. \tag{3}$$

Using this pure finance test, public provision is preferred if

$$\int_0^\infty c_t(g) e^{-rt} dt < \int_0^\infty p_t q_t e^{-rt} dt \tag{4}$$

and the PPP is preferred if the inequality is reversed.

The following Proposition shows when these two are equivalent.

PROPOSITION. *The pure finance test is equivalent to a full cost benefit test if the following hold:*

(i) $\int_0^\infty p_t q_t e^{-rt} dt = \int_0^\infty c_t(p) e^{-r_c(p)t} dt$
(ii) $v_t(g) = v_t(p)$
(iii) $r_j(g) = r_j(p), \quad j = v,c$
(iv) $r = r_c(p)$.

The result follows straightforwardly. If (i) holds then (1) becomes:

$$\int_0^\infty v_t(g) e^{-r_v(g)t} dt - \int_0^\infty c_t(g) e^{-r_c(g)t} dt$$

$$> \int_0^\infty v_t(p) e^{-r_v(p)t} dt - \int_0^\infty p_t q_t e^{-rt} dt$$

and if (ii) and (iii) hold then this reduces to

$$\int_0^\infty p_t q_t e^{-rt} dt > \int_0^\infty c_t(g) e^{-r_c(p)t} dt.$$

Finally, if (iv) holds then (1) is equivalent to (4).

If all four conditions hold then each of the conditions in the Proposition has a natural interpretation. Condition (i) is a restriction on competition. It only holds if the competition between the potential private sector partners for the PPP is such that there are no *ex ante* excess profits. Condition (ii) is a requirement on public and private benefits; stating that the quantity and quality of benefits are the same in the public project and the PPP. While this is unlikely to be the case in practice it is perfectly possible in theory to adjust the pure finance test to incorporate differences in quality. Conditions (iii) and (iv) relate to public and private sector discount rates. Condition (iii) states that the appropriate rate to discount the benefits (costs) should be the same whether the project is public or a PPP. In the context of the earlier discussion, (iii) does not seem an unrealistic requirement. However, (iv) is a far more powerful assumption since it requires the single discount rate used in the finance test to be equal to the discount rate that is appropriate for the cost stream in the PPP. The following Section shows that this is unlikely to be a sensible assumption and discusses the implications for public and private sector discount rates.

### 1.3. *Implications for Public and Private Sector Discount Rates*

Condition (iv) states that the single discount rates used in the financial test should be equal to the discount rate that is appropriate for the private sector's cost stream. It is tempting, but incorrect, to fall back on the introductory discussion in Section 1 to believe that the use of a single discount rate equal to private sector discount rate for costs is an innocuous assumption. Again it is helpful to interpret the financial test in terms of the road example. This shows clearly that the choice of a single public and private sector discount rate in the pure finance test cannot rely on the conventional argument.

The discount rate used for public sector provision is applied to the cost cash flow $c_t(g)$. This is the cash flow that represents the cost of building the road if it is built in the public sector. In contrast, the discount rate used for the private sector provision is applied to $p_t q_t$. This is not the equivalent cost of *building* the road with a PPP. It is the cash flow associated with the flow of benefits valued at the price in the contract. There is no reason to suppose that the risk characteristics are equivalent for these two cash flows; indeed there is every reason to suppose that they are not.

It is instructive to look at a special, albeit realistic, case to elucidate the point. This is where we restrict attention to the case where aggregate demand for the project is independent of the allocation of income within the community and the government uses a linear reimbursement schedule. The attraction of the former restriction is that in this case even if the choice of public or private provision affects income distribution, there will be no effect on aggregate demand. Aggregate demand is independent of the distribution of income if the indirect utility function can be characterised by the Gorman polar form. The Gorman polar form implies that the demand for a good must be of the form:

$$q_i = a_i(\mathbf{p}) + b(\mathbf{p})m_i \tag{5}$$

where $i$ denotes the consumer and $\mathbf{p}$ the vector of prices in the economy. In this case the revenue for the PPP can be represented:

$$R = p\Sigma_i a_i(\mathbf{p}) + pb(\mathbf{p})\Sigma_i m_i \tag{6}$$

(where $p$ is the price in the PPP contract) and the costs can be represented:

$$C = c\Sigma_i a_i(\mathbf{p}) + cb(\mathbf{p})\Sigma_i m_i + F \tag{7}$$

where $F$ is the fixed component of cost.

Using the Gorman polar form and a linear payment schedule, we can explicitly calculate the risk characteristics of these cash flows as measured by their beta (the weighted covariance between the cash flow and aggregate income). It is easy to show that the $\beta$ for the revenue cash flow is:

$$\beta_R = \frac{\text{cov}(R, m)}{\text{var}(m)} = \frac{\sigma_R}{\sigma_m} = p\Sigma_i b(\mathbf{p}) \tag{8}$$

and the $\beta$ for the cost stream is

$$\beta_C = \frac{\text{cov}(C, m)}{\text{var}(m)} = \frac{\sigma_c}{\sigma_m} = c\Sigma_i b(\mathbf{p}) \tag{9}$$

where $m = \Sigma_i m_i$.

Thus the ratio of the betas is equal to the ratio of price to marginal cost.

$$\frac{\beta_R}{\beta_C} = \frac{\text{price}}{\text{marginal cost}}. \tag{10}$$

There are two reasons to expect the price per unit in the PPP contract to be greater than the marginal cost. One is that fixed costs associated with PPP projects tend to be large. Again thinking of the road example, the marginal cost per vehicle is likely to be extremely small relative to the payment per vehicle to the partnership since the latter has to be sufficiently high to recoup the cost of building the road over the life of the contract. Hence the price marginal cost ratio may be very large. The second reason is that economic theory predicts that an optimal incentive scheme is almost certain to require the supplier to bear some of the risk of supply. Assuming that there are hidden actions, the harder it is to contract over quality and the greater the relationship between usage and quality then the more high powered the incentive scheme ought to be. Linear schemes of this sort are quite common in practice. Theoretically, it is unlikely that the exact payment scheme should be linear but in certain circumstances there are justifications for linearity; see Hart and Holström (1987) and Holström and Milgrom (1987). The general point, however, does not depend on this precise specification; we should expect to see a significant divergence between the private sector discount rates used to discount revenues and costs within a PPP.

Turning to the relevant discount rate for the public sector then it is clear from Section 1.1 that it is the cost stream that is discounted. In general, the public sector cost in the comparison should not be discounted at the same rate as the private sector. That is, the relevant beta for the public sector component of a pure finance test should be that given by (9) and the relevant beta for the PPP should be that given by (8).

## 2. Conclusion

This paper has argued that the standard practice of using similar discount rates for private and public provision in tests between public sector and PPPs is inappropriate. We have argued that lower discount rates should be used for the public sector than the private sector. Failure to do so will suggest that private provision is less efficient than public since the present value of private provision will be overestimated relative to public. It is important to emphasise, however, that the reason for the divergence between private sector and public sector discount rates is not related to the normal arguments in the literature. Even in a world of complete capital markets and no distortionary taxation, it is still appropriate to use a higher discount rate for the PPP than the public sector equivalent. This is a consequence of comparing the costs to the government of the two alternatives. This difference would disappear if the government chose to assess PPP by their costs of construction and maintenance not the cost of the contract for providing services to the public sector. Clearly, there are good reasons why this does not happen but the consequences for discount rates needs to be recognised.

This paper has focussed specifically on financial test for PPPs. However, the problem that we have identified is likely to be far more general. The cash flows that are discounted by state treasuries around the world tend to be cost cash flows in the sense that we are using them in this article. In contrast, any private contribution to the provision of services, when viewed by the government, tends to have some elements of revenue or net revenues built in. It follows that, although it may be legitimate to use the same rate for exact comparisons of similar cash flows between private and public sectors, in many instances the assessment procedures for private involvement in public services justifies the use of separate discount rates for the two sectors. Failure to recognise this is likely to prejudice private provision and favour too much public sector provision.

*University of Bristol*

## References

Arrow, K. (1965). 'Criteria for social investment', *Water Resources Research*, vol. 1, pp. 1–8.
Arrow, K. (1966). 'Discounting and public investment criteria', in (A. V. Kneese and S. C. Smith, eds.), *Water Research*, Baltimore, MD: Johns Hopkins University Press.
Arrow, K. and Lind, R. C. (1970). 'Uncertainty and the evaluation of public investment decisions', *American Economic Review*, vol. 60, pp. 364–78.
Bailey, M. J. and Jensen, M. C. (1972). 'Risk and the discount rate for public investment', in (M. C. Jensen, ed.), *Studies in the Theory of Capital Markets*, New York, NY: Frederick A Praeger.
Baumol, W. J. (1968). 'On the social rate of discount', *American Economic Review*, vol. 58, pp. 788–802.
Bentz, A., Grout, P. A. and Halonen, M. (2002). 'What should the state buy?', Working Paper no. 01/040, Centre for Market and Public Organisation.
Brealey, R. A., Cooper, I. A. and Habib, M. A. (1997). 'Investment appraisal in the public sector', *Oxford Review of Economic Policy*, vol. 13, pp. 12–28.
Diamond, P. A. (1967). 'The role of stock market in a general equilibrium model with technological uncertainty', *American Economic Review*, vol. 57, pp. 759–76.
Grout, P. A. (1997). 'The economics of the private finance initiative', *Oxford Review of Economic Policy*, vol. 13, pp. 53–66.
Harberger, A. C. (1968). 'On measuring the social opportunity cost of public funds', in *Proceedings of the Committee on Water Resources and Economic Development of the West; The Discount Rate in Public Investment Evaluation*, Denver, CO: Western Agricultural Economics Research Council.
Hart, O. (2002). 'Incomplete contracts and public ownership: remarks and an application to public-private partnerships', presented at the RES Conference, 2002, University of Warwick.
Hart, O. and Holström, B. (1987). 'The theory of contracts', in (T. F. Bewley ed.), *Advances in Economic Theory*, Cambridge: Cambridge University Press
Hart, O., Shleifer, A. and Vishny, R. W. (1997). 'The proper scope of government: theory and an application to prisons', *Quarterly Journal of Economics*, vol. 112, pp. 1126–61.
Hirshleifer, J. (1964). 'Efficient allocation of capital in an uncertain world', *American Economic Review*, vol. 54, pp. 77–85.
Holström, B. and Milgrom, P. (1987). 'Aggregation and linearity in the provision of intertemporal incentives', *Econometrica*, vol. 55, pp. 303–28.
Lind, R. C. (ed.) (1982). *Discounting for Time and Risk in Energy Policy*, Baltimore: Johns Hopkins Press.
Samuelson, P. A. (1964). 'Principals of efficiency: discussion', *American Economic Review*, vol. 81, pp. 191–209.
Sandmo, A. and Drèze, J. H. (1971). 'Discount rates for public investment in closed and open economies', *Economica*, vol. 38, pp. 395–412.
Solow, R. M. (1965). *Capital Theory and the Rate of Return*, Chicago, IL: Rand McNally.
Vickrey, W. (1964). 'Principals of efficiency: discussion', *American Economic Review*, vol. 54, pp. 88–92.

# Part V
# Experience Elsewhere

# [26]

# Public-Private Technology Partnerships

## Promises and Pitfalls

JOSEPH E. STIGLITZ
SCOTT J. WALLSTEN
*Stanford University*
*The World Bank*

*The U.S. government has a long history of supporting private sector research and development (R & D). The economic justification for government R & D support is clear. Primarily because of knowledge spillovers, profit-maximizing firms invest less than the socially optimal level of R & D. This market failure creates the possibility that government can help mitigate the underinvestment problem. Public-private technology partnerships are the newest approach to funding R & D. Technology partnerships include public funding of industry-led R & D projects and private research consortia, and collaborations between industry and government scientists. These programs hope to generate research that yields commercial products and innovations. This article discusses the rise of these programs, the theory supporting them, the types of research projects they must fund to be successful, the technical and political obstacles they face in funding these projects, and the evaluations of the largest partnership programs. This article concludes with policy recommendations, recognizing that these programs have potential but must overcome significant hurdles.*

**The U.S. federal government** has a long history of supporting private sector R & D. Indeed, the Constitution gave Congress the right to grant patents to "promote the progress of science." Until recently, however, most federally funded industrial R & D was directed at government needs, such as large weapons systems. Concerns about lagging U.S. productivity and increasing competition from U.S. trading partners in the mid-1980s and the subsequent end of the Cold War began to change the focus from government needs to government funding of commercial R & D. The end of the Cold War posed a challenge. Previously, Cold War research had funded a host of projects that eventually led to innumerable commercial projects of immense value. Although these projects were typically not undertaken to advance commercial technology, it was one of the clearly beneficial byproducts. Indeed, popular support for federal research undertakings such as the space program was maintained, in part, by frequent references to commercial spin-offs. With the end of the Cold War, the government began to put even more emphasis on research leading to commercially viable outcomes.

AMERICAN BEHAVIORAL SCIENTIST, Vol. 43 No. 1, September 1999 52-73

In 1993, the newly-elected Clinton administration put technology—and public support of private R & D in particular—at the center of its economic agenda, stating that "government can play a key role in helping private firms develop and profit from innovations" (Clinton & Gore, 1993).

Many types of public-private technology partnerships have been implemented in the last decade. These range from direct public funding of industry-led R & D projects, to public funding of private research consortia, to collaborations at the national laboratories between industry and government scientists. All of these programs share the goal of generating research that yields commercial products and innovations. The economic justification for these programs is clear. Theory predicts, and many empirical studies confirm, that profit-maximizing firms invest less than the socially optimal level of R & D. Government support of private R & D can help rectify this market failure. Sound theory does not always translate easily into sound policies. These programs must overcome enormous technical and political challenges if they are to succeed. Indeed, preliminary evidence on the effectiveness of these programs is mixed, at best.

In this paper, we first discuss the theory behind government support of R & D in general, and government support of industrial R & D in particular. We then discuss the rise of public-private technology partnerships over the past decade. Next, we consider the types of research projects these programs must fund if they are to be successful and the obstacles they face in achieving this goal. After the theoretical discussion, we highlight the largest and most prominent of these programs. This section also discusses the available evidence on the effectiveness of these programs. Finally, we conclude with policy recommendations, recognizing that these programs have potential, but that they also must overcome significant hurdles in order to be successful.

## WHY DOES GOVERNMENT FUND R & D?

Investments in R & D are crucial for economic growth, accounting for at least half of all increases in per capita output (Griliches, 1992). In fiscal year (FY) 1997, the United States spent about $205 billion on R & D. Industry provides the majority of R & D funds—approximately $133 billion in FY 1997. The federal government provides most of the remainder—about $67 billion in FY 1997, almost $20 billion of which went to industry. Table 1 provides a breakdown of U.S. R & D spending by performer and source of funds. Industry funds the majority of product-related research (i.e., applied R & D) whereas government funds the majority of fundamental (i.e., basic) research. Although much federal R & D is for specific government needs, government funding is crucial to economic growth because market failures cause firms, which act in their own best interests, to underinvest in R & D from society's perspective.

**TABLE 1: Source and Performers of R & D in the United States, 1997 (all figures in millions of dollars)**

| | Source of Funds | | | | | |
|---|---|---|---|---|---|---|
| *Performer* | *Federal Government* | *Industry* | *Universities and Colleges* | *Other Nonprofits* | *Nonfederal Government* | *Total* |
| Government | 16,450 | | | | | 16,450 |
| Industry | 20,787 | 130,631 | | | | 151,418 |
| Universities and colleges | 14,285 | 1,710 | 4,457 | 1,759 | 1,821 | 24,031 |
| Other nonprofits | 2,900 | 967 | | 1,653 | | 5,520 |
| Industry FFRDCs[a] | 2,273 | | | | | 2,273 |
| U & C FFRDCs[ab] | 5,405 | | | | | 5,405 |
| Nonprofit FFRDCs[a] | 644 | | | | | 644 |
| Total | 62,744 | 133,308 | 4,457 | 3,412 | 1,821 | 205,742 |

SOURCE: National Science Foundation, 1998.
NOTE: Figures are preliminary estimates.
a. FFRDCs: Federally-funded R & D centers.
b. U & C: University and college.

## THE PRIVATE SECTOR INVESTS TOO LITTLE IN R & D FROM SOCIETY'S PERSPECTIVE

Investments in R & D have very high returns and are a key component to economic growth. Under different assumptions, economic theory can explain why firms may underinvest or overinvest in R & D.[1] Empirical research, however, demonstrates that the private sector invests less than the optimal level in R & D. Jones and Williams (1997) estimate that actual total R & D spending in the economy is less than one quarter the optimal level. Underinvestment occurs because firms cannot appropriate all the returns to their R & D investments and because capital market imperfections may make financing R & D more expensive than other investments.

From the firm's perspective, R & D is like any other investment. The firm invests in R & D until the expected risk-adjusted private returns of the last research project equals its costs. Average returns on R & D to the firm are high—20% to 30%, on average—but the returns to society are even higher—often 50% or more.[2] These R & D spillovers occur as others use research results and extend them in directions the original innovator often could not have imagined. Spillovers mean that an innovator is compensated for only a fraction of the total returns on R & D. As a result, firms invest less in R & D than they would if they reaped all the rewards to their investments. In other words, some research projects that would yield positive net total benefits (i.e., the sum of private and social benefits less the project costs) are privately unprofitable because the investor does not see the social returns.[3] Without some intervention in the market, the private sector will not undertake these research projects, although it is in society's interest for them to do so.

In addition to investing in less R & D than society would like, firms may invest less than they want if they do not have sufficient access to capital for R & D. Capital market failures could arise if an innovator is reluctant or unable to provide financiers with enough information to evaluate a research project for fear of revealing too much about the proposed idea. Moreover, R & D cannot be collateralized, unlike investments in machines or buildings. Firms may therefore be forced to pay higher rates of interest on loans for R & D than charged borrowers financing other, collateralizable forms of investment, or they may have to rely more extensively on internal funds (see Hall, 1992; Himmelberg & Petersen, 1994). Because funds are fungible, firms with sufficient internal cash flow can, of course, resort to those funds for research, using collateral to finance investments in plant and equipment. The fact of the matter is that many high tech firms would like to invest more in research than they can finance through cash flow and collateralized loans. Schumpeter (1939) called attention to these constraints long ago. The evidence of the impact of changes in cash flow on R & D investment, however, must be interpreted with caution, because events that adversely affect cash flow may also adversely affect the firm's net worth and ability to bear risks (see, e.g., Greenwald, Salinger, & Stiglitz, 1991).

The fact that there is overall underinvestment in R & D does not mean that there may not be overinvestment in certain types of research. The most obvious example is alleged pharmaceutical research attempting to innovate around a patent. The objective of firms engaged in such research is not so much to produce a better drug (though that may be an unintended byproduct), but to divert the "monopoly rents" of an existing patent holder toward themselves. There can also be excessive expenditures in a patent race in which the marginal contribution—the earlier arrival of the innovation compared to when it would otherwise have arrived—may be small compared to the average return. This is a variant of the "common pool" problem. Some of the return represents the embodiment in the patent of commonly available knowledge.[4]

## TRADITIONAL GOVERNMENT SUPPORT OF R & D

The existence of a market failure opens up the possibility that government can help mitigate the underinvestment problem. The government has traditionally used many tools to promote science and technology. Some methods, such as the patent system and research tax credits, are indirect. The patent system— enshrined in the Constitution and probably the oldest tool for promoting R & D—increases the potential profits from an innovation. Because an innovation is costly to develop but often inexpensive to duplicate, the patent system grants a temporary monopoly to an innovator. Temporary monopoly rights provide an incentive to invest in research by creating the potential to profit off an innovation before others can use it. Patents, however, entail a high social cost.

Knowledge is a public good in the sense that the marginal cost of an additional individual using that knowledge is zero. There is thus a trade-off between static inefficiency, associated with the underutilization of knowledge, and dynamic inefficiency, associated with the underproduction of knowledge. That is, once knowledge has been produced, it is inefficient to prevent others from using it, but if anyone can use it without cost, there will be little incentive to undertake the investments necessary to produce that knowledge. The rules for intellectual property rights attempt to strike a balance, for example, by choosing the length of the patent's life and the breadth of the discovery the patent covers.

Research tax credits—a much newer device, having been implemented in 1981—decrease the cost of doing research to the firm by giving the firm a tax credit for a portion of its R & D expenditures.[5] A credit provides an incentive to increase R & D investment by reducing the cost of any research project, making any given project potentially more profitable. The R & D tax credit is actually a credit on incremental expenditures. As such, its impact on the long-run level of expenditures might be expected to be more limited. There are also concerns about whether all expenditures qualifying for the incremental R & D tax credit really are research and development (e.g., should marketing research really qualify for the tax credit). The R & D credit, of course, does not attempt to distinguish between research that has a high level of spillovers and research that does not.

The government also directly funds R & D. As noted above, the government funds the majority of basic research, where market failures are presumably greatest. Much of government support for basic research goes to universities and colleges. Basic research is crucial for long-run growth and is a key ingredient in more applied R & D. Commercial products and innovations, however, are rarely the stimulus for basic research and often come years after the research is completed. For that reason, and because commercial applications of basic research are rarely obvious, firms have little incentive to fund basic research on their own. There is little disagreement that government must take the lead in funding basic research and training scientists (presumably because the total returns to society from their activities are in excess of the returns they appropriate).

Much of government-direct R & D funding goes to applied R & D in industry, although the extent to which government should support industrial R & D is more controversial. Traditionally, most of this funding has been to satisfy government objectives like space, defense, and, especially recently, health research directly. Although market failures may be less extreme in applied R & D than in basic research, they still exist. Even the most applied R & D is inherently risky and can generate large spillovers.

Government support of R & D has generally been successful in helping to mitigate the underinvestment problem. Each dollar in research tax credit appears to generate more than a dollar in private R & D spending (Hall, 1993). Direct government spending also seems to stimulate additional private spending on both basic and applied research (Hill, 1995; Levy & Terleckyj, 1983; Robson,

1993). Although most federal R & D was not intended to yield commercial products for civilian use, it would often spin off into commercial use. As the Council of Economic Advisers (1995) noted, in this manner the government "supported the development and diffusion of jet aircraft and engines, semiconductor microelectronics, computers and computer-controlled machine tools, pharmaceuticals and biotechnology, advanced energy and environmental technologies, advanced materials, and a host of other commercially successful technologies."

This system for supporting R & D worked well when national security concerns generated sufficient support for funding myriad types of R & D. The end of the Cold War, however, decreased the demand for defense research and made national security a less compelling reason to support R & D. In addition, in the mid-1980s, the slowdown in U.S. productivity growth and the increasing competitiveness of U.S. trading partners led to a belief that the federal government should do more to help firms transfer research results in the laboratory to products in the market. These conditions led to a new push for public-private partnerships intended to support commercial R & D. Much of the groundwork for these partnerships was laid in the 1980s. The Clinton administration seized on these ideas and expanded public-private commercial R & D partnerships greatly, making them the centerpiece of its technology program.

The next sections discuss the rise of these programs, the largest such public-private partnerships, and the promises and pitfalls associated with this new approach to funding R & D.

## A NEW APPROACH: PUBLIC-PRIVATE TECHNOLOGY PARTNERSHIPS

Previously, we explained why some form of public support for research is desirable—without that support there will be underinvestment in R & D. There remains the question of what form that support should take. The concept of partnership has increasingly come into vogue. The concept suggests a relationship in which each partner is assigned specific responsibilities and given incentives and resources to fulfill those responsibilities. Partnerships work best when there are common shared objectives, but they may still be effective even when interests are disparate. When the partners have separate interests, however, more attention needs to be placed on the incentive-accountability structure. Public partnership policy is concerned with designing the terms of the partnership in ways that fulfill public objectives that are within the limits of available public resource constraints and that take into account private incentives and public political processes. The latter has received increasing attention. The government not only must have incentives to fulfill its commitments (responsibilities), but the public policy must be politically sustainable; that is, it must receive the necessary electoral support. (The problem of public commitment is especially important, because sovereign governments often cannot bind themselves with contracts in the same way that private parties, which rely on the government for contract enforcement, can).[6]

Partnerships in applied technology research generally take two forms. The first involves government funding of industrial R & D. The second involves government and industry scientists actually working together. The common theme of these two types of partnerships is promoting research, not necessarily to meet government objectives, but to help the private sector move research from the lab to the market. These programs are controversial. Proponents contend that they address a legitimate need—helping firms undertake research that is too risky or expensive for a firm to do by itself. Such research can lead to innovations that are net benefits to society, but would not have been profitable to the firm. Opponents contend that these programs result in government attempting to pick winners—second-guessing the market about which technologies will be successful.

Ironically, underlying the current drive for public-private partnerships is the widespread belief that government is not very effective in choosing good projects (i.e., picking winners) and managing research. The evidence for this perspective is far from clear. Certainly, government support and conduct (and dissemination) of agricultural and medical research is widely viewed as highly successful. Similarly, in the key area of telecommunications, government support has been vital, from the first telegraph line between Washington and Baltimore in 1842 to support of the Internet.

The close connection between firms that do research and firms that market gives some credibility to the view that the private sector may have a comparative advantage in the conduct of applied research. Today's technology partnership typically entails government support for research that is initiated and conducted primarily by the private sector. The point is that the rationale for government intervention is not that the government is better than the private sector at picking winners, but that there exist important spillovers, even for applied technology. The objective of the government is thus to identify winning projects that would be privately unprofitable but socially beneficial because of high spillovers.

Figure 1 can help us evaluate the effectiveness of a partnership. The figure shows the expected returns to research projects in two dimensions, social and private. The expected total returns to a project are the sum of the expected social and private returns. Government support can have several possible outcomes as follows:

- In some cases, government support goes to inframarginal projects—high return projects that would have been undertaken anyway (projects in Area C). In that case, the government support is just a transfer payment. It has no allocative effect (other than the distortions caused by raising the revenue).
- Some of the money may go to marginal projects (projects in Areas A and B—projects that firms will not undertake on their own). If the government cannot identify spillovers, then the subsidy causes firms to undertake some projects that are (at the margin) unproductive (i.e., projects in Area A, which have no positive spillovers), and also some projects that (at the margin) have a total return in excess of the

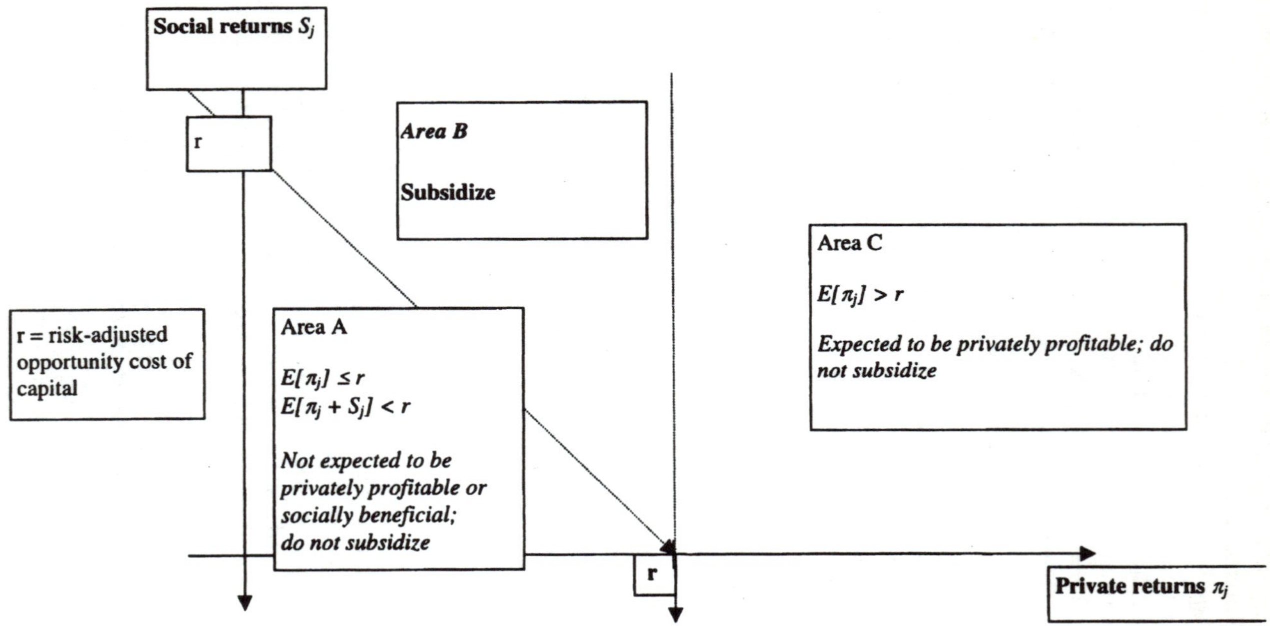


**Figure 1: Projects Targeted by an Optimal Government-Industry R & D Program**

opportunity cost of capital and would not have otherwise been undertaken (i.e., projects in Area B). The net social benefit in this case is ambiguous.

- If the government is very effective in identifying projects with social returns not captured by the private sector (i.e., projects in Area B), then the support unambiguously increases economic efficiency.

There are further ambiguities in the effects of government support. If there were no spillovers, limited available resources (e.g., key research personnel) for research, and if the government were worse than the private sector in picking winners, then the government would distort the direction of research into less productive areas. On the other hand, the reward structure for government research managers or project selectors and those in the private sector may be markedly different. The private sector participates in the upside potential of research projects—when successful they can reap tremendous rewards. The upside potential for public officials, however, is far more limited. There is, not surprisingly, more of a culture of risk taking in the private sector than in the public, partly as a result of these reward structures. The consequence is not that the government is bad at picking winners, but that it places too much attention on picking projects that have a high probability of success, foregoing projects that have even higher expected returns, but have a lower probability of success. To the extent that this is true, and that there are limited resources for research, government research support may lower expected returns.

## IMPLEMENTATION AND EVALUATION ISSUES

Consider again Figure 1. Recall that a government technology partnership program is more effective the better it can fund projects in Area B (projects with relatively high spillovers and low private returns). It is not clear how best to accomplish this goal. Most of these programs require industry to propose projects and the government to decide whether to subsidize them. Often, government subsidies are less expensive than capital from other sources, meaning that firms may be tempted to look to government before looking to other sources for financial support. In other words, there is no reason to believe that firms will propose only research projects in Area B (see Figure 1). Firms may be tempted to propose a project that falls anywhere in Figure 1 as long as they expect the subsidized project to be privately profitable. It is up to the government to determine which of these research projects would benefit society but would not be privately profitable without a subsidy. This means that government should not simply fund the best proposals it receives. Instead, it should fund the best among those that could not be funded elsewhere.[7]

Program managers who make funding decisions must reject not only projects of dubious scientific and technical merit, but also reject scientifically sound proposals that are very likely to yield commercial successes and therefore could be funded elsewhere. The obvious theoretical way to encourage this behavior is to build the proper incentives into these programs. Program managers should be rewarded for funding projects on the margin—those that are socially beneficial but would not be undertaken without a subsidy—and punished (or at least not rewarded) for funding inframarginal projects—those that firms would undertake without a subsidy.

In practice it is difficult to implement such a mechanism. First, observers must recognize that R & D is inherently risky, and any program that attempts to fund research projects that firms will not undertake will ultimately fund some projects that fail. Indeed, if the program funds only successful projects, it probably is not taking enough risks. But government-industry R & D programs—especially those aimed at commercialization—are controversial. Program supporters may be reluctant to allow many failures for fear that opponents will point to individual project failures as evidence of program failure. Likewise, managers may not feel comfortable rejecting the most promising proposals, either because they want to increase the chances of achieving commercial success or because it puts them in the position of rejecting proposals that are too good.

Second, the only way to implement an incentive mechanism of the sort mentioned above is to include a comprehensive evaluation mechanism as part of the program. That is, properly rewarding and punishing program managers is possible only if there is some way to detect what type of projects they fund. Evaluating technology programs is technically very difficult. A comprehensive evaluation would combine complicated scientific knowledge with economic analysis under conditions of uncertainty. In any event, as Adam Jaffe (1998) notes, technology programs have never been designed with economic evaluation in mind. Without some comprehensive evaluations, public debates on these programs tend to focus on easily measurable private returns and easily understandable anecdotal stories of project success and failure.

Even if the technical obstacles to conducting comprehensive evaluations can be overcome at a reasonable cost, political factors may decrease the likelihood that these programs can be implemented efficiently. The politics of technology spending are similar to those of other issues. Cohen and Noll (1991) point out that politicians face incentives to treat technology programs like they do any other government spending—as a way to reward constituents, not to correct market failures. Indeed, Cohen and Noll conclude that the "overriding lesson from the case studies is that the goal of economic efficiency—to cure market failures in privately sponsored commercial innovation—is so severely constrained by political forces that an effective, coherent national commercial R & D program has never been put in place" (p. 378). Politicians who favor allocating technology funds on the basis of constituencies may object to comprehensive evaluations, which have the potential to highlight funds allocated for reasons other than economic efficiency.

On the other hand, these programs cannot ignore constituency issues if they are to survive. Programs that attempt to select projects only on their economic and scientific merits may never develop a constituency and, thus, political support. Such programs may either be eliminated or changed to build support. This creates a potential Catch-22 situation: A program that allocates funds to reward constituencies may be popular, but will be less effective at correcting a market failure, whereas a program that attempts to correct a market failure may never develop a constituency and ultimately be canceled.

Finally, these programs raise other important questions that have yet to be dealt with fully. For example, how do we balance a firm's need for secrecy involving its research with society's desire to disseminate widely the results of publicly funded research and to evaluate the programs? Firms will not participate in these programs if results are immediately made available. On the other hand, making publicly funded research results available to only a few firms—which may profit enormously from them—puts the government in an awkward position. Moreover, the programs cannot be evaluated without access to information, and they are much more likely to be susceptible to political manipulation if not evaluated properly.

Another important question is how costs and benefits should be shared. Both to enhance private sector incentives and to enlist private sector judgments in making project selections, these partnerships are beginning to require greater equity contributions by the private sector. A common suggestion (e.g., Branscomb & Keller, 1998) is to require firms to bear costs in proportion to a project's expected private benefits. By requiring the private sector to put up considerable equity, it enlists the private sector in identifying winners, enabling government to focus on ascertaining the magnitude of spillovers. In addition, the reasoning goes, by contributing to project costs, the firm demonstrates its commitment to the project.

Although cost-sharing appears to be an attractive—and fair—proposition, in reality it raises many additional and as yet unanswered questions. First, estimating *ex ante* the private and social benefits of a project is a monumental task. The task is made even more difficult by information asymmetries. The firm will have far more information about the potential market success of an innovation than will the government, and the firm has an incentive to predict market success in a way that increases the probability of receiving a government subsidy. Second, cost sharing could have a perverse impact on the types of projects industry proposes to government. Although cost sharing may indicate a firm's commitment to a research product, it also indicates the firm's belief that the project is more likely to yield a commercial success. By requiring cost sharing, therefore, the government may actually be less likely to fund projects for which there is a market failure. Whether this hypothesis is true is yet to be seen. The point is that it is not necessarily true that cost sharing will increase program effectiveness. Cost sharing will affect incentives, but empirical analysis is necessary to determine precisely what the effects are.

In the following discussion, we will look more carefully at the impact of various government programs for the support of research. Unfortunately, many of these programs were started too recently and have funded too few projects to allow for reliable assessments. Moreover, although some of the analyses described below focus on the impact of the programs on the level of expenditure, few provide much insight into the more fundamental questions of the quality of research expenditures.

## GOVERNMENT-INDUSTRY R & D PROGRAMS: EXAMPLES AND EVALUATIONS

Much of the legislative groundwork for today's public-private technology programs was laid in 1980. The Stevenson-Wydler Technology Innovation Act of 1980 "granted broad authority to the Department of Commerce 'to enhance technological innovation for commercial and public purposes . . . including a strong national policy supporting domestic technology transfer and utilization of the science and technology resources of the federal government.' In addition to leveraging the economic impact of federal R & D investments, Stevenson-Wydler directed the federal government to conduct a wide range of research and cooperative activities to assess and improve American technological competitiveness" (Brody, 1996, p. 26). The Bayh-Dole, or University and Small Business Patent Procedure Act, of 1980 reformed government patent policy. Bayh-Dole allowed government grant recipients and contractors to retain ownership rights to government-funded innovations. The act also encouraged universities to license innovations to firms (National Science Foundation, 1998).

Although those key pieces of legislation were put in place in 1980, it was not until the mid-1980s that public-private technology partnerships began to materialize, and not until the Clinton administration took office that they became a central part of federal technology policy. The new administration believed that "only the private sector has the skills and abilities to manage the complex process of developing new technologies and bringing them to market, while . . . [the] government plays a vital role in enabling the private sector's efforts" (Executive Office of the President, 1996, p. 42). Indeed, a central tenet of the administration's technology policy was that "the Federal government must encourage the development, commercialization, and use of technology" (Executive Office of the President, 1996, p. 42).

Technology partnership programs come in two forms, direct government funding of private R & D and direct collaboration between government and industry scientists. The most prominent of the first type are the Small Business Innovation Research Program (SBIR Program), the Advanced Technology Program (ATP), and Sematech (which stopped receiving funds in FY 1997, but then entered into a partnership of the second type). The second type includes Cooperative Research and Development Agreements (CRADAs), the Partnership for a New Generation of Vehicles (PNGV), and the Manufacturing Extension Partnership (MEP). Table 2 shows funding for the SBIR Program, ATP, MEP, and

**TABLE 2: Funding for Government-Industry Technology Programs—A Partial List**

| | *Program (all figures in millions of current dollars)* | | | |
|---|---|---|---|---|
| *Year* | *SBIR*[a] | *ATP*[b] | *MEP*[c] | *PNGV*[d] |
| 1983 | 44.5 | | | |
| 1984 | 108.4 | | | |
| 1985 | 199.1 | | | |
| 1986 | 297.9 | | | |
| 1987 | 350.5 | | | |
| 1988 | 389.1 | | 5.0 | |
| 1989 | 431.9 | | 7.5 | |
| 1990 | 460.7 | 10 | 8.7 | |
| 1991 | 483.1 | 37 | 13.8 | |
| 1992 | 508.4 | 49.4 | 17.0 | |
| 1993 | 698 | 67.9 | 18.2 | |
| 1994 | 717.6 | 199.1 | 30.2 | Not available |
| 1995 | 948.9 | 340.5 | 74.2 | 223 |
| 1996 | 974 | 221.0 | 80.0 | 241 |
| 1997 | 1,269 | 253 | 95.0 | 263 |
| 1998 (estimated) | | 199 | 113.5 | 281 |
| 1999 (estimated) | | 269 | 106.8 | |

a. Source: Small Business Administration and authors' calculations.
b. Source: ATP (1998), Office of Management and Budget (1998).
c. Source: MEP (1998).
d. Source: Office of Management and Budget (1996, 1997).

PNGV from their inception through the present. We will next describe these programs and discuss the available evidence on their effectiveness.

## THE SBIR PROGRAM

The SBIR Program, established by the Small Business Innovation Development Act of 1982, was perhaps the first among the new wave of government programs intended to support private commercial R & D. This act required federal agencies with extramural (i.e., contract and grant) R & D budgets of over $100 million per year to set aside a certain percentage of that budget to SBIR Program grants. The set aside increased from 0.2% of the annual extramural budget in FY 1982 to 1.25% of the budget by FY 1986. By 1986, the SBIR Program budget was almost $300 million per year. The SBIR Program was renewed in 1992 and expanded dramatically. Congress increased the set aside to 2.5% of the agencies' extramural budget by FY 1997, causing SBIR Program funding to break the $1 billion mark that year.

SBIR Program grants are intended to encourage commercialization of innovations by small firms (i.e., firms with 500 employees or less). Eligible firms submit research proposals to participating federal agencies, which use a competitive review process to make funding decisions. Firms can first apply for up to

$100,000 to determine "the scientific and technical merit and feasibility of ideas." If successful, they can then apply for up to $750,000 to "further develop the proposed idea." Finally, the firm is expected to commercialize a product, although no additional SBIR Program funds are provided for that purpose.[8] The firm retains intellectual property rights to its innovation and all profits from commercialization, although the government retains a license for government use.

The U.S. General Accounting Office has reviewed the SBIR Program several times (e.g., U.S. General Accounting Office, 1989, 1992, 1995). These evaluations focus primarily on the commercialization rate of funded projects under the assumption that high commercialization rates imply a successful program. Such analyses ignore the possibility that some commercialized projects may not have required government support as well as the possibility that some projects that were not commercialized may have yielded large social returns. The focus on commercialization suggests that program managers may be rewarded for funding many successful projects. This system may induce managers to fund projects guaranteed to yield a commercial success. Firms may realize this and propose projects that they believe are more likely to yield a commercial success. As a result, the program could fund many very successful projects, but because they were selected on their expected probability of yielding a commercial success, these projects may not have needed government funding to begin with. Under that scenario, the program would support many successful projects, but would have no real economic impact.

Wallsten (1998a) found that firms that won SBIR Program grants reduced their own R & D expenditures by approximately the amount of the government grant, and that grants did not increase employment or sales. The results suggest that these government grants may crowd out a firm's R & D spending. That is, firms simply reduce their own R & D expenditures by the amount of the subsidy and put the money toward investments other than research. However, Lerner (1996) found that, for firms located in areas with high venture capital activity, those receiving SBIR Program awards increased employment more than those that did not receive the awards.

## THE ATP

The ATP, although not the biggest government-industry commercial R & D program in the government's portfolio, has attracted the most attention. The ATP was established under the authority of the Omnibus Trade and Competitiveness Act of 1988 and implemented by the Bush administration in 1990. According to this act, the ATP was established "for the purpose of assisting United States businesses in creating and applying the generic technology and research results necessary to (1) commercialize significant new scientific discoveries and technologies rapidly, and (2) refine manufacturing technologies" (Hill, 1998, p. 146). The ATP was initially funded at a relatively modest $10 million, slowly increasing to $68 million by FY 1993. The Clinton administration seized the ATP as a key component of its technology policy and increased funding to approximately $340 million by FY 1995. The ATP has been controversial, and funding has fallen since 1995, with only $181 million appropriated for FY 1999.

Like SBIR, firms submit proposals to the ATP for research aimed at ultimately commercializing a product.[9] According to the ATP (1998), it attempts to "foster enabling technologies that will lead to new, innovative products, services, and industrial processes. For this reason, ATP projects focus on the technology needs of U.S. industry, not those of government. The ATP is industry driven, which keeps the program grounded in real-world needs. Research priorities for the ATP are set by industry: for-profit companies conceive, propose, co-fund, and execute ATP projects and programs based on their understanding of the marketplace and research opportunities." The ATP also attempts to encourage firms to combine research efforts and thus funds many research joint ventures. Firms retain all intellectual property rights from any innovation.

The ATP is among the newest of these programs, and as such, few evaluations have been conducted. Preliminary evidence, however, is mixed. Yager and Schmidt (1997) examined the ATP's selection criteria and concluded that the ATP had no built-in mechanism to select projects that require government funding. The U.S. General Accounting Office (1996) surveyed firms that won awards and near winners firms that were rejected in the final stage of the competition. The U.S. General Accounting Office concluded that the ATP funded both marginal and inframarginal projects. Unlike many other government-industry R & D programs, however, the ATP has attempted to make economic evaluation a centerpiece of its implementation. The ATP holds regular conferences with economists and scientists in order to formulate ways to evaluate the program properly. In addition, recognizing that the program is new and itself an experiment, the ATP frequently rethinks the types of proposals it funds and how its funding should be allocated.

The ATP has faced more congressional opposition than any other technology program. In part, this opposition was simply the result of a Republican Congress attacking a program strongly identified with a Democratic president. But the opposition is not only the result of partisan politics. Some observers believe this opposition resulted, in part, because the ATP emphasized its role in mitigating market failure rather than in building a constituency. The ATP stated in 1996 that it aims to select "only those projects for awards for which it thinks the potential social rate of return . . . far exceeds the potential private rate of return on investment, and for which it thinks the private sector will either not do the project at all, or not within the critical time, or in the scale/scope necessary to realize the potential private benefits" (National Institute of Science and Technology, 1996, p. 4). In other words, the ATP's specific goal was to mitigate a market failure, not to reward or build a constituency. Because ATP had no natural constituency, it became an easy target for congressional critics of the administration, which had made ATP its flagship technology program.

The ATP's political problems also highlight another problem facing any government program that must reject some industry proposals and fund others. Although the program is sensitive to the problem of picking winners, by rejecting some proposals it ends up picking losers—firms that may be put at a disadvantage because they did not get government funds. This creates resentment between firms that did not receive funding. From 1990 to 1995, ATP received 2,210 applications and funded only 280 projects (ATP, personal communication, February 28, 1996). Even if all these projects were rejected on legitimate grounds, the large number of rejections creates a large number of potential program enemies.

## SEMATECH

Sematech was the first prominent example of government support of an industrial research consortium aimed at commercialization. Sematech is a government-supported industry consortium founded in 1987 to help shore up America's once-declining position in the semiconductor industry. The National Cooperative Research Act of 1984 paved the way for this consortium by loosening antitrust restrictions on industrial research collaborations. Sematech began as a consortium of 14 leading U.S. semiconductor-manufacturing firms. By participating in Sematech, otherwise competing firms pooled semiconductor R & D efforts. Participating firms are required to contribute 1% of their semiconductor revenues to the consortium, with a minimum of $1 million and a maximum of $15 million. Firms are also required to send engineers to Sematech's facility in Austin, Texas for at least half a year.

The federal government, through the Defense Department's Advanced Research Projects Agency (ARPA), provided approximately half of Sematech's annual $200 million budget through 1996. This direct subsidy ended in FY 1997. Sematech now has 11 domestic members and, now that it no longer receives funds from ARPA, has established a wholly owned subsidiary, International Sematech, with five foreign firms as members. Although Sematech no longer receives a direct subsidy, it has maintained a connection with the federal government by entering a partnership with Oakridge National Laboratory (partnerships of this sort are discussed below).[10]

Sematech is often credited with reversing the fortunes of the U.S. semiconductor industry, but that hypothesis is difficult to test. The Sematech model may have promise. For example, it is consistent with Paul Romer's (1993) suggestion of creating self-organizing industry investment boards. Such boards could "combine the government's efficiency at solving free-rider problems with the market's effectiveness in selecting practical problems that offer the highest rates of return" (p. 361). Here, too, we see difficulties in implementing theoretically sound ideas. Irwin and Klenow (1996), for example, found that firms involved in Sematech reduced their R & D expenditures by approximately $300 million per year. This reduction has positive and negative interpretations. On one hand, firms may have reduced spending on duplicative research. On the other hand, firms probably did not increase spending on high-spillover research. In addition, no research projects are completely duplicative—more than one firm working on similar problems may develop very different solutions or directions for future research.

**CRADAs**

Government-industry partnerships in which government and industry scientists work together for the purpose of commercializing a product is a new approach. The largest of these are CRADAs. CRADAs are formal agreements between the national laboratories and private firms. CRADAs are intended to help the national laboratories in their primary mission by building their technical capabilities and to help private industry by commercializing innovations produced in the labs (Cohen & Noll, 1995). Traditionally, the national laboratories facilitated technology transfer to the private sector by publicizing research results. By contrast, information from CRADAs is closely held, and the private partner retains intellectual property rights to any innovation. The Clinton administration initially wanted the national laboratories to devote 10% to 20% of their budgets to cooperative work with industry (Clinton & Gore, 1993). Unfortunately, data about CRADAs are exceedingly difficult to obtain. Available information reveals that the number of new CRADAs increased from about 500 in 1992 to over 1,100 in 1994 before beginning to decline in 1995.

CRADAs have not been subject to any comprehensive economic analysis. In part, this lack of evaluation is the result of a lack of access to data. As Cohen and Noll (1995) note,

> The government has been especially closed in providing solid information about CRADAs—a policy that was deliberately set in motion by the provisions of the enabling statutes that protect the confidentiality of the agreements. CRADA proposals and reports are exempted from the Freedom of Information Act, and the agreements bind the parties not to reveal any proprietary information brought to the CRADA or any research results that emanate from it, without their mutual consent. Whereas some agencies make the titles and partner identities available and, in some cases, the cost, agencies are not obliged to do so and will not if their partner objects. Moreover, none of the agencies responsible for managing the CRADA program regularly collects information about the extent of its CRADA activity, much less performance data about the joint project. Hence, nearly all the available information takes the form of raw 'CRADA counts' that do not differentiate between small, narrowly defined projects and massive, broad agreements with large industrial consortia. (p. 230)

Although the idea of CRADAs was initially popular across the political spectrum, implementation has led to many controversies. Most of them arise when a CRADA appears to be too successful. For example, the AIDS drug, AZT, was developed by Burroughs-Wellcome in a CRADA with the National Institute of

Health (NIH). Burroughs-Wellcome initially priced the drug at $2,000 to $10,000 per year. This led the NIH to develop fair pricing clauses for its CRADAs, but has been unable to determine what "fair pricing" means.[11]

### PNGV

Another large public-private partnership is the PNGV. This program began in 1993 as a collaboration between seven federal agencies, 20 federal laboratories, and the three big U.S. automobile manufacturers. The program's goal is "to develop an environmentally friendly car with up to triple the fuel economy of today's midsize cars—without sacrificing affordability, performance, or safety. The other two PNGV goals are (1) to significantly improve national competitiveness in automotive manufacturing, [and] (2) to apply commercially viable innovations to conventional vehicles" (PNGV, 1998). The PNGV has not received as much attention as other government-industry programs, although it receives over $250 million annually from the federal government.

The PNGV has not been subject to any economic evaluation. Although PNGV may have overcome many technological hurdles in its quest for a more efficient automobile, nobody has been able to investigate what the real effect of PNGV has been. Indeed, the National Academy of Sciences (1998) "found it difficult to assess the efforts and resources applied to the PNGV program because no funding plan was made available" (p. 11).

### THE MEP

The MEP is another part of the new push toward public-private technology partnerships. MEP is different from other programs in that it is not intended to produce any particular product. Instead, MEP consists of regional offices that provide small- and medium-sized firms with technical, technological, and business advice and help them form partnerships with other businesses or government agencies (MEP, 1998). Like some other programs, MEP began in 1988, but was very small for several years. In 1992, there were only seven MEP centers. By 1997, MEP had 70 centers and an annual budget of almost $100 million. Like CRADAs and PNGV, there have been no economic evaluations of MEP.

## CONCLUSIONS AND POLICY RECOMMENDATIONS

The end of the Cold War brought with it a need to rethink the way the United States funds science and technology. Support for basic research remains strong, and many have voiced their belief that government must continue to support R & D at universities and colleges. The question of how to support industrial R & D best has proven sticky. Government, and the Clinton administration in particular, has chosen to focus on government-industry R & D partnerships aimed at commercializing innovations. The administration has started a host of such programs and drastically increased funding to many others. These programs, however, remain controversial, and it is not yet clear that they can achieve their ambitious goal of mitigating a market failure.

The economics behind these programs is sound. Firms acting in their own best interests will invest less than the socially optimal level of R & D. By subsidizing some R & D, government can help mitigate this market failure. Sound theory, however, does not always translate easily into sound policy. Preliminary evidence on new government-industry technology programs suggests that they face a host of problems in terms of implementation, evaluation, and political support. Each of those issues impacts the other.

Checkered preliminary evaluations, however, should not necessarily be viewed as condemning either the programs or the idea behind the programs. Just as the outcome of R & D itself is inherently uncertain, so too is the outcome of an R & D program. Large firms undertake a portfolio of R & D projects, recognizing that some projects will pan out and others will not. Likewise, government programs to support industrial R & D should be viewed as a portfolio. Some of these programs may turn out to be successful whereas others will not. The failure of one program to generate benefits does not necessarily mean that another program cannot generate benefits.

## RECOMMENDATIONS

The large gap between private and social returns on R & D suggests that government-industry R & D programs, if properly implemented, could potentially yield enormous benefits. These programs are new, which means that we have a lot to learn about how they should be run. If we are to determine what works and what does not, the programs must include evaluation mechanisms. Unfortunately, the government agencies in charge of these programs tend to resist efforts to conduct comprehensive evaluations. As a result, we know very little about whether the programs are meeting their objectives.

Federal agencies should be more open toward evaluation and should give more thought to what success really means in the context of government-industry R & D programs. Simply noting that funded projects have a high commercialization rate does not demonstrate that government funding had any real impact. Likewise, a failed project does not mean that the program is a failure and a spectacular commercial success does not necessarily mean that the government should not have funded the project. To our knowledge, no program has been willing to release data that would facilitate a proper evaluation, much less actually implement the program in a way that facilitates evaluation.[12] For example, most programs are unwilling to release even the names of firms that applied to the program and were turned down. Without that basic information, it is nearly impossible to determine whether government funding had any real effect.

Agencies should also think carefully about the incentives facing managers who run these programs. Too much emphasis on commercialization may cause a manager to fund the most commercially promising proposals, which may be the very proposals that do not need funding. On the other hand, criticism of very large commercial successes may make managers reluctant to fund research that they feel has some small probability of being a tremendous commercial success (but would not be funded by the private sector alone). Comprehensive evaluations may help on this score—if managers are not judged just on commercialization then perhaps the debate will shift away from focusing on simple anecdotes.

Government-industry R & D programs are an innovative approach to solving a serious market failure. Whether the problems facing government-industry R & D programs can be overcome is still an open question. Much research needs to be done to determine how these programs can accomplish their goals. More thought needs to be given to the incentives affecting the behavior of politicians, program managers, and firms involved in these programs. If the problems can be overcome, these programs could contribute significantly to economic growth.

## NOTES

1. See Griliches (1992) for a discussion of underinvestment. See Reinganum (1989) for a discussion of factors that can lead firms to overinvest.

2. See Griliches (1992) and Nadiri (1993) for overviews of the literature on spillovers and returns to R & D.

3. Sometimes the term *social returns* embraces total benefits to society—the private returns as well as the value of spillovers. Here, we use the term in a more limited sense, to refer only to the benefits that are not appropriated by the innovator.

4. For discussions of these issues, see Stiglitz and Sah (1989) and Barzel (1995).

5. For a discussion of the R & D tax credit, see Hall (1993).

6. See Masahiko, Murdock, and Okuno-Fujihara (1997) for a general discussion.

7. See Wallsten (1998b) for a more in-depth discussion of this issue.

8. Initially, a Phase I award was worth up to $50,000 and a Phase II award was worth up to $500,000. Congress increased these amounts when it renewed the SBIR Program in 1992.

9. Although ATP has rules mandating small-firm participation, ATP competitions are open to firms of any size.

10. See Irwin and Klenow (1996) and Sematech (1998) for more information on Sematech.

11. Most of the information in this paragraph comes from Cohen and Noll (1995).

12. For example, Adam Jaffe (1998) notes that perhaps the best way to evaluate programs that solicit proposals is to randomize awards. Some percentage of selected projects would randomly not be funded and some percentage of rejected projects would be funded (with preliminary screening to ensure that truly ridiculous proposals were not funded). This randomization approach would generate control groups and help identify whether government funding was actually necessary in undertaking the research project.

## REFERENCES

Advanced Technology Program, National Institute of Science and Technology. (1998). [On-line]. Available: http://www.atp.nist.gov/atp/overview.htm.

Barzel, Y. (1995). Productivity change, public goods and transaction costs: Essays at the boundaries of microeconomics. In M. Perlman & M. Blaug (Eds.), *Economists of the twentieth century series*. Aldershot, U.K.: Edward Elgar Publishing, Limited.

Branscomb, L., & Keller, J. (1998). Towards a research and innovation policy. In L. Branscomb & J. Keller (Eds.), *Investing in innovation* (pp. 462-496). Cambridge, MA: MIT Press.

Brody, R. (1996). *Effective partnering: A report to Congress on federal technology partnerships*. Washington, DC: U.S. Department of Commerce, Office of Technology Policy.

Clinton, W., & Gore, A. (1993). *Technology for America's economic growth, a new direction to build economic strength*. Washington, DC: Executive Office of the President.

Cohen, L., & Noll, R. (1991). *The technology pork barrel*. Washington, DC: The Brookings Institution.

Cohen, L., & Noll, R. (1995). Feasibility of effective public-private R & D collaboration: The case of cooperative R & D agreements. *International Journal of the Economics of Business*, 2, 223-240.

Council of Economic Advisers, Executive Office of the President. (1995). *Supporting research and development: The federal government's role* [On-line]. Available: http://www.white-house.gov/WH/EOP/CEA/econ/html/econ-rpt.html.

Executive Office of the President. (1996). *Technology in the national interest*. Washington, DC: Author.

General Accounting Office. (1989). *Federal research: Assessment of Small Business Innovation Research Programs* (GAO/RCED-89-39). Washington, DC: Government Printing Office.

General Accounting Office. (1992). *Federal research: Small business innovation research shows success but can be strengthened* (GAO/RCED-92-37). Washington, DC: Government Printing Office.

General Accounting Office. (1995). *Federal research: Interim report on the Small Business Innovation Research Program* (GAO/RCED-95-59). Washington, DC: Government Printing Office.

General Accounting Office. (1996). *Measuring performance: The Advanced Technology Program and private-sector funding* (GAO/RCED-96-47). Washington, DC: Government Printing Office.

Greenwald, B., Salinger, M., & Stiglitz, J. (1990, April). *Imperfect capital markets and productivity growth* (Rev. 1991, March). Paper presented at the NBER Conference, Vail, CO.

Griliches, Z. (1992). The search for R & D spillovers. *Scandinavian Journal of Economics*, *94*, 29-47.

Hall, B. (1992). *Investment and research and development at the firm level: Does the source of financing matter?* (National Bureau of Economic Research Working Paper No. 4096). Cambridge, MA: National Bureau of Economic Research.

Hall, B. (1993). R & D tax policy during the 1980s: Success or failure? In J. Poterba (Ed.), *Tax policy and the economy* (Vol. 7). Cambridge, MA: MIT Press.

Hill, C. (1995, June 19). *Private funds are unlikely to replace cuts in public funds for R & D in the U.S.* (Available from the Institute of Public Policy, George Mason University, Fairfax, VA).

Hill, C. (1998). The Advanced Technology Program: Opportunities for enhancement. In L. Branscomb & J. Keller (Eds.), *Investing in innovation* (pp. 143-173). Cambridge, MA: MIT Press.

Himmelberg, C., & Petersen, B. (1994). R & D and internal finance: A panel study of small firms in high-tech industries. *Review of Economics and Statistics*, *76*, 38-51.

Irwin, D., & Klenow, P. (1996). High-tech R & D subsidies: Estimating the effects of Sematech. *Journal of International Economics*, *40*, 323-344.

Jaffe, A. (1998). Measurement issues. In L. Branscomb & J. Keller (Eds.), *Investing in innovation* (pp. 64-84). Cambridge, MA: MIT Press.

Jones, C., & Williams, J. (1997). *Measuring the social return to R & D* (Finance and economics discussion series). Washington, DC: Federal Reserve Board.

Lerner, J. (1996). *The government as venture capitalist: The long-run impact of the SBIR Program.* (National Bureau of Economic Research Working Paper No. 5753). Cambridge, MA: National Bureau of Economic Research.

Levy, D., & Terleckyj, N. (1983). Effects of government R & D on private R & D investment and productivity: A macroeconomic analysis. *The Bell Journal of Economics, 14*, 551-561.

Manufacturing Extension Partnership. (1998). [On-line]. Available: http://www.mep.nist.gov.

Masahiko, A., Murdock, K., & Okuno-Fujihara, M. (1997). Beyond the East Asian miracle: Introducing the market enhancing view. In A. Masahiko, H. Kim, & M. Okuno-Fujiwara (Eds.), *The role of government in East Asian economic development: Comparative institutional analysis* (pp. 1-40). New York: Oxford University Press.

Nadiri, I. (1993). *Innovations and technological spillovers*. (National Bureau of Economic Research Working Paper No. 4423). Cambridge, MA: National Bureau of Economic Research.

National Academy of Sciences, National Research Council. (1998). *Review of the research program of the Partnership for a New Generation of Vehicles: Fourth report.* Washington, DC: National Academy Press.

National Institute of Science and Technology. (1996). *Guidelines for economic evaluation of the Advanced Technology Program.* Washington, DC: Government Printing Office.

National Science Foundation. (1998). *Science and engineering indicators.* Washington, DC: Government Printing Office.

Office of Management and Budget, Executive Office of the President. (1996). *Budget of the United States government.* Washington, DC: Government Printing Office.

Office of Management and Budget, Executive Office of the President. (1997). *Budget of the United States government.* Washington, DC: Government Printing Office.

Office of Management and Budget, Executive Office of the President. (1998). *Budget of the United States government.* Washington, DC: Government Printing Office.

Partnership for a New Generation of Vehicles. (1998). [On-line]. Available: http://www.ta.doc.gov/pngv/introduction/intro.htm.

Reinganum, J. (1989). The timing of innovation: Research, development, and diffusion. In R. Schmalensee & R. Willig (Eds.), *Handbook of industrial organization* (pp. 850-908). New York: Elsevier Science Publishers.

Robson, M. (1993). Federal funding and the level of private expenditure on basic research. *Southern Economic Journal, 60*, 63-71.

Romer, P. (1993). Implementing a national technology strategy with self-organizing industry investment boards. *Brookings Papers: Microeconomics, 2*, 345-399.

Schumpeter, J. A. (1939). *Business cycles: A theoretical, historical, and statistical analysis of the capitalist process.* New York: McGraw-Hill.

Sematech. (1998). [On-line]. Available: http://www.sematech.org.

Stiglitz, J. (1988). *Economics of the public sector* (2nd ed.). New York: Norton.

Stiglitz, J., & Sah, R. (1989). Technological learning, social learning and technological change. In S. Chakravarty (Ed.), *The balance between industry and agriculture in economic development* (pp. 285-298). New York: Macmillan.

Wallsten, S. (1998a). Rethinking the Small Business Innovation Research Program. In L. Branscomb & J. Keller (Eds.), *Investing in innovation.* Cambridge, MA: MIT Press.

Wallsten, S. (1998b). *Can government-industry R & D programs increase private R & D: The case of the Small Business Innovation Research Program.* Unpublished doctoral dissertation, Stanford University.

Yager, L., & Schmidt, R. (1997). *The Advanced Technology Program: A case study in federal technology policy.* Washington, DC: AEI Press.

Pergamon

Technology In Society, Vol. 16, No. 4, pp. 389–402, 1994

0160-791X/94 $6.00 + .00

0160-791X(94)00017-4

# A New Model for Public–Private Partnerships

*Paul G. Apen, Brian C. Benicewicz, and Joseph R. Laia*

*ABSTRACT. In the United States, federal technology transfer programs, public–private initiatives, national centers for technology and manufacturing, research and development consortia, and university outreach centers have all been developed as public-investment-based solutions to enhancing economic competitiveness. Each of these activities has problems and shortcomings associated with it. In lieu of these traditional programs, an expanded, integrated, and self-sufficient model for public–private partnerships is proposed through which 503(c) nonprofit organizations can manage and operate technology extension programs for the state or federal government. This approach addresses small, medium, and large business in an integrated fashion in terms of nine sectors of economic competitiveness. Methods for acquiring and utilizing technology and accessing government markets are proposed. A unique method for obtaining self-sufficiency and growth is developed. The presented model leverages federal investments into an independent and self-sufficient, privately-funded partnership. This type of entrepreneurial approach to public–private initiatives has been conspicuously absent from the majority of existing federal and state funded technology programs. It is expected that this model will lead to a higher rate of return on public investment.*

Since 1987 the authors have been intimately involved in the development and transfer of technology from the public to the private sector. During this time at Los Alamos, they have managed government–industry

*Paul G. Apen is Section Leader for Polymer Sciences at Los Alamos National Laboratory. Dr. Apen received his PhD in Chemistry from the University of Michigan. Brian C. Benicewicz is Manager for Deposition Technologies, Polymer Sciences and Precision Manufacturing at Los Alamos. Dr. Benicewicz received his PhD in Polymer Chemistry from the University of Connecticut. Joseph R. Laia is Senior Manager for Deposition Technologies, Polymer Sciences, and Precision Manufacturing at Los Alamos. Dr. Laia received his PhD in Materials Science and Engineering from the State University of New York at Stony Brook.*

collaborative research projects worth in excess of 10 million dollars with companies such as DuPont, Dow, Pratt & Whitney, General Electric, and AT&T. The authors have worked with the State of New Mexico Economic Development Department and with regional industry networks to find ways to enhance small business competitiveness through technology transfer and utilization. The authors have also been active in establishing alliances between universities, national laboratories, and industry in collaborative research and development.

## *Introduction*

The recent attention paid by federal and state governments to the issues of technology policy, economic competitiveness, and free trade have led to a number of implementation plans. The major plans focus on the transfer of technology from the multitude of federal laboratories (726) to the private sector, commercial and dual-use technology programs, and the development of programs that utilize technology or manufacturing extension services. Numerous articles, commentaries, and congressional studies have been devoted to the issues of technology transfer, technology policy, and public–private partnerships in the US.[1–13]

Technology transfer from the public sector in the US can be traced to the passage of the Stevenson–Wydler Technology Innovation Act of 1980,[14] which requires federal laboratories to take an active role in disseminating technical information and established the Offices of Research and Technology Application at major federal laboratories. The Bayh–Dole Act of 1980[15] allows government-owned, government-operated (GOGO) laboratories to grant exclusive licenses to patents; furthermore, it provides universities, not-for-profit institutions, and small businesses with an opportunity to obtain titles to inventions developed with government support. Small businesses received further attention with the passage of the Small Business Innovation Development Act of 1982.[16] This law requires agencies to provide special funds for small business research and development (R&D) connected to the sponsoring agency's mission. Currently, one percent of the R&D budget of federal agencies is directed towards assisting small business through Small Business Innovative Research (SBIR) grants. Additional programs designed to assist small businesses have been developed, including the Small Business Technology Transfer (STTR) program, which allows federal laboratories to participate with small business in a program modeled after SBIR.[17]

The concerns of large business were addressed by the Cooperative Research Act of 1984.[18] This act eliminated many of the antitrust barriers that faced companies which wished to pool their resources and engage in precompetitive R&D. Numerous consortia, including the

Semiconductor Research Corporation (SRC), the Microelectronics and Computer Technology Corporation (MCC), and the National Center for Manufacturing Sciences (NCMS), have been established as a result of this legislation.[19] Each of these consortia consist of several companies engaged in precompetitive R&D in a broadly defined industry segment, such as the semiconductor, computer, microelectronics, communication, and transportation industries.

The Federal Technology Transfer Act of 1986[20] allows GOGO laboratories to make advance agreements with small and large companies concerning titles and licenses to inventions that result from Cooperative Research and Development Agreements (CRADAs). The Federal Technology Transfer Act of 1986 gives the directors of GOGO laboratories the authority to enter into CRADAs and negotiate licensing agreements.[21] The National Competitiveness Technology Transfer Act of 1989[22] grants similar opportunities to government-owned, contractor-operated (GOCO) laboratories. This act also allows information, innovations, and inventions brought into, and created through, cooperative agreements to be protected from disclosure for a period of up to five years. Finally, it was the intention of the National Competitiveness Technology Transfer Act of 1989 to provide a technology transfer mission for the Department of Energy's nuclear weapons laboratories.

Another noteworthy piece of federal legislation is the Omnibus Trade and Competitiveness Act of 1988,[23] which emphasizes the need for public–private cooperation and established centers for transferring manufacturing technology and industrial extension services within several states. The National Institute of Standards and Technology Authorization Act of 1989[24] addressed national technical needs by reconstituting the National Technical Information Services and by establishing a Technology Administration within the Department of Commerce (DOC). The DOC now has an expanded role and has become the focal point of the Clinton Administration's emphasis on technology development programs that have economic relevance.[25]

The Advanced Technology Program (ATP) and the Manufacturing Extension Program (MEP) at the DOC's National Institute of Standards and Technology (NIST) are designed to assist industry in developing commercially-relevant technologies through the government's funding of privately-directed R&D projects and the establishment of technology/manufacturing extension service centers. The Clinton administration proposes to increase funding for NIST's ATP and MEP programs from $287 million in fiscal year 1994 to $517 million in fiscal year 1995.[26] These programs are slated to be increased by a similar amount in fiscal years 1996 and 1997.

The dual-use Technology Reinvestment Project (TRP) at the Advanced Research Projects Agency (ARPA) also includes funding for such public–private initiatives. It is proposed that ARPA's total budget increase across all areas by $100 million to $2.7 billion in fiscal year

1995 and focus on dual-use technologies and public–private initiatives.[27] The proposed federal budget for 1995 includes a nine-agency, technology/manufacturing extension program initiative for which the budget has increased 10 percent to $2.1 billion.[28]

Technology and manufacturing outreach centers are becoming more common at universities as academics succumb to pressure from Congress and critics, and face a decrease in traditional funding. University scientists and engineers have been charged with becoming more "relevant" to society as a whole.

The majority of public–private initiatives and programs, national technology and manufacturing centers, technical alliances and consortia, Industry/University Cooperative Research Centers (IUCRCs), and university outreach activities have been unsuccessful at addressing private-sector opportunities and growth in a truly comprehensive manner. For example, federal technology transfer and utilization programs that access the national laboratories have been hampered by mismatches of capabilities, a lack of knowledge on the part of the public sector, misguided expectations on the part of the private sector, a lack of consistent government funding and commitment, and bureaucratic frustrations.[29]

The private sector encounters further roadblocks, including commercial rights agreements, product liability indemnification, and conflicts with US competitive rules.[30] According to Richard Marczewski of General Motors, who oversaw the signing of the largest single collection of CRADAs in the nation, the CRADA process at DOE is both ineffective and frustrating.[31] William Spencer, President and Chief Executive Officer of SEMATECH, explained after signing a five-year agreement with a DOE lab "the length of time it took to complete the negotiations and resolve issues raised by DOE was numbing."[32]

National centers, technical alliances, R&D consortia, IUCRCs, and university outreach centers also have their share of problems. Since most of these activities are funded by either the state or federal government, there is little or no incentive to directly address several important issues. For example, the incentive to bring new products to commercial markets is reduced because support for technical centers or outreach activities is provided by public funding. In addition, consortia and outreach centers typically have a broad agenda and less specific goals than individual companies. Secondly, consortia and outreach centers cannot deal effectively with intellectual property issues. This stumbling block can prevent companies from gaining true competitive advantages; as a result, it may be more difficult to bring new technologies and products to the marketplace. Finally, IUCRCs and university outreach centers are rarely self-sufficient: Most use public funding as a means of financing collaborative R&D, technical extension services, and information exchange. Self-sufficiency and long-term growth in the funding profile of this family of public–private initiatives are rarely addressed. Techniques for uniting capital investment with technology are rarely implemented.

Although several additional problems have been documented,[33] these are the critical issues. It appears that the true potential of US national resources — national laboratories, federal facilities, universities, nonprofit research institutions — is still unrealized. There are no true comprehensive models for managing, operating, and coordinating public–private partnerships in the US.

We propose an expanded, integrated, independent, and self-sufficient model for public–private partnerships. In this model, a 503(c) nonprofit organization manages and operates a manufacturing or technology extension program for a state or federal government. We will refer to the nonprofit 503(c) organization as a public–private Partnership, or PPP. This approach addresses small, medium, and large business in an integrated fashion in terms of productivity, technology, and education. This aspect of the model defines nine sectors of economic competitiveness.

The needs of the private sector, public sector, and small businesses are defined in areas vital to long-term economic growth in the US. Novel ways to acquire and utilize technology and to access government markets are described. Most importantly, a unique method for obtaining self-sufficiency and growth is proposed. The model can be supplemented with known and successful techniques for funding small start-up companies using venture capital investments. As a result, it can actively engage all of the vast resources of a particular locality (or country) in an expanded, integrated, and self-sufficient format and lead to a higher rate of return on public investment.

## *Sectors of Economic Competitiveness*

The factors that influence economic competitiveness are, in simple terms, productivity, technology, and education. Productivity enables one to more effectively utilize available resources. Concepts such as enhanced quality control, efficiency, proficient use of materials, just-in-time commitments, and information networking are examples of issues that fall into this category. For example, enhancements in quality and efficiency have allowed Motorola and Chrysler to again become competitive in the global market place.

Advanced or next-generation technology enhances products or services. Incorporation of new technologies can have a drastic effect on a product market by creating entirely new products while making others obsolete. An example of this is the incorporation of word processing and laser technology into the print media; this has had a drastic effect on the markets for typewriters and correction fluid. The incorporation of laser technology into the audio and video markets has had an enormous effect on the magnetic tape and electronics markets.

Education implies access to a skilled work force and to the knowledge base required to effectively utilize enhancements in productivity and technology.

The model we propose divides the segments of industry into three parts based on their size: small, medium, and large. If one constructs a matrix spanning the space of business size and factors influencing competitiveness, nine sectors of economic competitiveness can be developed, as shown in Table 1. These nine sectors of economic competitiveness are an extremely useful construct for evaluating federal initiatives and for determining the overall impact that a public–private program can have on the commercialization of new technologies and economic activity.

The majority of public–private programs, national centers, and university outreach activities, at least in the US, are largely biased towards one narrow region of the matrix. While these approaches may improve the business environment in a particular part of the country, all sectors of economic competitiveness should be considered for a truly comprehensive and effective program. In other words, by addressing and coordinating activities throughout all nine sectors of the matrix, vastly superior results could be achieved. This can be done by engaging small, medium, and large business in an integrated manner while utilizing the nation's vast scientific and engineering resources.

### *Private Needs, Public Needs and Small Business Needs*

Instead of taking the traditional approach of looking at the needs of small, medium, and large businesses separately, we consider in our model the collective private and public needs that will allow the PPP to comprehensively cover all nine sectors of economic competitiveness. The needs that the PPP should address in order to effectively engage all nine sectors are private needs, or the technology needs of large private companies driven towards significant consumer markets; public needs, or the requirements of the federal and state governments for goods and services which enhance the public good; and small business needs, or the specialized needs of small to medium-sized business.

The private needs may be thought of as the needs of medium to large businesses that have established markets and products and would like to

**TABLE 1. Sectors of Economic Competitiveness**

| | Productivity | Technology | Education |
|---|---|---|---|
| Small | 1 | 2 | 3 |
| Medium | 4 | 5 | 6 |
| Large | 7 | 8 | 9 |

enhance their competitive positions by utilizing public knowledge or facilities. This may be best described as *Technology Utilization.*

The public needs are real and seem to be overlooked in traditional public–private initiatives. For example, while the DOD needs and budget have decreased,[34] the federal requirements in areas such as environment, energy, nonproliferation, and drug interdiction have all increased significantly. Many technologies that have been paid for by the DOD exist but lack the traditional government market. These technologies may be suited to solving the national needs listed above. The DOD example is duplicated in DOE (defense R&D and super-conducting, super collider funding have decreased precipitously)[35] and NASA (space station and shuttle funding have decreased).[36]

The application of federally-funded, privately-developed, defense-related technology to solve problems of national need is *Technology Conversion.* This is a significantly different definition of technology conversion than is normally given; that is, using DOD-developed technology for nondefense public needs, as opposed to applying defense technology to the private sector. In our proposed model, transfer of defense technology to the commercial sector is covered by the technology utilization activity.

Small-business needs are perceived as particularly important because, as a whole, the small business sector has been the major contributor to the creation of new jobs in recent years. As a result, in order to enhance our manufacturing job base, there must be an infrastructure and organization that is supportive of entrepreneurs and provides small business with the necessary tools to enhance their economic competitiveness. The PPP model takes into account that small businesses and manufacturers must have access to techniques and concepts which increase productivity. In our model, we benefit small businesses by providing access to markets and recognize that this assistance must be provided in a coordinated manner and simultaneously leveraged with utilization and conversion activities. This series of activities is described as *small business enhancement.*

### *Technology Utilization*

In order to overcome the many problems associated with traditional federal technology transfer and utilization, we propose that the PPP act as an intermediary between private industry and the federal laboratories by matching, acquiring, and efficiently utilizing government-developed technologies for private industry. This effort should target medium to large businesses and require a cost for admission that could be paid in resources, such as manpower and facilities. This aspect of the technology utilization activity could be similar to current federal technology transfer programs and CRADAs. However, our approach takes on a unique perspective by developing government technologies in a way that will enable the PPP to become financially self-sufficient.

The federal or state government would directly award a PPP a contract for managing, operating, and coordinating a public–private initiative. The contract would include full funding and support for a series of projects to be subcontracted to laboratories and various R&D organizations. The PPP would act as the project coordinator between private industry and the government and directly fund projects at the national laboratories, defense laboratories, NASA laboratories, nonprofit research institutions, or universities. Federal agencies would not be directly involved in program selection, execution, or review. High-value-added processes and products with large commercial payoffs for private industry would be targeted. Since the PPP would directly fund the project at the government facility, it would own the intellectual property generated. This would be identical to current funds-in agreements between private companies and the national laboratories.

This is critical because it will enable the PPP to license the intellectual property to the participating company in a limited field-of-use arrangement. The licensing agreement would be negotiated on a case-by-case basis taking into account the amount of money and time invested, market size, profit margin, and impact of the technology. When the technology is successfully utilized by the private sector, a percentage of the revenues generated by the company would be returned to the PPP. For example, Amoco Chemical Company currently licenses a patent to produce purified terephthalic acid, an important industrial chemical precursor that nets the company tens of millions of dollars in revenues per year. If the right product and industry segments are chosen, this method of developing, acquiring, and licensing government technology would eventually fund the entire public–private program. Furthermore, a percentage of the revenues generated through licensing could be directed to colleges and universities for educational programs and scientific training, thus covering row three (sectors 7–9) of the matrix in Table 1.

The PPP will own the technologies developed and will be able to match large business needs, such as the need for small manufacturing partners, with existing small businesses in the region. If a small manufacturer does not exist, the PPP could act to stimulate and incubate a small business. Furthermore, since the PPP would own the intellectual property, it could spin-off newly developed technologies to other industry segments in broader fields and license such technologies to generate additional revenues.

This approach allows the investment made by the state or federal government to be maximized by generating a source of revenue for private, public, and small business needs in a coordinated fashion. This technology utilization activity would target specific industry segments of vital interest to the state(s) involved with the goals of generating maximum revenue for the PPP and sustaining economic activity. For example, a program in Michigan or Ohio might target the automotive industry, one in Texas or Louisiana might target the petrochemical industry, and one in North or South Carolina might focus on the textile industry.

The advantages of having a broker between industry and the federally-funded research institutions are, but not limited to, the proper management of the expectations of both parties, the careful evaluation of the applicability of government technologies to commercial markets,[37] and the reduction of bureaucratic red tape. Specifically, directly funding projects at federal research institutions would allow the PPP to critically evaluate available technologies and acquire only those technologies that meet shorter-term, high value-added market needs. This is in contrast to the current process in which collaborative R&D sets a broad agenda and drives the decisions of what is or what is not funded. In current federal programs, the time frame for technology development is generally long-term and the solutions are often driven by political decisions in which the return-on-investment is a minor consideration.

## *Technology Conversion*

Technology conversion is generally perceived as the application of defense-related technologies to new commercial markets. While this is an important and productive effort and is included in our model, there are untapped opportunities for small to medium-sized, defense-related companies to address national needs other than traditional DOD needs. Even though defense spending is declining,[38] the overall federal budget is not; instead, a great deal of the federal DOD/DOE/NASA/DOC resources are being channeled into areas such as environmental remediation and energy conservation. It is extremely difficult for small to medium-sized businesses to remain aware of the changes in policy, funding, new initiatives, and requirements necessary to participate in these programs. We propose that the PPP act as a window to government needs and markets. This would allow the conversion and application of federally-funded, privately-developed, defense-related technologies to other sets of public needs.

The objective for the PPP would be to match technologies available in small to medium-sized businesses with the aforementioned national needs, thereby generating contracts for regional businesses. In other words, the PPP would assist small to medium-sized businesses in finding and accessing new "national needs" markets. There would be no up-front cost for participating, only time would be required on the part of the business. The business would work with the PPP in identifying existing technologies and potential matches to new public needs and markets.

A primary focus could be the environmental restoration programs run by the DOE or DOD in which hazardous sites are monitored and decontaminated. For example, sensors developed by a small company for DOE or DOD applications may be ideal for monitoring hazardous waste sites. However, the small company may not have the resources nor the time to commit to research and understand these new markets, where they exist and how to access them. The PPP could easily gather that knowledge and be the bridge between small to medium-sized contractors and the federal government.

### *Small Business*

The PPP should focus on small business needs as well. The PPP would work to bring small manufacturers together with large industrial companies through its technology utilization activities and connect small businesses with national needs through its technology conversion activities. These are major components of the broadened and integrated model that we propose. The PPP should provide these services at no cost to participating small businesses.

In a manner similar to that used by many technical extension centers, small business services such as enhanced quality, efficiency, effective use of materials, just-in-time capital commitments and contracts, information networking, access to capital, and effective management techniques, should be made available to small businesses. The training and education component of the PPP would teach these productivity concepts to small-business owners. The PPP would assist small businesses in integrating these concepts and services in order to enhance economic competitiveness, increase small business survival rates, and, ultimately, create jobs. Small business owners would be educated as to regulatory and public policy issues that directly affect them.

The PPP would integrate manufacturing extension programs, university centers, and numerous technology alliances within the regions for the benefit of small businesses.

Finally, since capital is crucial to small business development during the initial stages of start-up, we also recommend a venture capital component that would follow the example of CONNECT® at the University of California, San Diego.[39] Forums would be scheduled to bring together small high-technology start-up companies with financial, legal, and managerial resources in order to enhance the success rates of small start-up companies.

### *PPP Structure*

Under our proposed scenario, the 503(c) organization — the PPP — would be an umbrella organization that integrates and coordinates the activities of the Technology Utilization Center (TUC), Technology Conversion Center (TCC), and Small Business Center (SBC) (Figure 1). Each center would provide leadership and oversight for the set of well-defined activities that we have described. A board of directors made up of industry, government, and university representatives would oversee and provide guidance to the PPP.

In order to effectively address all nine sectors, the three centers would have to coordinate and integrate their activities. TUC activities would span all nine sectors of the matrix in Table 1, with emphasis on sectors 7–9. TCC activities would target sectors 1–6 while focusing on both private and public needs. SBC activities would focus on sectors 1–3 and be leveraged by activities of the TUC and TCC.

### *Hypothetical Funding and Revenue Profile*

This model would be most effective with a staggered funding profile. For example, the hypothetical funding profile in Figure 2 shows an increase of $10 million per year from fiscal year (FY) 1 through FY3, and then a decrease of $10 million per year from FY4 to FY7. This would allow the PPP to ramp-up technology utilization projects by FY3 and FY4 and fund a different portfolio of high-value-added projects in a particular industry segment in each fiscal year. Technology utilization activities would require the bulk of the funding because these projects would have to be directly funded at various R&D institutions. Individual projects would last one to three years depending on the nature of the technology and the program. As a starting point, a possible funding breakdown for the PPP's activities would be 60% for technology utilization, 20% for technology conversion, and 20% for small business.

As FY4 approaches, the need for additional public funding would decrease as revenue streams from licensed technologies are realized. Figure 2 shows a projected and hypothetical revenue stream (solid line) from licensing agreements with private industry. This projected revenue stream assumes an aggressive growth rate of $10 million per year from licensing agreements. Figure 2 also shows the total revenue (solid

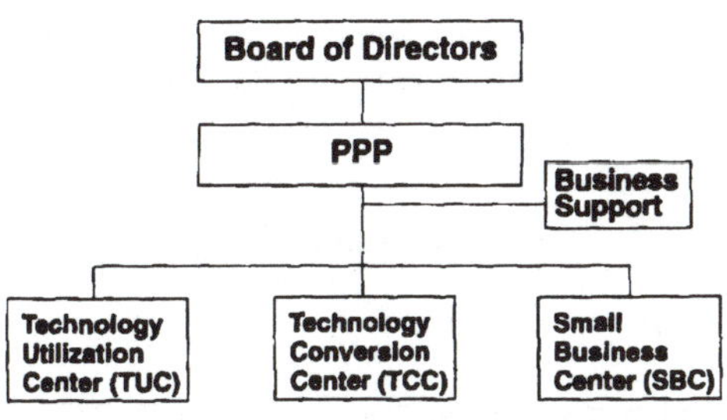


**Figure 1. Proposed Structure of the Model 503(c) Organization, PPP**

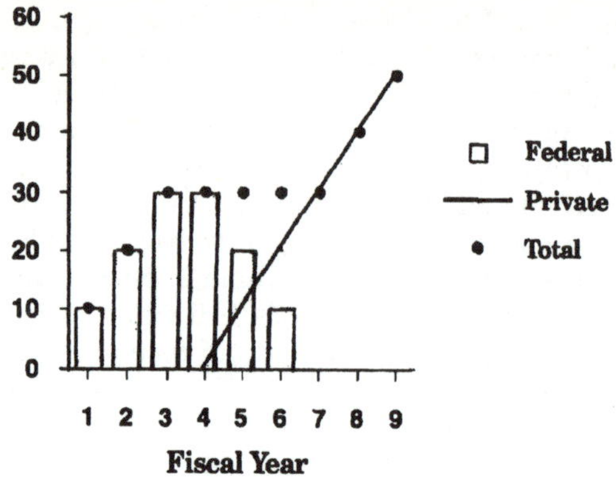


**Figure 2. Hypothetical Funding and Revenue Profile for a Self-Sufficient Public–Private Partnership**

circles) from both public and private funding of the PPP through the first nine years of the program. In this scenario, total revenues increase from $30 million in FY3–FY7 to $50 million in FY9. At the end of seven years, the PPP would be completely self-sufficient if the projects were chosen carefully to ensure significant market impact and minimal technical risk. At this point, public funding would be phased out. Revenues from licensing agreements would then finance the entire range of technology utilization, technology conversion, and small business activities.

### *Entrepreneurial Model*

Our model engages all nine sectors of economic competitiveness and attempts to do so in a self-sufficient manner. This is a key attribute of our model since the US Congress, the Administration, and state governments are looking to maximize the return on public funding of R&D, technology programs, and extension services. Our model leverages federal investments into a truly self-sufficient, privately-funded partnership. This type of entrepreneurial approach to public–private initiatives has been conspicuously absent from the majority of currently funded federal and state programs.

### *PPP Objectives*

The objectives of the PPP model can be summarized as follows:

1. self-sufficiency within seven years,
2. continued growth afterwards,

3. efficient extraction and utilization of federal technology,
4. effective conversion and deployment of federally-funded, privately-developed technologies,
5. small business creation and productivity enhancement,
6. improved education and training, and
7. job creation.

The first six objectives would always be directed toward long-term job creation and maintenance.

## *Conclusions*

We have outlined an expanded, integrated, and self-sufficient approach to enhancing economic competitiveness through the initial utilization of public resources. For the first time, a model that has self-sufficiency and growth as its primary goal is proposed for a comprehensive public–private partnership. Furthermore, small, medium, and large businesses are addressed in an integrated fashion in terms of sectors of economic competitiveness. This proposed model expands public–private partnerships into the nine sectors by defining private, public, and small-business needs in technical areas vital to the US. Each of the three focus areas — technology utilization, technology conversion, small business — has a productivity, technology, and education component. Finally, this program actively engages all of the vast resources of the US — national laboratories, defense and NASA laboratories, universities, national centers — in a coordinated fashion. We anticipate that a significantly higher return on public investment can be achieved using such a model.

## *Notes*

1. L. M. Branscomb (ed.), *Empowering Technology: Implementing a US Strategy* (Cambridge, MA: MIT Press, 1993).
2. E. Bloch and D. Cheney, "Technology Policy Comes of Age," *Issues in Science and Technology*, (Summer 1993), pp. 55–60.
3. D. L. Bodde, "On Guns and Butter: Reflections on Technology Transfer from Federal Laboratories," *Technology in Society*, Vol. 15 (1993), pp. 273–280.
4. J. Bingaman and B. R. Inman, "Broadening Horizons for Defense R&D," *Issues in Science and Technology*, (Fall 1992), pp. 80–85.
5. D. F. Burton, "A New Model for US Innovation," *Issues in Science and Technology*, (Summer 1992), pp. 52–59.
6. L. M. Branscomb, "Does America Need a Technology Policy," *Harvard Business Review*, (March–April 1992), pp. 24–31.
7. R. E. Gamory, "The Government Role in Science and Technology," *Technology in Society*, Vol. 14 (1992), pp. 357–362.
8. L. M. Branscomb, "Toward a US Technology Policy," *Issues in Science and Technology*, (Summer 1991), pp. 50–55.

9. A. Schriesheim, "Toward a Golden Age of Technology Transfer," *Issues in Science and Technology*, (Winter 1990–1991), pp. 52–58.
10. D. Osborne, "Refining State Technology Programs," *Issues in Science and Technology*, (Summer 1990), pp. 55–61.
11. S. Ramo, "National Security and Our Technology Edge," *Harvard Business Review*, (November–December 1989), pp. 115–120.
12. US Congress, Office of Technology Assessment, *Building Future Security: Strategies for Restructuring the Defense Technology and Industrial Base*, OTA-ISC-530 (Washington, DC: US Government Printing Office, June 1992).
13. J. Bingaman, J. Gansler, and R. Kupperman, *Integrating Commercial and Military Technologies for National Strength: An Agenda for Change*, (Washington, DC: Report of the Center for Strategic and International Studies Steering Committee on Security and Technology, 1991).
14. Public Law 96–480.
15. Public Law 96–517.
16. Public Law 97–219
17. Public Law 102–564.
18. Public Law 98–462.
19. *Technology Innovation*, Chapter 63 United States Code Annotated, Title 15 Commerce and Trade, Sections 3701 to 3715, prepared for the Federal Laboratory Consortium for Technology Transfer (St. Paul, MN: West Publishing Company, 1991).
20. Public Law 99–502.
21. *Technology Innovation, op. cit.*
22. Public Law 101–189, included as Section 3131 et seq. of DOD Authorization Act for FY1990.
23. Public Law 100–418.
24. Public Law 100–519.
25. W. Lepkowski, "Commerce's Mary Good Outlines Technology Policy Plans," *Chemical & Engineering News*, (October 18, 1993), pp. 19–20.
26. D. J. Hanson, B. Hileman, W. Lepkowski, J. R. Long, and P. S. Zurer, "Clinton's 1995 Budget Proposal Calls for Increases in R&D Funding," *Chemical & Engineering News*, (February 21, 1994), pp. 20–29.
27. *ibid.*
28. J. Long "Federal Budget Proposal," *Chemical & Engineering News*, (February 14, 1994), pp. 4–5.
29. C. Anderson, "Rocky Road for Federal Research Inc," *Science*, Vol. 262 (1993), pp. 496–498; D. J. Hanson, "Congress Moves to Reorganize Department of Energy Laboratories," *Chemical & Engineering News*, (June 14, 1993), pp. 31–32; J. D. Roessner, "What Companies Want from the Federal Laboratories," *Issues in Science and Technology*, (Fall 1993), pp. 37–42.
30. Hanson (1993), *op. cit.*
31. Anderson, *op. cit.*
32. Hanson (1993), *op. cit.*
33. Osborne, *op. cit.*; Roessner, *op. cit.*; W. M. Evan and P. Olk, "R&D Consortia: A New US Organizational Forum," *Sloan Management Review*, (Spring 1990), pp. 37–46.
34. US Congress, Office of Technology Assessment, *op. cit.*
35. "Fiscal Year DOE Budget Request Drops to $18.5 Billion," *DOE This Month*, (March 1994), pp. 3–4.
36. Hanson *et al.* (1994), *op. cit.*
37. Currently, government laboratory participation is funded directly by the federal government, so the true timely relevance of a technology to commercial markets is not always fully considered.
38. US Congress, Office of Technology Assessment, *op. cit.*; *DOE This Month*, *op. cit.*
39. CONNECT is a division of Extended Studies and Public Service at the University of California at San Diego, La Jolla, CA 92093-0176.

# [28]

# Public-Private Partnerships in U.S. Highway Finance: ISTEA and Beyond

The 1994 general elections—both national and state—appear to ratify a continuing trend towards seeking new relationships among levels of government and the private sector in both the financing and provision of public services. Within the transportation sector, efforts to reduce the federal deficit and improve governmental efficiency have energized subsequent efforts to reinvent the United States Department of Transportation (USDOT)—downsizing, devolution, deregulation, and consolidation. A central component of these efforts is programmatic elements designed to incentivize private capital and collaboration in the provision of highways.

*by Stephen C. Lockwood*

Already in 1991, the Intermodal Surface Transportation Act of (ISTEA) recognized the importance of increasing investment on the part of all levels of government and the need to attract investment capital to highway development from the private sector. Building on the experience of state-led innovation, principal features of ISTEA were provisions which encourage states to seek new resources for road improvements—both financial and entrepreneurial, including: permission to commingle conventional fuel and vehicle tax-derived funds with toll-backed revenues; extension of federal aid to cover private or quasi-public entities; and, flexibility for new funding mixes and financing instruments.

These legislative provisions have been strengthened by an on-going administrative commitment in the Federal Highway Administration (FHWA) to experiment with a more flexible application of federal aid and, more recently, by the potential for new legislation embodying additional programmatic reorganization that will bring them into even bolder relief.

While new approaches to highway finance are receiving more national political attention, they built on more than a decade of experimentation at the state and local level. Over the last 20 years, a range of innovations has focused on ways of drawing on sources of revenue other than increases in the conventional fuel and vehicle taxes.

TRANSPORTATION QUARTERLY, Vol. 49, No. 1, Winter 1995 (5-26)

Innovation has focused on three areas:

1. New revenue sources—other than traditional tax sources—principally tolls, value capture and cost-sharing with benefiting abutters, combined into new mixes with conventional revenues;

2. New roles for the public and private sector that support tapping of new resources, financial and entrepreneurial; especially increasing roles for the private sector beyond design and construction to include sharing in development, finance and even ownership; and

3. Financing structures and techniques that maximally leverage existing revenue sources and encourage private investment—both equity and debt.

Overall, the new legislative provisions and the range of experiments that are being undertaken by various states have increased the range of highway finance options available and brought with them opportunities for new relationships between the public and private sector. There are now more models available for combining revenue sources, financing structures and new forms of collaboration among public and private sector entities. As the basic relationships between federal, state and local governments continue to evolve, there are substantial opportunities for continuing innovation in highway finance.

## Traditional Highway Finance: an Intergovernmental Partnership

Institutional and financial roles in U.S. highway development are integrally related. Federal, state and local levels of government have evolved a partnership arrangement for the provision of highway transportation infrastructure. The role of the FHWA has, for over 75 years, been one of promotion of national interests through planning and standard-setting, research and technical support, together with capital grants to finance elements of the federal-aid system, especially facilities of national interest such as the Interstate System.

The 3.9 million mile American system is owned and operated by 50 states and 38,000 units of local government. In most states, public road ownership is divided between state and local governments, with states owning most of the higher level facilities and local government owning lower level facilities. However, there is a wide range of variation, from states which own virtually all public roads to states in which local governments own most of the public roads.

Within this hierarchical network of functionally-classified roads, there is an 945,000 mile Federal-Aid System comprised of the higher functional class components which carry a predominant share of the traffic (particularly longer interregional and interstate trips of special state and national interest). These roads receive preferential federal financial support. This system can be characterized as a state-owned, federally assisted system.

There is a strong post-World War II tradition of using user fees—motor fuel and highway use-related excise taxes, federal and state—as the principal means of financing the upper level road system (non-local roads). These fees are spent, largely by states, on a cost-reimbursable pay-as-you-go basis. This approach continues to dominate highway finance. At the same time, however, in rapidly growing regions where the demands for new highways are high, innovative approaches have been developed to supplement the conventional reliance on highway-user taxes.

In many industrialized countries, central government motor vehicle fuel tax and other vehicle-related revenues are considered as general purpose taxes. Transportation investments are made from general revenues, and transportation-related tax levels are set independently of transport sector investment requirements for the purpose of raising general revenues or achieve other policy objectives. This is not the case in the United States.

Major U.S. highways are financed mainly through federal and state motor fuel and highway vehicle-related excise taxes paid by the vehicle/highway user collected largely by the states. These taxes include flat fees to users (licenses and titles), taxes by amount of use (fuel) and taxes by type of use (motor carrier). These taxes are user charges, dedicated to highways, expended as they become available. Funds are apportioned to states for eligible uses as reimbursable grants.[1]

About 65% of revenues used by the public sector in expenditures on highways is derived from these user taxes through federal appropriations to states and specific project allocation at state and local governmental levels. These taxes are supplemented by general fund revenues in some states at both state and local government level. At the federal and state levels, highway investment levels are therefore substantially set by what is raised from users.

Table 1 shows the breakdown of 1993 highway funding by source and level of government. Currently states provide 52%, federal government 21% and local government 27% of the total funds used in highway transportation programs. The federal share has been decreasing in recent years. In 1992, the corresponding outlays by state and local government combined were $38 billion for capital, $22 billion for maintenance and $22 billion for administration ,law enforcement and finance.

**Federal funds:** Nearly all of the federal aid funds are derived from fuel taxes collected at the state level. These are retained in a separate federal account for exclusive use for transportation purposes—or as otherwise determined by Congressional legislation. This Highway Trust Fund was initiated in 1956 to support the recently-completed interstate highway system (funded 90% by federal aid) which is now being updated in terms of a larger National Highway System which, under current Administration proposals, will still receive federal funding preference.

The trust fund approach characterizes highway finance at the federal level as well as in most states. Its essential principles include:

- developing highways on a pay-as-

**TABLE 1: HIGHWAY RECEIPTS 1993 ($ MILLION)**

| *Financing source* | *Federal* | *State* | *Local Governments* | *Total* |
|---|---|---|---|---|
| User based: | | | | |
| Fuel and vehicle taxes | 15,776 | 32,743 | 1,085 | 49,604 |
| Tolls | | 3,147 | 485 | 3,632 |
| Beneficiary based: | | | | |
| Property taxes, assessments | | | 4,830 | 4,830 |
| Other taxes & fees | 240 | 1,643 | 1,105 | 2,988 |
| General funds | 1,371 | 1,655 | 9,690 | 12,716 |
| Investment income & Misc. | 817 | 2,093 | 3,065 | 5,975 |
| Bond proceeds (par value) | | 4,017 | 3,543 | 7,560 |
| Total | 18,204 | 45,298 | 23,803 | 87,305 |

Source: 1993 Highway Statistics, USDOT, FHWA, 1995.

you-go basis, rather than using toll-backed bonded debt finance;

- collecting user fees from vehicle classes in rough proportions to the costs imposed;
- dedicating transportation user fees to transportation purposes.

Historically, resistance to the diversion of receipts to non-transportation purposes or the imposition of policy-related surcharges has maintained very low tax surcharge (and thus, total fuel costs). However, this also magnifies the apparent impact of even a modest tax increase and thus increases political challenge of increases these taxes. Furthermore, the opportunity to accumulate unobligated balances in the Trust Fund has proved an attractive means of reducing the apparent federal budget deficit and has resulted in less than full utilization of the revenue stream. As a result, since 1985, the federal share of total highway funding has declined by 20%.

**State funds:** The majority (85%) of highway funds expended at state level come from fuel and vehicle taxes. This is in addition to federal grants to states in the form of formula appropriations from the federal Highway Trust Fund. But there is substantial variation by state, with some state programs being supported from general revenues and bond indebtedness, title fees or sales taxes. Twenty-nine states have dedicated user fees. In other states, part or all of the highway related revenues are placed in the general fund and may be available for non-transportation purposes, as is the case in many European countries. Aggregate fund support for highways, however, exceeds diversions of user fees.

**Local funds:** At local government level, property taxes are the main source of revenue for road investment. Revenues from these taxes are often supplemented by state aid for the funding of particular projects.

Collectively these institutional arrangements have assured a predictable source of income to support the federal-aid program. The financing methods have proved politically popular and stable because they are perceived to be relatively fair, difficult to evade, efficient to administer and reasonably related to use. In addition, the trust fund approach has also provided the federal and state highway authorities with an important measure of independence and insulation from budgetary tradeoffs. Indeed, European transportation agencies, traditionally wedded to the logic of general revenue allocations but now faced with the challenge of forging the continental highway system appropriate to the European Union, have recently been looking with greater interest at the U.S. approach, even as it undergoes serious reconsideration within the current debate in Congress.

## Innovative Highway Finance in the U.S.

During the last two decades, requirements for highway preservation and development have often outrun the willingness of federal, state and local governments to raise general revenues or impose increases in the fuel and other highway -use related taxes and fees. The rapid growth in jobs, especially in the service sector, and the accompanying suburbanization of employment, together with increases in female participation in the workforce, car ownership and disposable income led to a rapid increase in highway travel. The 1980s produced 30 million more commuters than the 1960s, and saw an overall increase in highway travel of over 35%. Three sunbelt states accounted for 30% of the nation's population growth in this period. Thirty metropolitan areas (predominantly in the south and west) added over 200,000 to their populations within

**TABLE 2: HIGHWAY FINANCING METHODS AND PARTICIPANTS**

| *Participants* | *Method* | *Level of Government* Federal | State | Local |
|---|---|---|---|---|
| *Direct Beneficiaries* | | | | |
| System users | Vehicle-related fees | x | x(1) | x |
| | Fuel taxes | x | x(1) | x |
| | Tolls | x | x | x |
| | Weight-distance fees | | x | |
| Property owners | Contributions | | x | x |
| | Benefit assessments | | | x |
| | Tax increments | | | x |
| | Impact fees | | | x |
| | Exactions | | x | x |
| Others | Vendor | | | x |
| *Indirect beneficiaries* | | | | |
| General public/ taxpayers | Head tax | | | x |
| | Sales tax | | x | x |
| | Income tax | | x | x |
| | Property tax | | | x |
| | Misc. fees | | x | x |

Note: (1) not dedicated in all states

seven years. Many of these areas had annual growth rates of over 5%, most of it concentrated in suburban areas with inadequate road systems. Congestion worsened, and heightened public demand for additional highway capacity.

Despite an overall increase in real highway expenditures, the revenues per road mile and vehicle mile of travel continued to decline. Highway user-related tax revenues failed to keep pace with increases in highway use, especially in the rapidly growing areas, and were further eroded by higher design standards, increased highway construction costs and increased fuel efficiency. Conventional revenues sources were committed to maintaining the maturing roadways as a first priority with decreasing revenues available for new construction.

In response, the 1980s saw several states in growing regions developing several new methods to augment tax revenues reflecting variations in the financial feasibility and local political acceptability. These innovations in highway finance can be best understood in the context of the complete spectrum of highway finance methods whereby beneficiaries of transportation improvements —both direct and indirect—are explicitly identified. The basic revenue sources commonly employed in highway finance are shown in Table 2, divided into three principal options :

- fees and taxes paid by users related to use (tolls and dedicated fuel or vehicle taxes),
- special fees or taxes paid by non-user beneficiaries (impact fees or property assessments paid by abutting property owners);
- payments by general public as indirect beneficiaries (general income/ sales taxes).

The innovations of the 1980s focused specifically on those methods that targeted direct beneficiaries most closely —tolling system users and developing various cost-sharing schemes with property owners. Each of these methods generated funds that could be mixed with conventional tax revenues to implement otherwise unaffordable projects. In addition, each method introduced potential institutional innovations—new roles and relationships among levels of government and between the public sector and private entrepreneurial entities.

The remainder of this section describes the principal innovations predating the federal initiatives crystallized by ISTEA and pursued in the most recent federal program reorganization efforts.

**Tolls.** Nationally, toll revenues have been a small proportion of total highway revenues - although significant in a few states. In the early nineties, toll facilities have accounted for 6.5% of the Interstate Highway System and carried approximately 7% of interstate traffic. Toll revenues constitute less than 5% of total highway revenues. The legal authority to develop toll highways is usually derived from state-enabling legislation and typically includes the issuance of tax-exempt bonds with various state or local government guarantees. Today, 29 states operate 37 toll roads and 44 toll bridges, with a total length of approximately 5,000 miles. In addition, there were 20 county and 27 municipal toll facilities, mainly bridges.

Use of tolls for major highway development declined during the period of Interstate system construction in the 1960s and 1970s. The low rate of toll project development can be explained in part by the competition from existing free roads and this approach to road provision to which must states are committed for major improvements. At the same time, stringent financial tests for the project finance of toll roads and the reluctance of the public to pay adequate tolls—especially when already paying into federal and state road funds through fuel and vehicle taxes (double taxation)—have inhibited widespread use of tolls.

Recently, however, toll facilities are undergoing a resurgence in the US, especially as urban facilities. As indicated in Table 3, there are about 250 miles of new toll road currently under construction at a cost of about $5 billion. An additional 1000 miles of toll road are in various early stages of development. Highway-related bond issues increased tenfold in the last decade to nearly $11B in 1993.

The advent of automatic vehicle identification (AVI) or electronic tolls may increase the viability of toll roads. Not only are the delays associated with urban toll road toll collection eliminated, but the automated billing may reduce popular opposition to tolling. Electronic tolls and traffic management systems (ETTM) are in increasingly widespread use in the U.S. on both state-wide systems such as Oklahoma and on specific urban facilities including those in Dallas, Houston, Orange County, Metropolitan New York and others.

Interest in tolls has also been spurred by increasing focus on the potential of congestion pricing to moderate congestion and air quality problems in some urban non-attainment contexts. Congestion pricing or time-of-day tolls are facilitated by ETTM technology which can control variable tolls by time of day or even by vehicle occupancy—as proposed for the financing mechanism for the SR 91 HOV/SOV lanes in Orange County. The on-going FHWA Congestion Pricing Pilot Program is supporting efforts in several urban areas to more fully test the public acceptability of introducing pricing to improve air quality and efficiency. However, there remain issues of enforcement, understandability, political acceptability, double taxation issues, as well as the impacts of diversion of

## PUBLIC-PRIVATE PARTNERSHIPS

### TABLE 3: NEW OR RECENTLY EXPANDED TOLL ROADS NATIONWIDE

| *State* | *Facility* | *Length (Miles)* | *Completion Date* | *Estimated Cost ($ Millions)* |
|---|---|---|---|---|
| California | San Joaquin Hills Corridor (TCA) | 15 | 1997 | $793 |
| California | Eastern Transportation Corridor (TCA) | 23 | 2000 | $630 |
| California | Foothill Transportation Corridor | 30 | 1999 | $746 |
| California | SR-91 Express Lanes | 14 | 1996 | $90 |
| Colorado | E-470 Beltway - First Segment | 5 | 1991 | $82 |
| Florida | Swaggers Expressway | 23 | 1986 | $178 |
| Georgia | Georgia State Route 400 | 10 | 1993 | $270 |
| Illinois | North-South Tollway | 17 | 1989 | $487 |
| New Jersey | New Jersey Turnpike | 10 | 1990 | $294 |
| Texas | Hardy Toll Road | 22 | 1987/1988 | $366 |
| Texas | Sam Houston Tollway | 28 | 1988/1990 | $436 |
| Texas | Dallas North Tollway Extension | 7 | 1987 | $124 |
| Virginia | Dulles Toll Road | 12 | 1984/1989 | $91 |
| Virginia | Dulles Toll Road Extension | 14 | 1996 | $190 |
| Virginia | Powhite Parkway Extension | 9 | 1988 | $88 |
| **TOTAL** | | **238** | | **$5,165** |

Source: IBTTA "List of Projects", June, 1993, plus author interviews

some traffic onto non-tolled, less developed routes, leading to traffic and safety concerns.

Financial technology has also had visible impact on the viability of toll roads. New financial products, lowered interest rates, tax exemption, government guarantees and attractive marginal rates have improved the market for toll-backed bonds. At the same time, the opportunities to combine toll-back debt with other revenues has increased the inventory of potentially toll-viable facilities. Recently constructed toll facilities in the U.S. such as the E-470 Beltway in Denver, Colorado, and the Hardy Toll Road north of Houston, Texas and facilities that are commencing construction (such as the San Joaquin Hills Transportation Corridor in Orange County, California) have required some degree of supplemental sources of funding to be financially viable (for example, donated right of way, dedicated developer fees, special district assessments, or public sector guarantees of toll revenues bonds) leading to increased interest in the commingling of funds and the cost-sharing approaches discussed below.

**Public/Private Cost-Sharing Options.** The shortage of conventional tax funds and the lack of financial or political feasibility of toll finance caused many state and local governments to consider tapping benefiting property owners as a supplementary source of highway funds. One approach is value capture—taxes or fees assessed to the windfall increases in private property value induced by public access improvements. This cost -sharing process can operate either through the property development process, or through assessing the beneficiaries of new infrastructure for a share of the improvement costs.

Local governments, through their land use and zoning controls, possess considerable leverage in negotiating such fees and exactions. States have been able to establish specific legal and institutional frameworks within which local governments, which already control land development, can develop cooperative cost-sharing arrangements with the private sector. Such revenues are particularly attractive since they represent sources not shared with other sectors. But the initiative in this has not been the exclusive preserve of the public sector. Since access improvements often increase the value of developable land, private entities have often been the initiator of cost-sharing arrangements.

The principal cost-sharing methods include private property owner contributions and institutionalized cost sharing (benefit assessments, tax increments, and impact fees). These are described below and illustrated in Table 4.

**Private property owner contributions:** Contributions cover the class of arrangements in which private property owners advance to the state or local highway agencies land for the right-of-way or cash against the cost of a new public facility. Variations include donations, exactions, negotiated contributions and developers' agreements. The major differences between them relate to the rationale and initiative for the contribution—whether required by the local government or offered voluntarily. Contributions are generally voluntary on the part of the property owners, made to advance the priority of a project by reducing its public cost, to mitigate impacts and enhance a private land development projects, or to provide special access to an existing or proposed facility.

**Institutionalized cost sharing:** Some states have established legal procedures to regularize systematic and simultaneous cost-sharing with multiple private parties whose properties are directly served (and benefited) by a transportation improvement.

Three methods are in use in the United States:

- Benefit assessment districts: Limited-purpose public authorities can be established within most states by local governments with the power to levy additional fees on property within their area to finance specific improvements. The level and structure of the assessment is expected to be commensurate with the benefits received. Revenues are collected on a one-off or (more typically) recurring basis, and are used either to fund bonds for highway construction, or to pay for operation and maintenance expenses;
- Tax increment financing districts: Within specifically defined benefiting areas, local government entities are permitted to divert regular ad valorem property or sales taxes to pay for all or part of specific transportation improvements. This form of taxation is created specifically for funding general obligation bonds without requiring a general referendum. The revenue available for investment is the increase in tax receipts over a pre-development base year level; it is placed in a special account to fund improvements or reimburse previous expenditures. Unlike impact fees, the tax increment is shared by all property owners in the district, and does not fall solely on new development. Unlike benefit assessment districts, there are no additional taxes;
- Traffic impact fees: Fees can be charged to property developers on the basis of the specific attributes of their developments, such as the amount of traffic generated. The fees are collected on a one-off basis by the sponsoring local government. Fees and assessments can be combined with conventional federal and state aid and/or with tolls to in

**TABLE 4: KEY CHARACTERISTICS OF PUBLIC/PRIVATE FINANCING TECHNIQUES**

| *Characteristics* | *Techniques* | | | | |
|---|---|---|---|---|---|
| | *Negotiated Exactions* | *Traffic Impact Fees* | *Benefit Assessment Districts* | *Property Tax Increments* | *Transportation Enterprises* |
| Improvement | Local | Area-Wide | Area-Wide | Area-wide | Project-oriented |
| Private Participant | Individual Property Owners | New Development | New Development | New Existing Development | Varies |
| Public Sector Authority | Zoning Subdivision | Police Power | Police Power | Redevelopment | Varies |
| Agency Administrative Burden | Low | High | High | Moderate | Low |
| Management Requirements | None | High | High | Moderate | None |
| Perceived Equity | Variable | Good | Problem | Potential Problem | Varies |
| Privatization | Low | Cost-sharing | Cost-sharing | Limited Cost Sharing | High/Variable |
| Voter Approval | Single Transaction | Ordinance only | Property majority | Area-wide | Private Initiative |
| Property Development Dependency | Moderate/Specific | High/General | High/General | Moderate/General | Moderate/Specific |
| Time Span | One-off | Continuing | Limited to Program | Limited to Program | Project-oriented |
| Revenue Predictability | Complete | Low | Low | Low | Varies |
| Ability to Support Bonds | None | Moderate | Moderate | Moderate | Moderate |
| Contributions | Cash, Land, Services | Fee | Assessment | Tax Increment | Varies |
| Revenue Potential | Low | High | High | Moderate | High |

Sources: *Understanding the Highway Finance Revolution*, AASHTO, 1987; *Public-Private Involvement And Toll Road Financing in the Provision of Highways*, TRR 1107, TRB, 1987; *Public and Private Partnerships for Financing Highway Improvements*, NCHRP Report 307, TRB, 1988, author interviews.

crease project feasibility.

The special fees, exactions and assessments used to defray the cost of new highway access are viewed in rapidly growing communities as a means of protecting existing residents and businesses from the financial burdens of accommodating new development, while simultaneously expanding the tax base. These financing methods often play an important role in metropolitan land use control and growth management policies. However, they introduce important public policy concerns regarding the introduction of bias into public priorities, and the shifting of risks and tax burdens. Equity among users is an important consideration. Some see cost sharing, particularly of the negotiated exaction type, as extortion. Others view such approaches as a legitimate and equitable means of recovering specific costs.

Combining property owner contributions, impact fees, tolls and federal and state tax revenues introduces a potential palette of revenues that can be tailored to fit a wide variety of circumstances. The various revenue sources can also be introduced in a strategic sequence: area-wide taxes followed by corridor impact fees followed by tolls. This generates the necessary front-end finance that can minimize the costs of toll-backed debt financing.

## Special Purpose Governmental Entities

As described above, there is now a rich palate of financing techniques from both conventional sources and from newer methods that tap both direct and indirect beneficiaries of road improvements. These new combinations of revenues require new institutional relationships in order to capture a degree of control or incentive for land-owners, developers or investors expected to participate financially. In response, state governments have created a range of semi-independent, quasi-governmental, special-purpose entities with various degrees of responsibility for project development and finance.

The common characteristic of these entities is a selective reduction of traditional state transportation agency roles in investment and implementation and an introduction of private sector entities into such roles. The access to the mix of revenue sources is made possible either by their local government make-up, strong private sector support, or both. Two major forms have emerged:

- limited function transportation development corporations and road districts with legal responsibility for specific functions such as right-of-way assembly, planning and design;
- independent transportation authorities generally comprising several local governments with or without direct state participation, with total project development responsibilities.

**Transportation development corporations:** Transportation development corporations (TDCs) are non-profit corporate entities chartered by states, acting for state or local governments for the purpose of developing major highway improvements. Such corporations have been formed at the initiative of private parties wishing to advance a project, and carry out the planning, engineering and right-of-way acquisition work at their own expense. The project is normally built by the state using state highway funds, but at a reduced public cost due to the donated rights-of-way and technical services However TDCs are also empowered to carry out construction work themselves using bond financing backed by a state agreement to buy back the facility after it has been completed.

**Road districts:** Road Utility Districts (RUDs) and County Road Districts

(CRDs) are also semi-autonomous legal creations of state governments, founded on the basis of private initiative. The Boards of Directors often consists of both public officials and private property interests. They are designed to expedite improvements in the county-level arterial and feeder road system. In addition to the normal powers of TDCs, they can raise funds through property assessments within specified districts.

**Independent Highway Authorities:** Independent highway authorities resemble conventional public toll authorities, but are applicable to projects where the start-up traffic is insufficient to fund the project by tolls alone. They are empowered to raise funds by a wide variety of financing techniques. Independent highway authorities are created by state enabling legislation, but unlike TDCs there is limited state involvement in project development or financing beyond the enabling legislation, although the state retains technical oversight of the project.

In one example of such an Authority and its capabilities, the California legislature authorized Orange County and several of the cities within the county to set up a public toll authority called the Transportation Corridor Agencies (TCAs). They are proceeding with three projects within the county. One of these facilities, called the San Joaquin Hills corridor, currently under construction, represents a $1.2 billion financing combining a $1 billion issue of toll road revenue bonds, about $111 million in State funds, $97 million in investment earnings, $39 million in subordinated debt by the private construction contractor, and $31 million in private development impact fees.

## Privatization

During the 1980s, in an attempt to supplement both conventional federal and state funds for road development, and also to tap private sector technology and developer initiative, several states experimented with public/private partnerships. These legal arrangements are based on a reallocation of the conventional roles in the development of new toll roads between the public agency sponsor and a private partner willing and able to finance, build and operate (and possibly own outright) the road.

In 1988-89, California and Virginia initiated the modern era's toll-financed concession programs—public-use toll roads conceived, financed and developed by private for-profit enterprises with state roles confined to right-of-way condemnation, limited protection from liability and competition and regulation of toll rates and profits. These projects have combined road developer's equity, adjacent property owners' land contributions and several forms of toll-backed taxable debt for their financing.

The principal feature of these privatization projects has been the complete separation, financially, from public financial support or guarantees and the introduction of bonded indebtedness free of the normal limitations of public sector credit limitations. These financings are project-based and non-recourse and, under current state and federal laws, returns are taxable. Financial programs generally involve a mix of equity and various layers of junior and senior debt marketed to the higher risk/high return investment community.

Private toll road projects in the U.S. have been structured as spatially and temporally limited concessions with specific roles for both state government and private franchisee identified. Concession holders are special purpose private profit-making entities that are mixes of investor, design, construction, management and technology companies.

Because private toll roads are still public use projects, the state or local government regulates safety, policing, design standards, and other government procurement and labor practices. However, economic regulatory approaches vary: the "Virginia model" treats the concession as a regulated private utility with the toll rate charged by the owner subject to state review; the "California model" concession is a finance, design, build and operate franchise in which returns on investment are regulated with toll rates left to the franchisee as a market matter.

Three basic types of public-private agreement have been used in the U.S. Under the build-own-operate (BOO) scenario, a private consortium agrees to finance, build, own, operate and collect toll revenues for access to the facility for a limited period of time. The Dulles-Leesburg Toll Road Extension (the Dulles Greenway) under construction in Loudoun County, Virginia, is an example of such a facility. Privately owned and operated, all pre-construction development costs have been at the expense of the owner. The road is being financed through toll-backed debt, substantial private equity and modest state sub-debt support. All of the right-of-way is either donated or has been purchased by the project sponsor.

The other basic types of public-private partnership arrangement in the U.S. involves a build-operate-transfer (BOT) or build-transfer-operate (BTO) scenario, differing only by the timing of the government's financial responsibility. Under BTO, the private consortium leases the facility from the government, operates it, collects toll revenues sufficient to retire project debt and earn a reasonable return on investment, after which ownership rights are passed back to the government.

Technically, although the government usually owns the facility from the first day of operations, full financial responsibility remains with the private consortium. The BTO scenario may be preferred to the BOT model when some form of government ownership of the facility is advantageous, and to ostensibly limit tort liability for the private consortia. A government-owned project is covered under sovereign immunity laws for tort, and this will avoid exposing the private consortium to uninsurable risk during operations.

The final important benefit of BTO is that, subject to certain conditions, it helps the private consortium avoid paying local property taxes on the facility (normal corporate income taxes, of course, still apply).Under either type of arrangement, a private consortium qualified by the government agency submits a competitive proposal and, if chosen, the consortium is allowed to proceed with negotiations that lead to the signing of a concession or franchise agreement. The concession agreement authorizes the private consortium to plan, design, finance, build, and operate a toll road for a limited time period (usually 20 to 40 years). After this period, ownership of the facility is transferred to the sponsoring government free of charge (under the former or BOT scenario), or the transfer can occur right after the completion of construction (under the latter or BTO scenario). Four concessions let by California in 1990 conform to this latter model. One project, on State Route 91 (SR-91) in Orange County, is the first of four franchises negotiated with Caltrans under Assembly Bill 680 (AB 680) to go to construction.

Prior to ISTEA, only a few states had passed laws permitting private profit-making entities to develop and operate toll roads. By the time of the passage of ISTEA, several other states were developing legislation authorizing private development of public/private toll facilities: Missouri (1990), Puerto Rico (1990), Arizona (1991), Florida (1991), and Texas (1991).

Table 5 indicates project examples of the principal innovative financing methods discussed in this section.

## The New National Transportation Policy

In the early 1990s the biennial studies of the condition and performance of the nations highways carried out by the FHWA indicated that the annual public capital investment of $40 billion/year in highways is not sufficient to cope with the accruing physical preservation needs of the mature federal-aid network (much less the remaining portions of the public road network), while also responding to deteriorating system performance as demand grows. Analysis of investment

**TABLE 5: EXAMPLES OF INNOVATIVE FINANCING METHODS**

| Project | Location | State | Approximate Value ($ mil.) |
|---|---|---|---|
| **Contributions/Donations** | | | |
| 1. Proffer System | Fairfax county | Virginia | 10 |
| 2. Friendswood | Houston | Texas | 11 |
| 3. North Central Expressway | Dallas | Texas | 60 |
| 4. Irvine Center | Irvine | California | 1 p.a. |
| **Benefit Assessment Districts** | | | |
| 1. Pleasanton Hacienda Business Park | Pleasanton | California | 200 |
| 2. Fort Collins | Fort Collins | Colorado | 0.5 p.a. |
| 3. Joint SW Denver Improvement Association | Arapahoe county | Colorado | 21 |
| 4. San Diego (city) | San Diego | California | 3.5 |
| 5. Moon Township Transportation Authority | Moon Township | Pennsylvania | 1.1 |
| **Tax Increment Financing** | | | |
| 1. I-74 Economic Development Area | Davenport | Iowa | 1.7 p.a. |
| 2. Maryland Tax Increment Financing | Prince Georges County | Maryland | 8.0 p.a. |
| 3. Boon Avenue | Brooklyn Park | Maine | 9 |
| **Traffic Impact Fees** | | | |
| 1. Transportation Corridor Fees | Orange County | California | 20+ |
| 2. Traffic Impact Fees | Palm Beach County | Florida | 12 |
| 3. Pleasanton Impact Fee Ordinance | Pleasanton | California | 80 |
| 4. Service Cost Recovery System | Loveland | Colorado | 2.2 p.a. |
| **Transportation Enterprises** | | | |
| 1. County Road District | Denton County | Texas | 8 |
| 2. E-470 | Denver | Colorado | 160 |
| 3. Grand Parkway | Houston | Texas | 56 |
| 4. Mopac Expressway | Austin | Texas | 30 |
| 5. San Joaquin Hills Transportation Corridor | Orange County | California | 270 |
| **Public/Private Partnerships** | | | |
| 1. Dulles Toll Road Extension | Loudoun County | Virginia | n.a. |
| 2. SR 125 | San Diego | California | n.a. |
| 3. SR 91 | Orange County | California | 410 |

Sources: See Table 4.

requirements suggested that a 20-30% increase is called for.

But fuel tax increases at the federal and state level continue to be politically difficult (although many states have raised their fuel taxes in the last five years). At the state and local level, increased reliance on general funds continues to be especially unpopular as a general tax revolt has taken hold, and the issue of additional debt is constrained by outstanding commitments and weak urban finances. Toll roads—despite renewed interest—are simply not financable on a non-recourse basis in more than a few locations. The search for alternative forms of highway finance has therefore taken on increased significance.

In 1991, the U.S. Congress passed new laws, representing the first major reorientation of the national transportation program in over a generation. The new policies reflected a broad consensus view of key national priorities and the appropriate governmental and sectoral roles. ISTEA introduced important changes into the federal aid highway program regarding planning, programming, new technology and other important elements.

ISTEA expressed a recognition of the need for an increase in investment on the part of all levels of government and the potential of attracting investment capital from the private sector. It was based on the proposition that full utilization of available federal revenues, if accompanied by increased state, local and private investment, could result in national highway expenditure approaching the levels necessary to preserve the major elements of the federal highway system and respond to critical capacity requirements.

Principal features of ISTEA were the provisions which encourage states to seek new resources—both entrepreneurial and financial. These provisions focus on three important opportunities:

- Commingling of Tax and Toll Funding—ISTEA permits states to co-mingle their apportioned federal highway tax funds with toll-backed bond revenues (and their own tax funds), breaching a long-standing U.S. tradition prohibiting tolls on roads utilizing federal tax funds. As a result of these options, highway projects which may not be feasible toll projects—public or private—can be subsidized with a state's federal funds.
- Leveraging Federal Aid—The potential for innovative finance introduced by ISTEA has generated concepts and experiments designed to capitalize on the use of loans, subordination and longer payback period to enhance the financial viability of toll road projects by making them attractive to private investors. Programs designed to leverage federal and state funds through issuing credit-enhanced tax-exempt or taxable debt also received considerable attention in more financially aggressive states.
- Public/Private Partnerships—Special emphasizes within ISTEA was also given to encouraging public-private partnership for the construction of toll facilities, by permitting a state to extend a loan or grant of federal aid to a private or quasi- public project sponsor in arrangements designed to be attractive to private capital (including investors seeking attractive taxable returns), recognizing that reallocation of the traditional roles of government and private enterprises regarding road finance, development and operation might encourage such investment.

To use these new provisions in federal law, most states must pass special conforming legislation. Since these new features are optional programs with no special additional federal funds— while at the same time introducing unfamiliar concepts and new procedures—state response has been slow, with several states having introduced required enabling legislation only within the last several months. Meanwhile, another round of federal program reauthorization may broaden yet further the options. Key issues associated with these opportunities are discussed below.

**Commingling of tax and toll funds.** Given today's construction costs, right-of-way uncertainties and environmental challenges, and given the general reluctance to charge toll rates substantially higher than experienced on like facilities elsewhere, many potential toll roads today may not be able to be self-financed. The financial challenges associated with advancing pure privatization toll road projects—entirely supported by toll revenues—can be overcome only in the most promising circumstances. The dependence on a single, projected revenue stream creates sufficient uncertainty with regards to construction, market and revenue risk such that completely non-recourse (i.e., fully self-financed) start-up toll facilities are increasingly difficult— especially since the U.S. investment community has little prior experience with such projects. Access to other forms of cost-sharing, revenue and credit are not only important, they are indispensable if privatization is to be more than a rare opportunity.

Governments—and local property owners—have, in the past, often supported toll roads by subsidizing them, or providing free or reduced-cost land, or even contributing some of their capital construction costs by outright cash, grants or loans. The importance of such support—public or private—to enhance the feasibility of start-up toll highways is increasingly evident.

**ISTEA expressed a recognition of the need for an increase in investment on the part of all levels of government and the potential of attracting investment capital from the private sector.**

ISTEA did not change the basic federal-aid highway mechanism: reimbursing states for expenses they will make on eligible projects. Rather, ISTEA expanded the types of projects that are eligible, the types of expenses that are eligible for reimbursement, and the identity of the facility owners. ISTEA permits states to commingle their apportioned federal highway tax funds with toll-backed bond revenues (and their own tax funds), Highway projects which may not be feasible as stand-alone toll projects—public or private—can now be subsidized with a state's federal funds. ISTEA also broadens the applicability of federal aid to include several categories of activity: 80% federal share for new construction of toll bridges, tunnels or approaches, and for reconstruction and conversion of existing bridges and tunnels to toll facilities; and 50% federal share for toll highways under the same conditions. ISTEA permits the tolls to be continued after construction costs have been recovered, thus providing a source of revenues not only for operation and maintenance, but also to fund other projects.

The legislation also permits loans, or other forms of credit enhancement, utilizing a state's federal funds, to be provided through the state to the toll road projects. These loans can be subordinated to senior debt and may have an extended repayment period. The importance of a federal loan appearing as subordinated debt in a transportation project financing is that its presence signifies to private debt holders (holders of the senior debt issued) that they will get repaid first in the event of a default. Together these features improve the political acceptability of partnerships as well as the marketability of the senior debt.

## Leveraging Federal Aid

The relaxation of the rigid reimbursible matching capital grant structure of the federal aid highway program introduced by ISTEA opened the door to more flexible use of federal funds to attract additional investment—both public and private. Administrative interpretations of ISTEA have introduced opportunities for states to experiment with increased flexibility in the applications of federal-aid funds such as: the ability to use private funds and right-of-way donations as part of the required state/ local funding match; phasing federal aid to increase project initiation rates, the use of federal aid funds directly to seed state transportation revolving loan funds; tests of congestion pricing to both suppress demand and generate revenues.

FHWA's Innovative Financing Test and Evaluation Project attracted over sixty proposals were received from the States and many of these proposals are undergoing further negotiation and will be implemented during 1994 and 1995. It is likely that further legislative actions will be taken at both the State and Federal levels to bring more financing techniques such as loan guarantees, revolving loan funds, and other credit enhancement mechanisms into active use.

The creation of a state-level transportation revolving fund is a natural extension of the loan repayment provisions under the Experimental Program. Under this type of scheme, loan repayments from an original federal-to-state loan generated by toll revenues would be collected and reloaned again and again, with the revolving fund growing in size as interest and principal payments and state grants are accumulated. The subsequent loan proceeds could then be used to repay the bondholders, and are not subject to any further federal requirements.

Current Administration and Congressional initiatives suggest that, as part of a reorganization and downsizing of USDOT, new federal legislation may be introduced to institutionalize the development of state infrastructure banks which in turn will facilitate state revolving loan funds and other loan enhancement mechanisms through direct seeding with federal aid. The revolving loan fund concept may enlarge the inventory of feasible tax-exempt toll-backed financings via the federal commingling subsidy or credit enhancement. However, by maintaining project funding within the existing public finance context, and relying on the existing tax-exempt investment market, such an approach would miss the opportunity to tap the large pool of institutional funds seeking attractive taxable instruments. Furthermore, reliance on the tax-exempt "window" would isolate new toll road development from the entrepreneurial energies, technical expertise and financial creativity of the private development and finance community. Fully capitalizing on the state infrastructure bank concept would require tax code modifications may also be needed to eliminate disincentives to private investment in public infrastructure projects introduced as part of the 1986 tax reform. These include lifting the private content caps for projects which want to utilize private and/or pension fund financing, providing the same type of tax exemption available to other modes and modifying to the tough arbitrage rebate rules so that transportation agencies could responsibility invest bond proceeds. These changes could have a dramatic impact on the leverage of state infrastructure banks. Figures 1 illustrates the potential of the loan provisions of ISTEA.

In the longer term, the thrust toward reinventing government in both the current Administration and Congress may also reenergize interest in the potential of establishing a national infrastructure bank. This concept, developed by a bipartisan commission and proposed in legislation last year, would be a new government-sponsored enterprise, for the specific purpose of providing credit support to toll projects. This support would be in the form of direct loans, bond insurance and development risk insurance. The corporation would securitize such loans, pooling them and selling them on the securities market. Backers of the concept assert that no federal guarantees or lines of credit would be necessary. A key objective of this proposal is to attract the large pool institutional investment funds an to involve the private sector in a broader rage of roles.

While a national infrastructure bank poses important challenges regarding its federal budget implications and raises some complex tax issues, international experience suggests that a degree of direct federal government intervention could play an important role in institutionalizing private investment in transportation infrastructure. Compared with today's federal involvement in road finance via a large scale federal grant program for construction, indirect financial assistance is a more modest—if unfamiliar—role, and perhaps one more appropriate to the new federalism that seems to have gained increasing general support.

**Public/Private Partnerships.** Special emphasis within ISTEA was given to encouraging public-private partnerships for the construction of toll facilities, by permitting a state to extend a loan or grant of federal aid to a private or quasi-public project sponsor in arrangements designed to be attractive to private capital (including investors seeking attractive taxable returns), recognizing that reallocation of the traditional roles of government and private enterprises regarding road finance, development and operation might encourage such investment. The ability to mix federal aid and private investment provides a broadened range of funding options that can be tailored through loans and/or grant mixes to increase the feasibility of otherwise financial infeasible toll road projects.

The loan provision substantially increases the political acceptability of a state entering into a partnership arrangement with private investor entities. This provision of ISTEA will also improve the ability of states to leverage scarce state and federal-aid funds with additional equity from the development community. However, as discussed above, additional tax-oriented legislation may be necessary to create a context where private investor/developers have significant opportunities.

If the tax-related barriers to private involvement in projects which comingle federal aid or support can be overcome, more prominant roles for private entities may be developed, as exemplified in the pre-ISTEA concessions. In such a context, there will still be important preconditions to the establishment of public-private/partnerships eligible for

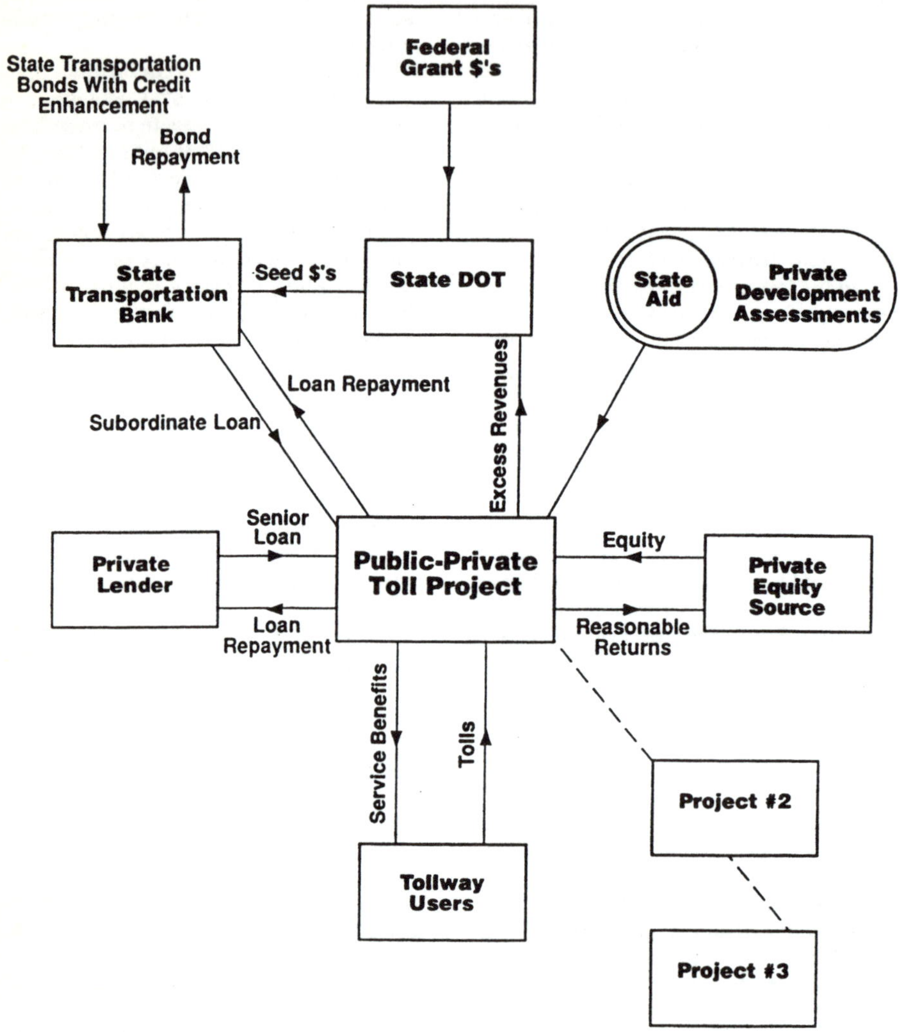


Source: Policy whitepaper "Toll Financing in Utah," Parsons Brinckerhoff.

**Figure 1. Leveraged loan plan.**

federal-aid funding to be established through a contractual agreement negotiated between the state and the private entity proposing to develop the facility. Through it, the state exercises its responsibilities of complying with all applicable statutory requirements under federal law, such as the environmental permitting and compliance process. This agreement would also include a description of the roles of the respective parties, would allocate responsibilities, and would contain details of the risk-sharing within the financial arrangements. ISTEA specifies only that the private developer/operator/sponsor is limited on his investment to a reasonable return on capital. All other terms of the contract are up to the state and the proposing parties and it may be expected that variations will evolve as states capitalize on their early experience.

To lure such up-front, at-risk capital investment, the private sector will expect a significant degree of control over project development and an adequate rate of return. Pre-ISTEA franchises provide instructive examples of the private sector perspective regarding allocation of roles, risks, and rewards that may be expected within partnerships that now also involve federal aid.

An example financial structure might include a mix of participants and features. A city could use general obligation bonds to partially fund right-of-way acquisition for a public-private toll road authority. The state department of transportation could maintain the system by utilizing state and/or local highway funds for this purpose. The road authority—public, private or mixed—could use a mixture of various kinds of debt and equity to construct the toll road supported by state loans of federal aid or other forms of federal aid based credit enhancement (such assistance is a reimbursable cost to the state). The state can thus use its remaining federal allocation, all of which would otherwise have been dedicated to constructing the project, on other projects (many of which are not suitable for tolling) and/or establish a revolving loan fund, seeded with state and federal aid and replenished from some part of project toll revenues. Federal dollars are thus used as a leverage to build more public projects per dollar appropriated. This blending of credits, credit support mechanisms, the sharing of the risks of project development and of operational risk, are increasingly trends in today's U.S. toll highway development.

Combined with conventional revenues and tolls, new forms of public/private cooperation will increase the resources available for highway improvements in rapidly growing areas, where the otherwise satisfactory conventional approaches are not sufficient.

## Conclusion: the New Array of Funding Models

Progress in implementing the flexibility provisions contained in ISTEA, i.e., the ability of states to mix federal, toll-generated and private funds, has been slow. It is an optional, not a mandatory program, and many sections and provisions are still unfamiliar to both state highway agencies and the private sector. However, some state highway agencies are beginning to use the provision of ISTEA. Conventional public toll authorities are also looking to use these provisions.

It is difficult to estimate the net contribution of new financing methods to total highway revenues so far. Certain forms of cost sharing are not recorded, while other forms are aggregated in state records. However national statistics, combined with estimates from a few states, suggest that the total value of non-conventional revenues including toll revenues, developer contributions, benefit assessments, impact fees and dedicated sales taxes, rights-of-way and other services may amount to between 6 and 8 percent of total receipts: $5-7 billion per year in the early 1990s.

Trends suggest that this proportion is increasing. States such as California, Florida, Texas, Colorado, New Jersey, Minnesota, Washington, Virginia, Pennsylvania, and Arizona, with a history of innovation and a need for increased revenues, are experimenting with a variety of approaches. California, for example, has estimated that over 30% of its highway revenues will come from unconventional sources by 1995.

Commingling and the leverage of revolving loan funds may have a substantial impact on the contribution of innovative finance to total highway funding. By way of example, Washington State is one of the first States to have passed conforming public-private venture legislation since the ISTEA passed in 1991. Taking advantage of the pre-ISTEA public private partnership experience in California, Virginia, and Arizona, Washington State designed legislation to solicit proposals from the private sector and select up to six transportation projects. The Washington State Transportation Commission approved six proposals to advance into negotiations representing over $2 billion of improvements to Washington's transportation system and include a park and ride capacity enhancement, two State corridor improvements using tolls, a congestion pricing program for the Puget Sound Region, and two enhancements using tolls for major bridges in the Puget Sound. Other states are following this example.

Over the last decade, accumulated state and municipal-level experience—combined with the new provisions of federal law (ISTEA)—have now generated a wide range of partnership structures as models for consideration in the U.S. There are five significantly different models, based on the institutional examples to date combined with the range of new funding options. Each model is a combination of an institutional arrangement and one or more funding sources, including conventional tax funding and conventional toll funding. The models are listed below, illustrating the potential combinations of revenue sources associated with each model owing to the sponsor jurisdiction (state vs. local government) or the involvement of the private sector.

Figure 2 indicates the combinations of revenue sources associated with the type of project sponsor. Each number indicates a discrete option. As can be seen. There are at least 10 distinct sub-options within the five basic modesl, all of which have project examples in the U.S. as illustrated in Table 5. These options are indicated with each of the five models with numbers that are keyed to the potential funding sources available to them:

1. Conventional public highway: public (state or local government) ownership with vehicle and fuel tax-based funding—justified through general system wide benefits utilized in:

- all states (1)
- almost all local government jurisdictions (4)

2. Conventional public toll highway: special-purpose public (state or local) authority ownership using government-guaranteed/tax exempt/toll-backed revenue bonds to construct and operate the facilities utilized in:

- some states (3)
- a few local jurisdictions (7)

3. Innovative public/beneficiary mix: public ownership with combinations of tax and/or toll-based funds plus cost-sharing with local property owners

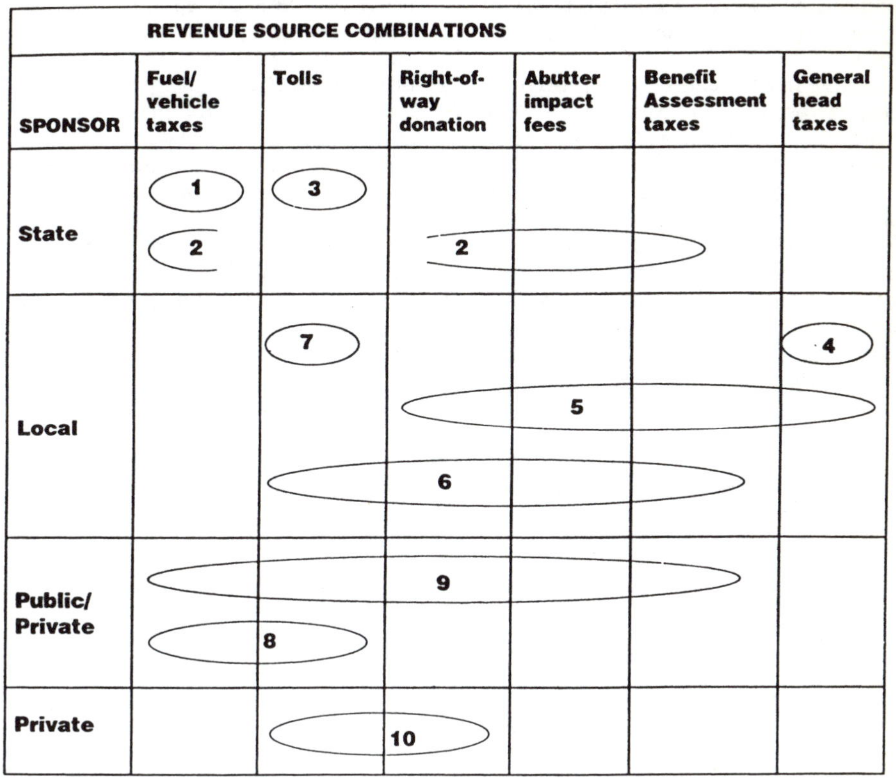


**Figure 2. Revenue source combination models.**

though contributions, tax-assessments or impact fees institutionalized in:

- transportation development corporations (2)
- road utility districts (5)
- local jurisdiction toll entity (6)

4. Public/private partnership: concession for private finance, development and operation with partial funding through toll-backed debt, but with public cost-participation through state or local government tax-based sharing costs of right of way, environmental studies and other pre-construction activities through:

- state-franchised public/private toll corporations (8)
- full public/private partnerships as permitted in ISTEA (9)

5. Privatization: private developer concession from state or local govern-

ment, financed entirely through toll-backed private equity and debt with or without voluntary local property owner contributions of right of way as a private toll concession (10).

ISTEA has introduced new provisions that are presumed to offer the degree of flexibility and incentives to induce additional state initiatives with new forms of funding and public/private partnerships. It is likely that the momentum of ISTEA will be further increased by federal program modifications providing additional incentives to states to capitalize on the potential of commingling and leveraging. More important, the accumulated state and municipal-level experience—combined with the new provisions of federal law—has now generated a wide range of revenue options, financing structures and partnership models for consideration. Within these models, the best financial technology must be tailored to project and market circumstances and the associated institutional and business mechanisms by which roles, risk and rewards are allocated must be structured. Capitalizing on this range of opportunities to develop new sources of funds and new forms of public/private collaboration presents exciting challenges to all the potential partners in the transportation sector.

**Acknowledgements**

Mr. Yuval Cohen, Chief Economist of Parsons Brinckerhoff made significant contributions to this paper.

## Endnotes

1. There is considerable on-going debate and research about both the equity of cost allocation to vehicle classes related to taxation and the degree to which vehicle users pay the full social cost of vehicle use, including not only road infrastructure and other public facilities but especially non-monetary costs such as environmental and delay externalities.

**Stephen C. Lockwood** is Vice President, Parsons Brinckerhoff, leading the firm's program development activities in the areas of congestion management, statewide multimodal planning and innovative public/private partnership approaches to mobility improvement in ITS. Before assuming his current position in 1993 he served for three years as the Senior Policy Official in the Federal Highway Administration and led FHWA's ISTEA task force. He previously served as the Executive Director of the Transportation Alternatives Group of the Transportation 2020 Consensus Program. As both an independent consultant/contractor and as an official of a major international engineering firm he worked on numerous transportation projects in the U.S. and abroad.

# [29]

# Public-Private Partnerships in the U.S. Prison System

ANNE LARASON SCHNEIDER
*Arizona State University*

*Prison policy is fundamentally different from virtually all other policy arenas in that prisons deliver punishment, rather than benefits, costs, or regulations. Within a prison, every aspect of an inmate's life is disciplined and subject to enhanced punishment at the discretion of guards and other personnel. Thus, special issues are raised when considering the appropriate role of the private sector in the management or ownership of prisons. Drawing from a theory of policy design, this study traces the emergence, demise, and reemergence of private involvement in prisons. Driven by hopes of creating prisons that could be self-sufficient, or even profitable, public officials periodically have turned to private entrepreneurs to build and manage these institutions. The study examines the claims made for and against private prisons including the "script" that purports to account for their reemergence in the 1990s and the empirical studies that have focused on costs and benefits of various types of public-private partnerships.*

**Public-private partnerships** in the operation of prisons have existed from the colonial period to contemporary times, although the extent of reliance on the private sector and the policy design models have varied somewhat. Drawing on ideas from policy design theory (Schneider & Ingram, 1997), this study will identify the characteristics of the partnerships, the reasons for private-sector involvement, the rationales and claims made by competing perspectives, and the consequences of private-sector involvement.[1]

Prison policy differs from other policy arenas in ways that have implications for the appropriate role of the private sector. First, prisons deliver punishment, whereas most policies deliver benefits or regulations. Other policies that impose costs—such as tax policy—may be unwanted or resented, but no other policy arena actually delivers punishment. Second, the target populations of prison policy are vastly different from most target populations—prisoners are not free, they do not make choices about most events in their daily life, they have virtually no political power, and they are socially constructed as deviant or violent by most of the population. Third, although many policy arenas offer some form of

**Author's Note:** *The author would like to acknowledge the valuable information provided by Terry Stewart, Director of the Arizona Department of Corrections. All points of view and interpretations of data, of course, are those of the author.*

AMERICAN BEHAVIORAL SCIENTIST, Vol. 43 No. 1, September 1999 192-208

political capital for elected officials, few, if any, offer such lucrative possibilities as prisons.[2] By inflicting harsh punishment upon criminals who are socially constructed as deviant, violent, and undeserving, elected officials can gain the accolades of the general public without incurring any noticeable political costs from those actually receiving the punishment. The monetary costs of mandatory long sentences are postponed to the future and spread across all taxpayers. Thus, it may be many years after legislation is passed before the full financial impact is felt. Finally, private-sector involvement in prison policy adds significant new target populations to the political arena by introducing businesses, corporations, and stockholders in publicly traded private prisons into the lobbying milieu. These groups have much to gain from a continued expansion of the number of prisoners available—that is, the prisoner "market."

Because of these differences, the politics of policy making may take on different characteristics, and the criteria by which policy should be evaluated must go beyond the usual reliance on effectiveness or efficiency to include the contributions of policy to justice, citizenship, and democratic institutions. It is one question to ask whether private involvement in prison management is more efficient on a per prisoner basis, but quite another question to ask whether the number of prisoners in society as a whole is efficient, or just, or appropriate in other ways for a democratic society.

## THE RISE AND DECLINE OF PUBLIC-PRIVATE PRISON PARTNERSHIPS

The three following basic types of partnerships have been apparent in the history of prisons in the United States: ownership of the facility in which the prisoners are kept; private use of prison labor and taking of profits from their labor; and private management of the facility, including the day-by-day supervision of prisoners.

Case studies of the emergence of prisons in the American states suggest that private involvement began through a convergence of interests among reformers, public officials, and local businesses (Shichor, 1995; Walker, 1980). Humanitarian reformers believed that prisons would be more humane than common forms of punishment in the American colonies—and later in the western frontier—which were death, branding, torture, or other physical punishment. The role of reformers was evident in the founding of the first prison in the Quaker colony of William Penn when the great law of 1682 banned the death penalty for everything except premeditated murder. This prison was a 5 feet by 7 feet cell. Later, the colony rented space from local businesses (Walker, 1980).

Public officials from the colonial period to the early 1900s believed that prisons could be self-supporting or even profitable for the state, and businesses were interested in sharing in those profits. Some states permitted a private individual or firm to build, manage, and handle the day-to-day operation of the prison itself, a system similar to the ones that have generated such intense debate in the 1980s and 1990s. Knepper (1990) reports that in 1825, Kentucky was not making enough money to support its growing prison population and was in desperate financial straits. A businessman, Joel Scott, paid the state $1,000 a year for the work of convicts in a 250-bed facility that he built and operated, with all profits kept for his own company.

In Louisiana (Walker, 1980), the state leased out the entire operation for 5 years and received $50,000 for the lease. Tennessee, in 1866, leased its Nashville prison to a furniture company for 43 cents per day per prisoner, reportedly because it was suffering from severe financial difficulties, and the number of prisoners had greatly expanded after the Civil War ended. California, in 1851, could not keep up with the increased crime attributed to the influx of settlers and was close to bankruptcy (Shichor, 1995), so the state leased its prison for 10 years to two local businessmen.

Oklahoma and Arizona not only viewed the prisons as potential profit-making entities for the state and for local businesses, but considered prisons to be an important part of the state's economic development program (Conley, 1980, 1981; Knepper, 1990). Oklahoma prisoners actually built McAlister Prison, which included an industrial factory and a 2,000-acre farm. Arizona's first territorial governor, Anson P. K. Safford, believed that a territorial prison would show that the territory was civilized and had a stable social environment sufficient to attract eastern businesses (Knepper, 1990). He was able to exploit the racial characteristics of prisoners—claiming that most of them were wild and dangerous Mexicans who preyed on travelers throughout the state, especially near the Mexican border. He also claimed that it would be the first profit-making state institution and that hard work was good for the health of prisoners (Knepper, 1990). Arizona eventually contracted with a private firm, the Arizona Canal Company, to take over the entire daytime operation of the prison. The prison provided all male convicts to the company for 10 years, for 70 cents per day, in the form of future water rights.

All of these forms of public-private partnerships eventually generated serious problems that produced opposition from business, labor, and humanitarian reformers. In some states, prisoners rioted or protested to such an extent that the partnerships were ended. For example, Tennessee ended its lease arrangement only a year after it began, apparently because the inmates burned the furniture factory. Subsequently, they built branch prisons and leased the prisoners to coal mining companies. In 1891 and 1892, free miners raided the prisons and set the prisoners free, reportedly because the competition was hurting them economically (Knepper, 1990). In Alabama, Knepper reported that opponents were worried that private leasing of prison labor would undermine the fundamental principle of restoring the prisoner's sense of obligation to a just society. They were worried that lessees would try to lengthen the sentences of good workers by giving bad reports about them.

Humanitarian reformers in Texas focused on what they viewed as excessive inmate deaths and injuries that were blamed on the private companies and the prisons they operated. California's contract system was accused of bid rigging, having a corrupt trustee system, selling of pardons, and other issues to the point that the Governor physically took control of San Quentin from the lessee—a former member of the legislature—and used the scandal for political advantage (Shichor, 1995). After a court had ruled that the takeover was illegal, the state had to buy the lease back from the private company for $275,000. In Oklahoma, businesses that did not have contracts joined with labor unions to oppose the prison industry system on the grounds of unfair competition (Conley, 1981).

New York passed legislation in 1842 that restricted the use of prison labor so much that it essentially ended public-private partnerships, and by the turn of the century, most other states had followed suit. Finally, in 1935, the social reform legislation initiated by the Roosevelt administration produced the Hawes-Cooper Act that authorized states to prohibit the entry of prison-made goods produced in other states. In 1936, the Walsh-Healy Act prohibited convict labor on government contracts that exceeded $10,000. In 1940, the Sumners-Ashurst Act made it a federal offense to transport prison-made goods across state borders, regardless of state laws. By the beginning of World War II, public-private partnerships in prisons were virtually nonexistent.

## THE REEMERGENCE OF PUBLIC-PRIVATE PARTNERSHIPS: PRIVATE PRISONS

Although prison industries have enjoyed a small resurgence, the most discussed form of public-private partnership today is the one popularly called private prisons, in which a private firm operates (and usually owns) a secure adult facility for prisoners and solicits contracts with local, state, or federal governments.[3]

These relationships are different and far more complex than those in the previously discussed historical period. The 19th century experiments with private involvement almost always involved local businesses. In the 1990s, the businesses are national and international corporations—some of which are publicly traded on one or another of the major stock exchanges. Although some of the private prisons have emerged as a result of contracts with the state in which they are located, the more common situation is that a private firm builds a prison in a state and simultaneously attempts to negotiate contracts with the home state—or any other state, county, or federal entity—for prisoners. The firm is usually paid on a per diem basis, either on the number of prisoners it houses for a particular entity or on the number of places it has reserved for that jurisdiction. In the past, the business paid the state for use of its prisoners; today, the state pays the business to manage the prisoners. Some state contracts, such as Arizona's, require that the Department of Corrections place a monitor on site to make critical decisions about disciplinary matters. Most of the state contracts require that private firms offer the service at 5% to 10% below what it would have cost the state. This, of course, creates complicated cost models involving a delicate balancing act between accounting principles and political realities. In Arizona and some other states, the state law actually includes a detailed description of what is to be counted or not counted in the costs of both private and public prisons (Prison Privatization Act, 1998). Arizona legislation requires that private prisons take out large insurance policies to reimburse state agencies that may have to intervene when an escape is in process or a riot occurs.

The growth of private prisons has been dramatic, as the number of places for prisoners in private facilities has increased from 1,345 (0.5% of all prisoners) in 1985 to 106,940 (8.5% of all prisoners) by December 1997 (Thomas, Bolinger, & Badalamenti, 1998). Thomas, Bolinger, and Badalamenti's *Private Adult Correctional Facility Census*, 10th edition (1997), listed 118 facilities located in 25 different states and Washington, DC; Puerto Rico; Australia; and the United Kingdom. The Private Prison Project at the University of Florida currently shows 162 facilities with 132,346 places (Thomas, 1999). Texas has 19 private prisons, the most of any state by far, as well as having the largest prison capacity and the highest number of actual prisoners held. Most of these prisoners, however, are not from Texas. In 1997, almost 6,000 prisoners from 14 different states were "outsourced" from their home state to a private prison located elsewhere. Most of the privately managed facilities are in the South (with 74, 41% of the total); this is followed by the West (with 32, 27% of the total). There are only 5 in the midwestern states, and only 1 of these has contracts that permit it to take prisoners from the state where it is located. There are only 4 in the Northeast, and none has contracts with its home state. The 5 facilities in the Northeast take local prisoners, federal prisoners, and out-of-state prisoners.

## SUBGOVERNMENT POLITICS AND THE GROWTH OF PRIVATE PRISONS

The Corrections Corporation of America (CCA) was the first corporation to enter the private prison business and currently is the largest one. In 1998, CCA officially became Prison Realty Corporation, and it, along with 10 other private prison businesses, is traded on a major stock exchange. The emergence of CCA is well worth describing here, for it is indeed a new model of public-private partnership in the prison business and it offers a fascinating case of subgovernment policy making.

CCA was well connected with political and financial leaders in Tennessee, and it had strong ties to experts in the prison business. One of the founders of Nashville-based CCA was Tom Beasley, a former chair of the Tennessee Republican party, and another was Nashville banker and financier, Doctor R. Crants. Another CCA founder, Don Hutton, was the former head of the American

Correctional Association—the association responsible for the accreditation standards of adult prisons (Shichor, 1995). Several high-ranking political officials in Tennessee owned CCA stock, including Honey Alexander (wife of the Governor, Lamar Alexander); the state insurance commissioner, John Neff; and the Speaker of the House of Representatives, Ned McWherter. He and Mrs. Alexander both divested themselves of CCA shares to avoid conflict of interest (Shichor, 1995; American Federation of State, County, and Municipal Employees [AFSCME], 1998).

In 1985, Tennessee reportedly faced a crisis in its criminal justice system (Folz & Scheb, 1989). The state was under a court order to reduce the number of prisoners from 7,700 to 7,019 within 3 months. The previous year, they had the highest rate of inmate-on-inmate violence of any state in the union. To complicate the situation further, Tennessee faced a significant budget shortfall and a rate of 450 new prison admissions for every 250 releases.

Realizing that Tennessee faced this kind of pressure, CCA offered to pay the state $100 million for a 99-year lease to operate the entire adult correctional system. CCA reportedly offered to invest $250 million in new facilities, and to receive $170 million per year to manage the system, which was approximately the size of the current state budget for prisons. According to the case study by Folz and Scheb (1989), Republican Governor Lamar Alexander was very interested, and it appeared that bipartisan support for privatization was substantial. A public opinion poll showed that 40% of the voters favored it, with 32% disapproving. Intense lobbying, however, scuttled the CCA proposal, with the most active opposition from the Tennessee State Employees Association; Tennessee Bar Association; Tennessee Trial Layers; American Civil Liberties Union; and AFSCME (AFSCME, 1998).

A much more modest bill was adopted during the 1986 session and signed into law, permitting private management of one new medium security facility. The restrictions written into this bill, however, were so unfavorable to business that there was only one firm bid on it (CCA declined). The first state contract in Tennessee was not granted until 1992 (to CCA), during the administration of Governor Ned McWherter, who was elected governor after Alexander. This contract was immediately challenged on conflict-of-interest grounds because another firm, U.S. Corrections Corporation, reportedly had submitted a lower bid (AFSCME, 1998).

CCA also contacted Texas officials in 1984 (Ethridge, 1990). Ethridge, in his doctoral dissertation, reports that Governor Mark White, a Democrat, viewed the private prison possibility as an opportunity to direct some business to a particular group of developers, and after CCA agreed to use those developers, White reportedly assisted CCA in gaining financial support from Merrill Lynch. Criticism about his close ties to the developers was deflected, Ethridge reports, by White's claim that private prisons were part of his economic development program for the state. CCA promised, among other things, a 20% savings in the costs of prison construction and operation. The legislation was passed with bipartisan support, according to Ethridge, although it was not passed until after White had left office and was succeeded by Bill Clements.

The policy-making context in Texas also was described as one of crisis and failed criminal justice policy (Ethridge, 1990). The total admissions to prison in Texas were twice the number of releases (Ethridge), the state had been found in contempt of court for not having obeyed previous orders to reduce overcrowding, Governor Clements reportedly faced a $231 million budget deficit for fiscal year 1986, and the estimates were that $400 million was needed to build enough prisons to meet the court mandate. The only person to speak against the legislation was the legislative coordinator for the Texas State Employee Union (Ethridge), who said that it was morally wrong and involved a fundamental conflict of interest because profit motives were not consistent with the best interests of prisons and the public. He was quoted as follows:

> Because prison contracts are structured on a per diem basis, the interests of the corporation will be to increase occupancy rates, to increase profits. . . . There is also a conflict of interest because corporate correctional officers will seek to maintain an ever increasing incarceration population and will lobby for tougher prison sentencing policies. (Ethridge, p. 82)

In 1987, Texas took the additional step of passing legislation that permitted local governments to contract for private facilities without having a vote of the people, which ordinarily would be required for any capital project. This may have contributed to the fact that Texas now has more private facilities (19) than any other state.

Privatization has also sparked old-fashioned partisan politics in some states. Arizona's Republican-controlled legislature passed legislation authorizing private prisons in 1985 and again in 1986, but both bills were vetoed by Democratic Governor Bruce Babbitt. Another bill was passed in 1987 and signed by Republic Governor, Evan Mecham, but Arizona's public employee union filed suit against the legislation on constitutional grounds and won. Republican-controlled legislatures again passed privatization legislation in 1988 that was vetoed by Democratic Governor, Rose Mofford, who had taken over as Governor after the impeachment of Evan Mecham. Privatization legislation finally succeeded in 1990, when it was approved mainly along party lines in the legislature and signed into law by Republican Governor Fife Symington. The partisan nature of private involvement in prisons is also documented by Gallagher and Edwards (1997), who found that states with Democratic governors and strong labor unions were more resistant to private prison industries.

The private prison subgovernment not only includes business leaders, state-elected officials, political party elites, and correctional experts, but also two influential social science researchers as well. The initial studies by both Logan and Thomas indicated that privatization had reduced the costs of prisons (Logan, 1990, 1996; Logan & McGriff, 1989; Thomas, 1997). Thomas is a member of

CCA's Prison Realty Corporation's board of directors, and his center at the University of Florida had been partially funded by the corporation (Thomas, 1999). Academics on the whole have been very cautious about the privatization of prisons, if not opposed to it (McDonald, 1990; Shichor, 1995; Sparks, 1994); thus, the emergence of research by well-respected academics that shows private prisons to be less expensive or higher quality has been important in legitimizing the arguments presented by businesses and policy makers.

## THE RHETORIC, CLAIMS, AND SCRIPT OF PRIVATE PRISONS

The most common script offered as an explanation for the growth of private prisons is that increasing crime rates, along with mandatory sentences and longer terms, have produced a rapid increase in prisoners. The increase in prisoners produced extensive overcrowding in secure adult facilities during the 1980s—a time when almost all states were faced with serious financial problems and budget deficits. These factors created a crisis in criminal justice policy, and public officials turned to the private sector to reduce the costs of prison operation.

As plausible as this scenario seems, it is simply inaccurate in some respects. There has been a virtual explosion in the number of persons sentenced to secure state and federal facilities, but it is very difficult to sustain an argument that the increase in prisoners has been the logical result of people committing more crimes than in the past. Data on the rate of imprisonment from 1925 to 1973 show that there was virtually no change in the rate of imprisonment, with the rate hovering around 100 prisoners per 100,000 people (Schneider, 1998). From 1973 to 1997, however, the rate increased to an all time high of 446 prisoners per 100,000 people (Bureau of Justice Statistics, 1998; Maguire & Pastore, 1994, 1996). If this were produced by an increase in crime, then one would expect the rate of crime commission to have increased in a similar way, but, except for drug crimes, this is not the case. In fact, victimization survey data on commission of violent crimes has been going down, not up, since 1973 when the first victimization survey was conducted (Maguire & Pastore, 1994). The uniform crime data on murder, which is the most serious and the most precise in terms of definition—shows an up-and-down pattern, certainly not a steady upward trend that could in any way account for the increase in prisoners (Bureau of Justice Statistics, 1998; Maguire & Pastore, 1995).

The increase in prisoners is accounted for by public policy changes, not changes in the propensity of people to inflict harm on others. The policy changes that produced the increase in incarceration and the overcrowding that results include longer sentences, mandatory sentences, three strikes you're out, no parole, no early release, and the huge increase in penalties for drug offenses. The point here is that turning to the private sector to build more prisons or to manage prisons so that the savings can be used to offset deficits, reduce overcrowding, or permit even more growth in incarceration is a policy choice made by elected public officials. There were other choices that could have been made. By the end of 1996, only 18 states had authorized contracts for private prisons within their state, and 32 had not. It must be emphasized that most states cannot prevent a private business from building a prison in the state and contracting with the federal government or with other states to take their prisoners. Unless a state passes legislation prohibiting the prison business, it is subject to finding one of these within its borders at some point in the future.

The policy choices available to states that are alternatives to privatization include reducing the scope of incarcerative sanctions, increasing the number of community-based alternatives, reducing the length of sentences, increasing the number of early release programs, or investing in prevention programs such as early childhood parenting and education.

The second part of the script is that the increase in prisoners produced overcrowding (which is supported by the evidence), and that overcrowding, combined with tight budgets, led public officials to turn to the private sector to build or manage prisons with the promise of a 5% to 20% savings. This savings, presumably, would permit the state to reduce its overcrowding. To examine this claim, I conducted an analysis in which the number of private prison contracts in the state is regressed on the three following possible explanatory variables: the extent of budget health from 1980 to 1986 (as measured by the difference between revenue one year and expenditures the next year, divided by expenditures; see Berry & Berry, 1992), the extent of overcrowding in the state and local prison systems, and the rate of incarceration (Schneider, 1998). The first two variables reflect the expectation that privatization was produced by the combination of an overcrowded prison system and the budget shortfalls characteristic of the 1980 to 1986 period. The third variable, rate of incarceration per 100,000, is a commonly used indicator for the punitiveness of the criminal justice system in the state.

The results show that budget health is statistically significant, but in the opposite direction of the prediction (beta = .36, $t = 2.64$, significance = .012). That is, states with larger budget shortfalls were less likely to turn to the private sector. Overcrowding had no significant relationship (beta = –.089, $t = -.66$). On the other hand, states with higher rates of incarceration were more likely to have private prison contracts (beta = .32, $t = 2.4$, significance = .02). The conclusion I draw is that increased privatization was driven by the same kinds of value orientations that produce more punitive criminal justice systems—a generalized sort of conservative, antigovernment, law and order ideology.

The purpose of this paper is not to offer a complete predictive model of the growth of private prisons, but only to examine the efficacy of the rationales that have been offered. Increases in the number of prisoners, overcrowding, and tight budgets were not causal factors that forced states to turn to private prison management. Instead, these trends required the states to confront the punitiveness of the criminal justice policies that had been produced in the decades after the 1960s. These trends established a context within which privatization could be promoted as a solution to a problem. In Kingdon's (1984) terms, it opened a window of opportunity in which a solution (privatization) found the problem that it could help solve.

In Schneider and Ingram's (1993, 1997) framework, privatization gave policy makers the opportunity to gain political capital through the appearance of doing something about the failed criminal justice system and simultaneously open up market opportunities for private business. It offered the attractive political opportunity to continue the negative social construction of prisoners and, at the same time, to develop a new positively constructed constituency of businesses, corporations, and stockholders who could profit from prisons. Support for private prisons also permitted officials to take advantage of the positive valance associated with downsizing government through privatization.

Policy makers in some states turned to privatization, others did not—at least not yet. The rationales used in states that adopted privatization could have been used with just as much credibility, if not more credibility, in states that resisted the privatization movement.

## ISSUES, COSTS, AND QUALITY OF PUBLIC-PRIVATE PARTNERSHIPS

The media coverage of private prisons has tended toward the dramatic, and it is usually unfavorable. More than one state has had the experience of a riot or escape from a private prison within its borders that houses persons who are from other states entirely. Local police and state highway patrol are expected to help quell the riot or find the escapees—at public expense. Ohio discovered that a private prison within its borders was taking prisoners classified as maximum security when they thought that the prison had agreed to only take minimum and medium security prisoners. However, these kinds of problems—riots, escapes, inmate-on-inmate violence—also occur in publicly managed prisons, and there have been far too few studies making reliable comparisons to draw the conclusion that private prisons are more subject to these sorts of problems than public prisons.

Most of the empirical research on private prisons emphasizes cost differences. Although fraught with methodological problems, the current studies are summarized in Table 1. For the most part, these studies show a slight advantage to the private prisons and illustrate (in Texas, at least) that a state may realize a reduction in per inmate cost, over time. It is interesting to note, however, that comparative data are available for only a handful of the private prisons. Following are some of the many methodological issues:

**TABLE 1: Summary of Cost Studies**

| State | Cost per Inmate per Day: Private | Cost per Inmate per Day: Public | Year (data) | Comment |
|---|---|---|---|---|
| Texas | $36.76 | $42.70 to $43.13 | 1990 | Study conducted by the Texas Sunset Advisory Commission compared four private prerelease minimum security prisons for males with hypothetical operation by the state (operational costs only) |
| | $33.95 to $33.61 | $39.79 to $38.64 | 1995 to 1996 | Texas Criminal Justice Policy Council report to the legislature in January 1997, for prisoners in the Texas Institutional Division (reported in Thomas, 1998) |
| | $27.91 | $28.96 | 1996 | Texas Criminal Justice Policy Council report to the legislature in January 1997, for prisoners in the Texas Jail Division (reported in Thomas, 1998) |
| California | $42.67 | $36.15 to $45.55 | 1991 to 1992 | Sechrest and Shichor (1993) compared three for-profit community correctional facilities, one operated by a private business, one by a local government, and one by a police department, both of the latter on a for-profit basis under contract from the state |
| Tennessee | $73.50 | $77.50 | 1985 to 1988 | Logan and McGriff (1989) compared two privately operated 350-bed facilities in Hamilton County, Tennessee (these cost figures assume full occupancy) |
| | $35.39 | $34.90 to $35.45 | 1993 to 1994 | Tennessee Select Oversight Committee on Corrections, 1995, studied one private, minimum-maximum security facility for men with two similar public facilities (U.S. GAO report considers this study to have the best methodology) |
| Washington (Tennessee data) | $33.61 | $35.82 to $35.28 | 1993 to 1994 | Washington's Department of Corrections Privatization Feasibility Study (Legislative Budget Committee for the State of Washington, 1996) used the same data from the Tennessee study of 1993 to 1994, but adjusted it as if the facilities were at full capacity |
| (Louisiana data) | $23.75 to $23.34 | $23.55 | 1995 to 1996 | Washington's Department of Corrections Privatization Feasibility Study (Legislative Budget Committee for the State of Washington, 1996) compared two private and one public mixed-custody facilities in Louisiana |
| Louisiana | | | | Archambeault and Deis (1996; quoted in Thomas, 1998) compared three large medium-maximum security prisons in Louisiana over 5 fiscal years, 1992 to 1996, and found cost savings of 11.7% for the 5-year totals |
| Arizona | $35.90 to $44.37 | $43.08 | 1995 to 1996 | Thomas's (1997) study of Arizona's costs produced an estimate of $44.37 for a private, 450-bed dual gender minimum security prison (Marana) when taking into account the state officials located at the site, but arrived at an adjusted cost of $35.90 after amortizing the costs of constructions, not including the taxes paid by the facility and other adjustments |

- How should indirect costs be allocated in the public and private facilities?
- Should the cost of the private and public facilities be based on the actual average daily population or on the number of places the facility is built to hold? What should be done if it is more than 100% full?
- Should the state costs associated specifically with privatization (e.g., having monitors on site) be counted as part of the cost of the private prison?
- Should in kind services provided by one public agency to another be added to the cost of the public prison (e.g., health or mental health programs)?
- Should services provided by the public sector to the private prison, such as capturing escapees or prosecuting inmates for violent acts on one another, be added to the private prison's costs?
- Should the taxes paid by private prisons be adjusted out, as Thomas (1997) has done in his cost studies, on the grounds that these are returned to the state?

In addition, the studies virtually never explain how or why the private prison manages to have lower costs even though they have the added responsibility of making a profit. There is a general perception that the reduced costs are at the expense of employee salaries. The methodologies also suffer because the comparisons, due to necessity, are of only one or two institutions and usually cover only 1 year of data. The natural variability in annual expenditures for any particular prison may be rather high from one year to the next, and differences as simple as the average age (experience) of employees may account for sizable cost differences between institutions.

Quality comparisons are even less common than cost analyses, although there have been some researchers who have made concerted efforts to develop a methodology with solid theoretical underpinnings for quality studies. Logan (1996) compared a New Mexico women's prison, operated under private contract with the prison that had previously housed New Mexico's women inmates, with a federal women's prison in West Virginia. He examined eight dimensions of service (security, safety, order, care, activity, justice, conditions, and management), each with six or eight separate indicators. The data included staff and inmate surveys as well as institutional records. He concluded that the private prison, overall, had a higher level of service quality, even though there were some interesting differences between staff and inmate assessments (with staff preferring the private prison and inmates preferring the public one).

Thomas' (1997) study of Arizona included several qualitative comparisons, but the fact that the private facility (Marana) housed a mixed gender population made comparisons risky. On most of the indicators, there were no differences, mainly because the time periods were so short that some of the more serious kinds of incidents (riots, inmate-on-inmate assaults or murders, staff abuse of prisoners) were not reported from any facility. The privately operated facility (Marana) had fewer jobs assigned per inmate than the medium security (level 2) public prisons (52 compared with 83), and was given lower ratings by the state's annual audits on most of the indicators. The private prison had an overall *good* rating, whereas all of the public facilities received an overall *excellent* rating. It is impossible to know whether these audit data reflect real differences in performance or system bias against private prisons.

Lanza-Kaduce, Parker, and Thomas (1999) conducted a comparative recidivism analysis for the Florida state legislature in which they compared the 12-month recidivism records of persons released from two privately operated facilities and those released from public facilities. The research design involved a sample matched-on-offense category (using 53 specific categories), race, number of prior incarcerations, and age. Multiple measures of recidivism were used, including rearrest, reconviction, and resentencing to incarceration as well as an overall indicator of any recidivism. There was a sample size of 198 in each group. With fewer rearrests (96 compared to 192), fewer reincarcerations (101 to 146), and fewer incidents of any form (172 to 237), the results clearly gave the edge to private facilities. There were similar differences in the severity of the recidivism offense. Finally, the study compared persons in the private facility who had completed their assigned programs and those who had not. The lower recidivism rates in the private prison, compared to the public prison, were due almost entirely to the fact that the private facility had more persons who completed their assigned rehabilitative programs. The noncompleters had recidivism rates almost identical to the persons from the public facilities—giving some powerful indication that successful completion of in-prison programs predicts the reduction of subsequent criminal activity.

A study of several Louisiana prisons (Archambeault & Deis, 1996) included a number of qualitative dimensions. The state-operated facilities were found to have higher quality in terms of preventing escapes, preventing sexual offenses, using urine testing, and having a wide scope of educational and job-related programs. The private facilities were found to have fewer critical incidents, a safer work environment for employees and prisoners, more effective discipline, and better access to programs for prisoners.

The design and methodologies of these studies indicate that on a localized, institutional basis, private prisons appear not to damage or harm the criminal justice system capacity of the state, and it may reduce costs without reducing service, or it may even improve service.

Another empirical question that needs analysis is whether public-private partnerships accentuate the pressure for an ever-increasing supply of prisoners, leading to longer sentences and more intrusive criminal justice practices. It would be naive to believe that private prison corporations are not involved in lobbying, and it would be equally naive to expect that they are only interested in capturing a larger market share from the public-sector prisons. In fact, possible conflicts between the two can be avoided if both work to ensure that there is a ready supply of prisoners to be housed. Prison as the punishment of choice has always been politically attractive, but it is limited due to its long-term cost. Even though the public may be easily swayed by the law and order rhetoric into believing that long prison terms are deserved by those who break the law, the public, nevertheless, does not like to spend money on people they perceive as undeserving, such as prisoners and would prefer to allocate those funds to education or other target populations. Hence, public-private partnerships that permit a large role for the private sector have the potential effect of bringing about a coalition between public and private providers of prisons with both advocating for increasing the scope of duration of prison sentences. Second, private management appears to cost less and therefore can be promoted by elected officials as a way of reducing the costs of the criminal justice system, even though the number of persons imprisoned stays the same or even increases.

The results of a regression analysis (see Schneider, 1998) indicate weak supports for these contentions, although the newness of private prisons and the complexities of the policy-making process are such that caution is in order. The results show that states with more contracts to private prison companies within their jurisdiction in 1996 had higher rates of incarceration per 100,000 in 1997 than states with fewer contracts (beta = .50, $t = 3.85$, significance = .000), even when budget health was controlled. This conclusion should be taken with caution, however, because the proportion of all prisoners who could be held in private facilities currently under contract or being built is still only about 8%. Furthermore, the time lag in the causal analysis is complicated. Decisions by a state to permit private prisons occur through several legislative sessions and may not result in any private prison contracts for several years after the authorization. The incarceration rate is the product of policy decisions over a long period of time, not simply during 1 year. It is possible that the rate of incarceration and the use of private contracts are both the product of an underlying conservative ideology, but it is also possible that political dynamics are being altered by the presence of private prisons in the state in such a way that the state can continue to increase the proportion of its population it is able and willing to place behind bars.

## CONCLUSIONS AND IMPLICATIONS

Public-private partnerships in prison operation is different from most other policy arenas because prisons deliver punishment, and there is no way to turn this into a technical administrative exercise devoid of discretion. When private owners or managers run a prison, they hire the guards and staff, and set the tone for how the prisoners are treated. There is enormous discretion exercised by the caseworkers who are in direct contact with prisoners. There are important differences between delivering service, benefits, treatment, or regulations to a target population and delivering confinement, orders, rules, discipline, and physical pain to a captive population that has no choice and no say in how they are treated.

In terms of the future of public-private partnerships in prisons, I believe this is a policy arena in which we would expect to find pendulum effects similar to those observed during historical experiments with private involvement. Extensive private involvement will give way to public delivery mechanisms that, in turn, will yield to private ones at some future time. A pendulum pattern in public and private delivery systems is expected because prisons are institutions that cannot be managed as effectively as expected by the media, political elites, or general public regardless of whether they are entirely under government control or whether they involve extensive privatization. Perhaps prisons will never be effective enough in producing public safety because public safety is more contingent on societal factors such as families, communities, schools, nonprofits, economic opportunities, and the absence of race and class discrimination. Institutions that cannot produce the level of performance expected and desired by the media, political leaders, and the public will move from the public sector toward partnerships with extensive private involvement, and then back toward the public sector, as the private gives up on them.

## NOTES

1. First, policy design theory emphasizes the substance of policy. What is being delivered to whom using what kinds of tools (incentives), with what rules, through which implementation structures, with what goals in mind (both symbolic and instrumental), with what rationales, and with what kinds of underlying assumptions. Second, policy design theory recognizes that policies emerge from a complex context involving the dynamic interplay between political power, social constructions (of events, people, facts), and the rationales that are used to justify various policy choices. Third, our theory of policy design posits the following four evaluative criteria for public policy: efficient problem solving, justice, citizenship, and democratic institutions. Policy design theory is intended to integrate interpretive (constructivist) perspectives with explanatory (positive) perspectives. Because this paper is intended mainly to analyze a particular kind of public-private partnership, the approach will reflect the theoretical underpinnings but not emphasize theory.

2. Political capital refers to the ability of elected officials to manipulate a policy arena to enhance their potential for reelection or election to higher office.

3. For a discussion of the reemergence of prison industries, see the lengthier version of this paper, Schneider, 1998.

## REFERENCES

American Federation of State, County, and Municipal Employees (1998). *Corrections corporation of America. Public employee, January, February* [On-line]. Available: http://www.afscme.org/afscme/press/pejf9809.html.

Archambeault, W. G., & Deis, D. R., Jr. (1996). *Private versus public prisons in Louisiana. Report to the National Institute of Justice* [On-line]. Available: http://www.uss.uconn.edu/~wwwsoci.

Berry, F. S., & Berry, W. D. (1992). Tax innovation in the states: Capitalizing on political opportunity. *American Journal of Political Science, 36*, 715-742.

Bureau of Justice Statistics. (1998). *Prisoners and prison capacity* [On-line]. Available: http://www.ojp.usdog.gov/bjs/pub.

Conley, J. A. (1980). Revising conceptions about the origin of prisons: The importance of economic considerations. *Social Science Quarterly, 62*, 249-257.

Conley, J. A. (1981). Prisons, production and profit: Reconsidering the importance of prison industries. *Journal of Social History, 53*, 259-275.

Ethridge, P. A. (1990). *An analysis of the policy process pertaining to the utilization of private prisons in Texas*. Unpublished doctoral dissertation, Sam Houston State University.

Folz, D. H., & Scheb, J. M. (1989). Prisons, profits, and politics: The Tennessee privatization. *Judicature, 73*, 98.

Gallagher, D., & Edwards, M. E. (1997). Prison industries and the private sector. *Atlantic Economic Journal, 25*, 91-98.

General Accounting Office (1997). *Private and public prisons: Studies comparing operational and/or quality of service* (U.S. GAO Letter Rep. GGD-96-158) [On-line]. Available: http://www.securitymanagement.com:80/library /000231.html.

Kingdon, J. (1984). *Agendas, alternatives and public policies*. Boston: Little, Brown.

Knepper, P. E. (1990). *Imprisonment and society in Arizona territory*. Unpublished doctoral dissertation, School of Justice Studies, Arizona State University.

Lanza-Kaduce, L., Parker, K. F., & Thomas, C. W. (1999). A comparative recidivism analysis of releases from private and public prisons. *Crime & Delinquency, 45*, 28-47.

Legislative Budget Committee for the State of Washington. (1996). *Department of Corrections privatization feasibility study*. Olympia, WA: Legislative Budget Committee.

Logan, C. H. (1990). *Private prisons: Pros and cons*. New York: Oxford University Press.

Logan, C. H. (1996). Well kept: Comparing quality of confinement in a public and a private prison. *National Institute of Justice Report* [On-line]. Available: http://www.uc.uconn.edu/~wwwsoci.

Logan, C. H., & McGriff, B. (1989, September/October). *Comparing costs of public and private prisons. A case study* (National Institute of Justice Research in Brief Rep. No. 216). Washington, DC: National Institute of Justice.

Maguire, K., & Pastore, A. L. (Eds.). (1994). *Sourcebook of criminal justice statistics*. Washington, DC: Bureau of Justice Statistics.

Maguire, K., & Pastore, A. L. (Eds.). (1996). *Sourcebook of criminal justice statistics*. Washington, DC: Bureau of Justice Statistics.

McDonald, D. C. (1990). The cost of operating public and private correctional facilities. In D. C. McDonald (Ed.), *Private prisons and the public interest* (pp. 86-106). New Brunswick, NJ: Rutgers University Press.

Prison Privatization Act, 128 Ariz. Rev. Stat. §§ 41-1609, 1681-1684, 1803. (1997).

Schneider, A. (1998, September). *Private prisons as public policy*. Paper presented at the American Political Science Association Annual Conference, Boston.

Schneider, A., & Ingram, H. (1993). Social constructions and target populations: Implications for politics and policy. *American Political Science Review, 87*, 334-347.

Schneider, A., & Ingram, H. (1997). *Policy design for democracy*. Lawrence: University Press of Kansas.

Sechrest, D., & Shichor, D. (1993). Corrections goes public (and private) in California. *Federal Probation, 57*, 3-8.

Shichor, D. (1995). *Punishment for profit: Private prisons/public concerns*. Thousand Oaks: Sage.

Sparks, R. (1994). Can prisons be legitimate? Penal politics, privatization, and the timeliness of an old idea. *British Journal of Criminology, 34*, 14-28.

Tennessee Select Oversight Committee on Corrections. (1995). *Comparative evaluation of privately-managed CCA prison and state-managed prototypical prisons*. Nashville: Tennessee Legislature.

Texas Sunset Advisory Commission. (1991). Information report on contracts for correctional facilities and services. In *Recommendations to the Governor of Texas and members of the seventy-second legislature* (chap. 4). Austin, TX: Author.

Thomas, C. W. (1997). *Comparing the cost and performance of public and private prisons in Arizona*. Phoenix, AZ: Arizona Department of Corrections.

Thomas, C. W. (1998). *Evaluating the potential public policy implication of correctional privatization by the state of Iowa*. Miami: University of Florida.

Thomas, C. W. (1999). *Private prison project* [On-line]. Available: http://web.crim.ufl.edu/pcp/census/.

Thomas, C. W., Bolinger, D., & Badalamenti, J. L. (1997). Private adult correctional facility census (11th ed.). *Private Corrections Project* [On-line]. Available: http://web.crim.ufl.edu/pcp/census/1997.

Thomas, C. W., Bolinger, D., & Badalamenti, J. L. (1998). Private adult correctional facility census (11th ed.). *Private Corrections Project* [On-line]. Available: http://web.crim.ufl.edu/pcp/census/1998.

Walker, S. (1980). *Popular justice: A history of American criminal justice.* New York: Oxford University Press.

[30]

# Private Capital in Water and Sanitation

DAVID HAARMEYER AND ASHOKA MODY

***Governments are drawing on private initiative and capital to address the deficiencies of water and sewage systems and the need for new facilities. What has their experience been and how can they encourage private investment?***

IN DEVELOPING countries, the water and sewage sector is generally financially and operationally weak. A World Bank study of municipal water projects in these countries found that revenues collected by utility companies cover only 35 percent of the cost of water. Unaccounted-for water (UFW)—the difference between net production of water and paid consumption—is in the range of 40–60 percent for many developing country utilities, compared with 10–20 percent for efficiently managed utilities. High rates of UFW reflect leakage as well as inability to bill and collect payments. Public water systems also tend to be overstaffed, often with 10 to 20 employees per 1,000 connections, compared with 2 to 3 employees per 1,000 connections required for efficient operations.

The disregard for commercial pricing and operational principles in the water sector has also prevented utilities from serving the poor. The rationale for continued subsidies has been undermined by findings that the poor often pay 10 times more for water than wealthier households because the poor do not have access to subsidized piped water and instead must rely on private vendors. The continued underpricing of water and wastewater services sends the wrong signals about the growing scarcity of water and the costs of meeting public health and environmental goals by investing in sewage collection and treatment.

The World Bank has estimated that developing countries' annual financial requirements for water supply and sanitation stand at $60 billion over the next decade. Yet the sector's fundamental problem arises less from the shortage of financial capital than from the lack of accountability in managing financial and operational resources. Water enterprises generally face weak internal (organizational) and external (regulatory) incentives to perform. The great challenge governments face is to improve these incentives.

Private capital and initiative can help accomplish operational efficiency and investment objectives if two stringent requirements are met: (1) projects must generate revenues that cover operating costs and debt-service payments, and earn a competitive rate of return on equity, and (2) risks that are internal (for example, construction and operation) and external (for example, regulatory and foreign exchange) to a project must be identified and clearly allocated to the parties that are in the best position to mitigate them. With their own capital at risk, lenders and investors have strong financial incentives to ensure that a project is built on time and within budget, and is operationally efficient. Uncovered political and regulatory risks require government attention—in particular, efforts to create and maintain a stable and predictable contractual environment—if projects are to attract private capital.

## Is the water sector different?

Like other infrastructure sectors, water and sanitation is characterized by large, sunk investments with long payback periods. But in contrast with the telecommunications and power sectors, there is little or no scope for introducing direct competition in any of the main operational segments—treatment, transmission, or distribution. The sunk investments and natural monopoly characteristics make the water and sanitation sector vulnerable to political expropriation and contracting problems. Also, the mismatch between domestic-currency revenue and international borrowing can create serious foreign exchange risks. Water and sanitation assets have additional institutional and economic features that differentiate them from assets in other infrastructure sectors and pose obstacles to achieving economic feasibility and proper risk allocation. These include the following:

• Increasing demand for public health services and a cleaner environment imply

**David Haarmeyer,**
*a US national, is a Consultant to the World Bank's Resource Mobilization and Cofinancing Vice Presidency.*

**Ashoka Mody,**
*an Indian national, is a Principal Financial Economist in the World Bank's Resource Mobilization and Cofinancing Vice Presidency.*

the need for establishing new regulatory structures, increasing investments, and raising prices.

• A highly fragmented industry structure results in the establishment of many small facilities, which often are under the control of financially inexperienced and uncreditworthy local government entities.

• The value of existing underground assets is often uncertain; consequently, workable and credible renegotiation procedures for investment plans and tariffs are critically important.

Largely as a result of these factors, contract and regulatory challenges have been widespread, and there have been fewer private projects in the water and sanitation sector than in the power or telecommunications sectors (see chart).

**Private infrastructure projects, by sector**

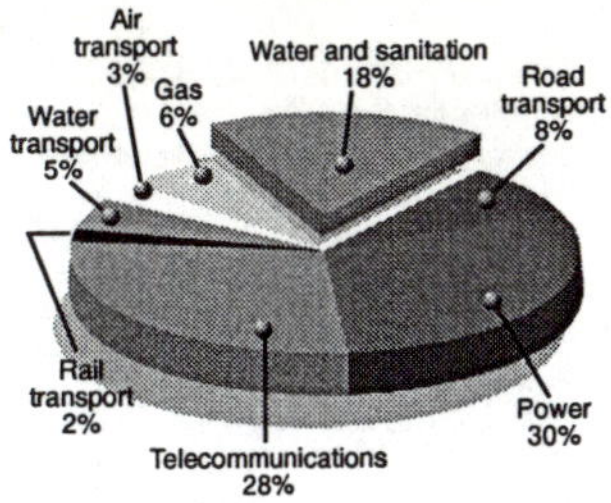


Source: World Bank, Private Infrastructure Project database.

## A variety of approaches

There is no one correct model for privatizing water and sanitation services, and there has been considerable diversity among countries' practices (Table 1). A private sponsor may take over an entire utility system (including the production, transmission, and distribution of the service). Alternatively, the utility's various segments can be split up (unbundled), with, for example, bulk water supply and water and wastewater treatment separated from the distribution to retail consumers.

Privatization of the sector has been limited in some countries, such as Chile—which has been in the vanguard of privatization in other sectors—and the United States, where all other utility services are, for the most part, privately provided. In contrast, certain African countries—Côte d'Ivoire and Guinea, for example—have long traditions of private participation in water and sanitation. Recently, Argentina and Malaysia have been at the forefront of developing countries in privatizing water services; in the developed world, the United Kingdom has led the way.

In some countries—Australia, Chile, and Thailand—governments have used corporatization strategies to transform water and sanitation systems into financially independent enterprises that operate along commercial lines. Especially in Chile, corporatization has been combined with short-term *service contracts* with private service providers—such contracts can be used to delegate responsibility to the private sector for providing a narrow service (for example, meter installation). Broader responsibility for the operations and maintenance (O&M) of a treatment facility or an entire water or sanitation system may be transferred to a private company with a fixed-fee *O&M contract*. With a *lease contract*, a private company is delegated responsibility for operations and tariff collection, but not capital financing.

Management and lease contracts have one major shortcoming: they do not assign full commercial risks to the operator—in particular, private capital investments are not at risk.

Long-term arrangements—build-own-operate (BOO) or build-operate-transfer (BOT) contracts for specific water supply/treatment projects (see box) and *full-utility concessions*—bring not only private management but also private investment. Projects under BOO/BOT contracts sell specific services to a municipal utility. In contrast, all facets of the system, especially distribution to consumers, become the private operator's responsibility under a full-utility concession. Assigning all the commercial risk to the private sector heightens performance incentives—but a predictable contractual environment is required to successfully attract private capital.

Table 1
**Allocation of responsibilities in alternative approaches**

| | Management contract | Lease contract | BOT/BOO[1] concession | Full-utility concession | Asset sale |
|---|---|---|---|---|---|
| | **Responsibilities allocated to** | | | | |
| Ownership | Public | Public | Public | Public | Private |
| Investment | Public | Public | Private | Private | Private |
| Operation | Private | Private | Private | Private | Private |
| Tariff collection | Public/private | Private | Public | Private | Private |
| | **Recent cases** | | | | |
| | Puerto Rico<br>Mexico City<br>Trinidad and Tobago<br>Antalya, Turkey | Guinea<br>Gdansk, Poland<br>North Bohemia, Czech Republic | Johor, Malaysia<br>Sydney, Australia<br>Izmit, Turkey<br>Chihuahua, Mexico | Buenos Aires, Argentina<br>Malaysia<br>Limeria, Brazil<br>Côte d'Ivoire<br>Macao | England and Wales |

Source: David Haarmeyer and Ashoka Mody, "Private Capital in Water and Sanitation," World Bank Discussion Paper, forthcoming.

[1] The abbreviation BOT denotes build-operate-transfer; BOO denotes build-own-operate.

## Case studies

Several examples illustrate how these alternative approaches work in practice, indicating both the potential for success and the nature of problems they encounter.

*Guinea*, a West African nation with a low per capita income, has achieved solid improvements in its water systems under a lease contract with a private operator. A subsidy arrangement was used to ease the transition to higher tariffs. Recently, however, coordination problems with the government have resulted from lack of clarity in the allocation of commercial risks. The high tariffs have also resulted in serious nonpayment problems.

*Mexico City* provides an example of an incremental approach. The government awarded 10-year management contracts for each quadrant of the city to four separate private companies. In three phases, the contractors are responsible for undertaking a census of the users and installing meters, billing and collecting tariffs, and rehabilitating the system. They are paid fixed fees by the government. Once the system is financially and operationally in order, the government is expected to award concessions. The devaluation of the peso in December 1994 caused serious financial strain—since operator fees and equipment purchases were denominated in foreign currencies—and set the program back.

A few countries have taken the bigger step of awarding concessions for operating an entire utility system. In *Argentina*, the city of *Buenos Aires* delegated the management and investment responsibility for its water and sanitation systems to a private consortium.

Under the terms of the 30-year concession, the consortium will invest $4 billion in upgrading, rehabilitating, and extending the systems. In three years, the private operator has brought dramatic operational and financial improvements through reduced UFW and higher bill-collection rates. This successful outcome can be traced to the significant steps the Argentine government took to ensure that the concession would be financially viable: raising tariffs prior to privatization, assuming the state water companies' liabilities, financing a voluntary retirement program, providing a guarantee that the concession company could cut off service to consumers for nonpayment, and creating an independent regulatory authority to prevent politicization of the concession. Soon after the award of the concession, however, tariffs had to be raised ahead of schedule because the government agreed with the operator's view that the physical state of the systems was worse than anticipated.

In *Malaysia*, the government signed a novel and ambitious 28-year concession with a private consortium to upgrade, rehabilitate, and extend the entire country's sewerage system. Although the estimated $2.8 billion contract was awarded in 1993, progress has been slow, primarily because of significant public and commercial backlash from tariff collection and tariff increases. Malaysia's experience points to the unique risk allocation issues raised by private provision of retail sanitation services in instances where these services have never been centrally provided before, the legal right to cut off service for nonpayment is absent, and sewerage and water services are billed separately.

A step beyond concessions is the full privatization of utilities' assets, which brings with it both the benefits provided by the assumption of full commercial risk and the discipline exerted by capital markets. The $5 billion public share offering of 10 regional water authorities in *England and Wales* in 1989 is the most prominent example of this approach. The British government's decision to sell these assets was influenced by a number of factors, including the $40 billion investment program the water authorities needed to undertake to meet the EU's environmental standards; the confidence in the new independent regulatory structure, and the existence of highly developed local capital markets. While successful in many respects, the privatization in England and Wales has been criticized for leading to rapid and substantial increases in tariffs and an absence of metering. More gradual privatizations are going on elsewhere—in *Thailand*, the East Water Company is expected to be listed on the Bangkok stock exchange during 1997.

## BOT/BOO projects: A step forward or a diversion?

Build-own-transfer (BOT) or build-own-operate (BOO) contracts shift the responsibility for financing, building, and operating discrete facilities, such as water or wastewater treatment plants, from the government to the private sector. These contracts are particularly attractive for countries with an urgent need to treat water or sewage but little capital to finance projects. Australia, Malaysia, Mexico, and, recently, China and Thailand have adopted this approach.

From the perspective of government officials, BOT/BOO contracts have two attractions: they are efficient mechanisms for rapidly organizing private capital and management to provide a narrow set of priority services, and they do so in a way that does not affect the overall utility system's organization and employees.

As this perspective suggests, the problem with BOT/BOO contracts is that they do not and cannot address a utility's fundamental operating deficiencies—leaks in the water distribution system, overstaffing, and poor tariff collection—and thus are not capable of transforming financially weak utilities into strong ones. Often because of these very same problems, many state-owned water utilities are not creditworthy, and consequently the implementation of BOT/BOO contracts requires a third party to provide credit support. Hence, by diverting attention from more fundamental problems, the use of BOT/BOO contracts may delay much-needed system-wide improvements.

## Financing private investment

Financing of BOT/BOO and full-utility concessions has followed the limited-recourse project finance model, which means that before providing debt finance, lenders appraise a project's ability to generate cash flow rather than the sponsor's balance sheet. The key mechanisms for attracting private capital are the underlying contracts and security agreements that identify a potentially secure revenue stream. The financial structure, sources of financing, and terms of lending for projects depend primarily on the risk and cash profiles of the project (Table 2).

***BOT/BOO projects.*** As for traditional independent power projects, the cash flows for BOT projects are contractually predetermined, often with government backing. Though construction risk exists, the absence of market risk—and, hence, the relative certainty of payment—means that BOTs/BOOs can be financially attractive and structured with more debt than full-utility concessions, whose cash flows may be less predictable. Also, construction risks can be mitigated when a discrete facility already generating cash flows is taken over for expansion by the private sector. This was the case of the 20-year BOT contract in *Johor, Malaysia* that covers responsibility for operating an existing treatment water plant and financing its expansion. As a result of the attractive cash flow profile of the project, the state government's strong commitment to privatization, and the availability of long-term local finance at reasonable rates, financing for the $284 million project was raised in record time—three months after the concession was signed.

***Full-utility concessions.*** Full-utility concessions can also be attractive to lenders, since existing revenue streams can be used immediately to service debt, thereby mitigating construction risk. In addition, over time, an established utility can benefit from both a steady flow of revenues from a diversified customer base and, if it integrates horizontally, from a diversified asset base. By creating a more robust balance sheet, these revenues may permit the utility to obtain financing internally as well as to use capital markets to sell long-term debt.

## Managing project risks

The considerable uncertainty regarding the asset value and the costs of rehabilitation and expansion in the water sector indicates that the regulatory risks faced by lenders and investors can be significant. Where the contractual and payment responsibility falls on financially weak municipal governments rather than on sovereign governments, political and regulatory risks are accentuated, and credit risks are created. Also, because water and sanitation projects rarely generate foreign

Table 2
**Cash flow and risk profiles of various approaches**

| | O&M [1] contract | Lease contract | BOT [1] concession | Full-utility concession | Asset sale |
|---|---|---|---|---|---|
| Time horizon | 2–5 years | 10 years | 10–20 years | 20–30 years | In perpetuity |
| Customer | Government | Retail customer | Government | Retail customer | Retail customer |
| Cash flow profile | Fixed-fee for service | Subject to market risk | Contracted payments due after construction | Subject to market risk | Subject to market risk |
| Construction risk | None | None | High | Low | Very low |
| Regulatory risk | None | Medium | Low | High | Very high |

Source: David Haarmeyer and Ashoka Mody, "Private Capital in Water and Sanitation," World Bank Discussion Paper, forthcoming.
[1] The abbreviation O&M denotes operation-and-maintenance; BOT denotes build-operate-transfer.

exchange, financing projects with foreign-currency-denominated debt exposes lenders to foreign exchange risk—the risk that exchange rate depreciation may prevent the timely repayment of hard currency debt. Consequently, finding long-term debt at reasonable interest rates can be especially difficult for water and sanitation projects.

Project risks have been managed or mitigated in different ways. First, to address sovereign risks, debt for privately financed water projects has tended to originate from commercial banks, export credit agencies (ECAs), and multilateral institutions (for example, the IFC was a source of direct loans and syndicated lending in Buenos Aires) owing to their ability to assess and mitigate these types of risks. Investors participating in capital markets are generally not able to do this, although established sewer and water projects should soon be able to tap capital markets. Second, lenders, as well as the government, gain comfort from the fact that equity is provided by experienced operators.

Finally, third-party and sovereign government credit support has been used to address municipal nonpayment risks. In *Chihuahua* and *Puerto Vallarta, Mexico*, credit enhancement provided by the federal development bank BANOBRAS was instrumental in the successful financing of two BOT wastewater treatment plants. Similarly, in the $800 million BOT project in *Izmit, Turkey*, the weak credit position of the city required the Turkish government to stand behind the local government's obligation to purchase water from the private bulk water producing company. And in Buenos Aires, the government of Argentina's guarantee to pay compensation if the concession should be terminated early was the chief form of security for lenders.

## Reducing risk

Sound due diligence, effective incentives, and credit enhancements are not sufficient. Ongoing mitigation of risk requires clear, predictable, and fair rules to secure long-term private capital at reasonable rates. For full-utility concessions and BOT/BOO contracts, the rules governing private participation are embedded in the concession agreement. This document acts as security for the significant amounts of capital and effort that project developers and lenders put at risk. Consequently, the credibility of this document—whether it can uphold the expectations of both parties—turns on the ability of a country's legal institutions to enforce contracts and arbitrate disputes fairly.

Three of the most important risks that concession agreements address are the timing and level of the investment program, how and when tariffs will be adjusted, and valuation of assets in case of early contract termination. Better information and smooth renegotiation and adjustment procedures are two important responses to these forms of uncertainty. Transparent and competitive bidding procedures have been shown to be efficient mechanisms for discovering information on appropriate performance targets, selecting qualified operators, and setting the right tariff levels.

The contractual and regulatory risk faced by private investors and operators increases as the level of involvement by private initiative and capital increases. Thus, the continuity and predictability of the contractual and regulatory framework is more critical for full-utility concessions than for BOTs (and for asset sales than for full-utility concessions). Countries with more developed administrative capacity, such as Argentina and the United Kingdom, have established independent regulatory authorities to achieve these important objectives. While the long-term solution is greater transparency and adequate adjudication mechanisms, in the near term, addressing these risks may require continued participation of multilateral and bilateral organizations through their assistance with the design of policy and regulation, and their provision of debt finance and partial risk guarantees.

## Conclusion

Successfully attracting and securing long-term private capital in developing countries' water and sanitation sectors depends on the simultaneous development of a number of institutions, including creditworthy local governments, independent regulatory agencies, and deeper and broader local capital markets. Nevertheless, depending on the political and economic realities facing a given water or sewage system, a variety of approaches are available to help it become an operationally efficient and financially self-sustaining commercial enterprise.

A few broad conclusions can be drawn from the limited but growing number of projects that have been structured with private capital:

- government political and financial commitment are essential;
- a contractual and regulatory structure that minimizes uncertainty and provides flexibility in renegotiation and operational autonomy is required;
- transparent competitive tendering is an important tool with which to generate information on asset values, tariff levels, and qualified operators;
- full-utility concessions and asset sales provide the broadest scope for operational and financial improvements; and
- where concessions and asset sales are not possible, utilities can be corporatized or operations and management contracts awarded to improve services and revenue streams in preparation for privatization.

F&D

*This article is derived from the authors' forthcoming World Bank discussion paper, "Private Capital in Water and Sanitation."*

# Lessons from the French Experience in Public and Private Partnership

**Dr Anne Ribault, Indecon International Economic Consultants***

Attention should be given to contract incentives and incentives within contracts, if lessons are to be taken from the French experience in Public and Private Partnership (PPP). This is because in economic terms PPP contracts are characterised by the granting of a temporary monopoly to a firm with long-term and specific investments, asymmetries of information between the firm and the public body, cost and quality requirements that cannot be monitored and pre-and post-contracting opportunism. Such contracts have the potential to contribute significantly to the efficiency and timing of infrastructure and other public service developments in Ireland. However, a rigorous evaluation of the economic, legal and technical aspects is essential if the public sector is to get a fair deal.

## INTRODUCTION

France has a long tradition of PPP dating from the 16th Century. Its present form was developed at the end of the last century for the purpose of building and operating the French railway system. PPP is currently used for infrastructure (such as highways, stadiums) and local public services, such as refuse collection, water provision or urban transport. This long experience permits a great awareness of the advantages and disadvantages of this type of organisation and above all its potential pitfalls in terms of pre- and post-contracting opportunism.

In one of his public addresses in relation to PPP, the Minister for Finance, Charlie McCreevy, stated that Public Private Partnership "could provide real opportunity – for the public sector to deliver key public services more efficiently, effectively and economically – for the private sector to share the risks and rewards for providing such services". To gain a better understanding of the key issues, it is useful first to examine the rationale for PPP and to analyse PPP contracts in economic terms. Later, examples of pre-and

* The author wishes to thank colleagues at Indecon for their comments, in particular Paddy McNutt, William Holmes-Batt, Gregory Swinand and Alan W. Gray. The usual disclaimer applies.

post-contracting opportunistic behaviour within the French experience are provided in order to highlight a number of lessons for the Irish situation.

## ECONOMIC RATIONALE BEHIND PPP

The rationale behind PPP is much the same all over the world. A wide range of factors as follows underlie its development. In the first instance, there is an increasing need for infrastructure due to increased wealth, urbanisation and environmental constraints. Secondly, public funds may be scarce and their opportunity cost can be expensive, whereas the PPP approach allows private investment to either crowd-in or crowd-out public funds. In fact, government financial and non-financial contributions can provide private contractors with a return on their investment when the project would have never taken place in in the absence of government intervention. Thirdly, governments can be risk-averse in relation to project delays, cost overruns, quality failures, or simply, price increases. Fourthly, all government levels may not have the technical expertise to deal with project management and operation. Finally, there is a general perception that private firms may be more efficient than public bodies, even though this perception has recently been challenged in France. [1]

## THE FRENCH EXPERIENCE

In France, PPP contracts are performed under *Délégation de gestion* contracts, that is to say, the public body's duties are transfered to a third party under two types of contract: C*oncession* and *Affermage* contracts. *Concession* contracts can be compared to BOT (Buy-Operate-and-Transfer) or DBOT (Design-Build-Operate-and-Transfer) contracts. The contractor chosen at the end of the tender process finances, builds and delivers the project for a specified number of years as agreed. The contractor also has to bear the cost of maintaining the project. At the end of the contract, the project is transferred to the public body. *Affermage* contracts, by contrast, can cover design and building, or even operations only, but do not cover project financing. The investment is publicly financed and publicly owned so that maintenance has to be provided by the public body (it is often contracted-out to the operating firm). Such contracts are awarded through a public tendering process. For small projects, the bids are price-based; for larger projects, tendering is based on the project design and price.

Concession contracts first appeared in France in the 1870s when the railway network was developed. They were later used in the development of water provision networks

[1] Cours des Comptes, 1997

and street lighting facilities. In the 1930s, local authorities could not afford the high cost of construction or extension of local gas, electricity and water networks so they were financed by private operators who charged service fees to end-users. As infrastructure was further developed in the 1950s and 1960s, PPP contracts became increasingly common. The majority of French highways were built under such schemes, for instance. In the 1980s, decentralisation made contracting-out easier, but it was the lack of public funds and the increasing need for investment in relation to EU environmental regulations that underpinned the last phase of PPP expansion.

However, a critical attitude progressively developed in the 1990s. The assumption that PPP was necessarily cheaper than public-only provision diminished as prices increased during the period of the contracts. Now, contracts are more carefully negotiated and enforced; and renegotiations take place when they are thought to be unfair.

At present, PPP covers a wide range of service provision at a national or local level in France. Highways, tunnels, bridges (often associated with tolling) are the most well known forms of PPP, but almost all local public services can be subject to PPP. In fact, sewage disposal, refuse collection and treatment (in landfill or incinerators), cable, urban transport (such as bus network or metro), sport facilities, school canteens, funeral services (as they have to be publicly provided) and water provision can be organised under *Delegation de Gestion* contracts. Water provision is the local public service with the greatest PPP element. In 1995, 75% of the population was provided with water under PPP contracts, as shown in Table 1.

**TABLE 1 POPULATION WITH PRIVATELY PROVIDED WATER IN FRANCE**

| Year | % of total population |
|---|---|
| 1938 | 25 |
| 1956 | 37 |
| 1970 | 48 |
| 1983 | 57 |
| 1995 | 75 |

Source: Defeuilley (1996)

The number of PPP private operators is limited, however. In 1995, two firms, Lyonnaise des Eaux and Generale des Eaux (now Vivendi), controlled 62% of the water distribution market and 36 % of the sewage disposal market (an area where PPP is still relatively limited but is expected to expand as strict EU regulations have to be applied). Both

52

**TABLE 2: PPP ASSESSMENT IN FRANCE OF RELEVANCE TO IRELAND**

| | FINANCE | KNOW-HOW | POLITICS | COST AND PRICE |
|---|---|---|---|---|
| Advantages | Private finance allows more flexibility<br><br>No opportunity cost of public funds (not an issue in the French context) | Management provides incentive to make productivity gains, R&D, economies of scale and/or scope<br><br>Fewer technical risks when the operator designs and builds the facility (if concession contract) | Private finance of public investment in case of concession contracts<br><br>Revenues if public facilities are sold to a private investor<br><br>The government does not bear the political risk of project delays, quality failures, price increase | Supposed or real cost efficiency<br><br>Supposed or real experience in project evaluation and cost monitoring |
| Disadvantages | The direct cost of public finance is cheaper because governments can have a higher credit rating<br><br>Possible bankruptcy of the private firm | Personnel employment status may be modified<br><br>Lack of control over investment decision<br><br>Possible lack of incentive to control costs when subject to price escalating mechanism | Possible political costs in implementing a PPP contract (privatisation fears and change of employment status for employees)<br><br>Possible collusion or corruption in relation to the allocation of the contract | Not necessarily the cheapest form of production organisation<br><br>Low level of competition in the market and vertical integration<br><br>Higher taxes |

firms also control 75% of the urban central heating market, 60% of refuse treatment, 55% of cable operation, and 36% of the refuse collection market. They are known as *multi-utilities* as they are horizontally diversified. As a result of vertical integration and a high degree of concentration in the market, it is argued that competition is limited if not infringed in some cases. Some commentators believe that, in the case of the water supply industry, firms have tacitly divided the market on a geographical basis.

## EVALUATION OF THE FRENCH EXPERIENCE

To evaluate the alternatives of public or private production of public services, four criteria are used as presented in Table 2. The first concerns access to funds and the cost of funds. The second criterion relates to technical and managerial know-how, that is to say, the ability to deliver the service efficiently in terms of quality and cost. The third evaluation criteria are the price and the cost of the provision of the public service. The last criterion concerns the political implications of contracting-out. More precisely, it is connected to two issues: the perception of the change of the public service organisation in terms of acceptance of the 'privatisation' process by the public/electorate; and the impact of the decision on the public budget, (local authorities' debt level is used to evaluate the quality of municipal management). PPP can also influence local authority balance sheets, as they can sell the project to the private firm.

A recent study by Kern and Vienne (1998) provides further information on the pros and cons of PPP. The authors surveyed 200 French local authority managers and local councillors. The former were asked why they chose not to contract-out local public services and to rank them on a scale from 1 to 5 (5 being the highest ranking). The results are summarised in Table 3 below.

**TABLE 3 EVALUATION OF PPP CONTRACTS FOR LOCAL PUBLIC SERVICES IN FRANCE**

| | |
|---|---|
| Technically, the local public service does not require any specific know-how | 50% |
| The monopoly position of the private operator would make things difficult | 49% |
| The public operation of the service is satisfying in terms of quality | 45% |
| One cannot really control the private operator | 43% |
| Contract length is too long | 41% |
| The decision is irreversible | 38% |
| Contracting-out is a form of privatisation | 36% |
| Public finance of the investment is cheaper | 34% |
| Users are reluctant or opposed to contracting out | 23% |

The PPP assessment indicates that local authorities have begun to recognise that there are some disadvantages inherent in contracting-out for infrastructure and public services. Some disadvantages are related to institutional features, such as taxation; others are connected to the nature of the contract relationship specified between the principal awarding the contract and the agent. The contractual relationship is analysed in economic terms in the following section.

54

## ECONOMIC ANALYSIS OF PPP CONTRACTS

The majority of PPP contracts award a monopoly franchise to a private firm following a public tender based on contract requirements and length. The economic analysis of PPP focuses on three areas, namely the competition issues arising from the awarding of such contracts, contract incompleteness and specific investment.

### *COMPETITION PROCUREMENT AND COMPETITION LAW*

In 1859, the English hygienist Chadwick advocated that "in absence of competition in the field ... competition for the field" would permit lower production costs. He suggested that services characterised by natural or institutional monopoly should be awarded to the lowest price firm believed to be able to provide the service throughout the contract life time. This argument constitutes the foundation of Demsetz's franchise theory (1968). According to this, the right to produce should be franchised and auctioned regularly so that the "rivalry of the market place disciplines more effectively than the regulatory processes of the commission". It is also stressed that the level of rent dissipation is inversely determined by the degree of collusion. This point was recently emphasised by the Irish Competition Authority in its Guidelines on the Detection and Prevention of Collusive Tendering on Public Sector Contracts when it stated: "Collusion will always result in higher prices. The cost of these higher prices must be borne by taxpayers and those who are affected because such behaviour diverts funds which could be used to provide other worthwhile services to the public".

### *INCOMPLETE PRINCIPAL AGENTS CONTRACTS*

PPP contracts typically involve long time-spans. It is noteworthy that the contract period may vary significantly from one project to another and from one country to another. Notably, in France, there is a perception that PPP contracts are shorter than in the UK. In relation to water provision and sewage, for example, the French government limits PPP to *affermage* contracts (there is no private financing) on the ground that such investments require over 30 years to recover the total cost involved. The local public service contract lengths recommended by the French Ministry of Internal Affairs are presented in Table 4.

PPP contracts are incomplete because contracting partners are not in a position to foresee all possible contingencies affecting the contracts; and even if they were able to do so, the cost of writing, negotiating, and enforcing such contracts would be too high in comparison to the potential benefits. Consequently, such contracts only take into account the likely contingencies needed to allocate the rights of the parties involved.

TABLE 4 RECOMMENDED LOCAL PUBLIC SERVICES LENGTH IN FRANCE

| Industry | Type of Contract | Contract Length |
|---|---|---|
| Water provision | Affermage | 12 years |
| Sewage | Affermage | 12 years |
| Refuse collection and treatment | Affermage | 5 years |
| | Concession | 10 years |
| Parking | Affermage | 6-15 yrs depending on specifications |
| | Concession | 6-24 yrs depending on specifications |

Long contract length and wide contract scope exacerbate information asymmetries. The private firm is responsible for project design, implementation and operation of the infrastructure or the service; the public body is able to monitor effectively the cost and quality requirements at each point of the production process. Information asymmetries distort contract enforcement procedures and the negotiating power of the parties allowing for contract opportunism.

***SPECIFIC INVESTMENT***

Under PPP, the material or immaterial investment supporting the service is tailored towards government needs over a number of years. These are also long-life investments and are difficult to relocate. Under such a contractual relationship, there is scope for opportunism once the parties have agreed to whatever contingencies they want to take into account and once they have decided upon the pay-off to each party. In fact, one party may try to take advantage of its contractual position to force the other to accept new contract terms (written or unwritten). Such hold-up situations may occur before the final contract is signed or even after.

## PRE- AND POST-CONTRACTING OPPORTUNISM

As stated, information asymmetries favour opportunism before and after the contract negotiation. Prior to the contract, they allow one party not to reveal its entire information set and to use its bargaining power to obtain an outcome in its favour. It also allows one party to exploit any loopholes to gain advantage over the other. In such situations, the other party may be forced to accept a worse situation in comparison to the terms agreed upon.[2] In other words, pre-contracting opportunism occurs when the contract is allocated and when the terms of the contract are negotiated. Post-contracting

[2] Milgrom and Roberts, 1992

opportunism takes place when the contract is performed and, finally, at the end of the contract.

***CONTRACT ALLOCATION***

At the tendering stage, public officials' investment decisions can be captured or even, in exceptional cases, driven by corruption. A number of examples of such behaviour are presented below.

- Investment capture takes various forms: from commercial advice, subsidiary involvement in preliminary evaluations and involvement of contract parties in decision processes. For example, a French utility gives its employees half a day off per week if they are members of a Municipal Council. Within this context, it has been suggested that some local authorities have de-nitrification water treatment plants when the level of nitrates in their water is far from being alarming.

- Bribery could also in selected cases influence local authorities in their choice of contracting firms. In France, some high-profile court cases in relation to PPP have resulted in prison sentences and civil penalties. However, such behaviour is now exceptional as tendering processes and political party funding are now carefully monitored.

***CONTRACT DESIGN***

Insufficient experience, lack of expertise and/or awareness of the potential pitfalls of PPP contracts weaken public bodies' bargaining position during negotiation. This phenomenon is not limited to small local authorities, as one might think. It also applies to major local authorities, national bodies and consortia financing projects. The financial troubles of the Channel Tunnel provide a good example of how poor evaluation and allocation of risks can result in huge cost overruns. The developer had no incentive to limit cost increases as they were borne by the operator.

The provision of an exhaustive list of opportunistic behaviour at the contract design stage is beyond the scope of this paper. However, four aspects of contract design can be highlighted: namely, choice of contract length, design of incentive and risk sharing schemes, definition of contingencies and contract enforcement.

**Choice of Contract Length** The choice of contract length can be affected by a government's political agenda. Political considerations may affect the discount rate used in the evaluation, the decision horizon and the objective function – minimising public expenditures, risks, price, construction delays, or maximising quality. Contract length specification is a challenging area, as several factors should be taken into account, including the following:

- The contract must be sufficiently attractive so that firms are competing for the project: a 'fair rate of return on investment' has to be expected otherwise firms will not participate in the tender.

- Potential costs, revenues and associated risks over the contract length need to be accounted for.

- The potential benefits from contract renewal need to be assessed, since new firms may enter the market, technical progress and/or cost-reducing investments may occur.

The majority of local authorities in France leave contract length decision to the final stage when contract terms are negotiated. However, contract length should be specified at the point of tender, on the grounds that private operators are likely to have a good idea of what is in their favour. Typically, two situations can arise. First, the private firm reduces the contract length to avoid increasing operating costs at the end of the investment life span. Secondly, at the opposite at the end of the scale, the operator may want to extend the contract length to increase profits or because of fears of competition.

**Incentive and Risk Sharing Agreements** In brief, the main issues in relation to incentives and risk sharing schemes are as follows. The public body awarding the contract must ensue that the contract provides an incentive to reduce price and cost over the contract life time and that the risks are shared without inducing high prices. In fact, the tendering process only allows the selection of the most effective firm on the basis of the tendering documents at a particular point in time. In designing the contract, a trade-off has to be made between the incentive to reduce cost and rent extraction in favour of consumers. For example, a contract with a price cap provides for participating firms to reduce costs as it allows a profit, but the cost reduction does not provide any benefit to the consumers or the public body. At the opposite end of the spectrum, cost-plus contracts do not provide the incentive to reduce costs as contracts specify that cost increases are supported by a third party. This phenomenon is exacerbated when the private firm is vertically integrated. In fact, cost increases supported by the third party can benefit a parent company in terms of profit. In brief, the contract must make sure that monopoly surplus is transferred to consumers over the contract length.

**Adaptation to Contingencies** Contingency adaptation mechanisms leave considerable scope for opportunism on the part of contract parties. Two aspects of such mechanisms are worth pointing out: namely, the definition of the price escalator scale to increase prices when production factor prices increase; and the definition of profit under a profit sharing scheme. Typically the escalator scale between date *0* and *t* has the following form:

$$\frac{P_t}{P_0} = a\frac{w_1}{w_0} + b\frac{f_1}{f_0} + c\frac{l_1}{l_0}$$

with $p$ = price of the service, $w$ = wage, $f$ = fuel index, $l$ = price of commodity and with $a + b + c = 1$. The choice of the price reference and its weight (respectively, $w$ and $a$, above) influence the outcome of the price escalating mechanism and therefore the profit of the firm operating the project. Two examples illustrate this point:

- In a six million euro leisure swimming pool project organised as a 22.5-year *concession* contract, the wage element of the price escalator was the wage index of technicians in the heat and freeze industry. This feature was not questioned by the local authority signing the contract, although it should have been. In fact, wage inflation is more likely to happen in that industry than in the leisure/sport industry.

- The weight of the indices should be re-evaluated over time. If a major operating cost such as labour is reduced over night, the local authority may wish to ensure that the wage share in the price index is reduced accordingly or partially to keep the incentive to reduce costs. This is of importance in inflationary periods as the price of the service would increase more than the real costs.

With a profit-sharing contract, a clear definition of the scope of the activities covered by the scheme is highly advisable: for example, failure to take into account retail space rents and retail outlet profits could alter the picture dramatically. In the swimming pool example, a bar may be opened! Designing a contract where all the major contingencies have been carefully evaluated is one consideration; another is contract enforcement.

**Contract Enforcement** Contract enforcement is very often loose. Several factors explain this: lack of expertise in detecting breaches of contract, lack of political will, high litigation costs and, finally, possible reluctance on the part of public bodies to admit their errors. These phenomena are more likely to occur at the end of the contract, especially when a contract will not be renewed or when the incumbent's chances of winning the new tender are limited. Another form of opportunism can arise at the contract renewal stage, whereby the incumbent firm may disguise or not release information in order to maximise its advantage.

## CONCLUSIONS

The scope for possible opportunistic behaviour in PPP contracting is impressive. One may wonder why such behaviour is so common when it is so obvious. The answer is simple: too little attention is given to evaluating incentives in contracts and incentives within the contracts by the authorities awarding them.

The Irish government took the decision to set up a small agency to deal with PPP contracting. This agency should not limit its expertise to investment decisions and contract negotiation, and it should ensure that there is no collusion at the tendering stage and that the contract is properly enforced. It should also carry risk profile assessments beyond the explicit risks in the contracts. This would allow contract negotiations on a more equal footing.

In addition, the Government should make sure that, where feasible, it has the expertise to take over the work of the private firms involved in PPP. This would increase its negotiation power and reduce the long-term, hold-up situation. Potential competition is essential to improve public service efficiency. The costs and advantages of projects managed by Government departments compared to PPP should be reviewed. Encouragement of maximum participation in PPP by Irish and international firms should also be vigorously pursued.

Furthermore, a comparison of public versus private operation would have two benefits: first, it would provide diversified information for yardstick comparison; secondly, it would limit the possible long-term effects of concentration in the utility market. PPPs have the potential to contribute significantly to efficiency and timing of infrastructural and other public service developments in Ireland. However, a rigorous evaluation of the economic, legal and technical aspects is essential if the public service is to get a fair deal.

## REFERENCES

Cours des Comptes, (1997), *La gestion des services publics de l'eau et d'assainissement.* Ed : Les éditions du Journal Officiel.

Competition Authority (1998), *Guidelines on the Detection and Prevention of Collusive Tendering on the Public Sector Contracts.*

Crain W, M. and Ekelunk R.B., (1976), "Charwick and Demsetz on Competition and Regulation", *Journal of Law and Economics*, 19.

60

Crampes Cl. and Estache A., (1997), *Regulatory trade-offs in the design of concession contracts*, CREMAQ, Université de Toulouse I.

Defeuille Ch., (1996), Le service public au defi de l'efficacité économique : les contrats de délégation de gestion des déchets ménagers. Doctoral Thesis Université Paris 7-Jussieu.

Demsetz H. (1968), "Why Regulate Public Utilities ?" *Journal of Law and Economics*, 11.

Farell Grant Sparks (1998), Public Private Partnerships Report for the Irish Ministry of Finance.

Kern B. and Vienne D., (1998), "Panorama de la gestion délégué en France", Internal Document, Arthur and Andersen, Paris.

Milgrom P. and Roberts J., (1992), Economics, Organisation and Management. Edition Prentice Hall.

Tirole J., (1999), "Concession concurrence et incitations". *Revue Economique et financière*, 51.

Troguer F., (1995), Services Publics : faire-faire ou déléguer ? Ed : Vuibert.

Williamson O.E., (1995), "The Economic Institutions of Capitalism", The Free Press.

The author wrote the article when she was working with Indecon / London Economics, an economic consulting firm.

# Part VI
# Risk Management

# [32]

## *Risk management*

# On the allocation of risk in construction projects

**S C Ward, C B Chapman and B Curtis**

*The willingness of contracting parties to take on risks is an important consideration in the allocation of project risks. A number of factors contribute to willingness to bear risks, but not all motivate conscientious, effective project risk management. A party's willingness to take on risk is reflected in the premium that he or she is able to charge for doing so. However, contractors face a number of difficulties in being able to price risk properly. The regarding of contractors as quasiinsurers suggests pricing rules that are analogous to insurance practice, and important complications associated with adverse selection and moral hazard.*

*Keywords: risk allocation, project risk management*

It is well known that project uncertainty and the allocation of associated risks to contracting parties have a substantial impact on project performance. This recognition has led several writers to argue for the systematic identification and assessment of all sources of risk for all projects[1,2]. The identification of risks as early as possible in a project's life is important, not only to enable project constraints and appropriate cost estimates to be determined, but also to focus project-management attention on ways of controlling and allocating risk[2].

In a construction context, risk analysis should be undertaken by the client to reduce uncertainty and risk, pursue efficiency, and check the risk/expected-cost balance. In addition, risk analysis should be used to determine how risks should be allocated to contracting parties. An analysis of risk should strongly influence the choice of method of payment and form of contract. Successful, appropriate allocation of risk presupposes an atmosphere of trust between contracting parties, and a clear, mutual appreciation of all relevant project risks and their effects. Subsequent risk analysis by other parties, including the management contractor, is appropriate, and the sharing of information about risks between parties is highly desirable[3].

High-quality project risk management requires the following preconditions:

- full specification of the project, and all associated risks,
- a clear perception of the risks being borne by each party,
- sufficient capability, competence and experience to manage the risks,
- motivation to manage the risks, which requires a clear linkage between a party's management of risks and the party's receipt of reward.

In short, the quality of project risk management is improved if risks are identified and evaluated in a systematic way, risks are allocated to the parties best able to control them, and parties who are expected to bear risk receive adequate reward for doing so.

This paper examines these ideas in more detail. First, some preliminary ideas about risk allocation that have general support are set out. Next, the implications of project risk allocation and the concept of willingness to take on risk are examined. A contractor's willingness to bear risk is considered, and related to the contractor's opportunity and ability to price for the project risks that he/she is expected to bear.

### SOME PRELIMINARY GUIDELINES

Max Abrahamson has suggested that it is proper for a contracting party to bear risk in any one of the following five cases[4]:

Department of Accounting and Management Science, University of Southampton, Southampton SO9 5NH, UK

- if the risk is of loss due to his/her own wilful misconduct or lack of reasonable efficiency or care,
- if he can cover a risk by insurance and allow for the premium in settling his charges, and it is most convenient and practicable for the risk to be dealt with in this way,
- if the preponderant economic benefit of running the risk accrues to him,
- if it is in the interests of efficiency to place the risk on him,
- if, when the risk eventuates, the loss happens to fall on him in the first instance, and there is no reason under any of the above headings to transfer the loss to another, or it is impracticable to do so.

These guidelines are a useful first step in addressing the problem of risk allocation, and they have received widespread support, but they do not provide a complete solution.

The first guideline deals with risks associated with unreasonable behaviour. The allocation of such uncertainties in the manner indicated must be uncontentious, but it is important for each party to recognize and deal with such risk as it relates to another party.

The second guideline deals with that set of project risks that can be externalized from the contractual parties. Insofar as the client ultimately pays the insurance fee, the issue of the allocation of insurable risks is only a question of who can obtain the cheapest cover. In an efficient insurance market, both parties are able to obtain cover at the same price, but, in practice, market inefficiencies may be important.

The third guideline recognizes that economic benefits and risks ought to be matched, but it does not provide guidelines as to how this should be done, or deal with the need for an adequate level of reward for taking on a particular risk, or differences in such rewards depending on willingness to take risk, which may be unrelated to the ability to take risk.

The fourth guideline recognizes the importance of efficiency, but there is some ambiguity about the nature of this: efficiency with respect to which contractual party, and with what objectives? Presumably, this guideline represents the widely accepted notion that 'risk should be allocated to the party best able to anticipate and control that risk'[5], but this may not be the party best able to bear it.

Taken together, the third and fourth guidelines suggest a fixed-price agreement for contractor-controllable risks, and a cost-reimbursable agreement for client-controllable risks, such as changes to designs. However, this is a naive interpretation, because it ignores the pricing of risks, and the differing attitudes to risk of the contractual parties. In addition, these guidelines offer little help in allocating risks that are uncontrollable, or controllable to a degree by more than one contractual party. The possibility of risk sharing is ignored.

The fifth guideline is a useful catchall, but does not resolve any of the difficulties noted above.

As Abrahamson has acknowledged[4]:

> One of the problems of the construction industry is that although decisions have to be made about allocating risks, in negotiating contracts and revising standard contract forms very little consideration has been given to basic principles, and what one might call a philosophy of risk is lacking.

Successful, appropriate allocation of risk along the lines proposed by Abrahamson presupposes an atmosphere of trust between contracting parties, and a clear, mutual appreciation of all relevant project risks and their effects. In the absence of one or both of these conditions, and given the limitations of these guidelines, it is perhaps not surprising that the debate about appropriate allocation of risks is often diverted to the investigation and clarification of the effectiveness of allocation mechanisms such as contract clauses[5].

## SOME IMPLICATIONS OF RISK ALLOCATION

The willingness of parties to take on risks is an important consideration in the allocation of project risks. Contractual allocation of project risks is essentially in the hands of the client. If the client is unwilling to bear a particular source of risk, he/she can pass this on to one or more of the other parties involved in the project, including the management contractor in a management contract if he so wishes. Of course, the client will pay a price for passing on this risk, although clients do not always fully appreciate the premium that they pay for this. Where a professional or contractor is aware that he/she will be required to bear a given type of risk, professional fees and tender prices will include an additional premium to reflect the expected cost of this risk, plus a contingency sum in most cases, plus a fee for the risk-bearing service. To the extent that a professional or contractor is unwilling to bear the given risk, a further increase in the premiums will be sought. The client may be unaware of the size of these premiums that are incorporated in prices tendered, although they may vary from contractor to contractor and represent a significant portion of the bids.

The client may also incur a further, additional cost via an impact on the project objectives of professionals' and contractors' behaviour over the life of the project. For example, quality may suffer, delays occur, or claims may arise that increase problems and potentially add to the project's cost.

Professionals or contractors who bear project risk have four basic response options:

- pass the risk on to a third party,
- continue to bear the risk, and manage it for profit, but accept liabilities,
- if a downside risk eventuates, try to recover costs from other parties, including the client,
- if a downside risk eventuates, meet liabilities reluctantly, walk away from the contract, or go bankrupt.

The bearers of a risk will be motivated to use the first

# Risk management

option, provided that this is cost-effective, irrespective of whether they bear the risk willingly or not, provided that they are sufficiently aware of these risks. Bearers of risk will generally be motivated to use the second option to the best of their ability. Arguably, to the extent that a contractor is an unwilling bearer of risk, the third and fourth options are more likely. In one major contractor's experience, if a contractor does take a risk that is realized, he will fight to get his money back any way he can[6].

If a professional or contractor is unaware that he or she bears a given type of risk, the third and fourth options are the only options, by default. The first option is a particularly undesirable strategy if the third party is unaware of what is happening, or is unwilling (but perhaps obliged) to bear the given risk, because the fourth option may be induced. In general, it ought to be in the interests of all parties to a project to ensure that the second option, the management of risk, occurs as far as is possible.

## WILLINGNESS OF PARTIES TO TAKE ON RISKS

The willingness of a contracting party to bear risk is dependent on the factors listed below:

- general attitude to risk,
- perception of project risk,
- ability to bear the consequences of a risk eventuating,
- ability to manage the associated uncertainty and thereby mitigate the risk,
- need to obtain work,
- perception of the risk/return tradeoffs of transferring the risk to another party.

General attitude to risk, the first factor, refers to a party's preference for different risk/return tradeoffs. One party may require a higher expected rate of return for taking on a given level of risk than another party. One organization may prefer low-risk, low-expected-return opportunities, while another may prefer high-risk, high-expected-return opportunities.

The perception of project risk, the second factor, is important. Obviously, a certain level of awareness of a given type of risk must be present if the issue of willingness or unwillingness arises. The point here is that perceptions may be incomplete, inaccurate, optimistic or pessimistic. In a cooperative project environment, perceptions should be based on the appropriate analysis of project uncertainty, and a clear understanding of the consequential risks to each party. If a risk is taken on with an inadequate understanding of that risk, then willingness to bear, manage and realize risk (the second response option) may turn to unwillingness and the third and fourth response options in due course. Clients who lack experience of the construction industry and building may be unwilling to take on any risk in the absence of any information about risks.

The ability to bear the consequences of a risk eventuating (the third factor) relates to the effect on the party's ability to meet the liability and continue in business. For example, a large organization involved in many projects may be able to diversify specific project risks away, and so accept them readily. However, it is also important to appreciate that some contractors, at some time, may take the view that, if they do not take the risk associated with low bids, they will certainly go out of business, and so believe that it is better for them willingly to take risks that, if realized, might put them out of business. The large organization that can distribute specific project risks has a real ability to take risks, while the contractor who is prepared to go bankrupt if a risk eventuates has a false ability to take risks. This issue is separate from that considered in relation to the first factor above, which implicitly assumes that all risks realized will be met.

A party will be more willing, all other things being equal, to bear risk if he/she feels able to manage the associated uncertainty, and thereby mitigate the risk (the fourth factor). Parties skilled in risk management ought to be comparatively more willing to bear risk. An important caveat is that the risk must be one that can be controlled by that party. A concern in developing an appreciation of project risks will be the extent to which the risks are controllable. Unwillingness to bear a given project risk might be due primarily to a perceived inability to control the given risk.

A party's need to obtain work (the fifth factor) will affect his/her willingness to take on risk directly. Competitive forces, or prestigious projects, may induce professionals and contractors not only to trim prices and risk premiums, but also to take on risks that they would otherwise prefer to avoid. Thus, one management contractor accepted a prestigious contract based on the Royal Institute of British Architects 1963 Prime Cost form of contract in which the management contractor remained wholly responsible for the working contractors. Although the company would have preferred a UK Joint Contracts Tribunal 1987 standard JCT 87 form of management contract, it took responsibility for the working contractors at a fee of 2%, with fixed preliminaries. Work was short at the time, and the project was seen as a prestige contract that would enable the company to develop its management contracting capability[6].

With respect to the sixth factor, a party may be willing to bear a risk in the first instance because the estimated costs of transferring the risk on to another party are lower than the premium earned for taking the risk from the client. For example, a management contractor may be prepared to accept liability for exceeding a 'guaranteed maximum cost', because the risk can be passed on to works contractors via suitable contractual terms[6]. Works contractors may fail to appreciate the significance of these terms, and therefore fail to price for them, or competitive forces may oblige them not to add a premium to their bids for taking on this risk.

Alternatively, a party, particularly the client, may be

willing to bear a risk because the perceived costs of transferring it to another party are considered to be too high. Professionals, contractors or insurers may require what the client considers to be excessive premiums, and so the client will retain the risk himself.

The willingness to bear risk is appropriate (in that it leads to conscientious management of risk) only insofar as it is based on a general attitude to risk (the first factor), an adequate perception of project risk (the second factor), a real ability to bear the consequences of a risk eventuating (the third factor), and a real ability to manage the associated uncertainty (the fourth factor). Willingness to bear risk may be inappropriate when it is due to inadequate perception of project risk, a false ability to bear the consequences of a risk eventuating, a need to obtain work (the fifth factor), and a false perception of the risk/return tradeoffs of transferring the risks to another party (the sixth factor).

## CLIENT WILLINGNESS TO RETAIN RISK

Client organizations are often quite unwilling to carry project risk. Moreover, clients have become increasingly influenced by their lawyers in determining the allocation of risk in construction contracts. Not surprisingly, lawyers advise their clients to obtain protection under their contracts for construction works[6]. Many clients still want the feeling of being safeguarded from having to carry risks, even with a management contract. Inexperienced clients are often advised by lawyers who do not generally understand the principles underlying management contracting, and they draft contracts that place some or all of the liability for cost and time overruns on the management contractor. For example, one management contractor received an invitation to tender for a contract using JCT 87 conditions, but with special clauses appended that assigned responsibility for the performance of works contractors to the management contractor[6]. This blatant inconsistency might have slipped through had not all the documentation been carefully checked. In any dispute, the special clauses would have taken precedence over the general clauses in English law. The contractor proposed to seek removal of the clause, or, failing that, to set a higher fee, or to withdraw. Experienced management contracting organizations avoid such contracts, but others bid keenly for them, and then get into difficulties. This has led to disillusionment with management contracting in some quarters.

Clients may be more willing to take on risk if they have experience of the construction industry and build frequently. For example, management contractors often ask works contractors to state separately what their bonding costs will be, so that the client can decide whether he/she should take the liquidity risk. Experienced clients weigh this decision up for each working contractor, whereas one-off clients normally expect full bonding to be provided[6]. Of course, it may be argued that there is no reason why a client should carry project risks if she/she does not wish to do so, provided that he is willing to pay for the privilege.

## CONTRACTOR WILLINGNESS TO TAKE ON RISK – PRICING FOR PROJECT RISK

The willingness of a professional, contractor or insurer to bear a risk, as based on the factors discussed above, is generally influenced by the premium that they are able to charge for doing so. Inability to charge a sufficiently high premium, owing to market forces, for example, may render a professional or contractor less willing to bear a given risk, and encourage the first, third and fourth risk response options, if they are obliged to bear a risk in the first instance. Consequently, as with any fixed-price contract with associated uncertainty, it does not necessarily follow that the party tendering the lowest premium is the party who should bear the risk.

As the managing director of a major contracting firm remarked, it is normal for the client to want a contractor to carry project risk, and, if the contractor is able to evaluate and price the risks, he/she may be happy to carry them.[6]. However, a contractor is often not able properly to evaluate and price risks. Even if the contractor is prepared to undertake appropriate analysis of project risks, lack of information about project uncertainties, and lack of time to prepare the tender, may preclude the proper evaluation of project risks[6]. Once the appraisal stage has been completed, and the design has advanced sufficiently for contractors to be invited to tender for the construction work, which can include the completion of major elements of design, a great sense of urgency normally becomes apparent. A project that may have taken several years to justify and prepare is parcelled up and handed to tendering contractors who are given just a few weeks to evaluate it from scratch and commit themselves to a price for building it. The tenderers may have been through an extensive and expensive prequalification exercise that is designed to determine their capacity to undertake the work. Having experienced the gratification of being considered acceptable, they would like to be allowed the time to study the tender documents in detail, and to consider carefully their approach to the work. Instead, they are normally faced with a tender-submission deadline that only permits a scanty appraisal of the complex construction problems and risks that are often involved. The following scenario is typical.

A site-assessment team, which may include a project manager, estimator, planner, geologist and representatives of specialist subcontractors, is assembled and despatched to the site with instructions to gather in all the method- and cost-related information needed for preparing the bid. This information, together with quotations from materials suppliers, subcontractors and plant companies, and advice on the legal, insurance, financial and taxation implications, is assessed by the estimating team working under great pressure to meet the deadline. Various construction techniques often have to be investigated and compared, and temporary

# Risk management

works proposals considered and designed. Lack of information on ground conditions, plant availability, materials supply, subcontractor capacity and many other important factors has to be overcome by further investigation and inspired guesswork. The contractual terms have to be explored to elicit the imposed risk strategy of the client. An assessment has to be made of the client's reaction to any qualifications in the bid. Possible claims opportunities must be evaluated.

In the absence of adequate time and information, any evaluation and pricing of potential risk exposure is likely to be on an *ad hoc* basis. A typical approach begins with the evaluation of risks by the questioning of experienced managers in the contractor's organization, and arrival at a consensus of the 'gut feelings' expressed. Working contractors attempt to assess their level of risk by looking at the overall programme, checking to see if it is very 'tight', considering the effects of delays by suppliers, and checking the basics for any extension of time. Few, if any, calculations or references to specific results on previous contracts are made, the rationale being that any such references are unlikely to be applicable to the circumstances of the contract in question, even if any relevant data exists. The chairman of the tendering organization ends up by 'pulling a figure out of the air' that is based on his/her feelings about the advice obtained.

Only special works contractors are likely to be in a position to price for a risk and negotiate for it to be identified explicitly. An alternative view is that 'contractors worthy of the name have the experience and capability to evaluate most risks with a sufficient degree of certainty on a broad approach, rather as insurers are able to evaluate insurable risks'[7].

## CONTRACTOR AS QUASIINSURER

Regarding contractors as quasiinsurers suggests pricing rules analogous to insurance law and practice. For example,

- If a contractor is to bear a risk, that risk ought to be identified, and the contractor given an opportunity to price it.
- All relevant information available to the client ought to be supplied to the contractor prior to contract, and ought not to be withheld.
- The basis of pricing should be on broad categories of risk, rather than related to small details.
- A contractor should not be expected to price risks that cannot be quantified with sufficient certainty, given the limited profit margins involved.

The first rule argues for the explicit identification of risks, at least by the contractor, and adequate time for a contractor to price these risks. Joint identification of risks by client and tendering contractors is desirable on efficiency grounds and to ensure that both parties are fully aware of the risks involved. If tendering contractors were simply given more time to tender without client involvement, they might or might not undertake adequate analysis of project risks. Clients ought to require tenders that clearly indicate the risk premiums associated with the major project risks. It is clearly more efficient for the client to undertake some aspects of the analysis of project risk, for example an analysis of ground conditions, to expedite the tendering process and to ensure all tenderers have similar information. The greater the detail provided by the client in relation to risks that are to be borne in whole or in part by the contractor, the less the contractor has to price for risk related to the contractor's uncertainty about what the project involves.

In the determination of the final bid figure, several other considerations are relevant[8]. The intensity of the competition from other contractors, the costs of financing, insurance and bonding, the financial status of the client, the terms of payment and project cash flow, and the level of the contingency allowance to cover risks, all affect the markup that is added to the prime cost of construction. Tendering contractors' risk analysis has a dimension that is additional to those of the client's risk analysis. Each contractor requires a bid that gives an appropriate balance between the risk of not winning the contract and the risk associated with possible profits or losses if the contract is obtained.

The second rule argues that clients should be obliged to disclose all information that might have a bearing on project risks. By analogy with insurance, disclosure by clients ought to be on an *uberrima fides* basis[7]. In a discussion of Barber's paper[9], it was pointed out that, under English law, an insurer under a contract to which *uberrima fides* applied had a right to disclaim for nondisclosure, even if the nondisclosure bore no relationship to the claim. If this were applied to construction contracts, the principle would be that the client would have to warrant the completeness and sufficiency of the information disclosed, and the contractor would be entitled to rely on it. There was general support during this discussion for the creation in the UK of a general duty of disclosure of information that was reasonably within the employer's knowledge and that was material to the project, including the design and implementation. The debaters considered that the creation of such a duty in the UK was necessary, even where a contract contained a provision such as Clause 12 of the UK Institution of Civil Engineers Conditions, as, under these conditions, clients sometimes feel inhibited from disclosing information that might subsequently be used as a basis for a claim.

The introduction of a general duty of this kind in the UK would seem to be helpful, but it would not, of course, act as a positive incentive to clients to undertake risk analysis. Clients would still need to be persuaded that this would be in their best interests. A duty to disclose to tendering contractors any risk analysis the client might undertake should not be regarded as a disincentive to carry out risk analysis. Indeed, clients might prefer to pass probabilistic information on to tendering contractors rather than to have them rely on spuriously precise data. In practice, the veracity of probabilistic data would be impossible to confirm after the event. Claims on the basis of misrepresentation of data would be impossible to substantiate. In these circumstances, the transfer of such data would be undertaken in the spirit of offering contractors a fair chance to price for project risk.

The third rule, that pricing should be on broad categories of risk, rather than related to small details, is a realistic approach. An important step in the performance of risk analysis is the identification of factors that can have a major impact on project performance. However, detailed risk analysis may be necessary to determine the relative significance of project risks. Pricing need not consider all project risks in detail, but it does need to be related to major sources of risk.

The fourth rule states that contractors should not be expected to bear risks that cannot be cost-effectively quantified with sufficient certainty, for example the risks of variable ground on a tunnelling project. In such cases, the price ought to be related to what is actually encountered[7]. If clients are unduly concerned about bearing such risks, then it will be appropriate for them to undertake the necessary in-depth risk analysis themselves, and to require tendering contracts to price for the risk on the basis of the client's risk analysis. The sharing of such risks is always an option.

It is important for clients to appreciate that, if contractors price for risk and play the role of insurer, this involves important complications associated with adverse selection and moral hazard that have been addressed by economists:

- Contractors who can provide honestly stated good-quality insurance may price themselves out of the market in relation to those who provide dishonestly stated poor-quality insurance at low prices, if sufficient clients are unable to distinguish between good and poor quality, and honesty and dishonesty. As Akerlof[10] argues, poor quality and dishonesty can drive good quality and honesty out of the market.
- If insurance is cheap, and, when a loss occurs, indemnity is easily recovered, carelessness is encouraged; a degree of pain is essential to keep the insured honest[11].
- Clients may become careless of actions, such as changes in plans, with which a contractor must cope to an extent that would not occur if the client bore the cost. Once insurance is in place, excessive demand for claims, analogous to Parsons' excessive carelessness, becomes inevitable, because the marginal cost of such behaviour is altered, and so rational behaviour requires a change in behaviour[12].

As Arrow argues, although the marginal cost of behaviour is altered by insurance given that there are no constraints on that behaviour, it is both possible and sensible to impose constraints[13]. Indeed, it would be sensible for the client to impose such conditions on himself in order to obtain appropriate insurance, which may not be forthcoming otherwise.

To quote Arrow[13],

> Because of the moral hazard, complete reliance on economic incentives does not lead to an optimal allocation of resources in general. In most societies alternative relationships are built up which to some extent serve to permit cooperation and risk sharing. The principal–agent relation is very pervasive in all economies and especially in modern ones; by definition the agent has been selected for his specialized knowledge, and therefore the principal can never hope completely to check the agent's performance. You cannot therefore easily take out insurance against the failure of the agent to perform well. One of the characteristics of a successful economic system is that the relations of trust and confidence between principal and agent are sufficiently strong so that the agent will not cheat even though it may be 'rational economic behavior' to do so. The lack of such confidence has certainly been adduced by many writers as one cause of economic backwardness.

## CONCLUSIONS

An underlying premise of this paper is that the quality of project risk management can be improved if project risks are appropriately allocated between contracting parties.

At first sight, appropriate allocation might be based on the willingness of parties to take on a risk. However, willingness to bear risk will only result in the conscientious management of project risks insofar as it is based on

- an adequate perception of project risks,
- a reasoned assessment of risk/return tradeoffs,
- a real ability to bear the consequences of a risk eventuating,
- a real ability to manage the associated uncertainty, and thereby mitigate risks.

Willingness to bear risk should not be a criterion for risk allocation when it is based on

- an inadequate perception of project risks,
- a false perception of ability to bear the consequences of risk eventuating,
- a need to obtain work,
- false perceptions of the risk/return tradeoffs of transferring risks to another party.

The willingness of a contracting agent to bear risk will generally be influenced by the premium that he/she is able to charge for this. However, experience of the construction industry suggests that tenderers are often faced with a tender-submission deadline that only permits a scanty appraisal of the complex construction problems and risks involved in a project. In the absence of adequate time and information, any evaluation and pricing of potential risk exposure may be on a perfunctory and *ad hoc* basis.

Regarding contracting agents as quasiinsurers suggests pricing rules analogous to insurance law and practice. This implies full disclosure of all relevant

# Risk management

information available to the client, and, in particular, disclosure by the client of all information that might have a bearing on project risks. It is important to appreciate that a contracting agent pricing for risk and playing the role of insurer involves important complications associated with adverse selection and moral hazard.

Effective project procurement requires that all parties involved understand and accept in an honest manner risks appropriately allocated to them, and that these risks are effectively managed. This requires explicit formal risk analysis. Whatever form of contract is adopted, there is a need for much more careful attention to risk analysis and management by all parties, and a need for a more cooperative attitude that avoids moral hazards.


## ACKNOWLEDGEMENT

This research was supported by SERC grant GR/E 48343.



*Chris Chapman is Professor of Management Science and Head of the Department of Accounting and Management Science at the University of Southampton. For about 15 years his consulting and research have centred on the management of risk. Most of his consulting has been concerned with large energy projects in the UK, and USA and Canada, but other concerns have included computer hardware and software systems, financial asset and commodity broking portfolio management. He holds a BASc in Industrial Engineering (Toronto), an MSc in Operational Research (Birmingham) and a PhD in Economics and Econometrics (Southampton).*

*Stephen Ward is a senior lecturer in Business Economics and Academic Deputy Director of the Management School at the University of Southampton, UK. Before joining the University in 1980, he worked in operational research with the National Westminster Bank, UK, and in merchandizing with Boots, UK. His research interests include project and contract risk management, strategic-investment appraisal and problem-solving methodology. He recently completed a UK Science and Engineering Research Council research contract on the roles, risks and responsibilities of management contractors in the construction industry. He holds a BSc in Mathematics and Physics (Nottingham University, UK) and an MSc in Management Science (Imperial College, London University, UK).*

*Bernard Curtis worked on site as a project manager on a variety of major civil-engineering schemes before becoming a lecturer in construction management. He now acts as a civil-engineering and building-works consultant and arbitrator, concentrating on contractual and project-management issues. His interest in improving the performance of the construction industry is pursued through his being a consultant research manager for CIRIA, a construction-management research monitor for the UK Science and Engineering Research Council, and a research fellow at Southampton University, UK.*


## REFERENCES


1 **Barnes, M** (and partners) 'Management contracting for health building – a comparative study' *Summary Report* UK Department of Health and Social Security (1984)

2 **Perry, J G and Hayes, R W** 'Risk management for project managers' *Build. Tech. & Manage.* (Aug/Sep 1986) pp 8–11

3 **Ward, S C and Chapman, C B** 'Extending the use of risk analysis in project management' *Int. J. Project Manage.* Vol 9 No 2 (1991) pp 117–123

4 **Abrahamson, M** 'Contractual risks in tunnelling: how they should be shared' *Tunnels & Tunnelling* (Nov 1973) pp 587–598

5 **Beard, J E** 'Risk allocation through contract clauses' *Proc. ASCE Symp. Managing Liability* ASCE, USA (1982) pp 49–60

6 **Curtis, B** 'Roles, responsibilities and risk in management contracts' *SERC GR/E 48343* (1989) (observations from interviews with senior management in client, professional and contracting organizations during above SERC funded research programme)

7 **Barber, J N** 'Risks in the method of construction' *in* Reference 9

8 **Ward, S C and Chapman, C B** 'Developing competitive bids: a framework for information processing' *J. Oper. Res. Soc.* Vol 39 No 2 (1988) pp 123–134

9 **Uff, J and Capper, P (Eds.)** *Construction Contract Policy: Improved Procedures and Practice* Centre of Construction Law and Management, King's College, London, UK (1989)

10 **Akerlof, G A** 'The market for "lemons": quality

uncertainty and the market mechanism' *Quart. J. Econ.* Vol 84 (1970) pp 488–500

11 **Parsons, T** *A Treatise on the Law of Marine Insurance and General Average* (Vol 1) (1868)

12 **Pauly, M V** 'The economics of moral hazard: comment' *Amer. Econ. Rev.* Vol 58 (1968) pp 531–537

13 **Arrow, K J** 'The economics of moral hazard: further comment' *Amer. Econ. Rev.* Vol 58 (1968) pp 537–538

[33]

# The U.K. Revolution in Public Procurement and the Value of Project Finance

ANTHONY FORSHAW

**ANTHONY FORSHAW** is a director of structured finance at Deutsche Bank in London.

The history of the private finance initiative (PFI) in public sector procurement in the U.K. has already been widely disseminated. This article briefly reviews the salient points in its development, introducing some of the innovations that radically affected the manner in which public contracts are now awarded. It concludes by setting out why project finance has become the financing option of choice for the PFI.

Officially, the PFI was launched in 1992 by the then Chancellor of the Exchequer, Norman Lamont. In reality, the State was changing the way it appraised infrastructure development and his Parliamentary announcement was only a stage in that process. It was followed by a series of policy statements and guidelines that continue to be issued and, significantly, have been supported by Governments of both principal political parties. The current Chancellor of the Exchequer, Gordon Brown, has expressed the view that:

> Through the PFI, the private sector is able to bring a wide range of managerial, commercial and creative skills to the provision of public services, offering potentially huge benefits for the Government. We are keen to see the PFI and other public/private partnerships succeed in delivering the necessary investment the country needs.[1]

The increasing importance of the new procurement and its involvement in many sectors of the economy is illustrated in Exhibits 1 and 2.

At the core of the PFI's development has been a fundamental reappraisal of the methodology for calculating the State's cost of capital procurement. In addition to the traditional analysis of the aggregate cost of a design and build contract (typically heavily specified prior to tender), a public sector project appraisal was expected, starting in 1984, to include:

1. capital cost of any buildings or equipment that need to be replaced over the appraisal period;
2. residual values of capital assets at the end of the appraisal period;
3. operating costs over the whole term of the appraisal;
4. other costs or benefits which can be valued in money terms, in the form of revenues, cost savings or non-marketed outputs;
5. measures or descriptions of those costs or benefits that cannot be valued in money terms.[2]

By requiring procurers, where possible, to embrace the fullest expectation of cost outcomes, public policy created an instrument that also measured risk. This is the logical consequence of testing different out-turn prices. Once this approach was

EXHIBIT 1
**UK PFI Dealflow**

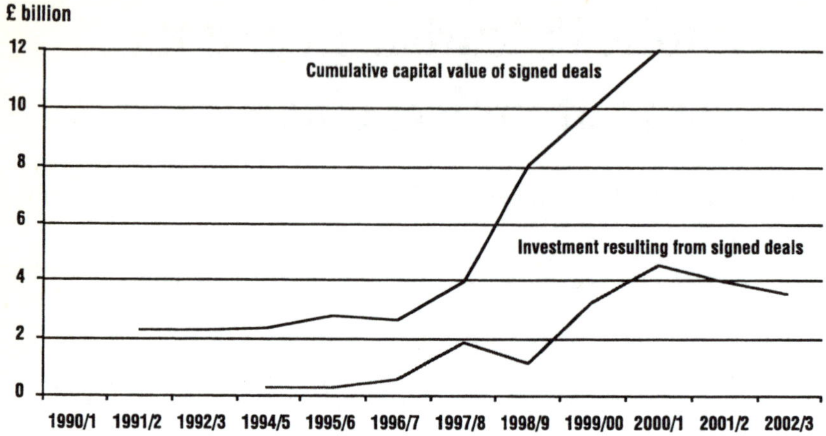


Source: HM Treasury [1998].

EXHIBIT 2
**Breakdown of PFI Sectors**

| Sector | Type of Asset | Contract Term | Typical Transaction Size |
|---|---|---|---|
| Accommodation | Refurbish/relocate Government offices | 20 years | £70m – £1.5bn |
| Railways | New light rail and high speed rail networks | 30 years | £90m – £3bn |
| Roads | Individual or linked new build and road widening schemes | 30 years | £50m - £300m |
| Prisons | New prisons | 25-27 years | £35m – £120m |
| Schools | New build and refurbishment of schools | 25-27 years | £15m – £150m |
| Defense | Equipment supply and maintenance and property new build and refurbishment | 15-25 years | £15m - £1.5bn |
| Healthcare | New hospitals | 30 years | £70m – £300m |
| Water | New/upgraded water treatment plants | 25-40 years | £10m – £80m |

Source: HM Treasury [1998].

**EXHIBIT 3**
**UK PFI Dealflow**

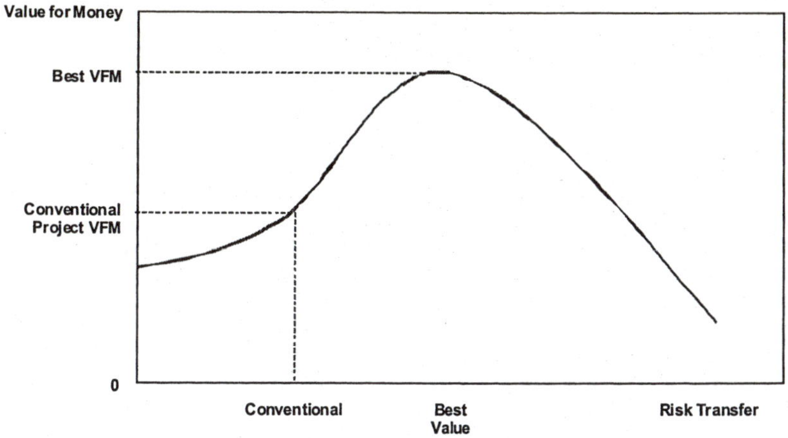


Source: Treasury Taskforce: Partnerships for Property [1998].

widely established, the State was able to apply historical data of actual versus forecast outcomes and conclude that public procurement would benefit if certain risks could be transferred to other parties. This thought process lay behind the now-overused PFI risk transfer graph in Exhibit 3.

This is intended as a graphic illustration of the failure of conventional procurement to generate true value for money because, where it might be cheaper in simple payment terms, it has failed to take into account other costs. These are, principally, the transferral of the risks left with the public sector under such procurement. The illustration is also intended to show that beyond a certain point, risk transfer will become inefficient if the risk taker is unable to absorb or price it properly.

A significant element in this methodology which comes to the fore in analysing the importance of project finance is that the forecast value of costs, over time, is discounted to present value terms to allow for comparison between different approaches. An example of this approach is set out in Exhibit 4.

A second key step in the PFI was to permit the private sector to tender more widely than previously. This also can be seen as a result of the conclusions regarding risk transferral. To manage the type of risks the public sector was eager to transfer, the private sector needed to be able to tender its own specifications for projects, subject to over-riding criteria such as health and safety and other public policy issues. This process has been described as the introduction of "innovation," and an illustration of how the State views this concept in relation to an actual project is set out in Exhibit 5.

From this point, the State had introduced a means whereby procurement decisions could be made after including an estimate of the cashflow effects of bad procurement. Instead of appraising the face value amount of a design/build contract, procurers now include an expectation that the exclusively public approach will result in over specification, poor project management, time delays and cost overruns, all on the basis of historic evaluation. Appraisals also typically include: valuations of the more rapid degradation of assets when retained by the public

## Exhibit 4
**Excerpt from a National Audit Office Project Review**

A comparison of the variability in the cost of each of the four bids with changes in key assumptions

Autolink's bid was likely to remain cheaper than that of its nearest competitor, UK Highways, under most circumstances. The diagram shows the extent to which most of the initial bids for the project varied with changes in key assumptions – such as construction timetables, traffic forecasts, interest rates and future levels of inflation. The length of road in each case illustrates this, while the figures in the lorries are the expected values of each bid, i.e., those costs which were assessed to be the most likely to occur in practice.

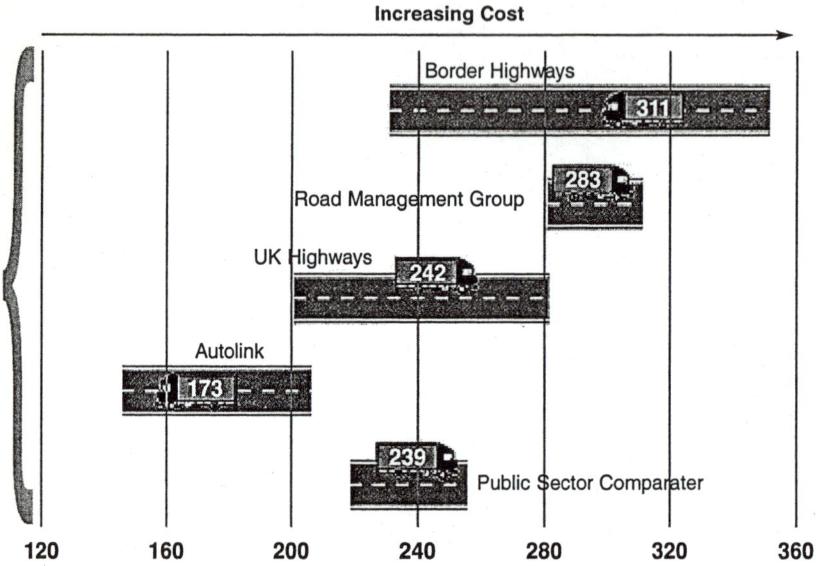


Source: National Audit Office, The PFI: The Contract to Complete the A74/M74 Motorway [1999].

sector; the greater operating expense of public sector maintenance organisations; and, the lower residual value amounts at the end of the expected useful life of assets retained in the public rather than private sectors.

This created the springboard for PFI insofar as the likelihood of the private sector achieving these benefits is the product of adequate risk transfer. In this context, the transfer of risks which make PFI valuable to the public sector comprise, inter alia, risks relating to construction, operations, upgrades, quality and demand. Further explanation of these risks is contained in Exhibit 6).

Project financiers immediately will recognise these risk categories and it is this familiarity that has led to the development of project financing for PFI projects.

The underlying asset class that the State has sought to finance under the PFI varies as illustrated earlier in Exhibit 2. However, State-supported infrastructure typically is long term in nature and, under PFI, the State has sought to match private-sector contracts to the

## EXHIBIT 5

**Excerpt from a National Audit Office Project Review**

Innovation by the private operator includes the design of the new motorway pavement incorporating a new road surfacing material.

The [Scottish Office] left it to the private operator to decide on pavement design and construction provided that a service life of at least 10 years following the end of the concession period would be achieved. [The winning bidder] varied the depth of the pavement by designing for the volume and type of traffic which will use each running lane and has used a surfacing material new to the United Kingdom, stone-mastic asphalt. [This was used] for the following reasons:

- It has lower road noise characteristics;
- It has superior drainage ability thereby reducing spray during wet conditions and improving visibility and safety; and
- It has a longer expected life than traditional surfaces, reducing the requirement for routine maintenance and renewal.

There is a risk that using such innovative pavement design will not result in the maintenance benefits which [the winning bidder is] expecting. In this instance, [it] must bear any additional costs should a more intense maintenance programme be required.

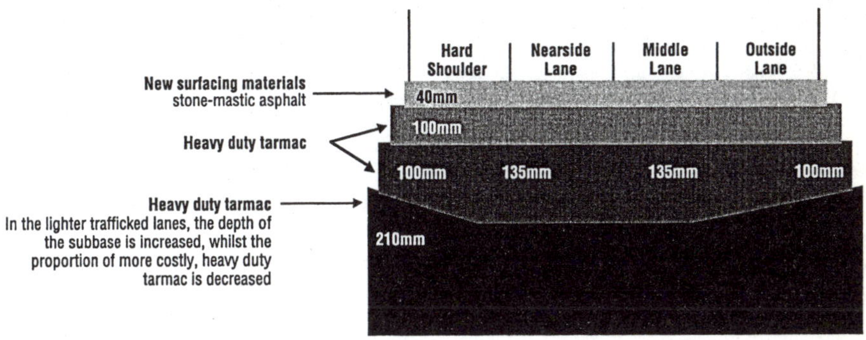


Source: "The PFI: The Contract to Complete the A74/M74 Motorway." National Audit Office, 1999.

period of usefulness normally associated with such an asset, although capping these contract periods where additional length is unlikely to generate value for money benefits. Typical concession period lengths are shown in Exhibit 2.

The State's discounted cashflow appraisal methodology, when applied to payment periods of this magnitude, significantly favors tenderers who defer payments to the tail end of the contract period. It also favors highly leveraged companies because the carrying cost of debt finance, even when structured on a limited or non-recourse basis, is less than the discount rate used by the public sector. On-balance-sheet debt or shareholder capital typically attracts a significantly higher cost of carry.

Consequently, winning tenders under the PFI needed to:

1. minimize sponsor equity;
2. maximize debt finance;
3. amortize debt to the maximum maturity available; and
4. typically accept the categories of risk enumerated in Exhibit 6.

EXHIBIT 6
**Key PFI Risks Taken by the Private Sector**

| | |
|---|---|
| **Construction Risk** | The risk that cost overruns or delays in construction impair the delivery of public services. |
| **Operating Risk** | The risk that cost estimates for routine maintenance are inadequately provided for in pricing the delivery of public services. |
| **Upgrade Risk** | The risk that major construction works will be needed over the period of a contract and will be inadequately provided for in pricing the delivery of public services. |
| **Quality Risk** | The risk that the service is not delivered to the standards expected at the outset. |
| **Demand Risk** | The risk that there will be no demand for a particular service in the future. |

Project finance has proven to be the tool most readily adaptable to this task and, with few, if any, exceptions, every transaction in PFI in the £50 million–£800 million transaction size range has been project financed. This is attributable to the specific resource that project finance lenders can deploy to undertake the analysis which is necessary to understand properly the nature of risks which can arise to single asset companies over very long periods. It is also attributable to many sponsors unwillingness to even consider the prospect of taking such risks. As a consequence of these two approaches project financiers are pricing long term risks more cheaply than sponsors, or other forms of finance, are willing to do, as reflected in the borrowing cost of debt compared to the target return on equity sought by sponsors. It is probably the subject of another article as to whether the project financiers have been correct in their appraisal, but it is possible to note that those PFI projects which a financier would consider to be performing badly, were financed on a full recourse basis, most notably in the Information Technology sector.

## ENDNOTES

[1]Source: Treasury Taskforce: Partnerships for Property, 1998

[2]Source: Economic Appraisal in Central Government: A Technical Guide for Government Depts.

*Engineering, Construction and Architectural Management* 1997 4 | **3**, 233–246

# Karachi light rail transit: a private finance proposal

S. FARUQI & N.J. SMITH
*Construction Management Group, Department of Civil Engineering, University of Leeds, Leeds, UK*

**Abstract** Light Rail Transit (LRT) systems have emerged as an attractive form of public transport both in industrialised as well as developing countries. This paper reviews the implementation mechanism of LRT projects proured by private finance, through Build Operate Transfer (BOT) type concession contracts. A case study approach is used to model an actual LRT project. The case study analysis shows that the uncertainty factor could be converted to monetary terms and the process would enhance ability of the decision makers to have a better understanding of the consequences of risks.

**Keywords** *light rail transit, PFI, risk assessment, transport*

## INTRODUCTION

Light Rail Transit (LTR) systems, the modern transformation of old trams, have emerged as an attractive form of public transport both in developed as well as developing countries. The implementation of LRT projects, as a means of improving the quality of urban life, has received great interest during the last two decades. The number of cities either planning, constructing or expanding this mode of travel is estimated to be more than 100 around the globe (Barry 1991).

Society is now re-assessing the role of the 'automobile' in the urban situation as being the biggest single contributor to congestion and pollution (Brew 1994). Although an efficient user of space, road based public transport services, typically using buses, are deteriorating; the vehicle stock of most cities is in poor condition, the overcrowing often reaches unacceptable levels during peak periods, and the increased pollution levels are becoming unacceptable (Wright 1990). In contrast, LRT systems provide a fast, safe and comfortable journey in modern vehicles with a reliable and frequent service that is also more environmentally efficient. Another fact, that the LRT system only requires a fraction of the capital and operating costs needed for heavy rail systems, has led to its selection as the most appropriate solution for traffic congestion in urban centres.

There have been major developments in technology and equipment, system planning and operational techniques; however a major objstruction in the implementation of these schemes is the availability of finance. Most of the earlier systems have been constructed and operated by the public sector because, experience worldwide has shown, only a few efficient LRT systems can cover their operating costs from fare box revenue (Wright 1994).

The governments in most of the developing countries are faced with enormous transport problems due to population explosions in the urban centres. However, the shortage of public funds to provide the infrastructure and the need for low fare rate to make the system affordable for the users, have increased the complexity of scheme procurement. Governments have been exploring innovative ways and techniques of funding infrastructure projects through private sector participation, and in recent years several cities in the UK have considered proposals for LRT projects through the Private Finance Initiative.

Private sector investment in major infrastructure projects has increased throughout the world since the 1980s. However, this involvement in the transport sector is mostly taking place in the shape of either privatisation of existing assets by the government or through construction of facilities that have lowest risk and are financially most attractive such as toll roads and bridges (Barry 1991). Various forms of innovative concession contracts, such as Build Operate Transfer (BOT), Design Build Operate and Maintain (DBOM), etc., have experienced limited success in the past for implementation of dynamic infrastructure, such as LRT systems, requiring large capital for construction and a reasonably high operating and maintenance cost (Merna & Smith 1996).

The World Bank's Private Sector Development Department (The World Bank 1995) has indicated that during the next decade, the greatest potential for private sector investments will shift from the power plant and telecommunication projects to transportation schemes mostly through new investments. The geographic pattern of these projections also indicates that the developing countries of the Asian continent have been the major beneficiaries in the last decade and these countries will continue to provide better investment opportunities in the coming years.

The governments of a number of countries are keenly interested in constructing LRT systems and private sector organizations are also seeking this new market. However, the low rate of successful BOT contracts has been a point of concern for all the parties. Negotiations for a number of projects have consumed considerable time and enormous expenses, before failing (Augenblick & Custer 1990). The main reason for this has been identified as a lack of proper understanding of risks and of balanced allocation between parties involved in the concession contract. With LRT projects in particular, a substantial investment in infrastructure reduces the commercial attractiveness and increases the risk.

The future of urban mass transit systems in each country, or for that matter for each city, will depend on a large number of factors. The economic development, growth in demand, government policies and available technology will particularly influence the choice. However, in the case of developing countries the staggering increase in urban population will result in enormous demand for urban mass transit. This anticipated future need can only be served if the existing bus fleets are at least doubled (Wright 1994).

The technology for bus priority systems is advancing and there is a pressure for higher capacity buses to meet the needs. Moreover, some studies indicate that exclusive busways can match the capacity of LRT systems and the busways are considered far more cost effective (Wright 1990). However, there is a limitation of space in urban streets to handle large fleets of buses. This restraint, coupled with greater concern for safety and environment, has enabled more countries to justify LRT in terms of the safety, comfort and speed it is able to offer. It is also expected that the growing worldwide interest in LRT is likely to promote technological advances in the future that may increase its cost effectiveness.

## LIGHT RAIL TRANSIT (LRT) SYSTEMS

The term 'Light Rail' refers to a wide range of electrically powered rail based public transport systems. At one extreme are trams or streetcars that operate on tracks and share the roadway with other users. At the other extreme are 'pre-metro' systems operated on exclusive rights-of-way with capacity reaching up to 35 000 passengers per hour per direction (Wright 1990).

A distinctive feature of LRT systems is that the passengers usually board from the road surface or from low platforms. Modern vehicles operate in single units or in short trains with faster speeds and high capacity. While parts of the network may be along shared city streets, the tracks are generally segregated from other traffic either at grade, on viaducts or in underground tunnel sections. The diversity of design options provides flexibility in coping with different right of way types that may vary from one part of the city to the next (Honduis 1995). This system also provides an opportunity for staging the construction thus facilitating an earlier stream of revenue from the system.

LRT projects offer development benefits which can make these projects politically acceptable, including:

- A clearly recognizable provision of a high quality public transport system, entirely new to most cities
- A fare structure nearly consistent with the exiting public transport fares
- Relief of demand for travel to a central business district by private transport
- Major opportunity for controlled urban redevelopment

The only clear disadvantage of an LRT system is the need for many passengers to change modes during their journeys, as these systems are generally confined to main traffic corridors as compared to a bus system which serves the entire road network (Barry 1991). Hence it is important for the success of the LRT system that careful planning is done for convenient interchange facilities and feeder network for the line.

## FINANCING PUBLIC TRANSPORT SYSTEMS

The commissioning of a new LRT system is likely to be one of the largest single investments undertaken by most cities. Hence it is vital that very careful consideration is given to the cost implications of each option. This section starts with a brief description of various elements of the total cost package. An understanding of these factors is important as it provides an insight into the possible variations in project cost with change in the design and operating characteristics.

The LRT project for the Caracas metro illustrates one of the problems. In Caracas, only 5% of the population regularly uses the underground metro, which was built at a cost in excess of US$1440m; that is equivalent to US$10 000 for each user. Meanwhile, the city spent an insignificant amount on public transport for the remaining 95% of the population. Hence in comparing options, the equity of wide variations in levels of expenditure needs to be considered (Wright 1994).

The cost characteristics of LRT systems vary considerably throughout the world. However, most LRT sytems lie between the two extremes, one being the bus system in which the operating costs predominate, forming about 85% with the other 15% covering depreciation and interest costs. The other extreme is underground metro systems in which the capital cost is enormous and operating costs form 25% whereas the other 75% covers the depreciation and interest costs (Wright 1990). For LRT systems operating costs are greatly influenced by the costs of labour, energy cost and materials used, whereas the capital costs are closely related to useful life of vehicles and infrastructure.

The important components of the total cost of an LRT system are briefly:

1 *Infrastructure costs* – these include civil work elements for the line structures, track work, stations and the depot and maintenance facilities. They may also include the cost of service diversion, environmental mitigation measures and cost of involuntary resettlement.
2 Depreciation and interest charges – each category of capital cost is assumed to be financed by a loan of varying terms, hence they should be annualised to represent the depreciation and interest charges over the loan repayment period.
3 *Equipment costs* – this component comprises all electromechanical equipment used by the system such as the power supply, signalling, communication, fare collection, etc.
4 *Vehicle costs* – the cost of vehicles varies considerably, depending on level of comfort, capacity, domestic or overseas manufacture, production-line or custom-built models.
5 *Operating and maintenance costs* – the estimation of the operating costs can be done by applying unit rates for following parameters:
   - *Distance-related costs* – for example energy, maintenance and servicing of vehicles. These costs are for the total of the distances travelled by the fleet of vehicles in operation and are expressed in terms of vehicle-kilometres. This element is mainly dependent on the energy cost of the country.
   - *Route related costs* – for example the maintenance of track, power supply, signals and stations. This is expressed in terms of costs per kilometre of route per annum or per day. This element is dependent on the sophistication of the equipment used and the frequency of the maintenance required by the manufacturers.

- *Time-related costs* – mainly consists of operating staff wages, measured in terms of the total number of hours run by the fleet of vehicles and expressed as vehicle-hours. In countries where the labour rates are low they are often associated with low productivity, hence the overall impact of this element remains same.

## Funding by users

Direct income for the public transport operators mainly consists of fare box revenue. In some cases the income from advertising and contract work is also sizeable, such as the Metro Manila system which gets between 2% and 3% of its gross income from non fare box sources (Razon 1994). Very few public transport services are viable relying entirely on direct income from users. A World Bank survey of 20 representative public transport systems revealed that direct income coverage for the total costs, that include operation, depreciation and interest costs, was 62% for bus operators and only 30% for urban rail systems (Wright 1994). This estimate matches the figures in Table 1, which shows various contributors for the operating cost component only of these systems. On average about 42% of the operating cost is recovered from fare box revenue; the systems receive about 44% in the form of grants and rest is raised by other means such as rents or sales tax.

Hong Kong MTR is regarded as the most successful mass transit system in the world recovering 100% of its operating cost from fare box revenue. The system has reached this distinction due to high affordability of users and very high ridership. Manchester Metrolink and the Ankara system are among the few successful LRT systems that are able to cover the operating costs from fares, if

**Table 1** Financing of urban mass transit systems, operating cost only (Contribution in percentage)

| City | Fares | Grants | Rents | Sales tax |
|---|---|---|---|---|
| Adelaide | 20.0 | 76.4 | 3.6 | |
| Amsterdam | 22.5 | 77.5 | | |
| Ankara | 70.0 | 26.0 | 4.0 | |
| Baltimore | 49.9 | 48.8 | 1.2 | |
| Brussels | 26.5 | 72.6 | 0.9 | |
| Calgary | 34.0 | 10.0 | 1.0 | 55.0 |
| Dallas | 35.0 | 1.0 | 0.0 | 64.0 |
| Edmonton | 40.2 | 7.8 | 5.5 | 46.5 |
| Grenoble | 51.0 | 40.0 | 9.0 | |
| Hong Kong | 100.0 | | | |
| Manchester | 73.5 | 22.9 | 3.6 | |
| Melbourne | 40.0 | 60.0 | | |
| Nantes | 46.8 | 51.2 | 2.0 | |
| Singapore | 52.0 | 44.6 | 3.4 | |
| Vancouver | 47.0 | 22.0 | 31.0 | |
| Average for 48 systems | 42.83 | 43.76 | 3.13 | 6.77 |

Source: Jane's Urban Transport Systems 1993. 'System' entries for each city.

depreciation and interest charges are not considered. However these systems also receive grants to participate in the subsidised fare schemes regulated by government. These are exceptions and most LRT systems rely heavily on grants, usually from government to cover the full operating cost.

### Government grants

When direct income does not cover the costs, it is usually supplemented by government grants and subsidies. The primary objective of government grants is to provide the users with a satisfactory level of servide at affordable prices (Barrow 1994). LRT private operators have the additional difficulties associated with building and maintaining track and infrastructure for their vehicles, which are not shared by competitors like private bus operators.

Governments in developing countries may choose to regulate fares and this requires the private sector to be reimbursed by subsidy. Government subsidies can also play an important part in capital intensive systems in which the interests of the private sector are being sought. The money from government reassures the investors of the government's commitment to the project and encourages private money to fund the element of the cost that could be recovered from users in the form of tolls or revenue. Capital subsidies could be in the form of capital grants, government equity and land or other assets provided at below market value. Occasionally these funds may be procided to the private operator from outside the country.

## CASE STUDY PROJECT; KARACHI LRT

This case study is based on a proposed project in a developing country, an LRT system in Karachi, Pakistan. The main features of the case study project can be summarised as:

- *Project* – Light Rail Transit (LRT) system
- *Facility* – Dynamic infrastructure
- *Procurement* – Invited bid
- *Revenue* – Market led
- *Competition* – International

Karachi ranks amongst the world's largest cities and it is the biggest industrial, commercial and financial centre in Pakistan. With an annual growth rate of 6%, the population of the city is projected to reach 14 million by the end of the century. It is spread over an area of 1300 $km^2$ and runs 40 km in the east-west direction and 30 km in north-south direction (Soomro & Shamin 1996). In spite of Karachi's significance in both nationally and regionally, the city is faced with serious inadequacies of infrastructure and services, including transport.

The urban form of Karachi is completely different from the cities of the developed countries. The socio-economic pattern is distinct because the affluent community has remained within the urban centre, close to scarcity of civic amenities, whereas planned and unplanned pockets of high-density, low-income housing clusters have grown up in the surrounding suburban area. Commuters from these settlements have to travel long distances to the central commercial and business districts which offer most of the employment opportunities. This unique travel pattern, where 65% of all passenger trips are served by public transport, creates a demand for a cheap and efficient public transport systems in the city. In spite of the enormous demand for public transport the city only has privately owned minibuses with medium and low capacity vehicles, adding to the congestion and number of accidents on the urban streets (Karachi Mass Transit 1990).

Against this background the Karachi Mass Transit Study was commissioned in 1987, with World Bank assistance, for the purposes of defining an appropriate system for Karachi. After three years of comprehensive study a multidisciplinary implementation plan was developed comprising a network of transitways. These transitways had been planned initially to be built as busways convertible to light rail after a few years of operation. However the implementation plan suffered considerable delays due to various political and financial changes and the government took the decision to propose an LRT system from the outset with a 40% government grant. The project was divided into three phases with phase 1 commissioned in the year 2000 the first priority, followed by phase 2 10 years later and phase 3 a further 5 years after phase 2.

## Case study data

Table 2 shows a construction programme comprising a list of activities, their estimated durations and starting months. The estimated monthly costs and revenues are also given. Some of the critical activities shown in this table, such as revenue and operation cost, were subdivided in order to produce more realistic results from a model of the project. A precedence network was used as the basis for the model, with cash flows considered annually over the concession period of 30 years. The costs and revenues of each activity are quoted in Pakistani Rupees; (the conversion rates in 1995 were UK£1 = Pak.Rs.54 and US$1 = Pak.Rs.32).

By assigning costs to the precedence network, the model was used to determine the profitability of the project. The key economic parameters are:

- Internal rate of return 12.32%
- Net cash balance Rs.43653m
- Maximum cash lockup Rs.11372m
- Cash payback period 11.69 years

A second analysis was performed to find out the effect of the government grant of 40% not being available. It can be seen from the economic parameters given below that the viability of the project will be severely affected as there is a significant decline in the IRR of the project, and an increase in payback time:

- Internal rate of return 10.60%
- Net cash balance Rs. 38543m
- Max. cash lock-up Rs. 11732m
- Cash payback period 14.01 years

240

*Faruqi, S. & Smith, N.J.*

**Table 2** Construction programme and estimated costs for LRT project

| Activity | Duration in months | Start month | Monthly cost/rev. |
|---|---|---|---|
| 1. Prepare Bid | 3 | June 1995 | 30.00 |
| 2. Negotiate Contract | 1 | Sept. 1995 | 15.00 |
| 3. Sign Implementation Agreement | 1 | Oct. 1995 | 1.00 |
| 4. Financing cost | 276 | April 1996 | 25.00 |
| 5. Right of Way acquisition | 6 | Dec. 1995 | 45.00 |
| 6. Land Provision for Depots | 2 | Jan. 1996 | 45.00 |
| 7. Design of Head Office/Control centre | 3 | May 1996 | 7.50 |
| 8. Design of LRT Line/Stations | 18 | May 1996 | 7.50 |
| 9. Design of Depot/Maint. facility | 3 | May 1996 | 7.50 |
| 10. Environmental Impacts mitigation | 24 | Nov. 1995 | 8.00 |
| 11. Involuntary resettlement | 4 | Nov. 1995 | 40.00 |
| 12. Utilities relocation | 18 | Nov. 1995 | 30.00 |
| 13. Construction of H.O./Control Centre | 12 | Dec. 1996 | 16.00 |
| 14. Construction of LRT Line/Stations | 24 | Oct. 1997 | 145.00 |
| 15. Construction of Depot/Maint. factory | 12 | June 1997 | 65.00 |
| 16. Power Supply/Signalling system | 18 | Dec. 1998 | 120.00 |
| 17. Rolling Stock | 24 | June 1998 | 165.00 |
| 18. Commission Phase-1 | 2 | Aug. 2000 | 4.00 |
| 19. Operate Phase-1 | 120 | Oct. 2000 | 11.25 |
| 20. Revenue Phase-2 | 120 | Oct. 2000 | 137.50 |
| 21. Construction Phase-2 | 36 | Sept. 2007 | 60.00 |
| 22. Commission Phase-2 | 1 | Sept. 2010 | 2.00 |
| 23. Operate Phase-2 | 60 | Oct. 2010 | 13.70 |
| 24. Revenue Phase-2 | 60 | Oct. 2010 | 187.50 |
| 25. Construction Phase-3 | 36 | Sept. 2012 | 35.00 |
| 26. Commission Phase-3 | 1 | Oct. 2015 | 2.00 |
| 27. Operate Phase-3 | 120 | Oct. 2015 | 16.25 |
| 28. Revenue Phase-3 | 120 | Oct. 2015 | 250.00 |
| 29. Revenue from other sources | 300 | Oct. 2000 | 9.25 |
| 30. Transfer to Principal | 1 | Oct. 2025 | 2.00 |

Further analysis of the project was conducted including the 40% government support loan. LRT projects are usually complex in nature and when they are negotiated as a concession contract the number of risk factors is increased. However, for the purposes of case study analysis the following risk factors were examined, having been identified as major sources of risk (Razon 1994; Ling 1996; Soomro & Shamim 1996):

- Total cost of construction (–40% to + 100%)
- Demand/ridership (–50% to + 50%)
- Fare level (–20% to + 30%)
- Operation and maintenance cost (0% to + 60%)
- Delay in rolling stock delivery (–100% to 0%)

## SIMULATION RESULTS

This section provides results of a sensitivity analysis and probability analysis based on these key variables.

### Sensitivity analysis

The spider plot shown in Fig. 1 illustrates the effects on IRR of the project due to changes in the individual variables. It can be seen that the inflation in revenue, rolling stock delivery and operating revenue are the most sensitive variables for the project. Inflation in revenue is showing the highest positive impact; a 40% increase

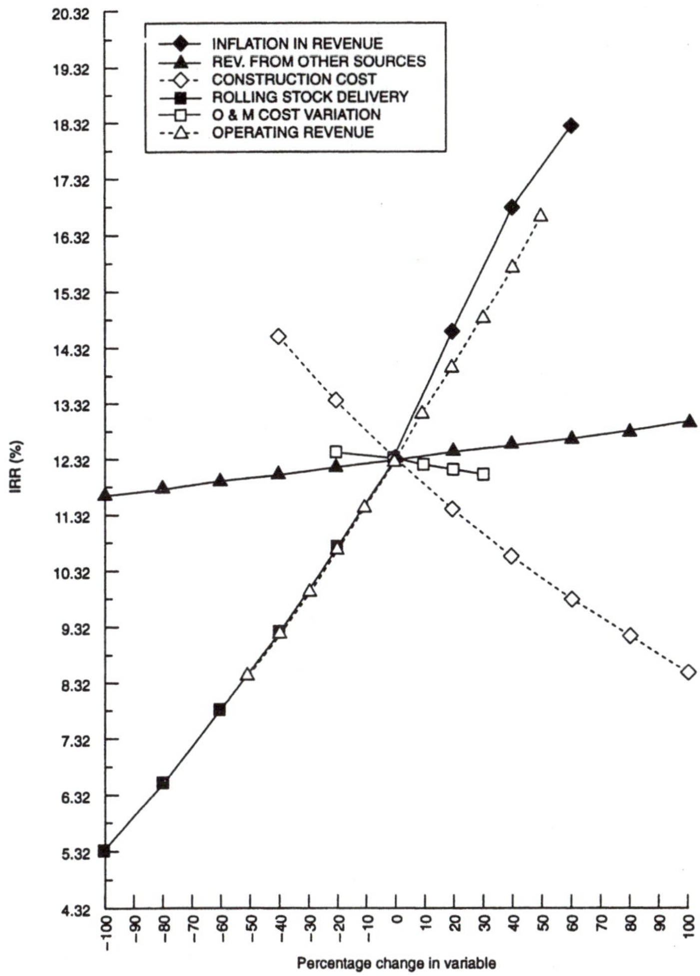


**Figure 1** Sensitivity analysis for the Karachi LRT.

in revenue inflation will result in an IRR of about 16.5%. The same effect could only be achieved by a 50% increase in operating revenue. A 50% decrease in the operating revenue will reduce the IRR to about 8.5%. The rolling stock can be identified as the single most critical element for the project completion. A delay of only 50% in its delivery will have the same effect on project viability as a 100% increase in the construction cost of the project. Revenue from other sources and operation and maintenance cost variation made negligible impact on the project outcome. A 100% increase in the non-fare based revenue will increase the IRR by only 0.75% and if there is no revenue from other sources than the IRR will be reduced by 0.6%.

The impact of variations in the operating revenue streams for three individual phases of the project was also tested. Figure 2 shows that revenue from phase 1 is most sensitive for viability of the project as during this period the debt servicing is taking place and any shortfall in revenue will impact the overall cost significantly. A 10% increase during this phase will increase the IRR of the project to more than 13%, whereas a 30% decrease will significantly decrease the IRR to less than 10%. The variation in revenue from phase 2 and phase 3 will not have such profound impact on the project outcome as revenue from phase 1. An increase of 10% in revenue of the last two phases will increase the IRR almost equally by about 0.5%. However, an important point to note is the decrease in their values, for 0a 30% reduction in the estimated revenue of phase-3 will have more adverse effect on the IRR than would phase-2.

## Probability analysis

A Monte Carlo type probability analysis was performed using the risk management software package, CASPAR. To investigate the combined effect of variables, probabilities of occurrence are assigned and triangular distribution is taken for the pessimistic, most likely and optimistic values. The cumulative frequency distribution is presented in Fig. 3, which illustrates that mean value of the IRR is 9.2% and the prediction of 12.32% IRR for the project in the base case is highly optimistic as there is 85% probability that IRR will be less than this value. A higher value of IRR is unlikely as using a 70% confidence interval the first and the last 15% values are neglected giving a range of 5% to 12.5%. The very low probability of achieving the predicted IRR suggests that the probability of occurrence of individual variables should be reduced by addressing the sources of risk with highest impact.

The analysis performed and results obtained demonstrate the importance of risk analysis. This process can be used as an effective tool to examine the effects of changes in different variables of the project, in a short time. Most of the results obtained in the simulation exercise followed the expected trend, such as the impact of increase in construction cost or decrease in operating revenue. However, the process has highlighted that individual variables such as delay in rolling

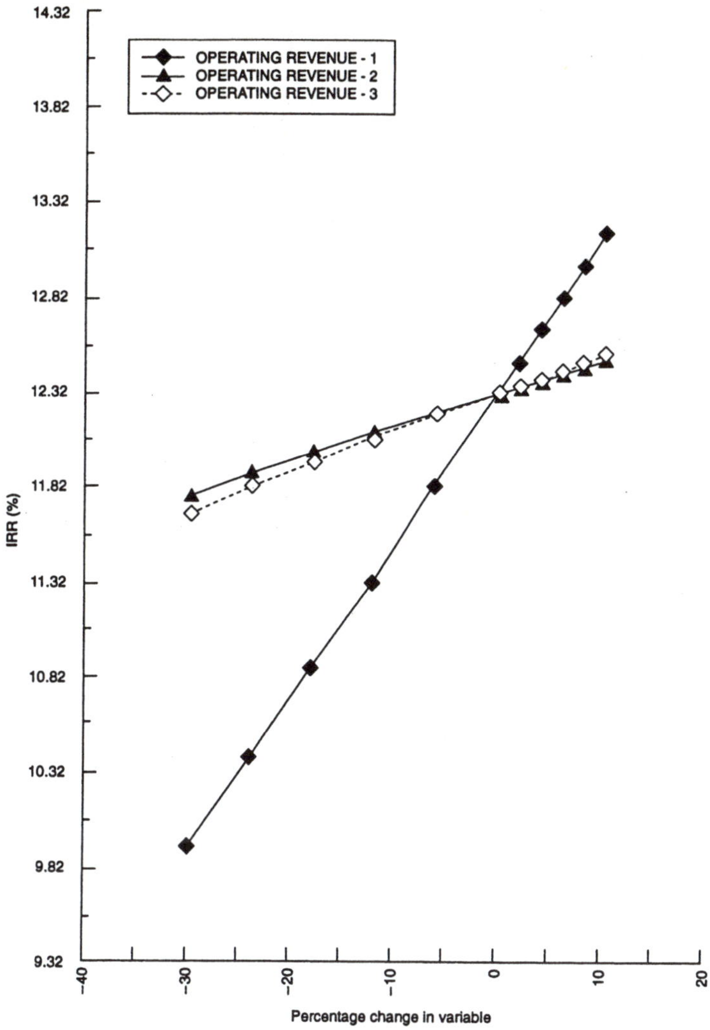


**Figure 2** Sensitivity of the operating revenue from phases 1, 2 and 3.

stock delivery can also be significant. Hence it is important that all such variables are identified and given due consideration, for success of the project. Operating revenue should also be considered separately for different phases of the project due to its varying effect.

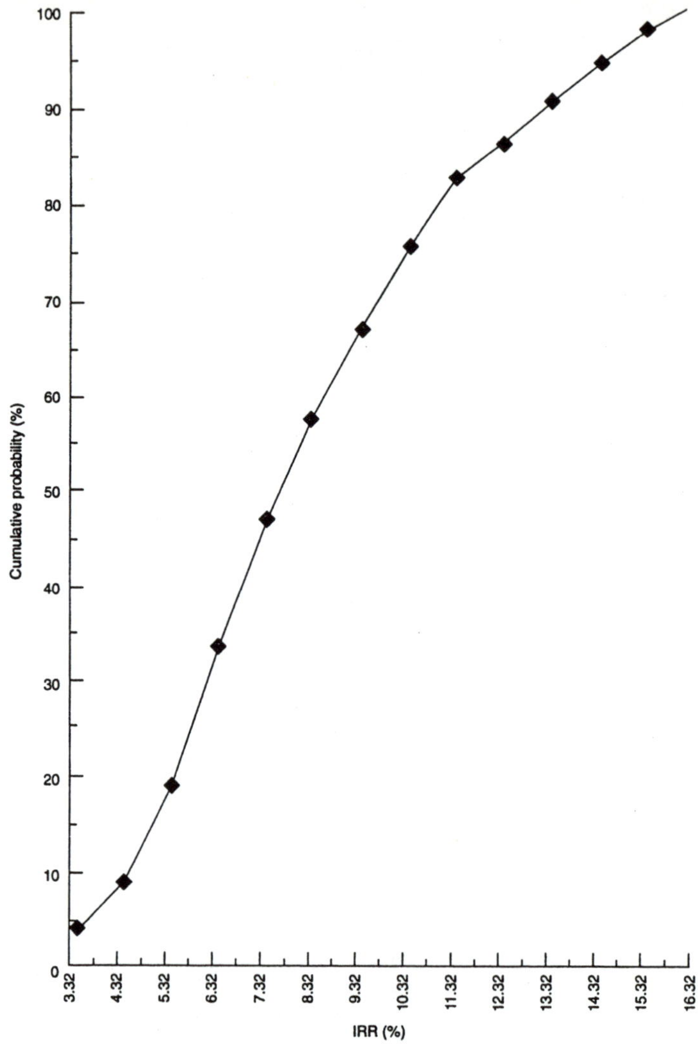


**Figure 3** Cumulative frequency distribution in terms of IRR for the Karachi LRT.

## CONCLUSIONS

The major factors influencing need for private sector financing of LRT projects have been identified as stiff competition between various sectors of the economy and cutbacks in public spending. Urban transportation projects have to compete with many other sectors for their share of the city and national budgets. With a general trend of reduced public sector investment in capital intensive infrastructure projects, LRT projects have little chance of getting implemented through traditional sources. Under these circumstances most countries are passing through a transition phase and neither the government nor the private sector alone is able to solve the ever escalating transport problems. Hence various forms of concession contract have been introduced, with a range of direct and indirect collaborative funding options to overcome this impasse, and keen interest is being shown by many governments. The Private Finance Initiative in the UK, ISTE Acts favouring public private partnership in the US, and similar schemes in most of the countries, show the moves taken by the respective governments to attract private finance.

An LRT project was selected as the case study, in Karachi, Pakistan. The major findings of risk modelling and simulations for the case study are:

- It was found that the government's contribution of 40% in the form of subordinated loans would substantially reduce the financing cost and was vital for the viability of the project.
- The delivery of rolling stock was identified as one of the most significant variables. A delay in this single activity could have a serious impact on the project's viability. It was identified that this risk should be minimised by addressing the vehicle design and specification issues early in the construction phase.
- The impact of variation in operating revenue streams for three individual phases gave different results. It was found that revenue from phase 1 was most sensitive as during this period the bulk of debt servicing is taking place and any shortfall in revenue would significantly increase the overall cost. Phase 2 was less sensitive than phase 3, which was affected by the cost of capacity expansion. This variable was dependent on the ridership forecast of the system and could be addressed by guarantee of a specified level of patronage, at least in the initial phase of the project.

### References

Augenblick, M. & Custer, B.S. (1990) *The Build, Operate and Transfer (BOT) approach to infrastructure projects in developing countries.* World Bank working paper WPS-498.

Barrow, M. (1994) Factors for successful Mass Transit Railway Projects. *Proceedings of Mass Transit Asia Conference in Singapore,* May 1994.

Barry, M. (1991) *Through the Cities; the Revolution in Light Rail.* Frankfort Press, Dublin.

Dockland Light Rail (1994) *Pre-qualification of Prospective Bidders.* Invitation document to design, finance, build and maintain DOCKLANDS Light Rail, Lewisham Extension Project. Dockland Light Rail Limited, UK.

Faghri, A., Hoel, L.A. & Joshua, S.C. (1996) A knowledge-based expert system for innovative transportation financing techn iques. *Micro Computers in Civil Engineering,* **11**, 141–150.

Honduis, H. (1995) How can tramways and light rail be made more readily affordable. *Public Transport International*, **3**, 71–77.

Hyderabad Light Rail (1994) Terms of reference for submission of implementation proposal for urban mass transit company. *Hyderabad Light Rail Transit System Project*, India.

Karachi Mass Transport (1990) *Final Report for Karachi Mass Transit Study*. Maunsell & Parsons Brinkerhoff.

Light Rail Transit Association (1996) *Light Rail and Modern Tramways*, April. Periodical of Light Rail Transit Association, UK.

Merna, T. & Smith, N.J. (1996) *Projects Procured by Privately Financed Concession Contracts*, 2nd edn, Vos 1 & 2. Asia Law and Practice, Hong Kong.

Razon, E.M. (1994) The Metro Manila Light Rail System; prelude to the future. *Proceedings of Mass Transit Asia Conference in Singapore*, May 1994.

Soomro, M.T. & Shamim, M.A. (1996) BOT funded projects in urban mass transport; experience and issues. *Proceedings of Transport Conference at Colombo*, March, 1996.

The World Bank (1995) *The private infra-structure industry; a global market of US $30 billion a year*. Note No. 45, private sector development department, The World Bank.

Wright, A.A. (1990) *Urban transit systems; guidelines for examining options*. World Bank Technical Paper No. 52.

Wright, A.A. (1994) *Public Transport in Third World Cities*. HMSO Publications, London.

[35]

# Risk Allocation in the Melbourne City Link Project

RAPHAEL HENRY ARNDT

RAPHAEL HENRY ARNDT is a Ph.D. candidate in the department of civil & environmental engineering at the University of Melbourne in Parkville, Victoria, Australia.

The A$1.8 billion (U.S.$1.2 billion) Melbourne City Link (MCL), currently under construction, is Australia's largest-ever privately funded public infrastructure project. The project sponsor is Transurban, a single-project company listed on the Australian stock exchange in 1996 and one of a handful of single-project companies publicly listed. Transurban has entered into a thirty-four-year concession with the state government of Victoria to build, own, and operate Victoria's first private toll road. At the end of this time, the project is to be transferred back to public control at no cost to the state.

## PROJECT FINANCIAL STRUCTURE

Because of an innovative financing structure, investors who paid A$500 for one Transurban security received A$499 in equity infrastructure bonds, which receive favorable tax treatment from the Australian commonwealth government; one share in the company; and one unit in an associated trust, also created for tax purposes. At the time of this writing, Transurban securities were trading in excess of A$1,300, which represents a 160% increase on the listing price. Construction of the Western Link (Tullamarine Freeway section) is on schedule to be completed in April 1999 and the Southern Link (SouthEastern Arterial #2 section) is ahead of schedule and expected to open in December 1999. Transurban has yet to begin generating revenue.

The total equity raised for the project is A$510 million. Of this, A$455 million is listed equity in Transurban, in shares and equity infrastructure bonds, and A$55 million is deferred equity from one of the contractors and the operator. Institutional investors subscribed to A$185 million of the stock prior to listing. The major investors include Transfield Infrastructure Investments Pty Ltd., the major developer and one of the major contractors; Hastings Funds Management Pty Ltd., an infrastructure investment company that administers both listed and unlisted unit trusts targeted at infrastructure investment; and Macquarie Corporate Finance Ltd., the lead financial advisor and arranger during the bid.

The total debt raised was A$1.32 billion, giving the project a debt-equity ratio of just under 0.75. Of this, A$865 million is traditional syndicated senior bank debt raised in two tranches for terms of seventeen and nineteen years with margins ranging from 150 to 170 basis points. The company used a separate, subordinated bank loan for A$150 million to fund the purchase of the electronic transponders motorists must place in their vehicles to use the road.

Finally, A$350 million was raised by an issue of CPI bonds. These are rated bonds at a fixed real interest rate; the nominal interest rate varies to reflect changes in inflation. As the toll revenue escalates with inflation, this form of finance provides Transurban with a

EXHIBIT 1
MCL Layout

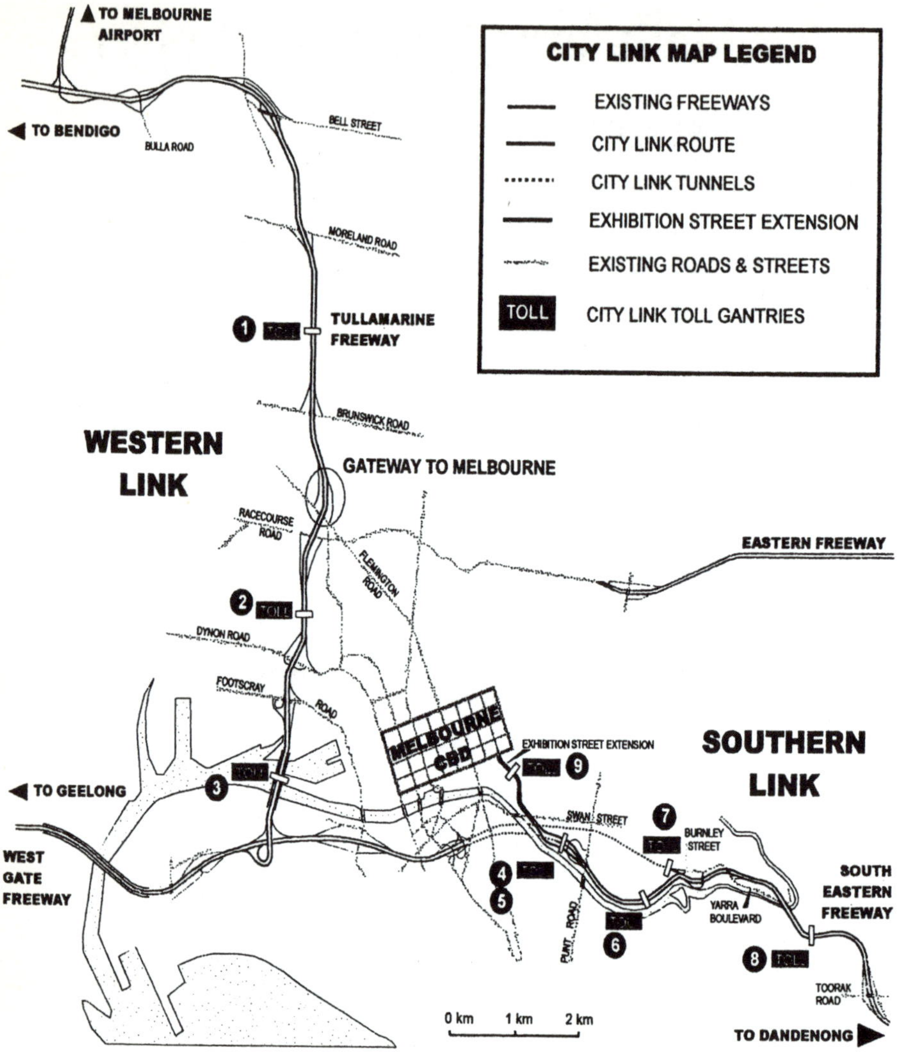

natural hedge for inflation.

## THE CONCESSION AGREEMENT

The concession agreement was hard fought, detailed, and expensive to negotiate, forcing the creation of novel risk-sharing mechanisms. In this project, the Victorian government achieved a more significant transfer of risk to the private sector than previously achieved for any Australian toll road agreement. This article discusses the major risks involved in the development of a new urban toll road such as the MCL and details how the risks were allocated to the parties. The risk profile is analyzed to determine where significant improvements have been made compared with past projects and where there may be room for further improvement as the market for private infrastructure projects matures.

The concession agreement for the MCL is likely to be used as the basis for many future large projects that are undertaken as public-private partnerships. The concession deed between Transurban (the sponsor) and the Victorian state government is publicly available in the Melbourne City Link Act 1995 ("Melbourne City Link Act" [1995]) and its associated amendments. The Victorian government holds this agreement up as a basis for future projects, including projects in industries other than roads, and the Victorian auditor-general has generally been favorable of the agreement ("Report of the Auditor General..." [1997]).

Projects such as the MCL are extremely expensive and time-consuming to negotiate. In this case, the successful tenderer had committed some $24 million by financial closure, including significant design costs (see Shepherd [1997]). Presumably, the losing bidder had also committed a substantial amount. As project tenderers cannot bear these high bidding costs indefinitely, firms seek to recoup costs accrued on unsuccessful bids when they win projects. These costs typically are factored into required rates of return and hence passed on to the community by way of reduced concession payments to the government or higher tolls to end-users when the firm is the successful bidder. The lessons learned in developing the MCL agreement should be shared and used as a starting point in future projects to reduce some of these transaction costs.

### Description of the Project

The MCL connects three of Melbourne's existing publicly funded freeways and allows traffic to bypass the Central Activities District (CAD). Previously, traffic approaching the CAD from the north (Tullamarine Freeway), the east (Eastern Freeway), the southeast (South Eastern Arterial), and the west (West Gate Freeway) had to pass through already congested city streets. The MCL widens and upgrades the Tullamarine Freeway (which serves the airport) and the South Eastern Arterial, and connects both of these formerly public roads with the West Gate Freeway. In all, about twenty-two kilometers of road is either being built or upgraded (*The Melbourne City Link Prospectus* [1996]).

This new urban toll road involves significant construction, including the widening of existing, formerly public freeways, new elevated sections, and major new bridges and tunnels under densely populated areas and the Yarra River. The tolling system for the project is completely automated, so there is no need for motorists to slow down approaching tolling plazas. A transponder in the car registers at tolling points and payment is transferred from the road user's account by direct debit, according to "user pays" principles.

### Project Timeline for Concession Agreement

Projects similar to the MCL have been contemplated in various strategic reviews of Melbourne's transport system since the mid-1950s. The Victorian government initially considered private-sector delivery and called for registration of interest in mid-1992.

It was not until mid-1994, however, that the state agreed to proceed with the project and issued a revised, output-based project brief to two short-listed bidders. At roughly the same time, the Melbourne City Link Authority was established to coordinate the government side of the process and facilitate any permits and approvals (see Megens [1995]). The Melbourne City Link Authority also has a role in reviewing the final bids, negotiating the concession agreement, and in monitoring the contracts and performance measures during the operations phase of the project.

Transurban was appointed as the preferred tenderer in mid-1995. The other tenderer, CHART Roads, was kept on "active reserve" status until financial closure was reached. CHART Roads was paid $3 million by the state government, partly compensating it for extra costs incurred due to the protracted bidding

**EXHIBIT 2**
**Project Timeline**

| | |
|---|---|
| **1992** | |
| April | Initial call for registrations of interest from the private sector. |
| May | Brief issued to interested parties. |
| July | Five proposals received. |
| September | Two bidders (Transurban and CHART Roads) shortlisted. |

Delay due to consideration of project financing requirements, particularly regarding the risks associated with electronic tolling and the impact of manual tolling on traffic diversion and space requirements.

| | |
|---|---|
| **1994** | |
| May | State agrees to proceed as a private-sector project due to advances in technology and problems with the fiscal impact of public funding. |
| August | Government decision to create the Melbourne City Link Authority. |
| September | Revised (output-based) project brief issued. |
| December | Melbourne City Link Authority established. |
| **1995** | |
| January | Bid submissions received. |
| March | Request for revised bids issued (both were nonconforming in the original format). |
| April | Revised bids received. |
| May | Recommendation of preferred bidder with the other kept on "active reserve." |
| | Government announcement of Transurban as preferred consortium. |
| July | Memorandum of understanding signed. |
| October | Concession deed signed. |

Source: *Report on Ministerial Portfolios* [1996].

process. In October 1995, the concession deed was signed, and, in March 1996, all of the conditions were met and construction began (Auditor General of Victoria [1996]).

This development process was extremely complicated and spanned a number of years. Large amounts of resources were used on both sides before a satisfactory agreement was reached.

## PROJECT RISKS

### The Victorian Government's Approach to Risk Allocation

In June 1994, the Victorian Department of Treasury released the *Infrastructure Investment Policy for Victoria* (IIPV), which superceded earlier policies covering private investment in the state's infrastructure. One of the main purposes of this policy is to facilitate private-sector investment in Victoria's infrastructure, both economic and social, by minimizing the costs of uncertainties faced by the private sector in pursuing project opportunities.

The IIPV provides guidelines for the types of projects that the government considers suitable for private-sector participation, along with a framework for the project development and tendering processes, attitudes toward intellectual property and unsolicited bids, and the government's approach to risk allocation.

In particular, the government intends to allocate risks to those parties it considers best positioned to assess and manage them. It recognizes that there is a link between risk assumed and expected returns for the project participant and intends to allocate these risks appropriately to reach the most effective solution for the state. The policy specifies that the risks associated with the design, construction, financing, and operation of an asset will generally be borne by the private sector. This philosophy has been adopted in the concession agreement for the MCL, which was implemented in accordance with the IIPV (see "Melbourne City Link Act" [1995, p. 139]).

### Risks Inherent in Urban Toll Roads

The performance of a toll road operating within a public road network can be affected by a range of risks. In this context, risks are defined as events that can influence the profitability or cash flow of the road. These can be broken into broad categories such as:

- Design and Construction Risks. Includes design suitability; obtaining necessary permits and approvals; the time and cost of construction compared with the budget; site characteristics, including environmental, archaeological, and heritage issues; and project completion and commissioning.

- Operating Risks. Production risks, including adequate tolling system operation, ability to penalize non-paying motorists, input costs, rates, and charges. Also risks associated with maintenance, service standards, meeting environmental standards, and maintaining required insurance.
- Market Risks. Traffic volume, growth of transport substitutes, availability of other revenue sources such as advertising, and the setting of toll levels subject to agreed caps.
- Sponsor Risks. Availability and structuring of finance, commercial risks such as required rates of return, tendering costs, and project viability, consortium risks including adequacy of documentation and the make-up of the project vehicle, and condition at transfer. Also includes the creditworthiness and suitability of the project vehicle and its individual parties.
- Sovereign Risks. Changes in legislation and government policy that affect the project.
- Network Risks. Access to the existing government road network and the feasibility of connecting to the existing infrastructure.
- External Risks. Force majeure events, interest rates, exchange rates, and inflation.

By the time the MCL agreement was negotiated, it was becoming generally accepted in Australia that the private sector would assume the design and construction, finance, and most operating and external risks. The critical elements were those risks that neither party was obviously "best positioned to assess and manage." The most significant of these risks for urban road projects are sovereign, network, and technology risks.

### Sovereign Risk

Australia is a federation of independent states, each with its own government. Additionally, there is a central commonwealth government, which is responsible for macroeconomic and fiscal policy, trade issues, and corporations, as well as general coordination of the various states. While state governments are responsible for providing much of the infrastructure, the commonwealth government levies income and business taxes. It returns some of these funds to the states as grants.

While most concession agreements are between a private-sector organization and a state government, the commonwealth government controls significant elements of the relevant policy and legislation. Hence state governments are not typically in a position to exert any control over changes to most taxation, subsidy and incentive schemes, and national development policies. State governments do, however, set some taxes and rates and set policy for urban transport systems such as roads and public transport.

### Network Risk

Traffic demand is probably the largest single risk for an urban toll road. Where there are many alternate routes available for toll-averse drivers, there is a tendency for those drivers to avoid tolls. This is particularly true for the MCL, which is one of the first urban toll roads to be developed as a BOOT (build-own-operate-transfer) project. The *Report on Ministerial Portfolios* [1996] reports that one study for the MCL estimated a 40% diversion rate if manual tolling was introduced. This figure was based on data for Melbourne's only other tolled road, the West Gate Bridge, for which the toll was removed more than a decade ago.

### Technology Risk

Urban toll roads are generally more constrained on right-of-way availability than interurban or country roads. This may preclude toll plazas altogether, as it did with the MCL. A fully automated tolling system therefore is required. Such a system had never been used on a real project at the time of the MCL negotiations.

## RISK ALLOCATION AND SHARING MECHANISMS

### Issues Where Optimal Risk Allocation is not Clear Cut

The government's philosophy in the MCL deal was to gain the best outcome for the community by allocating each risk to the party best able to deal with it. This provides incentives to use best management practices to reduce the probability of the risk materializing or "crystallizing," or to manage it effectively if it does crystallize.

Where no party is clearly best able to manage the risk, a transparent and fair system for risk allocation or risk-sharing must be found. This mechanism must be flexible over the life of the project and be able to cope with risks not yet envisaged. Often, significant resources are used in negotiating these risk-sharing arrangements. It is therefore useful to learn from the agreements reached in past projects.

### Traffic and Financial Models

In order to develop a risk-sharing mechanism, the parties to the MCL used a technique for measuring the effects of a risk materializing compared with the situation had the risk event not occurred. To achieve this, they developed two models. The base case financial model contains all of the assumptions and information used by Transurban in developing its business case, the proposed debt repayment schedule, and the predicted equity return. The base case traffic model is a computer-based model of the Melbourne transport system that has been used to generate the predicted traffic flows on the basis of a certain layout of the urban road network, public transport characteristics, and tolling regimes (see "Melbourne City Link Act" [1995, p. 94]).

These models are used as a basis for discussion regarding the financial effects of specified risk events. For example, when the models are linked, any change in circumstances, such as a modification in the publicly controlled traffic network, can be input and the changes in the project's cash flow and debt service requirements can be determined objectively. The models will be maintained and updated throughout the life of the project to accurately reflect the situation at any given time in comparison to the base case.

### Material Adverse Effect Regime

The material adverse effect (MAE) regime developed for the MCL is a tool that helps allocate and share risks. It also provides a mechanism for determining the size and nature of any settlement. The regime is designed to provide flexibility over the life of the project and has scope to allow for unforeseen risk events.

Before an event can be considered under the MAE regime, it must be identified. Only specified risk events for which the state has assumed at least a partial liability are covered. These events are listed in this article.

There are four stages in the MCL MAE regime. The first stage is the occurrence of an event that causes a risk to crystallize. It is then incumbent on Transurban to identify the situation and demonstrate that an MAE has occurred.

In the second stage, the parties agree that the event is material. This is defined as having an effect on the ability of a sponsor such as Transurban to repay the project debt in accordance with the amortization schedule or the level or timing of revenues and disbursements ("Melbourne City Link Act" [1995, p. 115]). This avoids wasting resources on minor disputes.

The third phase of the MAE procedure is "good faith" negotiation between the parties to resolve the issue leading to the MAE and to determine the likely consequences of the event occurring. In the event that no consensus can be found, the matter is referred for binding arbitration.

Assuming that consensus is reached, the final stage of the MAE procedure is to determine the level and form of compensation required. The agreed base case financial model and base case traffic model may be used to determine the effect of the MAE on the project's cash flow and projected returns. These models are a critical element of the MAE regime, as they provide an objective and agreed approach to determining the effects of any risk event on the project.

Typically, redress is to the extent that the debt servicing ability and the projected equity return to Transurban's investors is reinstated to where it was prior to the event. The form and method of redress is then determined and must be agreed upon by both parties from the following range of options ("Melbourne City Link Act" [1995, p. 158]):

- Amending the toll calculation schedule.
- Varying the concession period.
- Altering the risk allocation.
- Varying the rights of the state to receive payments.
- Requesting lenders to restructure project financing arrangements.
- Asking the state to make a financial contribution to the project.
- Any other method agreed upon by the parties.

Financial compensation is used only as a method of last resort in certain limited cases and where no other method of redress is available.

The variety of compensation methods allows the greatest possible flexibility in determining what action to take. Most of the options make calculating the actual compensation relatively easy, either in absolute or net present value terms. However, any attempt to alter the agreed risk allocation appears problematic and uncertain.

It is extremely difficult to assign probabilities to the occurrence of many of the risks and even more difficult to value them. This method of compensation is therefore only useful in trading off other crystallized risks for which there is a known and agreed financial value. In the interests of public accountability and transparency, it would be preferable for a direct compensatory payment to be made to Transurban rather than a nebulous trading of liabilities.

### Criticism of MAE Clauses

A number of recent Australian studies have examined the effectiveness of MAE clauses in allocating risks. The Industry Commission (Hepburn et al. [1997]) has criticized MAE clauses for restricting the flexibility of future governments to alter their policy without paying compensation to the private-sector parties involved. They also criticize the high transaction costs associated with administering such a clause.

> Material Adverse Effect clauses notionally [transfer] some of the cost of risk to the public in the form of a loss of flexibility — a loss of option value that potentially increases the cost of transport infrastructure in the future. There is also a potential for transaction costs to be incurred if the parties cannot quickly agree on whether a material adverse effect has occurred when the provisions are invoked (Hepburn et al. [1997, p. 12]).

Another recent inquiry also claims that BOOT agreements reduce government policy-making flexibility (see House of Representatives Standing Committee on Communications Transport and Microeconomic Reform [1997]).

> A BOOT agreement for a road project may prevent the government from developing public-transport services that would compete with the road or require the government to compensate the road operator in such circumstances (p. 114).

However, the dissenting report to that inquiry states

> The economic consequences for the government are identical whether the government retains the ownership of the tolled road or agrees to pay appropriate compensation to a private operator.

Had the road been developed as a publicly funded project, all the risks described in the MAE clause would have been retained by the public sector. MAE clauses merely set out those risks that are retained by the state, thereby transferring the remainder to the private sector. Secondly, the government does not lose flexibility when a project is publicly funded. Governments are free to make policy decisions, however, they must pay fair compensation to the project for any negative repercussions of a change in policy. Hence governments must assess all of the costs that will result from a change in policy.

This discipline is necessary for an efficient use of resources and often has been lacking or unclear in public-sector decision-making in the past. The requirement for compensatory payments enforces a rigorous, full network cost benefit analysis to be performed for new projects rather than merely a calculation on a single project in isolation.

It is true that there may be quite high transaction and monitoring costs associated with MAE clauses, and they may prove to be cumbersome years into the future. It is incumbent on the authors of these clauses to draft them in a manner that is as flexible as possible and that reduces monitoring costs as far as practicable. As greater experience is gained by all the parties involved, setup and monitoring costs are expected to decrease.

The many benefits that accrue from private-sector delivery should be traded off against the relatively high transaction and monitoring costs associated with operating an MAE clause to determine whether a BOOT delivery system is justified.

The apparent success of the MCL MAE regime is proof that these complex issues can be worked through and resolved to the requirements of governments, private sponsors, and the financial markets.

## THE MCL RISK ALLOCATION

### Agreed Risk Allocation

The risk allocation for the MCL generally follows the principles set out in the IIPV. That is, risks are allocated "to those parties which the Government considers best positioned to assess and manage" them. It is therefore not surprising to see Transurban bearing the risks associated with design, construction, financing, and operation.

Transurban is also responsible for all unidentified risks. In the words of the Auditor-General of Victoria:

> While certain project responsibilities and risks have been assumed by the State, substantial risks and exposures have been transferred to Transurban and the users of the City Link (see *Report on Ministerial Portfolios* [1996]).

In the case of the MCL, risks could be allocated to three parties: the private sponsor, the state, and the end-users on whose behalf the state negotiated. In order to achieve the most efficient outcome for the community, it is essential that all of the state's liabilities are included in any cost comparison made between a public-private partnership and a fully public development. It is therefore critical to understand the type and nature of the liabilities the state has accepted in the MCL deal.

### Design and Construction Risks

***Environmental.*** The state agreed to indemnify Transurban for most costs associated with an environmental impact statement (EIS) if one was required by the commonwealth government. In the worst possible scenario, Transurban could have terminated the agreement if the costs associated with complying with an EIS were too great. An EIS had already been done by the state for part of the project, and ultimately no further analysis was required.

The state has also agreed to compensate Transurban for costs it incurs in complying with a clean-up notice for any pollution or contamination on the site that preexisted the handover date and that Transurban could not reasonably have been aware of at financial closure. This is consistent with local legislation requiring the polluter to reinstate a site to its clean condition if that polluter can be identified. Alternatively, the owner of the site when the pollution occurred is deemed responsible. In this case, the state retains ownership of the project land.

***Heritage/Native Title.*** The state has accepted the risk of any impact of a native title claim by indigenous Australians or any action taken to safeguard or restore heritage buildings or sites within the project area. Under the commonwealth's proposed native title legislation, indigenous Australians can claim land rights or compensation over certain land under specific conditions. The details of the act are yet to be determined, and much uncertainty existed at the time the MCL was being negotiated. The state has acted to allay the concerns of Transurban and their financiers by removing this risk from their calculations. As the state is the owner of the land, it is likely that it would be held responsible for this risk anyway.

Heritage listings and directions are controlled by the state government. In this case, the parliament has excluded the MCL project area from the workings of the normal heritage protection procedures.

***Existing Structures.*** Certain existing structures were transferred from public ownership to Transurban, together with parts of the Tullamarine Freeway and South Eastern Arterial. A list of known faults in these structures was prepared and a specified amount was paid by the state to Transurban to repair them. Any future faults in the structures that were not listed are to be repaired by Transurban.

***Industrial Relations.*** Labor disputes have the capacity to disrupt the smooth running of the project, both during the development and the operating stages. The state has shared this risk by agreeing to compensate Transurban for any loss associated with disputes, either aimed specifically at state government policy, or due to opposition to the implementation of the project or other state projects. Other labor disputes remain the responsibility of Transurban.

At the time of financial closure there were a number of labor disputes directed at road projects and the government's road policy. For that reason, the private sponsor was not prepared to accept the risk of such disputes.

### Network Risks

This was one of the most contentious and difficult issues to resolve. Transurban recognized that the government had to retain the right to operate and manage Melbourne's transport network, including freeways and public transport. The private-sector sponsor and its bankers, however, had to have enough certainty to justify the traffic predictions and the project's financing on a non-recourse basis.

To mitigate this risk, the government has agreed not to discriminate between the MCL and other freeways in the state's transport system that are publicly owned and operated. This means that the laws controlling speed limits, safety procedures, and upgrades may be changed, but only so far as those laws and policies apply across the transport system. The state's ability to vary the nature and make-up of the public transport system is not hindered in any way. Changes in public transport routes and pricing are, however, subject to the MAE regime.

The state has accepted the obligation of maintaining the connecting roads to the MCL as it would for any other freeway. This is a good example of the state retaining a risk — the risk of retaining functioning connections from the MCL into the wider road network — that it is clearly better placed to control and manage than Transurban. Had the state insisted that Transurban bear this risk, either the project would have been unfinanceable, or Transurban would have charged the state (or the users of the MCL) an amount to bear that risk that is necessarily greater than the cost to the state for managing it internally.

The MAE regime is used as a tool to determine the level of compensation payable should the connecting roads fail to be maintained adequately and a material adverse effect to the project result.

The government also resolved to adopt certain agreed traffic management measures in the surrounding road network. These include allowing on-street parking in certain streets, downgrading certain roads, and even closing some existing roads. All of these changes were consistent with the government's broader aims for developing Melbourne's transport system and removing heavy traffic from local roads. The modifications, however, would also have the effect of causing the MCL to become more attractive to road users. Transurban has relied on these alterations to the road network in their traffic modeling. The state has therefore agreed to compensate Transurban if the agreed traffic management measures are not initiated by a certain date or of they are removed at some time in the future. Should the state institute further changes to the transport system that enhance the economic viability of the road, 50% of the additional benefits, net of increased costs, derived by Transurban are returned to the state. These benefits are determined using the base case traffic model and the base case financial model.

### Sovereign Risks

The state bears the risk of changes in state law that are detrimental to the project and that do not affect business generally. For example, the state has agreed to bear the risk of changes in state road or carbon taxes, fuel excise, or other environmental taxes but not for changes in payroll or sales taxes. The MAE regime is used to determine the effect of these potential legislative changes on the project's viability and to calculate the nature and amount of any redress.

The state, together with the toll road users, has accepted the risk of changes in commonwealth laws that discriminate against the project or that would not affect business generally. Again, this includes fuel excise and environmental taxes but may also include changes in the interpretation and application of Australia's taxation system that would not affect businesses generally. In this case, there is no option for financial compensation. Any compensation that is payable is limited to restoring the position of debt and equity that was projected in the base case model. The state's liability is limited to the loss of payments due under the concession deed. Other forms of compensation such as extending the concession term or allowing increased tolls above the regulated caps allocate this risk to the road's customers. Market forces will dictate whether those potential toll increases are sustainable.

In order to protect Transurban from changes in state government policy regarding private-sector investment, certain "acts of prevention" that hinder them from constructing, operating, or collecting tolls for the MCL are also covered by the MAE regime.

### External Risks

The risk of more traditional force majeure events is shared. This includes events such as natural disasters that are clearly out of the control of either party. If the event could have been insured against, Transurban must repair the damage. If this is not possible because the financiers have elected to use the insurance proceeds for debt repayment, Transurban may hand over the relevant part of the MCL to the state. If Transurban elects to repair the damage, the state has agreed to allow Transurban to restore its ability to repay the project debt and may provide redress to equity investors via the MAE regime to restore a specified minimum equity return. However, these forms of redress are limited to non-financial means and the maximum length of the concession period is capped at fifty-four years.

In the case of an uninsurable event, Transurban may similarly choose not to repair the affected part of the MCL if the equity return would fall below the lower of that projected in the base case model or the return that existed prior to the event. If the cost of reinstatement after any insurance proceeds have been applied exceeds a cap of A$450 million, Transurban may hand the affected part of the road over to the state at no cost. If the damage is repaired, then Transurban's investors will be able to seek redress under the MAE in a similar way to that for uninsurable events. Again, no financial compensation is payable and end-users may ultimately bear much of this risk. The same system applies to events that affect critical access routes to the MCL (which are publicly controlled) even if no damage is done to the MCL itself.

All the other risks, such as design and construction risks; financing risks, including interest rates; most operating risks, including the effectiveness of the previously untried automatic tolling system and the condition of the asset at transfer back to the government rest with the sponsor.

Most significantly, Transurban has explicitly accepted the risk of traffic demand, which Transurban considers the most critical risk to the project's viability once construction is completed (see *The Melbourne City Link Prospectus* [1996, p. 55]). There are no state-provided minimum usage or revenue guarantees.

### Contentious Risks for the State

The state's policy is to accept only risks it is best placed to control and manage. It adheres to the concept of risk-reward, in which the party assuming a risk should have access to associated rewards. Conversely, the party to whom the rewards flow should accept the risk. However, in a number of cases, as listed below, the risk regime for the MCL appears to depart from this philosophy.

***Network Risk.*** The state has rightly accepted the risk of changes in the state-controlled road network that connects to the MCL, adversely affecting MCL patronage. However, it is also important that this risk allocation be symmetrical. That is, if one party accepts the consequences of a downside risk, it should also gain the benefits of an upside risk.

The government has agreed to fully compensate Transurban under the MAE regime for any detriment to the project resulting from publicly sponsored changes in the transport network. However, if any modifications result in increased traffic volumes and profits for Transurban, only 50% of these are passed back to the State ("Melbourne City Link Act" [1995, p. 148]).

***Sovereign Risks.*** Again the state has rightly accepted the risk of discriminatory state policy or law adversely affecting the MCL. However, the state is arguably in no better a position to influence commonwealth government policy than Transurban with regard to taxation or other laws. Changes in commonwealth fuel excise taxes would influence many industries, including haulage, more directly than the MCL. It seems incongruous that Victorian taxpayers and road users have accepted this risk.

This risk allocation is also asymmetrical. Commonwealth laws could change to either increase or decrease the profitability of the project. If the project is enhanced by a change in policy that stimulates motor vehicle travel, the state derives no benefit from the contract other than through an imperfect, catch-all, superprofits clause. This clause allows some revenue-sharing with the state if profits far exceed those expected, or a reduction in the concession term if a certain, generous equity return is achieved.

***External Risks.*** The consequences of force majeure events are, by definition, outside the control of either party. The agreement should, however, provide the maximum incentive for both sides to avoid if possible, or else minimize any damage caused by these events. By agreeing to modify the concession agreement to allow Transurban to repay its debt providers and restore equity investors to some set level, albeit by non-financial means, the state has removed at least some of this incentive. If Transurban had been running any other business, its investors would be fully exposed to the risk of force majeure events. A return for bearing these risks is factored into standard market rates of return. This would ensure that the project sponsor takes all possible steps to design the MCL in such a way as to reduce the extent and cost of repairing any damage.

However, the state has ensured that Transurban's only options for redress are to pass on additional costs to end-users or to extend the concession period. Any increases in the tolls are subject to market forces. This puts Transurban in a situation similar to that of most other businesses following a force majeure event. The main difference here is that the business has partial monopoly characteristics and is subject to government regulation.

### Concession Note Scheme

The concession agreement requires Transurban to make certain payments to the state. These amount to A$95.6 million per year for the term of construction for the first twenty-five years of operation, A$45.2 million per year for the next eighteen years, and A$1 million per year thereafter.

**EXHIBIT 3**
**MCL Risk Matrix**

| | Government | Sponsor |
|---|---|---|
| **Design and Construction** | | |
| Design | | ✓ |
| Construction | | ✓ |
| Site | (✓) | ✓ |
| Approvals | (✓) | ✓ |
| Completion | | ✓ |
| **Operation** | | |
| Production | (✓) | ✓ |
| Asset Upgrade | | ✓ |
| Maintenance | | ✓ |
| Environmental | ✓ | (✓) |
| Insurance | | ✓ |
| **Market** | | |
| Demand/Volume | (✓) | ✓ |
| Revenue | | ✓ |
| **Sponsor** | | |
| Consortium | | ✓ |
| Commercial | | ✓ |
| Finance | (✓) | ✓ |
| Default | | ✓ |
| Condition at Transfer | | ✓ |
| **Sovereign** | | |
| Legislation | ✓ | ✓ |
| Policy | ✓ | ✓ |
| Residual Value | | ✓ |
| **Network** | | |
| Access Regime | ✓ | |
| Linked Infrastructure | ✓ | (✓) |
| **External** | | |
| Force Majeure | ✓ | ✓ |
| Financial | | ✓ |

Key: ✓ Majority of risk accepted. (✓) Partial risk accepted.

Instead of paying cash to the state, Transurban may choose to issue a *concession note*. This is effectively a promissory note redeemable only at the end of the concession period (a nominal thirty-four years) unless certain conditions are met. In order to redeem a note and obtain the payment, the real after-tax equity return at that date must be at least 10% per year and the payment must make up less than 30% of the previous year's distributable cash flow. As returns to equity are subordinate to debt, this also presupposes that all debt has been repaid or is not in arrears. No interest is paid on the concession notes (see *The Melbourne City Link Prospectus* [1996, p. 39]).

Although the main return to the state is obtaining a functioning motorway asset earlier than it could through public-sector delivery, and ultimately receiving that asset free of charge, the concession fees paid by Transurban also provide a return to the state on its direct investment in the project — mainly expenses for ancillary roadwork and landscaping. As the timing of the payment of the concession fees varies depending on the project economics, the present value of the concession fees can fluctuate substantially. As a result, at least part of the state's return is linked to the financial viability of the project. Hence the state is indirectly exposed to traffic flow and other risks that it has tried to transfer to Transurban.

It must be recognized that the private infrastructure industry in Australia is still in a formative state. As experience is gained, risk issues are becoming better understood by all of the parties involved and the private sector is increasingly willing to accept project risks. As will be discussed below, the MCL risk allocation is a significant improvement over that of previous projects. With further market development, governments can be expected to push the boundaries of risks that the private sector is prepared to accept and finance even further toward the theoretical optimum.

### Improvements over Previous Australian Toll Road Agreements

A number of other Australian urban roads have been developed as private/public partnerships. These began in 1989, with the signing of the agreement to develop the Sydney Harbour Tunnel, which was followed by agreements for the M4, M5, and M2 motorways in New South Wales (NSW).

The Sydney Harbour Tunnel agreement has been much criticized as a public underwriting of private-sector profits. The contract was structured in such a way that, while the private sponsor accepted some development, design, and construction risks, the majority of the financing, demand, and operational risks were left with the government. Indeed, the state government not only directly contributed to the costs of construction, but has also underwritten the revenue stream of the inflation-linked bonds (the main financing instrument), irrespective of the actual usage of the road (see "Private Participation in the Provision of Public Infrastructure" [1994]).

The M4 motorway was a relatively modest refurbishment and upgrade of an existing freeway by the private sector. The risk related to traffic demand was low, as the road already had established users. Although the sponsor has accepted the traffic risk in this case, the risk is not large and is further mitigated by the state agreeing to place the toll plaza in a section of the road adjacent to, but not within, the private-sector road. In fact, many of the toll payers do not even use the section of the M4 that was provided by the sponsor ("Private Participation in the Provision of Public Infrastructure" [1994]).

The NSW government provided funds for the construction of the M5 motorway near Sydney in the form of a low-interest loan. While the private sponsor again carries the design, construction, and traffic risks, the state bears much of the financing risk. Any other risks that are not explicitly defined are shared between the parties. There is no clear facility for the sharing of superprofits that may be caused by government modifications to the transport system, and which are extremely likely to occur. Indeed, already there are plans for a publicly funded extension of the project to outlying suburbs, which clearly would increase patronage on the connecting private road. The current state government chose to remove the tolls on both the M4 and M5 tollways by compensating road users for any tolls paid. Road users who register are sent a statement by the road operator listing their usage patterns for the time period in question. Users may then submit this statement to the government to receive a refund. The government compensates road operators for administrative and processing costs incurred by this system. The removal of tolling has increased the usage of the roads and provided windfall gains to the private-sector operators without the state receiving a pass-through benefit ("Private Participation in the Provision of Public Infrastructure" [1994]).

The M2 motorway was a more recent BOOT project in NSW, entered into in 1994. Risks associated with design and construction, finance, operation, and traffic flows have been transferred to the private sponsor. The state has agreed to provide compensation for changes in state and commonwealth taxation, local council rates, land acquisition, certain environmental issues, and public policies that have adverse effects as well as carrying the risk of general changes in the transport network. The force majeure risk is also shared in a similar way to that agreed to in the MCL. The rent payable to the government is subordinate to the finances of the project in a similar way to the concession notes scheme of the MCL. The state has agreed to indemnify the M2 for any increases in costs due to changes in state or commonwealth legislation "not reasonably foreseeable when the Project Deed was signed" (*M2 Motorway Prospectus* [1994]). This is arguably a much broader indemnity than that given by the Victorian government in the MCL project. In the words of the NSW Auditor-General:

> The [State] has handled risk allocation in a noticeably clearer way in these M2 arrangements than in previous arrangements for [the M4 and M5] Motorways and the [Sydney Harbour] Tunnel ("Roads and Traffic Authority — The M2 Motorway" [1995, p. 13]).

However, this agreement does not go to the same lengths as the MCL concession arrangements in sharing any gains accruing to the sponsors from favorable changes in the transport network or additional connections to the road.

> Where costs arise, some government concession is sought, but where benefits arise, they are to the profit of the developers ("Roads and Traffic Authority — The M2 Motorway" [1995, p. 36]).

The MCL agreement has shifted more risk to the private sector than in any previous Australian toll road. It has also created more symmetry in the acceptance of risk by the project parties. That is, in certain circumstances, the state receives a share of the benefits accruing from unforeseen risk events in the MCL deal, but not in the M2 project. One advisor to the Victorian government explained that

> The risk allocation [for the MCL] does mirror many of the aspects of the previous M2 toll road project but a closer reading of the documents indicates a further shift of risk to the private sector for projects of this type (Cunningham [1996, p. 76]).

### Areas for Future Improvement

There clearly has been a trend over time toward more clear, rational, and symmetrical risk allocation in Australian toll road projects, the MCL being the most recent example. However, as discussed, some of the risks in this project appear not to have been allocated to the parties best equipped to assume them, and not all of the risks have been allocated symmetrically.

The state government of Victoria is clearly not in a position to directly influence commonwealth government policy. The risk of changes in commonwealth government law and policy should be shared between the private sponsor and the state government. Future deals should adopt a sharing mechanism that provides adequate incentives to the private sector to reduce the effects of any changes. For example, the project could be financed in a way that reduces the potential effects of such changes.

Similarly, the risk of costs arising from an EIS should be shared so as to provide an incentive to the sponsor to design the project in the most environmentally sensitive way, while recognizing the state's influence in selecting the transport corridor.

Force majeure risks should be shared so as to provide the maximum incentive for the private sponsor to design the road to minimize any damage due to these events. The discipline of these cost benefit trade-offs is one of the features that make BOOT projects attractive to public decision-makers.

To create the maximum incentive to manage risks efficiently, risk allocation should be symmetrical. That is, if a party is exposed to a downside risk, it should also have the benefit of a related upside potential. In some aspects of the MCL deal relating to changes in the transport network and commonwealth law, this allocation is not fully symmetrical.

Finally, subordinating the concession payments to the project's financial situation is less than optimal. The risk of a project not meeting its financial projections is typically assumed by equity. By allowing some of its payments from Transurban to be deferred and reduced in present value terms, the state has removed some incentive for Transurban to manage its resources.

## CONCLUSION

In the MCL, Melbourne has received a significant and much needed integrated freeway system that would have been significantly delayed or probably never built — given the government's policy of fiscal restraint — if funding was restricted to traditional means. In spite of a complicated project, contained within an existing government-controlled traffic network, risks were allocated and risk-sharing mechanisms developed that were mutually acceptable to the sponsors, institutional investors, financiers, and the government.

This agreement is a significant improvement on previous, privately funded urban toll roads in Australia due to a greater degree of risk shifting to the private sector and a related reduction in contingent costs to Victorian taxpayers. There is greater symmetry in the risk allocation, which should result in greater effort to avoid potential risks and in better management of those risks that do arise.

Just as the MCL agreement improves on the deals made in previous projects, as the market continues to evolve the state can look to some areas to further reduce its liability. Its policy of allocating risks to those who are best placed to bear them could be applied more effectively and incentives for the private sector to avoid or better manage risk events could be increased.

## ENDNOTE

Assistance received from the Victorian Department of Treasury and Finance, the Melbourne City Link Authority, and Transurban City Link Ltd. in preparing this article is gratefully acknowledged. The author also thanks the Institution of Municipal Engineers of Australia for funding that made this work possible. All opinions expressed in this article are those of the author alone.

## REFERENCES

Cunningham, G. "Private Sector Investment in Infrastructure — The Melbourne City Link Toll Road Project." *Interdata Infrastructure Handbook 4*. KPMG Infrastructure Group, TFP Asia, 1996, pp. 75-78.

Hepburn, G. et al. "Private Investment in Urban Roads." Industry Commission, Canberra, 1997.

House of Representatives Standing Committee on Communications Transport and Microeconomic Reform. "Planning, not Patching: An Inquiry into Federal Road Funding." Canberra, 1997.

*Infrastructure Investment Policy for Victoria*. Victorian Department of Treasury and Finance, Melbourne, 1994.

Megens, P. "Melbourne City Link Authority Act 1994 — A New Approach to Private Sector Involvement in Public Sector Infrastructure in Victoria." *Australian Construction Law Newsletter*, 40 (1995), pp. 35-36.

"Melbourne City Link Act." Parliament of Victoria, Melbourne, 1995.

*The Melbourne City Link Prospectus*. Transurban City Link Ltd., Melbourne, 1996.

*M2 Motorway Prospectus*. Hills Motorway Ltd., Sydney, 1994.

"Private Participation in the Provision of Public Infrastructure: The Roads and Traffic Authority." Auditor General of New South Wales, Sydney, 1994.

"Report of the Auditor General on the Statement of Financial Operations 1996-1997." Auditor General of Victoria, Melbourne, 1997.

*Report on Ministerial Portfolios*. Auditor General of Victoria, Melbourne, 1996.

"Roads and Traffic Authority — The M2 Motorway." Audit Office of New South Wales, Sydney, 1995.

Shepherd, T. "Presentation to IEAust Transport Branch Seminar." Infrastructure for the New Millennium, Institution of Engineers Australia, Melbourne, 1997.

# [36]

PERGAMON

International Journal of Project Management 20 (2002) 107–118

INTERNATIONAL JOURNAL OF PROJECT MANAGEMENT

www.elsevier.com/locate/ijproman

# Evaluating the risks of public private partnerships for infrastructure projects

Darrin Grimsey [a], Mervyn K. Lewis [b,*]

[a] PricewaterhouseCoopers, Spring Street, GPO Box 1331L, Melbourne, Victoria, Australia
[b] School of International Business, University of South Australia, North Terrace, GPO Box 2471, Adelaide, Australia

Received 14 October 1999; received in revised form 16 May 2000; accepted 9 July 2000

**Abstract**

In many countries, limitations upon the public funds available for infrastructure have led governments to invite private sector entities to enter into long-term contractual agreements for the financing, construction and/or operation of capital intensive projects. For the public procurer, there is an obvious need to ensure that value-for-money has been achieved. To the project sponsors, such ventures are characterised by low equity in the project vehicle and a reliance on direct revenues to cover operating and capital costs, and service debt finance provided by banks and other financiers. Risk evaluation is complex, requiring the analysis of risk from the different perspectives of the public and private sector entities. This paper analyses the principles involved, drawing on practical experience of evaluating such projects to present a framework for assessing the risks, and using as illustration a case study of a waste water treatment facility in Scotland which is typical of most PPP projects. © 2001 Elsevier Science Ltd. All rights reserved.

*Keywords:* Public private partnerships; Infrastructure; Project finance; Risk analysis

## 1. Introduction

For most of the post-war period, government has been the principal provider of infrastructure (at least outside of the United States). Over the last decade, that position has begun to change. Faced with pressure to reduce public sector debt and, at the same time, expand and improve public facilities, governments have looked to private sector finance, and have invited private sector entities to enter into long-term contractual agreements which may take the form of construction or management of public sector infrastructure facilities by the private sector entity, or the provision of services (using infrastructure facilities) by the private sector entity to the community on behalf of a public sector body.

These arrangements often take the form of a build-operate-transfer (BOT) arrangement [1]. The acronym BOT was first used in the early eighties by Turkey's Prime Minister Targut Ozal [2]. However, the concept itself can be traced back to Hong Kong in the late fifties when a privatised vehicle tunnel was first talked about, and if regarded as a form of concession or franchise arrangement has even earlier origins. According to Monod [3], the first "concession" was granted in 1782 to Perrier in France and concerned water distribution, which in the context of this paper seems entirely appropriate.

In Australia, public/private sector infrastructure arrangements date back to the bicentennial year 1988. In the UK, the Private Finance Initiative (PFI) was introduced by the Conservative Government in November 1992, widening its privatisation and contracting out policies to incorporate the provision of infrastructure and public services by a hybrid approach of combined public and private sector funding [4]. Procurement was subsequently redefined as the provision of services rather than the ownership of assets, with partnerships sought on a range of projects and PFI promoted as a preferred procurement method — a position which did not change with the incoming Labour administration which in 1997 built on the initiative with Public Private Partnerships [5]. The European Commission, through its grant mechanism, is encouraging PPPs with projects so far in Portugal, Italy, Netherlands, Greece and Ireland [6]. The techniques have been adapted to promote investment both in local authority services and in infrastructure projects more generally elsewhere [7,8].

This paper analyzes the risks of PPP arrangements from the perspectives of the various parties. The character of

* Corresponding author. Tel.: +61-8-8302-0536; fax: +61-8-8302-0512.

*E-mail address:* mervyn.lewis@unisa.edu.au (M.K. Lewis).

0263-7863/01/$22.00 
PII: S0263-7863(00)00040-5

infrastructure investments and the nature of PPPs shape the riskiness of any individual project. Thus we begin by examining the nature of infrastructure and how PPPs are structured.

## 2. What is infrastructure?

Infrastructure is easier to recognize than define. Investment in infrastructure is thought to provide "basic services to industry and households" [9], "key inputs into the economy" [10], and "a crucial input to economic activity and growth" [7], although what is "basic", "key" and "crucial" varies from country to country and from one time to another (steel production was once regarded as essential infrastructure). Recently, the activities regarded as infrastructure investment include:

- Energy (power generation and supply);
- Transport (toll roads, light rail systems, bridges and tunnels);
- Water (sewerage, waste water treatment and water supply);
- Telecommunications (telephones);
- Social infrastructure (hospitals, prisons, courts, museums, schools and Government accommodation).

These share with other types of fixed investment (such as property development, office construction [11]) a number of common characteristics:

- Duration (infrastructure is long-lived, and has a long gestation process);
- Illiquid (the lumpiness and indivisibility of infrastructure projects makes for a limited secondary market);
- Capital intensive (projects are large scale and highly geared);
- Valuation (projects are difficult to value because of taxation and pricing rules and embedded options [12,13] and guarantees).

The result is that evaluation of the projects is a complex and specialised activity.

The litmus test used to be that infrastructure had to be provided by government-owned enterprises (the predominant approach in Europe) or by privately owned utilities subject to rate of return regulation (the approach in much of the United States). This conviction derived from a number of inherent features, such as the existence of:

- Network services, providing integrative activities which bind economic activity together;
- Public goods, from which it is difficult (and perhaps not desirable) to exclude non-payers (the non-excludability principle);
- Externalities, whereby benefits and costs are conferred upon those not a party to the transaction (e.g. spillovers);
- Natural monopolies, for which scale economies make it efficient to have only one provider (for example, of an electricity grid).

The trend away from public to private provision of infrastructure has been underpinned by a marked change in thinking and practice on these matters. There has been the perception, for example, that a move from 'taxpayer pays' to 'user pays' (i.e. from ability-to-pay to the benefit principle) in the provision of infrastructure services (water, power) is likely to be associated with a better economic use of the services. Many industries considered to be natural monopolies, e.g. electricity generation and telecommunications, have been broken up geographically into different regional firms or, with deregulation, separated into competitive (or potentially competitive) sectors vis-à-vis those sectors that remain natural monopolies (the distinction between power supply and high-voltage transmission, and between railway operation and rail track services). In those activities which have natural monopoly characteristics, substitution of price-cap regulation for rate-of-return regulation (i.e. fixing of maximum prices rather than the mark up over costs) has created strong incentives to reduce costs, while third party access to certain facilities that are not economic to duplicate has widened competition in the upstream and downstream markets served by the facilities. All of this has laid the groundwork for PPP arrangements.

## 3. PPP arrangements

Confusion sometimes exists between 'infrastructure financing' and 'infrastructure investment'. The former can arise from the privatisation of existing facilities, whereas infrastructure investment involves the development, operation and ownership either by the private sector alone or in a joint venture between government and the private sector entity. The distinction is analogous to buying an existing office block, already fully let, as opposed to developing a new site — the attendant risks are obviously quite different in the two cases.

Accordingly, PPPs can be defined as agreements where public sector bodies enter into long-term contractual agreements with private sector entities for the construction or management of public sector infrastructure facilities by the private sector entity, or the provision of services (using infrastructure facilities) by the private sector entity to the community on behalf of a public sector entity. They can take many forms and may incorporate some or all of the following features [14]:

- The public sector entity transfers facilities controlled by it to the private sector entity (with or without payment in return) usually for the term of the arrangement;
- The private sector entity builds, extends or renovates a facility;
- The public sector entity specifies the operating features of the facility;
- Services are provided by the private sector entity using the facility for a defined period of time (usually with restrictions on operations and pricing); and
- The private sector entity agrees to transfer the facility to the public sector (with or without payment) at the end of the arrangement.

A classic example of a BOT arrangement is the third Dartford Crossing of the River Thames linking two stretches of the M25 motorway circling London, to be operated (with virtually guaranteed toll income) by the vehicle company for up to 20 years, following which the facility will revert to the UK government. In Australia, projects such as the Sydney Harbour Tunnel and the City Link (linked motorways) project in Melbourne are also BOT arrangements.

With a BOO (build-own-operate) project, the private sector entity finances, builds, owns and operates an infrastructure facility effectively in perpetuity. An example comes from the water treatment plants serving parts of South Australia. These facilities are financed, designed, built and operated by a private sector firm to process raw water, provided by the public sector entity, into filtered water which is then returned to the public sector utility for delivery to consumers.

Although governments have been motivated into entering into PPP arrangements by the desire to reduce debt (and contain taxation), another consideration has been the benefits of sharing financial risks and rewards between public and private sector bodies. We now examine these risks.

#### 4. Risks

Much of the risk of a PPP project comes from the complexity of the arrangement itself in terms of documentation, financing, taxation, technical details, sub-agreements etc involved in a major infrastructure venture, while the nature of the risk alters over the duration of the project. For example, the construction phase of the project will give rise to different risks from those during the operating phase.

Some idea of the complexity is given in Fig. 1. The project concerned is the Almond Valley and Seafield (AV&S) project involving the construction and operation of a water treatment facility for East of Scotland Water (ESW), with a services contract over 30 years between ESW (the public procurer) and Stirling Water. There is also a separate operating agreement between Stirling Water and Thames Water, the private sector operator of the works. The project reached financial close in March 1999 and the figure sets out the links and key contractual arrangements between the parties involved.

From the viewpoint of the public procurer, there is an obvious need to ensure that money has been spent economically, efficiently and effectively. At its simplest, the Government seeks to utilise private sector finance in the provision of public sector infrastructure and services and thereby achieve value-for-money. Value-for-money, defined as the effective use of public funds on a capital project, can come from private sector innovation and skills in asset design, construction techniques and operational practices, and also from transferring key risks in design, construction delays, cost overruns and finance and insurance to private sector entities for them to manage. However, in some cases, the emphasis on risk transfer can be misleading as value-for-money requires equitable allocation of risk between the public and private sector partners, and there may be an inherent conflict between the public sector's need to demonstrate the value-for-money versus the private sector's need for robust revenue streams to support the financing arrangements [15].

From the perspective of the project sponsors, PPP (and PFI) is essentially project financing, characterised by the formation of a highly-geared special purpose company for the project vehicle and consequently a reliance on direct revenues to pay for operating costs and cover debt financing while giving the desired return on risk capital. Although there are exceptional cases such as the Hong Kong Harbour Tunnel which started making a profit four years after opening, these arrangements typically last for long periods and take a long time to generate a profit. It is therefore important to have a clear understanding of the principles of limited-recourse financing. PPP projects are viable only if a reliable, long-term revenue stream can be established. The risk that the predicted revenues do not materialise is the greatest risk to the commercial viability of a project.

This risk is borne by those providing finance or financial guarantees. Straight equity participation is generally low, only 5% of the total funding (£4.95 million out of funding of £99 million) in the case of the AV&S project. This situation is more starkly illustrated by the design–construct–manage–finance (DCMF) of a PFI private prison currently operating in Bridgend, South Wales which was funded with only £250,000 of equity constituting 0.3% of the total funding of £83.5 million. Subordinated debt is often regarded as the equivalent of equity, but this comprises only a further 14% of funds invested in the AV& S project.

110 D. Grimsey, M.K. Lewis / International Journal of Project Management 20 (2002) 107–118

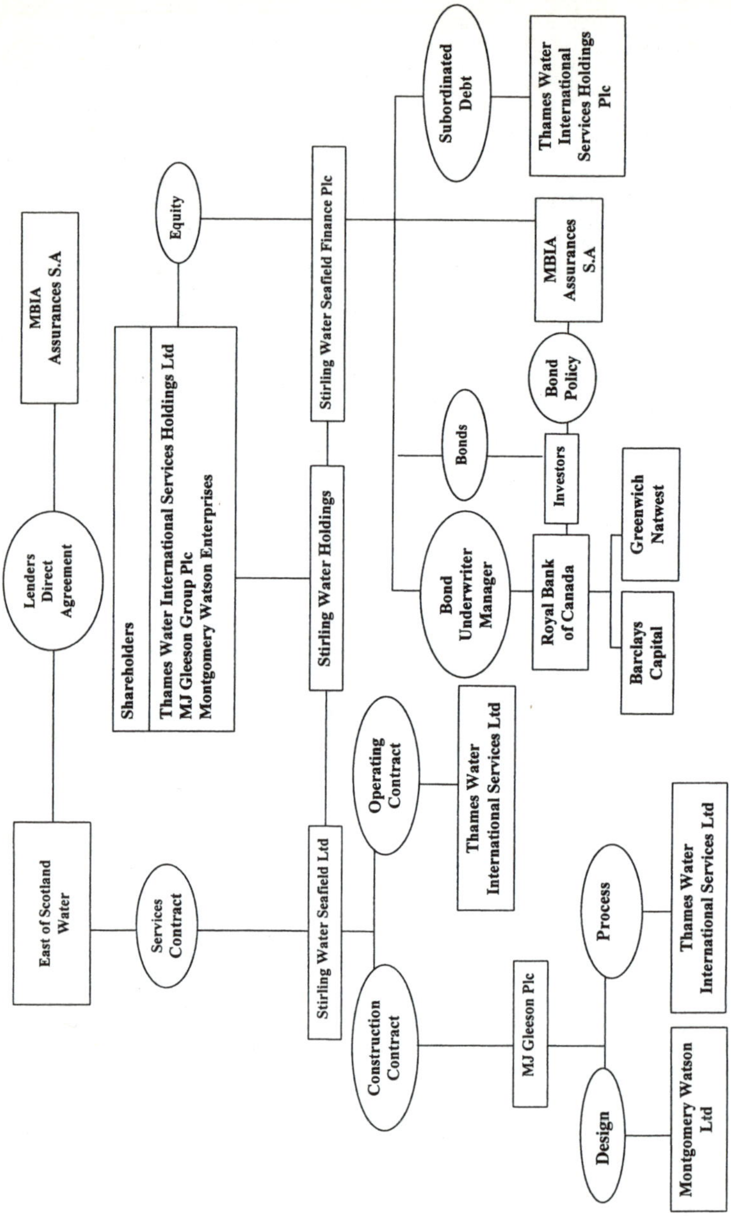


Fig. 1. Contractual arrangements in a PFI/PPP project.

Typically, the providers of finance look to the cashflow of the project as the source of funds for repayments. Financial security against the project company itself is not sought because the company usually has minimal assets and because the financing is without recourse to the sponsor companies. However, performance guarantees are often made available by the sponsor companies in favour of the lenders. Thus the key principle for large PPP projects is to achieve a financial structure with as little recourse as possible to the sponsors whilst at the same time providing sufficient credit support so that the lenders are satisfied with the credit risks.

What are the risks? At least nine risks face any infrastructure project [16–19]:

- Technical risk, due to engineering and design failures;
- Construction risk, because of faulty construction techniques and cost escalation and delays in construction;
- Operating risk, due to higher operating costs and maintenance costs;
- Revenue risk, e.g. due to traffic shortfall or failure to extract resources, the volatility of prices and demand for products and services sold (e.g. minerals, office space etc.) leading to revenue deficiency;
- Financial risks arising from inadequate hedging of revenue streams and financing costs;
- *Force majeure* risk, involving war and other calamities and acts of God.
- Regulatory/political risks, due to legal changes and unsupportive government policies;
- Environmental risks, because of adverse environmental impacts and hazards;
- Project default, due to failure of the project from a combination of any of the above.

Successful project design requires expert analysis of all of them and the design of contractual arrangements prior to competitive tendering that allocate risk burdens appropriately. For this purpose the risks can be broadly categorized as global or elemental [20]. Global risks are those risks that are normally allocated through the project agreement and typically include political, legal, commercial and environmental risks. Elemental risks are considered as those associated with the construction, operation, finance and revenue generation components of the project.

Most of these risks are common to any project financing activity, and apply with more or less force depending on the project concerned. With some PPP agreements, revenue risk and market risk might be low, indeed negligible. For example, the revenue from a toll bridge might be more assured than that of an oilfield, while a private prison is likely to operate with a higher occupancy rate (e.g. 100%) than a luxury hotel! At the same time, however, there is clearly the risk of losses arising from a changing political climate toward the provision of public services by the private sector, while the prices charged for many public sector services are politically sensitive and may be price-capped in some way.

Nevertheless, in principle, the risks of PPP projects seem little different from those of other project financing activities, and can be evaluated using much the same basic techniques. The critical question, as always, is whether revenue streams can cover operating costs, service debt finance and provide returns to risk capital.

Consider the case of infrastructure in the form of a power plant. Sponsors of the power project borrow money to build a generation plant. The sponsors contract to supply power to utilities, projecting that the contract revenues will suffice to pay debt service and generate profits. But risks abound. Will the plant actually be built on time? Will the plant work? And will the market value of the contracts enable participants to avoid an income shortfall? Can rates be raised to levels that more or less equal the utility's costs for providing electricity, an activity that has historically been regulated by government? None of these questions can sensibly be dodged or ignored in project evaluation.

Ultimately, the 'bottom line' (i.e. project default risk) is borne by the financiers, and when considering this scenario the uncertainties concerning future cash flows can be thought of as falling into two categories:

1. Moderate (and perhaps not so moderate) deviations from estimated cash flow projections, due to fluctuating prices, costs, timing delays, minor technical problems, etc.
2. Disasters to a project, due to a major cost overrun, downturn in the economy, change in legal rulings, alteration to the political climate, environmental disaster etc, which could lead to project failure and bankruptcy.

The difference here is not simply one of scale. Rather, the distinction we have in mind recalls that made by Frank Knight in his classic 1921 treatise [21]. Knight distinguished sharply between one type of situation, which he called "risk," and another situation altogether, which he named "uncertainty." In both cases, the actual future outcome is not predictable with certainty. But in the case of risk, the probabilities of the various future outcomes are known (either exactly mathematically, or from past experience of similar situations). In the case of uncertainty, the probabilities of the various future outcomes are merely "wild guesses" because

> the 'instance' in question is so entirely unique that there are no others or not a sufficient number to make it possible to tabulate enough like it to form a basis for any inference of value about any real probability in the case we are interested in. (p. 226).

Knight went on to argue that the main function of the 'entrepreneur' is to bear the brunt of this uncertainty of the future. The profits of enterprise ('pure profits' over and above interest payments on debt capital and/or dividend payments to shareholders) is a reward for facing this uncertainty.

However, the reality in the financing of projects is often quite different to that envisaged by Knight. For example, developers who put up blocks of offices or flats for future sale commonly set up a new limited company for each new building. This company borrows money and/or sells equity shares. If the building fails to make a profit, this particular company goes bankrupt. But the sponsor may survive. The successful entrepreneur is often one who knows how to shift the burden of uncertainty onto others, in particular investors and/or creditors, in such a way that he himself will survive, waiting for a more propitious time for others to again be persuaded to take chances with their money. As Blatt [22] puts it, the prudent entrepreneur reacts to true uncertainty by attempting to make others bear the consequences.

Clearly, an analysis of the nature of the risks [23–25] — and who bears them — is vital, and the evaluation of projects requires the use of several risk analysis techniques tailored to suit the interests of the various parties to the project. Nevertheless, the Knightian distinction remains. At least in theory, risk can be insured against, diversified, calculated with different probabilities, but true uncertainty or disaster scenarios are something else again. How are risks handled in practice? To answer this question we will look at risk analysis from the different perspectives of the parties to the AV&S project.

## 5. Risk analysis in practice

The AV&S project constitutes a major initiative being undertaken by ESW to improve the quality of the water within the River Almond and the Firth of Forth and to implement an alternative to the current practice of disposal of sewage sludge at sea. The project is driven by ESW's requirements to comply with its obligations under the Urban Water Treatment (Scotland) Regulations 1994. The project is just one of around ten PFI schemes currently in procurement with the three Scottish water authorities in order to comply with new regulatory standards to be in force by the end of December 2000. ESW alone has indicated that capital investment over 5 years of £850 million is required to achieve the required standard in its region.

Following a long procurement process of over 2 years, in March 1999 ESW entered into the Services Contract with Stirling Water pursuant to which Stirling Water agreed to upgrade and improve the treatment of waste water from the feeding catchments of Almond Valley and Seafield and to provide new arrangements as an alternative to the disposal of sewage sludge at sea. The main parties to the project and an indication of their connecting relationships are shown in Fig. 1, but in summary:

- ESW is the procuring entity and the authority responsible for providing water, collecting and treating waste water and disposing of sewage sludges within its region;
- Stirling Water is the special purpose company set up for the purpose of financing, constructing and operating the AV&S project;
- Thames Water, MJ Gleeson and Montgomery Watson are the project sponsors providing risk capital and acting respectively as the operator, contractor and designer to Stirling Water; and
- MBIA is providing the credit enhancement insurance policy so that the project can attain a credit rating of AAA. While institutional investors purchased the bonds, the MBIA policy unconditionally and irrevocably guarantees scheduled repayments of principal and interest under the bonds issued and therefore MBIA effectively assumed the role of senior lender.

Stirling Water funded the £99 million project from:

- £79.217 million of 27.5 year AAA rated credit — enhanced bonds paying a fixed coupon of 5.822%;
- £14.835 million of subordinated debt provided by Thames Water. The subordinated debt has the same term as the bonds and a similar interest rate; and
- £4.95 million of equity split between Thames Water (49%), MJ Gleeson (41%) and Montgomery Watson (10%). The internal rate of return on the equity was projected to be 16.56% nominal and 12.5% real at financial close.

## 6. Project risks

Stirling Water as the project vehicle has taken on certain construction and operating risks over the contract period but has allocated away contractually many of these risks to the construction contractor and the operator, as is usual under such arrangements. Stirling Water retained the risk that projected maintenance costs are exceeded, such as those arising from shorter than anticipated asset life spans, increased inflation on specific items of plant and machinery or the requirement to carry out unexpected repairs.

Once the plants are commissioned Stirling Water receives payment based on the volume of waste water treated. The payment mechanism is the key to the risk apportionment and is not like a normal PFI deal where the operator is paid on making the facility available. The contract is more akin to the UK's design, build, finance and operate (DBFO) programme for roads where shadow tolls are paid within payment bands (ie. defined levels of traffic volume), a structure in fact devised by PricewaterhouseCoopers. The aim of such a structure is to allocate a sufficient element of volume risk to the service company and also to limit the authority's exposure to an increase in payments arising from a greater than anticipated volume of waste water delivered. The AV&S payment bands are as follows:

- The first band for waste water treatment is for between 0 and 90,000 cu m pa and pays 13.883 p. This band is designed to generate sufficient revenue to cover fixed operating and maintenance costs and outstanding amounts due under the bond issue;
- The second band for waste water treatment is for between 90,000 cu m pa and 101,000 cu m pa and pays 9.2555 p. This band is designed to provide sufficient revenue to meet payments under the subordinated debt; and
- The third band for waste water treatment is for between 101,000 cu m pa and 107,000 cu m pa and pays 4.628 p. This band is designed to meet the shareholders' target investment returns.
- The fourth band for waste water treatment is for flows in excess of 107,000 cu m pa and is free of charge. This band is designed to cap the payments to be made by ESW.

Payment above the third band effectively is capped thereby limiting ESW's exposure to payments under the contract, while there is a separate rate for the treatment and disposal of imported sludge. The contract provides for payment to be subject to performance-related adjustments geared to any breaches in environmental discharge consent standards set by SEPA. A major concern for Stirling Water is the impact of the quality of the waste water delivered to the works by ESW upon the operator's ability to treat the waste water to a standard which results in the discharged waste water and sludge complying with the required consents. For this reason the contract contains a list of influent concentration levels. In the event that these are exceeded and as a result Stirling Water is unable to treat the waste water to the required standard, then Stirling Water will nevertheless be entitled to payment in full.

Stirling Water is protected through the contract against circumstances influenced by ESW that would impact on the volume of waste water such as the issuing of trade effluent discharge consents, the introduction of water metering or greatly increased capital investment in the sewerage infrastructure leading to a reduction of water infiltration to the sewers. However, under the payment mechanism, failure to achieve forecast levels of volume throughput or suffering larger than expected deductions for poor performance would result in lower than forecast revenues, which would impact on the equity return and may adversely effect Stirling Water's ability to make repayments of subordinated debt and even coupons on the bonds.

The proportion of the tariff indexed to the retail prices index (RPI) is 65%, applied to all three revenue-generating bands. The remaining 35% of the tariff is not subject to indexation but is fixed for the contract term. Proportionally this division approximates to the percentage of the nominal cash flow used to service the bond financing. However, it is possible that there will not be a precise match between Stirling Water's revenues and costs resulting in costs rising faster than revenue arising under the contract and this risk is borne by Stirling Water and its shareholders.

The risk of any adverse changes in law is an important element and on the AV&S project the risk is shared between ESW and Stirling Water over the first ten years of the contract. After this time, the risk is borne by ESW.

## 7. Risk analysis

Having sketched the key risks inherent in the project it is important to look at the nature and quantum of risk from the different perspectives of the main parties to the project. As a guide to the methodology employed, Fig. 2 provides a flow chart of the analytical approach. For each of the three major groups of entities, it summarises their risk perspective, the key variables, the major risks they face, and the risk analysis which is appropriate. There are several risk analysis techniques available ranging in complexity from simple expected cost analysis through sensitivity analysis and on to more complex probabilistic techniques involving computer-aided statistical sampling. The technique that should be used, as indicated, is largely dependent on the exposure of the party to the risk and the nature of the return expected by the party.

### *7.1. Procurer*

ESW, as the procurer, was only interested in the expected costs in the form of the payments they would have to make under the contract. In accordance with Government guidelines the projected payments to each of the bidders were discounted at 6% real and summed to derive the net present value (NPV) of each of the bids. From ESW's perspective, the risk analysis centred on establishing equality of treatment between bidders for bid evaluation and to facilitate a comparison with the public sector comparator in order to demonstrate value-for-money in NPV terms. The value-for-money criterion should establish the best means for achieving

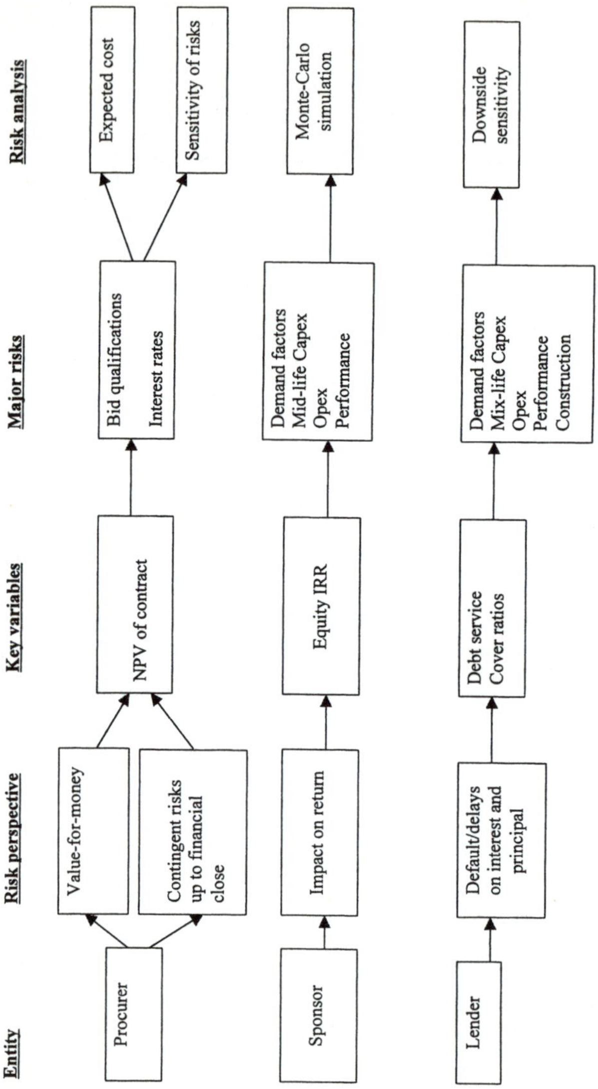


Fig. 2. Flow chart of analytical approach.

the required project function for the least cost. Part of the value-for-money analysis involves a comparison of the project against a traditional public sector procurement and operation route known as the public sector comparator. The main risks analysed from this perspective concerned the following issues:

- The contract was conditional on obtaining planning consent and a risk-sharing mechanism was agreed whereby ESW would pay for a proportion of the planning change costs through an adjustment to the tariffs;
- Stirling Water had qualified their bid in relation to passing the risk of costs resulting from finds, such as antiquities, being uncovered during the construction phase of the project back to ESW; and
- Bidders were also asked to calculate the impact of delay to the programmed contract signing date in terms of the acceleration costs necessary still to achieve the commencement date for the main period for waste water treatment of January 2001. ESW and its advisers made an assessment of the likely delay and adjusted the bids accordingly.

The risks were analysed by establishing the expected cost to ESW of these risks and adjusting the NPV of the bid. In the case of Stirling Water this resulted in approximately a one percent increase in the NPV of the bid. When compared with the competitors, this led to the conclusion that their bid provided ESW with the most economically advantageous proposal relative to the other bidders.

Under the Project Development Agreement, ESW also retained the risk of movements in the underlying interest rates up to financial close, a practice common to such projects. In this case, the specific risk is that any increase in the level of interest rates, and thus of the financing costs for the project, prior to financial close will result in a higher tariff being levied, while the discount rate used in the analysis is fixed at 6% real. Interest rate risk is generally difficult to quantify with any real precision. To get a feel for the likely impact of this risk, sensitivity analysis was carried out on the financial model that yielded the results shown in Table 1. The sensitivity analysis indicates that ESW were reasonably well protected against movements in the underlying interest rate with a moderate rate increase of 1% leading to an increase in the NPV of the cost stream of the project of 3.6% (the approximate gradient of the interest rate sensitivity relationship).

ESW also carry inflation rate risk to the extent that RPI deviates from that projected in the financial model. Whilst it is generally accepted that there is a link between interest rates and inflation the analysis looked at these independently since inflation rates may not be reflected fully in the inflation premia built into interest rates [26]. Like interest rates, inflation is difficult to predict and sensitivity techniques were again used. Table 2 shows the variation in the NPVs at inflation assumptions ranging from 2 to 6%. The NPVs are reduced at higher inflation rates partly because the debt element of the financing being serviced by the revenue stream of the project has not been indexed. The effect of discounting an element of the project's revenue stream fixed in nominal terms at a fixed discount rate of 6% real will lower the NPV of the debt element of the revenue stream at higher inflation rates and therefore lower the overall NPVs. The analysis demonstrates that ESW is well protected against the risk that inflation increases in the future.

It is widely acknowledged that sensitivity analysis is limited to indicating the potential effects upon an outcome, in this case the NPV, if a movement in the variable occurs. Critics of this form of analysis argue that unless some indication of how likely it is that a quantified movement will occur then this form of analysis is not of much use. This argument ignores the fact that some important economic variables cannot easily be quantified in terms of likelihood and extent of change. Who in the UK, for example, during the late seventies could have reasonably predicted that inflation would be 3% or less in the late nineties, a period of only 20 years — that is, 10 years less than the contract term in this case study? Under such circumstances, sensitivity analysis provides a useful tool for analysing these risks in terms of bid evaluation.

Table 1
Procurer: interest rate sensitivity

| Interest rate | % increase/decrease in NPV of expected cost stream from base case |
|---|---|
| Base case −1% | −3.3 |
| Base case −0.5% | −1.7 |
| Base case | Base case NPV |
| Base case +0.5% | +1.8 |
| Base case +1% | +3.6 |
| Base case +1.5% | +5.4 |
| Base case +2% | +7.5 |

Table 2
Procurer: inflation sensitivity

| RPI assumption (%) | % increase/decrease in NPV of expected cost stream from base case |
|---|---|
| 2 | +4.79 |
| 3 | +1.47 |
| 3.5 | Base Case NPV |
| 4 | −1.36 |
| 5 | −3.79 |
| 6 | −5.90 |

*7.2. Sponsors*

From the sponsors' perspective, the risk analysis centres around establishing the potential impact on the equity return. For the purpose of this exercise, the distinction between subordinated debt and equity is ignored because the degree of subordination gives subordinated debt virtually the same characteristics as equity. Subordinated debt is favoured in the UK because it enables the sponsors to extract cash from the project vehicle where dividends would be restricted by the profit and loss account and also because the interest is tax deductible. In order to review Stirling Water's financial proposals from the sponsors' perspective an analysis of the impact of the equity risks on the financial model had to take account of potential upside as well as downside risk.

A simulation exercise was therefore carried out using the following methodology. First, a realistic downside (and upside) case for each risk was defined by ESW's technical adviser Halcrow Crouch to establish a triangular risk distribution for each risk. The relevant risks for this analysis were:

- volume risk;
- the risk of mid-life capital expenditure and asset management costs being greater than forecast;
- operating cost; and
- operating performance.

Whilst construction delay is an important project risk it was not included. This was because the risk analysis looked at the risks from the project sponsors' perspective as equity investors in Stirling Water. For them, delay risk is dealt with contractually through liquidated damages contained in the construction contract and also business interruption insurance. Effectively, therefore, the risk resides with the construction contractor and the insurer and not with the project sponsors.

Second, having delineated the relevant risks for examination:

- a simulation exercise was carried out using the @RISK computer software package to determine the distribution of the relevant risks overall. Then, third,
- from this analysis an assessment was made of the impact on the blended equity/subordinated debt IRR.

The @RISK software package uses a Monte Carlo simulation process to perform a risk analysis. Simulation in this sense refers to a method whereby the distribution of possible outcomes is generated by letting the computer recalculate the financial model over and over again, each time using different randomly selected sets of values for the probability distributions contained in the spreadsheet model. In effect, the computer is trying all valid combinations of the values of input variables to simulate all possible outcomes.

A summary of the results of the quantitative risk analysis on the Stirling Water financial model is shown in Table 3. This analysis suggests that the sponsors are unlikely to achieve the base level rates of return, yet are taking a reasonable amount of financial risk commensurate with risk capital investments in such projects. Although the relevant risks modelled contained upside potential, the analysis also indicates that there is, overall, no likely financial upside for the sponsors. The main opportunity for financial upside comes from increased waste water volumes, but the payments made by ESW are capped as described earlier. Also, the procurer in this case was in a strong bargaining position; England and France have some of the largest water companies in the world and they were vying for a foothold in the relatively small Scottish market.

*7.3. Senior lenders*

For senior lenders the nature of non-recourse or limited recourse funding clearly carries a rather different risk or credit assessment than a conventional full recourse loan where the enforcement of security by the lender is additional to its ability to sue the borrower, and the lender can assess the value of the assets used as collateral. With project financing, the facilities often do not have a capital worth, in terms of a wide market, to which lenders would wish to attribute value. Lenders, of course, insist on having the opportunity to step in and rescue a failing project but they cannot simply sell off the asset to realise value. In contracts such as AV&S, the assets essentially take the form of the contract with the procuring authority. It is therefore understandable that senior lenders tend to take a pessimistic view where risk analysis is concerned. The key difference between the senior lenders and the sponsors is that for the senior lender holding debt rather than equity there is never any potential upside gain in the project, only downside risk that could reduce the ability of the borrower to make principal and interest payments under the loan agreement.

Table 3
Sponsors: equity/subordinated debt risk analysis

| Simulation | Decrease in blended equity IRR |
|---|---|
| Minimum simulation result | Base case −7.17% |
| 5% probability of returns being less than: | Base case −5.48% |
| 25% probability of the returns being less than: | Base case −3.9% |
| 50% probability of the returns being less than: | Base case −2.52% |
| 75% probability of the returns being less than: | Base case −1.47% |
| 95% probability of returns being less than: | Base case −0.57% |
| Maximum simulation result | Base case −0.06% |

Senior lenders therefore focus on cover to the income stream over the term of the loan and analyse risk to establish robustness by reference to cover ratios. The most important of these ratios are the loan life cover ratio (LLCR) and the annual debt service cover ratio (ADSCR). The LLCR provides a snap shot on a given date of the NPV of the projected cashflows from that date until retirement of the loan relative to the loan outstanding on that particular date. The ADSCR is an historic ratio that measures the cashflow for the previous year in relation to the amount of loan principal and interest payable for that period.

The sensitivities tested from the lenders' perspective are intended to capture the risks left with the service company rather than the project as a whole, taking account of the fact that it will seek to mitigate key risks by allocating them away contractually. The main instruments used for allocating risk will be:

- The Design and Construction (D&C) Contract which mitigates the Service Company's exposure to design risk and construction cost and time overrun risk; and
- The Operation and Maintenance (O&M) Contract which mitigates the Service Company's exposure to performance risk and operations and maintenance cost risk.

It is therefore crucial to the financial robustness of bids, given the highly geared financing structure envisaged, that these risks should be allocated away from the service company under strong contracts to suitable counterparties. However, even when risk is transferred contractually some residual risk will remain with the service company. For instance, if the operating costs turned out to be significantly greater than originally forecast it is conceivable that the service company could decide that it was in its best interests to share the pain with the O&M Contractor by agreeing to a price increase to absorb some of the increased cost, rather than running the risk of the O&M Contractor abandoning the contract. The operating expenditure (OPEX) and capital expenditure (CAPEX) sensitivities tested are intended to reflect this residual risk.

Table 4 below displays the results of the robustness analysis on Stirling Water's financial model. The ADSCR and LLCR (see earlier definitions of these cover ratios) only fall below the minimum requirement (ADSCR of 1.15 and LLCR of 1.15) under the OPEX, Flow and Combined Scenario. However, in no case do the ADSCR or LLCR fall below 1.0, which would indicate a default under the loan agreement. This analysis indicates to the senior lenders that the Stirling Water financing plan is reasonably robust to support the level of funding anticipated.

Table 4
Senior lenders: robustness analysis of cash flows

| Sensitivity | Change[a] (%) | ADSCR | LLCR |
|---|---|---|---|
| Base case financial model | – | 1.26 | 1.32 |
| Construction cost | +3 | 1.26 | 1.32 |
| OPEX | +12.5 | 1.08 | 1.15 |
| Downside flow | | 1.07 | 1.12 |
| Midlife CAPEX | +10 | 1.24 | 1.29 |
| Operational performance | −2 | 1.20 | 1.26 |
| Combined downside: downside flow plus midlife CAPEX | | 1.04 | 1.10 |

[a] As defined by ESW's technical adviser (see text).

Overall, the combination of risk analysis techniques used on the AV&S project demonstrated that:

- The project delivers value-for-money to the procuring entity ESW and satisfies the main government criteria for investing in capital projects;
- The project has reasonable but not excessive upside potential for the project sponsors and downside potential commensurate with the levels of return anticipated in the base case; and
- The downside sensitivity testing suggests that the project is sufficiently robust and financially stable from the viewpoint of lenders.

## 8. Conclusion

Project finance and PPP/PFI arrangements are founded on the transfer of risk from the public to the private sector under circumstances where the private sector is best placed to manage the risk. The general principles are common to all public sectors insofar as the projects seek to shift risk from the public sector to the supplier and offer a profit incentive to the private sector in return. However, the principal aim for the public sector is to achieve value-for-money in the services provided while ensuring that the private sector entities meet their contractual obligations properly and efficiently.

Value-for-money and risk transfer principles accepted, fundamentally PPP projects are viable only if a robust, long term revenue stream, over the period of the concession, can be established. A framework for investigating and carrying out an analysis of the risks has been outlined in this paper that systematically views project risk from the perspectives of the procuring entity, the project sponsors and the senior lenders. For a project to be successful, the differing (and conflicting) needs of these parties must be satisfied in the risk allocation process, and this would seem to have been achieved in the waste water treatment project used to illustrate the application of the framework.

## References

[1] McCarthy SC, Perry JG. BOT contracts for water supply. In: World water 89. Thos. Telford London: 1989.
[2] Augenblick M., Scott Custer Jr. B. The build, operate and transfer (BOT) approach to infrastructure projects in the developing countries. Working papers. World Bank, Washington: August 1990.
[3] Monod J. The private sector and the management of public drinking water supply. Washington: World Bank, 1982.
[4] Owen G, Merna A. The private finance initiative. Engineering, Construction and Architectural Management 1997;4(3):215–31.
[5] Mustafa A. Public–private partnership: an alternative institutional model for implementing the private finance initiative in the provision of transport infrastructure. Journal of Project Finance 1999;5(2):64–79.
[6] Horner R. Public private partnerships, the way forward. Irish Banking Review Summer: 1999; 25-34.
[7] East Asia Analytical Unit. Asia's infrastructure in the crisis, harnessing private enterprise. Canberra: Department of Foreign Affairs and Trade, 1998.
[8] International Finance Corporation. Project finance in developing countries. Washington:: The World Bank, 1999.
[9] Martini CA, Lee DQ. Difficulties in infrastructure financing. Journal of Applied Finance and Investment 1996;1(1):24–7.
[10] Threadgold A. Private financing of infrastructure and other long-term capital projects. Journal of Applied Finance and Investment 1996;1(1):7–12.
[11] Lewis M.K. Banking on real estate, In: Fair D.E., Raymond R. editors. The competitiveness of financial institutions and centres in Europe. Dordrecht: Kluwer, 1994.
[12] Dixit AK, Pindyck R. S., Investment under uncertainty. Princeton (NJ): Princeton University Press, 1994.
[13] Adam C. Embedded options in infrastructure projects. Journal of Applied Finance and Investment 1996;1(1):33–6.
[14] Peirson G, McBride P. Public/private sector infrastructure arrangements. CPA Communique 1996;73:1–4.
[15] Grimsey D, Graham R. PFI in the NHS. Engineering, Construction and Architectural Management 1997;4(3):215–31.
[16] Chapman CB, Ward SC. Project risk management — processes, techniques and insights. Chichester: John Wiley and Sons, 1997.
[17] Kerzner H. Project management, a systems approach to planning, scheduling and controlling. 3rd ed. New York: Van Nostrand Reinhold, 1989.
[18] Smith RC, Walter I. Global financial services. New York: Harper Business, 1990.
[19] Thobani M. Private infrastructure, public risk. Finance and Development 1998;36(1):50–3.
[20] Merna A, Smith NJ. Privately financed concession contract, Vols. 1 and 2. 2nd ed. Hong Kong: Asia Law and Practice, 1996.
[21] Knight F. Risk, uncertainty and profit. Boston: Houghton Mifflin, 1921.
[22] Blatt JM. Dynamic economic systems. New York: Sharpe, 1983.
[23] World Bank. Toolkits for private sector participation in water and sanitation. Washington: World Bank, 1997.
[24] Economic Committee APEC. Infrastructure development — conference summary and case studies. Singapore: APEC Secretariat, 1996.
[25] CEDA. Infrastructure and economic development. CEDA information paper no. 60. Committee for Economic Development in Australia, Melbourne: 1999.
[26] Lewis MK, Mizen, PD. Monetary economics. Oxford University Press, Oxford, 2000.

# Name Index

# The International Library of Critical Writings in Economics

1. Multinational Corporations
*Mark Casson*
2. The Economics of Innovation
*Christopher Freeman*
3. Entrepreneurship
*Mark Casson*
4. International Investment
*Peter J. Buckley*
5. Game Theory in Economics
*Ariel Rubinstein*
6. The History of Economic Thought
*Mark Blaug*
7. Monetary Theory
*Thomas Mayer*
8. Joint Production of Commodities
*Neri Salvadori and Ian Steedman*
9. Industrial Organization
*Oliver E. Williamson*
10. Growth Theory
(Volumes I, II and III)
*R. Becker and E. Burmeister*
11. Microeconomics: Theoretical and Applied (Volumes I, II and III)
*Robert E. Kuenne*
12. The Economics of Health
(Volumes I and II)
*A.J. Culyer*
13. Recent Developments in Macroeconomics
(Volumes I, II and III)
*Edmund S. Phelps*
14. Urban and Regional Economics
*Paul C. Cheshire and Alan W. Evans*
15. Modern Public Finance
(Volumes I and II)
*A.B. Atkinson*
16. Exchange Rate Economics
(Volumes I and II)
*Ronald MacDonald and Mark P. Taylor*
17. The Economic Value of Education: Studies in the Economics of Education
*Mark Blaug*
18. Development Economics
(Volumes I, II, III and IV)
*Deepak Lal*
19. The New Classical Macroeconomics
(Volumes I, II and III)
*Kevin D. Hoover*
20. The Economics of the Environment
*Wallace E. Oates*
21. Post Keynesian Theory of Growth and Distribution
*Carlo Panico and Neri Salvadori*
22. Dynamic Labor Demand and Adjustment Costs
*Giorgio Galeazzi and Daniel S. Hamermesh*
23. The Philosophy and Methodology of Economics (Volumes I, II and III)
*Bruce J. Caldwell*
24. Public Choice Theory
(Volumes I, II and III)
*Charles K. Rowley*
25. Evolutionary Economics
*Ulrich Witt*
26. Economics and Psychology
*Shlomo Maital and Sharone L. Maital*
27. Social Choice Theory
(Volumes I, II and III)
*Charles K. Rowley*
28. Non-Linear Dynamics in Economic Theory
*Marc Jarsulic*
29. Recent Developments in Experimental Economics
(Volumes I and II)
*John D. Hey and Graham Loomes*

30. Monopoly and Competition Policy (Volumes I and II)
*F.M. Scherer*
31. The Economics of Technical Change
*Edwin Mansfield and Elizabeth Mansfield*
32. The Economics of Exhaustible Resources
*Geoffrey Heal*
33. The Economics of Institutions
*Geoffrey M. Hodgson*
34. The Economics of Transport (Volumes I and II)
*Herbert Mohring*
35. Implicit Contract Theory
*Sherwin Rosen*
36. Foundations of Analytical Marxism (Volumes I and II)
*John E. Roemer*
37. The Economics of Product Differentiation (Volumes I and II)
*Jacques-François Thisse and George Norman*
38. Economic Growth in Theory and Practice: A Kaldorian Perspective
*John E. King*
39. Markets and Socialism
*Alec Nove and Ian D. Thatcher*
40. Recent Developments in the Economics of Education
*Elchanan Cohn and Geraint Johnes*
41. The Theory of Inflation
*Michael Parkin*
42. The Economics of Location (Volumes I, II and III)
*Melvin L. Greenhut and George Norman*
43. Financial Intermediaries
*Mervyn K. Lewis*
44. The Political Economy of Privatization and Deregulation
*Elizabeth E. Bailey and Janet Rothenberg Pack*
45. Gender and Economics
*Jane Humphries*
46. Macroeconomics and Imperfect Competition
*Jean-Pascal Bénassy*
47. Labor Economics (Volumes I, II, III and IV)
*Orley C. Ashenfelter and Kevin F. Hallock*
48. The Economics of Altruism
*Stefano Zamagni*
49. The Economic Analysis of Rent Seeking
*Robert D. Tollison and Roger D. Congleton*
50. Economics and Biology
*Geoffrey M. Hodgson*
51. The Economics of Ageing
*John Creedy*
52. Fiscal and Monetary Policy (Volumes I and II)
*Thomas Mayer and Steven M. Sheffrin*
53. The Economics of Information (Volumes I and II)
*David K. Levine and Steven A. Lippman*
54. Transaction Cost Economics (Volumes I and II)
*Oliver E. Williamson and Scott E. Masten*
55. Agricultural Economics
*George H. Peters*
56. International Debt (Volumes I and II)
*Graham Bird and P. Nicholas Snowden*
57. Economics and Discrimination (Volumes I and II)
*William A. Darity, Jr*
58. Business Cycle Theory
*Finn E. Kydland*
59. International Trade (Volumes I and II)
*J. Peter Neary*
60. The Money Supply in the Economic Process
*Marco Musella and Carlo Panico*

61. Small Firms and Economic Growth (Volumes I and II)
*Zoltan J. Acs*
62. Producer Cooperatives and Labor-Managed Systems (Volumes I and II)
*David L. Prychitko and Jaroslav Vanek*
63. Ethics and Economics (Volumes I and II)
*Alan P. Hamlin*
64. The Economics of the Family
*Nancy Folbre*
65. The Economics of Training (Volumes I and II)
*Orley C. Ashenfelter and Robert J. LaLonde*
66. Chaos Theory in Economics: Methods, Models and Evidence
*W. Davis Dechert*
67. General Equilibrium Theory (Volumes I, II and III)
*Gérard Debreu*
68. Economic Growth: Theory and Evidence (Volumes I and II)
*Gene M. Grossman*
69. Long Wave Theory
*Christopher Freeman*
70. The Economics of Communication and Information
*Donald M. Lamberton*
71. The Foundations of Public Finance (Volumes I and II)
*Peter Jackson*
72. The Theory of the Firm
*Mark Casson*
73. The Economics of Uncertainty (Volumes I and II)
*John D. Hey*
74. The Economics of Global Warming
*Tom Tietenberg*
75. The Development of Ecological Economics
*Robert Costanza, Charles Perrings and Cutler Cleveland*
76. Economic Growth in the Long Run: A History of Empirical Evidence (Volumes I, II and III)
*Bart van Ark*
77. The Economics of Productivity (Volumes I and II)
*Edward N. Wolff*
78. The Economics of Population: Key Modern Writings (Volumes I and II)
*Julian L. Simon*
79. Political Business Cycles
*Bruno S. Frey*
80. Cultural Economics: The Arts, the Heritage and the Media Industries (Volumes I and II)
*Ruth Towse*
81. Law and Economics (Volumes I, II and III)
*Richard A. Posner and Francesco Parisi*
82. Independent Central Banks and Economic Performance
*Sylvester Eijffinger*
83. Culture, Social Norms and Economics (Volumes I and II)
*Mark Casson*
84. Industrial Policy and Competitive Advantage (Volumes I, II and III)
*David B. Audretsch*
85. The Economics of Housing (Volumes I and II)
*John M. Quigley*
86. Economic Demography (Volumes I and II)
*T. Paul Schultz*
87. Trade and the Environment: Economic, Legal and Policy Perspectives
*Alan M. Rugman and John J. Kirton with Julie A. Soloway*
88. The Economics of Fiscal Federalism and Local Finance
*Wallace E. Oates*
89. Price Theory and its Applications
*Bernard Saffran and F.M. Scherer*

90. Women in the Labor Market (Volumes I and II)
*Marianne A. Ferber*
91. Market Process Theories (Volumes I and II)
*Peter Boettke and David Prychitko*
92. Input–Output Analysis (Volumes I, II and III)
*Heinz Kurz, Erik Dietzenbacher and Christian Lager*
93. Mathematical Economics (Volumes I, II and III)
*Graciela Chichilnisky*
94. The Foundations of Regulatory Economics (Volumes I, II and III)
*Robert B. Ekelund, Jr.*
95. The Economics of Marketing
*Martin Carter, Mark Casson and Vivek Suneja*
96. Service Industries in the Global Economy (Volumes I and II)
*J.R. Bryson and P.W. Daniels*
97. Economic Justice (Volumes I and II)
*Giorgio Brosio and Harold M. Hochman*
98. Foreign Exchange Intervention: Objectives and Effectiveness
*Sylvester C.W. Eijffinger*
99. Economic Anthropology
*Stephen Gudeman*
100. Consumer Theory
*Kelvin Lancaster*
101. The Economics of Famine
*Jean Drèze*
102. Microeconomic Theories of Imperfect Competition
*Jean J. Gabszewicz and Jacques-François Thisse*
103. The Economics of Executive Compensation (Volumes I and II)
*Kevin F. Hallock and Kevin J. Murphy*
104. The Foundations of Long Wave Theory (Volumes I and II)
*Francisco Louçã and Jan Reijnders*
105. The Economics of Commodity Markets
*David Greenaway and C.W. Morgan*
106. Corporate Governance (Volumes I, II, III and IV)
*Kevin Keasey, Steve Thompson and Mike Wright*
107. Economic Welfare: Concepts and Measurement (Volumes I and II)
*John Creedy*
108. Economic Forecasting
*Terence C. Mills*
109. Recent Developments in Game Theory
*Eric S. Maskin*
110. The Economics of Increasing Returns
*Geoffrey Heal*
111. The Economics of Corruption and Illegal Markets (Volumes I, II and III)
*Gianluca Fiorentini and Stefano Zamagni*
112. The Economics of Price Discrimination
*George Norman*
113. The Economic Theory of Auctions (Volumes I and II)
*Paul Klemperer*
114. The Economics of Regional Policy
*Harvey W. Armstrong and Jim Taylor*
115. Economic Integration and International Trade
*Carsten Kowalczyk*
116. The Political Economy of Science, Technology and Innovation
*Ben Martin and Paul Nightingale*
117. The Economics of Science and Innovation (Volumes I and II)
*Paula E. Stephan and David B. Audretsch*
118. Innovation, Evolution of Industry and Economic Growth (Volumes I, II and III)
*David B. Audretsch and Steven Klepper*

119. The Economics of Energy
(Volumes I and II)
*Paul Stevens*
120. Privatisation in Developing Countries
(Volumes I and II)
*Paul Cook and Colin Kirkpatrick*
121. The Economics of Tourism
(Volumes I and II)
*Clem Tisdell*
122. The Economics of Unemployment
(Volumes I, II, III and IV)
*P.N. Junankar*
123. Privatisation and Corporate
Performance
*David Parker*
124. Income Distribution
(Volumes I, II and III)
*Michael Sattinger*
125. International Finance
(Volumes I and II)
*Robert Z. Aliber*
126. Welfare Economics
(Volumes I, II and III)
*William J. Baumol and Charles A. Wilson*
127. The Theory of Trade Policy Reform
*Carsten Kowalczyk*
128. The Economics of Defence
(Volumes I, II and III)
*Keith Hartley and Todd Sandler*
129. The Economics of Property Rights
(Volumes I and II)
*Svetozar Pejovich*
130. Gender and Development:
Theoretical, Empirical and Practical
Approaches
(Volumes I and II)
*Lourdes Benería with Savitri Bisnath*
131. The Economics of Politics
(Volumes I and II)
*Dennis C. Mueller*
132. Economic Theory and the Welfare
State (Volumes I, II and III)
*Nicholas Barr*
133. The Regulation and Supervision of
Banks
(Volumes I, II, III and IV)
*Maximilian J.B. Hall*
134. The Political Economy of Monetary
Union
*Paul De Grauwe*
135. The Economics of Sport
(Volumes I and II)
*Andrew Zimbalist*
136. The Economics of Advertising
*Kyle Bagwell*
137. Regulation, Economics and the Law
*Anthony I. Ogus*
138. The Economics of Barter and
Countertrade
*Rolf Mirus and Bernard Yeung*
139. The Economics of Technology
Transfer
*Sanjaya Lall*
140. The Political Economy of
Development
(Volumes I, II and III)
*Amitava Krishna Dutt*
141. Macroeconomics and the Environment
*Mohan Munasinghe*
142. Happiness in Economics
*Richard A. Easterlin*
143. Speculation and Financial Markets
(Volumes I and II)
*Liam Gallagher and Mark P. Taylor*
144. Public Procurement
(Volumes I and II)
*Sue Arrowsmith and Keith Hartley*
145. The Economics of Intellectual
Property
(Volumes I, II, III and IV)
*Ruth Towse and R.W. Holzhauer*
146. Forecasting Financial Markets
(Volumes I and II)
*Terence C. Mills*
147. The Economics of Labor Unions
(Volumes I and II)
*Alison Booth*

148. New Developments in Exchange Rate Economics
(Volumes I and II)
*Lucio Sarno and Mark P. Taylor*

149. Long Term Trends and Business Cycles
(Volumes I and II)
*Terence C. Mills*

150. The Economics of Language
*Donald M. Lamberton*

151. The Economics of Migration
(Volumes I, II, III and IV)
*Klaus F. Zimmermann and Thomas Bauer*

152. Cost–Benefit Analysis
*Arnold C. Harberger and Glenn P. Jenkins*

153. The Economics of Budget Deficits
(Volumes I and II)
*Charles K. Rowley, William F. Shughart II and Robert D. Tollison*

154. Alternative Theories of the Firm
(Volumes I, II and III)
*Richard Langlois, Tony F. Yu and Paul Robertson*

155. The Distribution of Tax Burdens
*Don Fullerton and Gilbert E. Metcalf*

156. International Financial Integration
(Volumes I and II)
*Sylvester C.W. Eijffinger and Jan J.G. Lemmen*

157. The Economics of Structural Change
(Volumes I, II and III)
*Harald Hagemann, Michael Landesmann and Roberto Scazzieri*

158. The Economics of Poverty and Inequality
(Volumes I and II)
*Frank A. Cowell*

159. The Economics of Schooling
(Volumes I and II)
*Eric A. Hanushek*

160. Intra-Industry Trade
*Peter J. Lloyd and Herbert G. Grubel*

161. Economic Analysis of Regional Trading Arrangements
*Richard Pomfret*

162. The Principal Agent Model: The Economic Theory of Incentives
*Jean-Jacques Laffont*

163. The Economics of Business Strategy
*John Kay*

164. Recent Developments in Transport Economics
*Kenneth Button*

165. The Economics of Higher Education
*Clive R. Belfield and Henry M. Levin*

166. Constitutional Political Economy
(Volumes I and II)
*Stephan Voigt*

167. Economics and Religion
(Volumes I and II)
*Paul Oslington*

168. The Economics of Conflict
(Volumes I, II and III)
*Todd Sandler and Keith Hartley*

169. Cognitive Economics
(Volumes I and II)
*Massimo Egidi and Salvatore Rizzello*

170. Comparative Law and Economics
(Volumes I, II and III)
*Gerrit de Geest and Roger Van Den Bergh*

171. Personnel Economics
(Volumes I and II)
*Edward P. Lazear and Robert McNabb*

172. Empirical Industrial Organization
(Volumes I and II)
*Paul L. Joskow and Michael Waterson*

173. Multinationals and Public Policy
(Volumes I and II)
*Stephen Young*

174. Complexity in Economics
(Volumes I, II and III)
*J. Barkley Rosser, Jr.*

175. Time in Economic Theory
(Volumes I, II and III)
*Stefano Zamagni and Elettra Agliardi*

176. The Economics of Affirmative Action
*Harry J. Holzer and David Neumark*

177. Recent Developments in Environmental Economics
(Volumes I and II)
*Michael Hoel*

178. The Economics of Natural Hazards
(Volumes I and II)
*Howard Kunreuther and Adam Rose*

179. Recent Developments in Growth Theory
(Volumes I and II)
*K. Daron Acemoglu*

180. The Political Economy of Environmental Regulation
*Robert N. Stavins*

181. The Economics of Nonprofit Enterprises
*Richard S. Steinberg*

182. Recent Developments in Urban and Regional Economics
*Paul C. Cheshire and Gilles Duranton*

183. The Economics of Public Private Partnerships
*Darrin Grimsey and Mervyn K. Lewis*

184. New Economic Geography
*J. Vernon Henderson*

Future titles will include:

The Psychology of World Equity Markets
(Volumes I and II)
*Werner De Bondt*

The Economics of Crime
(Volumes I, II and III)
*Isaac Ehrlich and Zhiqiang Liu*

New Developments in Economic Sociology
(Volumes I and II)
*Richard Swedberg*

Spatial Economics
*Masahisa Fujita*

Recent Developments in International Trade Theory
*Rodney E. Falvey and Udo Kreickemeier*

The Economics of Deflation
(Volumes I and II)
*Pierre L. Siklos*

Recent Developments in International Investment
*Alan M. Rugman and Jing Li*

Recent Developments in Economic Methodology
*John B. Davis*

Open Economy Macroeconomics
*Norman C. Miller*

The Economics of Networks
*Michael L. Katz and Carl Shapiro*

The Economics of Contracts
*Lars A. Stole*

Recent Developments in Labour Economics
*John T. Addison*

Institutions and Economic Performance
*Masahiko Aoki*

Modern Classics in the Economics of Education
*Clive Belfield*

Imperfect Competition, Nonclearing Markets and Business Cycles
*Jean-Pascal Bénassy*

The International Monetary Fund and the World Economy
*Graham Bird and Dane Rowlands*

International Taxation
*Richard M. Bird and Michael Smart*

The Economics of Knowledge
*Robin A. Cowan*

Path Dependence
*Paul A. David*

The Economics of the Mass Media
*Gillian Doyle*

The Economics of Gambling and National Lotteries
*William R. Eadington*

The Economics of Transfer Pricing
*Lorraine Eden*

Financial Crises
*Douglas Gale and Franklin Allen*

The Economics of Association Football
*Bill Gerrard*

The Economics of Innovation Policy
*Bronwyn Hall*

Islamic Finance
*M. Kabir Hassan and Mervyn K. Lewis*

The Economics of Vouchers
*Caroline M. Hoxby*

The Economics of Free Trade
*Douglas A. Irwin and Arvind Panagariya*

The Economics of Organisation and Bureaucracy
*Peter M. Jackson*

Computational Economics
*Kenneth L. Judd*

Feminist Economics
*Mary C. King, Ann Mari May and Diana L. Strassman*

Cooperation, Competition and Collusion: The Economic Theory of Incentives
*Jean-Jacques Laffont*

The Phillips Curve
*Richard G. Lipsey and Robert Leeson*

The Economics of Biotechnology
*Maureen McKelvey and Luigi Orsenigo*

The Economic Role of the State
*Steven G. Medema*

Innovation and Economic Development
*Lynn Mytelka*

Forms of Capitalism: Comparative Institutional Analyses
*Ugo Pagano and Ernesto Screpanti*

The New Evolutionary Economics
*Jason Potts and Kurt Dopfer*

The Economics of Public Utilities
*Ray Rees*

The Economics of Modern Business Enterprise
*Martin Ricketts*

New Developments in Public Choice
*Charles K. Rowley, Robert D. Tollison and William F. Shughart*

Cartels
*Stephen Salant and Margaret Levenstein*

The Economics of the Hidden Economy
*Vito Tanzi*

The Economics of Leisure and Recreation
*Clem Tisdell*

Recent Developments in Evolutionary Economics
*Ulrich Witt*